FISCAL F

This comprehensive account of the principles and practices of fiscal federalism is based on the currently accepted theoretical framework and best practices. The traditional topics of assignment of responsibilities, intergovernmental fiscal arrangements, fiscal competition, and grants are covered in a unified framework with reference to actual practices followed in federations around the world. Special issues such as local government and the implications of natural resource issues are considered along with emerging issues such as governance, corruption, and the effect of globalization and the information revolution on the nation-state. The treatment is nontechnical and suitable for a wide variety of audiences, including scholars, instructors, students, policy advisers, and practitioners.

Robin Boadway holds the David Chadwick Smith Chair in Economics at Queen's University, Kingston, Canada. Before that he was Sir Edward Peacock Professor of Economics at Queen's, where he has taught virtually all his career. He is an Officer of the Order of Canada and a Fellow of the Royal Society of Canada, the Institute of Intergovernmental Relations, and the Center for Economic Studies and Institute for Economic Research (CESifo). Professor Boadway is a past president of the Canadian Economics Association and is Executive Vice-President of the International Institute of Public Finance (IIPF). He served as a Member of the Academic Panel in the Fiscal Affairs Department of the IMF and is currently on the Scientific Advisory Council of the Institute for Economic Research (IFO) in Munich. He has received the Harry Johnson Memorial Prize twice and the Queen's University Prize for Research Excellence. He has served as editor of the *Canadian Journal of Economics* and the *German Economic Journal* and is currently editor of the *Journal of Public Economics*. His books include *Public Sector Economics; Welfare Economics; Canadian Tax Policy; Intergovernmental Fiscal Relations in Canada; Equalization in a Federal State;* and *Intergovernmental Fiscal Transfers*, with Anwar Shah.

Anwar Shah is Lead Economist and Program Leader, Public Sector Governance Program at the World Bank Institute, Washington, D.C. He is a Member of the Executive Board of the International Institute of Public Finance, Munich, and a Fellow of the Institute for Public Economics, Edmonton, Alberta, Canada. Dr. Shah is also affiliated as Honorary Professor with the Southwest University of Finance and Economics, Chengdu, China, and Central University of Finance and Economics, Beijing, China. He has previously served as a staff member with the Ministry of Finance, the government of Canada, the government of Alberta, and the U.S. Agency for International Development, and he was the lead author for the Second Report of the UN Intergovernmental Panel on Climate Change. Dr. Shah was coordinator of the Global Dialogue on Fiscal Federalism conducted by the Forum of Federation in partnership with Governments in Federal Countries from 2005 to 2007. He has advised the governments of Australia, Argentina, Brazil, Canada, China, Germany, India, Indonesia, Mexico, Pakistan, Poland, South Africa, and Turkey on fiscal system reform issues. In the past, he taught graduate courses in natural resources and environmental economics at the University of Ottawa. He has published about two dozen books on governance and fiscal system reform themes and numerous articles in professional journals. His most recent edited books include *The Practice of Fiscal Federalism* and *Macro Federalism and Local Finance*.

Fiscal Federalism

Principles and Practices of Multiorder Governance

Robin Boadway

Queens University, Canada

Anwar Shah

The World Bank, Washington, D.C.

To Robaees Islam

For her inspiring leadership, guidance and encouragement.

Best,
Anwar

CAMBRIDGE
UNIVERSITY PRESS

CAMBRIDGE UNIVERSITY PRESS
Cambridge, New York, Melbourne, Madrid, Cape Town, Singapore, São Paulo, Delhi

Cambridge University Press
32 Avenue of the Americas, New York, NY 10013-2473, USA

www.cambridge.org
Information on this title: www.cambridge.org/9780521732116

First published 2009

Printed in the United States of America

A catalog record for this publication is available from the British Library.

Library of Congress Cataloging in Publication Data

Boadway, Robin W., 1943–
Fiscal federalism : principles and practices in multiorder governance / Robin Boadway,
Anwar Shah.
p. cm.
Includes bibliographical references and index.
ISBN 978-0-521-51821-5 (hardback) – ISBN 978-0-521-73211-6 (pbk.)
1. Intergovernmental fiscal relations. 2. Fiscal policy. 3. Decentralization in government.
4. Revenue sharing. I. Shah, Anwar. II. Title.

HJ197.B63 2009
336–dc22   2008045471

ISBN 978-0-521-51821-5 hardback
ISBN 978-0-521-73211-6 paperback

Contents

Contents

Preface

Globalization, the information revolution, and regional and ethnic conflicts have made it imperative for a large and growing number of countries around the globe to reexamine the roles of various orders of government to secure peace, order, and good government and to reposition their roles in improving social and economic outcomes and retaining relevance in the lives of their citizens. This reexamination has resulted in a silent revolution sweeping the globe, which is slowly but gradually bringing about rearrangements that embody diverse features of supranationalization, confederalization, centralization, provincialization, and localization. The vision of a governance structure that is slowly taking hold through this silent revolution indicates either a gradual shift from unitary constitutional structures to federal or confederal governance for a large majority of people or a strengthening of local governance under a unitary form of government. (In 2007 there were twenty-eight federal or quasi-federal and twenty decentralized unitary countries with a combined total of about two-thirds of the world's population.) This new vision of governance has also led to a resurgence of interest in fiscal federalism principles and practices as federal systems are seen to provide safeguards against the threat of centralized exploitation as well as decentralized opportunistic behavior while bringing decision making closer to the people. This book responds to this felt need by providing a synthesis of the literature on the theory and practice of multicentered, decentralized economic governance. The fiscal federalism principles and practices presented in this book may be of interest not just in federal countries but may also have important policy import for unitary countries interested in creating governments that work and serve their people.

This book is intended to encapsulate for a general reader the vast and diverse literature on the design and practice of fiscal constitutions – that is, how revenue raising, spending, and regulatory functions are allocated among various orders of governments and how revenue-sharing mechanisms and intergovernmental transfers are structured to ensure responsive, responsible, fair, and accountable decentralized governance. The motivation for the book has its origin in numerous requests for advice on the reform of fiscal systems sought from the authors over the past three decades by governments in both industrial and developing countries. Surprisingly, during these engagements almost all clients showed interest in seeking conceptual guidance and information on better practices on a broad set of similar questions. While the challenges these countries faced were somewhat similar, the solutions they discovered were often unique and local. Hence, it was felt that a book that documents these principles and practices not only would serve as a useful aid to future reform efforts but could also be of interest to the academic community in preserving such knowledge and advancing it to students and citizens at large.

The book represents more than two decades of work by the authors and their close professional associates. In particular, the authors would like to thank Sandra Roberts for her seminal contributions in updating the knowledge on fiscal federalism practices. The authors are also grateful to Scott Parris, Senior Editor at Cambridge University Press, for his encouragement for the completion of this book and to several anonymous readers for their thoughtful and incisive comments in helping improve the quality of this work. The authors are also grateful to Springer publishers for permission to reprint materials previously published in *International Tax and Public Finance* and to the World Bank for allowing us to liberally draw on works by the authors published by the World Bank.

Finally, our debt to our families for their unfailing support for this project is greater than we can express and hence, of necessity, is left unverbalized.

Robin Boadway
Anwar Shah
June 2008

PART ONE

DESIGNING FISCAL CONSTITUTIONS

Part I is concerned with division of fiscal powers in federal systems. Seven chapters are devoted to various aspects of assignment of spending, taxing, and regulatory powers among various orders of government.

Chapter 1 introduces basic concepts of federalism. It distinguishes between unitary and federal forms of constitutions and presents a stylized view of alternate models of federalism in theory and practice. It identifies the sources of inefficiency and inequity in a market economy and outlines the rational for public intervention. It argues that ultimately the assignment of powers in a federation and the optimal policies undertaken by each level of government depend on the same efficiency and equity considerations that determine the rationale for government intervention in the first place. Because federal economies consist of various autonomous jurisdictions, however, there are additional efficiency and equity considerations, some of which arise because decentralization has different effects on the fiscal capacities of different subnational jurisdictions, giving rise to fiscal inefficiencies and fiscal inequities. Others arise because of horizontal fiscal externalities, as the independent policies of governments at a given level have effects on residents or governments of neighboring jurisdictions. Still others arise when policies undertaken at a given level of government affect governments at another level, creating what are known as vertical fiscal externalities. The existence of these various effects will influence the case for decentralization, as they represent costs of decentralization that must be set against the many benefits. They will also determine the structure of fiscal arrangements that should exist between the various levels of government.

Chapter 2 is concerned with an examination of costs and benefits of decentralized governance. It evaluates the pros and cons of decentralization of spending, taxing, and regulatory responsibilities and highlights the theoretical and practical considerations and trade-offs policy makers must confront in making appropriate choices in centralization or decentralization of various service delivery responsibilities. An annex to this chapter provides a synthesis of empirical evidence on the impact of decentralization on service delivery performance and economic growth.

Chapter 3 highlights the assignment principles to guide the division of spending powers for specific services among various orders of government. It further reflects on additional problems that arise in coordinating decentralized provision of expenditure programs with national objectives. The chapter concludes by stressing that assignment of a service to a specific order of government does not necessarily imply public provision as the government could purchase such services from beyond government providers.

A common dictum to strengthen accountable, decentralized governance is to ensure that finance follows function. Chapter 4 highlights not only the principles and practices in assigning taxing powers to various jurisdictions but also the conceptual and practical difficulties in decentralizing taxing powers, especially those relating to mobile bases. It emphasizes the importance of a coordinated and harmonized tax system to ensure an internal common market and secure an economic union. It further provides guidance in achieving a harmonized tax system under decentralized governance.

Chapter 5 deals with the special issues that arise when natural resource endowments are allocated unevenly across a federation, which can cause both inefficiencies and inequities. In some federations, the problem is particularly pronounced because resource ownership resides with the subnational government. This decentralized ownership implies that resource revenues accrue directly to the subnational government, leading to potentially large net fiscal benefit differences across jurisdictions. In other countries where the federal government collects the revenues, resource-rich jurisdictions may feel that they are not getting their fair share of benefits. Of course, these tensions will be exacerbated if the federal government is perceived as using the resources unwisely or engaging in corruption. This chapter discusses public policy responses to mitigate these concerns in both unitary and federal nations, paying special attention to vertical and horizontal fiscal gaps in federal nations.

Chapter 6 is concerned with the role of local government in local governance. *Local government* refers to specific institutions or entities created to deliver a range of specified services to a relatively small geographically delineated area. *Local governance* is a broader concept and is defined as the formulation and execution of collective action at the local level. Local governance includes the diverse objectives of vibrant, living, working, and environmentally preserved self-governing communities. Good local governance is not just about providing a range of local services but also about preserving the life and liberty of residents, creating space for democratic participation and civic dialogue, supporting market-led and environmentally sustainable local development, and facilitating outcomes that enrich the quality of life of residents. The chapter is concerned with the conceptual underpinnings of the catalyst role in local governance that a local government could potentially play. It traces the evolution and analytical underpinnings of local governance as background to a better understanding of the comparative practices discussed in Chapter 7 and develops a model of local governance that integrates various strands of this literature.

Chapter 7 presents stylized models and institutions of local governance as practiced in different parts of the world during past centuries. It compares and contrasts the ancient Indian and Chinese systems of local governance with Nordic, Southern European, North American, and Australian models. The concluding section of this chapter provides a comparative overview of local government organization and finance in selected industrial and developing countries with a view to drawing lessons for future reform in developing countries.

ONE

Introduction to Federalism and the Role of Governments in Federal Economies

This monograph is a study of economic decision making by governments in a federation. A federation is simply a multilevel system of government in which different levels of government exist, each of which has some independent authority to make economic decisions within its jurisdiction. By economic decisions, we include a variety of things. Governments can acquire resources to provide public goods and services. Expenditures for these purposes can be of a current nature (e.g., hiring employees, purchasing materials) and a capital nature (e.g., buildings, infrastructure). Governments can raise revenues in order to finance services provided by the private or nonprofit sectors, such as hospitals, universities, or insurance. They can arrange to have resources redistributed among households in the economy. They can introduce regulations in the markets of the private sector so as to influence resource allocation there; or they can interfere with the pricing mechanism as an alternative way of achieving resource allocation or redistributive effects, such as through subsidizing or taxing certain activities. They can also attempt to influence the aggregate amount of activity that occurs in the economy both through budgetary actions and through changes in the amount of money and credit circulating in the economy.

BASIC CONCEPTS OF FEDERALISM

Constitutional divisions of powers among various orders of government fall into three categories: unitary, federal, and confederal.

Unitary Government

A unitary country has a single or multitiered government in which effective control of all government functions rests with the central government.

A unitary form of government facilitates centralized decision making to further national unity. It places a greater premium on uniformity and equal access to public services than it does on diversity. An overwhelming majority of countries have a unitary form of government. The city-states of Singapore and Monaco are single-tiered unitary governments. China, Egypt, France, Indonesia, Italy, Japan, Korea, New Zealand, Norway, the Philippines, Portugal, Sweden, Turkey, and the United Kingdom have multitiered governments based on unitary constitutions. Some unitary countries have decentralized responsibilities to lower orders of government (recent examples include Bolivia, Colombia, Indonesia, Italy, Korea, Japan, Peru, United Kingdom), and as a result some unitary countries (e.g., China, Denmark, Poland, Norway, and Sweden) are more fiscally decentralized than are some federal countries, such as Australia, India, and Malaysia.

Federal Government

A federal form of government has a multiorder structure, with all orders of government having some independent as well as shared decision-making responsibilities.[1] Federalism represents either a "coming together" or a "holding together" of constituent geographic units to take advantage of the greatness and smallness of nations. In a flat (globalized) world, it is increasingly apparent that "nation states are too small to tackle large things in life and too large to address small things" (Bell, 1987: 13–14). Subscribing to the "coming together" view of federalism, Daniel J. Elazar (1980) pointed out and elaborated that the word "federalism" has its roots in the Latin *foedus*, meaning "league," "treaty," or "compact." More recently, Robert Inman (2007: 530) noted that "the word 'federal' has come to represent any form of government that brings together, in an alliance, constituent governments each of which recognizes the legitimacy of an overarching central government to make decisions on some matters once exclusively the responsibility of individual member states." "Coming together" has been the guiding framework for mature federations such as the United States, Canada, and, more recently, the European Union.

---

[1] Federal countries (twenty-three in 2008) include Argentina, Australia, Austria, Belgium, Bosnia-Herzegovina, Brazil, Canada, Comoros, Ethiopia, Germany, India, Malaysia, Mexico, Micronesia, Nepal, Nigeria, Pakistan, Russia, St. Kitts and Nevis, Switzerland, United Arab Emirates, United States of America, and Venezuela. Nepal became a federal republic on May 29, 2008. In addition five more countries – Democratic Republic of Congo, Iraq, South Africa, Spain, and Sudan – have recently adopted constitutional provisions with federal features.

The alternative "holding together" view of federalism, also called "new federalism," represents an attempt to decentralize responsibilities to state-local orders of government with a view to overcoming regional and local discontent with central policies. This view is the driving force behind the current interest in principles of federalism in unitary countries and in relatively newer federations such as Brazil and India and emerging federations such as Iraq, Spain, and South Africa.

A federal form of government promotes decentralized decision making and, therefore, is conducive to greater freedom of choice, diversity of preferences in public services, political participation, innovation, and accountability.[2] It is also better adapted to handle regional conflicts. Such a system, however, is open to a great deal of duplication and confusion in areas of shared rule and requires special institutional arrangements to secure national unity, ensure regional equity, and preserve an internal common market.

Federal countries broadly conform to one of two models: *dual federalism* or *cooperative federalism*. Under dual federalism, the responsibilities of the federal and state governments are separate and distinct. According to William H. Riker (1964: 11), under such a system, (1) "two levels of government rule the same land and the people, (2) each level has at least one area of action in which it is autonomous, and (3) there is some guarantee . . . of the autonomy of each government in its own sphere." Under cooperative federalism, the responsibilities of various orders are mostly interlinked. Under both models, fiscal tiers are organized so that the national and state governments have independent authority in their areas of responsibility and act as equal partners. National and state governments often assume competitive, noncooperative roles under such an arrangement. Dual federalism takes either the *layer cake* or *coordinate-authority* approach. Under the layer cake model practiced in Mexico, Malaysia, and Russia, there is a hierarchical (unitary) type of relationship among the various orders of government. The national government is at the apex, and it has the option to deal with local governments either through state governments or more directly. Local governments do not have any constitutional status: they are simply extensions of state governments and derive their authority from state governments. In the

---

[2] Not all federal countries are decentralized and not all unitary countries are centralized. For example, Canada is highly decentralized, but Australia and Germany are centralized federations, as is indicated by the share of subnational expenditures in consolidated public expenditures. Nordic unitary countries are more decentralized than are Australia and Germany.

coordinate-authority model of dual federalism, states enjoy significant autonomy from the federal government, and local governments are simply handmaidens of the states and have little or no direct relationship with the federal government. The working of the federations of Australia, Canada, India, Pakistan, and the United States resembles the coordinate-authority model of dual federalism.

The *cooperative federalism* model has, in practice, taken three forms: interdependent spheres, marble cake, and independent spheres. In the interdependent spheres variety as practiced in Germany and South Africa (a unitary country with federal features), the federal government determines policy, and the state and local governments act as implementation agents for federally determined policies. In view of federal domination of policy making, state or provincial governments in this model have a voice in federal policy making through a second chamber (the upper house of the parliament). In Germany and South Africa, the second-order (state) governments are represented in the upper house of the national parliament (the Bundesrat and the Council of the Provinces, respectively). In the marble cake model of cooperative federalism, various orders of government have overlapping and shared responsibilities, and all constituent governments are treated as equal partners in the federation. Belgium, with its three territorial and four linguistic jurisdictions, has a strong affinity with this approach. Finally, in a model of cooperative federalism with independent spheres of government, all orders of government enjoy autonomous and equal status and coordinate their policies horizontally and vertically. Brazil is the only federation practicing this form of federalism.

The *competitive federalism* model is a theoretical construct advanced by the fiscal federalism literature (Salmon, 2006; Breton, 2006; Kenyon and Kincaid, 1991) and not yet practiced anywhere in its pure form. According to this construct, all orders of government should have overlapping responsibilities, and they should compete both vertically and horizontally to establish their clientele of services. Some analysts argue that such a competitive framework would create leaner and more efficient governments that would be more responsive and accountable to people.

Countries with a federal form of government vary considerably in terms of federal influence on subnational governments. Such influence is very strong in Australia, Germany, India, Malaysia, Mexico, and Pakistan; moderately strong in Nigeria and the United States; and weak in Brazil, Canada, and Switzerland. In the last group of countries, national control over subnational expenditures is quite limited, and subnational governments have considerable authority to determine their own tax bases and tax rates.

In centralized federations, conditional grants by the federal government play a large role in influencing the priorities of the state and local governments. In Australia, a centralized federation, the federal government is constitutionally required to follow regionally differentiated policies.

Federal countries also vary according to subnational influence on national policies. In some countries, there is a clear separation of national and subnational institutions ("executive" or "interstate" federalism), and the two orders interact through meetings of officials and ministers, as in Australia and Canada. In Germany and South Africa, state or provincial governments have a direct voice in national institutions ("intrastate" federalism). In the United States, regional and local coalitions play an important role in the Congress. In some federal countries, constitutional provisions require all legislation to recognize that ultimate power rests with the people. For example, all legislation in Canada must conform to the Canadian Charter of Rights and Freedoms. In Switzerland, a confederation by law but a federal country in practice, major legislative changes require approval by referendum. Such direct-democracy provisions indirectly reinforce the decentralized provisions of public services. In all federal countries, local government influences on the federal and state governments remain uninstitutionalized and weak.

Asymmetric Federalism

Countries with a federal form of governance do not necessarily treat second orders of government in a uniform manner. They often offer flexibility in accommodating the special needs or demands of constituent units or impose a federal will in certain jurisdictions. This adaptability may take the form of treating some members as less equal than others. For example, Chechnya in Russia and Kashmir in India enjoy lesser autonomy than do other *oblasts* and states; or the federation may treat some members as more equal than others by giving them wider powers, as is the case with Sabah and Sarawak in Malaysia and Quebec in Canada. Some federations offer constituent units freedom of choice to be unequal or more equal than others through opting in or out of federal arrangements. Such options are part of the arrangements offered by Canada, Spanish agreements, and the European Union's treaty exceptions for the United Kingdom and Denmark (see Watts, 1999).

Market Preserving Federalism

Barry Weingast (2006) has advanced a theoretical concept for comparative analyses of federal systems. Market-preserving federalism is put forth as an ideal form of federal system in which (1) multiple governments have clearly delineated responsibilities; (2) subnational governments have primary authority over public goods and services for local autonomy; (3) the federal government preserves the internal common market; (4) all governments face the financial consequences of their decisions (hard budget constraints); and (5) political authority is institutionalized.

Confederal Government

In a confederal system, the general government serves as the agent of the member units, usually without independent taxing and spending powers. The United States had a confederal system from 1781 to 1787. The United Nations, the European Union, and the Commonwealth of Independent States (CIS), which now consists of eleven of the former republics of the Union of Soviet Socialist Republics (USSR), approximate the confederal form of government. A confederal system suits communities that are internally homogeneous but, as a group, completely heterogeneous. The European Union, however, over time has consistently moved to assume a federal role.

Role of Government in Federal Economies

The instruments that governments use to undertake their economic activities include, broadly speaking, the following:

- *Expenditures on goods and services.* Governments may purchase labor, capital, goods, and services from the private sector in order to provide goods and services to their constituents. Such major expenditure categories as defense spending, transportation, schools, and hospitals are included in their menu of goods and services expenditures. In some cases, the public sector actually produces the goods or services. In others, it merely finances their provision by private producers or the nonprofit sector.
- *Transfers to individuals or households.* Government spending also includes transfer payments. These can be provided to households in the economy, for example, in the form of welfare payments, payments for disability, and payments to the elderly. These transfers might be administered through the tax system or through an agency responsible for delivering them to their intended recipients.
- *Subsidies to firms.* A particular form of transfer is a subsidy to firms in the private sector, whose purpose is typically to assist the firm's participation in the private sector in ways that facilitate government objectives.

- *Transfers to other levels of government.* In a federation, transfers can also be from one level of government to another. Most commonly, intergovernmental transfers go from higher-level to lower-level governments, but in some cases they go the other way.
- *Taxation.* Governments can, and do, use a wide assortment of taxes to raise revenues, such as individual and corporate income taxes, general sales taxes, payroll taxes, excise taxes, import and export duties, and property and wealth taxes, to name the main ones. Different levels of government may have access to different taxes and may share some tax bases.
- *User fees.* Revenues may be raised from charges that are related to services provided. Examples include water, garbage, and sewage charges; road tolls; licenses of various sorts imposed on individuals and businesses; user fees for parks and recreational facilities; fines; and charges for health and education services.
- *Borrowing.* In addition to raising revenues from taxation and charges, governments typically borrow money, especially but not exclusively for capital projects. Because the borrowed funds must be paid back in the future, they can also be viewed as postponed taxes. Lower levels of government may be restricted in what they are able to borrow.
- *Money creation.* Governments, through their central banks, may also be able to obtain some revenues through the creation of money. To the extent that the creation of money induces inflation (i.e., the money supply grows more rapidly than that needed to meet the growth in the volume of transactions in the economy), it is viewed by economists as being analogous to a tax, in this case a tax on holding money. Control of the money supply, however, is typically not seen primarily as a source of revenues but as a means of controlling the movement of aggregate economic activity by affecting interest and exchange rates.
- *Regulation.* Regulation is a nonbudgetary way of influencing the allocation of resources. It can take many different forms, including labor market regulation (hours of work, union formation, discrimination laws, occupational licensing, rules for layoffs, worker safety, etc.), capital market regulation (asset or liability rules for institutions, bankruptcy laws, insider trading rules, accounting requirements, etc.), and the regulation of goods and services markets (product liability, advertising rules, price and profit regulation for large firms, competition laws, communications regulations, environmental laws, regulation of natural resources such as fishing and forestry, etc.). In a federation, one level of government may have some regulatory control over another. An upper-level government may be able to override or disallow the

legislation of a lower-level government. It may also be able to impose mandates on the lower level of government, forcing it to provide certain types of services for its constituents.

- *Public corporations.* Governments may also engage directly in business-like activities, operating public firms that produce goods and services for sale to the public in industries that might be considered of national importance or in which it is felt that private competitive markets would not prevail. Some examples of such industries include transportation, communications, utilities, and aircraft production.

The ultimate concern in studying the economics of federations is how these various public-sector activities are to be divided among, or assigned to, governments. Which ones should be decentralized to lower levels? Which ones should be retained at the center? Which activities should be jointly undertaken? How should the division of responsibilities be written into the constitution? What influence, if any, should one level of government be able to exert on other levels? What institutional arrangements should be used to facilitate the interaction among levels of government? These are the sorts of questions that subsequent chapters address. They encompass what in fiscal federalism are referred to as the *assignment problem* – the assignment of taxation, expenditure, and regulatory responsibilities to various levels of government – and the *fiscal arrangements* – the design of intergovernmental fiscal relations. The key issue here concerns the optimal degree of decentralization of various public-sector decisions, an issue that we take up in the next chapter.

The assignment of functions is, of course, conditional on the sorts of roles undertaken by the public sector and also on the objectives of government intervention in the first place. It is worth beginning with a general discussion of the role of governments in a market economy and the special problems for governments that arise in a federal economy.

GOVERNMENT INTERVENTION IN A MARKET ECONOMY

The merits of leaving economic decisions to the private sector in a market economy have been well documented and are widely accepted by most economists. The argument is as follows. The decentralized nature of these private decisions and the competitive setting in which they are taken both contribute to efficiency in resource allocation. Moreover, the convention of private property and the right to the rewards from the use of one's person and property mean that there will be an incentive for such property to be put to its most productive use. In other words, the profit motive will typically have socially beneficial effects, rewarding effort and efficiency to the extent that it is allowed to proceed unfettered.

From this point of view, a necessary condition for government intervention in the market economy must be some form of *market failure*. Government intervention is called for when the benefits of collective decision making outweigh the losses from decentralized individual decision making. Whether intervention will be beneficial in any given circumstances will be a matter of judgment. For one thing, in the event that the private sector yields inefficient outcomes, there is no guarantee that the public sector can do any better. That is, there may be *public-sector failure* as well as market failure. For another, a main source of market failure involves the perceived unfairness of market outcomes. Different persons will disagree on the extent to which redistributive goals are important and on the extent to which governments can succeed in achieving them. Because redistribution is one of the key functions of government, this leads to disagreements over the role of government in the economy.

The usefulness of government intervention can be viewed from a *normative* or from a *positive* perspective. The normative point of view is unabashedly idealistic. It investigates how governments *ought* to act if they are acting in an ethical or benevolent manner, faithfully abiding by the wishes of their constituents. To the extent that governments do not actually behave ethically, the normative perspective can lead to overly optimistic views of the benefits of government intervention. It also suffers from an ambiguity as to what constitutes ethical behavior, or an ethical objective function, of government. Because ethics involves value judgments, different persons will disagree over what the government should strive to attain, especially when it comes to redistributive objectives. Moreover, if different persons do differ over what constitutes appropriate social preferences, it is generally not possible to find a political procedure that will reconcile them. It is a well-known result in welfare economics – Arrow's impossibility theorem – that individual preferences over social orderings cannot be aggregated into a single social preference ordering that satisfies certain seemingly innocuous requirements.[3]

---

[3] The requirements are: individual preferences over social outcomes are ordinal and non-comparable and come from an unrestricted domain (any preference orderings are permissible); the weak Pareto principle applies (if all households are better off in state A than in state B, state A must be socially preferred); the independence of irrelevant alternatives holds (the social ranking of two states is independent of the availability or ranking of other states); and no one individual's preferences (who is then effectively a "dictator") must determine social orderings.

Nonetheless, the normative framework constitutes a useful benchmark against which to judge government intervention. It can be thought of as the framework suitable for the policy adviser who wants to remove himself from the day-to-day political pressures of policy making and provide sound scientifically based policy advice. To provide such policy advice, one must necessarily adopt a normative criterion, especially with respect to equity or redistributive objectives and how to trade them off against possible conflicts with efficiency. For the purposes of this study, we adopt what can be viewed as a reasonably weak set of ethical judgments. One need not agree upon the exact degree of redistribution that governments should undertake to agree that some should be undertaken. As long as one is willing to accept certain minimal ethical judgments, one can use normative analysis fruitfully. These minimal judgments are sufficient to ensure that society has some redistributive motive. That is, there is some desire to redistribute from the better-off to the less well-off. Thus, if one accepts individualism (the primacy of individual preferences), the Pareto principle, the independence of irrelevant alternatives, the premise that all households should be treated anonymously and symmetrically (i.e., all persons should be treated alike – or given equal weight – regardless of their identity), and the premise that reducing inequality at least to some extent is a good thing, one is justified in evaluating social outcomes using a notional social welfare function that is increasing, symmetric and quasi concave in utilities. We have little need to use the formulation of a social welfare function in our discussion, but the value judgments we use as a basis for rationalizing redistributive arguments can best be understood by having a notional social welfare function of this sort in the back of our minds. A social welfare function that ranks alternatives solely on the basis of the utilities achieved by individuals in the society is referred to as a *welfaristic* social welfare function. It neglects nonutility aspects of different social states such as freedom of speech and religion, justice, and so on, except as they are reflected in levels of utility. These principles are obviously important, but it is assumed that their pursuit can be fostered independently of welfaristic objectives.[4]

We take it that there is wide enough agreement on these ethical premises to warrant using normative analysis in studying fiscal federalism. The exact form of the social welfare function that motivates us is not something that

---

[4] There is a vast literature on social welfare functions. For a nontechnical exposition, see Boadway and Bruce (1984). The argument that nonwelfaristic objectives should be important in formulating economic policy may be found in Sen (1977).

need concern us as long as we agree on its general features, as depicted here. The main open question concerns the degree of tolerance for inequality of real income levels, referred to as "inequality aversion" in the literature.[5] The degree of inequality aversion displayed by political decision makers is relevant both for the extent of government intervention in the economy and for the desired degree of decentralization. It is also one of the main sources of disagreement over the role of government in the economy, as will become apparent. Despite that, we can go a long way to discussing alternative approaches to fiscal federalism without specifying the exact amount of inequality aversion (as long as it is not negative).

The social welfare function perspective outlined here contains one further feature that is of immense importance in fiscal federalism. We have supposed that a social welfare objective should be symmetric and anonymous, so all persons are treated on a par. In a federal setting, this implies that all persons should be given equal weight *regardless of where they reside*. In a heterogeneous federation with differing degrees of well-being in different regions, this can be a contentious principle to abide by and apply in practice. However, we might regard this principle of equal weighting of all persons in the social welfare function as being a reflection of citizenship in a nation. It turns out that the equal weighting principle will be an extremely important consideration in designing a system of fiscal arrangements in a decentralized federation. Its acceptance necessarily involves a value judgment and is therefore a principle with which others may disagree.

The normative perspective is concerned mainly with the specification of the objective function that society should use to guide resource allocation and consequently with the relevant extent of redistribution. In our context, it is also used to suggest the appropriate assignment of responsibilities among the different levels of government. However, it is one thing to say what governments should do, and another to describe what they actually do. That is where the positive perspective comes in. It tempers the optimism about what can be expected from governments by emphasizing the ways in which government behavior can depart from that of a purely benevolent institution. The positive theory of government behavior is still far from complete, and one cannot use it for definitive answers. In

---

[5] Aversion to inequality can be framed in terms of utility levels or income levels. Even if there is no aversion to inequality in utility levels, there might still be aversion to inequality of income levels. For example, suppose the social welfare function is utilitarian: $W = \sum U(Yi)$, where Yi is real income. As long as the utility function $U(Yi)$ is strictly concave, there will be positive aversion to inequality in incomes, even though there is no aversion to inequality in utilities.

judging how actual government behavior departs from the ideal, there are two general types of considerations to take into account. One concerns the consequences of actual voting procedures as ways of taking collective decisions. The other involves inefficiencies of decision making within the bureaucracy of government.

In an ideal world, voting, as a means of taking collective decisions, should not necessarily be inconsistent with social welfare optimization. After all, social preferences should be based on the social values of individuals in the society. If persons vote according to their ethical values, there is no reason to second-guess the normative consequences that result, including the extent of redistribution that persons vote for. However, there are various ways in which voting outcomes, even in an ideal setting of direct democracy, can cause inefficient or inequitable outcomes. For one thing, majority voting is prone to giving intransitive orderings, which can translate into cyclical outcomes (the so-called Condorcet paradox), especially when more than one issue is being voted on at the same time. It also occurs when redistributive issues are at stake. As is explained later, when majority voting does lead to a unique outcome, it corresponds with the preferences of the median voter, typically with inefficient results. These are purely technical problems with majority voting, and they might not be as destructive as they first appear. The problems of cyclical majorities can be overcome to some extent by systems of representative democracy where voting takes place not issue by issue but over party platforms that consist of an aggregation of issues. The uncertain nature of voting outcomes can also reduce the chances of unstable voting outcomes, as the literature on probabilistic voting has shown.[6] However, voting systems are often far from ideal, especially in systems of representative democracy where ultimate decision-making authority rests with a small number of elected officials. The votes of elected officials, instead of truly representing their constituents, might be influenced by various forms of influence seeking, ranging from lobbying and log rolling to rent seeking and outright corruption, such as vote purchasing. In these circumstances, it is not at all obvious that the collective decisions of elected parliaments will correspond with the citizens' notions of ethical social orderings. For our purposes, this must be seen as a constraint on public-sector decision making that cannot be ignored.

The other main consequence of government decision making concerns the way in which collective decisions are implemented by the public sector.

---

[6] See, for example, the discussion in Mueller (1989) and the more recent analysis of it by Hettich and Winer (1999).

The latter constitutes a large bureaucracy that is not constrained or disciplined by the profit motive and free entry as in the private sector. Bureaucrats may be motivated largely by self-interest and may be hard to rein in. It may be difficult to monitor their effort and the use they make of resources, as well as their actual need for them. And, as with elected officials, they may be susceptible to the influences of rent seekers, lobbyists, influence peddlers, and so on. It is not hard to understand why some persons might adopt a pessimistic view of bureaucratic decision making and influence, the most extreme of which is the Leviathan model of the public sector whereby the objective of the bureaucracy is to maximize its size.[7]

Unfortunately, empirical evidence about the inefficiency and motives of the public sector is minimal. Much is based on opinion and conjecture rather than hard fact. Nonetheless, the possibility of significant inefficiency in the public sector and the consequent limits of public-sector benevolence is something that must be heeded in choosing among alternative degrees of decentralization within a federation. This is especially true in developing countries where the constraints imposed by electoral processes may not be as well established as in industrialized democracies, and where bureaucracies may be both less experienced in dealing with the complex issues facing public sectors and more susceptible to corrupting and rent-seeking influences. In addition, the administrative expertise may not currently exist at lower levels of government for undertaking what might otherwise be desirable amounts of decentralized decision making.

Given these caveats, it is still worth looking at the role of government from the benchmark of a normative perspective and then conditioning our views by taking a more positive perspective. The normative, or social welfare, perspective leads to identifying two general reasons for intervention, which correspond to two types of market failure. In turn, these two types of market failure correspond to two conceptually different steps involved in reaching the highest level of social welfare. The first is ensuring that the economy is operating on its *utility possibilities frontier*, that is, operating with economic efficiency. This requires seeing that gains from trade are exploited to the fullest extent possible consistent with the resources, technology, and constraints facing society. These constraints involve both institutional and informational constraints. We refer to this as the *efficiency* objective of economic policy. The second is ensuring that the "best" point on society's utility possibility frontier – that is, the point that yields the highest level of social welfare – is collectively chosen. This is

---

[7]   Brennan and Buchanan (1980) put this view most emphatically.

the *equity* objective of economic policy, because it involves making interpersonal comparisons of well-being. Moving along society's utility possibilities frontier necessarily involves making some persons better off and others worse off. This is a major part of what government policies do, so we must devote due attention to it.

The outcomes generated by a market economy alone will generally fail to satisfy both the efficiency and the equity objectives of policy; hence, there exists a potential role for government intervention. These failures are related to the failure of the so-called two fundamental theorems of welfare economics, which summarize the strengths of the competitive market mechanism.[8] The first theorem of welfare economics states that, in a certain set of idealized circumstances, private markets, if operating competitively, will yield a Pareto-efficient allocation of resources. That is, they will yield a point on the utility possibilities frontier where it is not possible to make one person better off without making someone else worse off. The second theorem of welfare economics states that any Pareto-optimal allocation of resources (i.e., any point on society's utility possibilities frontier) can be achieved by the competitive market mechanism combined with a suitable redistribution of resources among households.

It will be useful for our subsequent discussion of the assignment problem in federations to mention briefly some of the more prominent sources of inefficiency and inequity in the market economy. These market failures are the ultimate sources of the normative rationale for government intervention. We consider efficiency failures and equity failures in turn. This discussion can be brief because most of these items are well known from the public economics literature.[9] We can then spend more time considering the special problems of inefficiency and inequity in a federal setting.

Sources of Inefficiency in the Market Economy

Broadly speaking, inefficiencies occur because all opportunities for gains from trade have not been exploited to the fullest. This can be for technical reasons (e.g., having to do with the characteristics of goods), for institutional reasons (e.g., the nature and limitations of contracts), for informational reasons, or simply because of the inability of markets to coordinate properly the demand and supply sides of the market. A conventional list of types of inefficiencies is as follows.

---

[8] The notion of the two fundamental theorems can be attributed to Arrow (1951).
[9] See, for example, Atkinson and Stiglitz (1980) and Boadway and Wildasin (1984).

Public Goods

Public goods are those characterized by jointness of consumption and, in some cases, by nonexcludability. Jointness implies that more than one person can "consume" or obtain the benefits of the same good at the same time. Nonexcludability means that persons cannot be excluded from using the good, except perhaps at a high cost. The concept might apply both to consumer goods and to goods used as producer inputs. The standard examples of the former might be defense and foreign affairs, including foreign aid. Public producer inputs might include meteorological information and knowledge more generally. Nonexcludability leads to the free-rider problem – persons will have no incentive to pay for the use of the good if they cannot be excluded from using it in any case. Because of the free-rider problem, markets cannot be relied on to provide efficient amounts of public goods.

Although the existence of public goods is the standard rationale for government intervention in the public finance literature, relatively little of actual government expenditures are on public goods as such. Recognition of this is important for the assignment problem in federalism. Much of the traditional literature on fiscal federalism has focused on the provision of public goods as being the fundamental purpose of government expenditures. The case for decentralizing public expenditures then revolves around characterizing public goods whose benefits are limited either by geographic proximity, in which case they are referred to as *local or state public goods*, or by congestion (so that benefits per capita fall as the number of users increases), in which case they are *club goods*. Both cases of public goods are relevant for the assignment of functions because they might better be delivered at lower levels of government.[10] However, once it is recognized that government expenditures are much broader than spending on public goods, the relevance of this source of market failure diminishes in importance both as a rationale for government intervention and as a determinant of the appropriate degree of decentralization.

Externalities

Externalities might be viewed as resulting from a more limited form of publicness. They arise as special consequences of the joint consumption property in which private economic agents undertake activities that have benefits or costs for others without being priced. The absence of pricing

---

[10] The classic formulation of the assignment problem based on the local nature of public goods may be found in Breton (1965). See also Musgrave (1959) and Oates (1972, 2005).

reflects the fact that affected parties cannot be excluded easily from the benefits or costs of the activity in question. Typical examples include pollution, worker training, new knowledge acquired through research and development, and traffic congestion. Recent literature on growth theory – so-called endogenous growth theory – has also stressed externalities that might occur in a dynamic setting as a result of investment decisions. New knowledge may accompany new investment, and the benefits of this knowledge may not be fully appropriable to the investing firms. Similarly, on-the-job training and learning-by-doing may occur as firms produce over long periods of time. And the productivity of firms that deal with one another may be enhanced by the existence of larger concentrations of types of firms leading to so-called agglomeration and network externalities.

Governments may respond to the existence of externalities in various ways. They may assume responsibility for the provision of goods and services generating externalities (basic research, worker training). They may use corrective mechanisms such as taxes or subsidies of the private agents emitting the externalities, or they may impose quantity regulations on private agents (pollution controls). Because many externalities are limited geographically, decentralization of their control to lower levels of government is a possibility.

A more contentious type of externality that is sometimes said to arise from market activity concerns its perceived effects on social values. Thus, various societies might be concerned with the effect of certain types of products or private-sector activities on their culture or language, on their way of life, on the well-being of certain segments of the population (e.g., children, workers), on their health, or on the quality of their environment. There are thus a number of regulations in place to deal with these perceived effects. Examples include language legislation, product standards, labor regulations, and so on. These measures can be particularly important in multigovernment settings, especially where one government imposes regulations that can affect the activities of citizens in other jurisdictions. They will often result in restrictions on the free flow of products and factors of production across borders that might be interpreted as measures to protect local firms and workers. This outcome will be as important in federalism contexts as it is in international ones.

Economies of Scale
The minimum-cost output for a good or service may be large relative to the market being served, in which case competition will not prevail. In

these circumstances, firms might not be price takers, and free entry may not occur either because of the natural barriers to entry imposed owing to size or because of artificial barriers to entry imposed by existing firms (and/or government regulations). Private provision might result in an inefficiently low level of output and the existence of positive profits. Governments themselves may undertake to provide the good or service, either alone or in competition with the private sector, in an effort to attain a more efficient level of output; or they may regulate private provision by stipulating prices or rates of return that can be earned. Examples of each of these remedies may be found in industries like transportation, utilities, and communications in various countries.

Unemployed Resources

Problems of coordination in some markets, such as labor and capital markets, may cause resources to be unemployed. In the case of labor, the matching of skills to jobs might entail search processes that are inefficient, or imperfections in the ability to monitor their workers might lead firms to use the threat of unemployment as a device to discipline their workers. Such a threat is actualized by setting wages above their market-clearing levels at their efficiency wage levels.[11] With capital, many investments tend to be indivisible and to have benefits that are dependent upon investments taken elsewhere in activities that are interrelated. Thus, the suitability of any given investment project depends upon the others being undertaken. To the extent that investment decisions are taken independently, the wrong mix of projects could occur, with the result that there may be too much of one type of capital and too little of another.

Some literature indicates how these inefficiencies may be mitigated by government policies, such as unemployment insurance, wage or investment subsidies, or macroeconomic policies. However, there is considerable disagreement about the effectiveness of government policies for these purposes. Nonetheless, most governments tend to engage in them.

Absence of Markets

In some cases, the markets for engaging in certain types of trades simply do not exist, perhaps because there are not enough transactions to justify them, the objects being traded do not have enough homogeneity, or the

---

[11] The inefficiency of search unemployment levels was pointed out by Diamond (1981). Shapiro and Stiglitz (1984) have analyzed the inefficiency of unemployment with efficiency wages. A related source of inefficiency involves setting wages at too high a level to reduce costly turnover (Salop, 1979).

transactions costs are simply too high. A good example of this is the market for risk. Markets may simply be too thin both to trade away all possible diversifiable risks and to facilitate the trading of nondiversifiable risks among agents with differing aversions to risk. On the other hand, it may be that some forms of risk are induced by government action itself. For example, the absence of efficient private markets in unemployment insurance may be a result of the fact that the event being insured against – unemployment – may be at least partly under the control of the government. This can make unemployment an uninsurable risk.[12]

Limitations in the possibility to trade risks may also be of relevance in a federalism context. Regional jurisdictions may face the prospect of region-specific shocks that may or may not be diversifiable across other jurisdictions. If perfect markets do not exist for trading these risks with the other jurisdictions, forming a federation provides one way of facilitating such trading. Indeed, one of the roles of the federal government might be precisely to spread region-specific risks across component lower-level governments.

Imperfect Information

Markets may be inefficient because of asymmetric information problems. The two most common forms are moral hazard and adverse selection. *Moral hazard* refers to a situation in which one side of the market can take actions that affect the market outcome but that cannot be observed by the other side. Market outcomes will then involve a nonoptimal amount of such actions (at least when compared with what could be achieved given full information). *Adverse selection* occurs when participants on one side of the market differ from one another in some characteristics that are not observable to the other side. Such markets are also known to yield inefficient outcomes and perhaps even to preclude equilibrium outcomes.[13] These problems can occur in a wide variety of markets. Examples include the nonobservability of skills and effort in labor markets, imperfect knowledge about the underlying productivity of firms in capital or credit markets, the absence of knowledge about the quality of durable products, and the inability to distinguish high-risk persons from low-risk ones in insurance markets.

---

[12] See Boadway and Marceau (1994) for a model that demonstrates this possibility and the resulting need for public unemployment insurance.

[13] For a general discussion of moral hazard and adverse selection problems, see Hirshleifer and Riley (1992).

The general consensus in the literature is that in most cases, governments have little or no informational advantage over private-sector participants and therefore can do little to improve on the inefficiency of private markets. Given this, the government may be no more efficient at providing such things as health insurance and unemployment compensation than the private sector. On the other hand, mandating the purchase of insurance may be welfare improving in circumstances in which markets might not otherwise exist.[14] Still, governments commonly do provide (or finance) certain forms of insurance (health, disability, workers' compensation, unemployment insurance, etc.). However, this is more likely motivated by equity, or social insurance, concerns. Later, we consider equity arguments for the widespread tendency for these benefits to be publicly provided.

Time Inconsistency Issues

The preceding arguments for government intervention rely on the failure of private markets to allocate resources efficiently. To the extent that governments are benevolent and well informed, corrective policies could in principle be efficiency improving. There is, however, one type of circumstance in which even a fully benevolent and well-informed government might implement policies that lead to outcomes that are highly inefficient. It is worth considering this case because it in turn leads to a case for other policies that would otherwise seem unjustified. The circumstance can be briefly described as follows. Households and firms make decisions with both a long-term and a short-term impact. In the case of households, long-term decisions include savings, investment in human capital, and the purchase of durables. For firms, they include a multitude of investment decisions, such as investment in machinery and buildings. Farsighted governments, in setting their policies, would take due account of the effects of those policies on the long-run incentives of households and firms. For example, taxes on capital would not be set too high for fear that it would discourage capital accumulation and savings. But suppose governments cannot commit themselves to future policies. In these circumstances, governments will have the opportunity to change their policies after at least some households and firms have already made some long-run decisions: they have accumulated wealth or undertaken investments. Because these decisions have already been made, governments no longer need to worry about the disincentive effects of their policies. Even fully benevolent governments will not be able

---

[14] See, for example, Dahlby (1981). He shows that this will be the case if households are able to purchase voluntary supplements to compulsory insurance.

to resist imposing high taxes on existing wealth. Moreover, households and firms will correctly anticipate this in making their long-run choices. Expecting taxes on capital income to be high, they will restrict their investments accordingly. In the end, taxes on wealth and capital will be too high, and investment and savings will be too low.

Recognizing that this kind of problem of time inconsistency exists can go some way to explaining some of the policy phenomena observed in the real world. One is the tendency for taxes on capital and wealth to be higher than standard theory would predict that they should be. Another is to observe policies that can be explained as reasonable responses to the time inconsistency problem. There are significant examples of these outcomes. Up-front investment incentives, such as tax holidays, investment tax credits, and investment subsidies are widely used and could be interpreted as mechanisms for undoing the adverse consequences of high capital tax rates. Indeed, this is one of the few plausible explanations for observing the simultaneous existence of high capital tax rates and generous investment incentives in the same tax system. Systems of mandatory saving for retirement as well as mandatory education can also be explained on these terms. More generally, mandatory saving and mandatory insurance purchases can be interpreted as being in place to counter an opposite form of time inconsistency – that involving coming to the assistance of persons in distress as opposed to taxing those who have accumulated wealth. This is referred to as the Samaritan's dilemma problem. Persons who have the opportunity to take measures that will improve their prospects later in life are deterred from doing so because they anticipate that government will come to their assistance in the event that they become needy.[15]

This problem of time inconsistency is of relevance for federalism for two reasons. First, many of the policy instruments that might be seen as responses to time inconsistency issues, such as forms of social insurance, are often delivered by subnational levels of government. Second, a Samaritan's dilemma–type problem – or a *bailout problem* – can exist between levels of government. If a lower level of government knows that it will receive transfers from an upper level in the event that its fiscal resources fall below some standard level, it will have an incentive to exploit that possibility by making decisions that effectively increase the possibility of receiving federal assistance. This possibility explains, for example, why there may be significant restrictions of the ability of lower levels of government to borrow.

---

[15] Bruce and Waldman (1991) pointed out this motivation for either mandated or publicly provided social insurance.

Sources of Inequity in the Market Economy

Most public expenditure programs have an equity dimension to them, especially those in industrialized countries with their vast array of social programs. In fact, many important public programs are motivated primarily by equity concerns. One can think of three general sorts of redistributive spending programs – those intended to redress income inequality resulting from the ordinary workings of markets (inequality of outcome), those based on providing more equal opportunities to succeed (inequality of opportunity), and those based on compensating for inequality resulting from nonincome attributes or characteristics of different persons (social insurance). Governments address these three sorts of redistribution through a wide variety of policy instruments, some of which are intended to serve more than one goal. Consider each of the three types of redistribution in turn.

Unequal Incomes

The most obvious manifestation of inequity in a market economy is inequality in the distribution of incomes. Differences in the incomes obtained from participating in the market economy arise from many different sources, including natural abilities, inheritances, accumulated human capital, work effort, and luck in the marketplace. Virtually all economies attempt to redress income inequalities by redistributive policies of various sorts, through both money transfers and in-kind transfers.

Apart from the desired amount of redistribution being a matter of value judgment, redistribution based on income alone (and administered through the income tax system with its self-reporting approach) is of limited usefulness in achieving equity objectives. For one thing, income is a rather imperfect measure of economic well-being because, for example, it does not reflect nonmarket sources of utility such as leisure and household production. For another, individuals can readily manipulate their income for tax purposes by varying their behavior or by concealment. The main message to be taken from the extensive theoretical literature on the optimal income tax is that redistribution by income levels is a relatively limited policy instrument that needs to be supplemented by other instruments, such as targeted transfers based on need and employability, targeted in-kind transfers (e.g., housing, food stamps), and the provision of universal public services such as education.[16] Indeed,

---

[16] The usefulness of various policy instruments for redistributive purposes is fully discussed in Boadway and Keen (2000).

combined with a tax system that is only moderately redistributive or even approximately proportional, cash and in-kind transfers – whether targeted or universal – can make overall fiscal policy quite redistributive.

Equal Opportunities

Some of the attributes that determine incomes earned and therefore individual well-being are not immutable. The most obvious of these are labor market skills. Governments invest considerable amounts of resources into upgrading labor market skills, often on a universal basis. Universal public education is the most obvious of these, but others include labor market training, programs for developing entrepreneurship, and equal opportunity programs. One could even say that public health programs contribute to one's productivity in the marketplace. Most of these expenditures are on public services of a private nature and delivered to individuals. Thus, they are essentially like private goods and services delivered by the public sector outside the price system. We follow the common convention of referring to them as quasi-private goods. Bewley (1981) has referred to them as "public services" to distinguish them from public goods (which have the joint consumption property). We follow this convention as well.

The fact that the public sector is heavily engaged in providing essentially private goods and services to individuals turns out to be especially relevant for the extent of decentralization of the public sector to lower levels of government. It is often precisely these sorts of expenditures that are decentralized to subnational levels of government. At the same time, they are expenditure programs whose objectives are based on equity considerations, so they are of some interest nationally.

Social Insurance

In fact, there are differences between the abilities of individuals to earn income that are at least as important as sources of inequality in utility levels, and that can be, and are, used as bases for redistributive policies. Examples include health status, employment status, disability, location of residence, and date of birth. The characteristics possessed by each person are largely a matter of luck at birth. Redistribution based on these features is sometimes referred to as social insurance. If persons could purchase insurance against being unlucky in these characteristics, they would. Moreover, on actuarial grounds, such insurance would be to a considerable extent diversifiable. But persons obviously cannot buy such insurance because it could be purchased only after the event being insured against is revealed. Thus, they can be "insured" only after the fact by the public sector. The case for such social insurance must ultimately rest on a value judgment. But, as long as society's objective function exhibits some aversion to inequality, such social insurance should be provided.

This social insurance rationale might be viewed as the prime justification for public health insurance, unemployment insurance, assistance to the disabled, intergenerational transfers in favor of unlucky cohorts, and so on. These elements, too, make up a substantial proportion of public-sector budgets. And, because they tend to comprise services delivered to individuals rather than public goods, the decentralization of their delivery is a viable option to be considered, as we argue in the next chapter.

The recognition that there is a limit to the extent of redistribution that can be achieved through the income-based tax-transfer system, and that a substantial part of actual redistribution is achieved through the provision of targeted transfers, in-kind public services, and social insurance based on other personal characteristics, has important implications for an appreciation of the role of government and of the assignment of functions. For one thing, it helps explain why most studies of tax incidence, even those based on imperfect measures such as income, tend to show that taxes are only mildly redistributive. For another, it leads one to recognize that much of what governments actually do is redistributive in nature, if not in intent. The implication of this for the division of powers then depends upon one's view about what level of government should be responsible for redistributive measures.

Political Economy Considerations

The discussion so far relies on normative arguments about the role of government. Different persons will have very different views about how closely actual governments come to being benevolent social welfare maximizers, or whether they even take equity into account at all. The issue is difficult to resolve using casual observation. For one thing, governments are observed to do many sorts of things that are hard to justify on normative grounds, including regulatory activities, the subsidization and protection of certain activities, and the provision of certain goods and services that the private sector could provide more efficiently. Thus, far from being the social welfare maximizers of normative public economics, government decision makers may be controlled by self-interested bureaucrats or vote-maximizing politicians with relatively little interest in social welfare. On the other hand, it is also true that it would be very difficult to explain the extent of redistribution that takes place through the tax-transfer system, social insurance, social welfare programs, and in-kind transfers solely on the basis of a government representing the selfish interests of the majority or of rent-seeking interest groups. In fact, there is an entire spectrum of possibilities, ranging from the fully benevolent government to one that is purely selfish. The point on the spectrum chosen depends jointly on the preferences people express through their voting behavior and on how well political decisions take voters' preferences into account. Some well-known points on the spectrum are as follows.

Ethical Voting

It might be presumed that people vote according to their ethical preferences rather than their own self-interest. For example, it is well known that, from a purely private point of view, the act of voting is itself irrational. One way to explain voting behavior is by supposing that it is done without self-interest in mind.[17] To the extent that governments actually behave according to voters' preferences, this would imply that looking at them as social welfare maximizers has an element of truth to it. This sort of explanation would be consistent with the seemingly massive redistribution programs actually observed in the modern welfare state, which, as we have mentioned, are difficult to explain solely in terms of vote maximization or the self-interest of bureaucrats.

Altruistic Preferences

A milder form of equity is obtained by assuming that, though persons vote selfishly rather than ethically, their preferences include altruism toward the less well-off. This possibility would give rise to an exploitation of Pareto-improving transfers. Undoubtedly, altruism is a powerful motive, and one that could be used to explain redistribution undertaken by the public sector. Whether it can account for the full amount that one observes in practice would be difficult to determine. At the same time, from the perspective of recommending institutional arrangements for a federation, it does not really matter. Virtually all the normative analysis that we employ works equally well if the normative basis for the preferences in question is altruism rather than some social welfare function reflecting ethical preferences.

The Selfish Voter

If voters are purely selfish, a political system that obeys voters' preferences will redistribute toward the decisive voters, such as the median voter. Most

---

[17] Brennan and Lomasky (1993) have forcefully put forth this position.

models of voting would suggest that this would involve some redistribution toward the mean or lower mean, and would be consistent with some of what is observed.[18] It would still have difficulty explaining redistribution toward the least well-off persons, who are also often the least influential politically. Indeed, in practice, the least well-off persons (e.g., the disabled) receive substantial benefits from the public sector.

Pressure Group Influence

The political system may respond less to voters' preferences than to those of pressure groups and special interests. Consequently, as new groups are induced to form, this is likely to give rise both to policies favoring these groups and to wasteful rent-seeking behavior. Pressure group influence is more likely to explain special forms of treatment of well-defined groups than broadly based redistributive policies.[19]

The Leviathan

At the extreme end of the spectrum is the government that acts purely in its own interest relatively unconstrained by the voters. It is usually thought to be interested in maximizing its own size, constrained only by its ability to extract tax revenues from the taxpayers. To the extent that this behavior is true, it will have consequences for the assignment of powers in the sense that greater decentralization may reduce the ability of governments to increase their size wastefully.

One's view of the proper assignment of expenditure, tax, and regulatory powers to various levels of government will be influenced very much by the weight one puts both on equity considerations (i.e., one's aversion to inequality) and on one's view of the extent to which governments act in the interests of society as opposed to in their own interest. These will differ from observer to observer. As well, the conditions will differ systematically across countries. Thus, our discussion of the assignment of powers cannot give definitive answers to precisely how decentralized public decision making should be. Nonetheless, the case for decentralization is suggestive and persuasive enough to be able to make qualitative judgments in many cases.

[18] Standard models of political party competition – so-called Downsian models because they are based on the Downs (1957) notion of vote-maximizing political parties – typically predict redistribution from the ends of the income distribution toward the mean (Lindbeck and Weibull, 1993; Dixit and Londregan, 1996). Once ideology is added to the objectives of political parties, it is possible to obtain redistribution to the neediest members of society, but the source of ideology is not specified.

[19] See the analysis of special-interest politics by Grossman and Helpman (1996) and Dixit and Londregan (1996), and the discussion of these models in Boadway and Keen (2000).

EFFICIENCY AND EQUITY IN A FEDERAL ECONOMY

Ultimately, the assignment of powers in a federation and the optimal policies undertaken by each level of government depend on the same efficiency and equity considerations that determine the rationale for government intervention in the first place. However, the fact that federal economies consist of various jurisdictions means that there are a number of additional efficiency and equity considerations that are special to federal economies. Some of these considerations arise from the fact that decentralization has different effects on the fiscal capacities of different subnational jurisdictions, giving rise to what are referred to as fiscal inefficiencies and fiscal inequities. Others arise from the fact that the independent policies of governments at a given level have effects on residents or governments of neighboring jurisdictions, so-called horizontal fiscal externalities. Still others arise from the fact that policies undertaken at a given level of government affect governments at another level, known as vertical fiscal externalities. The existence of these various effects will influence the case for decentralization, as they will represent costs of decentralization that must be set against the many benefits. They will also determine the structure of fiscal arrangements that should exist between the various levels of government. Indeed, a main purpose of the fiscal arrangements is precisely to facilitate the decentralization of fiscal responsibilities in a way that minimizes the costs. That is a major theme of this book. Let us consider these efficiency and equity considerations in turn.

Efficiency Considerations in a Federal Economy

The achievement of efficiency in a market economy involves exploiting to the greatest possible extent the potential gains from trade, given the technical, informational, and institutional limitations of the economy. More precisely, in the literature on welfare economics,[20] the notion of efficiency is characterized as a situation in which the following conditions are being satisfied:

- *Technical efficiency.* Firms are producing outputs with the least required inputs.
- *Exchange efficiency.* All consumers face the same relative prices, so that the relative valuations placed by consumers on all goods, services, and inputs traded are the same across consumers.

---

[20] For a complete summary of welfare economics, including these conditions, see Boadway and Bruce (1984).

- *Production efficiency.* All producers face the same relative prices for their inputs and outputs, so the rates at which inputs will be transformed into products at the margin are the same across the private-sector costs, and the economy will be operating on the boundary of its "production possibilities frontier."
- *Overall efficiency.* Consumers and producers face the same set of relative prices in all markets, so the relative value placed on all pairs of products by consumers equals their relative marginal costs to producers.

A decentralized competitive market economy goes a long way to achieving economic efficiency. As we have seen, government intervention on efficiency grounds may be required to provide public goods, to internalize externalities, to ensure that resources are fully employed, to supplement missing markets, and to deal with the consequences of scale economies. In a federal economy, in which there are internal political boundaries and in which geographic differences exist, there are various other dimensions of economic efficiency that are important. Some of the more important of these are as follows.

The Internal Common Market

There are various gradations of economic integration among political jurisdictions, ranging from a free trade area, in which goods and services and possibly capital are free to flow across borders, to a customs union, in which a common external tariff exists, to a common market, in which labor is also free to move, to an economic union, in which various degrees of harmonization exist. A federation shares some important features in common with a common market or an economic union, although a federation is much more than either of these. In particular, a federation, unlike an economic union, has two distinguishing features. First, it has a central government that can legislate on matters that affect residents of all jurisdictions, and may even have some oversight over lower-level jurisdictions. Second, residents of the federation are citizens of the entire federation, which entitles them to some significant rights not just of mobility but also of equal treatment. These two features of a federation will be prominent in our discussion of the assignment of powers and the fiscal arrangements. For now, however, we concentrate on those features that a federation has in common with common markets or economic unions. We speak of the markets of a federation as comprising an *internal economic union* or an *internal common market*.

The internal common market of a federation has a number of characteristics. For ease of reference, where we are not referring to specific countries, we follow the convention of referring to the central government as the *federal* government, and to subnational governments as *state* governments.[21] Because there are no border controls in a federation, goods, services, labor, and capital are able to flow freely across state borders. A common external trade policy exists with the rest of the world. But internally, the states are able to engage in tax, expenditure, and regulatory policies within their own borders that can affect the cross-border flows of products and factors of production. A reasonable efficiency objective of a federation might be to attain the unimpeded and nondistorted flow of all goods, services, labor, and capital across political borders within the country.[22] There should be no barriers to movement imposed by governments within the federation, whether by taxes and subsidies, by regulation, by preferential procurement policies, or by the design of local public goods and services. Of course, there may be natural costs to trade, such as transportation costs, language, and so on. We are concerned instead with government-imposed barriers. The absence of these will contribute to resources being allocated efficiently within the federation.

In a federation in which decision making is decentralized, violations of the efficiency in the internal common market may be imposed by state governments either wittingly or unwittingly. In the former case, governments may use policies like taxes, subsidies, and regulations to improve

---

[21] Many of the same principles will also apply within a state, where the relevant subnational government is the municipal or local government. It is often the case, however, that local governments do not have the same degree of legislative independence as do state or federal governments. As well, the same principles we develop will also apply to nations that are not federations but nonetheless have multiple tiers of government. For example, countries like Japan and the Scandinavian countries are not federations, but similar issues of multijurisdictional fiscal interdependence apply between the national government and lower tiers, including regions, prefectures, or localities. Other countries, like South Africa, do not refer to themselves as federations but have multiple levels or spheres of government with some independence of legislative responsibility as well.

[22] Though the objective of the free flow of goods, services, labor, and capital across internal borders is widely accepted as a suitable objective for a federation, as for an economic union, it is well known that on second-best grounds this may not be a theoretically defensible objective. From the theory of customs unions we know that trade diversion from the rest of the world can offset some of the benefits of trade creation within the federation and that restrictions on the latter may be beneficial (Lipsey, 1970). However, in a federation, one is unlikely to have the information required to implement the optimal second-best policy. Moreover, to the extent that this is an issue, it is because there are barriers against the rest of the world. The problem would be resolved if barriers to international trade and capital flows were removed at the national level. Of course, this is what is happening in the real world with globalization of international markets.

local conditions at the expense of nonresidents. This is referred to as *interjurisdictional fiscal competition*, and it is discussed in more detail later. If all states engage in it, the result may be that all are worse off, akin to the outcome of tariff wars between countries. On the other hand, distortions may arise simply because states adopt differing policies in an uncoordinated fashion. After all, state fiscal policies cannot avoid being distortionary; almost all taxes necessarily are. If different states adopt different policy mixes, cross-border transactions will inevitably be distorted. The exception to this might be the case in which products and factors of production are so mobile that states are forced by competition to adopt similar fiscal policies as their neighbors. Such a high degree of mobility is unlikely to exist because mobility is costly.

The possibility of lower-level jurisdictions adopting policies that distort the efficiency of the internal common market has implications for the division of responsibilities. For example, the case for decentralizing some types of tax, expenditure, and regulatory policies may be compromised by the fact that they could lead to inefficiencies in the internal economic union. State responsibility for providing health, education, and welfare services might result in different standards nationwide or residency requirements that impede the free flow of labor across borders. Because most policies of lower-level jurisdictions have the potential for distorting the economic union, federations might have some other institutional arrangements in place for discouraging them.

Various possibilities exist. There may be a constitutional proscription on policies that distort the free flow of goods, services, and factors across internal borders. Such a measure would place in the hands of the courts the onus for enforcing the economic union, something that they may not be well suited to do, given that economic issues will be the determining factors.

Alternatively, the federal government could be given the responsibility for overriding the policies of state jurisdictions that are deemed to interfere with cross-border transaction or movements of labor or capital. This overriding could take the form of disallowing state legislation that is deemed to interfere with the efficiency of the internal common market or with other national objectives; or it could take the stronger form of the federal government's mandating the structure that state programs ought to take. Such a system, elements of which exist in many federations (e.g., the United States) runs the risk of making the state governments subservient to the federal government, always making them "look over their shoulder" before passing laws. This could detract from the full benefits of decentralization or, indeed, from the whole purpose of federalism.

The problem of cross-border distortions could also be addressed by agreements negotiated by the state jurisdictions themselves, similar to the system used in economic unions such as the European Union. Such agreements do not appear to have been used extensively in federations, though there has been a relatively weak one recently negotiated among the Canadian provinces with the participation of the federal government. The problem is that negotiation can be a costly process that leads to minimally acceptable outcomes, because virtually all states have a veto. Moreover, the enforcement of multigovernment agreements requires some adjudication or dispute settlement mechanism that can be acrimonious or ineffectual.

A final, more promising, solution, and one that has been used in many federations, is for the federal government to use conditional grants to encourage state jurisdictions to incorporate elements respecting the internal economic union into their policies. For example, the state governments could be encouraged to make the benefits of certain programs portable and not subject to residency requirements. Following the convention in Canada, this policy is referred to as the use of *the spending power* by the federal government. The spending power is a policy approach of more general interest, and we return to its use later. For now, we simply note that it has the advantage of being a policy that relies on the carrot rather than the stick, because it leaves the states ultimately responsible for enacting legislative measures as they see fit. The unfettered use of the spending power also runs the risk of excessive centralization and intrusion of the federal government in the jurisdictional spheres of lower-level governments, again running against the objectives of federalism. However, its use is politically constrained by the fact that a transfer of funds must accompany it.

These considerations about the appropriate response to the potential for fiscal decisions by state governments to distort the internal common market highlight a key difficulty in fiscal federalism. There are both benefits and costs to decentralizing fiscal responsibilities and benefits and costs associated with adopting measures to counteract violations of efficiency in the internal common market. The appropriate balance between those benefits and costs is inherently judgmental. One only has to look at experiences worldwide to see that different federations adopt very different remedies for this and other problems. We cannot therefore pretend to say what the best remedy is. Instead, our purpose is to set out as clearly as possible what the nature of the costs and benefits are, what the pros and cons of different remedies are, and what we might learn from the experience of mature federations.

The case for inducing harmonious and distortion-free policies by lower-level governments is subject to a couple of important caveats. First, in addition to the potential costs, there may also be significant benefits from lower levels of government competing with one another through their fiscal policies. That is, there may be benefits from noncooperative as opposed to cooperative behavior by lower-level governments. A body of literature associated with public choice economists takes the view that competition between governments is a good thing because it induces more efficient local government decision making, encourages policy innovation, reduces the size of government, and ensures that local governments act in the best interests of their residents. This claim may be used as an argument for decentralization. According to this view, what might be called the competitive federalism perspective,[23] the more decentralization there is and the fewer constraints on the policies of lower-level jurisdictions there are, the more efficient is the federation. Because of the assumed mobility of products and factors of production across borders, competition itself will minimize the use of distorting policy instruments. And any costs of distortions arising from uncoordinated policy making by lower jurisdictions will be far outweighed by the benefits of interjurisdictional competition. This view does seem to rely heavily on mobility to make interjurisdictional competition unobtrusive. As well, it abstracts from some of the other sources of inefficiency within a federation that we discuss elsewhere in this section. It might also be worth noting here that the use of the spending power need not detract unduly from the benefits of competitive federalism. Indeed, the spending power, if used unobtrusively, is the one federal policy instrument that allows for a suitable compromise between the benefits of decentralized decision making and the grosser forms of distortion to the internal common market that decentralized decision making might entail.

The second caveat is that not all distortions to the internal movement of goods, services, and factors of production should be viewed as a bad thing. For example, state or local public goods and services that are designed to suit the tastes of the residents may well differ across states, and this variety is a benefit of decentralized public service provision. Naturally, it will discourage in-migration of persons whose preferences for public service types differ. Similarly, laws governing the use of local languages or religious practices may impede the movement of labor and even of goods and services. More generally, the stringency of such things as labor laws,

---

[23] A good summary of this may be found in Breton (1994).

environmental laws, and product safety laws may differ from jurisdiction to jurisdiction, reflecting differences in tastes among provincial residents. These differences would seem to be desirable impediments to mobility, as prescribed in the famous Tiebout model (discussed later). The problem in practice is that, as in the international trade sphere, it is difficult to distinguish policies meant to cater to the special preferences of local residents from beggar-thy-neighbor policies intended to divert desirable resources from other jurisdictions. Thus, as with the case of competitive federalism, this uncertainty would suggest caution in interfering with the decentralized decisions of lower-level jurisdictions. This issue will arise over and over again in our discussion. Perhaps one lesson that can be taken from the international trade arena that would be helpful in the federalism context is that if distortionary policies are to be applied by state governments, they ought to abide by the analogue to the so-called national treatment criterion. That is, regulatory or fiscal policies or even procurement policies ought to be applied equally to all persons or firms transacting in the state, whether they are resident in the state or not. At least this would remove overt instances of preferential treatment.

Local Public Goods and Externalities

As mentioned earlier, the standard argument for public intervention in the economy is the provision of public goods and services. By the same token, the traditional argument for the decentralization of functions to lower levels of government is the fact that some public services are of a purely local or regional nature.[24] Efficiency in a federation requires that the level of local public goods in each locality be determined by comparing the benefits to all residents being served with the costs of provision. Residents of different localities will generally prefer different levels of provision. A decentralized federation has the benefit that each local government is able to provide the type and mix of public goods and services that its local residents prefer. Furthermore, if residents are relatively mobile, they should be free to move to the jurisdiction that best caters to their preferences. The Tiebout model has stressed the benefits of free migration ("voting with one's feet") combined with decentralized decision making in a federation in which some public goods are of a local nature and persons have different preferences. We have stressed that not all government expenditures are for public goods. Governments also provide many quasi-private goods or public services. Similar arguments about the benefits of catering to the

---

[24] Standard references include Musgrave (1959), Breton (1965), and Oates (1972).

tastes of local residents can be made in the case of these types of public expenditures. As well, some regulations may be local. For example, governments may use regulations to protect local culture or languages, which may be viewed as local public goods. In all these cases, the fact that the benefits of the policy instrument accrue mainly to local or state residents, along with the fact that preferences for these activities may vary from jurisdiction to jurisdiction, suggests that they should be local or state responsibilities.

On the other hand, the mere fact that different communities or regions have distinct preferences for the mix and amount of public goods and services does not imply that lower levels of government must provide them. In principle, it is possible for a central government to provide the appropriate level of locally differentiated public services. However, lower-level jurisdictions may have informational advantages and be more politically accountable to local residents compared with the federal government. Interjurisdictional competition may also make lower-level jurisdictions more responsive to local needs and preferences. We return to the arguments for and against decentralization on these and other grounds in the next chapter.

Interjurisdictional Spillovers

Public expenditure programs undertaken in a given jurisdiction are obviously meant to benefit the residents of that jurisdiction and are designed with that in mind. In practice, the beneficiaries of local or state public expenditures may not coincide with the residents of the locality undertaking the expenditure. Residents of neighboring jurisdictions may benefit from (or be harmed by) policies of a given jurisdiction. More specifically, there are said to be interjurisdictional spillovers, analogous to standard externalities among individual economic agents. They can be positive or negative according to whether the spillovers involve benefits to nonresidents or costs. Because state or local governments will have no incentive to take account of the spillover benefits they generate, or harms they impose for nonresidents, their decision making may lead to inefficient outcomes from the perspective of the nation as a whole. There will be an incentive for subnational jurisdictions to undertake too low a level of activity for those expenditure items that have positive spillover benefits and too high for those with spillover costs. Alternatively, to the extent that the activity involves providing a public service that is excludable, subnational jurisdictions may attempt to restrict access by residents of other jurisdictions.

There are many examples of interjurisdictional spillovers, both positive and negative. Both commercial and individual travelers who reside elsewhere may use roads in a given jurisdiction. Persons trained or educated in one jurisdiction may move to another and contribute their taxes elsewhere. Water or air pollution controls in one jurisdiction may have favorable effects on another. The jobless from one jurisdiction may move to another to collect welfare benefits. Persons who worked in one jurisdiction may retire in another one and obtain the benefits of public services provided there. As public-sector decision making becomes more decentralized, the incidence of interjurisdictional spillovers will increase. As mentioned, jurisdictions may respond by producing nonoptimal levels of public services or by imposing restrictions on the use of these services by nonresidents. Such responses can lead to limits on the amount of decentralization that might otherwise be desirable or to the decentralization being accompanied by measures that correct the spillovers.

Interjurisdictional spillovers can be analyzed in a way analogous to externalities in the private sector involving individual decision makers, such as households or firms. As is well known from the externalities literature, the spillovers can be "internalized" in a variety of ways, including by direct negotiation among the parties involved (the Coase solution), by taxation or subsidization (the Pigou solution), or by regulation involving quantity controls of mandates. In the context of fiscal federalism, the parties involved in the spillovers are lower levels of government. They could negotiate among themselves to internalize the spillover, possibly with compensation payments being paid from one state to another depending on the direction of the spillover; or the federal government might become involved in imposing remedies on the states to internalize interjurisdictional spillovers.[25]

In the case of positive spillovers, the federal government could implement subsidies to the state governments in the form of a conditional matching grant to encourage the states to undertake the appropriate amount of activity. If it were not so much a question of the amount of the activity but of its program design (e.g., the imposition of residency restrictions), conditional nonmatching grants could be used, with the full payment of the grant being conditional on certain design features being implemented. These uses of conditional grants are examples of the spending power in action.

It is much more difficult for the federal government to use taxation as a remedy in the case of negative spillovers. To tax a state government means forcing the state to pay moneys to the federal government, and that might be deemed to be contrary to the supremacy of the state legislature as the body solely responsible for raising revenues for the state's use. The other

---

[25] The same arguments apply at the state level with respect to its municipalities.

alternative is regulation, either imposing mandates requiring states to design and implement certain program requirements or disallowing state legislation unless it satisfies certain desirable norms. Such direct regulation of the states by the federal government may be viewed as incompatible with the constitutional division of powers in some countries or with the spirit of federalism. At most, the federal government may be able to declare void state laws that violate certain standards. In practice, at least in industrialized countries, the spending power is the most common form of influence the federal government has over the states' behavior; direct interference with state decisions is unusual.

Horizontal Fiscal Externalities

Interjurisdictional spillover benefits and costs arising from state expenditure programs represent but one way that the decentralized fiscal decisions of the states affect residents of other jurisdictions. State fiscal policies can affect the prices or incomes faced by nonresidents, or they can indirectly affect nonresidents by affecting the budgets of other state governments, especially the sizes of their tax bases. These direct and indirect effects of nonresidents' budgets or those of their state governments are referred to as horizontal fiscal externalities. Following Dahlby (1996), a simple taxonomic classification of them would include the following.[26]

Positive Tax Externalities: Tax Competition. Tax competition arises when the tax base is mobile across states. When the tax rate on a mobile base is increased, the size of the tax base will fall. Part of the fall might simply reflect elasticity in the supply of the base. But part might also reflect a movement of the tax base from one jurisdiction to another. Thus, an increase in capital tax rates will cause an out-movement of capital. An increase in income, payroll, or general sales tax rates will tend to provide an incentive for the out-migration of labor. An increase in an excise tax can cause a deflection of purchases to neighboring states – cross-border shopping. In each case, the tax base, and therefore the tax revenues, of neighboring states will rise and that rise will be perceived as a loss to the taxing state.

One way to characterize the effect of positive tax externalities is by the analytical device of the marginal cost of public funds (MCPF). The MCPF is a measure of the cost to the economy of extracting a marginal dollar of tax revenues. The idea is that an additional dollar of resources transferred by

---

[26] Recent surveys of horizontal fiscal externalities may be found in J. Wilson (1999) and Lockwood (2001).

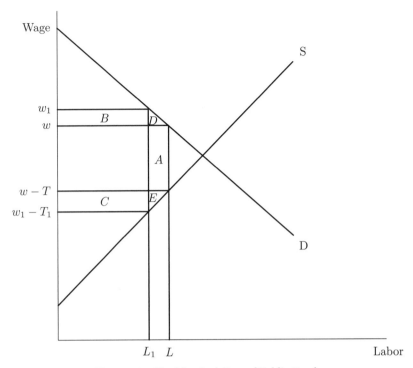

Figure 1.1. The Marginal Cost of Public Funds

taxation from the private to the public sector has a true cost of more than a dollar. The true cost includes not only the dollar's worth of resources transferred but also the increment in the deadweight loss because of the tax distortion. The latter arises because a tax levied on, say, labor income, drives a wedge between the before-tax and after-tax wage rates and prevents the economy from operating efficiently. The concept of the MCPF can be illustrated using Figure 1.1, which depicts the market for labor. The demand curve is labeled D and the supply curve S. In the initial equilibrium, the market wage paid by firms is w, while the after-tax wage is $w - T$, where T is the tax per unit of labor supplied. Suppose the tax is increased incrementally, causing the amount of labor traded in equilibrium to fall from L to L_1. The MCPF is the change in the social cost per unit of revenue raised, or

$$\text{MCPF} = (\Delta R + \Delta DWL)/\Delta R,$$

where ΔR is the change in revenue raised and ΔDWL is the change in the deadweight loss. Now, $\Delta R = C + B - A$, while $\Delta DWL = A + D + E$, or for a small change, $\Delta DWL = A$. Therefore, we can write

$$MCPF = (C + B)/(C + B - A) = 1/[1 - A/(C + B)].$$

This can be approximated by

$$MCPF = 1/[1 + (T\Delta L/L\Delta T) = 1/[1-\varepsilon],$$

where ε is the elasticity of the labor tax base with respect to the tax rate.[27] Estimates of the magnitude of the MCPF for standard tax systems range anywhere from 1.2 to 2.0 (Browning, 1975), and it can rise rapidly with the tax rate. A similar sort of expression applies for any tax base, where L can be replaced by whatever the tax base happens to be. It can be seen that tax bases that respond more to changes in the tax rate will have a higher MCPF. In the case of labor income, this responsiveness will be determined by the elasticities of the demand and supply curves for labor. Indeed, the more elastic either supply or demand is, the higher the MCPF will be.

The presence of positive tax externalities causes state governments to perceive the MCPF facing them to be higher than is the case from a social point of view. That is because part of the decline in the tax base – ΔL – is due to either labor's moving to another state (a shift in the supply curve) or firms' moving to other jurisdictions (a shift in the demand curve). In either case, the tax base is not lost to the nation because it is now in another state (if we assume no international mobility). This misperception causes states to set their tax rates too low on mobile factors. Because all states have the same incentive, competition effectively drives taxes down as states fear loss of tax base. In the end, tax rates are inefficiently low for the base, and little movement of the base across borders will occur. The tax competition effect is obviously more important the more mobile the tax base in question. Thus, capital and capital income taxes are more prone to tax competition than are taxes on labor income, which is far less mobile. The latter includes both payroll taxes and general consumption taxes, both of which are essentially taxes on the supply of labor. Specific excise taxes also have relatively mild tax competition effects. In this case, the mobility of the base involves cross-border shopping. The least mobile tax bases are those whose location is fixed, such as real property or natural resources, although capital used in conjunction with these fixed factors will itself be mobile.

One important type of positive tax externality occurs in the context of specific projects when regions engage in strategic tax competition or beggar-thy-neighbor policies to attract businesses. This strategy involves

---

[27] This is an efficiency approach to the MCPF. Equity considerations can also be incorporated, as in Dahlby (1998) or Sandmo (1998).

the use of tax incentives or subsidies to individual firms. The trouble with beggar-thy-neighbor policies is that all regions are likely to treat similar types of firms as being desirable and therefore are likely to provide competing tax incentives for them. In the end, no one region will succeed in providing a more favorable tax environment, so the allocation of firms across regions is not likely to be affected much. Instead, the firms receive favorable tax treatment no matter where they reside, which is a self-defeating outcome from the regions' point of view.

Negative Tax Externalities: Tax Exporting. Negative tax externalities arise from *tax exporting*, whereby part of the burden of a tax is borne by non-residents. This can occur when taxes are imposed on incomes generated in a region that accrue to nonresidents. Thus, business income taxes, taxes on natural resources, and withholding taxes on capital income may partly be exported. As well, taxes levied on products that are purchased by nonresidents can be exported. The MCPF is effectively underestimated, so there is an incentive to set tax rates too high.

Tax exporting can be severely limited by adjustments in relative prices. An attempt to tax nonresidents on their capital income earned in a region will be at least partly offset by the capital fleeing. Similarly, an attempt to capture tax revenue from the sale of products to nonresidents will be frustrated by a reduction in demand. In a small open economy that is a price taker on outside markets, tax exporting cannot occur. It may well be that the regions are in such a position.[28]

The existence of horizontal tax externalities is undoubtedly a fact of life, although their magnitude may be disputed. Options for the federation to deal with them are limited. They have implications for the assignment of taxes. It is widely accepted that, on efficiency grounds, taxes on mobile bases should be assigned primarily to the central government and those on less mobile ones assigned to regions. Thus, taxes on capital income, capital, and businesses would be mainly federal, whereas regions (and their municipalities) could access taxes on consumption, labor income, natural resources, and real property. Of course, assignment based on efficiency may well conflict with that based on equity or administrative considerations.

---

[28] Of course, in the short run, when capital has been installed, it will be possible to tax it without the capital fleeing. But such a policy is not sustainable in the long run, because capital owners will not want to install capital equipment if they expect that it will be taxed once in place. This is the problem of time inconsistency that will be referred to from time to time in this study.

Some of the consequences of tax externalities can, in principle, be addressed by cooperation among the states. Tax bases and tax rates could be harmonized by agreement, or by codes of conduct to preclude beggar-thy-neighbor policies. But binding cooperative agreements are difficult to achieve and are rarely effective in practice. They require not only unanimous agreement but also a dispute settlement mechanism that binds future legislative decisions, something that seems to be difficult to achieve in a decentralized setting.

Alternatively, fiscal arrangements between the central government and the states could address some effects of tax competition. Tax competition will be less the less tax room that the states occupy. This is an argument for a vertical fiscal gap. The central government may be instrumental in encouraging the states to harmonize their taxes on mobile tax bases, possibly by formal federal-state arrangements. Some authors (e.g., Dahlby, 1996) have suggested that the central government could use matching grants based on state tax effort to induce regions to internalize the tax externalities. This remedy has not been used and is probably impractical because it is virtually impossible to measure the magnitude of the externality associated with regional tax policies.

Positive Expenditure Externalities: Expenditure Spillovers. Interjurisdictional positive expenditure spillovers, which have already been discussed, constitute this category. The same discussion applies.

Negative Expenditure Externalities: Expenditure Competition. State expenditure programs may also induce movements of the tax base across jurisdictions. A prime example of this might be the provision of infrastructure or business services. The provision of such services increases firms' profits and attracts them to the state. States will be induced to overestimate the social value of these expenditures and will have an incentive to overspend in these categories. In addition to this overspending, the mix of public expenditures will tend to be skewed. Relatively too much will be spent on business services and too little on public goods and services affecting households.[29]

An important particular type of expenditure externality involves the strategic use of beggar-thy-neighbor policies. Regional governments may attempt to attract businesses using firm-specific infrastructure investments or outright subsidies. Procurement and regional hiring policies may discriminate against nonresidents. Residency restrictions may be put on

---

[29] Keen and Marchand (1997) make this point.

access to regional public services such as welfare, education, and health care. If they are effective, such measures will distort the internal economic union. But if all regions engage in them, they are likely to be self-defeating and ineffective. Preventing them involves the same considerations as in the case of tax incentives. It is hard to see how such measures can be effective without the participation of the federal government.

Regulation Externalities. Virtually identical arguments apply in the case where states impose regulations that affect nonresidents. Regulations can apply on all three major markets. Capital market regulations may restrict the free flow of capital among jurisdictions, for example, by favoring regionally owned capital. Similarly, labor market regulation may preclude persons from finding employment in other states. Different curricula across regional educational and training programs may make it difficult to pursue further education in another state. Different environmental or health and safety regulations may impose different costs on businesses across states. Regulations that buttress regional customs, culture, and language will typically favor residents. In all these cases, inefficiency is induced in the internal economic union by the relevant regulation. While some of the regulations may reflect legitimate social policy objectives, others constitute outright protection. Avoiding it therefore involves not only appropriate forms of cooperative agreement with or without the connivance of the federal government but also some judgment as to which sorts of discriminatory regulation are justified by social arguments.

Vertical Fiscal Externalities

Another source of inefficiency arising in a federation involves externalities between higher and lower levels of government.[30] The source of the inefficiency is that fiscal decisions made by the government at one level affect not only its budget but also that of the government at the other level. This effect occurs most clearly when the state and federal governments have access to the same tax base. Consider the case of the payroll tax. If the state government increases its payroll tax rate, it will presumably raise more revenue. If the tax base has some elasticity, however, it will shrink. Because the federal government occupies the same labor tax base, it will find its revenues shrinking as well.[31] Because the state neglects to take account of

---

[30] For a survey of vertical fiscal externalities, see Keen (1998).

[31] In fact, total tax revenues, both state and federal, might fall, implying that the federation as a whole is on the "wrong side of the Laffer curve," even if the state alone is not. Keen and Kotsogiannis (2002) have demonstrated this possibility.

this, the implication is that the MCPF it perceives is less than the true MCPF. To see this, recall the expression

$$\text{MCPF} = (\Delta R + \Delta\text{DWL})/\Delta R, \text{ or } \text{MCPF} = 1 + \Delta\text{DWL}/\Delta R.$$

The state government underestimates the aggregate fall in tax revenue $(-\Delta R)$ from a tax change because it neglects the fall in revenue to the federal government. Therefore, it underestimates the true MCPF. The magnitude of this negative vertical fiscal externality will be higher the more elastic the tax base and the higher the federal tax rate.

This same effect applies even if the states and the federal government do not occupy precisely the same tax bases. All the main broad tax bases – labor, income, and consumption – overlap to a considerable extent. Changes in the tax on any one of them will affect the size of the base of all of them. For example, changes in state payroll tax rates are likely to affect not only federal payroll tax revenues but also federal income and consumption tax revenues.

This tendency to underestimate the MCPF because of vertical fiscal externalities has a number of implications. It gives the states an incentive to raise too much revenue because it underestimates the cost of doing so. It especially encourages them to levy excessive taxes on bases that bear a high federal tax rate and are more elastic. On the other hand, to the extent that tax bases are mobile among states, the vertical fiscal externality offsets the tax competition effect that, as we have seen, tends to make states over-estimate their MCPFs.

As with the MCPF itself, there is some uncertainty about the magnitude of the vertical fiscal externality, although in a decentralized federation the expectation is that it can be reasonably large (Dahlby, 1994). There is certainly strong evidence that vertical tax interaction effects exist. Besley and Rosen (1998) found for the United States that increases in the federal excise tax on both cigarettes and alcohol caused states to increase their excise taxes significantly, indicating prima facie evidence of a vertical fiscal interaction. Hayashi and Boadway (2001) studied the interaction between the federal and provincial governments in Canada in the setting of their business income taxes. They also found that changes in the federal tax rate significantly affected provincial rates, but the sign was negative in this case. Of course, unlike cigarettes and alcohol, capital is highly mobile across regional borders so that vertical and horizontal externalities both apply.

In principle, the same kind of vertical externality also applies in the opposite direction. Changes in the federal tax rate will cause a loss in revenues to the state governments because their tax bases shrink. But there is good reason to suppose that this will not induce the federal government to set its tax excessively high. It is sensible to suppose that the federal government acts as a first mover or Stackelberg leader with respect to the states' tax policies.[32] If so, it will anticipate the effects of its tax policies on state behavior in setting its tax rates. (The states acting as followers take federal tax rates as given.) The federal government will therefore choose its tax rates to minimize the consequences of vertical fiscal externalities on the states. In very simple settings, this can involve the federal government levying only lump-sum taxes and turning over the responsibility for redistribution to the regions, contrary to standard prescriptions.[33] But, more generally, the federal government will set its tax rate too low to offset the tendency for the states to set theirs excessively. The end result will be that the total tax rate may not be excessive, but the allocation of total revenues will be inefficient. Specifically, too much revenue will accrue to the states rather than to the federal government.

From the point of view of the fiscal arrangements, little can be done to avoid vertical fiscal externalities altogether, apart from the federal government's vacating major tax fields entirely. As long as the federal government is imposing taxes, such externalities will exist. It is possible that sophisticated formulas for grants could be designed that penalize state tax effort by enough to offset vertical externalities. But, as of now, that approach is probably impractical as well as politically difficult to achieve.

These vertical externalities can in principle also arise on the expenditure side, though less directly (Dahlby, 1996). For example, an increase in labor training at the state level can increase the income tax base and generate tax revenue for the federal government. This form of externality would provide an incentive for states to provide too little of the expenditure relative to the efficient level. As with interjurisdictional spillovers, this could potentially be corrected using matching grants.

The fiscal federalism literature has also begun to consider the possibility of the states being first-movers in the policy interaction with the federal government. In this case, any given state government's policies are conditioned by how it expects the federal government will subsequently react. This, it turns out, leads to some rather unexpected results, results that arise because of the ability of the states to exploit the future behavior of the

---

[32] Hayashi and Boadway (2001) found weak evidence that the federal government is first mover in the setting of business income taxes in Canada.

[33] See the analyses of Boadway and Keen (1996) and Boadway, Marchand, and Vigneault (1998).

federal government. One result is an application of the so-called Samaritan's dilemma. Suppose that the federal government operates an equalization system that transfers funds to states according to some measure of
their residents' well-being – for example, average income or tax capacity.
(Such a system will be discussed in greater detail later in this study.) To the
extent that state government policies can influence such measures at some
cost to themselves, they will have an incentive not to incur the costs
involved in making themselves better off, anticipating (correctly) the
transfers that the federal government will make to them. The result will
obviously be an inefficient outcome. The real-world relevance of the
Samaritan's dilemma is obvious. Another result is in a sense the opposite
and is an application of what is known as the rotten kid theorem. If state
governments enact some expenditure programs that have benefits nationwide, left to their own devices they will tend to provide too low a level of
the programs because they are costly to provide. But, if the federal government tends to equalize after-tax incomes, states will have an incentive to
contribute efficiently to such programs because the expected transfer will,
to some extent, cover the marginal cost of an increased contribution.[34]

Fiscal Inefficiency
In a federation, the decentralized fiscal decision making of lower levels of
government can itself give rise to a particular form of inefficiency, referred
to in the literature as fiscal inefficiency. The problem arises because different governments at a given level are typically able to provide different
amounts of net fiscal benefits (NFBs) to their residents. NFBs are the
difference between the value of public services delivered by the lower-level
jurisdiction and their tax cost.[35] The existence of differences in NFBs
across jurisdictions means that the benefits of residing in one jurisdiction
relative to another include not only the relative earnings or productivity

[34] See the analysis of Caplan, Cornes, and Silva (1998). They show that if regions voluntarily
contribute to a national public good, a scheme in which the central government equalizes
fully regional disparities ex post will induce regions to provide the optimal amount of the
national public good. In contrast, if the central government moved first, regions will
contribute suboptimal amounts, and the central redistributive policy will be ineffective,
as described by the well-known Warr neutrality theorem. Models also exist in which
households move first, followed by central and regional governments. If the households
anticipate the equalizing policies that the governments will implement in the future, the
allocation of labor will be inefficient. Mitsui and Sato (2001) construct a simple example
in which households prefer to live in the largest community, which leads to concentrations of population that are too high.
[35] Net fiscal benefits are also sometimes referred to as fiscal residua (Buchanan, 1950). A full
characterization of the notion can be found in Mieszkowski and Musgrave (1999).

differentials between the two jurisdictions but also the differences in NFBs between them. To the extent that persons are mobile across states, they will allocate inefficiently because in equilibrium migration will equate the sum of earnings plus NFBs in the two states (net of any costs of moving) for the marginal migrant, while economic efficiency involves equating only earnings net of moving costs.

There are four main sources of NFB differentials in a federation – fiscal externalities, source-based tax capacities, state redistribution, and needs.[36] Consider them in turn.

Fiscal Externalities. Fiscal externalities arise in an economy with local public goods.[37] They result from the fact that persons entering a local jurisdiction do not take account of the fact that they jointly consume the local public good with other persons in the locality and reduce the tax burden to them from financing the public good. The classic case involves local public goods settings in which households are homogeneous and perfectly mobile across localities. If localities provided purely public goods to their residents and financed them with taxes on the residents, the size of the fiscal externality in each jurisdiction would simply be the per-person tax liability. If per-person tax liabilities differed across jurisdictions, there would be a fiscal incentive for inefficient migration.

Although this notion of fiscal externalities has figured prominently in the theoretical fiscal federalism literature, it is probably of much less importance in practice. This is partly because the phenomenon is not likely to be quantitatively significant, and partly because most local public expenditures are not on goods that are truly "public." For example, if public services or quasi-private goods were provided, there would be no fiscal externality in the simple example given here. The tax contribution made to the local jurisdiction by an in-migrant would just offset the cost of the additional public services that would be consumed, so there would be no fiscal externality. Only to the extent that the use of public services by in-migrants did not crowd out use by existing residents would there be an externality due to migration.

---

[36] For a more detailed discussion of these sources of NFB differentials and their relevance for policy, see Boadway and Flatters (1982b), Boadway and Wildasin (1984), and Boadway (2004).

[37] The notion of a fiscal externality was first discussed in detail in Buchanan and Goetz (1972) and analyzed in Flatters, Henderson, and Mieszkowski (1974). The circumstances in which lower-level government fiscal policies are likely to give rise to fiscal externalities are discussed in Boadway and Wildasin (1984).

Source-Based Tax Differences. A potentially more important source of fiscal inefficiency occurs from differences in NFBs across states. One way this can arise is from differences in access to source-based tax bases, especially taxes on resource rents or rents from other state-specific fixed factors but also such things as corporation income taxes and capital taxes. To the extent that state jurisdictions have the right to tax income generated on, say, resources, this can provide a valuable fiscal advantage from residing in states with large resource endowments. In effect, one acquires a share in the property rights of such resources merely by residency in the state. A state that has such large tax bases relative to another can provide public services at lower tax rates. This can cause fiscally induced migration and a misallocation of labor. It is not uncommon in federations for resource wealth to be concentrated in some states.

The same argument applies more generally to any of the other source-based taxes. Corporation income taxes or property taxes on businesses impose tax burdens that are independent of the residency of owners. States that have more business incomes generated within their boundaries have a greater ability to raise revenues on behalf of their citizens. Because citizens effectively obtain a claim on their share of these tax revenues, there is a purely fiscal incentive to migrate. Of course, given the mobility of capital, the extent to which states can obtain revenues from corporate taxes may be limited. To the extent that they exist and vary across states, though, they can be an important source of NFB differentials.

State Income Redistribution. The third source of NFB differences results from the redistribution inherent in state government budgets. For example, suppose state governments provide public services that are effectively quasi-private goods accruing in equal per capita amounts to all residents. Suppose also that they finance these public expenditures by a proportional income tax on all residents. Then, the budget has an overall redistributive effect. (Tax incidence studies seem to indicate that this is not too far-fetched empirically.) High-income persons obtain a negative NFB, while low-income persons obtain a positive NFB. If one compares across jurisdictions, persons in low-average-income states will have systematically lower NFBs than those in high-average-income states.

Moreover, suppose that all states impose the same tax rate. Then, the NFB differential across states will be the same for all persons, regardless of their income level. Because they pay the same income tax rate wherever they reside, the NFB differential is simply the difference in the level of public services provided in different states, which is in turn equal to the difference in per capita tax revenue collected in the state at the given tax rate. There will be a fiscal advantage for persons of all income types to live in jurisdictions with higher average incomes. Again, fiscally induced migration can occur from high-income to low-income states, resulting in an inefficiency of labor allocation.[38]

For future reference, notice that this NFB differential would be eliminated if equalization transfers were made among states so that all states could provide a comparable level of public services at comparable tax rates. In the example just given, this would require fully equalizing the ability to raise residence-based taxes. To the extent that the tax system is more progressive, more equalization would be required, and vice versa.

Differences in Needs. A final source of NFB difference results if we relax the assumption that public services are provided on an equal per capita basis. In fact, public services are likely to differ systematically across the population according to the needs of individuals. Young people are provided with schooling, the elderly require more health care, and so on. If states differ in their demographic makeups, they will have systematically different expenditure needs. For any given persons, NFBs will be higher the lower is the need for public expenditures. Again, these differentials could be neutralized by a system of equalizing interstate transfers that was based on differences in need.

In practice, these four sources of fiscal inefficiency will coexist. In each of these four cases, and therefore, in aggregate, an incentive exists for labor to be allocated inefficiently across the federation. There is some evidence that the quantitative magnitude of the inefficiency of fiscally induced migration may not be too great, even in a country like Canada where mobility tends to be relatively high.[39] Nonetheless, as we shall see later, the same sort of NFB differentials that gives rise to fiscal inefficiency also gives rise to a form of fiscal inequity in the federation, and the latter occurs without labor being mobile. Thus, a case can be made on both efficiency and equity grounds for eliminating these NFB differentials across lower-level jurisdictions. We shall see in more detail in a later chapter how this

---

[38] Buchanan (1952) was the first to point out the possibility that migration will be inefficient in these circumstances. For a detailed treatment of it, see Boadway and Flatters (1982b).

[39] See Winer and Gauthier (1982) and Day (1992). Watson (1986) has argued that the welfare costs associated with the estimates of Winer and Gauthier are very small, whereas L. Wilson (2003) has argued the contrary.

can be done by a system of equalizing transfers from the federal to the state government.[40] This is another example of the potential role of the spending power in a federation as a means of ensuring that the inefficiencies and inequities that might otherwise accompany decentralization are neutralized. In other words, the spending power facilitates decentralized decision making in a federation.

Tax Harmonization

Lower-level governments will (and should) generally have some independence in raising their own tax revenues. If revenue raising is done in an uncoordinated fashion, inefficiencies will typically arise because tax distortions imposed by the state or local tax system will differ across jurisdictions. These distortions can be a result of differential tax rates on capital or labor income causing a misallocation of these factors across jurisdictions, or different tax rates on the sale or production of goods and services, which will distort production patterns across jurisdictions. They may also come about because different jurisdictions choose to define their tax bases in slightly different ways. The magnitude of the distortions will depend upon the mobility of the tax base. Thus, differential tax rates on mobile tax bases like capital will be more distorting than those on less mobile tax bases like real property.

These sorts of distortions in a federation will be mitigated to the extent that tax systems are chosen in a harmonized manner. The harmonization can take the form of coordination among lower levels of government, or it can take the form of a higher level of government participating in the setting of tax policy for lower levels of government in a variety of ways. The latter will be most likely to occur when the two levels of government occupy the same tax base, or at least share its revenues. Federal participation in state tax policy in areas of common occupancy can include centralized administration of tax collection for both state and federal taxes, a centrally defined tax base that is used by both levels, or even a common rate structure applied to a common base. The lower level of government may be limited to setting the level of its taxes (e.g., by applying a surcharge on federal taxes), to choosing local credits and exemptions, or to defining the entire tax structure. The lower levels may or may not be involved in the tax policy chosen for the entire federation.

---

[40] Myers (1990) has argued that, for the case of fiscal externalities arising in a local public goods model, the federal government need not be involved. The states would make the required changes voluntarily. However, this will generally not apply when households are not identical.

The harmonization of taxes improves the efficiency of the internal common market by reducing the administration, collection, and compliance costs both for the private sector and for the tax authorities. It also reduces the possibility of double taxation or nontaxation of income earned by firms operating in more than one jurisdiction. And it reduces the possibilities for evasion and avoidance through such things as transfer pricing and financial transactions designed to reallocate tax bases to low-tax jurisdictions. It thus reduces the potential for wasteful tax competition among jurisdictions.

The benefits of tax harmonization of certain tax bases may come about to some extent without any formal agreement to do so. That is, competitive pressure may induce a certain amount of similarity among state tax bases. At the same time, similarity of tax bases is not sufficient to ensure efficiency. As mentioned, tax competition may take the form of beggar-thy-neighbor tax policies designed to attract factors of production from neighboring jurisdictions. If all jurisdictions do engage in tax competition, the result may be similar tax structures, albeit with inefficiently low tax rates and public service levels. From an efficiency point of view, it can be argued that harmonization is most important for taxes that impinge upon capital income; less important for taxes that are levied according to residency, such as labor income taxes and destination-based indirect taxes; and least important for taxes on real property. This means harmonization is less important in the indirect tax system than in the direct tax system. The main problem in the case of indirect taxes concerns the inability to enforce the residency provisions of the tax. Shopping across local borders can circumvent these. Given that there are no border controls, it is not obvious that anything can be done about this. In fact, because of the absence of border controls, there will be some competitive pressures for keeping sales tax rates and structures relatively similar. This will be important for our discussion of the assignment of taxes to jurisdictions.

The harmonization of taxes will serve to mitigate the inefficiencies arising from the use of different tax bases or rate structures. It will not undo differences in tax levels chosen by different states. However, differences in levels will also be mitigated to the extent that an effective system of equalizing grants is in place that reduces the NFB differentials across states. Even with full equalization, states may choose different tax levels because of differences in preferences for public services. Harmonization will still be beneficial in these circumstances because it will reduce the administrative, collection, and compliance costs borne by both the private and public sectors.

As we discussed previously, it can be argued that the existence of inter-jurisdictional competition can be as beneficial as coordination in the setting of tax policy. States will be induced not to adopt tax systems that are too different from those in other states, and they will also be encouraged to be efficient in their tax administration. On the other hand, where tax bases are mobile and where nonresidents may partly own them, the incentive exists for states to use tax policy in a beggar-thy-neighbor manner.

Expenditure Harmonization

There may also be some efficiency advantages from harmonizing public services delivered by local governments. Differences in the design of these programs could affect migration among jurisdictions. For example, the services offered to the poor may induce the in-migration of low-income persons. This possibility could induce local jurisdictions to engage in a type of wasteful expenditure competition whose aim was to attract desirable residents and repel less desirable ones. In aggregate, this effort will be largely self-defeating. There may be advantages from adopting common standards of service design so as not to discourage mobility. For example, educational standards across states could be standardized so that a common set of qualifications applies. Similarly, occupational licensing standards could be harmonized and made portable across states.

As well, as mentioned previously, some expenditure programs give rise to spillover benefits to residents of other jurisdictions who can take advantage of the services being provided. An example in industrialized countries is higher education. Residents of one state province may attend the universities of another state or province, thereby benefiting from expenditures made by the government of the latter. Transportation facilities and health services are other examples.

Finally, expenditure harmonization may be important vertically between government programs at different levels. Some programs will inevitably have some overlap, and harmonization will avoid costly duplication of effort. Examples might include regional development programs undertaken by two levels of government, or labor training and education programs.

Harmonization could be achieved by agreement among states, or by federal action. Again, perhaps the most viable method would be by the use of the spending power.

Other Sources of Inefficiency in Federations

There are other reasons, which are just coming to be studied by fiscal federalism scholars, why resources may be allocated inefficiently in a federation. The process of regional development might itself be character-ized by externalities that render market solutions inefficient. This phe-nomenon is something that geographers have long studied, but it has been slow to penetrate fiscal federalism theory, which tends to be based on conventional economic modeling. One argument, along the lines of Krugman (1993), is that there are economies of agglomeration, which enhance the efficiency of labor and capital markets as they become more concentrated. Information exchange is improved, and there is more opportunity for matching skills to jobs if the regional labor markets are larger. These agglomeration benefits are unlikely to be taken account of by those persons or firms choosing their locations.[41] The result is that resour-ces may not be allocated efficiently across regions. In fact, there might be multiple possible optima, depending on which locations grow to be large. In practice, historical factors determine which regions will grow and which will not.

Not only will the allocation of resources be inefficient in this context, but also government policies may themselves be detrimental to an efficient agglomeration of regions or urban areas. For example, equalizing grants may serve to perpetuate a dispersed population, when it would be more efficient to depopulate certain regions. Although this is a possible problem, there is simply not enough knowledge available to know how to deal with it.

Related to the agglomeration issue is the burgeoning field of endoge-nous growth theory, which also has regional implications. Endogenous growth theory posits that the growth of a given economy is determined partly by factors that are both endogenous to the economy in question and external to the decision makers in the economy. Thus, human capital investment and research and development (R&D) contribute to produc-tivity growth, but those undertaking them do not appropriate the rewards from these activities, so that too little is undertaken. For example, persons with high skills pass some of the knowledge and techniques associated with the skills on to other workers in the same regional labor market. An implication is that the in-migration of highly skilled workers will provide external benefits to existing workers, benefits that are not accounted for when location is decided. The result is that resources could be inefficiently allocated within a federation, and regional growth rates will not be as high as they could be.

---

[41] See also the recent analyses by Boadway, Cuff, and Marceau (2003), who analyze the consequences of labor market agglomeration effects for efficiency in the allocation of firms in a federal setting.

Again, the literature has not developed to the extent that policy pre-scriptions can be proposed on the basis of the models. But the possibility of these agglomeration and regional interaction effects being important leads one not to be too doctrinaire in adopting policies for a federation.

These examples of inefficiency in a federation have an influence on the assignment of responsibilities to different levels of government. They also give rise to arguments for intergovernmental fiscal arrangements in which higher levels of government retain some influence, if only via financial leverage, over the decentralized actions of lower levels of government. This arrangement, in turn, requires that higher levels of government raise more revenues than they need for their own purposes and transfer some to lower levels in ways designed to accomplish national objectives. This view is reinforced when sources of inequity in a federation are taken into account, to which we now turn.

Equity Considerations in a Federal Economy

Just as decentralized decision making in a federation gives rise to possible inefficiencies, it also gives rise to inequities. In addressing the sources of inequities, it is useful to make reference to the distinction that public finance economists have traditionally made between *horizontal equity* and *vertical equity*. The principle of horizontal equity says that persons who are equally well-off in the absence of government ought also to be equally as well-off in its presence. It is thus essentially a principle of "equal treatment of equals." This notion of equity turns out to be critical in the design of federal fiscal systems. Vertical equity is concerned with the appro-priate amount of redistribution from the better-off to the less well-off members of society. The extent of redistributive policies to achieve vertical equity will depend on both the constraints on redistributive instruments and society's aversion to inequality. This distinction between horizontal and vertical equity has been important in the literature on fiscal federalism.

In a federal state, the issue of equity introduces two main additional considerations that would not exist in a unitary state. One concerns ver-tical equity and the other horizontal equity. Consider them in turn.

Vertical Equity in a Federal State
With more than one level of government, the achievement of vertical equity becomes more complicated than in a unitary state. A major issue becomes which level of government is responsible for vertical equity. Those who use normative arguments to argue in favor of centralized responsibility do so

on the grounds that society's "social welfare function" ought to include all persons in the federation on a symmetric footing. In a sense, this is an implication of citizenship, or of equal treatment of equals. The argument is that in judging how much to redistribute from the better-off to the less well-off, it should not matter in which locality the persons reside. They would also argue that decentralizing responsibility for equity would result in a form of interjurisdictional competition that would result in too little redistribution. Each jurisdiction would have an incentive not to pursue redistribution, because it would tend to attract lower-income persons and discourage higher-income persons from in-migrating to the jurisdiction.

Those who favor some redistributive responsibilities for lower levels of government argue that there are distinctly local preferences for the extent of redistribution; namely, some localities may have a lower aversion to inequality than others. This is typically used as an argument for lower-level governments sharing the responsibility for redistribution with higher levels rather than the higher levels taking it on exclusively. Perhaps more telling is the argument that one's altruism is more pronounced for those residing closer to oneself. To the extent that altruism expressed through the political process is the ultimate rationale for redistribution, this might suggest that redistribution should be decentralized (subject to the proviso mentioned previously that beggar-thy-neighbor competition can induce inefficient amounts of redistribution).[42]

On the other hand, even if altruism is locally directed, that does not imply that it cannot be appropriately implemented by a central government, at least not as long as the degree of local altruism does not differ among localities. In the end, the appropriate sharing of redistribution responsibility between the federal and state levels of government is a matter for value judgment. In practice, both levels have fiscal instruments that can be used for redistributive purposes, so the issue is likely to be resolved through the political process.

Economists who take a more positive (public choice) view of the way governments behave often argue for decentralizing the redistributive function for other reasons. They see governments as engaging in too much redistribution because of the way in which collective decisions are taken.

Redistribution occurs, according to this view, because of the ability of purely selfish groups of persons being able to use the political system to

---

[42] Analyses of decentralizing redistribution in a world of local altruism may be found in Boskin (1973) and Pauly (1973). The former stresses the inefficiencies that can arise from fiscal competition over redistribution, while the latter emphasizes how centralized redistribution can be inefficient when preferences for redistribution are local.

their advantage, rather than because of the altruism of one group toward another. Thus, they would argue that redistribution is inefficiently excessive. Decentralizing the distributive function introduces interjurisdictional competition and effectively reduces the amount of redistribution that occurs. (Indeed, they apply the same argument to other functions of government as well as the redistributive one. For example, those who adopt the Leviathan perspective believe that government must be constrained from becoming too large and inefficient; decentralizing its functions in a federal system is one way to accomplish that.) More generally, economists who do not put a strong emphasis on redistribution tend to favor more decentralization of the redistributive function.

Of course, assigning responsibility for equity to one level of government or another is not a feasible option. Governments at all levels cannot avoid having an impact on the distribution of well-being because virtually everything they do will affect different groups differently. That is true for expenditures, for revenues, and for regulation. Thus, constraining different levels of government from undertaking redistributive functions must be done either by assigning functions appropriately or by allowing one level of government to influence the decisions taken by the other by regulation or financial incentive. This response turns out to be an important part of the way in which federal economies actually operate.

The consequences of the assignment of functions for vertical equity assume much greater importance once one recognizes the full extent of policy instruments that are used for redistribution. As discussed earlier, while economists have traditionally focused largely on the progressive tax-transfer system, in fact this component of the redistributive arsenal is arguably the least important. Much redistribution takes place through the provision of public services, through social insurance schemes, and through targeted transfers delivered outside the income tax system. It turns out, as we discuss further in the next chapter, that state-level governments are responsible for many of these items. Thus, in the absence of corrective measures, policies delivered by the states in a decentralized fashion will typically not satisfy national norms of vertical equity. This source of inequity is potentially important in a federal system and forms the basis for arguments for federal intervention.

Horizontal Equity in a Federal State

One of the most important considerations in designing a set of federal fiscal arrangements involves horizontal equity. In a federation with decentralized fiscal responsibilities, horizontal inequity is almost inevitable unless corrected explicitly. In the federalism context, horizontal equity is referred to as "fiscal equity," a term that goes back to Buchanan (1950). It is simply the notion of horizontal equity applied in a federal setting and is analogous to the concept of fiscal efficiency discussed previously.

In a decentralized federation, as we have discussed, different jurisdictions provide different NFBs to their residents. These NFB differentials come about from differences in source-based tax revenues (e.g., resource, property, and corporate taxes) and from the redistributive component of local government budgets operating through residence-based taxes. There may also be NFB differentials arising from differences in the cost and need for public services across localities. For example, localities with a higher proportion of children will need proportionately greater expenditures on education. If households can move easily, they will have an incentive to move to states with higher NFBs, resulting in an inefficient allocation of households across jurisdictions. But they cannot readily move (and this may be the more relevant case); therefore, households in different states will get systematically different NFBs from their state governments. As a result, otherwise identical persons will be treated differently by the public sector, specifically by the state governments. In other words, the actions of state public sectors, if left to determine their own expenditure levels using their own revenue sources, will violate the principle of horizontal equity in a federation.

As we discuss in later chapters, the existence of NFB differentials across lower-level jurisdictions, which is an inevitable consequence of decentralization of fiscal responsibilities, forms the main argument for a system of equalizing grants from higher levels of government to lower levels. The importance of such grants becomes greater the more decentralized the federation is. The argument for the use of grants to eliminate NFB differentials has a unique property. Because the existence of NFB differentials in a federation causes either fiscal inefficiencies or fiscal inequities, or more likely some combination of the two, their elimination is called for on both efficiency and equity grounds. It is one of those rare instances in economic policy analysis where efficiency and equity considerations do not conflict.

ADDITIONAL CONSIDERATIONS IN DEVELOPING COUNTRIES

A main purpose of this study is to investigate the desirability and the manner of decentralizing public-sector functions in developing countries, drawing on the experience of industrialized ones. Much of the theory of fiscal federalism that forms the basis for our analysis is based on the economies of federations in the developed world. It is worth briefly discussing some of the special features of developing countries that might temper the implications for decentralization in these countries drawn on the basis of experiences elsewhere. We do so first by outlining what some of those relevant special features are and then by briefly considering some of the sources of impetus for change.

Distinguishing Features of Developing Federations

Developing countries not only have lower per capita incomes, but their public sectors are less developed as well. We have noted that a major function of the public sector in Organization for Economic Co-operation and Development (OECD) economies is to achieve redistributive or equity objectives and that many of the policy instruments for addressing redistributive goals are decentralized to subnational governments. In developing countries, redistributive tax-transfer systems are much less prominent, and in some cases almost nonexistent. Universal social programs are uncommon, as are major social insurance programs. Thus, many of the arguments for decentralization relying on enhancing the efficiency of the delivery of public services do not have the same relevance.

The nature of public-sector intervention is quite different in developing countries. It tends to be much more oriented toward objectives of developing the economy rather than providing economic security. There is more participation of the government in the market sector of the economy, where state involvement can range from the use of state corporations in the provision of private goods and services, especially in tertiary sectors like transportation, utilities, and communications, but sometimes even in key sectors such as resource development. The state is also much more active in guiding investment decisions, not just through state investment but also by planning for the private sector and investment licensing. These sorts of activities, whether one might judge them to be good or bad, do not lend themselves readily to decentralization.

The public sector also faces different constraints and challenges on the financial side. Problems of debt and deficits are common. The means of raising revenues for the public sector are also considerably less developed than in OECD countries. Broad-based tax systems are less available as sources of revenues. While increasing numbers of developing countries have income, sales (e.g., value-added tax), and payroll taxes, the coverage is relatively limited compared to within OECD countries. Partly, this difference is a consequence of informal sectors being larger, but tax administration is sometimes less advanced and evasion is more rampant. As a result, tax mixes are quite varied, with much more reliance on indirect taxes than on direct ones. Again, this makes the decentralization of fiscal responsibilities more difficult.

Not only is the public sector less "developed" in developing countries, but so is the private sector. Factor markets, both capital and labor, are often thinner or even nonexistent for certain types of transactions. Thus, there may be fewer types of financial instruments, and the banking and equity sectors might be much less advanced so that financing is more difficult to obtain and more costly. Many workers may be employed (or self-employed) in the informal sector, where some of the protections afforded to workers may not be as available. Market regulations of the sorts found in OECD countries may not exist, such as competition laws, product safety provisions, workplace health and safety rules, environmental regulations, and bankruptcy laws. More generally, property rights may not be well defined for all types of assets. Again, this constrains the ability to decentralize fiscal responsibilities.

Finally, political and public administration factors constrain the case for redistribution. There may be a lack of democratic decision-making procedures and institutions or a lack of capacity to administer significant responsibilities at lower levels of government. In some countries there may be a fear of political instability from decentralizing decision-making authority, and some worry that subnational governments will be more corrupt as well. In the end, these political and administrative arguments may be the reason why developing countries tend to be much more fiscally centralized than OECD countries, including those in nonfederal or unitary nations. Of course, it can also be argued that decentralization would serve to overcome some of the deficiencies of subnational governments by providing them with administrative and political experience and inducing them into being responsible governments. The requirement to be responsive to their residents' needs might also reduce the extent of corruption and inefficiency. It might even be argued that some of the deficiencies of national governments might be countered by decentralization.

Sources of the Impetus for Decentralization

The gradual decentralization of fiscal responsibilities from national to subnational governments has been a common theme in many countries around the world. Although the process has differed greatly from country to country and is bound to reflect the particular institutional, political, and historical features of each one, there are some common factors that bear on many countries.

The first one is the enormous pressure arising from globalization – the opening up of world markets, accompanied by the rapid development of some developing economies and the revolution in communications. These changes have induced countries to seek to be more competitive, which in turn entails streamlining the public sector so as to reduce taxes and other government programs that might interfere with competitiveness.

Related to globalization is an increasing appreciation for market mechanisms and reliance on them. The end of the Cold War might have been interpreted as a victory of the capitalist ideal over that of the Soviet economy, which in turn led many countries to want to emulate the most successful of the capitalist countries. The belief in market mechanisms itself leads to a belief in decentralization as an organizing idea in the market economy. The same arguments for decentralization that are understood to yield benefits for the market economy can be used, as we shall see in the next chapter, to argue for decentralization in the public sector.

Advances in economic science themselves might take some credit for making the case for decentralization more compelling. In particular, the revolution in economic theory that has put the role of information at the center of economic analysis and interpretation has been influential. Some of the strongest arguments for decentralization center on information, in particular the fact that better information is available in a decentralized setting than in a centralized one. Coupled with this is a growing appreciation for the sorts of things that governments have come to do in the post–World War II era. Governments have come to be providers of economic security and vehicles for equal opportunity. Many of the instruments of the modern welfare state can more efficiently be delivered at subnational levels of government than at a federal level.

Finally, there is increased recognition that highly centralized public sectors are prone to be too big, too inefficient, and too unresponsive to the needs of their constituents.

TWO

The Decentralization of Government Authority

INTRODUCTION

The essence of federalism is the decentralization of decision making over some set of economic issues to lower levels of government. Decentralization is a very broad concept. All nations – even so-called unitary ones, with one main level of government that oversees all others – must of necessity engage in some sort of decentralization. For example, public services delivered to persons must at least be administered by agencies close to those being served. Thus, hospitals and schools must be administered by managers who have some degree of discretion over expenditure decisions; local services such as sanitation, water, recreation, and garbage are almost always delivered by local governments; welfare assistance and services are delivered through agencies employing social workers; and so on. What distinguishes federal nations from unitary nations is that the decentralization involves giving significant legislative authority to lower levels of government, as opposed to simply administrative authority. This definition is obviously rather loose. Nations that regard themselves as unitary states nonetheless allow local or regional governments considerable discretion in designing and delivering some public services. On the other hand, in some federal countries, central governments may have considerable power to override or direct legislative decisions of lower-level governments. Indeed, some countries that do not describe themselves as federations (e.g., South Africa) function as effectively as most federal countries do. These are largely semantic issues with which we need not be unduly concerned. In fact, one of the important considerations in federal countries is precisely how much power the central government ought to have to interfere with decisions of lower jurisdictions.

This chapter discusses the principles that are relevant in deciding how much legislative authority should be decentralized to lower levels of government. These principles guide what is referred to as the *assignment problem* in federations. What should be the general role of the federal, state, and local governments in the economy?[1] Who should be responsible for redistribution or for efficiency in the internal economic union? Which expenditure responsibilities should be assigned to each level of government? Which, if any, should be shared between levels? The same applies for tax responsibilities. Which level of government should be responsible for regulating activity in particular markets? What types of intergovernmental grants should be allowed? When, if at all, should one level of government be allowed to override the decisions of another? We address these types of questions in the following chapters. For now, we consider the general principles that might be used as a guide to answering these questions.

Although fiscal federalism is concerned with decentralizing decision making in the public sector, it is useful to begin by drawing an analogy with the private sector because economists take the decentralization of private-sector decision making for granted. The merits of decentralized decision making in the private sector are generally widely accepted. The decentralization of decision making to individual households gives them the opportunity to make choices that are in their best interests, given the resources available to them and the prices they face – choices about how much of various goods and services to consume and how much effort to exert and how to organize their households. Similarly, decentralizing decisions to firms permits production decisions that allow them to use inputs most economically and to produce outputs that maximize profits for their shareholders. Decentralized decision making gives firms an incentive to see that efficient amounts of effort are exerted by both workers and managers and provides an incentive to minimize the various sorts of monitoring and agency costs that naturally occur within organizations. In addition, decentralization improves technical efficiency both by reducing administrative overheads and by allowing information to be used more effectively. It allows for more innovation and enables decisions to be made by those closest to the ultimate users of the products of the economy.

In addition to ensuring that individual households and firms behave in the most efficient way from their own individual perspectives, decentralized decision making also induces efficiency in the way in which outcomes are determined as a result of the interaction of these agents on markets. Thus, in a competitive market setting, decentralization induces price-taking

---

[1]   As mentioned in the preceding chapter, unless we are considering specific countries, we adopt the convention of referring to the three main levels of government as the federal, the state, and the local governments throughout this book. In some cases, we can be content with considering two levels only.

behavior among firms and households, which generally leads to efficiency in the allocation of the economy's resources among alternative uses – the so-called first fundamental theorem of welfare economics discussed in the previous chapter. Such are the advantages of decentralized decision making in the private sector of the economy that they are now not questioned.

At the same time, there are limits to the extent of decentralization that is possible or desirable in the private sector. Economies of scale can be important in various senses and in a number of sectors. The least-cost output in some sectors may require large amounts of capital, as in transportation and utilities. Network and information economies might be important in some sectors, such as communications. Sectors for which research and development or risk sharing is important may benefit from scale economies. In the end, the advantages of decentralization must be set against those of scale in determining the optimal size of firms in various sectors and the optimal structure of decision making within firms. Nonetheless, given the advantages of decentralization, the onus of proof must be placed on those who would take actions to offset problems that might arise from decentralization.

Similar issues arise in the public sector where the institutions of decision making are not individual households and firms but different levels of government. There are advantages and disadvantages of decentralizing the various functions of government from higher (and larger) levels to lower (and smaller) levels. The literature on fiscal federalism is devoted in large part to analyzing the consequences of varying degrees and forms of decentralizing and to suggesting the desirable extent of decentralization in various contexts. Much of the literature draws on the practice and circumstances in industrialized countries, where federal systems of economic decision making have evolved over a long period of time. One of the main purposes of this study is to review some of the elements of the literature on fiscal federalism that have been formulated in the context of industrialized countries and to judge how they apply to the setting of developing and transitional countries where, by and large, decision making has been much more centralized.

The analogue with decentralization in the private sector is, of course, only an imperfect one. There are many differences between decision making in the two sectors. A key one concerns the objectives used for economic decision making. Private-sector firms are typically interested in maximizing profits. In the public sector, objectives may include the traditional normative goals of economic efficiency and redistributive equity that a benevolent government might use, as well as the more self-serving ones of maximizing political or electoral support and responding to the influence of bureaucrats and pressure groups.

The sorts of economic decisions that the public sector undertakes are also much different from those made in the private sector. The private sector sells the goods and services it produces on markets. The public sector, on the other hand, engages largely in nonmarket activities, which, broadly speaking, involves three sorts of things: spending, raising revenues, and intervening in the private sector by regulating its activities. Expenditures take the two main forms of the provision of goods and services (usually free of charge) and the making of transfer payments of various sorts to the private sector or to other levels of government. Some of the goods and services provided by the public sector are "public" in the sense discussed in the preceding chapter, but many, perhaps the majority, are of a private nature. These public services are *quasi private* – that is, private services that are not provided through the private pricing system. That a large proportion of government spending takes the form of transfer payments and the provision of quasi-private services reflects the fact that much what governments do is redistributive and that much of this redistribution takes place on the expenditure side of the budget. This has important implications for how one views the assignment of functions in a federation.

On the revenue side, although some revenues are obtained in the public sector by charges or user fees for goods and services provided or by money creation, the bulk of the revenue comes from taxation of one form or another (including future tax liabilities incurred through government borrowing). Tax systems are typically very complex, consisting of a wide variety of tax types, some broad based, others narrowly based, some levied on transactions, and others levied on individuals or firms. There is considerable scope for tax policies to be decentralized if the will exists to do it. Similarly, regulatory policies also take many different forms. They are often tempting policies for governments to engage in because they can accomplish similar objectives to taxation and subsidization but seemingly without requiring any revenues to flow through the public sector. The drawback of regulatory policies, however, is that the bureaucracy, often with considerable discretionary powers, must administer them. Government regulation can give rise to costly and capricious decision making, as well as the possibility for illicit activities.

It should also be remembered that in addition to the standard public and private sectors, there exists a nonprofit or voluntary sector that complements to some extent the functions of the public sector, particularly those involving redistributive objectives. In a developing economy in which the state has not built a substantial social safety net, the nonprofit sector is relied on to provide many of the social programs that governments normally perform in industrialized countries, including providing even basic services such as health care, housing, welfare services, and education. As economies develop and governments begin to provide the foundations of a welfare state, they tend to crowd out the nonprofit sector in the process.

Whatever might be the motivating forces guiding public-sector decision making, there are still advantages to be weighed against the disadvantages from decentralizing decision making to lower levels of government. Part of the purpose of this chapter is to outline what those advantages and disadvantages might be and to discuss in broad terms what overall roles different levels of government might be responsible for performing. In subsequent chapters, we discuss in more detail the assignment of specific functions to federal, state, and local governments. Here, we restrict ourselves to a discussion of principles.

It should be stressed at the outset that one should not be very precise or dogmatic about the ideal extent of decentralization. The degree and form of decentralization of various tax and expenditure decisions depends upon the political, economic, and institutional characteristics of the country in question, as well as on the role that its governments actually assume. Value judgments are involved as well as judgments about the way governments behave and the empirical effects that those government actions have on the economy. Thus, rational and reasonable people can disagree about the desired amount of decentralization. For that reason, we pose our analysis in the form of principles rather than precise prescriptions, though we, like others, have our own views about the role of government and the assignment of functions, views that will show through at times. These caveats about the judgmental nature of policy prescriptions are of special importance in the context of considering decentralization in developing countries, because, as we have mentioned, their features are somewhat different from those found in industrialized countries, where considerable decentralization has often become the practice after lengthy evolution.

We now turn to a general discussion of the principles involved in assigning of economic functions in a federation. The benefits and costs of decentralization are outlined, both for the expenditure and for the tax side of the public-sector budget. Decentralization can take varying forms. These range from assigning exclusive responsibility for a given function to a given level of government to situations of co-occupied responsibilities in which one level of government is able to influence the decisions made by another in varying degrees through mechanisms such as regulation, the power to override decisions, or financial intervention. To some extent, the amount of decentralization on the expenditure side of the government budget can be determined independently of that on the tax side, and the principles can be developed separately. Ultimately, we have to deal with reconciling the expenditure responsibilities and the revenue-raising capabilities of each level of government. That is the task of the system of intergovernmental fiscal relations. The fiscal relations between governments, especially the system of intergovernmental transfers, play a vital role in a federation. A properly designed system of transfers is what allows the benefits of decentralized decision making to be achieved without sacrificing national objectives of efficiency and equity.

THE DECENTRALIZATION OF FUNCTIONS IN A FEDERAL SYSTEM

As we have mentioned, the notion of an ideal assignment of functions is evasive because so much depends upon institutional considerations, value judgments, and empirical consequences that are hard to verify. These ambiguities arise from a number of factors. The political and social structure of the country might be such as to preclude the desired amount of decentralization. For example, countries with unstable regions may be reluctant to decentralize economic responsibilities for fear of inducing political instability, including impetus for secession from the federation. The extent of decentralization one favors also depends upon how one assesses the extent of the role that should be taken on by governments in the economy. Roughly speaking, those who wish to impose constraints on the size of government will likely want more rather than less decentralization. The relative role of central and lower levels of government will also be influenced by the degree to which governments are relied upon to redistribute income. Those who stress the redistributive role of government will generally favor more centralization than those who wish to restrain government redistributive activities will. This outcome is partly because of the possibility of redistribution being diminished by competing lower-level governments. It is also partly because redistribution objectives typically involve applying common standards for redistribution regardless of the states of residence of taxpayers and transfer recipients. Finally, the benefits of decentralization will depend on the responsiveness of economic activity to lower-level government decision making – that is, to what extent can state and local government policies influence (or believe they can influence) the level of economic activity attracted to their jurisdictions? That empirical question remains unanswered.

We are not able to resolve these issues because they depend either on value judgments or on unverified hypotheses about government behavior. The best we can do is to outline the sorts of considerations that need to be taken into account in deciding on which functions to decentralize and which to retain at higher levels of government. Ultimately, these amount to applying the conventional notions of efficiency, equity, and administrative effectiveness to a federal setting.

One useful perspective to take on the assignment of functions to higher or lower levels of government involves drawing a parallel between the role of markets and that of governments. Economists typically argue in favor of decentralized market solutions unless they can be shown to fail demonstrably. As discussed in the previous chapter, this is because of the well-known efficiency advantages of decentralized, private-sector, competitive decision making discussed in the previous chapter compared with the lack of incentives and bureaucratic decision-making procedures of government. Consequently, the onus for government intervention is typically put squarely on the shoulders of those who argue for it.

In the case of federal economies, it might similarly be argued that decentralizing economic functions to lower levels of government should be favored unless sound arguments can be advanced for centralized economic power. This has been referred to as the principle of subsidiarity. In our view, this principle is a useful methodological rule to adopt, and one we follow. The advantages of decentralized decision making in a federation should be clear from our subsequent discussion. The case for centralization will then follow from observing the circumstances under which decentralized public-sector decision making leads unavoidably to inefficiencies and inequities in the federation. Even in these circumstances, centralization need not entail exclusive responsibility for a particular area of policy making. A key message of this study is that the inefficiencies and inequities that may accompany decentralization can often be addressed with central government policies that are not so intrusive as to displace decentralized decision making and the delivery of services at lower levels of government. Consequently, we place considerable importance on intergovernmental fiscal relations, especially the system of transfers, as a means of facilitating decentralized decision making, while preserving efficiency, equity, and administrative effectiveness in the national economy and in the delivery of public services.

Our discussion in this chapter sets aside a potentially important issue for the assignment of powers in developing countries: the transition from one federal fiscal system to another. As we shall see, it is typically the case that decision making is relatively centralized in developing countries compared with the ideal. There may be various historical and political reasons for this. For example, the institutions that assume expenditure, revenue-raising, and regulatory responsibilities at lower levels of government – whether they are decision-making institutions or administrative and service-delivery institutions – are either nonexistent or not highly developed. The absence of such institutions implies that there would be a certain transition cost or learning period involved in decentralizing fiscal functions to lower levels of government. In each case, this transition cost would have to be set against the benefits of decentralization. But one should be cautious about using transition costs as the sole reason for avoiding decentralization, with all the longer-term benefits that it entails. As experience in developed countries indicates, once independent responsibility is given, lower levels of government often quickly and efficiently assume it.

The previous chapter dealt with the efficiency and equity roles of government in a market economy and with the special sorts of efficiency and equity considerations that arise in federal economies. To put the assignment of power issue in perspective, it is useful first to present the arguments for and against decentralization of responsibilities in a federation, both on the expenditure and on the tax side. Given the high degree of centralization of powers currently in existence in developing countries, this is a natural perspective to adopt. We then look at the roles of higher versus lower levels of government in general terms, given those special issues of efficiency and equity of federal economies. This approach enables us to set out some views about the overall roles of different levels of government in a federation and serves as a basis for our subsequent discussion of the roles of government in specific areas of government responsibility, which are taken up in the following chapters.

In what follows, our discussion is couched in terms of a federation with two levels of government. For expositional purposes only, the higher level is referred to as the federal government, and the lower level as the state government. In practice, all federations consist of a number of different levels of government, including federal, state, regional, county, municipal, and even some special-interest jurisdictions. The principles developed here can be readily extended to them.

The Pros and Cons of Decentralizing Expenditure Responsibilities

There are well-established arguments for decentralizing some of the economic functions of government to lower levels. As discussed in Chapter 1, some of these are related to the special problems of efficiency and equity that arise in federal economies. Others relate to the fact that lower levels of government may be better placed to perform certain functions. The main general arguments for decentralizing expenditure responsibilities to state governments are as follows.

State and Local Public Goods

Public goods – goods whose services are simultaneously consumed by a large number of persons and/or firms – can be distinguished according to the geographic extent of the benefits they deliver. At one extreme are national public goods, such as defense, foreign affairs, and control of the money supply. These goods are natural candidates for centralized provision. However, other public goods provide collective benefits to a more localized population. Of necessity, they must be provided separately in different locations across the nation. Although they could be provided to the various regions by a central authority, decentralization might be preferable for a few reasons. For one, the preferred amount and type of local public goods provided to a given locality depends on the tastes and needs of local residents. Local governments are likely to be in a better position to match their provision with local preferences. There may be more of a tendency for the federal government to implement expenditure programs that are uniform across the country, rather than those which cater to differentiated local preference and needs.[2]

Lower-level provision is also likely to be less costly. Administrative overheads should be lower because there are fewer levels of bureaucracy and because agency and monitoring costs are likely to be lower. Lower-level jurisdictions should be in a better position to identify and contract suppliers to provide the goods and services used in the provision of the public goods. Lower-level jurisdictions are also likely to face some competitive pressures from neighboring jurisdictions because of the mobility of resources across state boundaries, which can serve as a device for disciplining governments into cost effectiveness. It can also serve as a yardstick against which the local population can judge the type, quality, and cost of local public goods being provided.

Of course, it is unlikely that the ideal geographic extent of provision of any one local public good (to the extent that that can be meaningfully determined) will coincide with actual political borders in a federation. The optimal matching of jurisdictions with responsibility for providing local

---

[2]   In his classic treatise on the economics of federalism, Oates (1972) stressed this benefit of decentralization, which follows closely from the logic of the Tiebout (1956) model.

public goods would require a different-sized jurisdiction of each public good, resulting in a very large number of jurisdictions, with overlapping territories. This outcome is clearly not feasible on administrative and political grounds. As a result, the matching of jurisdictions with responsibilities for providing local public goods is likely to be imperfect, which may result in interjurisdictional spillovers that must be dealt with by appropriate policy instruments.[3]

Quasi-Private Goods and Services

We have already mentioned that relatively few of the goods and services provided through the public sector are public ones; most are quasi private, including some of the most important ones in terms of spending (e.g., schools, roads, hospitals). Similar issues favoring their decentralization apply here as in the case of local public goods. Given that these are ultimately services provided to individuals (or firms), their actual delivery will be administered through locally situated institutions or agencies regardless of which level of government is responsible for their provision. As with local public goods, the main beneficiaries of these locally delivered quasi-private goods are residents in the states involved. Decentralization to the states should allow the services to be provided in a way that best caters to local tastes and needs. State delivery should be more cost effective because administrative overheads and monitoring costs that would be incurred by a central bureaucracy are avoided. In terms of economic jargon, the agency costs associated with delivering the services should be less if lower-level jurisdictions are responsible for their delivery. These agency costs arise because government officials are not as well informed about the costs associated with delivering public services, costs that depend upon the severity of need of the local population, efficiency of management, effort exerted by workers in the agency, and so on. The argument is that lower-level governments are better informed and can monitor delivery agencies more effectively than higher-level governments, which are inevitably further away. Efficient provision and innovation should also result because of an element of competition induced among state levels of government providing similar services in parallel to their respective constituencies.

On the other hand, despite the benefits of decentralizing the provision of quasi-private goods to state governments, it may be useful for the federal government to retain a supervisory or oversight role if there are

---

[3] The seminal paper on the optimal matching of functions to jurisdictions is Breton (1965). See also the more recent version by Breton and Scott (1978).

advantages to harmonization of some of the design features of these goods. For example, if residents are mobile, harmonizing certain general features of the programs across state jurisdictions, such as portability and eligibility provisions, may be beneficial in order to ensure that labor mobility is not impeded and to guard against wasteful competition among states. Also, there is a limit to the amount of decentralization that is beneficial purely on cost-effectiveness grounds. Economies of scale in administering and delivering quasi-private goods and services could argue against decentralizing their provision all the way to the local level.

Perhaps most importantly, some of the main public services do more than simply cater to local preferences. They also fulfill important equity or redistributive objectives. Indeed, because they are quasi private, there is no market failure inherent in them requiring their provision through the public sector. Important public services such as health, education, and welfare services are typically provided through the public sector precisely because they are instruments of redistributive policy. They may provide social and economic security, foster equality of opportunity, or simply be in-kind transfers of services thought to be of particular importance to the needy. As such, the federal government will have a legitimate interest in how they are designed and delivered. The exercise of this interest need not preclude the services in question from being decentralized to state governments. But it does imply that measures might have to be taken to ensure that the state provision of these public services satisfies national norms of equity and efficiency. The issue of how to achieve the substantial benefits of decentralization without compromising national efficiency and equity objectives is one of the most important questions in fiscal federalism, and one to which we shall return. For now, suffice it to say that resolving this issue involves going beyond the simple assignment of responsibilities to the design of intergovernmental fiscal and institutional arrangements.

Targeted Transfers

Some interpersonal redistribution takes place through the income-tax-transfer system. But it is typically the case that transfers delivered to the poorest members of society are not. Rather, they are delivered by welfare agencies. There are various reasons for this. These transfers are often made on the basis of criteria that are somewhat more reflective of need than income is. Thus, ability to work is taken into consideration, as well as the need for particular types of expenditures, asset wealth, and living circumstances. The poor are typically not taxpayers, so would otherwise not be part of the income tax system. Their circumstances may change frequently, and their transfer payment would therefore need to change over the tax year. Finally, it may be preferable not to rely on the self-reporting and subsequent auditing mechanism used by the income tax system. In any case, transfers to the needy are based on prescreening by welfare agencies and are often subject to continual monitoring to verify changes in circumstances and sometimes to ensure that job search activities are being undertaken. These procedures are basically designed to reveal information, and their implementation clearly requires agencies that are as close as possible to the intended recipients. Decentralizing the responsibility for delivering targeted transfers to the lowest possible level facilitates the control of these agencies.

A special case arises with respect to transfers to the unemployed – unemployment insurance. This targeted transfer also requires direct contact with recipients. The complicating feature is that the need for unemployment insurance can depend upon shocks that might be to some extent independent across states. If so, there may be an argument for federal government involvement in unemployment insurance as a means of sharing risks across states. But this does not necessarily require federal provision. The advantages of decentralizing the provision of unemployment insurance to the states can be achieved without compromising the risk-sharing role that the federal government can serve. Designing the set of federal-state transfers that fund unemployment insurance payments so that they explicitly account for the different needs that states face in any given year can accomplish this. Such a judiciously designed system of fiscal arrangements can thus achieve the benefits of decentralization without incurring some of the costs.

Local Preferences for Redistribution

Preferences for redistribution may vary from one locality to another. Some jurisdictions may have more aversion to inequality than others, or different demographic or social characteristics may call for different degrees and types of redistribution being preferred in different jurisdictions. Some localities may prefer the use of certain types of in-kind transfers rather than cash transfers. This preference would suggest some decentralization of the provision of goods and services that are primarily redistributive. It might also support some state responsibility for the extent of redistribution accomplished through the tax-transfer system.

As with quasi-private goods and services, decentralization of other policy instruments for redistribution runs the risk of introducing distortions into the internal common market as well as wasteful and futile interjurisdictional tax or expenditure competition. It also runs the risk of compromising national redistributive objectives. In the end, some compromise must be reached between the pursuit of redistribution by the states and that done by the federal government. The nature of that compromise will vary with national circumstances and with the will or consensus that exists about the extent of redistribution that is desirable.

A word of caution is in order. Despite the impression that one gets from the traditional literature on fiscal federalism,[4] it is not possible to assign the responsibility for redistribution to one level of government or the other, or even to divide it easily into given shares. Virtually everything governments do has a redistribution consequence, if not an intention. In the end, redistribution is a shared responsibility, and mechanisms should be in place for the federal and state governments to pursue their respective redistributive objectives in a coordinated fashion.

Fiscal and Political Accountability

Generally, the decentralization of responsibilities may also induce more fiscal responsibility or accountability as well as more political accountability in the federation. The provision is at a level of government that is "closer" to the people served, and the government faces the discipline of persons or businesses leaving a jurisdiction that behaves irresponsibly (referred to as the exit option). Similar to interfirm competition in the private sector, inter-jurisdictional competition can be healthy and efficiency enhancing. Moreover, dividing responsibilities among levels of government in itself makes the responsibility for particular budgetary items sharper.

The argument for fiscal responsibility is especially valid to the extent that states must finance their expenditures out of their own-source revenues. It can be used as an argument for decentralizing the responsibility for raising the requisite amount to finance state public expenditures, at least at the margin. However, decentralization usually occurs in an asymmetric way: expenditure responsibilities are decentralized more than revenue-raising ones. The implication is that at least some state (and local) expenditures are financed by transfers from the federal government. As we argue in later chapters, there are sound reasons for such an asymmetric arrangement. Although the transfers themselves are indispensable for achieving national objectives in a federal system, they can detract from accountability both by blurring the financial accountability for public services in the eyes of the electorate and possibly by leading to adverse behavioral responses by the states.

---

[4] Good examples are Musgrave (1959) and Oates (1972).

An example of the latter is the so-called soft budget constraint problem discussed in the previous chapter. In the context of fiscal federalism, this refers to a situation in which lower-level jurisdictions anticipate that if they take budgetary actions that jeopardize their solvency or their ability to deliver necessary public services, they will be rescued ("bailed out") by federal funds.[5] This anticipation turns out to be correct, because the federal government finds it difficult ex post not to come to the aid of states that have behaved imprudently. This problem is a classic example of the time inconsistency of public policy and arises because of the inability of governments to commit to future actions. This inability to commit can provoke the federal government into imposing constraints on lower-level governments that restrict their ability to spend beyond their means. Thus, there may be limitations imposed on the ability of state and/or local governments to issue debt.

Another element of political accountability concerns the extent to which the political system can be subverted by self-seeking elements both within the government bureaucracy and outside. Those inside might be able to make decisions that enhance their well-being at the expense of the taxpayers, such as taking excessive perquisites, bloating the size of their bureaus, or even engaging in outright corruption. Taxpayers, through their elected representatives, may find it difficult to control this sort of behavior, if only because they lack the detailed information to detect it. Decentralization may serve to impose some discipline on the bureaucracy by exposing it to competition and standards that have been achieved in neighboring jurisdictions. By the same token, outside interest groups may be able to prey on the bureaucracy for special favors or *rents* that inevitably accrue from public-sector decisions. Again, decentralization may reduce the preponderance of rent-seeking activities by reducing the size of potential rents and making it less worthwhile to invest resources to obtain them.[6] Moreover, decentralization may make it easier to detect both bureaucratic largesse and rent seeking simply by putting decision making in the hands of lower-level political institutions.

Against these advantages of decentralization, there are also certain broad disadvantages. That is, there are some advantages to retaining at least some responsibility for the design and delivery of some public services at the center. Some of these have already been mentioned as caveats to the

---

[5] The soft budget constraint problem can also be applied to the propensity of governments to bail out both public and private firms. Qian and Roland (1998) have argued that decentralization can reduce the severity of this problem.

[6] For a formal analysis of this phenomenon, see Sato (1998).

benefits of decentralization. What follows is a list of some of the more important disadvantages of decentralization. These disadvantages form the basis either for assigning particular responsibilities to the federal government or, where the case for decentralization is compelling, for seeking ways to manage the decentralization so that national objectives are not unduly compromised.

Fiscal Inefficiency and Inequity

The most pervasive effect of decentralization results from the fact that different states may have different capacities to provide public services. That is, differential net fiscal benefits (NFBs) will typically result. As we have seen, if persons of a given type obtain different NFBs from two different states, either fiscal inequity or fiscal inefficiency will occur, or some combination of the two. If households are mobile, there will be an incentive to migrate between states on account of the NFB differentials, and the result will be that factors of production will be inefficiently allocated within the federation. On the other hand, if they are immobile, horizontal inequity will result. Either way, there will be a social cost to decentralization that is unaccompanied by compensating measures.

In the case of decentralizing expenditures, these differences in NFBs basically arise from differences in the need for public services. If an objective of government is to provide public services to identifiable groups of persons, such as the elderly (health), the young (education), or the needy (welfare), different states may have to incur quite different levels of expenditures to provide given levels of public services. In these circumstances, the tax costs for a taxpayer of a given income associated with providing these services – and thus NFBs – can vary significantly from one state to another.

As discussed in Chapter 1, there are caveats that must be made with respect to the relevance of NFB differences arising from different needs. First, the problem will arise only to the extent that the decentralized public services are not financed by benefit taxation. This seems not to be a serious concern. Most studies seem to suggest that state-level fiscal policies are at least mildly redistributive. A good approximation for OECD federations might be that the tax systems of state-level governments are roughly proportional.

Second, the fact that decentralization of expenditure responsibilities leads to differences in NFBs because of need should not be regarded as a telling argument against decentralization. Such differences can be readily compensated for by an appropriately designed set of fiscal transfers to the states from the federal government. We return in Chapters 9 and 10 to the issue of how to design such transfers.

Third, in a decentralized setting, NFBs differentials might arise even in the absence of differences in needs or tax capacities. That is because different states might choose to offer different levels of public services to their citizens, unlike, say, a unitary state. Indeed, one of the purported advantages of federations is to allow for diversity in state decision making. Nonetheless, a cogent argument might be made that needs-based differences are a concern and should be undone by equalizing transfers. The argument is that eliminating NFB differentials provides different states with the *potential* to provide comparable levels of public services at comparable tax rates. That they may not choose to behave in a common fashion might be regarded as a legitimate consequence of decentralizing fiscal responsibility. As discussed later, there may well be some other reasons of national efficiency or equity for encouraging states to provide some minimal level of services for some types of expenditures. But that would be over and above the issues associated with NFB differentials. The fact is that designing policies in a federation will always entail some compromise between the advantages of diversity arising from decentralization and the advantages for national efficiency and equity from states adhering to some common national standards. Different federations will resolve that compromise in different ways.

Interjurisdictional Spillovers

As discussed in Chapter 1, one of the efficiency issues arising in federal economies is the possibility of interjurisdictional spillovers resulting from decision making by lower-level jurisdictions. Public and quasi-private goods and services provided in one jurisdiction might generate benefits for the residents of neighboring jurisdictions. If left to their own, jurisdictions would systematically underprovide those goods and services that have positive spillovers and overprovide those with negative spillovers. Examples of positive spillovers include: the provision of transportation and communications facilities in one jurisdiction that are utilized by those in another; education and training programs that can attract those from other jurisdictions, or train persons who then migrate away from the jurisdiction in which the training has been obtained; welfare programs that not only affect the number of poor residing in a given jurisdiction relative to neighboring ones but might also appeal to the altruistic tendencies of those outside the supporting jurisdiction; pollution control programs whose benefits are not constrained by political boundaries; and recreational and cultural facilities that are available outside the community providing them.

The more expenditure responsibilities are decentralized, the more likely it is that interjurisdictional spillovers will arise, and the greater will be the extent of those spillover benefits. Consequently, there may be a greater misallocation of resources. Centralizing the provision of the spillover-generating program (i.e., not decentralizing its provision to lower jurisdictions) is one obvious way of internalizing the externalities. However, centralization of provision is not a necessary response to the problem of spillovers and may in fact be counterproductive. While spillovers would certainly be avoided that way, all the benefits of decentralization would also be forfeited. It is presumably better to find remedies that retain the considerable advantages of decentralized provision. One such way uses the power of the federal government to make conditional transfers to the states – the so-called spending power of the federal government. The federal government can influence the provision of spillover-generating activities by state governments through the use of matching conditional grants, or "shared-cost" grants, directed specifically at the program in question, with the magnitude of the matching rate chosen to provide the desired incentive. The use of matching conditional grants for this purpose has a long history both in the fiscal federalism literature and in practice. Many federations have had shared-cost programs in areas such as transportation, infrastructure, education or training programs, welfare schemes, and health care. However, their use is not without problem. For one thing, it is virtually impossible to know the "correct" rate of matching to apply because it is not possible to observe the extent of spillover benefits generated by a given expenditure program.[7] Thus, the matching rate must be chosen arbitrarily. In practice, rates are often quite high, typically 50 percent, and detractors argue that this provides an incentive for lower-level jurisdictions to overspend.

A key issue with the availability of shared-cost grants as a policy instrument of the federal government is that it provides the federal government with a potential instrument for interfering with the independence of decision making by state governments. It is argued that this distorts their priorities (to the extent that the cost sharing is not truly based on spillovers) and compromises the purpose of decentralization. The problem is that the spending power, once given, is difficult to constrain. The federal

---

[7] It might be argued that the impossibility to measure benefits of public expenditure programs applies more generally to all public goods and services. On the other hand, at least in the case of state and local public goods, the ability of citizens to "vote with their feet" provides one vehicle for lower-level governments to become informed about the benefits of their expenditures relative to their taxes. This is the message of the Tiebout model. Such a mechanism does not apply in the same way to spillover benefits.

government can effectively spend its revenues as it sees fit. In systems of government where parliaments or legislatures are supreme in spending decisions, it is hard to implement meaningful constitutional controls over the use of the spending power, even in ways that interfere with or influence state decisions. The political process itself must be relied upon as the discipline. This issue concerning the appropriate use of the spending power by the federal government to influence state budgetary priorities is by no means limited to the control of interjurisdictional spillovers. Indeed, as we argue, the spending power is an indispensable policy instrument for enabling the federal government to pursue its national efficiency and equity objectives in circumstances in which state expenditure programs have important national consequences. Indeed, the spending power is a sine qua non of an effectively functioning decentralized federation: it facilitates the decentralization process.

Finally, a very important feature of shared-cost programs is whether they are formula driven or discretionary. Ideally, grants from higher to lower levels of government should be based on objective formulas so that the recipient government retains as much independence of decision making as possible. Formula-driven grants also ensure that there is predictability about the stream of grants so that states can plan their expenditures rationally. However, in the case of shared-cost conditional grants, some amount of discretion by higher-level governments is inevitable, if only to determine what sorts of expenditures are eligible for sharing. The danger is that the granting government becomes too intrusive in attempting to influence the sorts and designs of expenditures subject to sharing. Such intrusion would also subvert the principle of decentralized decision making. The remedy for spillovers could turn out to be worse than the problem itself. Again, it is hard to imagine how higher-level governments could be prevented from acting this way, given the policy instrument of the spending power. The best protection against an overzealous federal government is the checks and balances of the political system itself, and the openness of the system of fiscal decision making to both the public and the press.

Conditional grants are not the only means available for correcting the spillovers that might arise in a decentralized federation. As with the correction of externalities in the market economy, the internalization of spillovers could, in principle, be accomplished by negotiations among lower-level governments in the manner of a Coasian bargaining solution. In this case, the federal government need not be involved at all. Intergovernmental negotiation is, however, a very ponderous process, especially because unanimous agreement would be required. The track record of bargaining among lower-level governments as a means of settling spillover problems or other interdependencies is very weak.

Alternatively, if the higher-level government has some regulatory power over the lower-level one, it could regulate the spillovers out of existence, for example by imposing mandates on lower-level governments that require them to behave in specified ways. In light of the concerns expressed previously about an overly intrusive higher-level government, this might not be an ideal solution. If anything, it might be applicable only at the state level of government in federations where the local governments are truly subservient to the state rather than at the national level where somewhat broader objectives are at stake.

Expenditure Competition

Not only can benefits from state public expenditures spill over onto those of neighboring jurisdictions; expenditures may also induce factors of production to relocate into the state from other states. This possibility is particularly relevant for three sorts of expenditures – business services, infrastructure, and subsidies. As discussed in the previous chapter, these are all examples of what we referred to as horizontal fiscal externalities. The use of these forms of spending gives rise to destructive (beggar-thy-neighbor) competition in such expenditures, as each jurisdiction treats the relocation of businesses from neighboring jurisdictions as a benefit to itself. These expenditures thus represent negative fiscal externalities that serve to provide an incentive for all jurisdictions to spend excessive and thus wasteful amounts of resources.

Once one puts expenditure competition in the context of other fiscal policy instruments, some caveats should be noted. First, to the extent that the expenditures are financed by taxes that themselves have externalities associated with them, the overall externality effect becomes less clear. The horizontal fiscal externality from the taxation might well be negative if the tax base is also mobile across jurisdictions, that is, if an increase in tax rate causes a loss in tax base to other jurisdictions. If the business expenditures are financed by such a tax, the incentive to overspend is countered.

Second, there may be other reasons for expecting that fiscal policies will inefficiently discourage private investment. A compelling one is the time inconsistency of capital taxation, also referred to as the holdup problem. The argument is that once capital is in place, governments will be inclined to tax it and find it difficult to resist this inclination. That being the case, firms will anticipate that capital tax rates will be excessive, and this possibility will discourage investment. A well-known way out of this problem is to provide up-front incentives to invest. The provision of business services is one such compensating policy. Thus, business competition may be beneficial in this context.[8]

A third factor to note concerns the mix of the public-sector budget. The fact that the provision of business services is accompanied by negative fiscal externalities while the delivery of public goods and services is not implies that relatively too much of the budget will be devoted to business services, subsidies, and infrastructure compared with that amount devoted to public goods and services.[9]

Economies of Scale

As in the private sector, scale economies provide an argument for provision of public goods or services by larger units of government. This would be the case where administrative overheads are large, such as, for example, the provision of labor-intensive public services to individuals in areas of education, health, and welfare services. In typical cases, it is not clear that this argument applies to the assignment of functions between the federal level of government and the states, because states in most countries would probably be large enough to exhaust most economies of scale. It is presumably more relevant between the states and their municipalities. Also, a judicial sharing of responsibilities in areas where administrative economies exist could allow the federation to reap the advantages of decentralization while taking advantage of scale economies. This consideration applies as well in the assignment of taxing powers, where the advantages of a single tax-collecting authority are significant.

For example, primary education could be shared between, say, the state and the local governments in a particular nation. The latter might be given full responsibility for building and operating schools within their jurisdictions, and partial financing for them can come from local sources. The state might be responsible for curriculum standards, teacher training, setting employment standards, and monitoring and testing school performance. Indeed, there might even be a three-way sharing of responsibilities in education, especially at higher levels where national standards of educational programs and student evaluation are important for maintaining efficiency in the internal economic union and for providing equality of

---

[8] Indeed, capital tax competition may also be beneficial for the same reason. For a model that analyzes this problem, see Kehoe (1989).

[9] Keen and Marchand (1997) study a federation in which state governments compete both in taxes and in business services. They show that in the Nash equilibrium a coordinated change by all states involving a revenue-neutral increase in public goods and decrease in business services would make all jurisdictions better off.

opportunity across the entire federation. This illustration is of particular relevance to the final two categories of drawbacks to full decentralization discussed next.

Before we turn to the remaining categories, there is one further advantage of size that is sometimes emphasized in discussions of the assignment of functions. States within a federation might be subject to idiosyncratic shocks. They may have differing industrial structures, or their populations may have different demographic compositions. If the risk is insurable, they may find it difficult to self-insure because markets are not available. Insurance may not be provided because of moral hazard associated with government decision making: governments have a high degree of influence over the consequences of economic shocks. Or governments may simply be too short-lived to have the foresight to engage in the long-term self-insurance against future idiosyncratic shocks. Moreover, even if they could self-insure to some extent, their risks may not be fully insurable. In these circumstances, it may still be advantageous for different states to trade risks with one another, especially if one is more prone to risk than another, or if they are of different sizes. In these circumstances, participation in a federation can serve to provide a vehicle for trading or sharing risks or for otherwise dealing with risk, implying certain tasks for the central government.

There are three general ways in which risks faced by states can be accommodated in a federation. First, states faced with adversity can adjust to it through mobility of labor and capital – workers who lose their jobs can migrate to neighboring jurisdictions, firms and their capital can relocate, and ready access can be had to broader capital markets to adjust to downturns. Second, national systems of taxes and transfers can help cushion the shock of a downturn. Indeed, this risk-sharing feature of national tax-transfer systems is a strong argument for keeping social insurance programs like unemployment insurance at the national level. Finally, one of the roles of equalizing interstate transfers, which are prominent in almost all multilevel nations, is precisely to insure states against adverse shocks. Of course, as with any insurance scheme, there are the dangers of moral hazard and possibly adverse selection that must be considered when designing transfer schemes in order to avoid their exploitation by the states. We return to the problem of designing transfer systems in Chapters 9 and 11.[10]

---

[10] Some recent literature has focused on these moral hazard and adverse selection problems of intergovernmental equalizing grants. See Persson and Tabellini (1996a, 1996b), Lockwood (1999) and Bordignon, Manasse, and Tabellini (2001).

Lack of Harmonization of Public Expenditures

For some types of services, some uniformity of program design may be important to ensure an efficient allocation of resources across states. For example, portability of pensions, absence of residency requirements for housing and welfare services, extent of coverage of types of services provided in social programs, and standardized education or trade qualifications make it easier for persons to move from one state to another, even though the actual rates of provision may differ across states. Harmonization may also reduce the ability of states to engage in wasteful beggar-thy-neighbor policies by using expenditures selectively to attract desirable types of factors, or repel undesirable types. The latter would include persons who use a lot of public services for whatever reason, such as the poor, the disabled or the elderly.

Again, the centralized provision of public services may not be necessary to achieve harmonization. The use of conditional grants to maintain national standards is often sufficient. In this case, because what is at issue is the design of the program rather than its size, the conditional grants need not be matching, nor need they be specific. They could be block grants of a fairly general nature whose relative size by state is based on some objective indicator of need that does not respond directly to actual program expenditures in the state (so as to avoid adverse incentives). The grants would, however, have general conditions attached to them that programs must satisfy in order for the state to be eligible for the full grant. States that failed to comply with the conditions could lose some part of the grant, presumably at the discretion of the federal government. This is another example of the usefulness of the spending power as an instrument for facilitating the decentralization of responsibilities while ensuring that national objectives are fulfilled.

The use of block grants to achieve expenditure harmonization goals is discussed in more detail in the next chapter. For now we simply note that, as with shared-cost programs, the possibility – indeed, perhaps the temptation – exists for the federal government to be too intrusive in its exercise of the spending power for this purpose. There is no easy way to ensure that the federal government will behave responsibly in this matter. One would hope that the political process could ultimately be relied on to be the enforcing mechanism.

The exercise of the spending power to achieve harmonization of the internal economic union and other national goals may or may not be related to an explicit constitutional assignment of responsibilities. That is, the federal government might use the spending power to support and influence program spending in areas of exclusive state jurisdiction as set out by the constitution of the federation. The spending power involves the granting of funds to the states, albeit conditional on the way in which the provinces spend those funds. It does not involve the federal government in legislating in the program areas that it is supporting. One might wish to restrict the federal government constitutionally in the way it exercises its spending power. For example, one might want to spell out in the constitution what sorts of objectives of the system the federal government is responsible for and can legitimately use the spending power to achieve. However, the danger exists that attempting to restrain the use of the spending power could result in gutting it altogether.

There are alternatives to the spending power, both more and less intrusive, as ways of inducing the preferred harmonization of state expenditure policies. The federal government could have the power to mandate the manner in which states provide particular public services or to strike down state legislation that does not conform to what is thought to be desirable. Though this would have the desired effect, it has the obvious disadvantage of detracting from the responsibility of the states for designing their programs as they see fit and not being overly accountable to the federal government. It also opens the prospect for the federal government to impose unfunded mandates on the states, that is, it requires them to provide certain types of public services without accompanying the requirement with a transfer of funds.

A less intrusive – and, in the abstract, ideal – way of achieving harmonization would be too use interstate agreements to secure some degree of harmonization among state programs, especially if there are mutual efficiency gains to be had from harmonization. Unfortunately, experience in existing federations does not give us much to go on. That may be because interstate agreements have not been given an opportunity to be used. Or it might be that the possibilities of negotiating binding and meaningful interstate agreements are relatively limited because of the costs of negotiation, the need to devise a mechanism to resolve disputes, and the requirement to achieve unanimity. The experience of economic unions like the European Union indicates the difficulties of relying on interstate agreements to achieve collective goals.

Compromising Federal Equity Responsibilities
Another important reason for the federal government to use its spending power to influence the behavior of the states concerns the federal

government's interest in redistributive equity across the nation. A substantial proportion of expenditures by governments are intended to achieve redistributive objectives. These include not only transfers based on incomes or demographic features of households but also spending on quasi-private goods and services (education, welfare services, housing, etc.) and social insurance schemes (health insurance, unemployment insurance, disability insurance, etc.). To the extent that the federal government has an interest in, and a responsibility for, equity across the nation, it will have an interest in the structure and extent of such programs. Indeed, this rationale is likely to be one of the most important for federal government intervention. Again, it is not clear that the exercise of federal responsibility in this area requires federal provision. Indeed, one of the underlying themes of this study is that the federal government can achieve many of its equity objectives in a federal system in which most services are delivered locally but where the federal government uses its financial and regulatory power to influence the design of state programs.

As we have seen, in the cases of quasi-private goods and services, some targeted transfers, and some forms of social insurance, there are compelling reasons for decentralizing responsibility for providing them to the states. These policy instruments must of necessity be provided by agencies close to where the target population resides. These agencies can work most effectively if state governments rather than the federal government assume control of them. They can better cater to local preferences and needs, can be better managed, can be more innovative, and can benefit from interstate competition. Ideally, to achieve the full benefits of decentralization, such as those of fiscal and political accountability and responsiveness to local needs and preferences, exclusive legislative responsibility for the design and delivery of such programs should be vested with the states. Yet, for the reasons stated previously, the federal government may well retain an interest in seeing that such programs conform to some basic standards of equity and harmonization. One way to reconcile these legitimate federal objectives with the benefits of decentralization is for the federal government to exercise some degree of oversight or influence over the way the states design the programs. The use of the spending power is a means by which the federal government can provide an incentive for the states to design their programs in conformity with national objectives. It would be preferable if the federal government were to use this power in a way that does not compromise the legislative responsibility of the states and the states' ability and incentive to use that responsibility to provide public services in the most effective and innovative way.

As previously noted, alternatives to the use of the spending power are possible. The federal government could exercise legislative authority over state programs by the use of mandates of disallowance. Alternatively, there could be voluntary agreements that are negotiated among the states. However, these might be even more difficult to secure where redistributive concerns are involved. Not only are such concerns likely to be valued differently by different states, but they are also almost certain to result in some states being "winners" and others being "losers" in the aggregate. This outcome would make a unanimous agreement almost impossible to achieve.

The choice of the degree of centralization versus decentralization on the expenditure side, and the precise means by which central governments achieve their desired influence, will vary from expenditure type to expenditure type. It will involve a trade-off between the benefits of decentralization, which include catering to local preferences, the ability to provide services at low cost, and creating incentives to innovate, against the benefits of centralization, which include the maintenance of an efficient internal common market, the achievement of national equity, the internalization of interstate spillovers, and the provision of national public goods and services. As mentioned, different observers will have different views about the ideal balance.

The Pros and Cons of Decentralizing Taxation Responsibilities

Similar issues arise when it comes to raising revenues. There are advantages and disadvantages to decentralizing the raising of revenues from various sources to lower levels of government. Of course, the decentralization of expenditure responsibilities itself suggests an argument for decentralizing some tax responsibilities as well so as to maintain some degree of fiscal accountability. However, it is important to recognize that the exact extent to which revenue-raising responsibilities are decentralized to state and local governments can, in principle, be done quite independently of the assignment of expenditure functions. What is especially relevant for fiscal accountability is that marginal revenues be raised by the lower jurisdiction (unless spillovers exist that can be used to justify some subsidy of particular expenditures), to assure that lower-level jurisdictions have some control over the amount of revenues raised and the size of their expenditure programs. That goal can be achieved even if lower-level governments do not raise enough revenues to cover all their expenditures but rely on transfers from higher levels of government, as long as the transfers are inframarginal (i.e., their magnitude does not depend on the actual amount of expenditures undertaken). This presumes that lower-level governments have de facto discretion over their expenditures as well.

Forms of Tax Decentralization

Tax decentralization can occur in various ways. One is by assigning particular tax bases exclusively to lower levels of government and allowing them to decide how much to exploit them. This form of decentralization typically entails not only local decision making but also local administration and collection of the taxes. However, lesser forms of decentralization are possible without necessarily compromising accountability. For example, tax bases and their revenues can be assigned to lower levels of government, but their administration can be operated centrally; or local governments may be assigned a property tax and retain all the revenues from its use, but the tax itself might be administered at the state level of government to take advantage of administrative economies of scale and to ensure a common set of procedures for property evaluation.

Alternatively, state and federal governments may jointly occupy tax bases, especially where broad tax bases are concerned. Then varying degrees of decentralized decision making and harmonization are possible. The federal government may be responsible for administration and tax collection both for itself and for the states, and it may be responsible for determining the base and possibly the rate structure. The states could then simply determine the level of taxes collected by applying their own tax rate as a surtax on the federal tax liability, a system sometimes referred to as piggybacking. This system combines the best features of tax harmonization with some degree of accountability for revenues raised in each state. States have ultimate responsibility for the amount of tax revenues they raise. A drawback of piggybacking is that state revenues are immediately affected by changes in federal tax rates. A reduction in the federal tax rate will presumably reduce federal tax liabilities and therefore reduce state tax collections. A problem could occur if federal tax rate changes are made with little advance notice, as is usually the case with budgetary measures,[11] but the states could avoid it if they were allowed to apply their tax rates to the federally determined base rather than to federal tax liabilities, a system referred to as a tax-on-base rather than a tax-on-tax system. More decentralized systems would allow the states to set their own rate structures

---

[11] A similar problem will also arise with changes in the federal tax base. But this is not as serious a problem because base changes occur less frequently than rate changes.

under a tax-on-base system. States might even be able to choose their own bases, at least within the limits allowed for by a common tax administration system.

In the limit, the two levels of government may simply co-occupy the same base but set and administer their own tax structures independently as they see fit. Even in this extreme case, to ensure that the same source of income is not double-taxed in more than one state, some minimal degree of harmonization across states is needed, usually in the form of rules for the allocation of tax bases to states. Under this very decentralized system some harmonization may also occur because of pressures of tax competition. This outcome will be more likely the more mobile the tax base is across states. We return to a more complete discussion of mechanisms of tax harmonization in later chapters.

Efficiency Costs of Tax Decentralization

While decentralization of taxing powers is desired mainly in order to induce political accountability into the federation, local jurisdictions may have particular preferences for certain features of the tax system, such as the degree of progressivity, the size of the public sector, or the set of tax preferences to use. Decentralization will allow these diverse preferences to be realized in tax policies. However, as with the decentralization of expenditures, the decentralization of tax responsibilities can give rise to various inefficiencies and inequities. Inefficiencies arise for two main reasons. Both involve distorting the allocation of mobile factors across states and therefore reducing the efficiency of the internal common market. The first occurs simply because decentralized tax policies distort the free flow of products and/or factors of production between states. The second occurs because tax decentralization inevitably leads to a situation in which different states have differing capacities to raise revenues and can therefore generate different NFBs for their residents.

Tax decentralization can distort the allocation of goods, services, labor, and capital in the internal common market because different states acting in an uncoordinated fashion choose individually to levy different tax rates. In the case of goods and services, cross-border trade is distorted as households and firms choose to make their purchases in the jurisdictions with the lowest tax rates on product transactions. To some extent, this problem is avoided if commodity taxes are levied on a destination basis, which is typically the case. Under such circumstances, the residents of a jurisdiction are expected to pay the tax rate applicable in their state of residence rather than the state of purchase. The problem is that the destination principle is difficult to sustain perfectly in a federation because there are no border customs controls. That is, cross-border shopping is difficult to prevent. In federations where cross-border shopping is not too costly, the pattern of production and consumption can be distorted if tax rates differ across jurisdictions. But in this case, tax differentials are unlikely to persist. States will compete in tax rates, and the result will be not only more uniform tax rates but also lower ones than would otherwise exist. That is, states will perceive revenue raising to be more costly than it actually is because part of the benefit of an increase in tax rates will be lost to neighboring jurisdictions.[12]

The problem of tax competition is likely to be less important for commodity taxes than it is for taxes on more mobile factors of production, especially capital and firms or entrepreneurs that are footloose. Mobile factors of production will tend naturally to locate inefficiently in the states with the lowest tax rates. Because capital is highly mobile, this would suggest that state taxes on capital within their jurisdictions may be potentially highly distortionary. Similarly, state income taxes can be distortionary to the extent that they have different average tax rates for more mobile segments of the population, such as highly skilled young persons and entrepreneurs. Given this, tax competition may result in considerable uniformity of tax rates across jurisdictions.

Even so, tax competition can itself result in a nonoptimal situation. As explained in Chapter 1, states will recognize the mobility of factors such as capital and will have an incentive to engage in beggar-thy-neighbor tax competition to attract them. The end result may well be uniformity of tax rates but at too low a level from the collective point of view of the states. These sorts of distortions will be less for taxes levied on less mobile factors of production, such as real property. In most federations, most persons will be much less mobile among jurisdictions than capital, though more so than real property and resources. Thus, taxes on persons, such as labor income taxes, income taxes based on residency, or general sales taxes, will generally impose less efficiency costs than those on capital. The exception, as mentioned, would be that segment of the population that is highly mobile, which might include the more highly skilled or entrepreneurial persons.

The second sort of inefficiency caused by the decentralization of tax responsibilities arises from differences in NFBs across states, one important source of which is differences in fiscal capacity. Different tax capacities

---

[12] There is a literature on commodity tax competition. Representative papers include Mintz and Tulkens (1986) and Kanbur and Keen (1993). Theoretical surveys may be found in Lockwood (2001) and J. Wilson (1999).

will result in lower NFBs in poorer states relative to richer ones and will induce too many factors to locate in the latter, resulting in inefficiency. Again, this can include the more mobile households as well as firms that are less tied to the state's resources. As we argue later, a way out of this problem that is consistent with decentralized tax responsibilities would involve corrective action by the federal government in the form of equalizing grants among states.

Equity Costs of Tax Decentralization

The decentralization of taxation responsibilities will also generally result in inequities from a national point of view. For one thing, differing degrees of progressivity will imply that, say, higher-income persons will face different tax burdens depending on their state of residence. From a national point of view, this outcome will be horizontally inequitable. As well, it will give rise to differing degrees of vertical equity across the federation. There will thus be a trade-off between the benefits of allowing state governments to implement their own local preferences for redistribution and nationwide horizontal and vertical equity. Also, if labor is mobile, tax competition among states can result in their competing away intrastate redistribution, even in circumstances in which such redistribution is desired by each state. Federal intervention may then be required simply to attain the extent of redistribution that states themselves would prefer.

In fact, this idea of interstate competition resulting in suboptimal redistribution is an old one in the fiscal federalism literature and accounts for the standard argument that redistribution ought to be a federal function.[13] This argument has been undermined by recent literature on vertical fiscal interaction. It has been suggested that when both the federal government and the states levy broad-based taxes, the states will underestimate the true costs of raising revenues. Increases in state tax rates that reduce the size of the base will cause federal tax revenues to decline, and this cost will not be taken into account by the federal government. The consequence is that states will have an incentive on this account to redistribute above the optimal level rather than the reverse. Whether the end result is too low a level of redistribution depends on the balance of horizontal tax

---

[13] This is the basis of the classical argument that redistribution should be a federal function in Musgrave (1959) and Oates (1972). See Boskin (1973) and Pauly (1973) for an early discussion of the consequences of tax competition for redistribution. A more recent analysis of competition in redistribution and the role of a federal government in correcting it may be found in Wildasin (1991).

competition, which tends to reduce redistribution, and vertical interaction, which tends to increase it.[14]

Even if states do not compete away redistribution and even if they engage in uniform redistributive policies, the decentralization of taxing responsibilities will generally give rise to fiscal inequities, which we have defined previously to be a form of horizontal inequity in a federation. Persons who reside in states with higher fiscal capacities will receive systematically higher NFBs from their state government, despite the fact that state policies incorporate comparable amounts of redistribution. The result is fiscal inequity. As with fiscal inefficiency, the remedy can involve a system of federal grants that do not compromise the ability to decentralize tax responsibilities. As we shall see later, one of the key functions of grants in a federation is precisely to compensate for differences in NFBs across states.

More generally, the extent of concern about the equity consequences of decentralizing revenue-raising responsibilities will depend on the role of the federal government in addressing the problem of redistributive equity. If one takes the view that equity is largely a federal responsibility, then those taxes which are best suited for redistribution should be centrally controlled. These include direct taxes on households, such as income and wealth taxes. Centralized control need not imply exclusive federal jurisdiction; state government piggybacking on federal direct taxes can be done with the federal government retaining control of the rate structure. Because transfers to persons are equivalent to negative direct taxes, the federal government might also control the structure of the latter. On the other hand, if one thinks redistribution is of less importance or thinks that there is a tendency for the federal government to over-redistribute, decentralization of fiscal responsibility can be a good thing. It can effectively constrain the amount of redistribution that takes place (subject to the caveat that vertical interaction can provide an incentive for states to redistribute too much).

The role of the federal government in the tax-transfer system becomes particularly important in a federation in which the provision of public services is highly decentralized to the states, which is not uncommon in practice. As we have pointed out in the first chapter, most important public services are essentially instruments for redistribution in the broader

---

[14] Johnson (1988 was the first to point out this vertical effect. Its consequences for redistribution have been analyzed by Boadway and Keen (1996) and Boadway et al. (1998). A general discussion of the offsetting effects of vertical and horizontal fiscal externalities may be found in Dahlby (1996).

sense. In addition to providing in-kind transfers, they also provide social insurance and foster equality of opportunity. They can therefore be viewed as part of the arsenal of policy instruments that are necessary for achieving important national equity objectives. Their decentralization to the state level is motivated largely by efficiency concerns. If the federal government is to retain some influence over national equity objectives, it must have the instruments with which to achieve these objectives. The less control they have over the provision of public services, the more they will need to rely on other instruments for redistributive purposes. Control of direct taxes and transfers is one such instrument. The use of conditional grants as a means of influencing how the states deliver these important public services is another. The latter plays a vital role in our discussion of federal-state fiscal policy in later chapters.

Criteria for Tax Assignment to Lower-Level Jurisdictions
When it comes to deciding which particular taxes to decentralize to the states and localities either exclusively or on a co-occupied basis, several factors are relevant. Some of these criteria may be conflicting for any given type of tax, so judgment is inevitable.

- The more mobile the tax base is across jurisdictions, the more difficult it is to decentralize its use to lower-level jurisdictions. For example, as mentioned previously, capital is highly mobile, so taxes that impinge upon capital income are not good candidates for decentralization. Because labor is less mobile than capital, taxes on labor income or consumption are more suitable for decentralization. Thus, payroll taxes and personal taxes on labor income could be decentralized. Similarly, taxes on consumption, either specific or general could be decentralized unless cross-border shopping is easy (subject to the provisos mentioned later about administrative costs). Taxes on real property and resources could also be decentralized.
- Taxes that are the most important for redistribution might be retained at the center, or at least the federal government might control their structures. These would include personal income and wealth taxes. States might be allowed to co-occupy these bases, although some degree of harmonization would be beneficial, especially to prevent distributive goals from being competed away.
- Tax bases that are very unevenly distributed among jurisdictions are less attractive for decentralization. They give rise to differences in fiscal capacity among states and therefore result in NFB differentials

that result in fiscal inefficiency and/or fiscal inequity. In principle, this inefficiency could be offset by an effective system of equalizing transfers among states, but more strain is placed on the equalization system the more uneven tax capacities are across states.

- Taxes that are the most difficult to administer, and easier to evade, might better be retained at the center. This policy might apply to some direct taxes such as those on personal and corporate income and wealth. It might also apply to value-added taxes that are difficult to administer on a multijurisdictional basis, as we discuss in more detail later.

- Taxes that should be harmonized with particular expenditure or regulatory programs should be at the same level as those programs. For example, taxes to correct for externalities might be at the level of government that is responsible for environmental control, taxes on petroleum might be administered at the level responsible for transportation, and earmarked taxes such as payroll taxes for social programs should be levied where the social program is delivered.

- Taxes that are on an uncertain revenue source might be kept at the center because the ability to spread risks and absorb shocks should be best at the federal level. At the same time, province-specific risk can be accommodated by the system of equalizing transfers. Indeed, that will be one of the roles of such transfers.

- Taxes that serve as benefit taxes are good candidates for decentralization. If they are related to benefits, they are unlikely to cause interregional distortions even if households are mobile. As we have mentioned, NFB differentials do not arise to the extent that taxes on residents are levied on a benefit basis.

These general principles are unlikely to give a clear prescription for tax assignment, and certainly not for the appropriate level of revenue raising by different levels of government. Some of them will be in conflict for some revenue sources. For example, taxes on resource incomes or revenues might be thought of as ideal for decentralization because resource bases are immobile across jurisdictions. At the same time, however, resources may be very unevenly distributed among jurisdictions so their decentralization might cause significant disparities in fiscal capacity by states. Thus, some resource bases might be decentralized and not others. Some judgment is inevitably involved.

To summarize, while fiscal accountability dictates that responsibilities for taxation be decentralized to allow state governments the ability to finance at least some of their own expenditures, this decentralization leads unavoidably to inequities and inefficiencies. Their magnitude is greater the higher the degree of decentralization. The solution may partly lie in retaining some control of the tax structure in the hands of the federal government, which will induce greater harmonization of the tax system among federal and state governments, thereby contributing to the efficiency of the national economy and reducing the costs of tax collection. Such control will also facilitate the federal government's pursuit of its redistributive objectives through the tax system. On the other hand, the federal government can undo some of the inefficiencies and inequities of decentralized tax systems, particularly those arising from NFB differentials across states, through its use of grants to the states.

THE OVERALL ROLES OF FEDERAL AND STATE GOVERNMENTS

These considerations of the benefits and costs of decentralization lead to a general prescription of the sorts of responsibilities for which the federal government might be best suited, those which should be left to the states and their localities, and those which might be shared by the two levels of government. We begin by outlining what general roles each level might assume. Then, in the next subsection, we turn to a summary of what these general roles imply for the assignment of more specific functions. Our discussion concentrates on outlining the general responsibilities of the federal government – that is, it considers the extent to which various roles should be retained at the center, the presumption being that other tasks should be decentralized. The logic of this approach is dictated by the reasoning indicated previously where we argued that, in the absence of a specific argument for centralization, decentralized responsibilities should be the rule. This is the principle of subsidiarity.

The reader should again be reminded that some judgment is involved in advocating a particular pattern of assignment of responsibilities to levels of government. Our views will not be the same as those of other well-informed observers. They depend upon a particular view of the role of government in the economy, the importance of redistributive equity and the policy instruments that might be used to attain it, and a general presumption of the way governments are capable of operating to achieve their objectives – assessments that must bear in mind the complexity of collective decision making and the political pressures that exist. Among economists who study fiscal federalism, our views would, we think, be regarded as reasonable.

At the most general level, the presumption we adopt is that the federal government should assume responsibility for important national efficiency objectives and national equity objectives. The former of these include the efficient functioning of the internal common market, the provision of national public goods, the internalization of spillovers within the federation, and relations with other nations. There are some caveats to this general rule. In some instances, the achievement of these objectives could be handled by interstate negotiation and agreement. An example might be interstate agreements or codes of conduct concerning local government regulations, such as procurement policies or fiscal policies that might violate efficiency in the internal common market. Such agreements are akin to international agreements like the World Trade Agreement, the North American Free Trade Agreement, or aspects of the European Union. Another example is that the states might share responsibility with the federal government for achieving parts of some of these efficiency goals, such as those concerning interstate spillovers.

Perhaps more controversial than its efficiency role is the role of the federal government in pursuing national equity objectives, including the definition of what these objectives are. It is controversial to the extent that different observers might put different weights on equity as an objective per se. The view we take is that to the extent that the pursuit of equity is accepted to be a legitimate role of government, the federal government can be assumed to be interested both in horizontal equity across the nation and in vertical equity across income groups. As well, there may be other broad equity objectives not easily captured by the notions of vertical and horizontal equity, which may be taken to refer to equalizing ex post the outcomes of the market economy. In the broader sense, national equity objectives might be taken to include equality of opportunity, which involves an ex ante notion of policy intervention. Social insurance objectives and the removal of economic insecurity also constitute a concern for equity. There may even be other equity objectives, such as those stressed by Sen (1985), which include the role of the state in providing citizens with the *capacity* to lead a rewarding and fulfilling life. These various equity objectives – horizontal and vertical equity, equality of opportunity, economic security – all have a national dimension to them and, in most federations, fall at least partly in the domain of federal responsibility. That does not preclude the states from having intrastate equity roles and even sharing in the responsibility for achieving national equity objectives. State involvement will be particularly relevant when some of the policy instruments that are critical for national equity are in the hands of the states.

How the sharing of responsibilities for national efficiency and equity objectives might be implemented in a federal setting is a key issue for the design of federal-state fiscal relations. Indeed, one of the main purposes of those relations is to facilitate the achievement of national objectives in a federation where significant fiscal responsibilities have been decentralized to the states. We elaborate on what is entailed by these general roles in a bit more detail in the following subsections, beginning with national equity.

The Federal Responsibility for Equity

The standard argument for assigning the federal government primary responsibility for equity is that all persons ought to be treated the same regardless of where they reside in the nation, and only the federal government can assure that this occurs. It is analogous to the technical notion in normative economics that all persons should "count" in the nation's social welfare function. Equivalently, it might be viewed as being a characteristic feature or even right of citizenship in the nation, a type of "equal treatment" convention. From the purely normative perspective, the equal treatment notion could be carried to an extreme. Persons residing in different regions would be given identical weight in society's preference ordering. In these circumstances, it would be natural to give the federal government sole or overriding responsibility for redistributive equity. A further consideration is that assigning equity to the federal government reduces the opportunity for state governments to engage in self-defeating interjurisdictional competition, which would prevent equity goals from being achieved in a decentralized federation.

The fact that all persons enter society's normative social welfare function with equal weighting does not imply that all persons of a given type (e.g., income, wealth) would be treated identically in all regions. For example, the efficiency costs of redistribution may be higher in one region than another, say, because it may be more costly to provide services in that region than in others. If there are such differential costs associated with different regions, even if all persons are given identical weight in the nation's social welfare function, otherwise identical persons will not end up being treated identically in terms of the fiscal benefits and costs that they face. Costs must be traded off against benefits. Thus, even in a unitary state, persons residing in different regions within the country will find themselves receiving different packages of public services simply because of differing costs of provision. The more substantive implications of the equal treatment norm apply when such cost differences do not exist. In this case, while a unitary state may provide common levels of public services and taxes throughout the nation, in a federation there may be violations of the strict horizontal equity norm.

The case for redistribution policies being partly differentiated by states can be based on at least three considerations, all of which draw on the reasoning of positive public economics. First, if one accepts the notion that ultimately redistributive equity implemented by actual collective choice procedures should be based on the altruism of those who are better off, the presumption of equal treatment for all persons regardless of where they reside no longer necessarily applies. That is because altruism may be geographically based: well-off persons in a given state may feel more strongly about supporting the less well-off in their own state than those in other states. Given that, as well as the possibility that tastes for redistribution can vary across states, the case for states assuming some responsibility for redistribution can be made.

The second argument for states having a role in redistribution is simply that it cannot be helped. The use of virtually any policy instrument given to the states will have distributional effects, and the states must make some distributional choice in deciding how to use it. A state role especially applies to the sorts of public services that one might like to see decentralized on efficiency grounds. It seems inevitable that some joint responsibility for equity will be the norm. Therefore, it would be infeasible to try and make redistribution the exclusive role of the federal government.

The third argument for decentralizing responsibility for redistribution to the states is based on the public choice notion that political processes lead governments to pursue "too much" redistribution, at least according to the viewer's idea of how much redistribution is "enough." So, for example, if one adopts a strictly altruistic notion of redistribution and believes that redistribution should be undertaken only to the extent that it is justified by altruism (i.e., that redistribution must be "efficiency-improving" in the sense of Hochman and Rodgers, 1969), it is quite reasonable to assume that the political system would yield "too much" redistribution, if only because of the preponderance of voters in lower-income groups. In these circumstances, decentralizing redistributive authority might be one way to constrain the amount of redistribution that governments engage in, if we assume that interjurisdictional mobility is sufficient to cause state governments to compete away at least some of their tendencies to redistribute. The drawback to this argument is that it might be difficult to prevent the federal government from redistributing, except by constraining its powers through constitutional strictures, and there are few examples of that being done in practice.[15]

Thus, there are arguments supporting a redistributive role for both the federal and the state governments. No clear-cut guidelines exist as to what amount should be trusted to the federal government and what might be given to the states. The view we take in this study is as follows. We recognize that the states may have some interest in redistributive equity. Moreover, given the amount of decentralization that we see as beneficial on other grounds, the states will undoubtedly be given policy instruments that enable them to undertake intrastate redistributive policies. At the same time, we take the position that there are significant national equity objectives for which the federal government should be responsible. Ultimately, if the notion of citizenship in a nation is to mean anything, it must include some degree of equal nationwide treatment from the point of view of redistributive equity, where the latter includes the various notions of equity mentioned previously – reduction of income-based inequality, accessibility of social insurance programs, and equality of opportunity. Thus, we take the view that decentralization should be accompanied by the retention at the federal level of the capacity to pursue national equity objectives. As we shall see, that implies not only retaining some instruments at the center that are critical for interpersonal redistribution but also being able to make interstate grants so that all states within the federation have fiscal capacities to pursue their own intrastate redistributional policies that are reasonably comparable.

Efficiency of the Internal Common Market

Parallel to concerns about the equity of the national economy are concerns about its efficiency. An important efficiency objective for the federation will be to facilitate the free and nondistorted flow of private-sector goods, services, capital, and labor within the common market of the federal economy. It is reasonable to assume that the federal government has a key role in ensuring this objective is pursued. The alternative is to turn over the responsibility for maintaining efficiency in the internal common market to the courts, or failing that, to rely on interstate agreements to preclude states from engaging in policies that distort internal transactions. The difficulty with the latter solution is that even if the states can come to a

---

[15] Arguments for restraining governments by constitutional limits in contexts more general than federal ones have been put by Brennan and Buchanan (1980).

negotiated agreement governing their conduct with respect to internal trade – and it is by no means obvious that an effective agreement can be negotiated – that agreement must still be enforced. Either the courts or the federal government itself must be relied on. Court enforcement of either a legislated agreement or a constitutional prescription concerning internal trade is bound to be problematic. It will inevitably involve the courts in making decisions that are of an economic policy nature. For, in evaluating restrictions on trade or discriminatory practice, there is always some judgment involved as to whether the practice is justified from the point of view of serving other social and economic objectives. For example, are local environmental regulations that interfere with internal trade justified or not? The same question arises with respect to labor regulations or product safety rules. Because political judgment is inevitably involved as well as national efficiency objectives, it seems unavoidable that the federal government should take on some responsibility for the efficiency of the internal common market, even in a highly decentralized federation. Decentralizing responsibilities to state governments is likely to interfere with this objective. There will be a natural tension between the rights of the states to undertake their policies as they see fit and the desire of the federal government to see that they do not exercise those rights in ways that unduly distort the workings of the internal common market.

Stating that efficiency in the internal economic union is a desirable objective of the federal government is one thing. Applying that principle is another. As we stressed earlier, the exercise of decentralized authority by the states that allows them to pursue legitimate state economic objectives cannot help but interfere with the efficiency of the internal economic union to some extent. Thus, one cannot regard the absence of distortions to mobility of goods, services, and factors of production to be an absolute objective. For example, in an ideal Tiebout world, the sorting of households into communities best suited to their tastes necessarily involves "barriers to mobility." The difficulties in applying the principle of free and undistorted interstate transactions are similar to the difficulties encountered in international and free trade agreements or economic union arrangements. Indeed, the problems are more difficult within a federation because of the ability of persons to reside in the jurisdiction of their choice. Nonetheless, looking at the details of such agreements might teach us some lessons. For example, the principle of national treatment would presumably be a minimal one to require states to conform to in designing their policies. National treatment requires that any policies applied within a jurisdiction must apply equally to all firms and individuals engaging in transactions within that jurisdiction, regardless of whether they are resident or not.

There will inevitably be trade-offs between the goal of efficiency of markets in the federal economic union and policies designed to meet the special tastes and needs of residents in each state. Thus, the federal role in pursuing this goal must somehow be tempered by the benefit of differentiated policies among regions. Here, as elsewhere, it would be helpful to have an assignment of functions that is not weighted too much in favor of federal intrusion on the one hand or state independence on the other. Ideally, there should be some institutional features of the federation that induce co-operative or partnership approaches between the levels of government.

Not only is the objective of efficiency in the internal common market an ambiguous goal, but the appropriate policy instruments for achieving it are also not clear. As mentioned, the requirement that state policies be nondistortionary and nondiscriminatory could be put into the constitution as a constraint on state laws, in which case it would be up to the courts to decide on whether interference with the internal economic union was justified in given cases. Because this would involve economic judgments, it is not at all clear that the courts are best suited for it. If it is to be a responsibility of the federal government, the way in which the latter should exercise the responsibility is not clear either. The federal government might be able to strike down or disallow state laws as in some federations, though this might be regarded as too heavy-handed a policy instrument. Or it might rely on the carrot of the spending power to provide an incentive for states to avoid excessive distortions in the internal common market. Our view is that this latter policy represents the most reasonable mechanism for pursuing efficiency in the internal economic union. How the federal government might be restrained from applying the spending power too intrusively is an important but still open question.

The desire to preserve the internal common market suggests various things about the assignment of regulatory powers. An important potential source of distortionary government decision making involves the regulatory power. Governments commonly impose regulations in markets for goods and services (e.g., as agriculture, transportation, and communications), in labor markets (e.g., professional licensing, union regulation, workplace safety, employment equity rules), and in capital markets (e.g., bankruptcy provisions, insider trading rules, pension rules). In many cases, these regulatory powers are used for protective purposes rather than as a way of improving the efficiency or equity of the market economy.

Decentralizing regulatory functions is almost certain to interfere with the efficiency of the internal common market and, for that reason, should be avoided to the extent that it is compatible with national customs. In diverse federations, it is inevitable that state governments will want to have some regulatory responsibility for safeguarding local culture, language, religion, and so on. The difficulty is in ensuring that these are not used in blatantly discriminatory and protective ways.

An aspect of efficiency in the internal common market involves macroeconomic policy, that is, policy for influencing the aggregate amount of economic activity, the movement of broad economic aggregates such as the money supply, the rate of inflation, the growth rate, and perhaps the relative extents of economic activity occurring in different regions of the country as a result of region-specific economic shocks. There is fairly general agreement that macroeconomic policies should be the ultimate responsibility of the federal government, though again state budgetary policies must necessarily have an effect on macroeconomic outcomes. The federal government should be responsible for the money supply and for credit conditions on capital markets, to the extent that an open economy has such influence. On the fiscal policy side, for the federal government to be effective requires some minimal amount of influence over tax rates and levels, as well as over the incentive structure that can be used to stimulate or retard economic activity. This outcome can best be achieved by ensuring that the federal government retains a dominant role in the key broad-based taxes in the economy. The federal government must also have the ability to facilitate the shedding of risks that states may face, given the possibility of shocks that can affect them selectively. There are many vehicles for spreading risks through the entire economy. The national tax-transfer system itself has the built-in ability to redistribute implicitly across states. In addition, the part of the federal-state transfer system that provides equalizing transfers can serve to insure state governments against adverse shocks. Also of importance is the fact that adjustment to regional shocks can be accommodated partly by factor flows between states. An important consideration in designing the fiscal arrangements is to ensure that the structure of federal-state grants does not preclude the reallocation of labor and capital across states where they are efficient. This flexibility will be particularly important where the shocks faced by states are of a permanent rather than a transitory nature.

A much more problematic area of macroeconomic management concerns the use of deficit finance and the ability to borrow, which is a general issue about the role of government encompassing more than its relevance for the assignment of powers. Some might argue that governments ought to face constitutional limits on their ability to borrow, mainly as a way to preclude current governments from passing on debt to successor governments and to future generations. The limits might apply generally to government budgets, or they might apply specifically to current expenditures only. Borrowing could be used to finance capital expenditures, provided proper principles of amortization and depreciation were applied. The limits could be applied on an annual basis or over longer (or shorter) time periods. Full consideration of the debate on this issue is somewhat outside the scope of our study. It involves such matters as: What precisely are the constraints on borrowing (e.g., balanced budget annually, over the business cycle, or borrowing within certain limits such as up to a specified debt-to-GDP ratio)? What is included in borrowing (e.g., the accumulation of public-sector liabilities through intergenerational transfers like unfunded public pensions that appear on the current account, or off-budget items such as social insurance schemes)? Who is to monitor and control government borrowing (presumably the courts, but will it be effective)? What if governments, given their legislative authority, simply ignore such limits? What about borrowing as an instrument of fiscal policy or of adjustment to exogenous shocks?

In other words, the concept of a limit to public-sector borrowing for the nation as a whole is not an easy one to put into practice. If the limits are defined simply by the issue of debt on capital markets, say, to finance current government operations, there are accounting ways of getting around the strictures. Moreover, defining the constraint by using formal debt issue is itself a rather narrow concept that does not even approximately capture the net liabilities one government passes on to future generations. For example, these liabilities would include, on the negative side, environmental degradation and the running down of natural resource wealth and, on the positive side, advances in technological knowledge and training of human capital. In the absence of a proper generational accounting system to begin with, it makes little economic sense to constrain governments in one particular element of that accounting[16] or to impose such constraints by constitutional fiat rather than by the political process. Given the latter, it is not obvious why legislation passed by one government ought to bind future governments. Thus, a skeptical economist needs to be convinced that extralegislative constraints can or should be imposed on the amount of borrowing that governments do.

---

[16] For a summary of generational accounting, see Auerbach, Kotlikoff, and Leibfritz (1999).

In the context of federalism, the issues are somewhat more complicated. What is at stake here is the ability of lower-level governments to borrow. There are various arguments that may be advanced for why lower-level governments ought to be constrained in their borrowing, or in their ability to run deficits. The arguments depend on what one views as the purpose of borrowing. On the one hand, it may be simply for macroeconomic purposes, especially to enable the government to make adjustments over economic cycles or to unexpected shocks. Some might argue that states (or their municipalities) do not need to borrow for stabilization purposes or as ways of adjusting to shocks because macroeconomic policy is best left to the center. This argument is given added impetus to the extent that a system of federal-state grants serves to insure states against adverse shocks. Borrowing, especially that done over a longer time horizon, might also serve as a way of making transfers across generations. Opponents of the use of state borrowing for this purpose might argue that while the use of intergenerational transfers is a legitimate policy instrument for pursuing equity or intergenerational social insurance, the achievement of intergenerational equity is best assigned to the federal government. More generally, states and their municipalities might be conceived of as financing their expenditures by the "benefit principle" rather than the "ability-to-pay" principle, even though this would run counter to the argument that some intrastate redistribution is a legitimate state policy objective. But this argument cuts both ways. To the extent that state expenditure is for durable goods (infrastructure) whose benefits accrue far into the future, the use of debt financing would be required in order to approximate the benefit principle. Some might argue for restricting state and local borrowing on the basis of distrust that the power would be used irresponsibly. Of course, such restrictions would contradict the very case in favor of decentralization, which is that lower levels of government are more accountable in delivering services to their residents.

Finally, two arguments based on political economy considerations merit serious consideration. Indeed, they may well constitute the main reasons for being cautious about state and local borrowing, or at least imposing some restrictions on it. The first is that the mobility of households among jurisdictions reduces the political constraints on the use of deficit financing.[17] The argument is that households resident in one state or locality will be more willing to agree to the deficit financing of current expenditures

---

[17] This argument has been put forward and analyzed in the context of a simple two-period model by Bruce (1995).

knowing that they can avoid the cost of repaying the debt so incurred by moving to another location. The second argument is that, given that states are to some extent financially subservient to the federal government (and localities to state governments), they may behave according to the expectation that they would be bailed out in the event of financial trouble or, less drastically, that if they acquire large debt service costs, the federal government will deem them to be more in need and thereby increase transfer payments to them. This is referred to as the soft budget constraint problem.[18] This argument is certainly convincing and is supported by the literature on time inconsistency, which stresses the difficulties a principal might have abiding by its announced long-term policies, especially if the principal is a government whose time horizon is limited by the requirement of short terms in office. The federal government might announce to its states that it will not bail out any state that gets into financial trouble in the future. But, when the future comes and a state has in fact put itself into difficulty, the federal government cannot avoid coming to its rescue. Moreover, states will be able to predict that eventuality and exploit it by being less cautious than they otherwise would be with their spending and borrowing.

If we assume that there may be an argument for restricting state and local borrowing, the issue is then how this might be accomplished. States might be precluded from borrowing at all, except for capital purposes. In the case of the latter, they may need to obtain the permission of another authority, be it the higher level of government or the electorate through a referendum. Alternatively, they may be restricted to borrow from the federal government, in which case the latter have more direct control over the amount and use of the borrowing. In any case, the issue is not a clear-cut one. Any monitoring or control role given to the federal government over state borrowing will inevitably come into conflict with the process of decentralization.

National Public Goods and Interjurisdictional Spillovers

The responsibility of the federal government for providing national public goods and addressing interstate spillovers are perhaps the least disputable sources of centralization of economic powers because they are based on efficiency grounds, on which most observers would agree. However, these responsibilities are also the least significant in terms of actual budgetary importance.

---

[18] See Wildasin (1997).

Even in these areas, there are a couple of things that make the federal role ambiguous. The first is that because the benefits of public goods and spillovers cannot be observed, there will be disagreement as to what the level of public benefits from a given public good, if any, is, and whether the political process resolves the issue appropriately. Some public choice theorists will argue that governments are bound to overprovide and be more intrusive and will therefore want to restrict the list of national public goods as much as possible.

The second is that some benefits of a national interest, including especially those which arise from internalizing interstate spillovers, can in principle be addressed by interstate agreement. We have indicated earlier some skepticism about the efficacy of relying on these agreements to deal with interstate spillovers. Similar concerns would apply even more strongly to providing national public goods where budgetary expenditures are involved. Thus, our view is that a federal role is indispensable in these areas.

There are various ways in which the federal government may exercise its jurisdiction so as to ensure that the benefits of national public goods and interstate spillovers are properly accounted for. One way is by federal government provision, which is the obvious solution for truly national public goods such as defense, foreign affairs, the control of the money supply, criminal law, and so on. However, there may be advantages from an efficiency point of view to decentralizing to the states the provision of public goods whose beneficiaries are mainly state residents but some of whose benefits also transcend state borders. In this case, the federal government can still induce the states to take account of spillover benefits without sacrificing the benefits of decentralization by providing grants to the states in support of such expenditures, but with conditions attached. The grants may be block grants with fairly general conditions setting out national standards, or they may be more specific in their conditions. The more detailed the accountability to the federal government that is required, the less will the benefits of decentralization be realized. The grants may also be of a matching nature in order to induce the states to provide enough expenditure on such goods.

In some circumstances, federal financial intervention may not be necessary. It may be sufficient for the federal government to impose regulations on state government behavior, such as regulations that preclude state decisions from interfering with the efficiency of the internal common market. The problem with this alternative is that it too can detract from the benefits of decentralization, one of which is to induce responsible and unconstrained decision making by lower levels of government.

Provision of Quasi-Private Goods and Services

A substantial proportion of government spending is on either quasi-private goods or services provided on a virtually free basis. Examples include education, health care, and local services. As mentioned previously, a strong case might be made for decentralizing the provision of these goods and services to state governments on the grounds that this will improve efficiency and accountability as well as the matching of local preferences and needs. At the same time, the provision of these public services may have implications for the efficiency of the common market and for national equity.

For example, state provision may be inefficient because of interstate competition in services designed to attract desirable residents. Also, there may be spillover effects associated with the use of state public services of this type. Residents of one state may be able to obtain the benefits of services provided by neighboring states by temporary or permanent movement between states. States may discount the benefits obtained by nonresidents and provide too low a level. More generally, the efficiency of the internal common market may be compromised if differences in public service provision preclude the free movement of resources among states.

As well as having possibly adverse effects on the efficiency of the internal common market, quasi-private goods and services have effects on national equity. As we have stressed earlier, many public services can be seen as devices for achieving redistributive goals delivered through the expenditure side of the public-sector budget. That is why, although they are private, they are typically provided free to residents or with a nominal user fee. The extent to which they serve as redistributive devices depends upon the details of their design, such as how comprehensive they are, their accessibility to the public, and what their eligibility requirements are. Significant differences in these sorts of design features may be viewed as violating national norms of equity. Moreover, these differences might be a result of beggar-thy-neighbor competition among the states.

Even though efficiency might dictate that quasi-private goods and services be provided by the states, it may be desirable that the federal government retain the ability to influence the way in which that authority is exercised. To the extent that the federal government has an interest in, and responsibility for, efficiency in the internal economic union and national equity, it will have an interest in seeing that the state provision of public services conform to some general norms or national standards. For example, they may wish to ensure that conditions of portability apply and that eligibility be the same for residents and nonresidents. By the same token, a federal interest in redistributive equity may entail, in addition to common portability and eligibility conditions, some harmonization of the comprehensiveness and quality of services as well as its accessibility. The latter might involve limitations on the use of user charges imposed on residents for the use of such services.

Given a federal interest in the general properties of state provision of quasi-private goods and services, the issue then becomes how do they best influence the states to abide by these features. The principles of decentralization (or subsidiarity) would suggest that the states be given as much independence as possible in designing, legislating and implementing these programs. There are two potential ways in which the federal government may be able to influence state provision. For one, the federal government may have the legislative power to override state laws that govern the provision of these goods and services, although that would seem to be inconsistent with giving the states the independent legislative responsibility for providing these goods, which is what arguments in favor of decentralization might suggest. Moreover, the power to override state legislation would be a rather heavy-handed means of intervention, and one that would compromise the ability of the states to design their programs in the most economical, accountable, and responsive ways.

The alternative instrument for policy influence might be the spending power, in this case the use of block conditional transfers. These would be effective ways of encouraging the states to implement programs that satisfy certain general conditions without directly interfering with the ultimate legislative responsibility of the states. Of course, one would want to look for ways of constraining the federal government from being too intrusive in the use of the spending power, something for which ultimately the political process may have to be responsible.

Tax Assignment and Harmonization

The general arguments in favor of decentralization apply with much greater force on the expenditure side than on the tax side of the budget. There are obvious administrative, collection and compliance economies from having a single large tax-collecting authority at the center. As well, the centralization of tax policy facilitates the achievement of national equity objectives by the federal government. Moreover, decentralizing tax powers leads to inefficiencies in the internal common market both because of the possible distortions imposed by state tax policies on the allocation of resources across states and because of the fiscal inefficiency that arises in a decentralized system when different states have different tax capacities. These factors have implications for the assignment of taxes to levels of government as well as for the role of the federal government in coordinating tax policies of lower levels of government.

In terms of tax assignment, the more "mobile" the base of a tax, the stronger is the case for its being centrally controlled. Thus, taxes on capital income and on stocks of movable capital should be assigned to the center. For equity purposes, federal control over direct taxes is important because these are the taxes best designed to address equity issues. Taxes that are difficult to administer on a decentralized basis, such as value-added taxes, are better retained at the center. And tax bases that are highly unevenly distributed across states could be kept at the center to preclude wide differences in fiscal capacity, unless equalizing federal-state transfers can offset them. This set of principles still leaves plenty of scope for decentralizing revenue-raising responsibilities.

It should be emphasized that the advantages of centralizing tax collection and tax policies need not entail that certain taxes be assigned exclusively to the federal government. There can be tax-sharing arrangements that combine federal collection and administration as well as federal control of the tax structure with states responsible for setting their own rate level alongside that of the federal government. Nonetheless, to ensure effective federal control, the federal government must retain a sufficiently large share of the tax room. Of course, tax sharing is quite different from revenue sharing under which the federal government turns over a predetermined proportion of the revenues of a given tax base to the states. Revenue sharing is emphatically not a method of decentralizing revenue raising to the states. Under it, the federal government retains complete control of tax policy. The states are passive recipients of a share of the revenues. Revenue sharing is better viewed as a form of federal-state transfers and will be dealt with as such later.

Despite the fact that there is considerable scope for the decentralization of revenue-raising responsibilities, the fact still remains that on economic grounds, the case for decentralizing expenditure responsibilities is likely to be greater.[19] The upshot is likely to be a situation in which the revenue-raising capacity of the federal government is greater than its expenditure responsibilities, and vice versa for the states. That is, there will be a fiscal gap, or vertical fiscal imbalance. This fiscal gap is not only a natural consequence of the fact that the case for decentralization is stronger on the expenditure side than on the tax side of the budget but also turns out to be a desirable and useful feature of federal systems to the extent that federal-state grants have a useful role to fulfill. That role is discussed later.

Transfers and Social Insurance

Along with the provision of public and quasi-private goods and services, transfer payments compose the bulk of government expenditures (especially in industrialized countries). These can be transfers to persons, transfers to businesses, or transfers to other levels of government. Some of these transfers, especially those to persons, are for redistributive purposes in the ordinary sense. Some are also for redistribution in the social insurance sense, such as unemployment insurance, health insurance, and public pensions. Others, such as those to businesses, are for industrial policy or regional development purposes. Those to other levels of government typically go from higher to lower levels. They serve both to close the fiscal gap and to accomplish the various objectives of intergovernmental transfers as discussed in more detail later.

Several factors bear on the assignment of responsibility for transfers. In the case of transfers to businesses, many economists would argue that they should not be used in the first place, especially if they are discretionary. But, given that they are used, they are likely to be more distortionary if used at the state level than at the federal level. This is because the objective of subsidies is typically to stimulate activity by firms, especially capital investment. Although there may be some scope for increasing the total

[19] In the recent theoretical literature on fiscal federalism, there has emerged an argument based on efficiency in favor of decentralizing revenue-raising capabilities (Boadway and Keen, 1996; Dahlby, 1996). The argument is based on the observation that state taxes impose a negative externality on federal tax revenues. For example, an increase in the state tax rate on, say, consumption will reduce the tax base, thereby reducing the tax take of the federal government. In other words, the marginal cost of public funds at the state level as perceived by the state is less than its true value. The states will be induced to set taxes too high, and the externality involved will be greater the smaller the share of state taxes relative to that of the federal government. On these grounds, the greater the responsibility given to the states for raising revenues, the less will be the size of the externality.

amount of business activity with subsidies, typically such activity is also mobile across states. Thus, part of the effect of the subsidy may be to divert activity from other states. In addition to distorting the efficiency of the internal economic union, the effect of such subsidies is to some extent self-defeating if used by all states at the same time. On the other hand, if capital really is perfectly mobile internationally, subsidies in one jurisdiction will not have any effect on neighboring jurisdictions and, in that sense, would not distort the allocation of capital across jurisdictions. They would succeed in attracting capital from international capital markets and thereby effectively end up subsidizing other immobile factors within the state jurisdiction, such as labor. In either case, one is left with an argument in favor of retaining the power to use subsidies at the center rather than allowing them to be used, or at least discouraging their use, by the states. This seems to be a clear case where competitive federalism is disadvantageous. How such a prescription might be put into effect is not clear. That is, it is not obvious how states could be precluded from using their general revenues for subsidizing firms to locate in their jurisdictions. Retaining the corporate tax at the center would rule out subsidies being run through that system, but it would not prevent state subsidy schemes that stand on their own. Some general proscription against measures that distort the internal common market would be necessary, either as part of the constitution of the nation or as a negotiated intergovernmental agreement. But some means of enforcing such an agreement is also necessary. This brings us back to the options available for achieving national objectives in a decentralized federation – a binding dispute settlement mechanism, enforcement by the courts, or federal enforcement by the spending power. The use of the spending power seems to be the most reliable among these options.

As for transfers to individuals, because most of them are for redistributive purposes, their assignment revolves around the extent to which the federal government assumes primary responsibility for equity. From an economic point of view, transfers are just negative direct taxes. One can argue that transfers should be controlled by the same level of government that controls direct taxes so that they can be integrated for equity purposes and harmonized across the nation for efficiency purposes. The case for integration at the central level is enhanced when one recognizes the several types of transfers that may exist to address different dimensions of equity or social insurance. There is an advantage of coordinating unemployment insurance with the income tax system or pensions with payments to the poor. Decentralizing transfers to the states will likely lead to inefficiencies in the internal common market, fiscal inequities, and interjurisdictional beggar-thy-neighbor policies. On the other hand, some transfers must be delivered by agencies of government because they must be targeted to particular segments of the population and that requires monitoring on the ground. Efficiency considerations might dictate that these be agencies of the state governments rather than the federal government. In this case, the federal government may have to find some means to ensure that the delivery of these targeted transfers satisfies the norms of national equity.

All this is, of course, predicated on wanting the federal government to have a dominant role in redistribution. This is a view to which we tend to subscribe. It is also one that seems to reflect the realities of many federations.

To summarize, the role of the federal government relative to state governments is governed by the national interest involved in providing national public goods and services, maintaining the efficiency of the internal common market, and pursuing redistributive equity nationwide. The importance of the latter determines to a great extent the degree of centralization of the federation. Equity objectives influence the role that the federal government should assume in the direct tax system and the system of transfers. They also have a bearing on the federal government's interest in the provision of quasi-private goods and services, many of which serve a redistributive function. And the federal government's interest in equity affects its use of the federal-state transfer system to influence the way in which state governments behave and to redistribute resources among states in an equalizing manner. In other words, the extent of the role of the federal government is largely determined by its interest or lack of interest in redistributive matters.

FEATURES OF THE OPTIMAL ASSIGNMENT
OF RESPONSIBILITIES

We have stressed that the search for an ideal assignment of economic functions to different levels of government is bound to be in vain. Different persons are likely to come to different judgments about such things as the way in which governments behave, the importance of competition among governments, the empirical effects of government policies on the allocation of resources, and the importance of equity as an objective of government. Nonetheless, on the basis of the preceding discussion of the advantages of centralization versus decentralization, certain broad prescriptions might be made about which functions should be decentralized. We outline here a view of the assignment of powers that we think would obtain the consensus of a spectrum of economists despite the judgments involved. It is presented in broad terms and serves as a context for the more detailed discussions of various policy areas in subsequent chapters.

General Principles

In general terms, the federal government should be largely responsible for stabilization policies, for addressing national redistributive equity objectives, for ensuring the optimal provision of public goods and services whose benefits transcend borders, and for the maintenance of an efficient and smoothly functioning internal common market in goods and services, labor and capital. The equity objective includes both horizontal and vertical equity and encompasses not only the redistribution of incomes but also social insurance and equality-of-opportunity objectives. Economic responsibilities should be decentralized to the states to the greatest extent possible consistent with these national economic objectives. The states should be responsible for the provision of goods and services of a local or state nature, that is, those whose beneficiaries are mainly within state borders. They might also share some responsibility for redistribution with the federal government. The reason for this is partly because states might have state-specific preferences for redistribution to their own needy, and those views may differ across jurisdictions, but also because many of the fiscal actions of the states will have unavoidable effects on equity, especially those arising from their expenditures. Moreover, many of the policy instruments decentralized to the state governments will be important ones for achieving equity and social objectives.

Expenditure Assignment

From these general principles follows a preferred assignment of expenditure responsibilities. The states would be responsible for the delivery of public services that are of a quasi-private nature, such as health care and insurance, education in all forms (including perhaps postsecondary and manpower training), welfare services, family and child support services, state transportation and communication services, local utilities and municipal services, and resource management (including local land management and environmental issues). The federal government, on the other hand, would be responsible for expenditures of a clearly national nature, including defense, foreign affairs, international trade, immigration, and the legal system. For stabilization purposes, the federal government should assume responsibility for the central bank and the currency. Transfers to individuals could be centralized to the extent that they are delivered through the tax system or are based on general criteria that are easy to observe (e.g., family size, age). On the other hand, if the transfers require detailed administrative oversight and monitoring, delivery might be more efficient at the state or local level. Following these principles would result in an assignment of expenditure responsibilities for goods and services provided through a public sector that is relatively decentralized.

At the same time, the federal government maintains an interest in the way in which the states exercise their expenditure responsibilities. For example, there are consequences for national efficiency and equity from the way the states design their expenditure programs. In the case of education, equity objectives may imply that equal opportunity and accessibility are important objectives. Efficiency might suggest some harmonization of curriculum standards and portability from one state to another. Similar arguments can be made to favor accessibility and portability of health care as well as a more or less comprehensive definition of the types of services covered by public health care expenditures. These objectives can be achieved, while maintaining the integrity of state delivery, by federal intervention in the form of conditional grants to the states; that is, by what we have called the spending power. If the spending power is used wisely, the benefits of decentralized decision making and delivery can be achieved alongside the harmonization of state expenditure programs to ensure that national equity and efficiency objectives are met. The spending power must be exercised in a way that is not too obtrusive and overbearing with respect to state decision makers, which requires only a minimal amount of accountability. In the absence of the spending power, complete decentralization of the provision of public goods and services to the state level could lead to wasteful expenditure competition and to substandard levels of efficiency and equity.

Regulatory Functions

To ensure a smoothly functioning internal common market, responsibility for regulatory functions that have effects crossing state borders should reside with the federal government. These functions include the regulation of international and interstate trade in goods and services (including such things as agriculture, communications, and transportation), environmental and resource use issues involving more than one state, and capital markets. The assignment of labor market regulation, including professional and trade licensing and employment practices, should also be at the federal level to maintain undistorted labor mobility in the internal common market.

At the same time, given that labor market circumstances differ from state to state, there might be some role for state participation in the regulation of these markets, provided that such regulation is not used in a discriminatory or distortionary way. On the other hand, the case for assigning to the federal government any role that may exist in regulating markets for capital, goods, and services is strong. In contrast to the case of public-sector expenditures, the assignment of regulatory responsibilities would thus be quite centralized.

It may be that the most effective way to exercise these regulatory responsibilities is through quasi-independent regulatory bodies, which may well have state representation. Even so, the federal government must maintain effective responsibility even if it chooses to exercise it using such bodies. By the same token, for some types of expenditures it may be sensible to form special-purpose bodies whose role is to deliver a particular type of public service. This choice may be appropriate for public services whose optimal delivery level is between existing levels of government, or those for which user fees or benefit taxes are the appropriate mode of financing. Examples of such bodies include local school boards, conservation or environmental authorities, local utilities, and transportation or communications bodies. They may be given varying degrees of autonomy when it comes to raising revenues and delivering services, and they may have varying degrees of political accountability. Also, they might represent a means of decentralizing economic decision making without decentralizing political authority and inducing political instability. The point is that one need not necessarily feel bound by the existing set of political jurisdictions.

Revenue-Raising Responsibilities

The assignment of revenue-raising responsibilities can be determined somewhat independently of the assignment of expenditure responsibilities, though accountability arguments can be used to limit that independence. The income tax system should be under the control of the federal government, although there is no reason why the states could not co-occupy the field preferably in a harmonized relationship. Federal dominance of the field assists in the fulfillment of the objectives of national equity because the income tax is one of the main instruments that can be used for redistributive purposes. Federal control of the income tax also serves to ensure that it will be harmonized across the nation so that administrative and compliance costs are minimized and resource allocations across states are not distorted by state tax provisions. It might also assist in the management of macroeconomic policy objectives.

Other direct taxes often used include capital taxes; taxes on wealth and wealth transfers (including bequests and inheritances); and resource, real-property, and payroll taxes. A strong case can be made for ensuring central control of the first two of these. Mobility considerations are paramount in the case of capital taxes and taxes on wealth, inheritances, and bequests. State taxation of capital either will be ineffective because of tax competition among states or will lead to distortions in the allocation of capital. Similarly, states are likely to compete away taxes on wealth, inheritances, and bequests, thereby reducing their effectiveness.

Resource taxes are an interesting case because arguments can be made for both centralization and decentralization. The problem with decentralizing them is obviously not one of mobility of the tax base but of the fact that resources tend to be distributed highly unevenly among states. From an equity point of view, one can argue that property rights to the bounty of natural resource endowments ought to rest with the national government to be shared among all citizens. Giving the states the right to tax resource rents leads to differential NFBs across states with the resultant fiscal inefficiencies and inequities that we have discussed earlier. Thus, a case can be made for federal assignment of the collection of rents for those resources which are of significant size and which are unevenly distributed among states. Common examples include oil and gas properties and significant mineral deposits.

At the same time, a case can be made for retaining state control over the collection of production taxes or royalties for other types of resources. Those of lesser importance such as small mines and quarries might be good sources of revenues for the states. The same might be said for timber properties. In the case of resource revenues, an additional consideration arises and that is the role of the government in managing, developing (including providing infrastructure), and conserving the resource. These are often functions whose primary benefits accrue to state residents. To the extent that state tax and royalty systems are useful for these regulatory purposes, decentralizing responsibility for them would be a good thing. If needed, the federal government could always provide general incentives for good resource usage by its spending power or its regulatory power, though it is not obvious that the federal government is in a better position to set such standards than the states themselves (unless there are cross-border issues involved in managing the resources).

The upshot is that resource tax assignment must be considered on a case-by-case basis. Because resources are immobile, resource revenues are good candidates for state taxation. Centralization becomes more important the more significant the value of the resource and the more unequally it is distributed among states. Even if states assume responsibility for resource taxation, there is still the option open to the federal government to correct for unequal distributions by equalizing grants to the states.

The fourth of these direct taxes, the real-property tax, is generally taken to be an ideal tax to assign to lower levels of government, especially municipal governments, given their immobile nature. The states can serve a coordinating and administrative function by assisting in the property evaluation process and even acting as a tax collector. At the same time, they can insure that different municipalities within their jurisdictions that have different property tax capacities can nonetheless provide comparable levels of services to their citizens. That is, the states can eliminate NFB differences within their borders just like the federal government can across states. However, for fiscal accountability purposes, it is important that local jurisdictions be able to set their own tax rates.

Finally among the direct taxes, it could be suggested that the federal government could have access to payroll taxes as well, because they are complementary with income taxes. On the other hand, because these are not important instruments for equity, there is no reason for federal dominance in the field. In fact, payroll taxes would make an excellent source of revenue raising for the state governments. They are typically single rate taxes applied on labor income only. As long as the rate difference is not too great across states, they are likely to cause little inefficiency because labor is much less mobile than capital. Payroll taxes are often used as earmarked sources of finance for social security programs. However, there is no reason not to use them as general revenue sources. On the contrary, their use as general taxes makes a great deal of sense in a developing-country context because of their relative ease of administration and broad base.

In the case of indirect taxes, the argument for central control is less compelling than it is for the case of direct taxes. To the extent that the decentralization of revenue-raising capacity is desired, indirect taxes are good candidates to be assigned to the states. In fact, the design of the indirect tax system itself depends on the extent of decentralization of taxes to the states. If the general sales tax is to be assigned exclusively to the states, it may be very difficult to administer on a multistage basis, such as a value-added tax (VAT). The system of crediting under a VAT would require that cross-border transactions be accounted for in order to be able to credit taxes paid on earlier stages of sales that cross state borders. With the possibility of differential state tax rates and different sets of exemptions, such an accounting becomes a difficult task. This means that decentralization of general sales taxation to the states may call for a set of single-stage retail sales taxes in each state. The benefits of a VAT in terms of administrative and economic efficiency would be lost. The base used by states would inevitably be narrower than is optimal, and the well-known problems of evasion and the inability to exempt taxes on capital purchases and exports completely would persist. More generally, the states would likely be forced to adopt consumption rather than income as a base for the tax (which may not be a drawback). Also, the ability to enforce the destination basis would be limited by the possibility of cross-border shopping among states, especially because in a federation there are no border controls.

The converse of this applies as well. If the general sales tax is centralized to the federal government, it could use a VAT and reap all its advantages. The simplest system would be one in which the states did not participate in the system in a way that gives them some discretion over their own rates and base. The system would be a uniform one with a common base and rate structure and a single tax-collecting authority. This would not preclude a form of revenue sharing for the proceeds of the tax, either on the basis of where the revenues were raised or on some other basis. Nor would it preclude some form of joint determination of the base and rates by the federal and state governments. However, this has the substantial disadvantage that the states have no discretion over their own revenue-raising authority.

An alternative is a VAT system in which the federal government sets the base as well as the list of exempt and zero-rated goods, but in which states can set their own individual rates. (If goods are exempt, they are not taxed on sale, and they are not eligible for tax credits for taxes paid on their inputs. If goods are zero-rated, they are not taxed on sale, but they are eligible for a credit on taxes paid on inputs.) As long as there is a single tax-collecting authority, such a system seems to be feasible albeit at some extra administrative cost. As we discuss further in Chapter 6, the additional administrative costs arise mainly from the tax treatment of interstate sales. Briefly, the problem is that under a standard credit-invoice VAT system, sales by a producer in one state to a producer in another would be taxed by the seller in one state and would be subject to an input tax credit for the buyer in another state. With state-level sales taxes, this would generally give rise to some net tax transfers among states. As well, if tax rates differed over states, there would be extra compliance costs for the firms, and, auditing by the tax-collecting agency would be complicated. Some of these problems can be avoided by revising the form of the VAT. One option is to adopt what is referred to as the deferred-payment method. Under this system, products exported to firms in another state would be zero-rated in the state of origin, so such sales would be purged of all state taxes. (Federal VAT would still apply.) When imported, no tax in the importing state is initially paid, unlike with a standard destination tax. However, when the importing firm sells products that have used the import as an input, the sale bears the full tax and receives no input tax credit. Thus, it is brought fully into the tax net of the importing state. Such a system has been shown to be feasible in Canada, albeit a country with a well-developed tax-collecting authority. Its application in a developing-country context may be more difficult. In any case, its feasibility in either context seems to depend for its effective administration on there being a federal VAT along-side the state one, as well as a single tax-collecting authority.[20]

Ultimately, the assignment of the general sales tax boils down to how much tax room the federal government should have relative to the states. The more decentralized the expenditure responsibilities to the states are and the more it is desired to decentralize some tax authority to them, the more beneficial it would be to decentralize sales taxes to them provided it can be done in an administratively feasible way. Of course, it is possible that separate federal and state sales taxes exist side by side in the same tax system.[21] The main point is that it is more important that the federal government have control of the income tax than of the sales tax.

Selective excises, such as those on tobacco, alcohol, fuel, entertainment, and communications, could readily be decentralized to the states, or co-occupied by both levels of government. The main efficiency issue concerns the possibility of cross-border shopping. In practice, this policy would restrict the ability of state governments to set widely differing rates. State excise taxes can also give rise to NFB differences to the extent that different states have different tax capacities for these taxes. If so, fiscal inequity will result, which the federal government will need to address with its grant structure.

---

[20] The case for a deferred-payment system has been made by Bird and Gendron (1998). They have argued that operating a VAT in a federal context is feasible and use the example of Quebec within the Canadian federation. However, Quebec is still the only province in Canada to operate its own VAT alongside the federal government. They have extended the argument to a developing-country context in Bird and Gendron (2001).

[21] It should be noted that if the states operate indirect taxes on a destination basis, including either general sales taxes or specific excise taxes, these taxes should be collected at the border on imports from other countries. Presumably this is the task of the federal government.

Overall, the states could occupy the indirect taxes fields (both general sales taxes and selective excises) and could have some access to direct taxes on residents (personal income and payroll taxes) jointly with the federal government. The states could also levy general payroll taxes. The federal government would be responsible for income taxes, major resource taxes, and taxes on capital income or wealth, with the exception of the property taxes. Wealth transfer taxes would also be centralized. Among these alternatives, virtually any realistic degree of decentralization of tax capacity to the states is possible and could be achieved by a combination of assignment of types of taxes and some tax sharing. User fees might also be a source of revenues. mainly for the state governments and their municipalities because the sorts of public services that are conducive to allocation by pricing are likely to be decentralized.

The issue of access of state and local governments to debt financing remains an open one. In a country with a highly developed political system and experienced and responsible lower-level governments that are financially independent of the federal government, the use of debt finance might simply be viewed as something for the state or local government to decide on, albeit constrained by capital market institutions. However, where lower-level governments are dependent on the federal government or have not developed the administrative capability for managing debt responsibly, some constraints might be placed on their ability to borrow. The danger is that whatever constraints are imposed, they will serve to undermine decentralized decision making and to retard the development of the capacity to behave responsibly. The ability to draw on debt finance is something that must be decided on an individual-country basis.

Despite the fact that it is feasible to transfer as much tax room to the states as one wishes, from an economic point of view it would also be desirable for tax rates to be such that the federal government collects more tax revenues than it needs for its own expenditure purposes. This imbalance is partly a consequence of the fact that the desired amount of centralization of taxes exceeds that of expenditures. For example, the federal government needs a large enough presence in the tax field to be able to pursue effective fiscal policy. We have also argued that the federal government should maintain enough dominance in direct taxes to be able to achieve tax harmonization and national equity goals. An excess of federal tax collections over expenditure responsibilities also allows for transfers of funds from the federal government to the states. These transfers have their own independent role in a federal economy with decentralized fiscal responsibilities, as we discuss in a later chapter.

APPENDIX TO CHAPTER 2

The Impact of Decentralization on Service Delivery and Economic Growth: A Synthesis of Empirical Evidence

Decentralized public governance continues to invite controversy and debate. Proponents of decentralization consider it a panacea for reforming the public sector in developing countries (Shah, 1996a, 1998a, 1998d, 2003, 2004a), whereas opponents consider it as a road to wreck and ruin (Tanzi, 1996). These disagreements primarily arise from perspectives on the potential impact of such policies in the institutional environment of developing countries. This annex provides a synthesis of the empirical literature on the impact of decentralization on service delivery and economic growth to inform this debate. The impact of decentralization on macromanagement and controlling corruption is covered in subsequent chapters.

Impact of Decentralization on Service Delivery
Recent studies have explored the impact of decentralization in various countries. In the following paragraphs, we have grouped these studies by their results - positive, negative, and inconclusive.

Positive Impacts. Alderman (1998 found that decentralization had a positive impact on targeting of social assistance in Albania. Bardhan and Mookherjee (2003) similarly found that decentralized management advanced poverty alleviation goals in West Bengal, India. The same results were confirmed by Galasso and Ravallion (2001) for Bangladesh. Eskeland and Filmer (2002) using cross-section data from Argentine schools found that decentralization of education led to improvement in school achievement scores. Faguet (2001) also found that decentralization in Bolivia helped improve consistency of public services with local preferences and quality and access to social services. Foster and Rosenzweig (2002) found that in India democratic decentralization led to improved allocation for pro-poor local services. Santos (1998) discovered the same effect in Porto Alegre, Brazil, with participatory budgeting. Isham and Kähkönen (1999) observed improvements in water services in Central Java, Indonesia, with local community management. King and Ozler (1998) observed that decentralized management of schools led to improvement in achievement scores in Nicaragua. Estache and Sinha (1995) using data on a cross section of industrial and developing countries found that decentralization leads to increased spending on public infrastructure. Huther and Shah (1998) and

Enikolopov and Zhuravskaya (2003) using cross-section and time series data for a large number of countries found that decentralization contributed to improved delivery of public goods provision. A joint study by the World Bank, Asian Development Bank, and the U.K. Department for International Development (World Bank, 2004b), utilizing survey data for six districts and twelve tehsil municipal administrations on the impact of 2001 local devolution in Pakistan, found that service delivery access for health and education uniformly improved in all sample areas whereas water and sanitation services showed improvements only in a few areas. Faguet and Sanchez (2006) carried out a comparative study of the impact of decentralization on educational outcomes in Bolivia and Colombia. They found that in Bolivia decentralization made government more responsive by redirecting public investment to areas of greatest need. In Colombia, decentralization of education financing improved enrollment rates in public schools. In both countries, investment shifted from infrastructure to primary social services. In both cases, smaller, poorer, more rural municipalities proved to be catalysts for improving educational outcomes.

Negative Impacts. Ravallion (1998) found that in Argentina poorer provinces were less successful in benefiting their poor areas and decentralization generated substantial inequality in public spending in poor areas. Azfar and Livingston (2002) did not find any positive impacts of decentralization on efficiency and equity of local public service provision in Uganda. West and Wong (1995) found that in rural China, decentralization resulted in lower levels of public services in poorer regions. A study of health services by the local governments in the Nigerian states of Lago and Kogi showed inefficient service delivery performance (Khemani, 2004).

Inconclusive Impacts. Several studies observed mixed or inconclusive impacts of decentralization. Azfar et al. (2000a, 2000b) concluded for the Philippines and Uganda that, while local governments do appear to be aware of local preferences, their response is often inadequate as they are hamstrung by procedural, financing, and governance constraints. Khaleghian (2003) using data for 140 countries found that, while decentralization improved the coverage of immunization in low-income countries, opposite results were obtained for middle-income countries. Winkler and Rounds (1996) reviewed Chile's experience with education decentralization and concluded that it resulted in improvement in efficiency of provision but also experienced decline in scores on cognitive tests. Elhiraika (2007), using provincial-level data for South Africa, found an inconclusive impact on service delivery of limited fiscal decentralization to provinces.

The Impact of Decentralization on Economic Growth

Several studies found a positive impact of decentralization on growth. Akai and Sakata (2002), using state-level data for the United States, concluded that fiscal decentralization contributed positively to U.S. growth. These results are further confirmed by Akai, Skata, and Ma (2003). Lin and Liu (2000) found that fiscal decentralization had a positive impact on China's growth. Thiessen (2000) found a positive and direct relationship between decentralization and growth for panels of high-income, Western European, and middle-income countries. Zhang and Zou (1997) found the same for regional growth in India. Martinez-Vazquez and McNab (2005), on the basis of international cross-section and time series data, found a positive impact of fiscal decentralization on economic growth through its direct positive influence on macroeconomic stability. Stansel (2005), using data for 314 metropolitan areas in the United States, found a negative relationship between the central-city share of metro area population and economic growth and a positive relationship between the number of municipalities per 100,000 residents and the number of counties per 100,000 residents and economic growth. Those findings provide support for the hypothesis that decentralization enhances economic growth. Atsushi (2005), using data for fifty-one countries, found a positive impact of fiscal decentralization on economic growth. Bodman and Ford (2006), on the basis of panel data for OECD countries, found a positive relationship between fiscal decentralization and physical and human capital accumulation. Akai, Nishimura, and Sakata (2007) examined the relationship between fiscal decentralization and economic growth by using state-level cross-section data for the United States, using a panel data set of the fifty states over the period of 1992–1997. They found that the relationship between fiscal decentralization and economic growth is not linear, so that the economic growth implication of fiscal decentralization depends on the structure of complementarity. Their analysis shows that the optimal degree of fiscal decentralization conducive to economic growth is higher than the average of the data in some cases, and hence further decentralization is recommended for economic growth.

Several other studies found that the impact of decentralization on growth is either negative or inconclusive. Davoodi and Zou (1998) and Xie, Zou, and Davoodi (1999), using various data sets for the developing countries, developed countries, and time series data of the United States, discovered that decentralization was associated with slower growth. Zhang and Zou (1998) found that fiscal decentralization in China contributed to lower provincial growth. Rodriguez-Pose and Bwire (2003) found a negative impact of decentralization on economic growth for Mexico and the United States but no impact for Germany, India, Italy, and Spain. Phillips and Woller (1997) and Martinez-Vazquez and McNab (2003) could not find a statistically significant relationship between fiscal decentralization and economic growth. Thornton (2007), on the basis of a sample of nineteen OECD countries, found that the impact of decentralization on economic growth was insignificant. According to Davoodi and Zou (1998) and Zhang and Zou (1998), the negative association between fiscal decentralization and economic growth may indicate that in practice local governments may not be responsive to local citizens' preferences and needs – for example, when local officials are not elected by local citizens and when local citizens may be too poor to "vote with their feet." For the case of China, the central government is constantly constrained by the limited resources for public investment in national priorities, such as highways, railways, power stations, telecommunications, and energy. Such key infrastructure projects may have a far more significant impact on growth across Chinese provinces than their counterparts in each province. This finding has some implications for other developing countries and transitional economies. The merits of fiscal decentralization have to be measured relative to existing revenue and expenditure assignments and the stage of economic development. The central government may be in a much better position to undertake public investment with nationwide externalities in the early stage of economic development. More important, if local shares in total fiscal revenue and expenditure are already high, further decentralization may result in slower overall economic growth.

Conclusions

Decentralization whereby local governments are empowered to make all policy and program decisions on behalf of their resident-voters represents a complex system of political, administrative, and fiscal autonomy and associated accountability mechanisms to ensure responsiveness and accountability to voters. In theory, such a system is expected to have positive impacts on the efficiency and equity of public service provision and provide an enabling environment to foster economic growth. In practice, these outcomes depend on the existing institutional arrangements (including power relations) and the coherence of decentralization policies to create the proper incentive environment for bottom-up accountability. The complexity of the system explains the myriad outcomes that we see in practice. Nevertheless, the empirical evidence presented here is broadly supportive of a positive influence of decentralization policies on service delivery and economic growth.

THREE

Expenditure Assignment

THE CASE FOR DECENTRALIZATION

In Chapter 2, we outlined the general principles of expenditure assignment and discussed in general terms the kinds of responsibilities that could be decentralized to the states. In this chapter, we consider expenditure assignment in more detail. The application of the general principles to specific types of expenditure functions is discussed, as well as some additional problems that arise in coordinating state provision of expenditure pro grams with national objectives.

It might be worth briefly recalling and summarizing the key arguments for decentralization of expenditures to put the following discussion into context. The following arguments constitute the case for decentralizing expenditure responsibilities. These have also been briefly discussed in earlier chapters.

Catering to Regional Preferences and Needs

The classic argument for decentralization (Oates, 1972) is that different states have different demands for types and levels of public goods and services. This variation may simply come from personal preferences of the residents themselves, perhaps arising from cultural differences or other sources of heterogeneity across states. Or it may come from more objective factors such as geographic differences (e.g., terrain, population density), demographic differences (age structure of the population), or relative price or cost differences. The presumption of the Oates decentralization theorem is that central provisions will tend to be uniform, so that efficiency could be improved if regional communities were allowed to provide their own local public goods and services to cater to local preferences and needs.

The famous model set forth by Tiebout (1956), written in the context of local communities rather than states comprising several communities, had gone one step further and argued that the makeup of communities themselves was endogenous and that decentralized decision making would facilitate the formation of optimal mixes of communities. The natural tendency for persons with similar preferences to congregate together would induce local governments, acting competitively, to provide efficient levels of public goods and services for their residents. While there is a grain of truth in the Tiebout view of competing local economies, the literal acceptance of the Tiebout hypothesis has been largely discredited. For one thing, mobility among communities is nowhere near the magnitude required to generate optimal communities, with the possible exception of intracity mobility. Even if mobility of households might be high, it is mitigated by the irreversibility of local capital and infrastructure. Indeed, the partial irreversibility of labor mobility itself poses difficult conceptual problems. If one takes the migration decision to be a long-run irreversible one, and governments can make budgetary decisions on a recurring basis, the Tiebout model and its consequences for optimal community formation break down.[1] The Tiebout model is too simplistic and one-dimensional. It turns out to be fairly simple to formulate Tiebout-type models in which either equilibrium does not exist (households would always want to move elsewhere) or, if it does, it would be inefficient or unstable (Bewley, 1981). Indeed, the existence of zoning laws is evidence that, in the context of cities, unfettered mobility of households and firms is not likely to result in acceptable outcomes. More generally, it is not clear that the Tiebout model of homogeneous communities is relevant for analyzing entities consisting of regions or states as opposed to communities. States necessarily serve a collection of communities. Even if mobility entailed the gathering of households into homogeneous communities, states would consist of a diversity of such communities. The literature has not formally addressed the implications of this for state-level decision making, except to say that public expenditures of purely local scope should be decentralized to the community level.

Nonetheless, the main message of the Tiebout model is a powerful one. In the face of heterogeneous communities, decentralized decision makers, constrained by the need to cater to potentially mobile households and firms, will strive to provide the best mix of public goods and services for

---

[1] In the extreme case where labor mobility is fully irreversible, and where households anticipate future local government behavior, households have an incentive to agglomerate in a small number of excessively large jurisdictions. This is analyzed in Mitsui and Sato (2001).

their residents that they can. Against this message must be set a number of considerations.

1. *Local public goods and services.* The message of the Tiebout model is really meant to apply only to public goods and services that serve local community residents. Because many important public programs that are candidates for decentralization to the states have benefits that are further flung than that, spillover effects will occur that will limit the efficiency of decentralizing decision making from the central government to the states. This constitutes the case for intermediate levels of subnational governments, like states.[2]
2. *Efficiency in the internal economic union.* Catering to regional preferences can conflict with the efficiency of the internal economic union. Different communities may have different preferences concerning environmental degradation, product safety, cultural and language protection, labor standards, and so on. These preferences might lead to policies that interfere with the free flow of products and factors across borders. As in the international sphere, some compromise must be made between the efficiency of the federal common market and the right to regulate local markets to achieve noneconomic objectives.
3. *Mobility considerations.* The extent of mobility may differ across different types of households or firms, in which case the most mobile command the most preferential policies. Thus, if low-income households are mobile, state redistribution policies may be suboptimal. If some firms are more footloose than others, fiscal policies will be adopted that favor them.
4. *Redistributive issues.* Profound issues arise with respect to the redistributive dimension of state fiscal programs. The residents of different states may have different preferences for redistribution, not only relative to each other but also relative to the federal government. An unavoidable conflict arises as to which level of government's preferences will prevail. The resolution of this conflict necessarily involves

---

[2] The seminal article on this is Breton (1965) who viewed the assignment problem as one of assigning functions to communities whose scope corresponded with the extent of benefits of the public goods being provided. As he pointed out, a perfect correspondence would be impossible, so that spillovers would be a necessary feature of multilevel governments. His analysis, like much of the earlier federalism literature, portrayed governments as providing mainly public goods, albeit ones that might be limited in geographic scope. As we emphasized in Chapter 1, public goods comprise but a fraction of actual government programs. Public services (quasi-private public goods) and transfers form the bulk of government expenditures.

a compromise, perhaps the most important of the many compromises that constitute an interdependent federal system of government. The extent to which federal versus state preferences for redistribution prevails depends on how decentralized the federal system is. Roughly speaking, the more decentralization, the more scope there is for federal and state redistribution policies to be in conflict. This possibility for conflict over redistribution is a key determinant of the desired extent and form of decentralization. It is also an important consideration in designing fiscal arrangements for an already decentralized system, a subject of later chapters.

Information Asymmetries

There are some spheres of policy making in which state governments (and their municipalities) may be better informed and therefore better able to provide public services effectively than the federal government. Consequently, states may have an advantage in catering to the preferences and needs of state residents when determining the optimal amounts of public goods and services to provide. Equally important are the information issues associated with administering public programs and delivering both public services and targeted transfers. Such programs are typically delivered on the ground by agencies whose administrators are local managers, social workers, and the like. The agencies themselves may be part of the public sector, but in some instances they are private or nonprofit agencies contracted by the government to administer the services. Examples of the latter might include hospitals, child welfare agencies, and nonpublic schools.

Whether or not they are public agencies, they are accountable to the relevant government's public sector, so their performance has to be monitored. This oversight gives rise to discrepancies, because the motives governing agency decision making will generally differ from the government's objectives. In addition, the agencies themselves are subject to standard "agency problems" of management and control: managers cannot manage efficiently because they cannot perfectly observe relevant characteristics of those under their control.

One such agency problem, analogous to the adverse selection in insurance contexts, is that agencies serving different populations may have systematically different costs of delivery.[3] If the bureaucracy does not know

---

[3] The consequences of this for the structure of grants have been analyzed in Boadway, Horiba, and Jha (1999) and Lockwood (1999).

these costs precisely, it is not clear how much funding is required to run the agency. For example, what are the costs of running a school in a high-income neighborhood relative to a deprived one? If that is not known, the result is that resources will necessarily be wasted. It is argued that state governments may be better able to monitor the true costs of providing such public services than the federal government, if only because they are closer to the source of delivery and need only monitor those within their jurisdiction.

Another problem is analogous to moral hazard. It may be difficult to monitor the effort that providers of public services are putting out, and it may be difficult to ensure that they are targeting the services (or transfers) to the intended population. Programs like unemployment insurance, disability benefits, and welfare are intended for particular groups and may be contingent on those groups satisfying some conditions (e.g., searching for work, taking training). Again, in the absence of careful monitoring, this is likely to lead to significant waste.[4] For the same reasons as previously noted, state governments may have an advantage at such monitoring.

These arguments apply not only to public services provided to households and firms but also to transfers targeted to persons on the basis of nonincome information. The distinction between these transfers and those delivered through the tax-transfer system is important. The latter can be administered using the self-reporting procedures of the income tax system, for which delivery by the central government is efficient. But targeting involves monitoring for initial and ongoing eligibility, for which decentralization might be more efficient.

Finally, decentralization may itself reduce the administrative costs of delivering services by cutting down the number of layers of bureaucracy. This constitutes a further argument for decentralization in addition to that arising because state governments are better informed.

These information-based arguments are relatively powerful ones in a world where administrative costs are an important part of the costs of delivering some programs. They apply with much more force to public services that are delivered to persons or firms than to large-scale transfer programs that can be delivered through the tax system, for which there may be significant economies of scale. Indeed, many of the arguments for decentralization have the feature that they apply especially to the provision of public services and targeted transfers. It is therefore not surprising that

---

[4] For an analysis of the effects of monitoring on the delivery of unemployment insurance and welfare, see Boadway and Cuff (1999).

in many federations the delivery of public services are much more decentralized than the system of taxes and transfers. Even in otherwise unitary nations, the delivery of public services is often devolved to regional or local governments. As we have mentioned in earlier chapters, examples include the Scandinavian countries and Japan, where public expenditures are actually highly decentralized, although often with significant central control. Likewise, in China in 2003 local governments were responsible for 70 percent of total government expenditures (Dong, 2007).

To repeat a point that recurs throughout this study, these arguments for decentralization are based on efficiency considerations. Many of the important public services that states provide have an important equity dimension – examples of health, education, and welfare come immediately to mind. The federal government may therefore have an interest in how well and at what level the services are delivered. If decentralization were unaccompanied by other measures, state governments acting independently might well design their programs in ways that do not satisfy national norms of equity. A role of the fiscal arrangements is to address this issue.

Innovation and Cost-Effectiveness in Public Programs

Decentralization may lead to improvements and innovations in program design and program delivery because of the opportunities and constraints faced by state-level decision makers. When there are many states, perhaps in competition with one another, there are more opportunities for innovations in program design and delivery, and, once improvements do occur, other jurisdictions can imitate them.

The existence of neighboring jurisdictions can itself have a salutary effect on service delivery. Yardsticks for delivery costs will become available that will serve to discipline a given jurisdiction. Citizens and politicians alike will have the opportunity to compare the costs of delivering public services in neighboring jurisdictions and will expect their own state public sectors to be as cost-effective. Such mobility as there is will also induce states to deliver their services in an efficient way. Of course, such competition may have its downside as well, as states engage in destructive competition, an issue that potentially gives rise to federal intervention.

Political Economy Arguments

Public choice economists are prone to using market analogies to judge public-sector outcomes. They regard political competition induced by decentralization to be a force for greater efficiency improvements compared with centralized fiscal decision making.[5] The arguments are not always fully articulated in an economic model, and they are sometimes difficult to substantiate, but they have some intuitive plausibility. A common notion of political competition is based on the Tiebout-type presumption that households and firms, especially desirable ones, are mobile across jurisdictions. This mobility constrains competing governments from excessively high tax rates or public service levels. Of course, this argument can cut both ways. Given that it might be the better-off households that are the most mobile, competitive reductions in the level of public programs and especially in their progressivity may make it more difficult to achieve redistribution objectives. This is why proponents of decentralization are often identified with those who wish to constrain government's ability to redistribute.

As described in Chapter 1, an extreme form of this argument is based on the presumption that governments are essentially self-serving Leviathans intent on aggrandizing themselves at the public's expense. In the well-known version of Brennan and Buchanan (1980), governments maximize their size. Decentralization can serve to tame the Leviathan by constraining the ability of the government from extracting resources from an unwitting electorate.[6] This argument too relies on interjurisdictional mobility as the source of the constraint: firms and households can exercise their exit option.

Political economy arguments also come in other forms. A common argument is that lower-level governments are more "accountable" because they are "closer to the electorate." Political accountability might be enhanced by decentralization because it is possible to identify given public programs with given levels of government, and given tax dollars with given expenditures. But the accountability argument is not clear-cut. There is no compelling evidence that lower levels of government are more accountable to their electorates. In fact, given that the glare of national media publicity is typically directed at the federal government, one could argue just the opposite. Moreover, one could also argue that the lines of responsibility get blurred rather than clarified as one decentralizes responsibilities.

A final political economy consideration concerns the effect of decentralization on antisocial political behavior – rent seeking, influence peddling or outright corruption. It is argued that decentralization reduces the

---

[5] See the discussion and further references in Breton (1994).

[6] An elegant demonstration of this may be found in Edwards and Keen (1996).

possibilities for such behavior, perhaps by reducing the size of the rewards for engaging in it.[7] Also, save for certain spillover effects, decentralized corruption is more likely to affect fewer people. Generally, the consequences of corrupt state behavior would be confined to their particular state or region whereas a corrupt federal government's actions would be more likely spread throughout the entire nation. On the other hand, decentralization might make it easy to engage in corrupt practices if there is a closer relation between the bureaucracy and local constituents. The jury is still out on the relationship between decentralization and corruption.

Other Considerations

The four classes of argument just outlined are perhaps the most persuasive general arguments for decentralizing responsibility for expenditure programs to the states. In actual federal economies, other factors come into play. The level of development is particularly relevant in the context of developing countries. The kinds of public services that are prime candidates for decentralization to the states are also the services that are more comprehensively provided in industrialized countries, such as universal health insurance, education and welfare, and targeted transfers.

Historical, political, and constitutional factors help determine the feasible and desirable extent of decentralization. Constitutional provisions may restrict the extent to which fiscal responsibilities can be decentralized, and constitutional change may be difficult to pursue. There may be concerns about the consequences for stability of the nation if fiscal responsibility is decentralized. These concerns may be particularly important where states differ substantially in terms of wealth, culture, language or other characteristics that could represent latent nationalism. The extent of decentralization must obviously be tempered by such country-specific considerations. One argument that is frequently used as a counter to decentralization is that the states do not have either the administrative capability of providing public services or the political experience required to make responsible fiscal decisions. This is largely an argument about the costs of adjustment. It is no doubt difficult for lower-level governments suddenly to be handed responsibility for providing major public services when they have had no experience in doing so in the past. In these circumstances, the move to a more decentralized system of government requires a period of transition in which persons are trained, systems of decision

---

[7] A formal analysis of this may be found in Sato (1998).

making and accountability are put in place, and experience is gained, perhaps with errors along the way. Funds presumably need to be provided for such a transition. Recognizing that a transition will be required and may be costly is important. The long-run benefits of decentralization should be set against the transitional costs. Instantaneous gratification is not the norm. It is sometimes all too easy to dismiss decentralization by arguing that the states are incapable of assuming the responsibility of independent government. Proponents of decentralization must forcefully make the case for decentralizing from the status quo by arguing that an investment in the transition will pay off in the medium run.

South Africa is an example in which the transitional period is formally recognized, even as implementation is delayed. Its constitution explicitly recognizes the need to develop lower-level administrative capacity and to transfer responsibilities once that capacity exists. Provinces with sufficient administrative skills are entitled to implement national legislation in certain fields. Similarly, a municipality with the relevant administrative capacity must be assigned responsibility for local government matters in the provincial sphere. Despite these constitutional provisions, however, no actual reassignment has taken place. Indeed, the provincial role was strengthened in 2003 when the constitution was amended to allow, and in some cases compel, provincial governments to intervene in cases of municipal financial crises (Steytler, 2005). Similar issues of financial instability and inadequate subnational administrative capacity help contribute to the dominance of the central government in the Brazilian federation. The Brazilian constitution of 1988, for example, retains the right of the central government to intervene if state or municipal finances need reorganization (Souza, 2005).

In the economics literature and as discussed in earlier chapters, a major source of inefficient government decision making arises because of the so-called time inconsistency problem, which typically leads to excessive government taxation and spending. Unlike with many public choice explanations for excessive government, this one applies even if governments are fully benevolent. It arises essentially because of the inability of governments to be able to abide by long-term commitments. If a government announces a policy that has long-run effects, it will presumably want to take account of all the long-run consequences of it, especially the effect it has on the long-run decisions of its residents. However, once time has passed, and firms or households have committed themselves to long-run decisions and cannot undo them, the government will have an incentive to renege on its previously announced policy. For example, taxes on capital will discourage investment, and governments would prefer not to implement them at high levels. However, once investment is in place, it is to some extent irreversible. The government has an incentive to levy high tax rates on it. This kind of argument has been used to explain high tax rates on capital and wealth, as well as the tendency of governments to accumulate debt and run down the funds of public pensions, and to bail out declining or inefficient industries. Decentralization and the resultant political competition it induces might serve as an antidote to these tendencies.[8]

ASSIGNMENT BY TYPE OF EXPENDITURE

With these general principles as a background, we can look now at specific categories of public expenditures with a view to assessing their candidacy for decentralization. A representative assignment of responsibilities consistent with the discussion in the following paragraphs is presented in Tables 3.1, and a comparative assignment in twelve federal countries is summarized in Tables 3.2.

Public Goods

The traditional public finance literature takes the provision of public goods as being the main function of government in terms of addressing market failures – what is referred to as the "efficiency" branch of government. Because of their joint consumption and nonexcludability properties, public goods suffer from the free-rider problem, which entails that provision must be compulsory and based on collective rather than market decision making. The early literature on fiscal federalism simply gave public goods a geographic dimension and attempted to align expenditure functions in accordance with the area spanned by the public good in question. Thus, local governments would be responsible for local public goods, state governments for "regional" public goods, and the federal government for national public goods. In the earlier models of fiscal federalism, this defined the scope of local and state decision making, along with whatever revenue-raising responsibilities were decentralized.

---

[8] For an argument that decentralization can provide some discipline against governments bailing out inefficient firms, see Qian and Roland (1998). By the same token, decentralization might serve to mitigate the time consistency problem of capital income taxation. Kehoe (1989) has argued that coordinated capital income tax policies among countries can in fact exacerbate the problem.

Table 3.1. *Representative assignment of expenditure responsibilities among various orders of government*

Function	Policy, standards, and oversight	Provision and administration	Production and distribution	Comments
Interregional and international conflicts resolution	U	U	N,P	Benefits and costs international in scope
External trade	U	U,N,S	P	Benefits and costs international in scope
Telecommunications	U,N	P	P	Has national and global dimensions
Financial transactions	U,N	P	P	Has national and global dimensions
Environment	U,N,S,L	U,N,S,L	N,S,L,P	Externalities of global, national, state, and local scope
Foreign direct investment	N,L	L	P	Local infrastructure critical
Defense	N	N	N,P	Benefits and costs national in scope
Foreign affairs	N	N	N	Benefits and costs national in scope
Monetary policy, currency, and banking	U,ICB	ICB	ICB,P	Independence from all levels essential; some international role for common discipline

Interstate commerce	Constitution, N	N	P	Constitutional safeguards important for factors and goods mobility
Immigration	U,N	N	N	U because of forced exit
Transfer payments	N	N	N	Redistribution
Criminal and civil law	N	N	N	Rule of law, a national concern
Industrial policy	N	N	P	Intended to prevent beggar-thy-neighbor policies
Regulation	N	N,S,L	N,S,L,P	Internal common market
Fiscal policy	N	N,S,L	N,S,L,P	Coordination possible
Natural resources	N	N,S,L	N,S,L,P	Promotes regional equity and internal common market
Education, health, and social welfare	N,S,L	S,L	S,L,P	Transfers in kind
Highways	N,S,L	N,S,L	S,L,P	Benefits and costs vary in scope
Parks and recreation	N,S,L	N,S,L	N,S,L,P	Benefits and costs vary in scope
Police	S, L	S,L	S,L	Primarily local benefits
Water, sewer, refuse, and fire protection	L	L	L,P	Primarily local benefits

Note: U = supranational responsibility, ICB = independent central bank, N = national government, S = state or provincial government, L = local government, P = nongovernmental sectors or civil society.

Table 3.2. *Summary statistics on division of powers in twelve federalism countries*

Expenditure category	Number of countries with shared and/or subnational assignment	
	Responsibility	Provision
Defense	0	0
Foreign affairs	0	0
International trade	0	0
Currency banking	0	0
Interstate trade	0	0
Immigration	1	0
Air and rail	4	4
Unemployment insurance	1	2
Environment	7	8
Highway	8	8
Education	11	11
Natural resources	8	8
Social welfare	9	10
Industrial and agriculture	9	9
Police	10	10
Health	9	11
Residual functions	2	2

Note: Sample countries include Australia, Brazil, Canada, Germany, India, Malaysia, Nigeria, Russia, South Africa, Spain, Switzerland, and the United States.
Source: Compiled from country case studies in Shah (2007a).

This schema, though conceptually neat and completely noncontroversial, is an incomplete and unsatisfactory representation of federal economies in the real world. For one thing, public goods cannot be compartmentalized into local, regional, and national and assigned accordingly. Their geographic reach did not coincide with political boundaries. There was likely to be overlapping benefits. Thus, the assignment of functions was bound to be unclear, and decentralization to "arbitrary" political boundaries was likely to lead to spillovers of benefits among residents of overlapping jurisdictions.[9] Of course, this outcome could be accommodated in the theory of fiscal federalism by adding conditional matching intergovernmental grants to the arsenal of upper-level governments. Perhaps more important is the fact that relatively few public expenditure programs fall under the rubric of public goods. Major functions like defense, foreign affairs, justice, the

[9] This was the essence of Breton's (1965) influential view of the assignment problem in federations.

environment, cultural and communications policy, and control of the currency can be thought of as programs whose benefits are public. Most of these are national, with the exception of regional elements of environmental policy or cultural policy, and are naturally assigned to the national level of government. The enforcement of criminal justice may be to some extent decentralized to lower levels of government, although cooperation and information exchange among governments is obviously important here. In Brazil, for example, municipal safety is a state responsibility, while the federal government has jurisdiction over most organized crime activities. In practice, a lack of coordination has hampered police work in municipalities, causing some observers to call for a stronger role by the central government and closer cooperation between all levels of government (Rezende, 2007). There are also some purely local functions that can be thought of as at least partly public, such as fire protection, water and sanitation, roads, parks, and libraries. Again, there is little dispute about the assignment of these to local governments. (There is dispute about the optimal means of provision, whether by the public sector or contracted to the private sector, but that is different from the assignment function.)

Identifying public goods at the state level of government is somewhat more difficult. Elements of environmental and cultural policy come to mind, as already mentioned. Public health programs have a public benefit component to them, especially those involved with communicable diseases. Some forms of public-sector infrastructure, such as transportation facilities, also come to mind. Although there are elements of joint consumption to these, they are treated as a separate category here.

The bulk of state-level expenditures are not public goods in the traditional sense originally characterized by Samuelson (1954). Instead, they fit into one of the following categories.

Public Services

A significant proportion – perhaps the majority – of public expenditures on goods and services are not for public goods but for quasi-private goods, what we are referring to as public services. Large-scale expenditure programs involving education, health care, and social services are of this sort, as explained in Chapters 1 and 2. Given the private nature of these services, quite different issues arise in their assignment. The dichotomy between local and national public goods does not apply because there are no natural geographic limitations to their provision. Given the essentially private nature of these services, one cannot rely on traditional efficiency-type market failure arguments to justify public responsibility for their provision. Instead, as we have suggested in earlier chapters, the public sector assumes responsibility for providing public services largely for redistributive reasons. These redistributive reasons may be broader than the traditional income-based redistribution, including such concerns as equality of opportunity and social insurance. These two features result in a situation where the case for decentralization is largely based on efficiency arguments, but the programs being decentralized have a redistributive dimension that is likely to be of national interest.

Public services are delivered directly to households on an individual basis. The case for decentralization rests on the argument that this delivery is more efficiently accomplished if it is the responsibility of a lower level of government, say, the states. State governments are able to identify the special needs and preferences of their own citizens and tailor the public service programs to them. They may be better able to monitor the agencies that provide the services on their behalf. And state provision may lead to more innovation and cost-effectiveness as a result of the interjurisdictional competition that inevitably arises (if only via yardstick competition).

At the same time, decentralization might not be warranted as far down as the local level. There are some economies of scale of providing public service programs, and some benefit to be had from a reasonably harmonized system of programs within states. Thus, it is not surprising that a major function of state-level governments is precisely the provision of major public service programs in the broad areas of health, education, and welfare. Indeed, one of the main reasons why systematic differences exist in the extent of decentralization between industrialized and developing federations is simply that health, education, and welfare programs are of relatively more importance in the former.

The extent of decentralization of public services to state governments can be controversial. Unlike with state and local public goods, public services fulfill major equity objectives. Moreover, their design can have implications for the efficiency of the internal economic union. The scope of public services decentralized to the states can vary across federations, and the extent of decentralization for a given public service can vary as well. Major elements of education are decentralized to the states (the previously mentioned efficiency arguments apply). In most federations, state governments provide primary and secondary education. On the other hand, postsecondary education may be provided federally, especially in nations where student mobility tends to be high. At the same time, even where the states provide education, they may be constrained to do so according to national standards of curriculum, teacher qualification, and so on. The attempt to induce states to abide by national standards in the design of their education systems reflects a natural desire to combine the advantages of decentralized decision making with the achievement of national equity and efficiency objectives. But it is also fraught with difficulties. The imposition of national control via such things as teacher training, national wage scales, curriculum requirements, school design, and the like naturally detracts from state fiscal responsibility and blurs accountability. The management of joint federal-state objectives in the provision of public services is one of the most contentious issues in fiscal federalism.

The situation with health care is similar. Its provision is also often decentralized to the states. At the same time, certain elements may be retained at the center (e.g., research, doctor training), and there may be standards of program design to which the states must conform. In health care, as in education, there will be a tension between the desire to decentralize fiscal responsibility to reap all the advantages of decentralized decision making and the desire to maintain federal control so that national equity objectives are taken into account in program design. Health care is in fact much more complicated because there is a much less well-defined demarcation between the scope of services provided by the government and those for which citizens are individually responsible. But there is also much more scope for state innovation, given the speed of change of health technology.

The assignment of responsibility for the delivery of welfare services varies across federations. It is generally more likely to be retained at the federal level than either health or education, perhaps because the advantages of decentralized provision are not nearly as prevalent. There is less scope for innovation, and informational problems may not be as severe. Welfare services may be much more prone to interjurisdictional competitive pressures than health care and education, especially given the much narrower (and less influential) base of their clientele. Moreover, welfare services might be more closely integrated with the tax-transfer system that is typically in the hands of the federal government. Nonetheless, it is fairly common for welfare services to be decentralized to the states (along with welfare payments). There are special needs that may differ from state to state, and there are advantages to state control of the agencies that deliver these services.

Social Insurance

The provision of economic security has come to be a major function of the modern state, although one from which there has been some retreat in recent years. The massive buildup of the welfare state that occurred in the early postwar period is thought by many to have been responsible for the deficit and debt problems faced by many countries in the 1980s. There has also been concern that the universal provision of economic security had an adverse effect on incentives.[10] Thus, there has been a move toward retrenchment and rationalization. In many countries, social programs have become more targeted and less universal, especially as countries try to cope with the fiscal consequences of higher unemployment rates and the coming demographic change due to an aging population. These issues have also put some strain on fiscal arrangements in federations because state-level governments provide many programs aimed at providing economic security.

In considering the assignment of social insurance functions, many issues must be addressed. First and foremost is to identify what is the proper government role in providing social or economic insurance. Two alternative types of social insurance can be distinguished. The first involves the nation providing insurance against unexpected adversities that, for some reason, are not insured by the private sector. Examples of this include unemployment insurance, disability insurance, workers compensation covering injury on the job, and that part of health insurance that deals with unforeseen ill health. The reasons for market failure can be many, including moral hazard, adverse selection, informational asymmetries favoring the suppliers of insured services, scale economies, administrative costs, and, in the case of unemployment insurance, the fact that the event being insured against is at least partly under the control of government. Economists disagree on the exact causes and severity of market failure and on the issue of whether the government can do any better than the market at overcoming market failure. They also worry about the incentive/insurance trade-off that is necessarily present when governments cannot monitor perfectly the cause of an individual's economic distress. Regardless of that, in virtually all industrialized countries, government is heavily involved in the provision of this form of economic insurance.

The second form of social insurance relates to adverse outcomes that are uninsurable, especially those which are revealed at birth. Specifically, persons may be born with characteristics that put them at a disadvantage relative to others. They may be disabled, prone to serious illness, or unlucky in their time or region of birth. Indeed, one can look at the general problem of redistribution per se as being one of social insurance. Persons

[10] See the recent analysis by Sinn (1995).

may be born with different abilities, skills, or productivities that lead to different degrees of economic success regardless of their work effort.[11] Social insurance of this form is obviously uninsurable by the private sector. The extent to which the public sector should insure against bad luck at birth is a matter of value judgment, given the equity-efficiency trade-off involved. But again, governments in many countries, especially industrialized ones, are heavily engaged in the provision of social insurance. Universal health insurance is common, as are disability pensions, social security (public pensions), and programs of regional equalization.

The question then becomes which level of government should be responsible for providing social insurance of these forms. The arguments for decentralization apply directly here. State-level governments should have an advantage at tailoring social insurance programs to suit the needs of their residents, at targeting the programs to those for whom the programs are intended, and at overcoming agency programs. And the efficiency with which they go about the provision of their programs should benefit from interjurisdictional competition. Thus, it is not surprising that many social programs are assigned to state-level governments in federations.

There are disadvantages of decentralizing the provision of social insurance to the states. Different states may face very different needs for social insurance because of the demographic makeups of their populations or because of events that have affected their development. In the case of the first form of social insurance, states may face idiosyncratic risks that could be partially pooled across states by central provision. State provision might also have some adverse side effects. Interjurisdictional competition that may induce states to reduce the level of protection they provide to those adversely affected might be particularly detrimental for the second form of social insurance. Also, different states might simply choose very different forms of social insurance, leading to uneven levels of coverage across the nation and thereby detracting from efficiency and equity in the internal economic union.

The balance of advantages to disadvantages of decentralization may differ from one form of program to another. Disability insurance and workers compensation are often decentralized, reflecting that fact that monitoring and agency issues may be relatively important. The

---

[11] The traditional theory of income redistribution, as seminally propounded by Mirrlees (1971), relies on differences in such abilities. A general survey of the theory and practice of redistribution may be found in Boadway and Keen (2000).

involvement of higher-level governments varies. In Canada, provinces have jurisdiction over labor relations in the sectors they regulate (Knopff and Sayers, 2005). In Germany, job safety is a municipal responsibility carried out on behalf of the *Land* government. The *Länder* retain the right to provide legal supervision and to evaluate the effectiveness of local measures. If municipalities ignore their instructions, the supervisory bodies can take over an activity (Kramer, 2005). In India, overall labor welfare, including work conditions, workers compensation, and employer's liability, are on the concurrent list, with the exception of a few industries assigned solely to the union (mines, oilfields). Indian states have responsibility for the disabled and unemployable (article 246 of the Constitution of India). In Brazil, services to the disabled are a shared responsibility (Souza, 2005). Health insurance is also often assigned to the states for the same reason. In Canada, health care is solely a provincial responsibility. In many federations, health care is a shared responsibility; examples include Brazil, Mexico, South Africa, and Switzerland. In the United States, the federal government provides health care targeted to older individuals (Medicare) while sharing responsibility for health care for the poor (Medicaid) (Fox, 2007). Unemployment insurance is sometimes decentralized and sometimes centralized. Monitoring is important, but so are the possibilities for idiosyncratic risk. Public pension schemes are almost always retained at the federal level. They are relatively easy to administer, and they might be prone to interjurisdictional competition. In Brazil, as in the United States, social security is an exclusively federal responsibility (Souza, 2005). In India, old-age pensions are on the concurrent list, although the union and state governments are responsible for the pensions of their employees (Majeed, 2005; Constitution of India). China is unusual in that unemployment benefits and pensions are assigned to local governments. These expenditure responsibilities can exceed the financial resources available (Mountfield and Wong, 2005).

Given that the case for decentralization is strong, it is not surprising that many social insurance schemes are decentralized to the states. At the same time, measures can be undertaken to offset the adverse consequences that might otherwise come from decentralization. In particular, equalizing federal-state transfers can be used to compensate for differences in needs among states. The federal government can also attempt to induce states to harmonize their programs to some minimal national standards by the use of block grants with general conditions attached.

The delivery of social assistance in Brazil illustrates several of these points. Social assistance is assigned primarily to local governments; state and federal governments are to provide technical and financial support. In practice, the responsibility is shared almost evenly between the state and local levels. Federal control is exercised through earmarked grants that fund social services at the state and local level. These grants assumed greater importance after economic crises eroded subnational tax bases. However, efforts to coordinate service delivery between the state and municipal levels have been unsuccessful. The lines of authority are not clear. Complementary legislation allowed states to establish coordinating metropolitan regions. This legislative assignment conflicts with the constitutional autonomy of municipalities. The result is metropolitan regions that lack real authority and service delivery characterized by conflicting policies, administrative overlap, and uneven access to services. The Brazilian example underscores the importance of clear assignments of responsibility (Rezende, 2007).

Transfers to Individuals

Transfers to individuals are components of the overall redistributive policy of governments. They can take many different forms, but we can distinguish three broad categories of transfers to individuals. The first and most general are demogrants, lump-sum transfers of a given amount to all persons of a given demographic category. Common categories are by age, including universal transfers to the elderly and to families according to the number of children. Demogrants induce minimal inefficiency in the private sector because of their lump-sum nature, but at the same time they are very expensive relative to the amount of redistribution they deliver.

The second category consists of transfers delivered through the income tax system. These are sometimes referred to as refundable tax credits and are essentially equivalent to a negative income tax system. Both the size of the transfer and the tax-back rates are matters of policy choice. An important feature of these transfers is that they are administered by the income-tax-collection system, so their size can be conditioned on income as well as other tax variables. Typically, one has these transfers in mind when referring to the "tax-transfer system." Although economists have long favored negative income tax systems, only recently has their use become widespread in industrialized countries. Their introduction is partly associated with the retreat from the universal welfare state. It is also a reflection of the fact that income tax administration and record keeping has become much more streamlined and responsive to change with the advent of computerization. At the same time, a major problem with transfers delivered through the tax system is that they are relatively inflexible. They must be based on income data stretching over the previous tax-reporting year. It is difficult to use them to meet the needs of those whose circumstances change more frequently.

The third category complements the previous two: transfers that are targeted to individuals according to their particular circumstances and needs. They encompass the welfare or social assistance transfers made to the needy, including the long-term unemployed, single parents, and those unable to work. Administered by agencies responsible for identifying and targeting the transfers as well as monitoring recipients for continued need, the transfer programs may have significant eligibility conditions attached to them, such as the requirement to be engaged in job search or training activities, or even the requirement to perform work in return for the transfer (i.e., workfare programs).

The assignment arguments differ for these types of transfers. In the case of demogrants, there are no particular advantages to decentralization. The programs are relatively easy to administer, and there may even be economies of scale involved. Federal provision ensures that a uniform transfer is available nationwide.

Federal control is also evident in the case of transfers delivered through the income tax system. Typically, the federal government administers the income tax system and controls its base and rate structure, presumably with national standards of vertical equity in mind. At the same time, a state role in income-based transfers is possible if desired. Just as states might piggyback onto the federal income tax system by selecting their own surtax rates, so they could be allowed to choose state-specific refundable transfers alongside those of the federal government. Of course, this ability to choose will generally entail that different standards of redistribution apply across states. Nonetheless, this may be judged to be desirable to allow for the possibility that citizens of different states have different collective preferences for redistribution.

Targeted transfers are strong candidates for decentralization to the states. These transfers rely for their delivery on local agencies whose role is to identify the needy and monitor them for continued eligibility. The case for decentralizing control of the agencies and the programs they administer is especially strong, for all the reasons we have mentioned previously. In Canada, targeted transfers to individuals are a provincial responsibility (Boadway, 2007b). In India, responsibility for implementing programs of social and community services – in particular, poverty alleviation – rests with local governments. However, while they are given funds to implement these programs, local governments have little real flexibility (Rao, 2007).

In the United States, intergovernmental grants focus on equalization across individuals. The decentralized delivery system is well illustrated by two major social insurance programs: welfare (Temporary Assistance for Needy Families [TANF]) and health care for the poor (Medicaid). Both programs are administered by states but funded by federal grants. The TANF grant is a block grant, whereas Medicaid transfers match between one-half and three-quarters of a state's Medicaid costs. The state programs are subject to federal rules. However, a state can apply for a waiver in order to vary its program. The possibility of experimentation is considered a positive benefit of this system (Fox, 2007).

Transfers to Businesses

Transfers to business seem to be endemic to most countries, despite the disfavor with which economists look on them. The problem is that, while there may be some sound reasons in theory for selective transfers to business, identifying the circumstances in which transfers are justified is difficult. The transfers inevitably tend to be used for protectionist or blatantly political ("pork barrel") reasons.

The main theoretical argument for transfers relies on there being some externalities associated with business activities. Research and development activities may yield spillover benefits to others in the economy. The new growth theory literature has stressed the externalities associated with process innovation, investment, learning-by-doing, and training.[12] The presumption is that the extent of these externalities varies across firm types, implying that transfers might be targeted as well. The problem is that by their very nature externalities are difficult to measure, so it is not clear to whom the subsidies ought to be directed. Moreover, it is difficult ex post to verify if the subsidies have been properly directed, so accountability is an issue. There might be a case for general support of R&D activities of firms, and most governments do provide such support. But specific subsidies are prone to be used for political purposes. Brazil has pursued a strategy of supporting broadly applicable research. Technical innovations developed at a federal agricultural research body enabled rural areas in the underdeveloped North and Northeast regions of the country to establish highly productive farms (Rezende, 2007).

---

[12] A comprehensive survey of the new growth theory and its implications for policy is found in Aghion and Howitt (1998).

Another form of business transfers that is perhaps more justifiable is the provision of insurance. There may be instances where private insurance markets fail to provide efficient levels of insurance, and the public sector steps in. For example, the agricultural industry may rely on the public sector for crop insurance and insurance against natural disasters. This public role may simply be a case of the so-called time inconsistency of government policy, an application of the Samaritan's dilemma, discussed in earlier chapters. The argument is that governments will always come to the aid of those who suffer serious adversities, regardless of whether they have insurance. If this is understood to be the case, businesses will under-insure themselves. In these circumstances, public provision (or compul-sory insurance purchase) can be beneficial.[13] There seems to be no good reason for decentralizing the transfers to business to state governments. Indeed, a bigger problem may be to prevent states from using them. Such transfers are prime candidates to be instruments for the states to use to engage in beggar-thy-neighbor competition for firms and to otherwise distort the internal economic union. The main advantages of fiscal decen-tralization do not apply with much force. Of course, there are also prob-lems with business transfers being an instrument of the federal government. It too can engage in pork-barrel politics, and may be even more prone to do so, given the larger pool of revenue available to it.

Infrastructure

Government expenditures on goods and services may be either current or capital. The latter component may reflect capital goods that are used in the provision of public goods and services, such as hospitals, schools, govern-ment buildings, and military hardware. The assignment of responsibility for those types of capital expenditures goes hand in hand with the assign-ment of provision for the relevant public service. Canadian provinces are responsible for both hospitals and health care, for example, whereas the Constitution of India assigns hospitals and dispensaries to the states along with public health (Knopff and Sayers, 2005; and article 246 of the

---

[13] This phenomenon is analyzed by Bruce and Waldman (1991) and Coate (1995). It also applies to social insurance programs directed at individuals. It can be argued that public pensions are largely justified on similar grounds. Households do not save for their own retirements anticipating that the government will provide for them if they have inad-equate savings. This turns out to be the case, so it is reasonable for the government to react by mandating savings for retirement through provident funds or public pension schemes.

Constitution of India). Of course, even if the public service is decentralized, the federal government may have an influence on capital spending associated with providing the service via conditional grants. Thus, federal grants in support of state education programs may include a component that is specific to school construction.

Some forms of capital spending by the public sector involve providing infrastructure that is used by the private sector, either firms or households. Transportation facilities are a good example of this. Governments are involved in the provision of roads, airports, waterways, public transit, and sometimes railroads. They may provide major communications facilities. Municipal water and sewage systems are typically government provided, as are irrigation projects. There is a lively debate about the extent to which the public sector should provide infrastructure facilities of this sort and also about the form that public-sector intervention, if justified, should take. Most infrastructure facilities could, in principle, be provided by the private sector, with or without regulatory oversight by the public sector. The relatively large size of such facilities, and their natural monopoly and strategic natures typically leads to some form of government intervention.

The issue is what level of government should be responsible for which elements of infrastructure. Generally speaking, the assignment of responsibility for infrastructure is straightforward. In some cases, decentralization is the obvious solution. Where the infrastructure is purely local, as in the case of local roads, water supply, sewage, and irrigation, the advantages of decentralization are obvious. Local control is likely to be more cost-effective as well as more suited to the needs of the users. Projects whose benefits are more widespread, such as motorways, waterways, airports, and major communications facilities, might be left to the federal government. In Germany, for example, the federation is responsible for air traffic, railways, and highways, while municipalities have independent planning and administrative responsibilities for water, power, waste disposal, and local roads (Kramer, 2005). In South Africa, public transport is a concurrent responsibility, whereas provincial roads and traffic are exclusively provincial, and local roads and street cleaning are the exclusive responsibilities of local government (Gonzalez, 2005).

The issues at stake are more of an efficiency nature, so the tendency for conflicts to arise is relatively small. The federal government may be involved with the state governments when it comes to financing – an issue we take up in more detail in Chapter 9 – but the case for federal intervention in state infrastructure programs is not strong. Nonetheless, there may be some reluctance by the federal government to allow states discretion over infrastructure programs. These programs might be viewed as serving partly or only political objectives. In fact, decentralization to the states may be a means by which such political tendencies are countered. Interstate competition may serve to reduce the tendency for waste in the provision of infrastructure.

Public Enterprise

Governments may also be prone to operating their own business enterprises, especially where the business involves significant scale economies. Public ownership is common in utilities, communications and broadcasting, transportation, postal services, and sometimes even industrial enterprises, like oil or automobiles. The use of public enterprise as a policy instrument is highly debatable, and economists in particular tend to take a dim view of it. However, governments often view public enterprise more benignly.

As with infrastructure, issues of decentralization tend to be fairly straightforward. Public enterprises can be owned by either the federal government or the states. If the users of the product being sold are localized, as in the case of local utilities or local transportation enterprises, state involvement is called for. Indeed, state responsibility may itself serve to counter some of the worst possible consequences of public ownership per se by injecting a form of competition into the marketplace. On the other hand, many of the more important public enterprises, such as communications and transportation firms and the postal service, are bound to be more national in scope.

EXCLUSIVE VERSUS SHARED ASSIGNMENT

In many areas of expenditures, both the federal government and the state governments have an interest in the design and delivery of programs. It might be desirable to decentralize provision to the states for all of the reasons we mentioned earlier. But, at the same time, the programs in question might impinge on issues of national concern. Efficiency in the internal economic union might be at stake, or the programs may be important components of a national equity strategy. It might be important to harmonize the basic features of the programs, while leaving discretion to the states for the specifics. There may also be overlaps or interjurisdictional spillovers in the coverage of some programs (e.g., environmental programs) that call for federal participation or oversight.

These issues of program overlap and shared objectives can be handled in various ways. Some of them we have dealt with already. The following is a more general summary of the kinds of mechanisms that are available, and are used in practice, to balance the advantages of decentralization against the interests of the national government.

Exclusive State Responsibility with Federal Oversight

At one extreme, the states may be given exclusive legislative responsibility in areas assigned to them. In the case of some state expenditure responsibilities, such as health, education, or social insurance, the design and delivery of these programs may impinge upon national efficiency or equity concerns. These national concerns can be dealt with in various ways while maintaining the integrity of exclusive provincial legislative responsibility. A rather blunt means is by constitutional mandate. It is blunt because it cannot include requirements of current policy concern, and its enforcement may well involve the courts, which may not be suitable where economic objectives are involved.

Alternatively, the federal government may hold the power of disallowance. If used reasonably and with prior negotiation, the threat of disallowance can induce the states to design policies that respect national objectives and, where necessary, are harmonized to national standards. The danger, however, is that the power of disallowance could be used in a heavy-handed way. If so, it can serve as a device for ensuring that the will of the federal government is adhered to in detail, thereby voiding the benefits of decentralized legislative responsibility.

The federal government may also have the power to impose mandates on the states, basically dictating what the states must legislate. This version of the power of disallowance is more proactive and has correspondingly more potential for abuse. If the federal government is able to mandate the design of state programs, it can effectively use that power to usurp responsibility from the states. The power of the mandate can be effective as a device for imposing minimum standards on state programs. What is important is that its use be limited to that. We return to the use of mandates later.

Finally, the federal government may use the carrot rather than the stick to induce the states to take national objectives into account. The appropriate instrument for this would be the use of conditional grants, or the spending power, which is perhaps the most common method used to reconcile decentralization with the achievement of national objectives.

Ideally, the conditions associated with the use of the spending power should be restricted to general ones rather than those involving detailed program design. Thus, conditional block grants are generally more appropriate for achieving broad national objectives than specific conditional grants. As well, it is typically not necessary to use matching provisions for this purpose. As with the previous instruments, the use of the spending power is open to potential abuse by the federal government. That is, the federal government could use it in a way that is too intrusive in areas of state responsibility. However, it could also be argued that the spending power is less open to abuse than the powers of disallowance or mandate. That is, because there are actually federal tax moneys involved, it is costly for the federal government to attempt to impose its will. Moreover, if exclusive legislative responsibility lies with the states, that in itself will limit the extent to which the terms of conditional grants can impose detailed legislative requirements on the states.

Our general presumption is that the spending power offers a flexible way for the fiscal arrangements to combine truly decentralized responsibility with the achievement of national objectives. The spending power must, however, be sanctioned by the constitution. That will vary from country to country.

In Canada, the federal spending power is implicit in the constitutional assignment of revenues and expenditures, which gives the central government greater tax revenues than required expenditures. The spending power is used in fields such as education, health care, and welfare, which are solely provincial responsibilities. For example, provinces cannot impose minimum residency requirements on entitlement programs such as health and welfare (Boadway, 2007b). The degree of control exercised through the spending power has varied. In recent decades less restrictive transfers became more common, as provinces sought to occupy their constitutional fields and the federal government sought to control its debt. For example, the Canada Health and Social Transfer, a grant based on population, replaced cost-sharing transfers based on provincial expenditures (the Established Programs Financing and the Canada Assistance Plan) (Knopff and Sayers, 2005). The Social Union Framework Agreement was negotiated between the federal government and the provinces to further refine the use of the spending power. The federal government is now required to give advance notice of its use (Boadway, 2007b).

In Germany, the *Länder* have sole responsibility for education. However, the federal role is increasing. The central government has exerted a strong influence on the design of the tertiary education system and has planned national standards at the primary and secondary levels (Joumard, 2003). A cooperative solution has evolved to address issues of service delivery. *Länder* policy is coordinated through the Education Ministers' Conference, with the result that educational qualifications and courses are virtually uniform throughout the country. This conference is not mandated in the Basic Law but is one of many forums that was developed to coordinate policy (Kramer, 2005).

In India, public health and hospitals are state responsibilities. The union government influences outcomes through a number of channels. As part of its occasional subject-specific working groups, the union government has established a Central Council of Health and a Central Council of Indian Medicine. These councils were intended to study and discuss issues of common interest, in order to make recommendations for coordinating policy across governments. The union government also plays a more direct role in health care as the control of infectious or contagious diseases is a concurrent responsibility (Majeed, 2005; Constitution of India).

In Australia, the central government does not intervene directly in policy or spending decisions by states or territories. Instead, its influence is exerted through fiscal channels. Funding tied to a specific purpose or objective has been used to further national priorities in health, education, and housing (Morris, 2007).

Shared Jurisdiction

In some areas of responsibility, the federal government and the states may share jurisdiction, perhaps because the constitution has not assigned the responsibilities or because there are both national and local dimensions to it. Thus, highways may be both federal and state. There may be state and federal universities. Environmental policy may be both state and federal. In some cases, joint legislation may lead to no difficulties. However, in others it could lead to conflicts and contradictions or to administrative complexities and overlapping regulations. Such conflicts might be resolved by negotiation. That may prove to be difficult, especially where there are a large number of state governments involved. Here again, the federal government could make use of the spending power to harmonize state and federal policies.

With Federal Paramountcy
Some of the difficulties in reconciling conflicting federal and state policies can be resolved by having one level or the other paramount. If the federal

government is paramount, that implies that state legislation will be applicable only to the extent that the federal government does not override it. This assorting of institutional provision can be another effective way to allow legislative responsibilities to be decentralized to the states while ensuring that national objectives are taken into consideration. As with other means of reconciling decentralization with the achievement of national objectives, there is the danger that the federal government will maintain too zealous a grip on effective decision making.

Shared jurisdiction with federal paramountcy also offers the advantage of a flexible instrument than can be applied selectively state by state. Thus, it allows for asymmetric federalism in which states differ in their responsibilities. This flexibility may be a desirable feature in federations where certain states have unique cultural, linguistic, or historical features that warrant them being treated differently. Examples of asymmetric federalism include Canada, Spain, and Malaysia, all of which have one or more state-level governments that exercise more fiscal responsibility than the others.

For this provision to be feasible, the constitution must allow for it, and that will depend upon the country in question. Most federations with concurrent powers retain federal paramountcy in those fields; examples include Australia, Brazil, Canada, Germany, India, Mexico, Nigeria, South Africa, Switzerland, and the United States. Whether the federal government dominates concurrent fields depends on individual country features.

The Brazilian constitution of 1988 established a symmetrical federal system whose concurrent powers include health, social welfare, and education. As noted earlier, primary responsibility for basic health care, primary education, and social assistance was assigned to local governments, with higher levels providing technical and financial assistance. In practice, state and local governments share the responsibilities almost equally. The federal government is directly involved in higher education and more sophisticated health care. Consistency in health care and primary education is encouraged through federal guidelines and resources. Indeed, its control of financing allows the federal government to play a dominant role. Earmarked federal grants have become the main source of funding for social services. States have very little control over resources in their budgets. Municipalities are somewhat more independent, with a large share of their budgets coming from general purpose grants. (Souza, 2005; Rezende, 2007).

Mexican federalism is also symmetrical, with shared responsibilities that include education, health, and the environment. Formal coordinating mechanisms were created through federal laws. These bodies include representatives of all relevant levels of government: federal, state, and, if appropriate, municipal. In practice, the federal government dominates and subnational governments play a subordinate role (Gonzalez, 2005).

In India, union law prevails in concurrent fields, which include social security, unemployment, labor welfare, and education. Various fields were moved from the state list to the concurrent list in an effort to improve national symmetry. The spending power is also used to ensure greater uniformity. Finance Commission grants are one tool for controlling and coordinating states' welfare programs (Majeed, 2005).

In Germany, most legislation falls into the concurrent sphere, with federal law taking precedence in cases of conflict. However, limits can be imposed. The federation can assume responsibility for a field, and effectively block conflicting *Land* laws, only when it is deemed necessary to ensure unity (legal or economic) or to fulfill the constitutional requirement of equivalent living conditions throughout the federation. The Federal Constitutional Court has ruled against the central government in some cases (Kramer, 2005).

With State Paramountcy

Paramountcy might instead rest with the states. In this case, federal decision making can be effective only if the states choose to allow it. It might be argued that state paramountcy is the most reasonable way to guarantee that the benefits of decentralization are achieved without federal usurpation. As with the case of federal paramountcy, state paramountcy allows for asymmetric federal arrangements.

State paramountcy presumably makes it more difficult to ensure that the federal government be able to act as the overseer of national economic and social objectives. On the other hand, the use of the federal spending power need not be ruled out in this case. In one of the few examples of explicit concurrent jurisdiction found in the Canadian Constitution, "old-age pensions and supplementary benefits" are assigned to both the provincial and federal governments, with provincial laws having precedence (Knopff and Sayers, 2005).

MANDATES

As we have mentioned, mandates are one method by which the states can be induced to design their expenditure programs (and perhaps taxation systems as well) so as to respect national economic and social objectives. Mandates can differ according to their nature as well as according to how they are imposed and enforced.

With respect to their nature, we can distinguish two types of mandates, negative and positive. These correspond with negative and positive integration measures when it comes to coordinating decision making in an internal economic union of even an international trading agreement. Negative mandates refer to prohibitions imposed on states from designing their programs so that they violate basic efficiency and equity principles of the internal economic union. Thus, states might be precluded from incorporating discriminatory elements into their programs or restricting the mobility of goods and services, labor, and capital across jurisdictions. In the United States, for example, the federal government imposes conditions on how states issue driver's licenses and register voters (Fox, 2007). As noted earlier, Canadian provinces cannot impede labor mobility in the design of health or welfare programs (Boadway, 2007b).

Positive mandates are those which require states to initiate programs in certain areas, or to design their programs in ways that advance national economic or social objectives. For example, states may be mandated to provide schooling of a certain type and level to all children of a given age in their jurisdiction. Or they may be required to provide health services of a certain minimum standard to their residents.

With both types of mandates, the conditions and obligations on the states may be more or less general. As we have repeatedly argued, the more detailed are the obligations imposed on the states, the less their discretion and therefore the less likely it is that the benefits of decentralization can be realized. The most important national objectives are rather general ones (e.g., norms of equality of opportunity, levels of schooling, accessibility and comprehensiveness of health services, minimum levels of social assistance, efficiency in the internal economic union). Within these general principles, there is considerable scope for individual program design at the state level. Achieving an ideal balance between nationally mandated standards and individuality of program design is not a simple matter. Given the natural tendency for the federal government to be excessively intrusive, one might advocate erring on the side of decentralization wherever possible. In any case, communication between the two levels of government is extremely important. As well, it is desirable that the states have sufficient financial independency so as not to be reliant on the federal government for the bulk of their funding.

The responsibility for imposition and enforcement of mandates can also vary. Mandates may be imposed by the constitution, in which case they are likely to be fairly general. The enforcement may then lie either with the courts or with the federal government. Court enforcement is likely to be rather blunt and imperfect, especially because the mandates will have a policy as well as a judicial aspect to them. Courts may not be the best vehicle for trading off the benefits and costs of achieving varying degrees of compliance. The federal government is likely to be more effective at enforcing the mandates. As we have mentioned, that can be done using either the stick (dictating to the states the relevant program designs) or, preferably, the carrot (conditional transfers).

The federal government may also be responsible for imposing the mandates in the first place. The major issue then becomes how to ensure that it does not do so in a way that subverts the exercise of fiscal responsibility by the states. The effect of mandates on subnational budgets can be sizable. In the United States, a recent estimate calculated that federal mandates for a set of programs, including significant educational reforms, imposed costs tens of billions of dollars greater than the funding provided. The Congress is required to estimate the costs of its mandates, but the federal government does not fully fund them (Fox, 2007). In China, the central government required increases in local government spending in numerous sectors. For example, educational expenditures were expected to reach 4 percent of GDP by the year 2000, while spending on science increased to 1.5 percent of GDP. Meeting these requirements was nearly impossible with budgeted funds. The result was an increased reliance on surcharges, fees, and other extrabudgetary funds. On average, local governments use these funds to finance almost half their expenditures. The lack of transparency of these funds, and the often regressive nature of the user fees, are concerns (Mountfield and Wong, 2005). Some centralized activities can act as unfunded mandates, constraining the flexibility of subnational governments. In South Africa, for example, centralized labor negotiations and agreements have limited decentralized decision making (World Bank, 2003). In some federations, quasi-independent advisory bodies exist whose purpose is to make recommendations about federal-state fiscal arrangements, including mandates and conditional grants. Provided they are at an arm's length and that they command the respect of decision makers, they can be effective at guarding against the excessive use of federal intervention in areas of state responsibility.

PRIVATE PROVISION OF PUBLIC GOODS OR SERVICES

Finally, it should be noted that government responsibility for public goods and services does not imply public provision. There is a spectrum of institutional ways for public services to be delivered to citizens. At one extreme, the public sector might finance and provide the public services using public servants. At the other, the services could be provided by the private sector – including the nonprofit sector – with minimal intervention by the government. The intervention could be restricted to providing financial assistance or to regulating the terms of provision. In between, there are varying degrees of public-private partnership. The government may contract with private agencies to provide certain services. Thus, some social services may be provided by nongovernmental agencies. And local services might be contracted out to private firms. The professionals who are involved in provision may be hired on a contractual basis rather than being public servants. Doctors might be an example of this. In the case of social insurance, the government may act as insurer of services provided by the private sector.

The existence of these various institutional arrangements for the delivery of public goods and services does not necessarily change the responsibility that governments bear for that delivery. Governments can influence the manner in which the services are delivered by some combination of financial incentives and regulation. Most of the principles of decentralization and its reconciliation with national objectives remain relevant, even if private institutions or agencies are vehicles for delivery. In the United States, for instance, much health care is privately provided. The responsibility for regulating these providers is shared across all levels of government (Fox, 2007).

FOUR

Revenue Assignment

Decentralizing revenue-raising responsibilities is one of the most unsettled issues in fiscal federalism. The dispute concerns the extent and method of decentralizing expenditure responsibilities, with relatively little debate about its merits. It is common in federations to decentralize the provision of major public services in areas of health, welfare, and education, as well as the provision of public goods and services of purely state or local concern, such as roads, water, and sanitation.[1] Some of these programs are of national importance. Federations differ considerably, however, in the extent to which they accompany expenditure decentralization with revenue-raising responsibilities. For example, in Canada and the United States, provincial or state levels of government enjoy considerable revenue-raising autonomy with access to virtually the same broad-based taxes as the federal government. On the contrary, in Australia and Germany, while the states and *Länder* are responsible for delivering health and education services, they rely heavily on transfers from the federal government for their financing and have no direct access to income or general sales taxes. In both cases, they share sales tax revenues with the federal government through revenue-sharing arrangements, but this leaves them with no independent revenue-raising discretion of their own.

The reason for this disparate situation is that the case for decentralizing revenue-raising responsibilities is much less clear-cut than for expenditures. Perhaps the strongest political argument is that of accountability, a notion that is not easy to formulate or verify. The argument is that state governments will be more accountable to their own electorates and will use

---

[1] This is true even in nonfederal nations. For example, the Scandinavian countries as well as Japan decentralize the provision of health and education, and in some cases welfare, to lower levels of government.

their funds more efficiently and judiciously the more responsible they are for deciding on their own revenues. This response would seem to be especially true at the margin: if the amount of federal-state transfers is unresponsive to state expenditure levels, incremental revenues must be raised locally so that state governments will effectively have control over the size and allocation of their budgets.

A further argument for decentralizing revenue-raising responsibilities is that, if the federal government finances state spending, there will be an unavoidable tendency to use its fiscal weight to unduly affect the form of that spending. This can have two adverse consequences. First, the federal government may be tempted to use its spending power too intrusively and to be too heavy-handed in influencing state spending priorities. Federal control would detract from the true decentralization of expenditure responsibilities to the states. Second, because the federal government's priorities change from time to time, as well as the state of its finances, the states may be subject to unannounced unilateral federal funding changes, which would adversely affect the ability of the states to plan and budget over the longer term.

These sorts of considerations enhance the case for decentralizing revenue-raising responsibilities to the state level, the level at which the growth of public spending has been the greatest over the past few decades, at least in OECD countries. The downside is that the decentralization of taxation responsibilities carries the potential for serious compromises of the efficiency and equity of the internal economic union. Taxes on mobile factors of production can distort the allocation of labor, capital, and businesses and can induce wasteful tax competition among states. Decentralization of direct taxes (and transfers) can also lead to destructive competition, which can undermine societal redistributive objectives, and to very different standards of redistribution among states, compromising national equity objectives. If states differ considerably in the size of their tax bases, decentralization of taxing responsibilities can lead to large differences in the ability of states to provide public services, which itself can be a source of fiscal inefficiency and inequity. The decentralization of tax responsibility can also lead to significant administrative costs. Taxpayers will be subject to another layer of tax authority to which they must report, leading to an increase in the complexity and compliance costs of the tax system and the undermining of its integrity. Finally, if the decentralization of revenue raising is too selective in terms of the tax bases that may be used by state governments, the result could be inefficient and inequitable tax structures. The main message here is that, given the relatively large expenditure responsibilities that state governments in a modern federation are likely to assume, access to some broad-based tax would seem to be necessary in order to achieve a reasonable level of state revenue-raising capacity. If states are dependent on excise taxes or resource taxes, for example, and are left with narrow tax bases, they will be tempted to use them excessively to the detriment of the tax system as a whole.

If we take as given the extent to which expenditure responsibilities are at the state level, each federation obviously needs to find its own suitable balance between the benefits and costs of decentralizing taxation responsibilities. This chapter outlines the principles that might be used to guide the choices that countries might make. We also address the question of which types of taxes and other charges are most suitable for use by lower levels of government, either on an exclusive basis or shared with higher levels of government. Governments rely on a wide variety of revenue-raising instruments to meet their revenue needs. These include direct and indirect taxes, general and specific taxes, business and individual taxes, taxes on trade, licenses, user charges, and so on.

It should be stressed at the outset that the decentralization of taxing responsibilities need not, indeed should not, be undertaken in a vacuum. The adverse effects of giving states access to new tax bases can be mitigated in two important ways. First, it can be accompanied by measures that serve to coordinate state tax systems with one another and with the federal government. Second, the differential benefits that tax decentralization can afford to states with relatively high tax bases can be offset by an effective system of equalization transfers.

We begin with a review of the general principles of tax assignment, which we have already seen in outline form in Chapter 2. We then consider how these principles might apply to each of the common types of taxes and fees typically levied. Following that, we address some of the issues arising from joint occupancy of given tax bases by more than one level of government and discuss the means for harmonizing taxes both vertically and horizontally.

GENERAL PRINCIPLES OF TAX ASSIGNMENT

The assignment of taxes by jurisdiction depends partly on the mix of various taxes used in the nation overall, that is, the extent of reliance on broad taxes like income taxes, wealth taxes, payroll taxes, general sales taxes, and excise taxes. In the theory of public economics, the issue of the ideal tax mix even in a unitary nation has not been widely developed.

Governments almost universally employ balanced tax systems that spread the burden of raising taxes across a large number of types, a policy that keeps the tax rates on any one base relatively low. An interesting feature of such systems is that many of the different taxes implicitly apply to basically the same bases, or at least overlap to a large extent. For example, general sales taxes, payroll taxes, and income taxes have bases that overlap considerably. Indeed, in present value terms, they are almost the same. They differ mainly in how they treat capital income, which in many countries is a relatively small part of the tax base. From the point of view of standard efficiency and equity criteria, one should be able to choose the most preferred general tax base and make do with a single general tax, thereby economizing on costs.

Yet, no governments behave that way. They typically use different tax types to raise revenues from similar bases. The usual reason given for this is that administrative and compliance considerations play an important role. A mix of taxes keeps the rate on any one tax low, thereby reducing the incentive to evade or avoid the tax. Furthermore, by using a mix of taxes, taxpayers who would otherwise be able to avoid taxation of one type are caught in the net of another, making the tax system fairer overall.[2] The importance of the various taxes in the overall mix remains, however, a matter of judgment rather than something that can be deduced from the principles. For our purpose, we simply take it as given that governments will desire to employ a mix of taxes.

These same general considerations apply in determining the mix of taxes in a federal economy. However, there is now the additional consideration of how that mix should be allocated among levels of government in a way that ensures both the best mix of taxes nationwide and the best assignment of taxes by level of government. Moreover, the assignment and mix must be determined in a way that generates a desirable division of revenue-raising responsibility between federal and state levels of government. The goals of achieving the appropriate mix of taxes, tax assignment, and division of revenue-raising responsibilities must be accomplished simultaneously. Given this, the assignment of taxes cannot be decided on abstract criteria

---

[2] For a preliminary analysis of the optimal tax mix based on this type of argument, see Boadway, Marchand, and Pestieu (1994). In the optimal-tax literature, the issue of whether it is useful to supplement a nonlinear income tax with a set of commodity taxes has been addressed by Atkinson and Stiglitz (1976) and Edwards, Keen, and Tuomala (1994). However, this is not an analysis of the tax mix in the sense in which that term is being used here, which refers to the relative levels of tax rates of different taxes. Instead, it analyzes the structure of marginal tax rates: any given structure is compatible with a large number of different levels.

independently of these broader issues of the tax mix and the assignment of responsibility of functions. For example, assigning a limited number of tax sources to state governments might result in their having to set rates on those taxes which are too high from the point of view of the desired tax mix. Either more taxes have to be assigned to them, or there has to be joint occupancy of tax bases by the state and federal levels of government. This tax dilemma has occurred in many federations, and it calls for special measures to coordinate the use of tax bases simultaneously by the two levels of government, an issue we treat in more detail later in this chapter.

As with the choice of tax mix, the choice of tax assignment to state and federal governments is not a clear-cut matter. Standard efficiency and equity arguments have to be tempered by administrative and compliance considerations, and the exact assignment depends upon informed judgment. We can, however, outline the economic principles that come into play in deciding which taxes to assign to lower levels of government. They include efficiency of the internal economic union, national equity, minimization of collection and compliance costs, and fiscal accountability. We consider these in sequence, and then turn to some more specific principles to which these general criteria give rise.

Efficiency of the Internal Common Market

The internal common market, or internal economic union, will be functioning efficiently if all resources and commodities (labor, capital, goods, and services) are free to move from one region to another without impediments or distortions imposed by policy. Note that this does not preclude impediments from other sources. For example, transportation costs represent a natural impediment to the free movement of resources and commodities, and therefore an economic cost of cross-border transactions. The fact that they cause the cost of similar commodities to differ across states does not imply any inefficiency in the internal common market. Similarly, local cost conditions (e.g., climate, terrain) may make the cost of living different across states. However, this difference does not reflect any inefficiency of resource allocation within the nation, and therefore does not call for corrective action on efficiency grounds. There may be some equity arguments for redressing inequalities arising from differential costs of living across states, but they will have to be traded off with inefficiencies induced in interregional resource allocation in the usual way.

Decentralized tax systems can interfere with the efficiency of the economic union in three ways. For one, the uncoordinated setting of taxes is likely to result in state tax systems that differ either in their rate structures or in the definition of their bases. This can lead to a type of transaction bearing different tax rates in two states that gives an incentive, based on taxes alone, for transactions to occur in the lower-tax state. This incentive then leads to distortions in markets for resources and commodities that are mobile across states, especially capital and tradable goods.

Second, differences in tax structures can also increase the administrative and compliance costs of the tax system. If firms operate in more than one state and face different tax structures in each, they will incur additional costs from having to conform to two different tax structures. Indeed, some transactions might end up being taxed in both states at the same time (or in neither) if the rules for the allocation of tax bases differ across states. Moreover, multijurisdictional firms will typically have an incentive to tailor their accounting and financial practices in order to shift their tax bases from higher- to lower-tax jurisdictions. Such adjustments can occur through transfer pricing operations within vertically integrated firms, by issuing debt in high-tax jurisdictions to finance operations in low-tax ones (to take advantage of interest deductibility provisions), or through other tax planning strategies designed purely to minimize taxes. These tax planning strategies, in addition to causing firms to alter the real decisions they take for tax reasons, require managerial, accounting, and legal resources that could otherwise be put to more productive uses.

These issues of tax-imposed distortions on resource allocation within the federation and tax planning will be mitigated by tax competition if state governments recognize that resources are mobile. Competitive pressures should tend to cause taxes to be more uniform than they otherwise would be. At the same time, a third problem may arise if states do recognize that their tax policies will influence resource allocation across states: they may engage in socially wasteful beggar-thy-neighbor policies to attract resources to their own states. If all jurisdictions engage in such policies, the end result may well be uniform state tax systems. But it will also likely be tax systems that will have inefficiently low taxes (or high subsidies) on mobile factors. This outcome provides a strong argument for retaining taxes on mobile factors at the federal level of government.

National Equity

The tax-transfer system is obviously one of the main instruments for achieving redistributive equity. As we have discussed earlier, the argument for making equity a primary federal objective is simply that all persons ought to enter into society's "social welfare function" on an equal basis; that is, all citizens should count equally for redistributive equity purposes. The presumption is that the federal government is the only level that can take actions to ensure that residents in different regions are treated equitably. This view may be tempered if states have different tastes for redistribution, if redistribution is based on altruism that works most strongly on an intrastate basis, or if centralized decision making is not guided by normative criteria. In these circumstances, states may legitimately share the responsibility for redistributive equity and pursue their own equity objectives alongside those being addressed by the federal government. Even in this case, however, national equity considerations suggest that the federal government has a role in equalizing the potential ability of the states to provide comparable services at comparable levels of taxes, whether they choose to do so or not.

Because so much of what governments actually do from a fiscal point of view is redistributive, the extent to which states are viewed as being responsible for redistribution is clearly an important determinant not only of the assignment of taxes but also of the ideal amount of fiscal responsibility decentralized to the states. As usual, state responsibility is a matter of judgment, institutions, and history, and can differ considerably across countries.

To the extent that equity is viewed as being a federal policy objective, decentralized taxes can interfere with the achievement of this goal. As with the efficiency case, uncoordinated state tax policies may unwittingly induce arbitrary differences in redistributive consequences for residents of different states. If labor is relatively immobile, persons of different income levels will be subject to different redistributive policies depending on their state of residence. At the same time, to the extent that labor is mobile across states, the states may engage in perverse redistributive policies using both taxes and transfers to attract high-income persons and repel low-income ones. Beggar-thy-neighbor redistributive policies are likely to be offsetting with respect to resource allocation if all states engage in them simultaneously. But they will result in less redistribution than would occur in their absence.[3] Of course, those who abhor redistribution by the government, or think that there is a tendency for political processes to over-redistribute, will prefer decentralized redistributive policies for precisely the same reason. Excessive redistribution is obviously likely to

---

[3] For an early analysis of this, see Boskin (1973). For recent general treatments of the limits that mobility places on redistribution by competing governments, see Wildasin (1991) and Christiansen, Hagen, and Sandmo (1994).

be more of a problem for those taxes that are redistributive, as well as for transfers.

The upshot of this discussion is that if redistribution is viewed as being a major federal government responsibility, tax instruments that are suitable for redistribution, such as income and wealth taxes, should be under federal control. This policy does not preclude the states from having access to these instruments for their own sources of revenue. However, in that case, there are advantages to the co-occupation being instituted in a harmonized fashion. As discussed in more detail later, income tax harmonization arrangements can be devised in a way that preserves the uniformity of the base and a single tax-collection authority, while allowing states the leeway to select their own tax levels, and possibly even their own progressive tax structures.

Administrative and Compliance Costs

As referred to in our earlier discussion of efficiency and equity criteria, the decentralization of revenue raising can also serve to increase the costs of collection and compliance, for both the public and private sectors. To begin with, there are fixed administrative costs associated with collecting any tax that will be borne for each tax type used by the states. These costs can be mitigated by joint collection mechanisms where the federal government is involved, but only to the extent that states are willing to make their taxes conform enough to make joint collection worthwhile. As well as the costs of collection borne by the government, taxpayers themselves will also have to incur costs of compliance for all taxes levied. In the case of taxes jointly collected by both the federal and state levels of government, such as income taxes or sales and excise taxes in some cases, the burden of compliance on taxpayers can again be reduced by joint collection machinery so the taxpayer does not have to file separate returns.

The possibilities for evasion and avoidance will also increase with decentralization for some types of taxes, especially where the tax base is mobile or straddles more than one jurisdiction. In the latter case, there will need to be rules for allocating tax revenues among jurisdictions. In their absence, some tax bases may face either double taxation or no taxation at all. As we have seen previously, interstate tax differences can induce firms to engage in tax planning whose purpose is to shift tax liabilities from high-tax to low-tax states. Government auditing procedures may also be distorted for those tax bases that involve transactions across state boundaries. Auditors may be more vigilant when it comes to auditing nonresidents or transactions whose tax revenues partly accrue to other jurisdictions.

Few general principles emerge from considerations of administrative and compliance costs. Perhaps the most important one is that tax structures should be chosen to be as simple as is compatible with achieving the other goals of the tax system. In some cases, this principle implies making bases as broad as possible and rates as low as possible, so as to reduce incentives for the tax system to distort transactions and reporting as much as possible.

Fiscal Accountability

In addition to assigning particular taxes to levels of government, the division of revenue-raising responsibilities in the aggregate between levels of government – the so-called division of the tax room – is also relevant. Of course, this division is not something that can be prescribed constitutionally or otherwise dictated outside the legislative authority of the governments involved. Instead, it is determined endogenously by the independent setting of tax rates by the two main levels of government. The federal government is often seen as the leader in this regard. The revenue-raising responsibilities and abilities of the states will be affected by the level of rates set by the federal government on broad tax bases, as well as on the amount the federal government chooses to transfer to the states (i.e., the size of the fiscal gap). Nonetheless, the ability of the states and localities to raise their own revenues is partly dependent on the types of tax bases to which they have access.

The general principle to be followed in determining state revenue-raising responsibility and ability is that of fiscal and political accountability. The idea is that fiscal accountability is greater the more jurisdictions are required to finance their expenditures from their own revenue sources. Accountability should make them more vigilant and cost-conscious, as well as enhancing their independence. They have to account only to themselves (or their electorates) for the expenditures they make. To foster accountability, access to revenue sources should be matched as closely as possible to revenue needs. Tax instruments intended to further specific policy objectives should be assigned to the level of government that has the responsibility for such a service. Thus, progressive redistributive taxes, stabilization instruments, and major resource rent taxes would be suitable for assignment to the national government, while tolls on intermunicipal roads are suitably assigned to state governments. More generally, considerable flexibility in the ability to raise own-source revenues can be obtained by allowing states access to some of the same broad-based taxes that are used by the federal government, such as general sales taxes, payroll taxes, or income taxes. In a sense, the former two are ideal for use by state governments because they are relatively nondistortionary and are not taxes of redistributional importance. However, there might be limitations on the ability of states to use them. In countries with a federal-level VAT, it may be feasible but quite cumbersome to allow states to have access to the same base, although they could still use single-stage sales taxes. Payroll taxes may already be used as sources of revenues earmarked for particular social programs. In such circumstances, the fiscal accountability criterion would suggest allowing state governments to have access to taxes that are traditionally regarded as more suitable for national administration, such as personal income taxes. The best approach would retain the ability of the federal government to set a uniform income tax structure. As an example, state governments might be allowed to piggyback on the federal income tax system by setting surtax rates on the federal income tax.

FACTORS RELEVANT FOR ASSIGNING TAXES TO STATES

These criteria for judging how much tax decentralization is desirable are still very general. In order to make them more applicable to actual tax assignment issues, it is worth setting out more specific economic factors that should be taken into consideration in deciding on which taxes to make available to state governments. We set aside for the moment the issue of whether states should be given exclusive use of particular taxes or whether they should share those taxes with the federal government.

Mobility of the Tax Base

Tax bases that are more mobile are less suitable as state tax bases than those which are less mobile, all other things being equal. The reason is that state taxes applied to mobile bases give rise to spillover effects on other states – or horizontal fiscal externalities – which can lead to inefficiencies in the allocation of resources among states. These inefficiencies can take two forms.

The first is that, if state tax systems are chosen in an uncoordinated manner, they are likely to have different structures. Different production and consumption activities will face different tax rates in different states, with the result that resources will be misallocated among states because of the tax distortions. It might be argued that competition among states will induce states to select tax structures that conform with one another to some extent. But this same competition can also lead to inefficiencies of the second sort.

The second inefficiency arises because states will have an incentive to use tax-transfer policies intentionally to influence the allocation of activities to their own states, trying to attract desirable businesses and high-income taxpayers and to discourage activities and persons viewed as being a drain on the state economy. This sort of beggar-thy-neighbor activity is self-defeating to the extent that all states engage in it, and if they do not, it leads to an inefficient geographic allocation of resources.

Presumably the most mobile tax bases are capital income and footloose entrepreneurs and firms. Workers should be less mobile, although not completely immobile, especially those with skills in high demand. Real property is relatively immobile, at least once in place. Similarly, natural resources are immobile, though the capital needed to develop them might not be. Finally, commodity tax bases are also relatively immobile. If commodity taxes are levied on a destination basis, they are very similar to taxes on the residents themselves; they are therefore, as immobile as the residents. On the other hand, if the destination basis can be circumvented by cross?border shopping, that effectively makes the tax base more mobile.

The Suitability of the Base for Redistributive Purposes

Some taxes, like income taxes, are an important part of the tax mix for equity purposes. Their base and rate structure can be chosen according to societal norms for redistribution. To the extent that one views redistribution as being a federal government function, the determination of the structure of these taxes ought to rest primarily with the federal government. Wealth taxes may also fulfill redistributive roles, and even some types of excise taxes do as well, such as those on luxury products.

Even if the federal government is seen as having a predominant role in redistribution, the states may have legitimate redistributive objectives of their own. If so, it may be reasonable to allow them to have some access to taxes like the income tax that can be used for redistribution. However, the pursuit of redistributive policy by the states may well be self-defeating. To the extent that either high- or low-income persons are mobile, the objectives of state redistribution can be frustrated by interstate fiscal competition, what has been referred to aptly as the "race to the bottom."

Actual tax systems are notoriously nonprogressive. That is, governments rely relatively little on the tax system for achieving their redistributive objectives. There may be good reason for this, such as the adverse incentive effects of high marginal tax rates or the extent to which high tax rates elicit evasion and avoidance activities. Nonetheless, an aspect of the income tax system that is important in redistribution is the delivery of transfers to the lowest-income persons. Although many redistributive transfers are delivered separately from the income tax system (e.g., welfare, public pensions, unemployment insurance), the use of refundable tax credits delivered through the income tax system is becoming more prevalent in OECD countries. In principle, both federal and state governments could use the income tax system for that purpose, albeit in a coordinated way.

Unequal Distribution of Tax Bases

As we have mentioned in Chapter 2, one of the potential sources of inefficiency and inequity arising from fiscal decentralization occurs because different states are endowed with relatively different tax capacities. If states are left to raise their own revenues, some will be better able than others. This discrepancy gives rise to what we have referred to as differences in net fiscal benefits (NFBs). To provide a given level of public services, different states will have to apply different tax rates. Or, conversely, for comparable tax rates, different states will be able to provide differing levels of public services.

The literature has stressed that differences in NFBs across states, that is, differences in per-resident benefits from state public services less per-resident tax costs, can cause both inefficiencies and inequities in the internal economic union. The inefficiencies arise because mobile factors of production and businesses have an incentive to migrate to states with larger per capita tax bases for fiscal reasons alone. The inequities reflect a failure of horizontal equity within the federation: otherwise identical persons are treated differently by the public sector depending on where they reside.

These considerations might suggest that decentralizing tax bases that are highly unevenly distributed across jurisdictions can lead to inefficiencies and inequities in the federation. An example of this might be taxes on major natural resources. On the other hand, these sorts of problems can be avoided to the extent that a system of federal-state equalization transfers is in place, such as those which exist in Australia and Canada. What one needs to be aware of is the fact that the more decentralization there is, the more demand will be placed on the equalization system. The political support for maintaining equalization may wither as states become more and more responsible for raising their own revenues. We return to this later in the chapter.

The Breadth of the Tax Base

Serious devolution of fiscal responsibility requires that states have access to tax bases with the capacity for raising relatively large amounts of revenue, that is, broad tax bases. If states rely too much on narrow tax bases, tax rates on those bases may well be pushed much too high compared with other tax bases. There are relatively few broad taxes to choose from. The three main ones are income, sales, and payroll. It seems that if states are to raise substantial revenues, they need access to at least one of these major tax bases. There is the issue of whether one is enough. If the states occupy only one of these tax bases, there is the danger that the overall mix of taxes in the federal and state tax systems taken as a whole will become too skewed in favor of the tax base that the states occupy.

Elasticity of the Tax Base

In addition to being mobile, tax bases may be more or less elastic, that is, responsive to the tax rate. The elasticity of the tax base with respect to the tax rate is an important consideration when deciding on the appropriate tax rate. From an efficiency point of view, the higher the elasticity, the lower the tax rate should be, because the greater is the deadweight loss from increasing tax rates. In a federation, the effect of the elasticity of the tax base as a factor constraining states from setting excessive tax rates can be muted by what are referred to as vertical fiscal externalities.[4]

The argument, which was recounted in Chapter 1, is a subtle one and is worth recalling. Suppose the state and the federal governments both occupy some common tax base. In assessing the effects on tax revenues of an increase in the state tax rate, a state will take into account the fact that the increase will reduce its tax base – either because the base is elastic or because it is mobile among states – and a reduced tax base will reduce its own revenues. But, to the extent that the tax base is elastic, this same reduction in base will also reduce federal tax revenues obtained from the same base, and the state will not take this into account. There will thus be an incentive for states to overextend their tax rates on elastic tax bases.[5] It is not at all clear how this problem can be avoided.

---

[4] These are discussed in more detail in Boadway and Keen (1996) and Dahlby (1996).

[5] Technically, the states are said to underestimate their "true marginal cost of public funds." It might also be the case that the equalization system exacerbates this problem. In the Canadian case the equalization system is determined by a province's tax base. Any reduction of the tax base is at least partly offset by an increase in equalization payments for those provinces receiving them. This further provides an incentive for provinces to impose excessive tax rates. See Smart (1998) for this argument.

Recently, Dahlby and Wilson (2003) showed that the sign of the vertical fiscal externality can go either way, depending on whether the tax base is defined as being before or after taxes. For example, consider the payroll tax. If its base is defined as being before-tax wages, an increase in state taxes can increase the size of the base even if labor supply is discouraged. That is, pretax wage payments may rise with an increase in state taxes. Then, if the federal government applies its tax to the same base, its revenues will rise. State tax increases will therefore have a beneficial effect on the federal budget, and states will therefore overestimate the marginal social cost of raising revenues. They will have an incentive to set taxes too low, thereby reinforcing the effects of horizontal tax competition. Such vertical externalities, whether they have positive or negative external effects on the federal government's budget, seem to be an unavoidable consequence of fiscal decentralization.

User Fees and Benefit Taxes

Many of the problems of inefficiency and inequity rising from decentralizing tax responsibilities are avoided to the extent that the taxes reflect the benefits of the public services that they are intended to finance. In a system of pure benefit pricing, there are no NFB differentials across provinces because all persons receive from the public sectors services whose benefits are reflected in the tax price they pay. This suggests that taxes that are levied largely on the benefit principle are suitable for decentralizing to state and, especially local governments.

Examples of taxes whose bases approximate the benefit principle include property taxes, some excise taxes, and user fees. Taxes of this sort may well be important for financing public services of a local nature, but they are unlikely to be sufficient for major public services in the areas of health, education, and welfare. An exception might be payroll taxes earmarked for social insurance programs, like workers' compensation or pensions.

Further Administrative Cost Considerations

For some taxes, the administrative costs associated with their decentralization might be significant, especially if both the federal and state governments jointly use the taxes. Taxes with complex bases, like income taxes, impose significant compliance costs on taxpayers if levied by one level of government, let alone two. These problems are compounded for taxpayers who, like businesses, obtain income in more than one state.

Sales taxes can also be difficult to decentralize. If they are multistage sales taxes, like value-added taxes (VATs), the fact that many interfirm transactions take place across borders makes the allocation of tax revenues and credits among states very difficult to enforce, especially if different states have different tax rates. VATs are ideally suited for jurisdictions that have border controls. The absence of such controls between states makes the administration of a fully decentralized VAT system almost nonviable. Some of these problems can be overcome, as we shall see, if the federal government occupies the VAT alongside the states, and a single tax-collecting authority exists. Lesser problems can exist for single-stage sales taxes. Cross-border sales make the precise application of the destination principle difficult and also make it difficult to ensure that local firms are treated on a par with out-of-state firms. That is because with single-stage taxes, it is difficult to avoid taxing business inputs purchased by firms.

The one broad-based tax that is easy to decentralize is the payroll tax. Its structure is usually very simple, and compliance is relatively straightforward, given the use of payroll deductions. Wealth or capital taxes can also be administered relatively easily at the state level, although these are unlikely to be major revenue sources.

Given these considerations, what do they imply for the assignment of individual taxes? We turn to that question next.

ASSIGNMENT BY TYPE OF TAX

The relevance of each of the above principles varies from tax type to tax type. It will also depend on how much responsibility for revenue raising has been devolved to the states. In this section, we consider how the principles apply to each of the main types of taxes. Where relevant, we note particular issues and practices in OECD and developing countries. Of course, there may be institutional impediments to the ability to assign taxes freely according to economic principles. In particular, national constitutions may restrict the ability of either the federal government or the states from assuming responsibility for certain types of taxes. That possibility will obviously depend upon the country in question. It may also be the case that the federal government can override state policies, including tax policies, in certain countries, where the overriding is justified by national objectives, such as the maintenance of an efficient internal economic union or the achievement of equity objectives. Thus, for example, the interstate commerce clause in the U.S. Constitution allows the federal government to strike down state laws that interfere with interstate trading.

Finally, the feasibility and desirability of allowing states to have access to some taxes may depend upon the existence of arrangements for harmonization of tax structures across states or between states and the federal government in cases where taxes are co-occupied. We return to the issue of tax harmonization in the next section.

Personal Income Taxes

Income taxes applied to individuals (or households) are the sources of revenue in many OECD countries. Their importance is much less in developing countries where the complex tax-collection machinery has not been fully developed and where many taxpayers have yet to experience the self-reporting required to administer the tax. Presumably as development proceeds, income taxes are liable to become more and more important sources of revenues. The importance of the income tax is its role as a redistributive or at least fair tax. Unlike other taxes, the rate structure can be chosen to be as progressive as desired. The income tax forms an important part of the tax mix in countries with mature tax systems.

A broad-based income tax includes in its base income from a wide variety of sources, regardless of the use to which it is put. There is, however, ongoing debate about how comprehensive the tax should be. Three components of particular concern are capital income, business income, and inheritances. In addition, there is debate about how progressive the rate structure should be. Each of these debates is relevant for the issue of decentralization. To the extent that capital income, business income, and inheritances are included in the base, the case for decentralization is weakened. These potentially mobile bases would lend themselves to tax competition among states.

The main argument for dominant federal involvement in the income tax concerns redistribution. The income tax is the main tax that is available for addressing equity objectives. Given the presumed interest of the federal government in national equity, the income tax should be an important part of its tax mix. Assignment of personal income taxes to the states runs the risk of national equity objectives being violated. States could choose different degrees of progressivity in their rate structures, at least partly driven by beggar-thy-neighbor state policies that compete away redistribution. They could also choose much different sets of exemptions and credits as a way of favoring (or disfavoring) certain types of taxpayers, especially mobile ones. Moreover, as we have mentioned, because capital income is typically a component of these taxes, there is a possibility that capital markets will be distorted. State income tax regimes could give preferential treatment to capital income generated within the state. Because capital income can be earned both within the state and outside, compliance and collection costs, and the possibilities for evasion, are likely to increase substantially as responsibility for personal income taxes are decentralized. For all these reasons, it is preferable that primary responsibility for the personal income tax rest with the federal government.

Similar arguments apply for other direct taxes on persons, such as taxes on personal wealth and on wealth transfers (e.g., estate taxes). Indeed, the case for centralization of these is perhaps even stronger, given that their bases are highly mobile and that they are very effective instruments for pursuing equity.

By the same token, subsidies to persons delivered through the income tax system, which are essentially negative direct taxes, might also be federally levied and integrated with the income tax system. The extent to which such subsidies can be delivered through the tax system is limited. Most major subsidy programs are delivered by special agencies, such as unemployment insurance or welfare agencies, because these subsidies are typically based on characteristics of recipients other than their incomes, characteristics that often require close monitoring. This need poses a major dilemma for national redistributive policy because, as we have emphasized, these subsidies are good candidates for decentralization to the states. Unlike with the tax system, it is not feasible for the federal government to control them directly. Indirect means, like the use of conditional grants, must be used. Nonetheless, significant transfers can be delivered through the tax system using refundable tax credits. These transfers are becoming more common in OECD countries as they gradually move from universal to more targeted transfers. Retention of control of the income tax at the federal level is important for enabling the federal government to be able to deliver these redistributive transfers.

At the same time, there may be legitimate arguments for states' having some leeway for implementing their own within-state redistributive goals. States may differ systematically from one another in their population makeups, giving rise to different preferences for redistribution. The issue is how this might be accomplished without compromising national equity objectives or making the tax system too complex administratively. One way to do so is to allow states to co-occupy the income tax field, but in a way that maintains an appropriate degree of harmonization. We deal with this in more detail in the next section. For now, we simply note that it is feasible to let the states choose various state-specific redistributive elements, such as credits to certain types of taxpayers or even a state rate structure, while maintaining a common base and ruling out state measures that distort the internal common market or discriminate against nonresidents. Such a system likely requires that the federal government must maintain a dominant position in the income tax field so as to have the moral authority to ensure that harmonization is respected.

In applying these principles to developing countries, it should be noted that in low-income agrarian societies and lower-middle-income countries, the coverage of the personal income tax is quite limited. Its role as a redistributive element of the fiscal system is further clouded by widespread tax evasion. Shah and Whalley (1991) have argued that, when one considers the rural-urban migration effects associated with a tax on urban incomes, as well as the reverse redistribution effects of the income tax through the bribe system, the personal income tax may not be viewed as a progressive element of the tax structure in lower-middle-income countries. Under such circumstances, an exclusive federal role for the personal income tax is difficult to justify. Further, many of the services provided by subnational governments in developing countries could not be regarded as directly related to property, and many are redistributive. Although the federal government may impose a progressive income tax structure, subnational governments should be given access to flat charges on the federal base. That way they will have access to a broad-based tax source that will become increasingly important and will, at the same time, have responsibility for the amount of the revenue that they raise.

To the extent that states are allowed access to personal income tax revenues, the allocation of the tax base across states becomes important to ensure that each person is taxed only once. In principle, tax allocation according to place of residence should be preferred over one that does it by place of employment. However, establishing place of residence may be difficult if persons move during the tax year. Assigning proportions of a tax base to each state according to the share of a tax year spent in the state would be complicated. Countries with decentralized income tax systems usually assign residency to a given state for the entire tax year according to residency on a given date (e.g., the last day in the year). This issue, again, must be dealt with by the system of harmonization.

Practice in developing countries varies. China has assigned personal income taxation to the provincial-local governments, while retaining control of the determination of its base for the central government. In most other developing countries, the determination of the personal income tax base and rate is a central responsibility, whereas tax administration is occasionally shared with subnational governments. In Russia, the income tax is a federal tax, collected (as are all taxes) by the federal Tax Ministry (Salikov, 2005). In Mexico, the Supreme Court recognizes the income tax as a concurrent tax, although most revenue is collected by the federal government. An exception is the tax for low-income individuals, the "regime of small taxpayers." States and municipalities collect and retain this revenue, although a percentage is paid to the federal government in some instances. To allocate income across jurisdictions, individuals pay taxes in the state where they work or where their employer is located (Gonzalez, 2005). Exceptions are India, where this tax field is co-occupied by the federal and state governments. The central government taxes non-agricultural income and wealth, while states can tax agricultural income and wealth. This distinction has created difficulties. States have found it politically infeasible to tax agricultural incomes, creating an opportunity for evasion. Farmhouses are popular investments in the vicinity of major urban areas. Eliminating the distinction in the origin of personal income is one issue in discussions of reforms in India (Rao, 2007b). In Brazil, states are allowed a supplementary rate on the federal base. Nigeria is unusual insofar as the federal government collects only a limited share of income taxes. It has access only to taxes paid by the armed forces, external affairs employees, and residents of the Federal Capital Territory. The predominance of state-level income tax collection hinders redistribution. In some cases, state governments control instruments other than the income tax that may affect income redistribution. In Brazil, for example, the taxes on inheritances, gifts, and supplemental capital gains are state levies. Estate duties in Nigeria are a state-level tax (Ayua and Dakas, 2005). In Russia, local governments are assigned the tax on inheritance. The Tax Code of the Russian Federation allows them to set the rates as well as to establish privileges for groups of taxpayers (Salikov, 2005).

Corporation Income Taxes

As with the personal income tax, the case for making the corporation income tax a federal responsibility is a strong one. For one thing, the corporate tax can be viewed partly as an adjunct to the personal tax or, more precisely, as a withholding device for the personal tax. It taxes at the source shareholder income that could otherwise be reinvested in the corporation and escape immediate taxation. To the extent that the corporate tax serves this withholding purpose, it is better levied at the same level as the personal income tax so that it can be integrated easily. In an open economy, the corporate tax also serves as a useful device for obtaining revenues from foreign corporations, especially those which are able to obtain tax credits from their home governments. Again, the federal level seems the most appropriate one for this purpose. In Switzerland, the confederation government is in principle restricted to indirect taxes. However, it may impose direct taxes on net profits and on corporate capital and reserves for limited periods of time. These taxes are regularly extended. The current direct federal tax is in effect through 2006, with maximum rates established in the Swiss Constitution (Schmitt, 2005). More to the point, because the corporate tax base is capital income within a jurisdiction, decentralizing it to the states would jeopardize the efficient functioning of capital markets. It would give rise to the possibility of wasteful tax competition to attract capital at the expense of other jurisdictions. Its use by a state would also invite the implementation of measures that discriminate against corporations based in other states. In the United States, the federal government maintains a role in the state use of corporate income taxes because of these potential problems. Court rulings have determined when corporate income can be taxed within a state. Congress has also used legislation to preempt state-level taxation that it feels could hinder interstate commerce (Fox, 2007).

Administrative simplicity also favors centralizing the design and administration of the corporate tax. Because many corporations operate in more than one jurisdiction at the same time, tax administration in a multijurisdiction setting can be a complicated matter. For any given jurisdiction, the appropriate share of the tax base must be allocated to that jurisdiction, and the taxing authority must have some way of monitoring the firm to ensure compliance. With complete independence of taxing authorities, this would be difficult. The firm may well have an incentive to engage in transfer pricing or financial and book transactions to shift its profits across borders to reduce its tax burden. The firm itself will have an increased cost of compliance if it faces different tax regimes in different jurisdictions. There are nonetheless some federations in which subnational governments are allowed access to corporate taxation, such as Canada and the United States. In such cases, tax bases are typically allocated among provincial or state jurisdictions according to methods of formula apportionment that attempt to minimize the administrative and incentive problems associated with determining tax shares. Common methods include allocating tax revenues of a given corporation among jurisdictions according to a mix of shares of the firm's payroll, revenues, and possibly capital stocks. In the United States, most states use a variant of the federal definition of corporate income for tax purposes. Although taxable corporate income is allocated across jurisdictions by formula, the specifics vary by state. In practice, the differences lead to increased compliance costs (Fox, 2007).

Thus, the case for centralizing the corporate tax is very strong. The same might be said for other taxes that effectively fall on corporate capital, such as capital taxes. By symmetric arguments, subsidies to corporations should be centralized, given the obvious tendency for lower levels of government to use them to attract capital in competition with other jurisdictions in ways that might be distorting or discriminatory.

Of course, not all tax competition need be wasteful. It could also serve to improve the efficiency of lower-level governments by imposing a form of marketlike discipline on them. Some of the adverse effects of tax competition could be avoided if the states were subject to commitments not to use them to distort the internal common market or to discriminate against nonresident businesses. The latter is equivalent to the so-called principle of national treatment in international trade policy, whereby all capital within a state is afforded the same treatment regardless of the residency of its owners. Implementing such a scheme would require either a binding and enforceable commitment among states with respect to their tax policies or the ability of the federal government to enforce such policies through the carrot (grants policies) or the stick (mandates or disallowance). In either case, the integrity of the internal common market would seem to be much easier to enforce if the federal government maintains a dominant position in the corporate income tax field. More generally, it would be preferable to restrict the field to the federal government alone, although this may not be possible where the constitution allows state access to income taxation.

In most developing countries, the determination of the corporate tax base and rate structure is a federal government responsibility. However, collection and administration is sometimes decentralized. In the Philippines, the business tax is an important source of local revenues, accounting for an average 29.8 percent in 2002. The rates are determined by the central government (Taliercio, 2005). Administration of the corporate tax is a joint responsibility of national and subnational governments in Pakistan and the Russian Federation. In China, corporate tax collection is divided among federal, provincial, and local governments (although the federal government retains sole authority to set the base and rates). The provincial and local governments are responsible for collecting taxes from provincially and locally owned enterprises, respectively. The federal government collects taxes on its own enterprises as well as on foreign-owned enterprises and all domestically owned private enterprises. Indeed, this pattern of the federal government setting the base and rate structure combined with some decentralization of collection applies to all major taxes in China, including sales and excise taxes. In Indonesia, business taxes are levied on specific sectors, such as hotels, restaurants, and advertising. An increasing number of subnational governments impose these types of taxes, creating the potential for distortions at the local level (Taliercio, 2005). In some cases, subnational governments control instruments that may affect capital mobility. In India, for example, the capital transactions tax is a state instrument.

General Sales Taxes

Sales taxes are good candidates for decentralization to the states, especially if significant revenue-raising responsibility is required. Nonetheless, sales taxes are centralized in some federations. In Switzerland, only the confederation government can levy a value-added tax or special consumption taxes (Schmitt, 2005). In South Africa, provinces and municipalities are prohibited from levying a value-added tax or a general sales tax (Steytler, 2005). Typically, general sales taxes are levied on consumption goods, defined with varying degrees of inclusiveness, and on a destination basis. As such, they are essentially general taxes on the residents of the taxing jurisdiction. Given the relatively low degree of mobility of households, they are likely to be much less distorting than, say, taxes on mobile bases like capital (at least as long as investment goods are not included in the base). Because general sales taxes are not significant instruments for redistribution, little is lost from an equity point of view from decentralizing them to the states.

Some distortions and administrative problems, however, are likely to arise from state sales taxes. The main source of inefficiency has to do with cross-border shopping. Residents of states with high sales tax rates will have an incentive to shop in states with lower tax rates to reduce their tax burdens. Given the absence of border controls in a federation, this outcome will be difficult to avoid. As a consequence, tax competition will likely result in rate levels and structures that do not vary greatly across jurisdictions. On the surface of it, this might pose a problem for poorer jurisdictions that might otherwise need higher tax rates to finance their basic services. However, this disadvantage would be mitigated if an effective system of equalizing transfers from the federal government were in place, as discussed in the previous section, so that states could provide comparable public services at comparable tax rates.

There are, however, some serious administrative issues with state sales taxation, especially if there is no federal sales tax with the potential for a single tax-collection authority. If the state sales taxes take the form of subnational, credit-method, value-added taxes, the taxation of interstate transactions creates potentially major administrative difficulties. Such transactions can be taxed either on a destination basis (taxing final consumption), such that imports are taxed and exports are zero rated, or on an origin basis (taxing production), such that imports are exempted from taxation, while exports are fully taxed in the state of origin (i.e., not zero-rated). The origin basis has the advantage that cross-border sales need not be monitored as closely. But because origin-based sales taxation is analogous to taxing production, interstate differences in tax rates – which one must expect if states are truly exercising independent revenue-raising authority – translate into inefficiencies in the allocation of production across states. The use of the destination basis for a VAT requires applying taxes appropriately at state borders within a federation, including crediting for taxes paid on intermediate business inputs in selling jurisdictions. In the absence of border controls, reliance must be placed on self-assessment by firms being taxed. Not only will this add to compliance costs, but also enforcement may be difficult unless auditing information flows freely across borders. Having a single federal administration will certainly make things simpler, but the complexity involved in firms keeping track of their input credits on a state-by-state basis is significant. It could work as an impediment to the free flow of goods and services within the nation.

There are some possible alternatives to the strict application of the destination principle. One is to adopt the so-called *restricted origin principle*, where interstate trade is taxed on the origin principle and international trade on a destination basis. This solution would work well if subnational units had uniform rates of VATs and if trade flows within and from outside the country were not too uneven across states (see also Cnossen, 1998). Inefficiencies could result if the taxation basis differed across jurisdictions; for example, state governments might be tempted to use an origin basis for their state taxes rather than a residency one.

A second alternative is the *clearing house method*. Here, exports are not zero-rated but are subject to full taxation in the state of origin. The importing firm, when paying taxes in the state of destination, then claims full credit for taxes paid to the exporting jurisdiction. If this method is applied to all cross-border transactions, the likely result will be an imbalance on taxes owing between states, because taxes levied by exporting states are credited against taxes in the importing state despite having been paid elsewhere. This balance is settled by a system of interstate payments. Such a system certainly simplifies tax compliance for private traders, especially if there is a single tax-collecting authority. However, it complicates matters for the tax authorities because it must keep track of interstate tax liabilities. In practice, the balancing payments are often based on some crude indicators of state tax liabilities, like aggregate consumption.

A third alternative is to use the so-called *deferred-payment method*, which is able to finesse the interstate crediting issue. It does this by zero-rating from state VAT sales to taxpaying firms in other states. At the same time, importing firms are not immediately taxed. Instead, they enter the tax system only when they are resold by the importing firms. Such a system insures that imports are eventually fully taxed in the importing state, as must be the case under the destination principle. The system is not foolproof and has really been applied only in the case of one province in Canada. But experience there indicates that it is feasible, at least as long as one can rely on the self-reporting method of tax payment backed up by reasonable auditing. The latter is certainly facilitated by having a central tax-collecting authority. The main problem with the system is the same as with any sales tax system – that it is difficult to ensure that cross-border sales to consumers (and other final users) are taxed properly. Ideally, exports to consumers should be taxed at the rate applicable to the state of destination, but this may be difficult to enforce. The problem may well become more difficult with the advent of electronic commerce. In a federation with several states, all of which charge a different sales tax rate, compliance itself becomes complicated, especially when one recognizes that interstate sales are treated much differently than international sales. The viability of such a system in a developing-country context remains to be seen.[6]

---

[6] The deferred-payment system is applied on a limited basis in the Canadian federation. The province of Quebec implements its own VAT-type system alongside that of the federal government (which applies nationwide). Firms engaging in transactions between Quebec and the rest of Canada must pay the Quebec Sales Tax (QST) on all purchases in Quebec along with the federal Goods and Services Tax (GST). Firms who have paid the QST on their inputs then obtain a credit on subsequent sales whether the sales are in Quebec or not. Sellers in Quebec who have purchased inputs outside Quebec obtain credit for the GST only. Firms pay the tax on a self-assessment basis, subject to the usual auditing provision. Bird and Gendron (2001) have argued that this is a feasible system in any federal setting. In Canada, only the Quebec government has adopted its own independent VAT. If several other provinces did so as well, the system may not prove to be as simple as in the one-province case. Brazil also operates a VAT system at the subnational level but not jointly with the central government. It is effectively an origin-based system with all its difficulties.

But the most common practice when state sales taxes are used is to avoid these problems by employing single-stage sales taxes, despite the inefficiencies that they entail. Under a single-stage sales tax, it is difficult to avoid a cascading of the tax through purchases of taxed business inputs, especially if the tax is levied at the retail stage. Systems in which taxes paid on purchases from registered dealers are credited toward or exempted from later levies reduce the incidence of this problem at some administrative cost, but do not eliminate it entirely. A related issue is the difficulty in ensuring that sales to buyers outside state boundaries have been purged of taxes on intermediate inputs. These same problems arise at the federal level and are typically addressed by adopting a multistage VAT. Under a VAT, taxes on business inputs are eliminated by the system of crediting for input purchases, while under the destination principle, exports are given full credit for taxes paid and imports are fully taxed. As noted previously, adopting the same remedy at the state level is difficult because of the absence of border controls. Furthermore, because states are inevitably much more open than entire countries, the administrative complexities of operating a system of taxing and crediting on all cross-border transactions would be high and would likely constitute a significant distortion on interstate trade. For these reasons, single-stage state sales taxes may well be preferred in a developing-country context, at least until viable alternatives, like the deferred-payment method, have been tried and tested.[7]

Quite apart from these difficulties of dealing with cross-border transactions by both producers and consumers, separate state sales taxes entail an additional layer of administrative machinery on the government side, and additional compliance costs for businesses that are required to collect the tax. These costs are especially high in a system in which there are sales taxes at both the federal and state levels of government. In the United States, companies can face widely divergent tax regimes as sales taxes are levied on a destination basis. For example, Colorado allows local governments to establish both the base and rates for their own sales taxes. In Virginia, on the other hand, the state government determines both. The potentially high compliance costs led the Supreme Court to rule that a company must have a physical presence in a state before it can be required to collect sales tax for that state (Fox, 2007).

---

[7] For a contrary view, see Burgess, Howes, and Stern (1995), who have advocated a system of state VATs for India. And we have already mentioned Bird and Gendron (1998), who recommend a dual VAT system involving both the federal and provincial governments, at least for developed federations.

The practical difficulties associated with the subnational administration of a multistage sales tax are well illustrated by the Brazilian experience. In Brazil, the federal government levies a manufacturer-level sales tax called the Imposto Sobre Produtos Industrializados (IPI); states are assigned a broad-based credit-method VAT (the Impostos Sobre Circulação de Mercadorias e Prestação de Serviços (ICMS)) at a 17 percent rate); and municipalities administer a services tax, the Imposto Sobre Serviços (ISS). Under the ICMS, interstate sales are taxed on the origin principle (at a 12 percent rate for North-South and a 7 percent rate for South-North transactions), and international trade is taxed on a destination basis. Thus, in domestic trade, relatively less-developed northern states are given preferential treatment. In international trade, as most of the imports are destined for the southern states and a disproportionate amount of exports go through the northeastern states, most of the revenues are collected by the richer states, and export rebates are given by poorer states. Another emerging area of major potential interstate conflict is the use of the ICMS as a tool for state industrial development. Some northeastern states are offering fifteen-year ICMS tax deferral to industry. In a highly inflationary environment such as that of Brazil, unless such tax liabilities are indexed, they have the potential to wipe out much of the ICMS tax liabilities. A separate source of conflict is the classification of emergent information technology industries, such as communications and software. If they sell goods, they are subject to the state-level ICMS; if they are service providers, municipalities can levy the ISS. The interjurisdictional disputes between states and municipalities continue (Rezende, 2007).

Recognizing these difficulties, China introduced a centrally administered VAT with proceeds to be shared with the provinces. Effective January 1, 1994, the provinces are given 25 percent of VAT revenues and the federal government the remainder. India is facing major difficulties in reforming its sales tax system. At the present time, sales taxes are assigned to the state level; the federal government administers excise taxes, and the proceeds are shared with the states; and the octroi is a local tax on inter-municipal trade. While these tax assignments are exclusive, in practice there are overlaps that contribute to the complexity. The central manufacturing excises have evolved into a central value-added tax (CENVAT) at the manufacturing stage. Thus, production is taxed by the center, while the sale of the goods is taxed by the states, essentially sharing the same base (Rao, 2007a). Sales taxes are administered on narrow bases: the number of rates varies by state from six in Orissa to seventeen in Bihar and Gujarat. Some states consider the sales tax an important element of redistributive policy. To reform the existing sales tax structure, a broad-based national value-added tax has been proposed, but this is strongly opposed by the states. The states are also dissatisfied with the centrally administered excise tax because it limits their powers of taxation. The federal government prefers to raise additional revenues from administered prices rather than from excises because the proceeds from excises have to be shared with state governments. The octroi tax on intermunicipal trade is a source of significant revenues for local governments and remains popular in spite of its antitrade bias.

Other possible inefficiencies of state sales taxation are related to administrative problems, which are certainly likely to be present in developing countries. One has to do with the fact that the broader the base, the more difficult it is to enforce compliance. To get a fully general consumption base, including both goods and services, it would be practically necessary to collect the tax at the level of final sales to the consumer, the retail stage, under either a single stage or a VAT system. This requirement increases the compliance costs considerably because the number of taxpaying firms could be extremely large. In practice, having an exemption for small firms mitigates this problem. However, in developing countries, a reasonable exemption could encompass a large number of firms narrowing the tax base considerably. Furthermore, enforcement of the tax becomes very difficult if it is applied at the retail level, and evasion is likely to be high. Some of these difficulties can be avoided by levying the tax at an earlier stage, though again at the cost of making the base much narrower.

Excise Taxes

Specific excise taxes are also good candidates for decentralization to the states, perhaps even better than general sales taxes, although they have much less potential for raising revenues. (Obviously, we are not including customs duties and export taxes in this category, because they should clearly be federal responsibilities.) Specific excises are unlikely to cause significant impediments to the efficiency of the internal economic union or major misallocations of labor and capital if they are levied on a destination basis. They simply become a form of taxation of residents and are unlikely to be significant enough to cause migration. If they were levied on an origin basis, this might not be the case. Businesses could avoid the tax by moving elsewhere, unless the product taxed depended upon a local resource. An example of the latter might be taxes on oil and gas, to which we return later when discussing resource taxes.

From an efficiency point of view, there are two problems with excise taxes. For one, as with sales taxes, they will give rise to cross-border shopping problems, possibly on a large scale, given that the taxed goods may be cheap to transport. Tax competition is likely to reduce the importance of this, especially if the fiscal capacities of the states are not too different and/ or if equalizing transfers further reduce discrepancies.

The second possible problem arises from the fact that excise taxes distort the markets for the goods being taxed. This distortion can be significant if states must rely on excise taxes for a large part of their revenues. Of course, it could be argued that, for some goods, at least some differential tax is justified on the basis of externalities. Alcohol and tobacco taxes are good examples of this, and gasoline taxes might also be so considered.

Excise taxes may have an adverse effect on equity to the extent that they are levied on goods consumed by lower-income persons. However, this need not be a telling problem as long as the federal government has at its disposal other tax instruments for addressing redistributive issues on a broader basis, such as the income-based tax-transfer system. There might, however, be other federal policy objectives that are affected by excise tax policy. For example, the federal government may have a concern with health policy, the effectiveness of which may be influenced by cigarette and alcohol taxes, or with pollution and road use, where gasoline taxes become relevant.

The federal and provincial levels could jointly occupy excises on alcohol and tobacco, as both health care and the prevention of accidents and crimes are usually shared responsibilities in most federations. Games of chance and gambling usually fall within the purview of state and local governments, and therefore taxes on betting, gambling, racetracks and lottery revenues would be suitable for assignment to subnational governments only.

Taxation to control environmental externalities such as congestion and pollution could be suitably imposed by the level of government having the responsibility for curtailment of such externalities. Accordingly, carbon taxes to combat global and national pollution issues should be a federal responsibility. All levels in their own sphere of authority could levy BTU taxes, taxes on motor fuels, and congestion tolls. Effluent charges to deal with interstate pollution should be a federal responsibility. Intermunicipal pollution would be a state responsibility, but the responsibility to deal with intramunicipal pollution should rest with local governments. Parking fees to influence intermodal choices and thereby regulate local traffic congestion should be a local responsibility.

Relative to other taxes, the administrative problems associated with decentralizing excise taxes are less severe. The difficulties of eliminating taxes on business inputs and on exports that plague general sales taxes do not apply with the same force here. Collection costs may not be excessively high for either the sellers or the government. Enforcement should be no greater a problem than with other taxes, especially if the rates are neither too high nor too varied across the federation.

A large variation in excise tax assignment prevails in developing countries. In some countries, such as Indonesia and Mexico, they are centralized. Indonesia has undertaken some decentralization. Law 34 of 2000 assigns motor vehicle registration and transfer and fuel taxes to provincial governments. City and regency governments can levy excises on such activities as hotels, entertainment, advertising, and parking. However, rates cannot exceed the maximum established in the legislation (Taliercio, 2005). In others, such as Bangladesh and Argentina, they are decentralized. In a large majority of developing countries, excise taxes are co-occupied by national and subnational governments – for example, in Malaysia, Nigeria, and Thailand. In Thailand, gasoline and tobacco taxes are part of subnational governments' own-source revenues (Taliercio, 2005). In the Russian Federation, the 1998 tax code assigned excises to the federal government and highway, transport, and gambling taxes to regional governments. Regional legislatures determine tax rates for their assigned taxes (Salikov, 2005).

Payroll Taxes

Payroll taxes are typically used in industrialized countries for financing social insurance schemes, especially those limited to employees. The sorts of programs for which payroll taxes are often earmarked may be those which are decentralized to state governments (workers compensation, health care), in which case they should be obvious sources of state revenues. However, they can be a useful adjunct to general revenue financing as well. In either case, they are ideal candidates for state revenue sources. Payroll taxes are relatively easy to administer because they can be collected with minimal cost through payroll deduction. Their base is ultimately almost equivalent to that of general sales taxes and overlaps considerably with the income tax base. Because it is a very broad base, it is relatively nondistortionary. Indeed, to the extent that they are perceived as being payments for social insurance benefits, they may be virtually distortion free. Provided their rates do not differ significantly across states, they are unlikely to cause significant distortions in the internal common market.

In addition to causing very little distortion of internal labor markets, payroll taxes have minimal redistributive effects. They are not a necessary component of federal redistributive policy instruments, and any adverse effect they may have on income distribution can be easily offset by other taxes at the federal level. In fact, given the properties of payroll taxes, it is perhaps surprising that they are not the tax bases of choice for decentralization to the states.

One alleged drawback of payroll taxation is its effect on employment. Payroll taxes have been referred to as "taxes on jobs," especially by the business sector. This claim is surely a misnomer. A fully general tax on labor income should have no more effect on employment than a sales tax or income tax. To the extent that labor markets function freely, payroll taxes will be passed back to labor and have virtually no effect on employment if labor supply is relatively inelastic. This assertion might not be true to the extent that wages are institutionally determined. For example, union bargaining may preclude workers from bearing payroll taxes resulting in wages set above the market clearing level. Or minimum wages may go up in response to increases in payroll taxes. However, empirical evidence in developed countries suggests that, at least in the long run, payroll taxes are borne by workers, with little effect on employment.[8]

In many industrialized federations, subnational governments use payroll taxes. Examples include Australia (where the states are precluded from using the other main broad-based taxes – income and sales), Canada, and the United States. They are rather less prevalent in the developing world, exceptions being in many Latin American countries. Perhaps because the proportion of the labor force in the organized sector of the economy is still relatively low in many developing countries, imposing a payroll tax on them might discourage further organization. Nonetheless, given the benefits of using payroll taxation, there is the potential for greater use of this tax instrument by subnational governments in developing countries, especially as the development process proceeds.

Resource Taxes

The case of taxes on resources is an interesting one because it brings the two economic criteria, efficiency and equity, into direct conflict. On the one hand, because resource endowments are immobile across jurisdictions, state taxes on resources, if designed properly, should not distort

[8] In the Canadian context, see, for example, Abbott and Beach (1997).

the internal economic union. Indeed, taxes on resource rents would in a sense be an ideal tax because they would have no efficiency effects whatsoever.[9] The administrative costs associated with state resource taxes would not be excessive either, and the taxation of resources goes hand in hand with their management, which is often more efficiently done at the state level. At the same time, resources tend often to be distributed very unevenly across states in a given country. In these circumstances, decentralizing resource taxes to the states would result in significant differences in tax capacities, thus creating fiscal inefficiencies and inequities.

In an ideal world, the decentralization of resource revenues to the states would be accompanied by a set of equalizing federal provincial transfers to alleviate the NFB differences that would otherwise result. However, full equalization of tax capacities is rarely implemented and might be especially politically difficult if the resource revenues are distributed very unequally among states. In these circumstances, one might opt for maintaining federal control of those resources which are more likely to be important and unequally distributed, such as oil and gas and mining, while decentralizing others that are less important, such as quarrying and perhaps forestry.

In practice, resource tax bases tend not to coincide with rents, and thus resource taxes do have efficiency effects. They often distort capital and employment decisions. States might be tempted to use them as instruments to attract economic activity to their jurisdictions, thereby violating the efficiency of the internal economic union. Thus, what could ideally be a fully efficient source of state revenue could turn out to be a highly distortionary tax type. In these circumstances, the case for decentralized control is weakened.

Some resource taxes, however, such as royalties and fees and severance taxes on production and/or output, are designed to cover costs of local service or infrastructure provision and could be assigned to local governments. In addition, subnational governments could also impose taxes to discourage local environmental degradation. This rationale explains the practice in Canada, Australia, and the United States of having state-level governments (and in the case of the United States, local governments as well) impose such taxes on natural resources. In Australia, states cannot tax the production of resource products, but they collect royalties on the use of resources within their own borders and within the three-mile territorial sea (Saunders, 2005). In Germany, neither the Basic Law nor *Land*

---

[9] For a general discussion of the way in which resource taxes could be designed to capture rents, see Boadway and Flatters (1993).

constitutions grant any government formal ownership or tax authority over natural resources. However, private companies working oil and gas fields in northern Germany pay extraction fees to the *Land* where these fields are located (Lower Saxony and Schleswig-Holstein). These fees are counted as revenue when horizontal equalization payments are calculated (Kramer, 2005).

Resource taxes in most federations are typically a responsibility of the central government. In Mexico, a federal concession or authorization is required to exploit natural resources, and taxes on petroleum products are exclusively federal (Gonzalez, 2005). In Nigeria, the federal government has exclusive ownership of oil and solid minerals (Ayua and Dakas, 2005). One exception is Canada, where provinces have access to resource revenues generated within their boundaries, a feature of the Canadian federation that has given rise to much political conflict during the postwar period. Another exception is India, where such taxation is solely a state responsibility. In Malaysia, resource taxes are a shared responsibility between federal and state governments. In a few developing countries, such as Colombia and the Russian Federation, tax administration is decentralized to subnational governments. In Indonesia, the mining of selected minerals can be taxed by cities and regencies, although the maximum rates are set by Law 34 of 2000 (Taliercio, 2005).

Property Taxes

Taxes on real property are usually the mainstays of municipal finance, and with good reason. Real property is immobile across jurisdictions, so the efficiency costs of using it as a tax base are low. Moreover, it can be argued that many benefits of local public services accrue to property owners, so the tax serves as a sort of benefit tax. Of course, there are costs incurred in administering property taxes, and considerable discretion is involved in arriving at property values for the purposes of taxation. Thus, there is an argument for having the states play a coordinating role in administering property taxes, though not necessarily in setting local rates. In Canada, for example, a single provincial agency assesses property values, while local governments apply their own rates (Boadway, 2007b). In the United States, property taxes are primarily a local government levy and generate nearly three-quarters of local revenues. States have intervened when sharply rising property values increase the tax burden. Michigan lowered property taxes in 1994, for example, and replaced the revenues with a 2 percent increase in the state sales tax. Texas and New Jersey are among the states currently evaluating alternative sources of local funding, to reduce reliance on property taxation (Fox, 2007). In South Africa, on the other hand, national legislation was proposed to harmonize municipal property tax rates through the Property Rates Act of 2004 (Steytler, 2005).

Just as different states may have different fiscal capacities and can provide different levels of NFBs to their citizens, so municipalities have different fiscal capacities, particularly with respect to real-property tax bases. The case for equalizing transfers among municipalities within states is as strong as that for similar transfers across states. Of course, it is likely to be the states that make the transfer, rather than the federal government. In industrial countries, a common practice regarding property development is for local governments to require developers to provide basic infrastructure in a new subdivision – the so-called practice of gold plating or exactions. Such a practice has potential applications in developing countries as well.

The assignment of property taxes varies across developing countries. In Indonesia, property taxes are a responsibility of the central government. In Brazil, China, and the Philippines, the responsibility is shared among federal, state, and local governments. In China, for example, local governments set the tax rate on urban land use subject to legislated maximums and minimums (Taliercio, 2005). In Russia, real estate taxes and taxes on the property of organizations are regional levies. The revenues from the tax on organizational property are shared between the regional and local budgets. Local governments can tax land, individual property, and the acquisition of property. In all cases, the taxes are collected by the federal Tax Ministry (Salikov, 2005). Property taxation is a state-local responsibility in Argentina, Malaysia, and Pakistan. In most other developing countries, such as Bangladesh, Colombia, Mexico, Nigeria, Papua New Guinea, and Thailand, it is solely local responsibility. Only municipalities collect real-property taxes in Mexico, although arrangements can be made to have the state administer and collect the tax in exchange for a share of the revenues (J. Gonzalez, 2005). Thus, significant potential exists for the decentralization of property taxes in developing countries. Colombia has successfully experimented with a tax on urban property value increases (valorization tax) to finance infrastructure investment projects that were responsible for the improvements in property values. The city of Jakarta, Indonesia, is experimenting with a betterment levy to finance urban infrastructure improvement projects.

Developing countries also frequently levy agricultural land taxes. Taxes based on land area, the market value of agricultural land, the productivity potential, and market access of the land have been used as a source of central government revenues in many developing countries. These taxes are more suitable for assignment to local governments.

Pricing for Public Services

A potentially important source of funds for publicly provided services that are private is the pricing of those services by such things as user fees and licenses. These are especially relevant for local and some state public services because these are often private. The case for pricing of public services is clearest where the service in question is not provided publicly for redistributive reasons. Many local services are of this sort, including water, garbage, local utilities, and recreational facilities.

An advantage of pricing for public services, in addition to its pure revenue-raising role, is that efficient use of the services can be promoted. This can be useful both for rationing available supplies and for determining how many resources to devote to providing the service. That is not to say that pricing is distributionally neutral in these cases. Indeed, many of these services are necessities and form an important part of consumption by lower-income persons. However, in an economy with a well-developed public sector, distributive objectives are probably better left to higher levels of government rather than being a component of each public service provided.

On the other hand, some important quasi-private public services are provided by the public sector largely for redistributive reasons, including health and education. Relying heavily on user fees to finance these services would seem to contradict this objective, although that does not preclude limited amounts of pricing, for example, to cut down on overuse of medical services.

In any case, these sources of revenues are likely to be more important to lower levels of government, whose services tend to be private. User pricing should not have an adverse effect on resource allocation. Nor is it costly to administer because it is simply an application of the fee-for-service principle. And, as mentioned, any adverse effects on equity can be addressed more effectively by policies of a more general nature applied by higher levels of government.

User fees are common in the Philippines. There are more than thirty-three types of charges on services ranging from animal registration to garbage collection. Subnational governments in Thailand levy charges on medical services and child care, trash collection, public utilities, and mass transportation. In Indonesia, charges for health services are the most significant user fees at the provincial level. In Vietnam, user fees are virtually the only own-source revenue for subnational governments. Fees include road tolls and some charges for schools and hospitals (Taliercio, 2005).

In summary, this discussion of the assignment of taxes makes it clear that the case for decentralizing taxing powers is not as compelling as that for decentralizing public service delivery.

Lower-level taxes can introduce inefficiencies in the allocation of resources across the federation and can cause inequities among persons of different jurisdictions. Collection and compliance costs can also increase significantly. These problems seem to be more severe for some taxes than for others, so the selection of which taxes to decentralize must be done with care. In the end, a balance must be reached between the need to achieve fiscal and political accountability at the lower levels of government and the disadvantages, from a national point of view, of having a fragmented tax system. In virtually all countries, the balance involves a fiscal gap between adjacent levels of government.

The trade-off between increased accountability and increased economic costs from decentralizing taxing responsibilities can be mitigated by the fiscal arrangements that exist between levels of government. We have already mentioned the fact that the system of fiscal transfers can serve to reduce the fiscal inefficiencies and inequities that arise from different fiscal capacities across states. In addition to this, some of the fragmentation that would otherwise occur from decentralizing taxes can be mitigated by joint occupation and harmonization of taxes among different jurisdictions. That will be discussed in the next section.

Federal-State Co-occupation of Tax Bases

Taxes need not be exclusively assigned to one level of government or another but may be occupied simultaneously by both. Examples exist in which income taxes are levied by both federal and state governments (the United States, Canada), general sales taxes are levied by both federal and state governments (Canada), payroll taxes are levied by both federal and state governments (Canada), and excise taxes are levied by both federal and state governments (Canada, the United States). Indeed, even municipal governments may share income or sales tax bases (as in the United States and the Scandinavian countries). Allowing co-occupation of tax bases is an effective way of decentralizing tax responsibility to the states without sacrificing the harmonization of the system.

The co-occupation of tax bases can be done with varying degrees of coordination. At one extreme, there may be no formal coordination in the sense that both levels of government set their own policies independently. Even in this case, tax policies will not be completely unrelated. For any given tax base, there is a limit to the extent to which it can be exploited for revenue purposes. The amount of tax room available for one level of government will depend on the amount that has been occupied by the other. The division of the tax room can affect the degree of harmonization in an otherwise uncoordinated system. For example, the greater the pro- portion of the tax room occupied by the federal government, the more likely it is that the states will adopt tax structures that are similar to those of the federal government. This similarity may be important for tax bases, like the income tax, that are instruments for achieving national objectives. Indeed, determining the amounts of tax room of various taxes the federal government should occupy is an important policy decision in a decentral- ized federation. In the United States, for example, roughly 80 percent of all income tax revenues are generated by the federal government tax. Given this large federal role, most states start with some variant of the federal definition when calculating their individual income tax base (Fox, 2007).

Alternative forms of coordination of co-occupied tax bases can exist. At the least there may be an exchange of taxpayer information and other auditing information, agreements on the formulas for the allocation of tax bases among jurisdictions, and agreements on the bounds of tax rates for sales and excise taxes. Common bases, or even common rate structures, may be agreed upon. Common tax-collection machinery may be adopted. In the limit, there may be highly centralized tax systems with agreed-upon tax sharing formulas. The next section considers in more detail the design and consequences of different degrees of coordination and harmonization.

Table 4.1 presents the main arguments for assignment of the various taxes to the three main levels of government – federal, state, and local. A broad view of the extent of decentralization of tax bases in a sample of twelve federal countries is presented in Table 4.2.

TAX HARMONIZATION AND COORDINATION

The harmonization of tax systems in a federation, like the system of inter- governmental transfers, is a means by which the advantages of decentral- ized fiscal decision making can be accomplished without excessively jeopardizing the efficient and equitable functioning of the national econ- omy. In this section, we discuss first the purpose of tax harmonization

Table 4.1. *A Representative assignment of taxing powers*

Types of tax	Determination of base	Determination of rate	Collection and administration	Comments
Customs	F	F	F,I	International trade taxes
Corporate income tax	F,U	F,U	F,U,I	Mobile factor, stabilization tool
Resource taxes				
Resource rent (profits and income) tax	F	F	F,I	Highly unequally distributed tax bases
Royalties, fees, charges; severance taxes; and production, output, and property taxes	S,L	S,L	S,L,I	Benefit taxes and charges for state-local services
Conservation charges	S,L	S,L	S,L,I	Intended to preserve local environment
Personal income tax	F	F,S,L	F,I	Redistributive, mobile factor, stabilization tool
Wealth taxes (taxes on capital, wealth, wealth transfers, inheritances, and bequests)	F	F,S	F,I	Redistributive
Payroll tax	F,S	F,S	F,S,I	Benefit charge, such as social security coverage

(*continued*)

Table 4.1 (*continued*)

Types of tax	Determination of base	Determination of rate	Collection and administration	Comments
Multistage sales taxes (value-added tax)	F	F,S	F,I	Border tax adjustments possible under federal assignment; potential stabilization tool
Single-stage sales taxes (manufacturer, wholesale, and retail)				
Option A	S	S,L	S,L,I	Higher compliance cost
Option B	F	S	F,I	Harmonized, lower compliance cost
"Sin" taxes				
Excises on alcohol and tobacco	F,S	F,S	F,S,I	Health care a shared responsibility
Betting and gambling taxes	S,L	S,L	S,L,I	State and local responsibility
Lotteries	S,L	S,L	S,L,I	State and local responsibility
Racetrack taxes	S,L	S,L	S,L,I	State and local responsibility
Taxation of "bads"				
Carbon tax	F	F	F,I	Intended to combat global or national pollution
Energy taxes	F,S,L	F,S,L	F,S,L,I	Pollution impact may be national, regional, or local

194

Motor fuels tolls	F,S,L	F,S,L	F,S,I	Tolls on federal, provincial, and local roads
Effluent charges	F,S,L	F,S,L	F,S,I	Intended to deal with interstate, intermunicipal, or local pollution issues
Congestion tolls	F,S,L	F,S,L	F,S,I	Tolls on federal, provincial, and local roads
Parking fees	L	L	L	Intended to control local congestion
Motor vehicles				
Registration, transfer taxes, and annual fees	S	S	S	State responsibility
Driver's licenses and fees	S	S	S	State responsibility
Business taxes	S	S	S	Benefit tax
Excises	S,L	S,L	S,L,I	Residence-based taxes
Property tax	S	L	L	Completely immobile factor, benefit tax
Land tax	S	L	L	Completely immobile factor, benefit tax
Frontage and betterment taxes	S,L	L	L	Cost recovery
Poll tax	F,S,L	F,S,L	F,S,L,I	Payment for local services
User charges	F,S,L	F,S,L	F,S,L,I	Payment for services received

Note: U = supranational agency, F = federal, S = state or province, L = municipal or local government, I= independent revenue administration agency supervised by multiple orders of government.

Table 4.2. *Summary view of subnational tax assignment in twelve federal countries*

| | Number of countries with subnational determination of | | |
Type of tax	Base	Rate	Tax collection and administration
Customs	1	1	1
Income and gifts	5	6	5
Estates	4	5	4
Corporate	3	3	3
Resource	3	3	3
Sales	4	4	4
VAT	3	3	3
Excises	4	6	5
Property	9	11	10
Fees	7	8	8
Residual powers	2	2	2

Note: Sample countries include Australia, Brazil, Canada, Germany, India, Malaysia, Nigeria, Russia, South Africa, Spain, Switzerland, and the United States.
Source: Compiled from country case studies reported in Shah (2007a).

from a general perspective and then outline some of the alternative ways in which harmonization can be achieved ranging from the most to the least harmonized.

The Objectives of Tax Harmonization

The need for tax harmonization arises because of the desirability of decentralizing revenue-raising responsibilities to the states. Uncoordinated tax setting by states can give rise to deleterious effects for the internal economic union of the federation, and tax competition can lead to inefficient state fiscal systems. Tax competition can be beneficial by encouraging cost-effectiveness and fiscal accountability in state governments. It can also by itself lead to a certain amount of tax harmonization. At the same time, decentralized tax policies can cause certain inefficiencies and inequities in a federation as well as lead to excessive administrative costs. Tax harmonization is intended to preserve the best features of tax decentralization while avoiding its disadvantages.

To recall some of our previous discussions, inefficiencies from decentralized fiscal decision making can occur in a variety of ways. For one, states may implement policies that discriminate in favor of their own residents and businesses relative to those of other states, thereby preventing nonresidents from competing against local interests. They may also engage in beggar-thy-neighbor policies intended to attract economic activity from other states. Inefficiency may also occur simply from the fact that distortions will arise from differential tax structures chosen independently by state governments with no strategic objective in mind. Inefficiencies also can occur if state tax systems adopt different conventions for dealing with businesses (and residents) that operate in more than one jurisdiction at the same time. The results can be double taxation of some forms of income and nontaxation of others.

State tax systems may also introduce inequities into the tax system. Different states may have differing degrees of progressivity in their tax structures, and these may differ considerably from national equity norms of the federal government. To the extent that one views the federal government as being responsible for redistributive equity, this makes its task more difficult. States may also be induced by competitive pressures to implement tax measures that appear to be regressive from a national perspective. For instance, the mobility of either high-income or low-income persons would encourage them to set tax structures that are less progressive than they would otherwise be.

Administrative costs are also likely to be excessive in an uncoordinated tax system, especially if the states and the federal government both occupy a given tax field. Taxpayer compliance is costly because of the need to deal with more than one different tax system. Auditing and collection costs are likely to be higher as well, as taxpayers may be able to engage in tax avoidance by cross-border transactions of a book nature, and authorities cannot obtain information from operations in other jurisdictions. In addition, the auditing priorities of state governments may themselves become skewed in favor of generating revenue from nonresidents or from residents doing business outside the jurisdiction.

Tax harmonization is intended to eliminate some of these excesses. At the same time, a harmonized tax system can serve as a useful complement to the system of intergovernmental transfers. For one thing, taxes that are harmonized vertically can be used as devices for getting revenues to state governments through tax sharing. For another, if taxes are harmonized across states, equalizing transfers based on tax capacities of states are easier to implement.

The importance of tax harmonization varies by type of tax. Taxes on businesses, such as corporation income taxes, are good candidates for harmonization to the extent that state governments use them. They apply to a mobile tax base and would otherwise pose significant administrative costs if left uncoordinated. Personal income taxes would also benefit from some harmonization. Compliance costs to taxpayers and collection costs to governments could be reduced. Distortionary treatment of capital income could be mitigated. In addition, national equity objectives could be addressed through harmonization measures. The case for harmonizing sales and excise taxes is less compelling. The main inefficiencies here result from cross-border shopping problems, and those are likely to be handled by tax competition among jurisdictions. There could be some administrative savings by having a coordinated system of sales taxes between the federal government and the states to reduce the compliance cost to sellers and to economize on auditing by the tax authorities. Some form of harmonization would be virtually mandatory should the states attempt to operate a VAT system. In this case, harmonization alone is unlikely to overcome perfectly the problems of dealing with cross-border transactions in a federation without border controls. For other tax bases, such as payroll taxes, property taxes, and user fees, the advantages of harmonization would seem to be minimal.

Methods of Tax Harmonization

Varying degrees of tax harmonization are possible depending on the degree of decentralization within the tax system. The following are listed in decreasing order of centralization, focusing largely on systems of harmonization that encompass both the federal government and the states.

Revenue Sharing

Greater harmonization generally entails less decentralized decision making. The extreme form of harmonization is revenue sharing, whereby the states are given a predetermined share of the revenues from a given tax source. The federal government determines the tax base and rate structure (perhaps in consultation with the states) and simply agrees to share a certain proportion of it with the states. What must be decided are both the share going to the states as a whole and the allocation among states. A pure revenue-sharing system might be one in which the revenue sharing applies on a state-by-state basis, so that a state's share depends simply on the amount of the tax originating from within that state, the so-called principle of derivation. In Pakistan, for example, the 1973 constitution mandates the sharing of major taxes collected by the central government.

The excise duty, royalties, and surcharges on gas; the royalty on crude oil; and the profits from hydroelectricity are shared among provinces on the basis of origin (Rao, 2007a). In Mexico, the Fiscal Coordination Act of 1978 established an extraconstitutional system in which the states forgo the levying of particular taxes in exchange for a share of the funds collected by the central government. The shares approximate what the states would have collected on their own. These major concurrent taxes include income and sales taxes (J. Gonzalez, 2005). But there is nothing to preclude other formulas for distributing the revenues. In Germany, for example, revenue-sharing funds are allocated using equalization principles as well as the "principle of local yield." The *Länder* as a group receives 42.5 percent of the revenues from the income and corporation taxes. That share is divided among individual *Länder* on the basis of the amount of taxes collected by revenue authorities within the territory. The *Länder* as a group receives 55 percent of revenues from the VAT, which are allocated on an equal per capita basis, which is a simple form of equalization. The German Basic Law details the equalization procedure, which takes these initial distributions into account (Kramer, 2005). Belgium uses both derivation and equal-ization principles in sharing personal income tax revenues. The central government collects and redistributes them to the communities and regions that compose the federation. The language-based communities receive a proportion of income tax revenues based on their contributions. The territorially defined regions receive shares based on fiscal capacity. A region with personal income tax revenues below the national per capita average receives an equalization transfer. Since 2002, the regions have been given some tax autonomy. Regions can introduce lump-sum increases or decreases in the amount of personal income tax collected; however, steps were taken to limit competition. The regional adjustments are set at 6.75 percent of that region's personal income tax collections. The Special Law of 2002 also prohibits the regions from "unfair tax competition." It is expected that a precise definition will be negotiated over time (Deschouwer, 2005).

From an economics point of view, revenue sharing is really equivalent to a system of unconditional grants, albeit one whose magnitude is tied to revenues raised from a particular tax source. Virtually any type of tax could be shared in this way. The tax being shared is completely harmonized so that a fully uniform tax structure is achieved, and national equity and efficiency goals can be pursued at minimal administrative cost. But this harmonization is done at the expense of decentralization of fiscal decision making. States really have no independent taxing responsibility, although they presumably could be consulted collectively about the terms of the revenue sharing, and maybe even about the structure of the tax being shared. On the other hand, revenue-sharing formulas might take out of the hand of the federal government part of the ability to take unilateral actions that will adversely affect the states – at least, those which operate through changes in the grant structure. The federal government can still affect the size of the revenue-sharing pool by changes in the structure of the tax whose revenues are being shared.

Given that revenue-sharing schemes essentially leave the states with little taxing power, it is presumably suitable only for those tax sources that are otherwise deemed to be unsuitable for decentralization. Multistage sales taxes might fit in this category. In Canada, there is a revenue-sharing system in effect for the VAT between the federal government and three provinces. But it is then not clear what purpose is served by revenue sharing as opposed to federal-state grants. The states are still exposed to federal unilateral decision making with respect to tax structure, and they are also exposed to the uncertainties associated with fluctuating tax revenues. If one of the purposes of grants were to insure state treasuries against fluctuations in their tax bases, revenue sharing would clearly be dominated by a grant system whose formula yields more-stable funding to the states.

Moreover, there can be adverse incentives built into revenue-sharing systems. As has been alleged in the case of some federations that use revenue sharing, the incentive of the federal government to use a tax base subject to revenue sharing will be diluted relative to other tax bases simply because the federal government gets only a fraction of the revenues it obtains from shared bases. Revenue sharing as a way of getting more revenues to state governments – as opposed to being a method of tax harmonization – is discussed more fully in the next chapter.

State Surtax
The advantages of a single system can be retained, while allowing the states some responsibility for revenue raised in their jurisdiction by letting the states impose surtaxes on existing federal taxes. This practice is also referred to as piggybacking on federal taxes. In this case, the federal government determines both the base and rate structure for a particular type of tax and chooses the rate level so as to generate the amount of revenue it needs from the tax. The states then piggyback on the federal base and rate structure by setting their own independent state tax rate – or surtax – to apply to federal tax liabilities that would determine how much revenue is

owing to the state. The federal government collects the state surtax on behalf of the state and passes on each state's share of the revenue to them.

There is a need to agree to an allocation formula to determine the distribution of the federal tax base among states. In the case of personal income taxes, it could be based on the residence of taxpayers. For corporate taxes, the allocation formula might be based on some measure of the amount of profits generated in each state, but a precise measurement is difficult, given that many corporate activities affect profits across the nation (e.g., administrative overheads, research and development, advertising). Furthermore, allocation by profits would provide an incentive for corporations to engage in book transactions in order to take their profits in low-tax states. Allocation formulas actually used tend to be based on such things as the share of payrolls in each state, the share of revenues, the share of capital stock, or some combination of those. Sales and excise surtaxes could be allocated simply according to the destination principle, and payroll taxes could be allocated according to the wages paid to workers in the state.

The surtax system combines a high degree of harmonization of the base, rate structure, and collection machinery with the devolution of some revenue-raising responsibility to the states. It is ideally suited to personal and corporate income taxes where such harmonization is desired for reasons of national equity and efficiency.

However, the surtax can have some disadvantages as well. Federal changes to either the base or the rate structure will affect not only its revenues but also those of the states. In most cases, these effects will not be anticipated by the states, so they cannot make timely countervailing changes in their surtax rate to offset the revenue changes induced by federal action.

Also, the states may feel constrained by an inability to use the base or rate structure for policy purposes. This restriction will be more relevant the more important the surtax is as a source of state revenues, and the higher are state tax revenues from the harmonized tax relative to those of the federal government. Their inability can be mitigated to some extent by allowing states to implement their own tax credits alongside the surtax. This system was used in Canada until recently. The federal government continued to set the base and rate structure and administered the credits for the provinces. Provinces were constrained to implement credits that were not discriminatory and did not interfere with the efficiency of the internal economic union. However, as the provinces occupied more and more of the income tax room, they demanded more autonomy in setting tax policy. Provinces are now able to adopt the somewhat more decentralized scheme discussed next whereby they are able to set their own rate structures to apply to the federal base.

In the case of sales taxes, such a system might constrain the type of tax operated by the federal government. For example, if the federal government wished to operate a VAT, it would be administratively costly to allow the provinces to piggyback onto it while setting their own VAT surtaxes independently (let alone their exemptions). As we have mentioned, the process of crediting that is entailed by a VAT would be cumbersome for intermediate transactions across state borders. These problems may well be overcome as viable methods for operating federal-state combined VATs, such as the dual VAT used in Canada, prove to be administratively feasible in developing countries. In fact, this outcome would be ideal, given the inherent advantages to the VAT as a general sales tax system. An alternative would be to have the states levy single-stage sales taxes with the same final base as the federal VAT and a common collection procedure. The problems with monitoring cross-border transactions would disappear, but many of the advantages of a VAT would be lost (e.g., purging final sales of state taxes levied on inputs at earlier stages). Thus, further work and practice with multilevel VATs would be highly desirable for the future of taxation in federations.

Tax on Base System

State surtaxes can be viewed as a tax-on-tax system, whereby the state tax applies on the federal tax liabilities. It keeps intact the base and rate structure chosen by the federal government (albeit in consultation with the provinces). An alternative is to retain a common base but to allow the states to select their own rate structures. This plan can include not only the system of tax brackets but also any tax credits that form part of the progressivity of the tax system. Maybe even some state-specific exemptions from the tax base could be allowed. States could also participate in collection procedures (e.g., auditing). Indeed, they may have a great interest in doing so if their tax structures include certain items of interest to them but not to the federal government (e.g., tax credits, allocations of tax revenue to their jurisdiction).

This system continues to have the advantages of a single tax-collecting authority, and the common base facilitates compliance. It also allows the states more flexibility in designing their tax policies, including the degree of progressivity, to suit the preferences of their residents. It also avoids the large spillover effect that the federal government imposes on state revenues when it changes its tax rates. As long as the federal government retains enough tax room, it can still have the moral or political authority to select the base and can use the tax system for national social and redistributive objectives. Thus, this tax-on-base system might be suitable for a decentralized federation.

At the same time, some advantages of harmonization are necessarily sacrificed. As states obtain more autonomy in the choice of their tax structures, the possibility that they will use it in ways that distort the internal common market or discriminate against out-of-state residents and businesses is enhanced. As well, the national tax structure becomes fragmented so that different standards of redistributive equity might apply in different states. This fragmentation simply reflects the inevitable trade-off that exists in this and other contexts between the advantages and disadvantages of decentralization.

During the late 1990s, Canada revised its personal income tax-collection agreements. These bilateral agreements between the central government and a province follow a common template. The system changed from tax-on-tax to one in which provinces determine their own rate structure on the federal tax base. Participating provinces have full discretion over the size of tax brackets and the use of tax credits, while the federal government acts as the sole tax-collection authority. In practice, various tax structures were chosen, with some provinces implementing a flat tax. Many provinces reduced the progressivity of their tax systems. Only one province elected not to participate and runs its own income tax system (Boadway, 2007b).

In this system, the federal government acts as the facilitator for achieving harmonization. It sets the rules, presumably in consultation with the states, and induces the states to participate. The inducement involves both the provision of tax-collection services for the states and some financial incentive to join by making tax room available to the states. If the federal government is not using the tax source under consideration, harmonization must involve interstate cooperation. That is notoriously difficult, not just to achieve, but also to maintain. There seem to be few examples of interstate binding agreements in any area, let alone tax harmonization. Such agreements involve not just several governments bargaining among one another to achieve a unanimous consensus; it must also involve mechanisms for binding future governments as well as a dispute settlement procedure for enforcing the agreement. These things are all very difficult to achieve. Experience in interjurisdictional agreements in a decentralized federation like Canada is instructive. Attempts to formulate interprovincial agreements, even those involving federal government participation, in basic areas like removing interprovincial trade barriers or agreeing on terms of a social union, have proved to be fairly fruitless. Tax harmonization will be much easier to accomplish in a setting where the federal government is in a position to set the agenda and to encourage compliance by a combination of rewards, financial incentives, and quid pro quos.

Uncoordinated Tax Decentralization

The extreme case is where states enter a tax field in a purely uncoordinated manner, regardless of whether the federal government occupies the same base. Each state chooses the tax structure and rates that best suits itself, subject only to the constraints imposed by interjurisdictional tax competition. Because this form of decentralization leaves the states with the most independence, it presumably results in the most accountability. But there are obvious drawbacks, which we have discussed previously. Uncoordinated tax setting can lead to inefficiencies and inequities in the internal economic union, as well as excessive collection and compliance costs.

These drawbacks will be less severe for some taxes than for others. Taxes on very immobile factors such as natural resources and real property might be cases where coordination is less important. Even for these immobile tax bases, though, the incentive to develop resource properties or to locate business properties in a jurisdiction might be influenced by tax rates and tax incentives. Uncoordinated state payroll taxes are also relatively immune to efficiency problems because labor is relatively immobile. Broad-based sales taxes are slightly more problematic. Only single-staged sales taxes can realistically be decentralized to the states, and these inevitably have inefficiencies built into them that are exaggerated in a state economy with no border controls.

Decentralizing income taxes, both personal and corporate, in an uncoordinated manner leads to significant problems with efficiency, equity, and administrative ease. In addition to the possibility that these taxes distort the interstate allocation of resources and lead to self-defeating tax competition, taxpayers whose activities overlap jurisdictions are faced with the prospect of complying with different tax systems and dealing with different tax administrations. This situation can cause problems for both the tax administrators and the taxpayers. Tax administrators may find it difficult to ensure compliance when taxpayers are free to reallocate their activities across jurisdictions. Sometimes this can be done by paper transactions, such as transfer pricing and switching financing from one jurisdiction to another. Ambiguities with determining how a taxpayer's income is allocated among states can lead to double taxation or nontaxation of some income if states adopt different methods of allocating taxable income to their own jurisdiction.

Additional problems occur if the federal government co-occupies the same tax bases with the states. With two levels of government setting tax rates and defining their tax structures independently, compliance costs for firms are heightened. Moreover, vertical fiscal externalities may be significant if the tax base has some elasticity: each jurisdiction will have no incentive to take account of the effect on the revenues of the other when setting its own tax rates. If the federal government occupies the same tax base as the provinces, little substantial state fiscal independence is lost by agreeing at a minimum to a single tax-collecting authority.

In deciding on whether to pursue federal-state tax harmonization, one must weigh the benefits of harmonizing with the costs, and this decision may come out much differently for different taxes. The benefits are clear-cut: harmonization improves the efficiency and equity of the tax system in the federation as a whole; reduces the opportunities for destructive fiscal competition, while retaining the advantages of healthy forms of competition and accountability arising from decentralized fiscal responsibility; and reduces collection and compliance costs. The costs are that states must have somewhat less autonomy in decision making compared with a fully decentralized system, though not necessarily less than if they relied on grants from the federal government; that states might not be able to implement legitimate local redistributive objectives using the tax system; that a single tax-collecting authority might be less responsive to state interests than a state one would be; and that the states would be open to unexpected and unilateral changes to the tax base or rate structure, which would affect their budgets. How these benefits and costs trade off against one another will depend on the type of tax in question. We have argued that the harmonization of income taxes is highly desirable. For taxes like payroll taxes, taxes on resources, excise taxes, and property taxes, the net benefits are somewhat less apparent. For these tax types, running a fully decentralized and uncoordinated state tax system would not be too damaging. The case of sales taxes is problematic. The ability to decentralize state taxing responsibility, harmonized or not, is contingent on the form of the tax. A single-stage tax is relatively easy to decentralize, and the need for harmonization is not compelling. But, by the same token, the choice of a single-stage form is itself problematic. A multistage sales tax is acknowledged to be immensely superior to a single stage form on grounds of efficiency, though perhaps less so from the point of view of collection and compliance costs. But with such a tax, it is very difficult to decentralize decision making to the state level, even in a highly harmonized setting.

The Crucial Role of Equalization

It is worth repeating a point that has been made earlier. To the extent that states become more self-reliant in raising their own revenues, they will be able to raise differing amounts per capita because they have different tax capacities. In itself, this ability will cause fiscal inefficiencies and inequities as a result of taxpayers in different jurisdictions obtaining differing net fiscal benefits from their state governments. Unless actions are undertaken to offset this, the benefits of decentralized decision making will be accompanied by distortions and horizontal inequities in the internal economic union. The remedy is relatively straightforward. Decentralization of revenue-raising responsibilities should be accompanied by a system of equalization of revenue-raising capacities designed to ensure that different states have the potential for financing comparable levels of public services at comparable tax rates. The term "potential" is used because states need not be compelled to behave uniformly: that would contradict the basic premise of federalism.

Tax harmonization and equalization should be seen as complementary parts of the general system of federal-state fiscal relations. To the extent that tax capacities among states are equalized, so that states have the potential to select comparable tax systems, harmonization should be easier to achieve. At the same time, having state tax systems that are harmonized facilitates the equalization of tax capacities, especially if equalization is achieved using the so-called representative tax system approach. As we discuss in more detail in Chapter 9, the representative tax system approach calculates the tax capacities of the states by determining how much revenue would be raised in each state when a common tax rate is applied to a representative tax base in each state. The definition of the representative tax base used in this calculation is made much easier to the extent that states have agreed on harmonized tax bases.

FIVE

Natural Resources Ownership and Management in a Federal System

INTRODUCTION

Natural resource endowments in a federation are typically allocated very unevenly across the federation. To the extent that subnational jurisdictions have access to revenues generated directly or indirectly from resource exploitation, both inefficiencies and inequities can occur. In some federations, the problem is particularly pronounced because resource ownership resides with the subnational government. This decentralized ownership implies that resource revenues accrue directly to the subnational government, leading to potentially large net fiscal benefit differences. An example of this is Canada, where natural resources are owned by the provinces, although the federal government can also obtain some tax revenues through its income and sales taxes. In other cases, management is at the subnational level, although revenues are more centralized. Even in this case, uneven economic development can occur, which puts strains on the federation. Moreover, there may be tensions between subnational governments where natural resources are located and the federal government that collects the revenues if the former feel they are not getting their fair share of benefits. Of course, these tensions will be exacerbated if there is a perception that the federal government is not using the resources wisely or if there is outright corruption.

Many issues arise in federations where natural resource endowments are significant. First, there is the issue of managing the rate of exploration, extraction, and processing of the resources. Typically, the government at one level or another exercises oversight and control of resource management, which involves establishing property rights to resources with some regulation of the use of those property rights. Thus, private firms may acquire property rights in return for paying some price to the government and, as a result, gain significant revenues. Alternatively, the property rights might be retained by a public corporation or by a joint venture between the public and private sectors. Then, as production proceeds, governments obtain revenues by some combination of royalties, taxes, and public corporation profits, including profit sharing. These revenues, along with those obtained from the sale of property rights, can represent significant amounts to the relevant level of government.

The manner in which revenue schemes are designed can lead to various inefficiencies. To the extent that the base for collecting revenues deviates from economic rents from the resources – either expected or ex post – resource exploration, extraction, and processing might be inefficient. There is a body of literature that studies alternative forms of resource revenue collection, ranging from the auction of leases, taxes, or royalties on production, income taxes, and profit sharing.[1] We need not be too concerned with revenue collection here because what are relevant are the consequences of such revenues for the federal system. The use of these revenues is what generates much of the concern. For one thing, a large influx of natural resource revenues can be disruptive to the real economy depending on how they are used. The "resource curse" or "Dutch disease" phenomena reflect the fact that there are various ways in which natural resource revenues can affect the development of an economy.[2] An active resource sector itself draws factors of production from other productive sectors, especially those more likely to generate productivity gains. This can be exacerbated by improvements in the currency value if resource revenues are spent. Reallocation of productive factors to regions in which the resources happen to be located can also have interregional and inter-industry effects, which can be reinforced if subnational governments use revenues proactively to attract economic activity from the rest of the country.

Finally, natural resource revenues are particularly prone to volatility. Resource prices fluctuate in world markets, generating uncertainty that different levels of government may cope with differently. Moreover, because revenues are bound to be temporary in the case of nonrenewable resources, forward-looking policies are important, and these may be more difficult to achieve in a decentralized setting.

---

[1] For surveys of issues involving the taxation of natural resources, see Heaps and Helliwell (1985) and Boadway and Flatters (1991). The distorting effects of resource tax regimes can be estimated by using the concept of marginal effective tax rates. For an application of this to nonrenewable resources, see Boadway et al. (1987).

[2] The effect of natural resources on growth and development is analyzed in Sachs and Warner (1999, 2001).

The case of Canada illustrates some of the problems in a stark form, and we refer to that case from time to time in this chapter.[3] An important feature of the Canadian federation in recent years has been the rapid rise in oil and gas revenues in western Canada, especially Alberta. Petroleum prices have become high enough to warrant significant extraction of crude oil from the so-called tar sands, where extraction is much more costly than for conventional oil deposits. A major reallocation of economic activity and workers to the west has resulted, causing an unprecedented horizontal imbalance between Alberta and the rest of the provinces that is beyond the capability of the equalization system to address. The effects of this resource boom and the manner in which the revenues are being used have the potential for inducing considerable restructuring of industry in other provinces, possibly at great cost. This is especially true in the poorer parts of the country from which much manpower is being attracted, but even the manufacturing heartland in central Canada is vulnerable.

In what follows, much of our focus is on problems associated with the consequences of relatively large natural resource endowments because that is where the major concerns arise. As mentioned, this circumstance can generate problems whether the country is a federation or not. It will be useful to focus initially on problems that arise in a unitary-nation context, those normally associated with the resource curse. How to deal with the resource curse is still an open question in the literature. However, measures can be taken to mitigate the damage. As we have learned from the Norwegian case, careful management of natural resource revenues can shield the economy from the consequences of volatile cash flows that are disruptive in the short term. Simply holding the revenues in a fund, investing the fund in foreign assets, and drawing on that fund only to the extent that it generates income will ensure that induced financial effects will be largely suppressed. However, not all governments are able to exercise the self-discipline required to save all resource revenues. Even if such a fund can be sustained, the real effects of a resource boom cannot be avoided entirely. Interindustry adjustments are inevitable, as are interregional ones, to the extent that the resources are not evenly spread across the country.

In a federal context, these problems are magnified. Resource-rich regions will have a greater ability to raise revenue and, if uncorrected, this will lead to fiscally induced migration from other regions. Some regions will have greater financial ability to provide given levels of public services,

---

[3] The discussion of the Canadian case draws heavily on Boadway (2007a).

the classic source of fiscal inefficiency and inequity that we have encountered repeatedly in earlier chapters. These can be thought of as the passive consequences of unequal resource revenues. There is a further problem in a decentralized federation. Subnational governments in resource-rich regions now have a source of revenues that they can use to attract economic activity to develop their own provinces, to some extent at the expense of other provinces. This temptation to use resource revenues for region-building purposes can lead to excessively rapid resource development, too little saving of resource revenues, and a building up of infrastructure to attract nonresource industries to regions that have no natural industrial location advantage apart from being where natural resources happen to be found.

These issues pose enormous challenges for managing natural resources in a federal system, which is not well suited to dealing with asymmetric and large concentrations of natural resources in a limited number of regions. Indeed, economic policy analysis gives us relatively little guidance on how to design policies to deal with such a situation, whether in a federal context or not. Even in a unitary nation, the issue of the optimal regional pattern of development and infrastructure investment is not well understood. In a federal context, the issues are even more complicated because of the incentives that exist for subnational governments with high fiscal capacity to engage in strategic region-building policies to the partial detriment of other regions. Given that, much of the discussion to follow is speculative and based on suggestive arguments that have not been theoretically vindicated or empirically verified.

THE SETTING

Natural resources differ from other industries in that they are endowments that are given to a nation and are location specific. That is, the activity involved with exploration and extraction is by definition not mobile across regions or nations, unlike with other goods and services production. Of course, there may be locational advantages to industrial production that influence where production does or should take place. Moreover, the development of natural resources uses factors of production in competition with other industries, so to that extent production activity is itself mobile. Within a country, natural resource endowments can vary by region as well as by type. It may well be the case that different types of resources (e.g., petroleum, minerals, fisheries, forestry, water) are concentrated in different regions but that overall the diversity in endowments cancels out, so that revenue-raising capacities do not differ much. In this case, many of the special problems that arise in federations do not apply. However, in many federations or decentralized nations, some regions tend to be resource rich and others resource poor (e.g., Australia, Canada, Malaysia, Nigeria, South Africa, and the United States).

Different types of resources pose different problems for regional development. Nonrenewable resources by definition will run out, so management of the speed of development is important. Renewable resources in principle can operate in perpetuity but will do so only if properly controlled. Resource endowments may be very uncertain both in size and in value. Exploration investment must be undertaken to discover deposits of petroleum and minerals and will be affected by public policies. The price may be quite volatile and difficult to predict so potential revenues will be uncertain. This inherent riskiness of natural resources is made more pressing by the fact that resource development tends to be relatively capital intensive. The life of natural resources tends to span many generations, so some account must be taken of the intergenerational consequences of resource depletion, if only implicitly.

Of particular importance in a federation is the assignment of ownership and responsibilities for natural resource management and development. As we discussed in earlier chapters, there are conflicting arguments about this. On the one hand, because natural resources are immobile, it makes some sense to decentralize the responsibility for management and regulation of their development and even for revenue raising. For example, resource development requires specific types of infrastructure, such as transportation and utilities in the often-remote areas where the resources are located. The provision of such infrastructure is typically a subnational function. On the other hand, the often highly uneven distribution of natural resources across regions and their volatility in value supports central control of revenue raising. The practices vary from federation to federation partly because of the historical determination of property rights. Thus, where federations are formed from previously separate jurisdictions that become states, those states may retain the ownership of public property rights that they previously enjoyed. In this case, the revenues of the ownership of natural resources accrue to subnational governments along with the responsibility for managing development. Even so, the central government will typically have some ability to raise revenues using other tax instruments. In these circumstances, the division of revenues between the central and subnational governments will be the outcome of separate decisions by the two levels of government. The more revenues the central government raises from, say, income taxes on natural resource firms, the more difficult will it be for the subnational governments to raise revenues. In what follows, we allow for different degrees of decentralization of revenues but typically assume that subnational governments can influence resource development through infrastructure investments and regulatory means.

There are some other characteristics of natural resources that are worth mentioning because they are relevant for some of the subsequent discussion. Natural resource commodities, whether processed or not, are typically traded on international markets, and resource production may be dominated by foreign-owned firms, perhaps in sharing arrangements with local producers. This arrangement implies that there will be direct effects of resource activity on international markets, including currency markets. Natural resources will be subject to varying degrees of further refinement and processing activities and will typically require special facilities for transporting the products to market. This also contributes to the capital intensity of resource development. There will be downstream economic activity related to resource development, such as refinement and other processing, as well as transportation or transmission. Resource development will have an effect on the quality of the environment that needs to be accounted for. Finally, there will be inevitable social consequences of resource development for the local populations where it takes place. For example, in Canada these consequences include the indigenous aboriginal communities whose life-styles may be disrupted by resource development.

Natural resource development differs from manufacturing development and gives rise to special unique policy challenges. Many of these challenges call into question the principles of regional economic development, which are not well understood by public finance specialists. They have been the subject of study by economic historians and economic geographers (Krugman, 1995a, 1998), though relatively few general principles of economic policy have emerged. The fiscal federalism dimension of natural resources has yet to be fully scrutinized. For that reason, much of what we discuss is suggestive.

To put issues of fiscal federalism and resources in perspective, it is useful as a benchmark to begin by setting aside federalism issues and considering the consequences of natural resource booms for economic policy in a unitary but geographically diverse nation. This approach is useful for highlighting the special problems that can be attributable to federalism as opposed to the natural resource development per se.

NATURAL RESOURCES IN A UNITARY NATION

The unitary nation we consider consists of a number of regions. One of those regions, call it Petrolia, is endowed with a substantial amount of oil and natural gas. The exact amount is uncertain, but the known reserves are large and valuable owing to high world prices. To focus on problems of adjusting to natural resource shocks, it is useful to suppose that prices have risen recently causing the value of the resource stocks to be much higher than in the recent past. Other regions may also have natural resource endowments, but they are much more limited in value and do not give rise to large differences across regions.

We proceed by first considering how the advent of a region-specific resource boom will affect the private sector, particularly the kinds of adjustments that must occur. Then we turn to the challenges faced for public policy choices by the government of the unitary nation.

Private-Sector Adjustments

Suppose Petrolia experiences a sudden increase in the value of its already substantial oil and gas reserves because of a rapid increase in the world price of oil and natural gas. Similar issues would arise from resource booms of other sorts, such as new mineral discoveries. Indeed, our discussion could also apply in reverse to regions facing negative economic shocks, such as a sudden collapse in world prices for a natural resource or the depletion of resource stocks, such as fish or minerals. The first response is for an increase in the level of development of the resource through extraction, processing, transportation, and further exploration. Given that the resource boom is relatively large, this entails in the first instance the attraction of substantial amounts of labor and capital to Petrolia, although the details will differ for the two types of resources. There will also be an increase in the purchase of intermediate inputs from various sources.

If we assume that Petrolia has limited excess labor available, much of the influx of labor will come from other regions and perhaps from international sources as well to the extent that immigration is possible. Because most of the labor will have been employed in other industries, some retraining will be necessary, especially for workers who must work on machinery specific to the oil and gas industry or management workers who must learn about the oil and gas business. Of course, for some workers, their skills will be general enough to adapt to local needs, such as those involved in manual labor, transportation, and some forms of white-collar work. Given the need to attract workers from other regions and industries, wages will presumably be bid up. Other regions will suffer from a decline in economic activity, although the increase in wage rates will be an offsetting factor.

The increase in demand for capital will be particularly pronounced because resource production is highly capital intensive. Some of the machinery and equipment required will be produced in other regions, thereby ensuring that some of the benefits of the resource boom will be diffused across other regions. Some may also be imported, which would in itself put downward pressure on the value of the nation's currency. However, given that much of the output of the resource sector is exported, this offsetting effect on the import side mitigates the consequences of the exchange rate increase that would otherwise occur.

The increase in real investment would be accompanied by an inflow of financial capital. To the extent that the nation's capital markets were open to international ones, much of the increased demand for financial capital would come from abroad, especially if resource firms were international ones. This would also offset exchange rate effects that would come about from the sale of resource products. Even so, if national capital markets are to some extent segmented from international ones because of transaction costs or nation-specific risks, some of the increased demand for capital would come from finance that would otherwise go to other regions.

The upshot of these adjustments in labor and capital markets is that all regions would face some adjustments. Petrolia's population will rise because of interregional and international migration. Because these will be predominantly working-age persons, the average age of residents will fall and the proportion of the population in the work force will rise. As mentioned, the demand for labor will cause wage rates to increase substantially, especially if it is costly to move to Petrolia, and there may well be significant labor shortages in the short run. The change in population will cause property values to rise, given that it takes time to adjust the housing stock. This will, of course, contribute to the pressure on wage rates. Other industries will also flourish, including those which provide goods and services to the oil and gas industry as well as to the increased population. The larger population may itself induce industry diversification because of agglomeration economies that result from a larger work force with higher skills. This will reinforce the increase in industrial activity in Petrolia.

At the same time, there will be offsetting reductions in the labor force and industrial activity in other regions, although the offsetting will be less than complete. These regions will lose the most mobile workers, who tend to be relatively young, as well as high skilled entrepreneurial and managerial persons. The loss in labor force will be dampened by the fact that some of the workers might come from international migration. Because the oil and gas industry is capital intensive, the amount of labor needed directly for that industry will be limited. However, many of the nonresource industries that experience growth in Petrolia will be much more labor intensive, including the service sector and construction sectors. The resulting need for migrants will ensure that wage rates rise, thus putting pressure on industries in other regions, including the manufacturing and high-technology sectors where much of the productivity growth occurs. Some workers may relocate only temporarily, or even engage in commuting while maintaining their permanent residence in other regions. This will be especially true for those attached to their original region who may find it difficult to relocate permanently to Petrolia in possibly remote and less attractive areas. This possibility of temporary migration serves as an effective adjustment mechanism that reduces the long-term costs of adjusting to the resource boom.

From the point of view of the whole nation, an important impact of the oil and gas boom is on the real exchange rate. Pressure for the real exchange rate (the real price of foreign currency) to fall comes from the fact that much of the oil and gas produced is sold abroad and also because foreign investment flows in to help finance the industry's expansion. These serve to increase the supply of foreign currency. On the other hand, some demand for foreign currency will be induced by imports of intermediate goods and capital equipment used in industries in Petrolia; by an increase in demand for imports because of increases in domestic income; and, potentially more important, by an increase in demand for foreign financial assets as domestic savings increase. The change in domestic savings is critically affected by how the net revenues (rents) generated by oil and gas sales are used. To the extent that they are saved, particularly in foreign assets, exchange rate effects due to increases in oil and gas sales abroad will be considerably mitigated. On the other hand, if the rents are spent, additional pressure may be put on industries elsewhere in the country depending where the revenues are spent. Because oil and gas rents are likely to be substantial, this effect is likely to be important. Oil and gas rents will be shared by the industry and by the government of the unitary nation; whether they are saved is heavily influenced by how the government disposes of its share. Both the share of resource rents going to the government and the extent to which the government saves them are important policy issues.

The upshot for the nation as a whole is that the resource boom will cause some shift in industrial activity from nonresource industries to the resource industry and the largely nontraded sectors used to support it. To the extent that the declining industries are those where innovation and productivity growth are likely to occur, one source of the resource curse will be prominent (Sachs and Warner, 1999, 2001). The curse will be exacerbated to the extent that the real exchange rate falls (and the real wage rate rises). These factors will be relevant in assessing policy responses, both in the unitary-nation setting and in the federal one considered later.

As an inevitable by-product of these adjustments to the resource boom, interregional income disparities will be created or increased. Per capita income in Petrolia will rise substantially relative to other regions. Incomes in the latter may rise or fall depending on the offsetting effects of relocation of labor and capital to meet the demand of the oil and gas boom and the fact that some industries in other regions will be able to sell intermediate inputs and consumer goods in Petrolia. Capital owners elsewhere may earn higher incomes to the extent that they have a stake in Petrolia's industries. Despite the outflow of labor, unemployment may increase in other regions if the real exchange rate changes make it more difficult for existing producers to sell their products. The extent of the change in per capita incomes and employment will depend in part on how freely labor flows from one region to the other in response to economic incentives. The more costly migration is, the greater will be the disparities in income and unemployment that have to occur to accommodate the shift in the demand for workers. Finally, the increase in the average age of the population in other regions will have important consequences for government policy.

Consequences for the Public Sector

The adjustments of the private sector to a resource boom will necessarily have an impact on the government, even in the unlikely event that the government does not adjust its policies. We first summarize what that impact might be and then turn to likely or desirable policy responses by the government. For now we continue to assume the country is a unitary nation whose policy responses will take account of the regional effects of the boom. Later we look at the additional issues that arise when the country is a federation. This hypothetical separation between unitary- and federal-nation responses serves as a useful pedagogical device for emphasizing the particular problems that resource booms pose for federations.

The government of the unitary nation will raise revenues and provide public goods and services nationwide. Presumably, the revenue system will be based on a tax system that applies uniformly to all residents and firms in all regions of the nation. Public goods and services will also be provided nationwide, but there may be regional differences because of differences in costs of provision. Otherwise, residents would be entitled to a relatively common level of public services, such as education, social insurance, and health care, wherever they reside. Among the revenue sources for the national government would be revenues from natural resources that would consist of some combination of revenues from the sale of rights to private firms to explore and develop natural resources, profits from any public resource corporations, and direct taxes of various sorts on natural resources.

These revenues from resources might go into the general revenue fund along with other tax revenues. Or, in the case of nonrenewable resources, a portion of them may be held in a dedicated fund to be saved for future use. The decision about the disposition of natural resource revenues is of relevance for how the national economy is affected by the resource boom, as we have seen. The potentially adverse consequences for other industries will be dampened if the revenues are saved. This will especially be the case if they are saved in foreign assets so that real exchange rate effects are minimized.

The resource boom will affect national revenues and expenditures more generally. Income and sales tax revenues will increase as national output grows. Corporate tax revenues will increase, especially from resource-related sectors. The distribution of tax revenues by region will change, but because all are consolidated in national revenues, that will be of little consequence. On the expenditure side, regional effects will be important. The migration of labor and economic activity from other regions to Petrolia will require a shift in supply of public services to accommodate changes in need. These changes will reflect changes in the age structure induced by migration.

There will also be redistributive consequences of the resource boom that will be accommodated by the fiscal system. Changes in the distribution of personal income across regions will be dampened by the progressive tax system. The system of social protection, which includes unemployment insurance and welfare transfers, will serve to insure persons who have been displaced by the dislocations cause by the interregional shift in economic activity. Along with the adjustments in public services in different regions, a great deal of social insurance will be brought to bear in dealing with the redistributive consequences of the resource boom. The fact that the national fiscal system applies is of relevance for our discussion of fiscal federalism and means that there is an implicit form of interregional equalization taking place that provides interregional insurance: the revenues raised from Petrolia will implicitly be redistributed via the national budget to help finance public services and transfers in other less-fortunate regions.

Finally, there will also be a need for adjustments in the provision of infrastructure in different regions. The national government will have to decide the amounts and forms of infrastructure investment that should be made in Petrolia to accommodate the increased economic activity, as well as to facilitate subsequent economic development. These investments will target transportation and communications for the resource industry itself and for supporting industries. There will also be a need to provide for an expansion of local utilities, water and sewage, and schools and hospitals to accommodate the increase in population. More ambitiously, there may be a need to provide investment in human capital, through either training or higher education, although this may be more effectively done elsewhere in the nation. A more difficult decision is how much to invest in expanding and diversifying Petrolia's economy beyond its resource base. Of course, at the same time as public investment is increasing in Petrolia, it will be decreasing elsewhere.

Policy Responses in the Unitary Nation

The consequences of a resource boom for both the private and public sectors invite a policy response by the government, owing to its obligations with respect to the resource industries. The government commonly enjoys some form of property rights over natural resources and so necessarily must decide how to exercise those rights. Decisions can concern the quantity of rights to sell or lease to the private sector, control over the intensity of exploration and extraction, and the provision of infrastructure that accompanies resource development. In addition, the government must decide how to use the resource revenues that it collects and how to respond to changes that occur in other sectors and regions of the economy as a result of the resource boom. All these things involve difficult policy choices even in the absence of the complications faced in a federal system where policies must be coordinated by governments. Decisions must be based not only on considerations of economic efficiency and economic growth at the national level but also on consequences for economic development in the different regions of the nation. Moreover, because the resource boom will create losers as well as gainers, weighing one against the other involves difficult equity judgments. In this section, we outline the policy issues that would be faced by a hypothetical unitary-nation government that endogenizes outcomes for all regions. Even in this context, the optimal policy response to a resource boom is an open question, and there is not a lot of academic literature to draw on for answers. We can at least outline various factors that must be taken into account.

Suppose the price of oil and gas rises significantly, leading to a rise on the value of the natural resources with which Petrolia is endowed. The overarching policy decision facing the nation in responding to this rise in prices is how fast to search for and develop sources of oil and gas. This difficult decision is affected by a number of factors, some of which are not known with certainty. One concerns expectations about future oil and gas prospects, which, despite standard predictions about an upward trend, are notoriously volatile and respond to events such as weather and political upheaval. Even knowing future prices is not sufficient because the rate of success of exploration investment is itself uncertain. The decision about how rapidly to develop natural resources must also deal with legitimate concerns about the costs of industrial and regional adjustment throughout the country, especially given the fact that other industries include those whose potential for technological progress and innovation is greater than natural resources. There is also the need to consider the environmental consequences of resource development, including the degradation of the landscape, the depletion of water supplies, and the effect on woodlands and wildlife. Unlike industrial adjustment, these changes can be cumulative rather than transitory. As a result, there will inevitably be social and cultural consequences of resource development, including the impact on aboriginal and other vulnerable communities. New communities must also be created in the knowledge that they may last only as long as the life of the nonrenewable resource. And, as mentioned, one of the most difficult judgments is how to deal with the competing claims of present and future generations, given that the development of nonrenewable resources entails the depletion of the amount of national wealth left for future generations. The implication of these effects of resource development is that the decision about how rapidly to proceed involves more than standard economic cost-benefit analysis.

Once the rate of resource exploration and development has been chosen, the next issue is how much of a share of natural resource revenues should accrue to the public sector, and what policy instruments should be designed to capture them. The design of instruments to divert a share of natural resource rents to the public sector in the most efficient way has been widely studied, and there is some consensus among economists. Expected rents can be collected before exploration or production takes place through the sale of exploration rights and development leases or through public-private equity sharing agreements. Alternatively, rents can be diverted to the public sector as they are earned through appropriately designed rent taxes. The proper mix of these mechanisms is not clear, and governments typically use a mixture. In principle, the sale of leases through competitive auctions should collect all expected rents, which might be reasonable to the extent that the property rights to the resources belong to the public. However, the sale of leases typically does not extract all expected rents. For one thing, the sale may not be at a competitive price, given that there may be a small number of large potential buyers. As well, there may be considerable uncertainty about the value of resources covered by the lease, so a significant risk premium is required. More important, buyers of leases will correctly anticipate that their profits will eventually be subject to taxes, and these will be capitalized into the price of the lease. In the case of taxes imposed on profits or revenues, it should be possible in principle to design their bases to reflect economic rents so that efficient resource development is achieved. For example, taxes on the cash flow of resource firms will be equivalent to rent taxes.[4] In practice, natural resource taxes often deviate from rents. Resource firms are often given very favorable deductions for exploration and development, thereby encouraging excessive investments in these activities. In addition, government-imposed royalties or severance taxes on revenues (perhaps net of current costs), rather than on economic rents, will distort the extraction decision.

Resource booms will lead to a sizable influx of funds into public revenues. The next issue is what should be done with these funds. They could be saved and drawn down gradually in the future. In this case, a decision must be made about the kind of assets to hold and at what rate to draw the assets later. Alternatively, some or all of them could be spent. The spending could be on current government goods and services, or it could be on infrastructure and regional development or diversification projects. One useful model for dealing with natural resource revenues is that found in Norway, where enormous amounts of oil and gas are being extracted from the North Sea.[5] There, all public-sector petroleum revenues from sales of

---

[4] A cash flow tax includes all revenues and allows a full deduction for investments (but no deduction for capital costs or depreciation). Tax bases that are equivalent to a cash flow tax are discussed in Boadway and Flatters (1991).

[5] A summary of Norwegian oil policy may be found in OECD (2005).

exploration licenses and tax revenues from producing firms are saved in the so-called Government Pension Fund – Global (until 2006, called the Petroleum Fund of Norway). The fund is invested in foreign assets, suitably diversified, and only the capital income generated from the fund is available for current government use. Thus, the assets are kept intact. Obviously, maintaining such a system requires a high degree of discipline and foresight by the government, and the Norwegian case is unique in that regard. Other countries have not been able to resist the temptation to spend substantial parts of their natural resource revenues, and this shortcoming, as we suggest, may be a particular problem in federations. Even in Norway, the government is under pressure to spend some of the fund revenues to relieve taxpayers of high tax rates. The Norwegian system has a number of advantages. It facilitates intergenerational wealth sharing; it avoids the creation of excessive current demand on the domestic economy; it shields the domestic economy against major changes in the industrial structure, the resource curse, or Dutch disease; it reduces exchange rate appreciation that might be detrimental to the domestic economy; and it shelters the government from volatility that characterizes resource revenues. But, as mentioned, implementing the Norwegian system entails a level of commitment that few governments show evidence of satisfying.

Complementary to designing a system for taxing the rents from resources directly, it is important to have in place a corporation income tax system that is as nondistortionary as possible so that investment is allocated efficiently among different uses. In public finance terms, the tax system should be designed so that marginal effective tax rates are reasonably uniform across industries and regions, where the marginal effective tax rate is the corporate tax rate applicable to the marginal investment of a given type. This tax should be combined with a corporation tax whose components serve the main purpose of the corporation tax as a withholding system applicable to shareholder profits. The intention is to avoid sheltering corporate income within the corporation to postpone taxes as well as to withhold against nonresident shareholders. It is the withholding motive that justifies having positive taxes on equity income in the first place. It is clear that the current business tax systems around the world do not satisfy these ideals. For example, as the Technical Committee on Business Taxation (1998) ("The Mintz Committee") documented for the case of Canada, the Canadian business tax system favors the resource sector by its system of generous write-offs for exploration and development, while discriminating against the service sector, which is one of the main sources of innovation and productivity growth. Similar structural problems may be found in business taxes elsewhere in the world.

The design of a national tax–transfer–social insurance system is also relevant as a means of addressing the consequences of resource development for individual workers and their households in all regions. This system serves a purely redistributive motive as well as providing social protection against adversities of various sorts. Its elements include the progressive income tax, employment insurance, disability transfers, and welfare. Designing these systems must take due account of the trade-off between social insurance and the incentive that potential workers might have to seek employment both in their place of residence and in other regions. This is the classical equity-efficiency trade-off that involves important value judgments as well as judgments about the role of the state – as opposed to other institutions, such as family, friends and community, and charitable organizations – in providing social insurance.

The social protection system involves more than transfers and social insurance. It also involves choosing of public service levels in areas like health, education, and social services. These are every bit as redistributive in intent and effect as the progressive tax-transfer system. Indeed, one could argue that much more redistribution takes place through public services than through transfers. This issue in the context of a resource boom in Petrolia is how to adjust the levels of public services there and in other regions in response to the changes in regions' populations and their possible dispersion into remote areas where resource development is taking place. In particular, decisions must be made by the unitary nation's government about how fast hospitals, schools, colleges, and universities should be expanded in Petrolia and consolidated in other regions in response to population adjustments. The issue partly turns on citizens' expectations about their rights to basic public services, or what might be called their social citizenship rights. In a unitary nation, one might expect social citizenship rights to be defined on a national basis, so that as an ideal, comparable levels of public services should be available to citizens in all regions, just like comparable taxes apply. However, even in a unitary nation, public service levels might justifiably differ across regions because the costs of providing comparable levels of services differ considerably. In most countries, city dwellers receive higher levels of many public services than do rural dwellers, reflecting differences in the cost of provision. Even so, persons in comparable settings in different regions might be entitled to comparable treatment: rural residents in Petrolia might expect comparable access to health and education as rural residents in other regions. Translating that into a specific program of responses to rapid changes in population resulting from an oil and gas boom in Petrolia is a matter of judgment and is not independent of the desired rate of development of the natural resources themselves. In any case, the redistributive nature of the tax-transfer system and the system of social insurance, combined with the fact that public services would be funded from national general revenues, implies that there would be a large amount of implicit interregional redistribution resulting from policy responses to an oil and gas boom in Petrolia.

A further difficult decision that cannot be avoided by the unitary government is the extent of infrastructure investment to provide to service resource activities and remote populations. This affects the extent to which labor can be attracted to Petrolia and reflects a conscious decision about the speed and extent of resource development. How much of this infrastructure development should be financed by resource revenues themselves is also an important policy question.

The most difficult policy issue involves not how many productive factors of various kinds to devote to resource development, but how much infrastructure and other investments ought to be undertaken to attract other activities that might diversify Petrolia's industrial structure. This includes whether proactive policies should be undertaken to encourage upstream activities, such as refining and processing of the resources. More ambitiously, should public investments be made to diversify horizontally into related industries or, more ambitiously, to create such things as industrial parks and universities, whose presence might promote all sorts of industrial activity, including those of lasting value like manufacturing and high-tech industries. Economics offers little guidance as to the ideal allocation of industrial activity across regions and especially the extent to which resource-rich regions should be diversified industrially. Are there agglomeration effects that should be exploited? Should Petrolia be diversified just because it already has a lot of resource activity and presumably a critical mass of workers for a potentially thick labor market? Is Petrolia necessarily a good place to foster diversification, that is, is it a good growth node? Urban economic development specialists recognize that the agglomeration of labor and the diversification of activities within urban areas can serve as engines of economic growth because of spillovers among activities feeding off one another. Similar considerations might apply to regional development. Agglomeration economies might serve to boost economic development in regions that have previously stagnated. The question is, Where should such agglomeration growth nodes be encouraged? It is not at all clear that the location of valuable deposits of natural resource wealth should itself dictate the location of nodes for the development and growth of diversified economic activity. On the contrary, natural resources are often located in remote areas that have no otherwise natural advantages for economic development.

These are all difficult policy issues that even a unitary-national government must confront. Neither economics nor other relevant disciplines give unambiguous guidelines for policy, especially with respect to efficient agglomeration. Decisions about where to focus regional economic development initiatives cannot rely on the usual marginal analysis that economics often emphasizes. The process of economic development involves scale economies and potentially multiple equilibria, and there are no easy answers as to which one to choose. The point is that there are policy imperatives that arise from resource booms quite apart from those which are special to federations. Moreover, there is no presumption that a national government will have any monopoly on good policy judgment, even if it is benevolent.

NATURAL RESOURCE ISSUES IN A FEDERATION

As the preceding discussion indicates, even in a unitary nation many difficult policy issues must be addressed when different regions are endowed with widely differing amounts of natural resources. We have emphasized especially the adjustment to shocks in the value of the resources, but persistent differences in the value of resource endowments also require long-term policies. In adjusting to a resource shock, both efficiency and equity issues are involved in deciding not only the pace of exploration and development of the resource, the level and speed of adjustment of infrastructure spending that should accompany the resource boom, and the extent to which interregional and international migration to the regions should be encouraged but also the manner in which the system of taxes, transfers, social insurance, and public services should be changed in response to the various dislocations that will occur in all regions. Resolving these policy issues involves making some judgment about the expected future path of resource prices; how much diversification of activity should be encouraged in the resource-rich region; what weight should be given to the social and environmental costs of resource development; and, most difficult, how the fruits of the resource boom should be shared among residents of all regions and between present and future generations.

These same problems obviously also apply in a federation when one region benefits from a major resource boom. But the fact of decentralized fiscal decision making in a federation and the additional element of intergovernmental transfers add even more complications. In this section, we discuss the further issues that arise when the nation is a decentralized federation where subnational governments have significant amounts of policy and fiscal discretion. An important distinction now must be made between the two cases where natural resources are owned by the federal government and where they are owned by the subnational governments. In many federations, the truth is somewhere in between, with some shared jurisdiction for natural resources and its proceeds. Focusing on the two extreme cases will be sufficient for understanding the intermediate case.

Federal Ownership of Natural Resources

Consider first the case in which the federal government owns the resource revenues and obtains the direct revenues from them. Otherwise, the federation is a decentralized one in the sense that the states have authority to raise their own revenues from standard tax sources and are responsible for providing public services in their jurisdictions, including important ones like education, welfare services, and health care. As we discuss further in the next subsection, assuming away state ownership of natural resources removes an important dimension of problems associated with natural resource booms, that is, the large interstate fiscal disparities to which state resource ownership gives rise. Even in the absence of such concerns, various other issues arise in a federal context. State ownership of resources serves to exacerbate these problems. Along with an otherwise decentralized federation, we suppose that there is in place a set of federal-state transfers that serve all the standard purposes of such transfers discussed in earlier chapters. In this context, we imagine once again one of the states, Petrolia, owning a significant amount of oil and gas and benefiting from a shock in prices.

Even without resource revenues accruing to Petrolia, the economic impact of the oil and gas boom will generate significant fiscal capacity differences between it and other regions. Wage rates will be bid up, and per capita incomes will be higher in Petrolia than the national average. This will translate into a higher per capita revenue-raising capability in Petrolia than elsewhere. The federal-state fiscal transfer system will tend to mitigate these differences to the extent that it is equalizing, which we suppose to be the case. But unless the transfer system fully equalizes both the above- and below-average states, some fiscal disparities will remain. Indeed, in many equalization systems that are financed out of federal general revenues, below-average states will be brought up to some standard of fiscal capacity by federal-state transfers, but above-average states will not be brought down.

At the same time, there would also be changes in the need for state public services in Petrolia and the rest of the nation. Migration from other regions will cause increases in population in Petrolia and reductions elsewhere, and public services would have to adjust accordingly. However, because the migration would involve mainly younger, healthier working-age persons, the relative need for public services per capita would rise in some regions elsewhere (especially poorer ones) and fall in Petrolia. This would be offset to the extent that in-migrants to Petrolia locate in remote areas where the costs of providing public services are higher. In principle, a system of equalization could deal with these changes in the expenditure requirements as well as changes in revenue-raising capacities, but not all actual systems do so. They effectively assume that expenditure requirements are equal per capita, implying that demographic adjustments and cost of provision changes are not accounted for.

On balance, the shift in economic activity from the other regions to Petrolia would likely exacerbate differences in the ability of states to provide comparable levels of public services at comparable levels of taxation. As the fiscal federalism literature stresses and as we have discussed earlier, such differences can lead to both inefficiencies and inequities (Boadway and Flatters, 1982a, 1982b; Boadway, 2006b). Inefficiencies arise to the extent that persons and businesses are encouraged to migrate to take advantage of higher levels of public services at lower tax costs (higher net fiscal benefits). Of course, many other factors are likely to be drawing persons to Petrolia, such as the prospect of higher-paying jobs. Nonetheless, empirical evidence suggests that fiscal factors have some influence on migration decisions.[6] This is not to say that there should not be significant migration into Petrolia from elsewhere but, if there is, it should reflect productivity factors rather than purely fiscal ones.

The changes in fiscal capacity among states can be thought of as a passive consequence of the oil and gas boom in the sense that they arise even if state governments do not change their fiscal stances. However, states everywhere are not likely to stand pat in the wake of an oil and gas boom in Petrolia. State fiscal policies are not taken in isolation but reflect an awareness of the competition that exists for valuable mobile resources and businesses. Fiscal competition is generally taken to be one

---

[6] This issue has been studied in Canada, where interprovincial migration is significant. Empirical estimates of the effect of fiscal benefits on interprovincial migration can be found in Winer and Gauthier (1982), Day (1992), and Day and Winer (2006). The efficiency consequences of these responses are estimated in L. Wilson (2003) and suggest that the magnitude is relatively large.

of the healthy features of a federation. It enhances the efficiency and accountability with which states provide public services for their citizens and it encourages innovation. However, these benefits from fiscal competition presume that the states are on reasonably equal footings in their abilities to engage in fiscal competition. Where one state has a significant fiscal capacity advantage over the others (after equalization), the full benefit of fiscal competition can break down.

In the context of a major oil and gas boom in Petrolia, fiscal competition likely favors Petrolia with its much higher fiscal capacity, and the competition can take various forms. Fiscal measures might be taken to attract good workers to Petrolia, and other states might find it difficult to respond. By the same token, fiscal policies, using both tax policy and infrastructure, might be used to attract businesses to the state. Even in the absence of state-owned resource rents, Petrolia can be expected to engage in state-building activities that will attract industrial activity away from other regions. Given that the differential fiscal capacity benefit that Petrolia enjoys is a result of its endowment of oil and gas rather than some natural industrial advantage, the ability to use its superior fiscal capacity to engage in beggar-thy-neighbor industrial policies can lead to an inefficient pattern of industrial location. More generally, given that part of the costs of adjustment to resource development are borne by other regions, there may be an incentive for a single region to develop resources too rapidly.

Other sorts of inefficiencies can arise from decentralized decision making, such as nonharmonized tax-transfer systems, distortions in the internal economic union, and spillovers of benefits or costs of state expenditure programs. Most of these are not unique to natural resource booms. In the case of an oil and gas boom, some particular sources of interstate inefficiencies can be identified. One is that coordination among states is required to transport oil and gas across state boundaries. Another is that the heavy use of water and electricity in the process of extracting oil and natural gas from less accessible locations could affect the supply of water and electricity in neighboring states and territories. There could also be environmental spillovers across state boundaries.

From an economics perspective, a case can be made that the federal government has a role in addressing the inefficiencies and inequities resulting from an oil and gas boom in a particular state. This role could involve redistributive interstate transfers, the use of the federal spending power to influence state behavior via conditional grants, federal taxation and spending policies that might mute the consequences of inefficient state building, and serving as a coordinator to induce cooperative behavior among states.

It is clear, however, that the difference in fiscal capacities induced by a region-specific resource boom combined with the state-building policies that might emerge in a state like Petrolia will pose enormous challenges for conventional federal-state fiscal arrangements. These include the need to adjust public service levels across states and respond to fiscal capacity differences, as well as to mitigate the effects of the inevitable state-building tendencies in Petrolia. As we have argued, the expectation that Petrolia would use its fiscal capacity advantage in a proactive way to foster industrial development and diversification of the Petrolia economy would cause a reallocation of industry to Petrolia from other regions over and above that resulting from fiscal capacity differences and fiscally induced migration alone.

Standard arguments about the responsibilities of the federal government in an otherwise decentralized federation would justify federal policy concern about the consequences of a significant shift in industrial activity from other regions to Petrolia induced by differential fiscal capacities. Even though the states are responsible for providing important public services to their residents, the federal government does assume some responsibility for matters of national concern, including regional economic development and the need to ensure that citizens in all regions are provided with acceptable levels of public services.[7] What is not clear is how the federal government can adequately fulfill this responsibility. It cannot for example, restrain state-building development policies in one state that come at the expense of other states. As mentioned, standard systems of federal-state equalization are likely to be insufficient. Although they undo some of the most egregious fiscal capacity differences among states by making transfers to less-well-off states, they are typically unable to equalize high-fiscal capacity states down. Nor do equalization systems deal with adjustment problems or with the effect of state building in Petrolia on the other regions, especially those which are the least well-off. Some federal policy instruments are useful, such as the nationwide system of progressive taxation and social insurance. Moreover, in this setting where it obtains the public's share of resource rents, it has enough resources to pursue a national infrastructure strategy, although the details of how it should do so are not at all well developed. The federal government can continue to play an important role in facilitating the harmonization of state fiscal policies,

---

[7] In some countries, these responsibilities are spelled out in the constitution. In Canada, for example, the federal government is responsible along with the provinces for regional development, equality of opportunity, and ensuring that comparable levels of basic services are available to all citizens in the country.

as long as it maintains a dominant position in raising important types of tax revenues and assumes a major role in financing social programs delivered by the states. These responsibilities continue to be important national objectives independent of an oil and gas boom. But coordinated decision making in other areas, such as environmental policy, cross-border spillover issues with respect to water, and aboriginal policy, is also important.

State Ownership of Natural Resources

Consider now the additional problems that arise when natural resources are owned by subnational (state) governments. This is the case, for example, in Canada where significant disparities exist in provincial endowments of resources, particularly oil and gas. The possibility that natural resources might be owned by the states rather than the nation as a whole exacerbates the problem of dealing with a major resource boom concentrated in one state and makes it more difficult for federal fiscal policy to respond. In addition to all the policy challenges posed previously, state ownership of resource revenues leads to the following concerns.

First, the usual problems created by differential state fiscal capacities are greatly intensified. Revenues from oil and gas might significantly increase Petrolia's fiscal capacity relative to those of all other states, including those which might be more industrially advanced. Depending on how the system of federal-state equalizing transfers treated state natural resource revenues, these differentials may still be substantial after transfers. Equalization systems differ considerably in terms of how they treat the revenue-raising capacity of states. Even in the Canadian case where natural resource revenues have until recently been fully included in the calculation of provincial fiscal capacity, the equalization system does not come close to eliminating fiscal capacity differentials arising from oil and gas revenues because it is a gross system that redresses only the below-average fiscal capacities of the nonresource provinces. As a consequence, the major oil- and gas-producing province, Alberta, is left with a revenue-raising capacity twice as large as its nearest provincial rival after equalization.[8] In this system, in which revenues are treated as current additions to revenue-raising capacity, Alberta's ability to raise revenues per capita is of the order of twice that of Ontario. Even if the standard used to determine the level of equalization of the receiving provinces were to be increased significantly – and

---

[8] See the estimates provided in Expert Panel on Equalization and Territorial Formula Financing (2006: 8–9).

it is by no means clear that such an outcome is politically feasible or affordable by the federal government – Alberta would still be left with a considerably higher revenues-raising capacity than the national average. The result is a substantial source of horizontal imbalance arising from the subnational ownership of resources, and the same can apply in any federation for which this is the case. If these resource revenues are used by resource-rich states like Petrolia for current purposes, the purely fiscal incentive created for persons and businesses to migrate to Petrolia are substantial. Although there is some dispute over the relative magnitude of fiscally induced migration in federations, evidence in Canada suggests that interprovincial migration as a result of the current oil and gas boom is sizable.[9] Moreover, the demographics of migrants are bound to be relatively favorable to receiving states, which makes the horizontal imbalance more pronounced.

Related to these effects of the oil and gas boom on fiscal capacity disparities is the fact that, even under generous systems of federal-state equalization, the transfer system becomes strained. This is especially the case the more decentralized are revenue-raising responsibilities in areas other than natural resources. The greater the share of taxes raised by the states, the greater the degree of fiscal disparity in state revenue raising even without resource revenues, and the fewer the financial resources the federal government has to fulfill its equalization responsibilities. The affordability of the equalization system will become even more acute with the increase in disparities resulting from the oil and gas boom in Petrolia as well as possible lesser resource booms in other selected states. The affordability problem could be mitigated to the extent that the federal government could use its general taxing power to obtain a substantial share of revenues from natural resources. For example, to the extent that the corporate tax system is based on rents, the federal government could exploit that. However, for whatever reason, governments tend to favor natural resources in their business income tax systems, mainly by giving generous write-offs for exploration development and processing investments. In a context where the states own the natural resources, there may be additional reason for the federal government to be cautious with respect to its own desire to obtain a share of resource revenues. The affordability problem has been magnified by the fact that, for various reasons, the federal government has chosen not to exploit fully its ability

---

[9] Recent work on the long-run welfare consequences of fiscally induced migration in Canada suggests that it is quantitatively significant (L. Wilson, 2003).

to obtain resource revenues through the income tax system.[10] We return briefly to these issues in the final section.

With affordability being threatened, the sustainability of even a comprehensive gross equalization system becomes tenuous. Despite the importance of equalization as a federal policy instrument for dealing with fiscal inefficiencies and inequities arising from decentralization, its sustainability requires a nontrivial national consensus about the extent to which the nation constitutes a "sharing community." How much are residents in the nation as a whole willing to commit to ensuring that residents of all states can enjoy comparable levels of public services at comparable levels of taxation regardless of the source of disparities? To put it another way, how far does national social citizenship as opposed to state social citizenship extend? Does a nation define its sharing community primarily at the national level or at the state level?[11] These become open questions when disparities of fiscal capacity become wide.

Perhaps the most critical and compelling consequence of state resource ownership is the intensification of asymmetric fiscal competition among states. Petrolia clearly has the resources to engage in infrastructure and other forms of spending designed to diversify its economy and engage in state building, to a large extent at the expense of other states. Whether this state building constitutes efficient development is certainly questionable, because it is based not on any economic geography rationale but simply on the availability of resource revenues to finance state building. A priori, one might expect that state building is not efficient, because it is at the initiative of one state and based on its interests alone. However, other states are necessarily affected. How Petrolia might be persuaded to take account of other states' interests is not obvious because the federal government has limited ability to influence it. The issue is quite similar to that which has animated the debate about cities. Those who worry about neglecting the existing cities as potential sources of growth should doubly worry about too many resources being devoted to building up infrastructure in Petrolia simply because it has oil and gas revenues. No economic imperative

---

[10] As has been well documented for the Canadian case (Technical Committee on Business Taxation, 1998), the existing system of business taxes provides preferential treatment to the resource industries through its generous treatment of exploration and development expenses. In addition, federal revenue losses occur through the deductibility of provincial resource levies from the federal corporate tax base and, until recently, through the toleration of income trusts in the resource sector.

[11] The concept of social citizenship and the sharing community and their relevance for the fiscal arrangements are discussed in Banting and Boadway (2004).

suggests that the best place for economic development is where large amounts of oil and gas are located.

Of course, these effects arising from fiscally induced migration of economic activity and asymmetric fiscal competition are very much dependent on resource revenues being treated as general revenues and available for spending on infrastructure and economic development rather than being saved by the resource-rich state. To the extent that Petrolia were to go the Norwegian route, many of the problems resulting from state ownership of resource revenues would evaporate, although those arising from disparities per se would still abound.

The best response of the federal government to these problems is not clear. It is not feasible to meet the asymmetric capacities for state building simply by enhancing equalization because full net equalization is far from feasible. That is not to say that the treatment of resource disparities under equalization is not an important issue. But that alone is not sufficient to meet the challenge of responding to the possible inefficient consequences of state building that follow a significant resource boom. This all implies that the way in which the federal government deals with fiscal balance in light of the new reality is critical. The final section discusses the more modest issue of what feasible measures might be taken by the federal government to address the fiscal balance issue given the policy feasibilities that might exist in a decentralized federation. The more ambitious agenda of how the federation as a whole could respond to the possibility of regional resource booms probably requires cooperative action of both levels of government, which is a notoriously demanding requirement in a decentralized federation.

FEDERAL RESPONSES TO A NATURAL RESOURCE BOOM

In this final section, we step back and consider the broader issues of federal policy in the wake of a resource boom that causes major fiscal disparities among states in a federation. These disparities can be put into a broader context of fiscal imbalances in a federation. It is useful to distinguish two dimensions of fiscal imbalance, although the two are interdependent: horizontal and vertical. The concepts of fiscal imbalance are not precisely defined, but they nonetheless serve as a useful device for organizing one's thoughts about broader fiscal federalism policies.[12] Vertical fiscal

---

[12] A practical discussion of vertical and horizontal imbalance in a federation may be found in Boadway (2006a), on which this discussion draws. For an attempt to develop the concept more theoretically, see Boadway and Tremblay (2006).

imbalance arises because federal and state governments are simultaneously making decisions that affect one another. The federal government chooses how much revenue to raise, how much to spend, and what level of transfers to make to the states. The states make their own plans to raise revenues and provide public goods and services. Vertical fiscal imbalance arises if these two sets of decisions are not consistent with one another in a normative sense. That is, it arises if, given the expenditures that are in some sense ideal for the two levels of government, and given the way the tax room is shared by the two of them, the level of transfers is not adequate for the states to balance their budget. Whether or not there is a vertical fiscal imbalance depends on one's view about the ideal levels of spending at the federal and state levels of government as well as the appropriate division of revenue raising between them, and those are bound to be ambiguous. Even so, the idea of a vertical fiscal imbalance is conceptually an important one and has animated recent fiscal federalism debate in Canada, as an example. (See the Commission on Fiscal Imbalance, 2002, and the Advisory Panel on Fiscal Imbalance, 2006.)

The case of horizontal fiscal imbalance is less ambiguous but still somewhat judgmental. Horizontal fiscal imbalance exists if the different states in a federation have differing fiscal capacities or ability to provide comparable public goods and services at comparable tax rates. A precise definition would specify what levels and types of public goods and services and what forms of taxation should be included in the comparison, which is problematic given the very different choices states might themselves make. Moreover, it might be questionable whether all such differences should be eliminated in decentralized federations in which states are diverse in terms of geography, history, language, culture, or religion. Although these may preclude a precise definition of horizontal fiscal imbalance, most persons will agree that large variations in fiscal capacity constitute some degree of imbalance.

The debate over fiscal balance in a federation takes on heightened importance in light of the asymmetries resulting from the oil and gas boom in our hypothetical state of Petrolia. Both the horizontal and the vertical dimensions are then relevant in the sense that, for the federal government to deal with the large disparities in fiscal capacity through its equalization system, a rebalancing of revenues vertically would be necessary. In turn, measures taken to rebalance the federation vertically have consequences for the horizontal balance, and achieving horizontal balance necessarily implies some constraints on the direction and magnitude of vertical rebalancing. More generally, rebalancing has important implications for the efficiency and equity that can be achieved in the economic union of a diverse nation and will have longer-term effects on the evolution of the federation. The treatment of natural resources is at the heart of the fiscal balance debate. Despite the interdependency of the horizontal and vertical dimensions, it is useful to review the issues surrounding them sequentially.

Horizontal Balance with Natural Resource Disparities

As we have discussed, the consequences of a natural resource boom in Petrolia are first and foremost the creation of fiscal disparities among states. This will be true whether the ownership of resources resides with the states or with the federal government. In the case of Petrolia, the horizontal balance debate revolves around the extent to which state natural resource revenues should be equalized. To fully address the equity and efficiency concerns that disparities in resource revenues are likely to cause, one might argue for complete equalization of state resource-revenue capacity. Only then would the net fiscal benefit differences resulting from the resource boom be eliminated. Apart from detailed issues involved in designing such an equalization system, other concerns could be raised about fully equalizing resource revenues.[13]

The first concern is the property rights or constitutionality argument. It revolves around the inevitable conflict that arises between the state ownership of natural resources and the equalization of those resource revenues by a federal equalization scheme. The argument that state ownership of natural resources precludes full equalization of their revenues because equalization amounts to undoing that resource ownership is not fully persuasive on a couple of grounds. First, state ownership of tax revenues applies equally well to all its revenue sources and not just resources, and few would argue that this compromises the case for revenue equalization more generally. Moreover, equalization does not constitute taxation of resource revenues, although equalization transfers are conditioned on a state's ability to raise resource revenues. The federal government does, in fact, impose taxes directly on natural resources activities through its income and sales tax systems, and this imposition has not been ruled out by state ownership arguments.

---

[13] This issue has been much debated recently in Canada in connection with the oil and gas boom in Alberta. The pros and cons of equalizing natural resource revenues have been carefully set out in the Expert Panel on Equalization and Territorial Formula Financing (2006). For more detailed discussion of these points, see Boadway (2005a, 2005b, 2006a).

The second argument is that of affordability. It suggests that, because the federal government has no direct access to resource revenues (e.g., royalties, sale of leases), this makes fully equalizing them infeasible. The argument is that only a proportion of resource revenues should be equalized. There are two responses to this. The first is that the federal government does, as we have mentioned, have access to revenues generated by resources using conventional income and sales taxes. Indeed, it could, if it so chose, obtain significantly more revenues from resource industries than it does now by reforming the business tax system. As mentioned, few governments fully exploit the opportunity to tax resource rents through the corporation income tax system. Second, to the extent that affordability is an issue, it should be addressed by changing the standard to which equalization-receiving states are equalized rather than changing the proportion of resource revenues that are equalized. It is straightforward to show that changes in the standard entail equal per capita changes in entitlements for all states, so that the standard at least maintains horizontal balance among equalization-receiving states. Proportional reductions in resource equalization will work to the detriment of resource-poor states.

The third argument considers the consequences of equalizing natural resources when some of them are also situated in poorer states. The presumption is that if natural resources are to be equalized, the principle should apply to all such resources and not just those located in rich states like Petrolia. The argument is that full equalization of resource revenues discourages equalization-receiving states from developing their natural resources. This incentive problem is overstated. In federations where natural resources have been subject to equalization, such as Canada, there is no evidence that such equalization has had any effect on the rate at which resources are exploited by the states. Moreover, there are theoretical arguments against this incentive story. Once resources have been discovered, whatever equalization adjustment there is will occur whenever they are developed. There is thus no advantage in postponing development. Any disincentive that exists will apply at the stage of discovery and not development.

A fourth, and potentially serious, problem with equalizing natural resource revenues is the difficulty of measuring the revenue-raising capacity of particular resources. Different resource deposits will have different capacities for raising revenues given their different costs of extraction, and this variation makes the use of a representative-tax-system approach difficult. Some have argued on this account that actual revenues rather than revenue-raising potential might be a better basis for equalization (Expert Panel on Equalization and Territorial Formula Financing,

236 Designing Fiscal Constitutions

2006). The problem with using actual revenues is that they exacerbate incentive problems because actual revenues depend on tax rates chosen by the states. In these circumstances, the inclusion of only a portion of resources revenues in the formula is almost mandatory. A way of getting around the measurement issue that does not have drastic implications for incentives is to use a so-called stratification approach by which revenues are disaggregated into groups with more comparable revenue-raising capacities. This is done to some extent in the current equalization systems that use the RTS approach (e.g., Canada, Australia).

Finally, there is the argument put by Courchene (2004) that because it is costly for state governments to earn resource revenues – owing to the need to provide dedicated infrastructure and other business services – resource revenues should not be fully equalized. The problem with this argument is that it is a piecemeal approach that deviates arbitrarily from the principle of revenue equalization for particular revenue sources, and it ignores the fact that exploiting or developing many other revenue bases incurs costs. For example, the health and education systems certainly contribute to the size of the earnings capacity on which personal and corporate tax bases depend. It would therefore be discriminatory to treat natural resources differently on these grounds.

The upshot is that these objections to full equalization of resource revenues would lead to proposals that result in a system that arbitrarily and systematically harms states that are resource-poor. Not only does this fail to alleviate the major source of fiscal capacity differences among states; it also facilitates the role of natural resource endowments as a major determinant of economic development.

Dealing with Vertical Balance

Let us now cast our gaze somewhat broader and consider the issue of vertical fiscal imbalance, which becomes a concern in two sorts of circumstances. First, as federations become more and more decentralized, maintaining vertical balance is important. The gradual decentralization of federations is an ongoing phenomenon. The relative importance of the kind of public services provided by subnational governments, such as health care and education, is increasing, and the issue arises as to how much of the financing should come from provincial own-source revenues as opposed to those of the federal government. Second, federations are sometimes subject to shocks that affect the fiscal situation of the federal government and the states. Thus, if states are subject to shocks that lead to a sudden deficit situation, the issue is whether the federal transfer system should respond, and if so how. Similarly, if the federal government suffers a fiscal shock, it may choose rightly or wrongly to share that shock with the states. More generally, a vertical fiscal imbalance may have gradually built up over the years as a result of a federal fiscal system that was not appropriate for the evolving situation.

One way to approach the vertical imbalance issue is to ask what would be a suitable vertical balance in the long run. The issue of vertical balance boils down to the extent to which states should obtain their revenues from own-source taxes instead of from federal transfers. Suppose a federation is a representative one with a reasonable degree of decentralization. The states are responsible for a significant amount of expenditures in the provision of public services to their citizens and also have a significant amount of own-source revenue, including that from broad tax bases. At the same time, the federal government makes considerable transfers to the states, partly for equalization purposes and partly to maintain a harmonized system, of revenue and expenditure harmonization. Suppose also that the states are arguing for more fiscal autonomy and less reliance on federal transfers, in part to reduce their vulnerability to arbitrary federal changes in transfers and to reduce the extent to which the federal government can impose conditions on the transfers. Of course, the federal government likely argues against that. What, if any, changes in vertical balance ought to be made.

In essence, there are three options for approaching the vertical balance issue. One is to maintain the status quo, which entails keeping federal transfers to the states roughly as they are in proportion to state spending, while taking account of the fact that state spending is likely to continue rising disproportionately over time. The second is to turn over tax room to the states and at the same time reduce federal transfers to accede to state desire for more autonomy. The third is to do the opposite: increase the tax share of the federal government and with it the level of transfers. The second alternative is the one that is attractive from the states' point of view, at least those states that are not too dependent on the federal government. It may also be attractive if the federal government has used its transfer power in too intrusive and unpredictable a way in the past. Although the relationship with the natural resource issue is somewhat tenuous, it is worth outlining why this might not be a good idea. On the contrary, I suggest that the third alternative may be preferred.

There are three main arguments for turning over tax room to the states and making them more self-sufficient. The first one is accountability.

The argument is that states will be more accountable for their spending to the extent that they are required to raise their own revenues to finance it. The second is that turning over revenue-raising power to the states and reducing federal transfers, particularly in support of state social spending programs, will reduce the ability of the federal government to use transfers to influence state decision making. Not only would avoiding use of the spending power enable states to pursue their priorities in an unfettered way, but it would also avoid the kind of abrupt and unexpected changes in transfers to the states that might occur if the federal government suddenly faces some fiscal shock and reduces transfers dramatically. The final argument is that turning over tax room to the states might actually be a way of encouraging them to harmonize their taxes systems. For example, these arguments have been used in Canada to support the suggestion that the federal government should turn over some or all of its sales tax to the provinces, whose sales taxes are not well harmonized (Commission on Fiscal Imbalance, 2002; Poschmann and Tapp, 2005; Smart, 2005). Arguably, the harmonization of provincial sales taxes is the most important step that could be taken to improve the efficiency of the Canadian economic union and the competitiveness of Canadian industries.

There are, however, compelling counterarguments to further decentralization of revenue raising to the states. The accountability argument is not very convincing and really amounts to an argument of faith. There has been no good argument made as to why states should be more vigilant spending general revenues from their own sources than from federal transfers. Both are fungible once they are received. Moreover, accountability already exists for marginal increases in revenue because they must come from additional taxes raised in the state. Perhaps more important, in the case of broad-based taxes like the sales tax, states simply do not use tax rates, especially sales tax rates, to fine-tune their budgets. Instead, they essentially take as given whatever revenues come in at their given tax rates. Why they should treat those revenues differently from unconditional revenues received as transfers is not clear. If one took the accountability argument seriously, one would have to suppose that serious accountability problems also accompanied windfall revenues obtained from natural resources, and no one makes that argument.

Similarly, the argument that turning over tax points to the states facilitates tax harmonization by giving them more of a stake is highly wishful thinking. On the contrary, it almost certainly makes tax harmonization more difficult. Tax harmonization in the past has occurred only when federal governments have been dominant revenue raisers. Revenue sources that are concentrated at the state level are typically the most disharmonized in federations, resource taxes being among the most obvious. Moreover, when the federal government has vacated particular sorts of tax room to the states, the taxes have often become less harmonized. A case in point is the personal income tax in Canada. In the extreme, when the federal government turned over the inheritance tax to the provinces in Canada, it gradually disappeared. There is no particular reason to suppose that the states would unilaterally choose to increase the degree of harmonization of any of their major taxes in response to a reduction in federal tax rates. The advantages of harmonization have been well known to them for some time now, and they have chosen not to act.

Equally important, in the case of sales taxes where the value-added tax is now the dominant and preferred form, it is not clear that a harmonized VAT is administratively feasible in a federal system in which the states have real discretion over their own tax rates. The absence of border controls makes it very difficult to administer the credit and invoice procedure when taxes are different in all states. (See a more detailed discussion in Boadway, 2006b.) It is true that models exist by which decentralized value-added taxes could be implemented.[14] However, they have yet to be applied in any context, including the European Union. In Canada, it is true that the Quebec Sales Tax (QST) operates as a decentralized VAT harmonized with its federal counterpart. But it is not clear that extending the QST system to other provinces would be reasonable on administrative grounds. To put it differently, it may be feasible to run a decentralized and harmonized VAT system, but given its administrative costs, there is a preferred alternative discussed later that would avoid these administrative costs.

Another counterargument to the decentralization of tax room to the provinces is that greater fiscal disparities would be created among provinces and the pressure on the equalization system would increase. To maintain the existing structure of equalization, the size of the transfers would have to increase. Affordability concerns would become more intense, and the sustainability of equalization at its current level would be jeopardized. These concerns are particularly apt in a context where resource revenues are owned by the states.

Finally, a rebalancing of the federation that entailed less federal-state transfers would render the ability of the federal government to influence the states by attaching conditions to transfers – the spending power – less

[14] For some options, see Keen and Smith (2000), McLure (2000), and Bird and Gendron (2001).

effective. One can have different views about the role of the federal spending power, and one could certainly argue that it has the potential for being abused or used in noncooperative ways. Nonetheless, the federal spending power remains an important policy instrument. It is the only one that is available to the federal government to fulfill its legitimate policy interest in national efficiency and equity. Even if federal transfers were largely unconditional, the mere existence of significant federal-provincial transfers would give the federal government a meaningful seat at the intergovernmental interaction table and afford it some legitimacy in persuading states of the merits of coordination and harmonization of policies. But it also allows the federal government to engage in spending projects that foster national development, such as investment in infrastructure, human capital, and the cities. This might be useful for counterbalancing state-building policies by the states.

A Suggested Option

The preceding discussion argues against further decentralization of revenue raising to the states in a federation in which the states already have access to broad revenue sources. In other words, it argues against moves in the direction of reducing or eliminating the vertical fiscal gap. On the contrary, a strong case can be made that the most important objectives of the fiscal federation can be achieved by maintaining a strong federal presence in both the raising of revenues and the giving of transfers. It is fitting to end this chapter on a somewhat polemical note by arguing for a particular form of rebalancing of a federation in favor of enhancing federal revenue raising, although it goes somewhat against the recent emphasis on as much decentralization as possible as an objective of fiscal federalism. The option is designed with a federation like Canada or the United States in mind, where the states or provinces raise much of their revenues by sales and income taxes.

The preferred option would take the following form. The states would vacate the sales tax field completely and the federal government would take up the tax room with a new or enhanced national value-added tax. By definition, this would harmonize the sales tax system, thus achieving a sought-after source of efficiency improvement. The loss in state sales tax revenue would be made up with an explicit revenue-sharing agreement with respect to the national VAT revenue. (The exact sharing proportions need not be proposed here: it is the principle that is important.) The revenue-sharing component could be allocated among the states in a variety of ways, though the cleanest way might be an equal per capita allocation. By doing it that way, no further equalization would be required.

The consolidation of the VAT at the national level with its revenues shared at specified rates with the provinces is precisely the method that is used in Australia and in Germany. It is also similar to the system that is currently used for three of the provinces in Canada that participate in the harmonized sales tax system. The latter is a revenue-sharing scheme with the revenues being allocated to the three provinces using the derivation principle. In this case, the revenues then become provincial sources of revenue that are fully equalized, which makes them analogous to an equal per capita transfer. As argued, accountability is not sacrificed. The states obtain general revenues according to their share of the VAT revenues allocated to them, just as under a more decentralized system of revenue raising they obtain general revenues according to the state tax revenues that they receive. They have neither more nor less control over the revenues in either case. Such a rebalancing of the tax system would leave the system of federal-state transfers intact, including those which are used to support and influence state social program spending. There may still be some desire to reform the process by which such transfers are determined and changed so as to induce the federal government to use the spending power as responsibly and predictably as possible.

Of more immediate relevance, the rebalancing reforms suggested would not resolve the major issues arising from an oil and gas boom that we suppose occurs in Petrolia or those which might arise in other states in the future. The best that can be said is that the rebalancing would not exacerbate the problem. The main way of mitigating the consequences of the oil and gas boom involves actions that only Petrolia can take. In particular, to the extent that net state oil and gas revenues are placed in a dedicated savings fund and the capital is not drawn down, the main problems will not arise, where net refers to after costs of providing necessary business infrastructure to the resource industry. If a Norwegian-style savings fund were set up whereby *all* net state oil and gas revenues are deposited in it and the fund treated as a perpetuity whose capital income is available for current use, the problems would not arise. It seems unlikely that such a scenario will occur given the strong incentives that exist for state building or, more precisely, the lack of incentives for Petrolia to consider the consequences of its actions for other states. Perhaps that is all the more reason for the federal government to pursue its own infrastructure and human capital development strategy.

SIX

Local Governance in Theory

We will strive increasingly to quicken the public sense of civic duty, that thus . . .
we will transmit this city not only not less, but greater, better, and more beautiful
than it was transmitted to us.
– Oath of office required of council members in the ancient city of Athens

LOCAL GOVERNMENT AND LOCAL GOVERNANCE

Local government refers to specific institutions or entities created by national
constitutions (Brazil, Denmark, France, India, Italy, Japan, Sweden), by state
constitutions (Australia, the United States), by ordinary legislation of a higher
level of central government (New Zealand, the United Kingdom, most countries), by provincial or state legislation (Canada, Pakistan), or by executive
order (China) to deliver a range of specified services to a relatively small
geographically delineated area. *Local governance* is a broader concept and is
defined as the formulation and execution of collective action at the local
level. Thus, it encompasses the direct and indirect roles of formal institutions of local government and government hierarchies, as well as the roles
of informal norms, networks, community organizations, and neighborhood associations in pursuing collective action by defining the framework
for citizen-citizen and citizen-state interactions, collective decision making, and delivery of local public services.

Local governance, therefore, includes the diverse objectives of vibrant,
living, working, and environmentally preserved self-governing communities. Good local governance is not just about providing a range of local
services but also about preserving the life and liberty of residents,
creating space for democratic participation and civic dialogue, supporting
market-led and environmentally sustainable local development, and facilitating outcomes that enrich the quality of life of residents.

Although the concept of local governance is as old as the history of
humanity, only recently has it entered the broad discourse in the academic

and practice literature. Globalization and the information revolution are forcing a reexamination of citizen-state relations and roles and the relationships of various orders of government with entities beyond government – and thereby an enhanced focus on local governance. The concept, however, has yet to be embraced fully by the literature on development economics, because of the long-standing tradition in the development assistance community of focusing on either local governments or community organizations, while neglecting the overall institutional environment that facilitates or retards interconnectivity, cooperation, or competition among organizations, groups, norms, and networks that serve public interest at the local level.

Several writers (Bailey, 1999; Dollery and Wallis, 2001; Rhodes, 1997; Stoker, 1999) have argued that the presence of a vast network of entities beyond government that are engaged in local services delivery or quality-of-life issues makes it unrealistic to treat local government as a single entity (see also Goss, 2001). Analytical recognition of this broader concept of local governance is critical to developing a framework for local governance that is responsive (doing the right thing – delivering services that are consistent with citizens' preferences or are citizen focused), responsible (doing the right thing the right way – working better but costing less and benchmarking with the best), and accountable (to citizens, through a rights-based approach). Such analysis is important because the role of local government in such a setting contrasts sharply with its traditional role.

This chapter traces the evolution and analytical underpinnings of local governance as background to a better understanding of the comparative practices presented in Chapter 7. The next section outlines analytical approaches to local governance that can be helpful in understanding the role of governments and comparing and contrasting institutional arrangements. It further develops a model of local governance that integrates various strands of this literature. This model has important implications for evaluating and reforming local governance in both industrial and developing countries.

CONCEPTUAL PERSPECTIVES ON LOCAL GOVERNANCE AND CENTRAL-LOCAL RELATIONS

Principles and Theories

Several accepted theories provide a strong rationale for decentralized decision making and a strong role for local governments, on the grounds of efficiency, accountability, manageability, and autonomy.

Stigler (1957) identifies two principles of jurisdictional design: (1) the closer a representative government is to the people, the better it works; and (2) people should have the right to vote for the kind and amount of public services they want. These principles suggest that decision making should occur at the lowest level of government consistent with the goal of allocative efficiency and that order of government should have *home rule* – that is, complete autonomy in decision making on local services. Thus, the optimal size of jurisdiction varies with specific instances of economies of scale and benefit-cost spillovers.

The Principle of Fiscal Equivalency
A related idea on the design of jurisdictions has emerged from the public choice literature. Olson (1969) argues that if a political jurisdiction and benefit area overlap, the free-rider problem is overcome and the marginal benefit equals the marginal cost of production, thereby ensuring optimal provision of public services. Equating the political jurisdiction with the benefit area – the principle of fiscal equivalency – requires a separate jurisdiction for each public service.

The Correspondence Principle
A related concept is proposed by Oates (1972): the jurisdiction that determines the level of provision of each public good should include precisely the set of individuals who consume the good. This principle generally requires a large number of overlapping jurisdictions. Frey and Eichenberger (1995, 1996a, 1996b, 1999) have extended this idea to define the concept of functional, overlapping, and competing jurisdictions (FOCJ). They argue that jurisdictions could be organized along functional lines, while overlapping geographically, and that individuals and communities could be free to choose among competing jurisdictions. Individuals and communities express their preferences directly through initiatives and referenda. The jurisdictions have authority over their members and the power to raise taxes to fulfill their tasks. The school communities of the Swiss canton of Zurich and special districts in North America follow the FOCJ concept.

The Decentralization Theorem
According to this theorem, advanced by Oates (1972: 55), "each public service should be provided by the jurisdiction having control over the minimum geographic area that would internalize benefits and costs of such provision," because local governments understand the concerns of

local residents; local decision making is responsive to the people for whom the services are intended, thus encouraging fiscal responsibility and efficiency, especially if financing of services is also decentralized; unnecessary layers of jurisdiction are eliminated; and interjurisdictional competition and innovation are enhanced.

An ideal decentralized system ensures a level and combination of public services consistent with voters' preferences while providing incentives for the efficient provision of such services. Some degree of central control or compensatory grants may be warranted in the provision of services when spatial externalities, economies of scale, and administrative and compliance costs are taken into consideration. The practical implications of this theorem, again, require a large number of overlapping jurisdictions.

The Subsidiarity Principle

Taxing, spending, and regulatory functions should be exercised by lower levels of government unless a convincing case can be made for assigning them to higher levels of government. This principle evolved from the social teaching of the Roman Catholic Church and was first proposed by Pope Leo XIII in 1891. Subsequently, Pope Pius XI highlighted the principle of subsidiarity as a third way between dictatorship and a laissez-faire approach to governance. The Maastricht Treaty adopted it as a guiding principle for the assignment of responsibilities among members of the European Union (EU). This principle is the polar opposite of the *residuality principle* typically applied in a unitary country, where local governments are assigned functions that the central government is unwilling or thinks it is unable to perform.

Implementation Mechanisms

Achieving the optimal number and size of local jurisdictions requires the operation of community formation processes and the redrawing of jurisdictional boundaries.

- *Voting with feet.* According to Tiebout (1956), people consider tax costs and the public services menu offered by a jurisdiction in deciding where to live. Thus, voting with feet leads to the formation of jurisdictions, creating a market analogue for public service provision. Oates (1969) argued that if people vote with their feet, fiscal differentials across communities are capitalized into residential property values. This conclusion has been refuted by formal tests of allocative efficiency proposed by Brueckner (1982) and Shah (1988a, 1989a, 1992)). Both tests suggest that optimal provision of public services is not ensured by voting with feet alone but depends also on rational voting behavior.

- *Voting by ballot.* This line of research suggests that collective decision making may not ensure maximization of the electorate's welfare, because citizens and their governmental agents can have different goals.
- *Voluntary associations.* Buchanan (1965) postulates that the provision of public services through voluntary associations of people (clubs) ensures the formation of jurisdictions consistent with the optimal provision of public services.
- *Jurisdictional redesign.* An important process for community formation in modern societies is redrawing the boundaries of existing jurisdictions to create special or multipurpose jurisdictions.

Roles and Responsibilities of Local Governments: Analytical Underpinnings

There are five perspectives on models of government and the roles and responsibilities of local government: traditional fiscal federalism, new public management (NPM), public choice, new institutional economics (NIE), and network forms of local governance. The federalism and the NPM perspectives are concerned primarily with market failures and how to deliver public goods efficiently and equitably. The public choice and NIE perspectives are concerned with government failures. The network forms of governance perspective are concerned with institutional arrangements to overcome both market and government failures.

Local Government as a Handmaiden of a Higher Government Order: Traditional Fiscal Federalism Perspectives

The fiscal federalism approach treats local government as a subordinate tier in a multitiered system and outlines principles for defining the roles and responsibilities of orders of government (see Shah, 1994b, for such a framework for the design of fiscal constitutions). Hence, one sees that in most federations, as in Canada and the United States, local governments are extensions of state governments (*dual federalism*). In a few isolated instances, as in Brazil and South Africa, they are equal partners with higher-level governments (*cooperative federalism*), and in an exceptional case, Switzerland, they are the main source of sovereignty and have greater constitutional significance than the federal government. Thus, depending on the constitutional and legal status of local governments, state governments in federal countries assume varying degrees of oversight of the provision of local public services. In a unitary state, subnational governments act on behalf of the central government. Therefore, a useful set of guidelines for the assignment of responsibilities for local public services in a unitary state would be that policy development and standards of service and performance are determined at the national level, implementation oversight is carried out at the state or provincial level, and services are provided by the local governments or by the metropolitan or regional governments.

In all countries, the production of services can be public or private, at the discretion of local or regional governments. Responsibilities for public services other than such purely local ones as fire protection could be shared, using these guidelines.

The assignment of public services to local governments or to metropolitan or regional governments can be based on considerations such as economies of scale, economies of scope (appropriate bundling of local public services to improve efficiency through information and coordination of economies and enhanced accountability through voter participation and cost recovery) and cost-benefit spillovers, proximity to beneficiaries, consumer preferences, and budgetary choices about the composition of spending. The particular level of government to which a service is assigned determines the public or private production of the service in accordance with considerations of efficiency and equity. Large metropolitan areas with populations in excess of 1 million could be considered for subdivision into a first tier of municipal governments of smaller size responsible for neighborhood-type services and a second tier of metropolitan-wide government providing areawide services. The first-tier governments could be directly elected, and elected mayors of these governments could form the metropolitan council at the second tier. Two-tier structures for metropolitan governance have been practiced in Melbourne, Australia; Vancouver, Canada; Allegheny County, Pennsylvania, United States; and Stockholm, Sweden.

In industrial countries, special-purpose agencies or bodies deliver a wide range of metropolitan and regional public services, including education, health, planning, recreation, and environmental protection. Such bodies can include library boards; transit and police commissions; and utilities providing water, gas, and electricity. These agencies deal with public services whose delivery areas transcend political jurisdictions and are better financed by loans, user charges, and earmarked benefit taxes, such as a supplementary mill rate on a property tax base to finance a local school board. If kept to a minimum, such agencies help fully exploit economies of scale in the delivery of services where political boundaries are not consistent with service areas. A proliferation of these agencies can undermine accountability and budgetary flexibility at local levels. Accountability and responsiveness to voters are weakened if members of special-purpose bodies are appointed rather than elected. Budgetary flexibility is diminished if a majority of local expenditures fall outside the control of local councils.

Table 6.1 provides a subjective assessment of how various allocative criteria favor local or metropolitan assignment and whether public or private production is favored for efficiency or equity. The criteria and the assessment presented in this table are arbitrary; practical and institutional considerations should be applied to this analysis, and the reader may well reach different conclusions using the same criteria.

Private-sector participation can also take a variety of forms, including contracting through competitive biddings, franchise operations (local government acting as a regulatory agency), grants (usually for recreational and cultural activities), vouchers (redeemable by local government with private providers), volunteers (mostly in fire stations and hospitals), community self-help activities (for crime prevention), and private nonprofit organizations (for social services). Thus, a mix of delivery systems is appropriate for local public services. In most developing countries, the financial capacities of local governments are quite limited. Fostering private-sector participation in the delivery of local public services thus assumes greater significance. Such participation enhances accountability and choice in the local public sector. However, assigning responsibility for the provision of service to a specific level of government does not imply that government should be directly engaged in its production. Limited empirical evidence suggests that private production of some services promotes efficiency and equity.

Fiscal federalism literature also provides guidance on financing choices for local governments. Four general principles require consideration in assigning taxing powers to various governments. First, the *economic efficiency* criterion dictates that taxes on mobile factors and tradable goods that have a bearing on the efficiency of the internal common market should be assigned to the center. Subnational assignment of taxes on mobile factors may facilitate the use of socially wasteful beggar-thy-neighbor policies by regional and local governments to attract resources to their

Table 6.1. *Assignment of local public services to municipal and regional or metropolitan governments*

Public service	Allocation criteria for provision							Allocation criteria for public versus private production		
	Economies of scale	Economies of scope	Benefit-cost spillovers	Political proximity	Consumer sovereignty	Economic evaluation of sectoral choices	Composite	Efficiency	Equity	Composite
Firefighting	L	L	L	L	L	M	L	P	G	P
Police protection	L	L	L	L	L	M	L	P	G	G
Refuse collection	L	L	L	L	L	M	L	P	P	P
Neighborhood parks	L	L	L	L	L	M	L	P	G	G
Street maintenance	L	L	L	L	L	M	L	P	P	P
Traffic management	L	M	L	L	L	M	L	P	P	P
Local transit service	L	M	L	L	L	M	L	P	P	P
Local libraries	L	L	L	L	L	M	L	G	G	G
Primary education	L	L	M	M	L	M	M	P	G	P,G
Secondary education	L	L	M	M	L	M	M	P	G	P,G
Public transportation	M	M	M	L,M	M	M	M	P,G	G	P,G
Water supply	M	M	M	L,M	M	M	M	P	G	P,G

(continued)

Table 6.1 (*continued*)

| Public service | Allocation criteria for provision | | | | | | | | Allocation criteria for public versus private production | |
	Economies of scale	Economies of scope	Benefit-cost spillovers	Political proximity	Consumer sovereignty	Economic evaluation of sectoral choices	Composite	Efficiency	Equity	Composite
Sewage disposal	M	M	M	M	M	M	M	P,G	P,G	P,G
Refuse disposal	M	M	M	M	M	M	M	P	P	P
Public health	M	M	M	M	M	M	M	G	G	G
Hospitals	M	M	M	M	M	M	M	P,G	G	P,G
Electric power	M	M	M	M	M	M	M	P	P	P
Air and water pollution	M	M	M	M	M	M	M	G	G	G
Special police	M	M	M	M	M	M	M	G	G	G
Regional parks	M	M	M	L,M	M	M	M	G	G	G
Regional planning	M	M	M	L,M	M	M	M	G	G	G

Note: L = local government, M = regional or metropolitan government, P = private sector, G = public sector.

Source: Shah (1994b).

250

own areas. In a globalized world, even central assignment of taxes on mobile capital may not be very effective in the presence of tax havens and the difficulty of tracing and attributing incomes from virtual transactions to various physical spaces. Second, *national equity* considerations warrant that progressive redistributive taxes should be assigned to the center, which limits the possibility of regional and local governments following perverse redistribution policies using both taxes and transfers to attract high-income people and repel low-income ones. Doing so, however, leaves open the possibility of supplementary, flat-rate, local charges on residence-based national income taxes. Third, the *administrative feasibility* criterion (lowering compliance and administration costs) suggests that taxes should be assigned to the jurisdiction with the best ability to monitor relevant assessments. This criterion minimizes administrative costs as well as the potential for tax evasion. For example, property, land, and betterment taxes are good candidates for local assignment because local governments are in a better position to assess the market values of such assets. Fourth, the *fiscal need* or *revenue adequacy* criterion suggests that to ensure accountability, revenue means (the ability to raise revenues from own sources) should be matched as closely as possible with expenditure needs. The literature also argues that long-lived assets should primarily be financed by raising debt, so as to ensure equitable burden sharing across generations (Inman, 2006). Furthermore, such large and lumpy investments typically cannot be financed by current revenues and reserves alone (see Box 6.1).

These four principles suggest that user charges are suitable for use by all orders of government, but the case for decentralizing taxing powers is not as compelling as that for decentralizing public service delivery. This is because lower-level taxes can introduce inefficiencies in the allocation of resources across the federation and cause inequities among people in different jurisdictions. In addition, collection and compliance costs can increase significantly. These problems are more severe for some taxes than others, so the selection of which taxes to decentralize must be made with care, balancing the need to achieve fiscal and political accountability at the lower levels of government against the disadvantages of having a fragmented tax system. The trade-off between increased accountability and increased economic costs from decentralizing taxing responsibilities can be mitigated by fiscal arrangements that permit joint occupation and harmonization of taxes to overcome fragmentation and by fiscal equalization transfers that will reduce the fiscal inefficiencies and inequities that arise from different fiscal capacities across regional and local jurisdictions.

Box 6.1. Key Considerations and Tools for Local Government Finances

Key Considerations

The overall objective of local governments is to maximize social outcomes for residents and provide an enabling environment for private-sector development through efficient provision of public services. This requires that local financing should take into account the following considerations:

- Local government should limit self-financing of redistributive services.
- Business should be taxed only for services to businesses and not for redistributive purposes.
- Current-period services should be financed out of current-year operating revenues and future-period services should be financed by future-period taxes, user charges/fees, and borrowing.
- Residential services should be financed by taxes and fees on residents.
- Business services should be financed on site/land value taxes and user charges. Profit, output, sales, and movable asset taxes may drive business out of the jurisdiction.

Tools for Local Finance

- *Local taxes* are for services with public goods characteristics – streets, roads, street lighting.
- *User charges* are for services with private goods characteristics – water, sewerage, solid waste.
- *Conditional, nonmatching, output-based grants* are from national- or state-order governments for merit goods: education and health.
- *Conditional matching grants* are for spillovers in some services.
- *Unconditional grants* are for fiscal gap and equalization purposes.
- *Capital grants* are for infrastructure if fiscal capacity is low.
- *Capital market finance* is for infrastructure if fiscal capacity is high.
- *Development charges* are for financing growth with higher charges for developing land on local government boundaries.
- *Public-private partnerships* are for infrastructure finance but keeping public ownership and control of strategic assets.

- *Tax increment financing districts* are to deal with urban blight. For
  this purpose, the area should be designated for redevelopment and
  annual property tax revenues frozen at previtalization levels. For a
  specified period, say fifteen to thirty-five years, all tax revenues
  above base are used for redevelopment. Capacity improvements
  are undertaken through municipal borrowing or bonds against
  expected tax increments.

Source: Inman (2006); Shah and Shah (2006).

The fiscal federalism perspectives presented previously are helpful, but
in practice they have resulted in some major difficulties – especially in
developing countries – because the practice seems to emphasize fiscal
federalism's structures and processes as ends rather than as means to an
end. These structures and processes were designed as a response to market
failures and heterogeneous preferences, with little recognition of government failures or the role of entities beyond government. The NPM and the
NIE literature (synthesized in the following paragraphs) sheds further light
on the origins of these difficulties. This literature highlights the sources of
government failures and their implications for the role of local government.

Local Government as an Independent Facilitator of Creating
Public Value: New Public Management Perspectives
Two interrelated criteria have emerged from the NPM literature in recent
years: determining what local governments should do, and how they
should do it better.

In discussing the first criterion, the literature assumes that citizens are
the principals but have multiple roles as governors (owner-authorizers,
voters, taxpayers, community members); activist-producers (providers of
services, coproducers, self-helpers obliging others to act); and consumers
(clients and beneficiaries) (see Moore, 1996). In this context, significant
emphasis is placed on the government as an agent of the people to serve
public interest and create public value. Moore (1996) defines public value
as measurable improvements in social outcomes or quality of life. This
concept is directly relevant to local and municipal services, for which it is
feasible to measure such improvements and have some sense of attribu-
tion. The concept is useful in evaluating conflicting and perplexing choices
in the use of local resources. The concept is also helpful in defining the role
of government, especially local governments. It frames the debate between
those who argue that the public sector crowds out private-sector investments and those who argue that the public sector creates an enabling

environment for the private sector to succeed, in addition to providing basic municipal and social services.

Moore (1996) has argued that, rather than diverting resources from the private sector, local governments use some of the resources that come as free goods – namely, resources of consent, goodwill, Good Samaritan values, community spirit, compliance, and collective public action. This argument suggests that the role of public managers in local governments is to tap these free resources and push the frontiers of improved social outcomes beyond what may be possible with meager local revenues. Thus, public managers create value by mobilizing and facilitating a network of providers beyond local government. Democratic accountability ensures that managerial choices about creating public value are based on broader consensus by local residents (see Goss, 2001). Thus, the local public sector continuously strives to respect citizen preferences and to be accountable to them. This environment, focused on creating public value, encourages innovation and experimentation, bounded by the risk tolerance of the median voter in each community.

The main current of the NPM literature, however, is concerned not with what to do but with how to do it better. It argues for an incentive environment in which managers are given flexibility in the use of resources but held accountable for results. Top-down controls are thus replaced by a bottom-up focus on results. Two NPM models have been implemented in recent years. The first model is focused on making managers manage. In New Zealand, this goal is accomplished through new contractualism, whereby public managers are bound by formal contracts for service delivery but have flexibility in resource allocation and choice of public or private providers. Malaysia attempts to achieve the same through client charters, under which public managers are evaluated for their attainment of specified service standards (Shah, 2005c).

The second model creates incentives to let managers manage. It applies the new managerialism approach, as used in Australia and the United States, whereby government performance in service delivery and social outcomes is monitored, but there are no formal contracts, and accountability is guided by informal agreements. In China and the United Kingdom, autonomous agency models are used for performance accountability. Canada uses an alternative service delivery framework: public managers are encouraged to facilitate a network of service providers and to use benchmarking to achieve the most effective use of public moneys. The emerging focus on client orientation and results-based accountability is encouraging local governments to innovate in many parts of the world (Caulfield, 2003).

Local Government as an Institution to Advance Self-Interest:
The Public Choice Approach
Bailey (1999) has conceptualized four models of local government:

- A local government that assumes it knows best and acts to maximize the welfare of its residents conforms to the *benevolent despot* model.
- A local government that provides services consistent with local residents' willingness to pay conforms to the *fiscal exchange* model.
- A local government that focuses on public service provision to advance social objectives conforms to the *fiscal transfer* model.
- A local government that is captured by self-interested bureaucrats and politicians conforms to the *Leviathan* model, which is consistent with the public choice perspectives.

In the same tradition, Breton (1995) provides a comprehensive typology of models of government. He distinguishes two broad types of government. The first embodies the doctrine of the common good, and the second acts to preserve the self-interest of the governing elites. The second type can assume either a monolithic or a composite structure. In a monolithic structure, local government is subject to capture by bureaucrats or interest groups. Also, local government may maximize economic rents for dominant interest groups (as in the Leviathan model) or may advance compulsion or coercion. If the self-interest model assumes a composite structure, it may encourage Tiebout-type competition among local governments.

The public choice literature endorses the self-interest doctrine of government and argues that various stakeholders involved in policy formulation and implementation are expected to use opportunities and resources to advance their self-interest. This view has important implications for the design of local government institutions. For local governments to serve the interests of people, they must have complete local autonomy in taxing and spending and be subject to competition within and beyond government. In the absence of these prerequisites, local governments will be inefficient and unresponsive to citizen preferences (Boyne, 1998). Bailey (1999) advocates strengthening exit and voice mechanisms in local governance to overcome government failures associated with the self-interest doctrine of public choice. He suggests that easing supply-side constraints for public services through wider competition will enhance choice and promote exit options and that direct democracy provisions will strengthen voice (see also Dollery and Wallis, 2001). The NIE approach discussed later draws on the implications of opportunistic behavior by government agents for the transaction costs to citizens as principals.

The Government as a Runaway Train: NIE Concerns with the Institutions of Public Governance

The NIE provides a framework for analyzing fiscal systems and local empowerment and for comparing mechanisms for local governance. This framework is helpful in designing multiple orders of government and in clarifying local government responsibilities in a broader framework of local governance. According to the NIE framework, various orders of governments (as agents) are created to serve the interests of the citizens as principals. The jurisdictional design should ensure that these agents serve the public interest while minimizing transaction costs for the principals.

The existing institutional framework does not permit such optimization, because the principals have bounded rationality; that is, they make the best choices on the basis of the information at hand but are ill informed about government operations. Enlarging the sphere of their knowledge entails high transaction costs, which citizens are not willing to incur. Those costs include participation and monitoring costs, legislative costs, executive decision-making costs, agency costs or costs incurred to induce compliance by agents with the compact, and uncertainty costs associated with unstable political regimes (Horn, 1997; Shah, 2005a). Agents (various orders of governments) are better informed about government operations than principals are, but they have an incentive to withhold information and to indulge in opportunistic behaviors or "self-interest seeking with guile" (Williamson, 1985: 7). Thus, the principals have only incomplete contracts with their agents. Such an environment fosters commitment problems because the agents may not follow the compact.

The situation is further complicated by three factors – weak or extant countervailing institutions, path dependency, and the interdependency of various actions. Countervailing institutions such as the judiciary, police, parliament, and citizen activist groups are usually weak and unable to restrain rent seeking by politicians and bureaucrats. Historical and cultural factors and mental models by which people see little benefits to and high costs of activism prevent corrective action. Furthermore, empowering local councils to take action on behalf of citizens often leads to loss of agency between voters and councils, because council members may interfere in executive decision making or may get co-opted in such operations while shirking their legislative responsibilities. The NIE framework stresses the need to use various elements of transaction costs in designing jurisdictions

for various services and in evaluating choices between competing governance mechanisms.

Local Government as a Facilitator of Network Forms of Local Governance

The NIE approach provides an evaluation framework for alternative forms
and mechanisms of local governance. It specifically provides guidance in
dealing with government failures in a hierarchical form of public governance. The framework is also suitable for examining local government
involvement in a partnership of multiple organizations. Dollery and Wallis
(2001) extend the NIE approach to these issues. They argue that a structure
of resource dependency vitiates against collective action in the interest of
the common good because of the tragedy of commons associated with
common pool resources. This scenario results in failures in horizontal
coordination in a multiorganization partnership.

One possible solution is to introduce a market mechanism of governance, whereby a contract management agency enters into binding contracts with all partners. However, this solution is unworkable because the
potential number of contingencies may simply be too large to be covered
by such contracts. A second approach to overcome horizontal coordination, the so-called hierarchical mechanism of governance, relies on institutional arrangements to clarify roles and responsibilities and to establish
mechanisms for consultation, cooperation, and coordination, as is done in
some federal systems. Such institutional arrangements entail high transaction costs and are subject to a high degree of failure attributable to the
conflicting interests of partners.

Given the high transaction costs and perceived infeasibility of market
and hierarchical mechanisms of governance for partnerships of multiple
organizations, a network mechanism of governance has been advanced as a
possible mode of governance for such partnerships – the kind to be managed by local governments. The network form of governance relies on
trust, loyalty, and reciprocity between partners with no formal institutional
safeguards. Networks formed on the basis of shared interests (interest-
based networks) can provide a stable form of governance if membership
is limited to partners that can make significant resource contributions and
if there is a balance of powers among members. Members of such networks
interact frequently and see cooperation in one area as contingent on cooperation in other areas. Repeated interaction among members builds trust.
Hope-based networks are built on the shared sentiments and emotions of
members. Members have shared beliefs in the worth and philosophy of the

network goals and have the passion and commitment to achieve those goals. The stability of such networks is highly dependent on the commitment and style of their leadership (Dollery and Wallis, 2001).

Local government has an opportunity to play a catalytic role in facilitating the roles of both interest-based and hope-based networks in improving social outcomes for local residents. To play such a role, local government must develop a strategic vision of how such partnerships can be formed and sustained. But then the local government requires a new local public management paradigm. Such a paradigm demands that local government separate policy advice from program implementation and assume a role as a purchaser of public services but not necessarily as a provider of them. Local government may have to outsource services with higher provision costs and subject in-house providers to competitive pressures from outside providers to lower transaction costs for citizens. It also must actively seek the engagement of both interest-based and hope-based networks to supplant local services. It needs to develop the capacity to play a mediating role among various groups.

A Synthesis: Toward a Framework for Responsive, Responsible, and Accountable Local Governance

We have reviewed ideas emerging from the literature on political science, economics, public administration, law, federalism, and the NIE with a view to developing an integrated analytical framework for the comparative analysis of local government and local governance institutions.

The dominant concern in this literature is that the incentives and accountability framework faced by various orders of government is not conducive to a focus on service delivery consistent with citizen preferences. As a result, corruption, waste, and inefficiencies permeate public governance. Top-down hierarchical controls are ineffective; there is little accountability because citizens are not empowered to hold governments accountable.

Fiscal federalism practices around the world are focused on structures and processes, with little regard for outputs and outcomes. These practices support top-down structures with preeminent federal legislation (i.e., federal legislation overrides any subnational legislation). The central government is at the apex, exercising direct control and micromanaging the system. Hierarchical controls exercised by various layers of government have an internal rule-based focus with little concern for their mandates. Government competencies are determined on the basis of technical and administrative capacity, with almost no regard for client orientation, bottom-up accountability, and lowering of transaction costs for citizens. Various orders of government indulge in uncooperative zero-sum games for control.

This tug of war leads to large swings in the balance of powers. Shared rule is a source of much confusion and conflict, especially in federal systems. Local governments are typically handmaidens of states or provinces and given straitjacket mandates. They are given only limited home rule in their competencies. In short, local governments in this system of "federalism for the governments, by the governments, and of the governments" get crushed under a regime of intrusive controls by higher levels of governments. Citizens also have limited voice and exit options.

The governance implications of such a system are quite obvious. Various orders of government suffer from agency problems associated with incomplete contracts and undefined property rights, as the assignment of taxing, spending, and regulatory powers remains to be clarified – especially in areas of shared rule. Intergovernmental bargaining leads to high transaction costs for citizens. Universalism and pork-barrel politics result in a tragedy of commons, as various orders of government compete to claim a higher share of common pool resources. Under this system of governance, citizens are treated as agents rather than as principals.

On how to reverse this trend and make governments responsive and accountable to citizens, the dominant themes emphasized in the literature are the subsidiarity principle, the principle of fiscal equivalency, the creation of public value, results-based accountability, and the minimization of transaction costs for citizens, as discussed earlier. These themes are useful but should be integrated into a broader framework of citizen-centered governance, to create an incentive environment in the public sector that is compatible with a public-sector focus on service delivery and bottom-up accountability. Such integration is expected to deal with the commitment problem in various levels of government by empowering citizens and by limiting their agents' ability to indulge in opportunistic behavior.

Reforming the institutions of *citizen-centered local governance* requires agreement on basic principles (Table 6.2). Three basic principles are advanced to initiate such a discussion:

- *Responsive governance.* This principle aims for governments to do the right things – that is, to deliver services consistent with citizen preferences.

- *Responsible governance.* The government should also do it right – that is, manage its fiscal resources prudently. It should earn the trust of residents by working better and costing less and by managing fiscal

Table 6.2. *Key elements of citizen-centered governance*

Responsive governance	Responsible governance	Accountable governance
Has subsidiarity and home rule	Follows due process:	Lets the sunshine in:
Has direct democracy provisions	• Principle of *ultra vires* or general competence or community governance	• Local government bylaw on citizens' right to know
Has budget priorities consistent with citizens' preferences	• Procedure bylaw • Local master plans and budgets • Zoning bylaws and regulations • Funded mandates	• Budgetary proposals and annual performance reports posted on the Internet
Specifies and meets standards for access to local services	Is fiscally prudent:	• All decisions, including the costs of concessions, posted on the Internet
Improves social outcomes	• Balanced operating budget • Golden rule for borrowing	• Value for money performance audits by independent think tanks
Offers security of life and property	• New capital projects specifying upkeep costs and debt repayment	• Open information and public assessment
Offers shelter and food for all	• Fiscal rules to ensure sustainable debt levels	Works to strengthen citizen voice and exit:
Has clean air, safe water, and sanitation	• Major capital projects that are subject to referenda	• Citizens' charter
Has a noise-free and preserved environment	• Maintenance of positive net worth	• Service standards
Offers ease of commuting and pothole-free roads	• Commercially audited financial statements	• Requirements for citizens' voice and choice
Has primary school at a walking distance	Earns trust:	• Sunshine rights
Has acceptable fire and ambulance response times	• Professionalism and integrity of staff • Safeguards against malfeasance	• Sunset clauses on government programs
Has libraries and Internet access	• Streamlined processes and e-governance	• Equity- and output-based intergovernmental finance
Has park and recreation programs and facilities	• Complaints and feedback acted on • Honest and fair tax administration	• Citizen-oriented performance (output) budgeting
	• Strict compliance with service standards	• Service delivery outputs and costs

(continued)

Responsive governance	Responsible governance	Accountable governance
	• Citizen-friendly ouput budgets and service delivery performance reports	• Citizens' report card on service delivery performance
	• Participatory budgeting and planning	• Budget, contracts, and performance reports defended at open town hall meetings
	Works better, costs less:	
	• All tasks subjected to service delivery test – competitive provision involving government providers and entities beyond government	• All documents subjected to citizen-friendly requirements
	• Financing that creates incentives for competition and innovation	• Open processes for contract bids
	• Comparative evaluation of service providers	• Mandatory referenda on large projects
	• Public sector as a purchaser through performance contracts but not necessarily a provider of services	• Steps taken so that at least 50 percent of eligible voters vote
	• Managerial flexibility, but accountability for results	• Citizens' boards to provide scorecard and feedback on service delivery performance
	• No lifelong or rotating appointments	• Provisions for popular initiatives and recall of public officials
	• Task specialization	• Bylaw on taxpayer rights
	• Budgetary allocation and output-based performance contracts	
	• Activity-based costing	
	• Charges for capital use	
	• Accrual accounting	
	• Benchmarking with the best	
	• Public scrutiny of general administration costs	
	• Boundaries that balance benefits and costs of scale and scope economies, externalities, and decision making	
	• Boundaries consistent with fiscal sustainability	

Source: Shah and S. Shah (2006); Shah and F. Shah (2007).

and social risks for the community. It should strive to improve the quality and quantity of and access to public services. To do so, it needs to benchmark its performance with the best-performing local government.

- *Accountable governance.* A local government should be accountable to its electorate. It should adhere to appropriate safeguards to ensure that it serves the public interest with integrity. Legal and institutional reforms may be needed to enable local governments to deal with accountability between elections – reforms such as a citizens' charter and a provision for recall of public officials.

A framework of local governance that embodies these principles is called *citizen-centered governance* (Andrews and Shah, 2005a, 2005b). The distinguishing features of citizen-centered governance are citizen empowerment through a rights-based approach (direct democracy provisions, citizens' charter); bottom-up accountability for results; evaluation of government performance as the facilitator of a network of providers by citizens as governors, taxpayers, and consumers of public services.

The framework emphasizes reforms that strengthen the role of citizens as the principals and create incentives for government agents to comply with their mandates (Table 6.2).

The commitment problem may be mitigated by creating citizen-centered local governance – by having direct democracy provisions, introducing governing for results in government operations, and reforming the structure of governance, thus shifting decision making closer to the people. Direct democracy provisions require referenda on major issues and large projects and require that citizens have the right to veto any legislation or government program. A "governing for results" framework requires government accountability to citizens for service delivery performance. Hence, citizens have a charter defining their basic rights as well as their rights of access to specific standards of public services. Output-based intergovernmental transfers strengthen compliance with such standards and strengthen accountability and citizen empowerment (Shah 2006c).

Implications for Division of Powers within Nations: Role Reversals for Central and Local Governments

The framework described previously has important implications for reforming the structure of government. Top-down mandates on local governance will need to be replaced by bottom-up compacts. Furthermore, the role of local government must be expanded to serve as a catalyst for the formulation, development, and operation of a network of both government providers and entities beyond government. Local government's traditionally acknowledged technical capacity becomes less relevant in this framework. More important are its institutional strengths as a purchaser of services and as a facilitator of alliances, partnerships, associations, clubs, and networks for developing social capital and improving social outcomes. Two distinct options are possible in this regard, and both imply a pivotal role for local governments in the intergovernmental system: local government as the primary agent, subcontracting to authorities in local, state, and federal or central governments and engaging networks and entities beyond government; and local, state, and national governments as independent agents.

Option A: Local Governments as Primary Agents of Citizens. In this role, a local government serves as a purchaser of local services, a facilitator of networks of government providers and entities beyond government, and a gatekeeper and overseer of state and national governments for the shared rule or responsibilities delegated to them. This role represents a fundamental shift in the division of powers from higher to local governments. It has important constitutional implications. Residual functions reside with local governments. State governments perform intermunicipal services. The national government is assigned redistributive, security, foreign relations, and interstate functions such as harmonization and consensus on a common framework. The Swiss system bears close affinity to this model.

Option B: Various Orders of Government as Independent Agents. An alternative framework for establishing the supremacy of the principals is to clarify the responsibilities and functions of various orders as independent agents. This framework limits shared rule. Finance follows function strictly, and fiscal arrangements are periodically reviewed for fine-tuning. Local governments enjoy home rule, with complete tax and expenditure autonomy. The Brazilian fiscal constitution incorporates some features of this model, albeit with significant deviations.

Feasibility of Options. Option A is well grounded in the history of modern governments and is most suited for countries with no history of internal or external conflict in recent times. It is already practiced in Switzerland. War, conquest, and security concerns have led to a reversal of the roles of various orders of governments and to a reduction in local government functions in more recent history. Globalization and the information revolution have already brought pressures for much larger and stronger roles

Table 6.3. *The role of a local government under the new vision of local governance*

Old view: Twentieth century	New view: Twenty-first century
Is based on residuality and local governments as wards of the state	Is based on subsidiarity and home rule
Is based on *ultra vires*	Is based on community governance
Is focused on government	Is focused on citizen-centered local governance
Is agent of the central government	Is primary agent for the citizens and leader and gatekeeper for shared rule
Is responsive and accountable to higher-level governments	Is responsive and accountable to local voters; assumes leadership role in improving local governance
Is direct provider of local services	Is purchaser of local services
Is focused on in-house provision	Is facilitator of network mechanisms of local governance, coordinator of government providers and entities beyond government, mediator of conflicts, and developer of social capital
Is focused on secrecy	Is focused on letting the sunshine in; practices transparent governance
Has input controls	Recognizes that results matter
Is internally dependent	Is externally focused and competitive; is ardent practitioner of alternative service delivery framework
Is closed and slow	Is open, quick, and flexible
Has intolerance for risk	Is innovative; is risk taker within limits
Depends on central directives	Is autonomous in taxing, spending, regulatory, and administrative decisions
Is rules driven	Has managerial flexibility and accountability for results
Is bureaucratic and technocratic	Is participatory; works to strengthen citizen voice and exit options through direct democracy provisions, citizens' charters, and performance budgeting
Is coercive	Is focused on earning trust, creating space for civic dialogue, serving citizens, and improving social outcomes
Is fiscally irresponsible	Is fiscally prudent; works better and costs less
Is exclusive with elite capture	Is inclusive and participatory
Overcomes market failures	Overcomes market and government failures
Is boxed in a centralized system	Is connected in globalized and localized world

Source: Shah and S. Shah (2006); Shah and F. Shah (2007).

for local governments (see Shah 2001). Although most governments have done some tinkering with their fiscal systems, the radical change recommended here is not being considered anywhere. The unlikelihood of overcoming path dependency – a tall order for existing institutions and vested interests – makes such reform infeasible. Under such circumstances, option B may be more workable, but here the clarity of responsibilities may not be politically feasible, for the will to undertake such bold reforms is lacking. Piecemeal adaptation of this model will nevertheless be forced on most countries by the effects of globalization and by citizen empowerment, facilitated by the information revolution.

CONCLUDING REMARKS

We have presented a brief overview of the conceptual and institutional literature on local governance. A synthesis of the conceptual literature suggests that the modern role of a local government is to deal with market failures as well as government failures. This role requires a local government to operate as a purchaser of local services, a facilitator of networks of government providers and entities beyond government, and a gatekeeper and overseer of state and national governments in areas of shared rule. Local government also needs to play a mediator's role among various entities and networks to foster greater synergy and harness the untapped energies of the broader community for improving the quality of life of residents. Globalization and the information revolution are reinforcing those conceptual perspectives on a catalytic role for local governments.

This view is also grounded in the history of industrial nations and ancient civilizations in China and India. Local government was the primary form of government until wars and conquest led to the transfer of local government responsibilities to central and regional governments. This trend continued unabated until globalization and the information revolution highlighted the weaknesses of centralized rule for improving the quality of life and social outcomes.

The new vision of local governance (Table 6.3) presented here argues for a leadership role by local governments in a multicentered, multiorder, or multilevel system. This view is critical to creating and sustaining citizen-centered governance, in which citizens are the ultimate sovereigns and various orders of governments serve as agents in the supply of public governance. In developing countries, such citizen empowerment may be the only way to reform public-sector governance when governments are either unwilling or unable to reform themselves.

SEVEN

Local Governance in Practice

Local governance historically predates the emergence of nation-states. In ancient history, tribes and clans established systems of local governance in most of the world. They established their own codes of conduct and ways of raising revenues and delivering services to the tribe or clan. Tribal and clan elders developed consensus on the roles and responsibilities of various members. Some tribes and clans with better organization and skills then sought to enlarge their spheres of influence through conquest and cooperation with other tribes. In this way, the first Chinese dynasty, the Xia, was established (2070 to 1600 B.C.) (see Zheng and Wei, 2003). A similar situation prevailed in ancient India, where in the third millennium B.C. (about 2500 B.C.) a rich civilization was established in the Indus Valley (now Pakistan). This advanced civilization placed great emphasis on autonomy in local governance and enshrined a consensus on division of work for various members of the society. This emphasis led to the creation of a class society in which each member had a defined role: upholder of moral values, soldier, farmer, tradesperson, worker. Each community formed its own consensus on community services and how to accomplish them.

Native American tribes in North America and tribes and clans in Western Europe also enjoyed home rule. Subsequent conquests and wars led to the demise of these harmonious systems of self-rule in local governance and to the emergence of rule by central governments all over the world. This development (roughly around 1000 B.C. in Western Europe) ultimately led to the creation of unique systems of local governance and central-local relations in most countries. Those systems can nevertheless be classified into the following broad categories for analytical purposes.

ALTERNATIVE MODELS OF LOCAL GOVERNANCE AND
CENTRAL-LOCAL RELATIONS

The Nordic Model

In the fifteenth century, Denmark, Norway, and Sweden were ruled by a Danish king. Residents in those countries contributed to the king's coffers but were allowed to run local affairs autonomously (Werner and Shah, 2005). In the absence of central intrusion, the seeds for a locally run, client-oriented, welfare state were sown. As a result, local governments assumed most functions of the state, while the central government largely assumed a ceremonial role and foreign relations functions. Local governments therefore assumed responsibility not only for local service delivery but also for social protection and social welfare functions. Local governments in Nordic countries served their residents from cradle to grave. They delivered property-oriented as well as people-oriented services.

In modern times, the central governments in Nordic countries have assumed wider regulatory and oversight functions, but the predominance of local government – more than 30 percent of gross domestic product (GDP) in Denmark – and its autonomy are still preserved because of citizen satisfaction with local government performance. The Nordic model emphasizes small local governments (average jurisdiction of fewer than 10,000 inhabitants) that are primarily self-financing. In Denmark and Sweden, nearly 75 percent – and in Norway, 64 percent – of local expenditures are financed from own-source revenues. Personal income taxes (piggybacking on a national base) are the mainstays of local finance (almost 91 percent of tax revenues), and property taxes contribute a pitiful 7 percent of tax revenues.

The Swiss Model

The origins of the Swiss Confederation can be traced to the defensive alliance signed by the cantons of Uri, Schwyz, and Unterwalden in 1291. Before that event, the Swiss territories were under the control of independent local governments (cantons). This tradition of local government domination continues in the Swiss system today: local governments enjoy autonomy not only in fiscal matters but also in such areas as immigration, citizenship, language, and foreign economic relations.

This tradition of strong local government is further strengthened through direct democracy provisions in the Swiss constitution, including people's initiatives, referenda, and petitions. The people's initiatives empower citizens to seek a decision on an amendment that they want to make to the constitution. A people's initiative may be formulated as a general proposal or as a precisely formulated text whose wording can no longer be changed by parliament or the government. For such an initiative to be considered, the signatures of 100,000 voters must be collected within eighteen months. A popular majority and a majority of all cantons are required for the acceptance of such an initiative.

Through the referenda provision, the people are entitled to pronounce their judgments on matters under consideration by the legislature or the executive or matters on which a decision has already been made. In the latter case, the referendum acts as a veto. Federal laws and international treaties are subject to optional referenda, provided that 50,000 citizens request it within 100 days of the publication of the decree. Under the petition provision, all eligible voters can submit a petition to the government and are entitled to receive a reply. Switzerland consists of twenty-six cantons and 2,842 communes. Each canton has its own constitution, parliament, government, and courts. The communes are handmaidens of the cantons. They perform some delegated tasks such as population registration and civil defense, but they have autonomous competencies in education and social welfare, energy supply, roads, local planning, and local taxation (see Switzerland, 2003).

The French Model

In the French model, the primary role of local governments is to allow citizens at the grass-roots level a sense of political participation in decision making at the national level. The system embodies the thinking of Rousseau and Voltaire on rationality and social cohesion and that of Napoleon on a sense of order and an unbroken chain of command. The national government and its agencies represent the apex of this system, with an unbroken chain of command through regional and departmental prefects to chief executives and mayors of communes at the lowest rung of the system. There is a similar chain of command through line and functional ministries. Therefore, the model is sometimes referred to as the *dual supervision* model of local governance.

The system permits *cumul des mandats* (concurrent political mandates or holding multiple offices or positions concurrently) to provide elected leaders at lower echelons with a voice at higher levels of governments. Public service delivery remains the primary responsibility of the national government, and its agencies may be directly involved in the delivery of local services. The average size of local government jurisdiction is small (covering fewer than 10,000 inhabitants), and local governments have a limited range of autonomous service delivery responsibilities. Local governments use a mix of local revenue instruments and rely significantly on central financing. This model, with its focus on strong central command and dual supervision, proved very popular with colonial rulers from France, Portugal, and Spain, as well as with military dictators, and was widely replicated in developing countries (Humes, 1991).

The German Model

The German model emphasizes subsidiarity, cooperation, and administrative efficiency. It entrusts policy-making functions to the federal level and service delivery responsibilities to geographically delineated states and local governments, to which it gives a great deal of autonomy in service delivery. All purely local services are assigned to local governments. The average local government covers 20,000 inhabitants, and local expenditures constitute about 10 percent of GDP. General revenue sharing serves as a major source of local finances.

The British Model

The British model has elements of the French dual supervision model. It emphasizes a stronger role for centrally appointed field officers and sectoral and functional ministries in the provision of local services. Local governments must coordinate their actions with these officials. Local governments are given substantial autonomy in purely local functions, but they can access only a limited range of revenue instruments. Local governments play a dominant role in such property-oriented services as road maintenance, garbage collection, water, and sewerage and a limited role in such people-oriented services as health, education, and social welfare. Property taxes are the mainstay of local governments. Local governments typically derive two-thirds of their revenues from central transfers. They do not have access to personal income taxes. The role of the chief executive is weak, and local councils play a strong role in local decision making. The average local government is large, covering about 120,000 inhabitants, and local expenditures account for about 12 percent of GDP (McMillan, 1995, 2008). In former British colonies, the role of field officers was strengthened to provide general supervision and control of local governments on behalf of the central colonial government.

The Indian Model

India had one of the oldest traditions of strong self-governance at the local level. In the pre-Moghul period, local government was in operation more extensively in India than anywhere else in the world. Small villages and towns were regulated by custom and community leadership, with authority normally vested in an elders' council headed by a *sarpanch* or *number-dar*. The apex institution was the *panchayat*, with responsibilities for law and order, local services, land management, dispute resolution, administration of justice, provision of basic needs, and revenue collection. These institutions enabled each village and town to function harmoniously.

Subsequent wars and conquest led to a weakening of local governance in India. During the Moghul period, panchayats were required to collect central taxes, but local government autonomy was not disturbed (Wajidi, 1990). During the British Raj, with its central focus on command and control and little concern for service delivery, the system of local governance received a major setback. Powers were centralized, and loyalty to the British regime was rewarded with land grants, leading to the creation of a class of feudal aristocrats who dominated the local political scene on behalf of the British government. The central government also appointed roving bureaucrats to run local affairs. Since independence in both India and Pakistan, centralized governance has been maintained, while small steps have been taken to strengthen local autonomy. In India, feudal aristocracy was abolished through land reforms, but in Pakistan, such reforms could not be carried out. As a result, in areas of feudal dominance in Pakistan, local self-governance led to capture by elites.

The Chinese Model

The Chinese model places strong emphasis on making provincial and local governments an integral and dependent sphere of national government. This is accomplished in two ways: through democratic centralism, which integrates the local people's congress with the national People's Congress through a system of elections, and through dual subordination of local governments, whereby provincial and local governments are accountable to higher-level governments in general, but the functional departments are also accountable to higher-level functional agencies and departments. The personnel functions are also integrated among various orders of government. Because of its integrative nature, the model permits a large and expansive role for provincial and local governments in service delivery. The average local government jurisdiction is very large. Subprovincial local government expenditure constitutes 51.4 percent of consolidated public expenditures. Subprovincial local governments employ 89 percent of the total government work force. Some clearly central functions such as unemployment insurance, social security, and social safety nets are assigned to provincial and local governments. Local autonomy varies directly with the fiscal capacity of a local government, with richer jurisdictions calling their own tunes, while poor jurisdictions follow the pied piper of higher-level governments.

The Japanese Model

The local government system introduced in Meiji Japan in about 1890 had elements of the French and German models. It emphasized centralized control, as in the French model of local governments, through the Ministry of Interior appointing heads of regional governments (governors of prefectures), who controlled local districts and municipalities. The local government simply implemented policies determined by the central government. During the post–World War II period, direct elections of governors, mayors, and councils were introduced. The practice of agency delegation (German model) was retained, and local governments were expected to perform functions mandated by the central government and its agencies. The Ministry of Home Affairs, which had a supportive role for local governments, was introduced in 1960 (Muramatsu and Iqbal, 2001). Income taxes are the mainstay of local government finance, contributing 60 percent of own-source tax revenues, followed by property taxes (about 30 percent) and sales taxes (about 10 percent of total tax revenue).

The North American Model

In the early period of North American history, local communities functioned as *civic republics* (Kincaid, 1967) governed by mutual consent of their members. The framers of the U.S. Constitution did not recognize local governments. The Civil War led to the centralization of powers in the United States. Subsequently, the formal institutions of local government were created by states. The judiciary further constrained the role of local government through recognition of Dillon's rule: local governments may exercise only those powers explicitly granted to them under state legislation. Subsequently, most states have attempted to grant autonomy to local governments in discharging their specified functions through *home rule* provisions (Bowman and Kearney, 1990).

Local governments in Canada are faced with circumstances similar to those in the United States. Thus, the North American model recognizes local government as a handmaiden of states and provinces but attempts to grant autonomy (home rule) to local governments in their specific areas of responsibility – predominantly delivery of property-oriented services. Local governments perform an intermediate range of functions. The average jurisdiction of local government in the United States is about 10,000 and in Canada about 6,000 inhabitants. Property taxes are the dominant source of local revenues. Local government expenditures constitute about 7 percent of GDP (see McMillan, 1995, 2008).

The Australian Model

The Australian constitution does not recognize local governments. It is left to the states to decide on a system of local governance in their territories. Most states have assigned a minimal set of functions to local governments, including engineering services (roads, bridges, sidewalks, and drainage), community services (old-age care, child care, fire protection), environmental services (waste management and environmental protection), regulatory services (zoning, dwellings, buildings, restaurants, animals), and cultural services (libraries, art galleries, museums). Local governments raise only 3 percent of national revenues and are responsible for 6 percent of consolidated public-sector expenditures. Property taxes (rates) and user charges are the mainstay (about 70 percent) of revenues, and central and state grants finance about 20 percent of local expenditures. Transportation, community amenities, and recreation and culture command two-thirds of local expenditures. Local government in New Zealand bears a close resemblance to the Australian model.

LOCAL GOVERNMENT ORGANIZATION AND FINANCE IN INDUSTRIAL COUNTRIES

We have already noted the broad diversity in approaches to local governance in industrial countries. This section provides a few key comparative indicators on local government organization and finance in countries of the Organization for Economic Co-operation and Development (OECD).

Legal Status of Local Governments

The legal status of local government varies across industrial countries, with local government deriving authority from national constitutions in

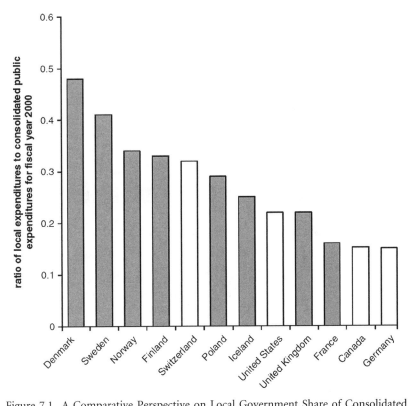

Figure 7.1. A Comparative Perspective on Local Government Share of Consolidated Public Expenditures, 2000. *Note:* X-axis presents ratio of local expenditures to consolidated public expenditures for the fiscal year 2000. White bars represent federal countries. *Source:* Shah (2006c).

Denmark, France, Germany, the Netherlands, and Sweden; from state constitutions in Australia, Switzerland, and the United States; and from national legislation in the United Kingdom and New Zealand and from provincial legislation in Canada. It is interesting that there is no clear pattern in the autonomy and range of local services provided by local governments deriving their status from national and state constitutions. However, local governments that are created through legislation are significantly weaker.

Relative Importance of Local Governments

The relative importance of local governments in industrial countries is compared using two indicators: share of consolidated public-sector expenditures (Figure 7.1) and local expenditures as a percentage of GDP

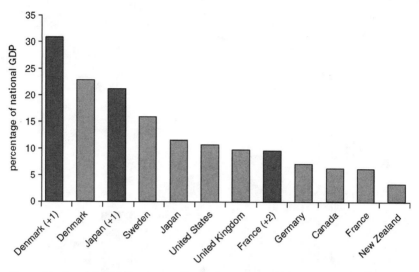

Figure 7.2. Local Expenditures as a Share of National GDP, 2001. *Note:* France (+2) includes municipalities, regions, and *départements*; Japan (+1) includes cities and prefectures; Denmark (+1) includes municipalities and counties (*Amtskommuner*). *Source:* Shah (2006c).

(Figure 7.2). On both indicators, Nordic countries are the leaders; the United Kingdom and United States are in the lower ranges; and Canada, France, and Germany are in the lowest range. Local government in Denmark stands out, claiming about 50 percent of total expenditures, which account for about 30 percent of GDP. Among the industrial countries, Australia is an outlier with local expenditures accounting for less than 3 percent of GDP.

Population Size Covered by Local Governments

There are wide variations in the number of municipal governments, with as few as 74 in New Zealand and as many as 35,906 in the United States. Table 7.1 provides the distribution of municipalities by size category for several industrial countries. Similarly, the median size of a municipal government jurisdiction in 1998 was smallest in Iceland (1,160 people) and largest in the United Kingdom (about 160,000) (see Table 7.2 and Scottish Office, 1998). In a large majority of industrial countries, the average municipal government jurisdiction covers fewer than 20,000 people.

Table 7.1. *Size distribution of municipal governments in industrial countries according to year of lateral census*

Number of inhabitants	Canada (2001)[a]	Denmark (2002)	France (1999)	Germany (2001)	Japan (2000)[b]	New Zealand (2002)[c]	Sweden (2003)	United States (2002)[d]
0–499	1,975	0	21,038	3,680	0	0	0	0
500–999	1,023	0	6,763	2,521	0	0	0	18,013
1,000–9,999	1,786	134	7,957	6,097	1,557	14	73	14,057
10,000–49,999	308	125	802	1,348	1,220	40	175	3,125
50,000–99,999	51	12	82	109	224	12	30	461
100,000–499,999	33	3	32	70	206	8	9	219
500,000–999,999	6	1	3	10	11	0	1	22
1,000,000 or more	2	0	2	3	12	0	0	9
Total no. of municipalities	5,184	275	36,679	13,838	3,230	74	288	35,906

[a] The high number of small Canadian settlements is based on the fact that all First Nation of Native American bands are affiliated. For example, 1,052 Native American reserves and 5 Nisga'a villages are included in this survey.

[b] Japan includes all *shi*, *machi*, *mura*, and *gun*. Moreover, the *ku*-area of Tokyo is counted as one *shi* and the population of Okinawa-*ken* is excluded.

[c] Besides the 74 territorial authorities, New Zealand also has 1,860 area units, which are very small settlements.

[d] United States includes all cities, municipalities, towns, and townships. Moreover, the 2002 figure presents only the total number of all local authorities that have fewer than 1,000 inhabitants.

Source: Shah (2006c).

Table 7.2. *Average populations per local authority in OECD countries*

Median population of municipal government	Countries (listed in ascending order of population)
1,000–5,000	Iceland, France, Greece, Switzerland, Luxembourg, Austria, Spain
5,000–10,000	Canada, United States, Italy, Germany, Norway
10,000–15,000	Finland
15,000–20,000	Belgium, Netherlands, Denmark, Australia
30,000–35,000	Sweden, Portugal
35,000–40,000	Japan
40,000–50,000	Ireland, New Zealand
100,000+	United Kingdom

Source: Shah (2006c).

Local Spending Responsibilities

There is no uniform model, except that property-oriented services are provided at the local level in almost all countries. In infrastructure, Australian local governments command 27 percent of total expenditures, compared with 62 percent in the United Kingdom and 47 percent and 41 percent in the EU and the OECD. People-oriented services show more variation. In education, local government has no role in Australia but takes up more than 60 percent of expenditure share at local levels in Canada, the United Kingdom, and the United States. In the OECD, it averages about 46 percent. In health, local governments have no role in Australia and the United Kingdom but a predominant role in Denmark (about 92 percent); EU and OECD average expenditure shares are 28 percent and 19 percent, respectively. Most industrial countries have significant higher-level intervention in social services and unfunded mandates to local governments in environmental protection.

Overall, local governments in Nordic countries perform the maximal range of local services, encompassing a wide range of people- and property-oriented services. Local governments in Southern Europe and in North America fall in a median range and are more focused on property-oriented services. Australian local governments are engaged in the most minimal property-oriented services (primarily "roads and rubbish").

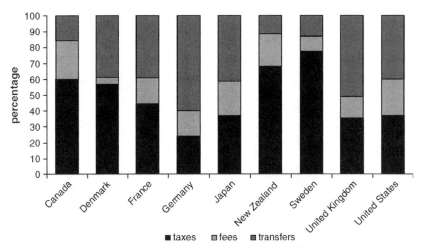

Figure 7.3. Composition of Operating Revenues for Local Authorities, 2001. *Note:* The shared taxes in Germany and Japan are consolidated under transfers. Moreover, local borrowing is excluded from this survey. *Source:* Shah (2006c).

Local Revenues and Revenue Autonomy

Income taxes, property taxes, and fees are major revenue sources for local governments. In Belgium, Denmark, Finland, Germany, Iceland, Japan, Luxembourg, Norway, Sweden, and Switzerland, more than 80 percent of tax revenues are derived from taxes on personal and corporate incomes. In contrast, in Australia, Canada, Ireland, the Netherlands, New Zealand, the United Kingdom, and the United States, property taxes contribute more than 80 percent of local tax revenues. Austria, France, Greece, Italy, Portugal, and Spain rely on a mix of local tax sources, with Spain drawing about 40 percent of tax revenues from sales taxes. For the EU as a whole, income taxes dominate, followed by property taxes, sales taxes, and fees. On average in industrial countries, 50 percent of local revenues come from taxes, 20 percent from user charges, and 30 percent from transfers from higher levels (see McMillan, 1995). Figure 7.3 illustrates the composition of local operating revenues, and Figure 7.4 shows the composition of tax revenues for selected countries.

Table 7.3 shows that intergovernmental finance is relatively less important in Austria, Canada, Denmark, Finland, New Zealand, and Sweden, whereas in most OECD countries the share of grant-financed local expenditures is quite large (see Figure 7.3). This large share of grants indicates that, in many OECD countries, local governments typically perform

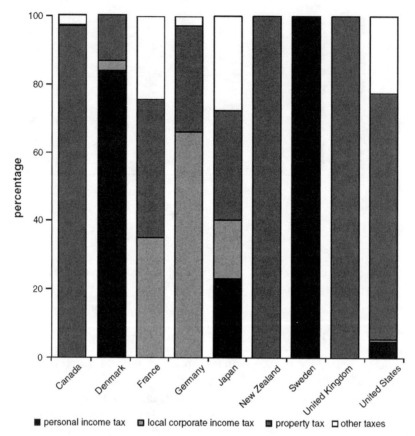

Figure 7.4. Composition of Local Tax Revenues, 2001. *Note:* The shared taxes in Germany (personal income tax and value-added tax) and in New Zealand (fuel tax for the regional councils) are excluded. *Source:* Shah (2006c).

agency functions for higher-level governments and have only a limited range of locally determined responsibilities. General-purpose, formula-based grants using fiscal capacity and need factors dominate in most OECD countries, with the exception of Finland, New Zealand, and the United States. In those three countries, specific-purpose transfers assume greater importance in local finances

In most countries, airports, parking, water, sewerage, and garbage collection are financed predominantly by fees, whereas social services are primarily financed from general tax revenues and grants. Infrastructure finance relies on a mix of sources that include own-source revenues and reserves, charges, fiscal transfers, borrowing, and public-private partnership

Table 7.3. *Intergovernmental transfers as a share of local government revenues in OECD countries in 2000*

Transfers as a percentage of total local revenues	Countries (listed in ascending order of the share of transfers)
10–20	Finland, Sweden, Denmark, New Zealand
20–30	Canada, Austria
30–40	France, Japan, Australia, United States
40–50	Ireland, Norway, Belgium, Germany
50–60	Spain
60–70	Greece, Portugal
70–80	Italy, United Kingdom, Netherlands

Source: Shah (2006c).

arrangements. In most countries, significant help is available from higher-level governments in facilitating access to the credit market for local governments.

Facilitating Local Access to Credit

Local access to credit requires well-functioning financial markets and creditworthy local governments. Although those prerequisites are easily met in industrial countries, traditions for assisting local governments by higher-level governments are well established. An interest subsidy to state and local borrowing is available in the United States because the interest income of such bonds is exempt from federal taxation. Needless to say, such a subsidy has many distortionary effects: it favors richer jurisdictions and higher-income individuals, it discriminates against nondebt sources of finance such as reserves and equity, it favors investments by local governments rather than autonomous bodies, and it discourages private-sector participation in the form of concessions and build-own-transfer alternatives. Various U.S. states assist borrowing by small local governments through the establishment of municipal bond banks. Municipal bond banks are established as autonomous state agencies that issue tax-exempt securities to investors and apply the proceeds to purchase the collective bond issue of several local governments. By pooling a number of smaller issues and by using the superior credit rating of the state, municipal bond banks reduce the cost of borrowing to smaller communities.

In Canada, most provinces assist local governments with the engineering, financial, and economic analysis of projects. Local governments in Alberta, British Columbia, and Nova Scotia are assisted in their borrowing through provincial finance corporations, which use the higher credit ratings of the province to lower the cost of funds for local governments. Some provinces, notably Manitoba and Quebec, assist in the preparation and marketing of local debt. Canadian provincial governments on occasion provide debt relief to their local governments. In Western Europe and Japan, autonomous agencies run on commercial principles assist local borrowing. Municipality Finance of Finland is owned by the association of local governments and provides debt pooling for municipal governments. Similarly, Kommun Invest of Sweden is owned by the association of local governments but privately managed to provide credit to local governments. Credit Communal de Belgique is jointly owned by Belgian central and local governments, and deposits are the main source of finance. Dexia in France is privately owned and raises resources entirely though bond issues. The Banco de Crédito Local in Spain is also privately managed and uses bond finance. In Denmark, local governments have collectively established a cooperative municipal bank. In the United Kingdom, the Public Works Loan Board channels central financing to local public works.

An important lesson from industrial countries' experience is that municipal finance corporations operate well when they are run on commercial principles and compete for capital and borrowers. In such an environment, agencies allow risk pooling, use economies of scale better, and bring to bear their knowledge of local governments and their financing potential to provide access to commercial credit on more favorable terms (see McMillan, 1995).

Some Conclusions

Historical evolution, as well as the current practice of local governance, is instructive in drawing lessons for reform of local governance, especially in developing countries. There is great diversity in practice in local governance in industrial countries, but there are also some common strands. The diversity is in the institutional arrangements, which have evolved incrementally over a long period. This evolution has resulted in diverse roles for local governments and diverse relations with central governments across countries. In Nordic countries, local government serves as the primary agent of the people, whereas in Australia, that role is entrusted to state governments, and local government has a minimal role in local affairs.

No uniform model for local government size, structure, tiers, and functions exists across OECD countries. There are, nevertheless, some interesting common features. First, most countries recognize that finance must follow function to ensure that local governments are able to meet their responsibilities efficiently and equitably. Second, home rule is considered critical to meeting local expectations and being responsive to local residents. Therefore, local governments must have significant taxing, spending, and regulatory autonomy, and they must have the ability to hire, fire, and set terms of reference for employees without having to defer to higher levels of governments. Only then can local governments innovate in management by introducing performance-based accountability and innovate in service delivery by forging alternative service delivery arrangements through competitive provision, contracting, and outsourcing wherever deemed appropriate. They can also facilitate a broader network of local governance and harness the energies of the whole community to foster better social outcomes. Third and most important, accountability to local residents has been the factor most critical to the success of local governance in industrial countries. This accountability is strengthened through democratic choice, participation, transparency, performance budgeting, citizens' charters of rights, and various legal and financing provisions that support wider voice, choice, and exit options to residents.

LOCAL GOVERNMENT ORGANIZATION AND FINANCE IN DEVELOPING COUNTRIES

The conceptual literature argues for a strong role for local governments in local development, improving public services and quality of life at the local level. It would therefore be instructive to learn about the role of such governments in developing countries. The following paragraphs provide a bird's-eye view of local government organization and finance in twelve selected developing countries.

Legal Status of Local Governments

The legal status of local governments varies across developing countries. In Brazil, Chile, India, South Africa, and Uganda, local governments have a constitutional status. In Bangladesh, Indonesia, Kazakhstan, and Poland, local governments were created by national legislation, in Argentina by

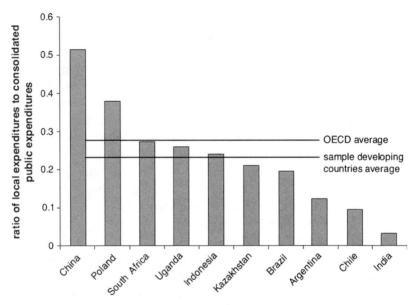

Figure 7.5. A Comparative Perspective on Local Government Share of Consolidated Public Expenditures. *Note:* The data are the latest available for each country: 1997, Poland; 2001, Chile, Indonesia, and South Africa; 2002, India; and 2003, Argentina, Brazil, China, Kazakhstan, and Uganda. *Source:* Shah (2006d).

provincial legislation, and in China by an executive order of the central government. It is interesting to note that there is no clear pattern in the autonomy and range of local services provided by local governments deriving their status from national and state constitutions or legislation. However, local governments that are created through legislation, in general, are significantly weaker – with the notable exception of Poland.

Relative Importance of Local Governments

The relative importance of local governments in developing countries is compared using two indicators: share of consolidated public-sector expenditures (Figure 7.5) and local expenditures as a percentage of GDP (Figure 7.6). According to both criteria, local governments in China command the largest share – more than 51 percent of consolidated public expenditures and 10.8 percent of GDP – whereas in India, it is the smallest share – 3 percent of the expenditures and 0.75 percent of GDP. The rank order of some countries, however, is not consistent across both criteria. For example, South Africa

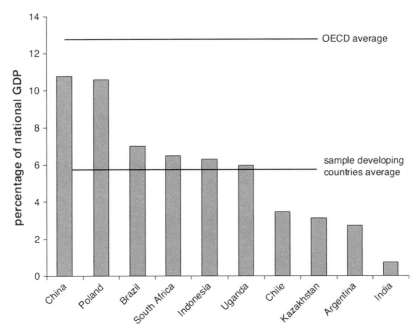

Figure 7.6. Local Expenditures as a Share of National GDP. *Note:* The data are the latest available for each country:1997, Poland; 2001, Chile, Indonesia, and South Africa; 2002, India; and 2003, Argentina, Brazil, China, Kazakhstan, and Uganda. *Source:* Shah (2006d).

does better than Brazil on the first and worse on the second criterion. On average in sample countries, local government expenditures amount to 23 percent of consolidated public-sector expenditures and 5.7 percent of national GDP. Comparable figures for a sample of OECD countries would be 28 percent of consolidated expenditures and 12.75 percent of GDP. Thus, local governments' role is large, but in comparison with central and intermediate governments in developing countries and local governments in OECD countries, it is relatively much smaller in most developing countries – with the exception of China and Poland. In China, subprovincial local governments employ 38.7 million people and account for 89 percent of total public employment.

Population Size Covered by Local Governments

The number and median size of municipal governments vary widely in the sample countries. Uganda has only 70 municipal governments, whereas China has 43,965 (Table 7.4). The mean population covered by municipal

Table 7.4. *Size distribution of municipal governments in developing countries*

Number of inhabitants	Argentina (2001)	Brazil (2002)	Chile (1992)	China (2004)	India (2001)	Indonesia (1990)	Kazakhstan (2002)	Poland (2003)	South Africa (2001)	Uganda (2002)
0–4,999	1,770	1,365	269	43,258	230,161	1,237	7,660	604	0	0
5,000–9,999	→	1,316	16	→	16,115	62	201	1,049	4	1
10,000–19,999	360	1,342	40	→	5,536	→	81	731	16	0
20,000–24,999	→	989	→	→	→	→	→	→	7	0
25,000–49,999	24	→	→	→	1,386	7	→	→	36	6
50,000–99,999	→	309	→	→	498	→	7	54	61	6
100,000–199,999	→	123	→	→	388	6	18	22	67	9
200,000–499,999	→	82	→	374	→	→	→	13	52	31
500,000–999,999	→	20	→	283	→	→	→	5	25	15
1,000,000 or more	→	14	→	50	35	→	1	→	14	2
Total number of municipalities	2,154	5,560	325	43,965	254,119	1,312	7,968	2,478	282	70

Note: An arrow indicates that the value is an aggregate and covers the range indicated.
Source: Shah (2006d).

Table 7.5. *Average population per local authority in sample developing countries*

Country	Average population per local authority
India, rural	3,278
Kazakhstan	4,331
Indonesia	5,915
Argentina	14,972
Poland	18,881
Brazil	30,099
Chile	64,592
India, urban	68,027
China	107,334
South Africa	238,839
Uganda	373,321
All sample countries	79,000

Source: Table 7.4 (this volume).

government is fewer than 10,000 people in Kazakhstan and more than 100,000 people in China, South Africa, and Uganda. Argentina and Poland have mean populations of less than 20,000, and Brazil has a mean municipal government population of about 31,000. Municipal governments in Chile and urban India have mean populations between 60,000 and 70,000 (Table 7.5).

Local Spending Responsibilities

Local governments vary in their responsibilities across developing countries. China grants most extensive expenditure responsibilities to local governments. In addition to traditional local and municipal services, local governments in China are responsible for social security (primarily pensions and unemployment allowances) and have a much larger role in local economic development than local governments in other countries. Local governments' role in delivering local services is minimal in India and South Africa and largely focused on delivery of municipal services. In Kazakhstan, all local services are shared central-local responsibilities; local governments do not have independent budgets and have no fiscal autonomy. Education and health account for nearly half of local government expenditures in Argentina, Brazil, Chile, Indonesia, Kazakhstan, Poland, and Uganda. In Uganda, education alone accounts for about 40 percent of local expenditures. In India and South Africa, municipal services (e.g., water, sewer, and garbage) and municipal administration

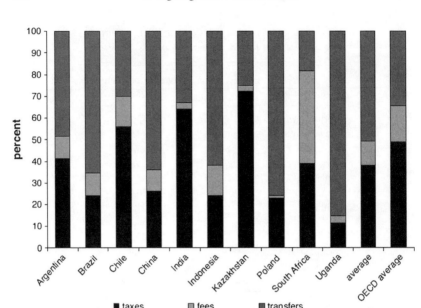

Figure 7.7. Composition of Operating Revenues for Local Authorities. *Note:* The data are the latest available for each country: 1997, Poland; 2001, Chile, Indonesia, and South Africa; 2002, India; and 2003, Argentina, Brazil, China, Kazakhstan, and Uganda. *Source:* Shah (2006d).

dominate local expenditures. In China, education, municipal administration, justice, and police account for nearly half of local expenditures.

Local Revenues and Revenue Autonomy

Local governments in sample countries raise 39.6 percent of revenues from taxes, another 9.5 percent from fees and charges, and the remaining 50.9 percent from higher-level transfers (Figure 7.7 and Table 7.6). Comparable figures for OECD countries are 49 percent for taxes, 16.6 percent for fees, and 34.4 percent for transfers. The role of fiscal transfers is much larger than average in Uganda (85.4 percent), Poland (76 percent), Brazil (65.4 percent), Indonesia (62 percent), and China (58 percent). The sample countries have diverse revenue structures. On average, they raise 32 percent of tax revenues from property taxes, 15 percent of revenues from personal income taxes, 4 percent from corporate income taxes, and the other 49 percent from a large number of small taxes, fees, and charges. In comparison, OECD countries raise 54 percent of local revenues from property taxes, 23 percent from personal income taxes, 14 percent from corporate taxes, and 9 percent for

Table 7.6. *Intergovernmental transfers as a share of local revenues in developing countries, 2003*

Transfers as a percentage of total local revenues	Countries (listed in ascending order of the share of transfers)
10–20	South Africa
20–30	Kazakhstan, Chile
30–40	India
40–50	Argentina
60–70	Indonesia, Brazil, China
70–80	Poland, Uganda

Source: Shah (2006d).

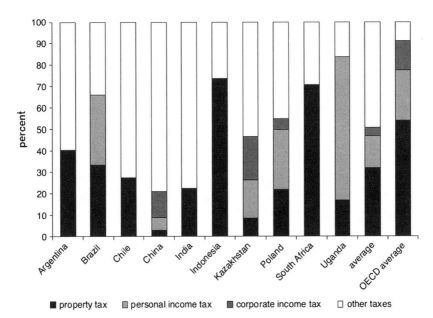

■ property tax   ▨ personal income tax   ■ corporate income tax   □ other taxes

Figure 7.8. Composition of Local Tax Revenues. *Note:* The data are the latest available for each country: 1997, Poland; 2001, Chile, Indonesia, and South Africa; 2002, India; and 2003, Argentina, Brazil, China, Kazakhstan, and Uganda. *Source:* Shah (2006d).

sundry taxes. Thus, local governments have a much greater reliance on property and income taxes in OECD countries than in developing countries. Property taxes raise only 3 percent of local revenues in China and 74 percent in Indonesia (centrally administered property tax) (Figure 7.8).

For all developing countries, revenues from property taxes amount to 0.5 percent of GDP compared with about 2 percent (1 to 3 percent) of GDP in industrial countries. This finding suggests that property taxes may represent significant untapped potential for further exploitation. User charges are a significant source of revenues, but often such charges are poorly designed and administered and do not satisfy equity and efficiency principles or provide special safeguards for the poor. Autonomy in local tax base determination and administration is significant in Argentina, Brazil, and Poland; is limited in other countries, and does not exist in Kazakhstan. Overall, the degree of tax centralization in the sample countries is far greater than would be dictated by economic principles or political accountability considerations.

Sample countries in general follow a formula-based approach to general-purpose transfers. Nevertheless, the transfers are often not well designed compared to principles and better practices laid out in Chapter 8. China, Indonesia, Poland, and South Africa attempt to use fiscal capacity and fiscal need measures in their fiscal equalization transfers, whereas most other countries have revenue-sharing programs with multiple factors that work at cross-purposes. The practice of fiscal equalization transfers is welcome; however, none of the sample countries use explicit equalization standards that determine both the total pool and the allocation of these transfers. As a result, the transfers do not achieve jurisdictional fiscal equity goals. Specific-purpose transfers are usually ad hoc and do not create incentives to safeguard their objectives. In particular, none of the sample countries practice output-based fiscal transfers to set national minimum standards of basic services and to enhance local accountability to citizens for results or performance. Thus, the reform of fiscal transfers to ensure equitable and accountable governance remains an unfinished task.

Facilitating Local Access to Credit

Local borrowing from capital markets is permitted in most of the sample countries with the exception of China, Chile, and Indonesia. In China, however, central government may borrow or issue bonds on behalf of local governments, and local enterprises owned by local governments can also borrow directly from the capital markets. In Argentina, Brazil, and Poland, local borrowing from domestic and international capital markets is allowed but constrained by fiscal rules to ensure fiscal prudence and debt sustainability. In South Africa, most such borrowing takes place from public agencies such as the Infrastructure Finance Corporation and the

Development Bank of Southern Africa. The central government in South Africa provides regulatory oversight of all such borrowing and has the authority to intervene if a local government fails to meet its debt servicing obligations. South Africa has enacted a comprehensive framework for fiscal prudence at the local level, including provisions for declaring bankruptcy. In Kazakhstan, local governments can borrow only from the central government.

Large infrastructure deficiencies in developing countries call for significant access to borrowing by local governments. But local access to credit requires well-functioning financial markets and creditworthy local governments. In developing countries, undeveloped markets for long-term credit and weak municipal creditworthiness limit municipal access to credit. Nevertheless, the predominant policy emphasis of the central government is on central controls. Consequently, less attention has been paid to assistance for borrowing. In a few countries, such assistance is available through specialized institutions and central guarantees to provide greater municipal access to credit. These institutions are typically quite fragile, not likely to be sustainable, and open to political influences. Interest rate subsidies provided through these institutions impede emerging capital market alternatives. Furthermore, these institutions fail to smooth the transition to a market-based capital finance system.

Thus, in developing countries, the menu of choices available to local governments for financing capital projects is quite limited, and the available alternatives are not conducive to developing a sustainable institutional environment for such finance. Such limitations exist because macroeconomic instability and lack of fiscal discipline and appropriate regulatory regimes have impeded the development of financial and capital markets. In addition, revenue capacity at the local level is limited because of tax centralization. A first transitory step to provide limited credit market access to local governments may be to establish municipal finance corporations run on commercial principles and to encourage the development of municipal rating agencies to assist in such borrowing. Tax decentralization is also important to establish private-sector confidence in lending to local governments and sharing in the risks and rewards of such lending. Central government bailouts and guarantee of subnational debt should, however, be ruled out through enactment of comprehensive frameworks of fiscal responsibility and fiscal insolvency, as was done in Brazil and South Africa recently. Transparency in local budgeting and independent credit-rating agencies are also essential to smooth the transition to a market-based approach to subnational lending.

Some Conclusions

Recent years have seen positive developments regarding local governance in developing countries. Local governments are increasingly assuming a larger role in public services delivery. However, with the exception of a handful of countries such as Brazil, China, and Poland, local governments continue to play a very small role in people's lives. They typically are bounded by the principle of *ultra vires* and allowed to discharge only a small number of functions, which are mandated from above. They have limited autonomy in expenditure decisions and hardly any in revenue-raising decisions. Their access to own-source revenues is constrained to a few nonproductive bases. Political and bureaucratic leaders at the local level show little interest in lobbying for more taxing powers and instead devote all their energies to seeking higher levels of fiscal transfers.

As a result, tax decentralization has not kept pace with political and expenditure decentralization. Hence, one does not find many examples of tax-base sharing, and even the limited existing bases available to local governments are typically underexploited. Fiscal transfers typically account for 60 percent of revenues in developing countries (51 percent in sample developing countries) as opposed to only 34 percent in OECD countries. This distinct separation of taxing and spending decisions undermines accountability to local citizens because local leaders do not have to justify local spending decisions to their electorates.

Local self-financing is important for strengthening governance, efficiency, and accountability. Although most countries have opted for formula-driven fiscal transfers, the design of these transfers remains flawed. They do not create any incentive for setting national minimum standards or accountability for results and typically do not serve regional fiscal equity objectives either.

Local governments also typically have very limited autonomy in hiring and firing local government employees. In a number of countries with decentralization, such as Indonesia and Pakistan, higher government employees are simply transferred to local levels; financing is then provided to cover their wage costs. This approach limits budgetary flexibility and opportunities for efficient resource allocation at the local level.

Overall, local governments in developing countries typically follow the old model of local governance and simply provide directly a narrow range of local services. The new vision, with the local governments assuming a network facilitator role to enrich the quality of life of local residents, as discussed earlier in this chapter, is yet to be realized in any developing country.

PART TWO

REVENUE SHARING AND FISCAL TRANSFERS

Matching revenue means with expenditure needs as closely as possible for various orders of government is a desirable goal to strengthen accountable governance. In practice, such a goal is not realized because of greater difficulties in decentralizing taxing powers than expenditure responsibilities and the desire to leave the federal government with some room for the use of spending power to influence subnational policies to achieve national objectives. Several chapters in this section address the use of these important fiscal tools in securing a common economic union.

Mismatch between the revenue means and expenditure needs or vertical fiscal gap, usually for lower orders of government, is a common occurrence in federal countries for reasons discussed earlier. Such gaps can be mitigated through a transfer of a predetermined share of federal revenues either on a tax-by-tax basis or from a specific or general pool to subnational governments. Chapter 8 discusses the pros and cons of revenue sharing and assesses the usefulness of alternate revenue-sharing mechanisms.

Chapter 9 details the instruments of intergovernmental finance available to exercise the federal spending power. It highlights the incentives, accountability implications, and potential impacts of various instruments and associated designs. The chapter discusses the use of performance-oriented transfers to achieve results-based accountability while preserving autonomy and flexibility of decentralized decision making. The chapter then presents the economic rationale of federal-state-local fiscal transfers and discusses grant design issues to advance equity and efficiency objectives of such transfers.

Intergovernmental fiscal transfers finance about 60 percent of subnational expenditures in developing countries and transition economies and about a third of such expenditures in OECD countries. Beyond the expenditures they finance, these transfers create incentives and accountability mechanisms that affect the fiscal management, efficiency, and equity of public service provision and government accountability to citizens. Chapter 10 reviews the practices of intergovernmental finance, with a view to drawing some general lessons of relevance to policy makers and practitioners in developing countries and transition economies. The chapter provides guidelines for grant design and describes the objectives and design of fiscal transfers in various countries around the world. In developing countries and transition economies, fiscal transfers focus largely on revenue-sharing transfers, with little attention paid to serving national objectives. The chapter cites examples of simple but innovative grant designs that can satisfy grantors' objectives while preserving local autonomy and creating an enabling environment for responsive, responsible, equitable, and accountable public governance. Its concluding section highlights some lessons of relevance to current policy debates in developing countries and transition economies and lists practices to avoid as well as those to emulate in designing and implementing grant programs.

EIGHT

Revenue Sharing

The vertical fiscal gap (VFG) in a federation reflects the difference between revenue means and expenditure needs of states. This gap is usually filled by the revenues raised by the federal government that are made available to the states to finance their expenditures. There are two broad ways this transfer of funds can take place: by assigning a predetermined share of federal revenues to the states, or by making federal-state transfers whose magnitude is based on criteria other than federal revenues. The first is revenue sharing, which is the subject of this chapter, while the second falls under the general rubric of federal-state transfers. The distinction is a conceptual one only, because they both amount to a transfer of funds, and both share some common characteristics. Nonetheless, the term revenue sharing tends to refer to a specific method of calculating transfers to the states according to the sharing of federal revenues, so we follow common practice in treating them as separate entities.

The structure of revenue-sharing systems varies by country, and it is useful to set out a taxonomy of forms. One feature that most revenue-sharing systems share is that the transfers involved are typically unconditional. That is, their use is at the discretion of the state governments that receive them. This is by no means a necessary feature of revenue sharing but one that is commonly used. Revenue sharing is usually only one component of a broader system of transfers. Where the federal government wants to use its spending power to impose transfers on recipient governments, it will do so through conditional transfers designed for that purpose (and discussed further in the next chapter).

The basic structure of revenue sharing can be described by three components: the type of federal revenues to be shared, the proportion of those revenues that will go to the states as a whole, and the allocation of the shared revenues among the states. The revenues to be shared can be narrow or wide. The revenue source can be single, such as a broad-based tax that the states do not have access to (e.g., income or general sales taxes), or it can be a set of federal taxes. Of course, the larger and more diverse the federal revenue sources to be shared, the smaller the rate that needs to be applied to achieve a given size of revenue transfer, and the less volatile will be the revenues the states receive.

The proportion of the revenues that go to the states will presumably be chosen with regard to the size of state expenditure responsibilities relative to the adequacy of their own-source revenues. Of course, this will be a matter of judgment, because there is no well-defined notion of either the size of state expenditure responsibilities or the ability of states to raise their own revenues. The federation will adjust to whatever sharing rule is adopted, and the amount shared can usually be adjusted if it is found that states are having difficulty meeting their obligations.

The allocation of revenues among states can follow different rules. At one extreme is the *principle of derivation* whereby revenues are transferred to states in accordance with where the federal revenues were raised. In this case, there is no redistributive element incorporated into the transfers at all. The funds might be transferred using a simple equal per capita rule, which will be implicitly redistributive. States that have higher-than-average per capita tax bases will implicitly be transferring to those which are below average. More generally, the revenues might be disbursed according to the principles of equalization developed more in the next chapter. Each state's share will reflect both its tax capacity relative to other provinces and its need for funds to finance the provision of some standard level of public services. Which of these formulas is appropriate depends on what other federal-state transfers exist alongside revenue sharing. If revenue sharing is the main means for getting unconditional funding to the states, it ought in principle to be designed to meet the objectives of federal-state transfers, which include some equalizing component.

Finally, the mechanism for determining the type of revenues to be shared and their amount can vary from country to country. The formula can be to some extent constitutionalized. Thus, the constitution might stipulate which federal tax revenues must be subject to revenue sharing (e.g., Germany, Argentina). Alternatively, revenue-sharing structures might be based on the advice and recommendation of quasi-independent bodies that exist in some federations (e.g., Australia, India, South Africa). Depending on the country involved, these bodies may have more or less clout in determining the final outcome. But the most common practice is for the federal government itself to determine the revenue-sharing formula, taking into account its own political and economic objectives. This has the advantage of making the federal legislature explicitly responsible and accountable for the system. But it has the potential disadvantage of subjecting the formula to frequent change, perhaps as frequent as the annual federal budget.

THE PROS AND CONS OF REVENUE SHARING

Revenue sharing is widely used by federations around the world. The main arguments for it use are straightforward. These are recounted first, followed by some of the drawbacks with revenue sharing.

Arguments for Revenue Sharing

Revenue sharing represents a simple way to get a reasonably secure and growing amount of revenues to the states. As mentioned previously, revenue-sharing formulas are quite simple and transparent. For a given revenue-sharing base, one needs to define only the sharing proportion and its allocation to the states.

Standard revenue-sharing systems provide transfers in a lump-sum and unconditional way to the states. The states are left with full discretion over how to spend them. This facilitates the decentralization of fiscal responsibility and contributes to the efficiency of the federal system. The states are accountable to their own constituents via the legislative process for the manner in which they provide public services. Moreover, as long as the states have reasonable sources of their own revenues, they can determine the size of their expenditure programs. Revenue-sharing transfers will be inframarginal sources of revenues.

At the same time, revenue sharing can be a very flexible policy instrument. In addition to closing the fiscal gap, it can be designed to accomplish other objectives of federal-state transfers. For example, it can have an equalizing effect on state revenues. In Switzerland, a portion of selected federal tax revenues is shared on the basis of the financial strength of the cantons, as part of the confederation's support of financial equalization (Schmitt, 2005). In Indonesia, the central government administers all shared taxes, which can include an element of redistribution. Property tax revenues, for example, are allocated primarily to the originating region (80 percent), but a portion is also distributed among all the regions (Taliercio, 2005). It could also in principle have elements of conditionality, similar to those found in block grants. Of course, the more of these features are incorporated into the revenue-sharing system, the more complicated it becomes, and the more it becomes open to federal discretion. This can detract from the independence of state fiscal decision making.

The use of revenue sharing, like the use of other forms of federal-state transfers, allows expenditure responsibilities to be decentralized to the states, while retaining major revenue raising at the federal level. Thus, it can be seen as a way of facilitating the effective decentralization of fiscal responsibilities to the states and preserving a fully harmonized tax system. In Australia, for example, the federal government collects all revenues from the income and goods and services taxes. The sole federal use of the income tax began in the Second World War. In the late 1990s, the states agreed to forgo additional taxes in exchange for a commonwealth agreement to allocate goods and services tax (GST) revenues to them. These shared revenues (general revenue funds) are distributed among the states in proportion to population, with an equalizing factor adjustment taking into account revenue capacity and expenditure needs (Saunders, 2005).

The fact that revenue sharing is formula based further contributes to the effectiveness of decentralization. A general principle of decentralization is that its effectiveness is enhanced to the extent that transfers are formula based rather than discretionary. The existence of discretionary grants leaves open the opportunity – often seemingly irresistible – for the federal government to exercise too much control over provincial spending priorities. Revenue-sharing systems can provide some discipline against that. This is especially important when the states rely on federal transfers for a significant proportion of their funding.

Drawbacks of Revenue Sharing

For all its simplicity and effectiveness in getting funds into the hands of the states with a minimum of intrusion, revenue sharing has some drawbacks, especially if relied on excessively. The main issue concerns the fact that, while states are left with considerable discretion in the use of revenue-sharing funds, they have virtually no discretion over the amount of funds they receive. If revenue sharing is seen as an alternative to other forms of federal-state transfers, this is no drawback. But revenue sharing is often a feature of federations that leave little revenue-raising responsibility to the state governments. In Mexico, for example, the central government collects most of the important taxes. About 60 percent of federal tax revenues are shared. Subnational governments are heavily dependent on federal revenue transfers. In 2003 an average of 95 percent of states' revenues came from transfers; at the municipal level the figures ranged from 50 to 98 percent (J. Gonzalez, 2005). In these circumstances, revenue sharing must be assessed against the alternative of assigning tax sources to the states. As we saw in the previous chapter, states can be given access to broad-based tax sources in a way that does not disrupt the integrity of a single tax base and tax-collecting authority, such as by the use of surtaxes on federal tax liabilities. Enhancing the ability of the states to raise their own revenues can increase the accountability of state governments for their fiscal performance.

Another potential drawback to revenue-sharing schemes is that the formula determining the state's revenue allocation bears little relation to actual state expenditures. In particular, given the sharing formula, state revenues will grow at the rate of growth of the federal tax sources being shared. This may differ considerably from the rate of growth of state expenditure responsibilities. In most federations, significant responsibilities in education, health, and social services are at the state level, and these are among the most rapidly growing expenditure areas. State expenditures might rise especially rapidly in developing countries, where programs in these areas are in the process of becoming established, where decentralization is being undertaken, and where the states may be responsible for significant infrastructure programs. Of course, in principle, revenue-sharing rates can be adjusted to account for this, but that is much less flexible than giving the states direct discretion over more of their own revenue raising.

A final potential drawback to revenue sharing is that it exposes the states to the risk associated with unanticipated changes in the federal tax base. This is especially, but not exclusively, the case when the revenue-sharing base is relatively narrow. It is often argued more generally that one of the roles of the federal government is to provide insurance against idiosyncratic risk facing the states. Whether this is true might be a matter of dispute. One might expect that the states could insure themselves against idiosyncratic risks by using capital markets for borrowing and lending, at least if the risks are not correlated over time. To the extent that the states must rely on the federal government to fulfill a risk-sharing function, revenue sharing is not a suitable device. Far from protecting the states from risks that they might face from internal sources, it actually exposes them to some of the risks faced by the federal government. This suggests, as with many of the previous arguments, that revenue sharing should be at best one of many comparable components in the system of federal-state fiscal arrangements.

MECHANISMS OF REVENUE SHARING

We have already outlined in general terms the different forms that revenue-sharing systems might take. In this section, we take a slightly more detailed look at the properties of these forms.

Revenue Sharing by Base

In principle, revenue sharing could apply to any tax base occupied by the federal government. However, there seems to be little justification for sharing narrow tax bases such as excise taxes. Narrower bases do not get reasonably large revenues into the hands of the states, which is a main objective of revenue sharing, and are less likely to yield a secure source of revenues. Thus, attention can be restricted to the various broad-based taxes, including income, payroll, general sales, property, and perhaps significant resource taxes.

Income Tax
The income tax is the largest tax base and potentially the largest revenue source available to governments. In OECD countries, it accounts for a substantial amount of tax revenues, although its potential has not been realized in most developing countries. It is typically collected at the federal level. As we have seen, there are good arguments for retaining a single tax-collection agency with a common base and perhaps a common rate structure. Indeed, in many countries it is only at the federal level that administrative machinery exists to collect the tax and ensure compliance. Being a large base, it yields a reasonably steady stream of revenues, although it is naturally subject to cyclical fluctuations. It would therefore seem to be a suitable candidate for revenue sharing, at least in countries that are able to exploit the base.

The real issue with the income tax is whether access to its revenues is best accomplished by a revenue-sharing mechanism. As we have discussed in the previous chapter, it is feasible to give states direct access to the income tax by allowing them to piggyback on the federal government's income tax by imposing surtaxes. (Indeed, the states could even be allowed to impose a tax directly on the base of the federal income tax.) Such a mechanism accomplishes much the same as revenue sharing in the sense that the states obtain a proportion of federal revenues, but it has the advantage that each state can choose the surtax rate it imposes. This allows the states to tailor the rate to suit their own needs and preferences and enhances the responsibility and accountability of the state governments.

The use of a surtax as an alternative to revenue sharing is more restrictive in one sense. The revenues thus collected accrue to the states according to the principle of derivation. Revenue sharing is more flexible in the sense that the funds that are shared can be allocated in a more redistributive way. That is, they can be used to accomplish some of the other objectives of transfers, such as equalizing the ability of the states to provide a given level of public services. If states are allowed to use surtaxes, there would need to be a complementary system of transfers that accomplishes these other ends. The requirement for such a system is the price that necessarily has to be paid in order to get revenue-raising responsibility into the hands of the state governments, which itself is a laudable objective.

Payroll Tax

Similar considerations apply in the case of payroll taxes. The base for payroll taxes is slightly narrower than the income tax, but it is still a large potential revenue raiser. Revenue sharing could generate sizable amounts of revenue for the states, which could be allocated among them in order to achieve objectives other than simply closing the fiscal gap.

The case for allowing states direct access to payroll taxes, however, is at least as strong, and probably stronger, than for the income tax. We have argued in the previous chapter that the payroll tax is an ideal tax for decentralization to the states. It is broad-based, is relatively easy to collect by payroll deduction (at least for reasonably sized employers), demands less harmonization, and generates less fiscal externalities than other tax bases. Even if the states are not ready to administer their own payroll taxes, they could piggyback on the federal payroll tax. In addition, to the extent that the payroll tax is earmarked to financing particular state spending programs (e.g., pensions, unemployment insurance, workers compensation), it becomes de facto a state tax. So it is not clear why one would choose to use it for revenue sharing rather than as an own-source revenue for the states.

If payroll taxation were used by the states instead of revenue sharing, it would again have to be accompanied by a system of transfers designed to achieve the other functions of transfers. Otherwise, revenue sharing could be used for that purpose.

General Sales Tax

General sales taxation is a mainstay of tax revenue for most countries. It is especially important for developing countries. Moreover, most countries have recognized the advantages of adopting the value-added tax (VAT) as the preferred form of sales taxation. The VAT is a broad-based tax that can be applied as far up the chain of production as the retail stage. The method of crediting businesses for taxes paid on their inputs and the ability to purge exports of taxes while taxing imports fully makes the VAT a neutral form of taxation. It favors no one industry over another, and it treats domestically produced goods on a par with imports. Moreover, the input credit mechanism creates the means by which compliance with the tax can be enhanced.

Unlike with direct taxes on income or payrolls, the VAT does not lend itself as readily to state participation. If states were allowed to set their own VAT rates or surtaxes alongside the federal VAT, the system would become much more complex and difficult to administer (though perhaps not impossible, as we have discussed in Chapter 4). The VAT is more of a candidate for revenue sharing than income or payroll taxes, especially because the VAT is a reasonably stable tax base.

The main issue with applying revenue sharing to the VAT concerns the choice between revenue sharing as a means of getting transfers to the states and formula-based unconditional transfers. The latter have the advantage that the formula for determining the amount of the transfer and its escalation can be based more directly on the needs of the states rather than on federal tax revenues. For example, they could be based on some measure of the amount of funds that would be required to finance a standard level of state public services and could escalate according to some index of state expenditure needs. On the other hand, these calculations are not straightforward to do.

The case for adopting a formula-based method of transfers rather than one determined at the discretion of the federal government is strong. There may be political arguments for using a revenue-sharing system rather than a transfer system as a means of achieving a stable formula. That is, a revenue-sharing formula may be more sustainable than a transfer formula. There will be less opportunity to change the formula from year to year and therefore less temptation for political decision makers to do so.

Resource Taxes

In some countries, resource revenues are major sources of government revenue, for example, if the country is endowed with large mineral or oil and gas deposits or sizable forests. In these circumstances, as we have argued, there are significant advantages to having the federal government be the revenue-raising authority, especially if the distribution of the resource wealth is very uneven across states. Given the magnitude of the revenues, and perhaps some notion that as a common resource the states might have some claim to sharing their property rights, resource revenues might be a natural candidate for revenue sharing. For example, the Mexican constitution includes a provision for the federal government to share with states revenues from the "special taxes" levied on exclusively federal sources of revenue. These include taxes on petroleum-based products and forestry exploitation. It is further expected that the states will share these revenues with municipalities (J. Gonzalez, 2005).

As with the other major taxes, there are pros and cons of applying revenue sharing to resources. On the pro side, revenue sharing might be a superior way of getting resource revenues into the hands of the states than allowing the states to have direct access to them. If the resources are unevenly distributed across states, states would obtain very different amounts of revenue. In principle, the disadvantages of this could be offset by an equalization system. However, such a system might be difficult to sustain politically, as the experience of federations that assigns resource revenues to states attests (e.g., Canada). Moreover, equalization schemes intended to undo the uneven distribution of resource revenues inevitably induce adverse incentive effects upon the states. The amount of resource revenues that a state collects is partly determined by state policies with respect to resource development. States might be reluctant to develop resource properties if the additional resource revenues generated for them end up being taxed away through the equalization system. These problems do not apply if resource revenues (and resource management) are in the hands of the federal government and the revenues are shared with the states. The sharing formula can ensure that all states obtain a "fair" share of the revenues regardless of which states the revenues come from.

On the other hand, there are disadvantages to revenue sharing. The standard one that the states do not have any discretion over their revenues applies. As a revenue-sharing base, resource revenues also have the disadvantage of being unstable because they depend on resource prices. To the extent that the federal government is better able to pool the risk of fluctuations in commodity prices, it would be preferable to base transfers on a more stable formula than a share of resource revenues.

Other Issues with Specific Revenue Sharing

Among other considerations related to revenue sharing applied to specific tax types, one concerns the incentives that revenue sharing imposes on the federal government. If the federal government obtains only a fraction of the revenues it collects from a particular base, that will provide a disincentive for it to use that base relative to others. Not only that, the federal tax-collection agency may be less vigilant in administering the tax, choosing to devote more of its scarce compliance resources to other types of taxes. A classic example of disincentives created by sharing specific taxes is India. The Constitution of India originally mandated the sharing of revenues from nonagricultural income taxes and union excise duties collected by the center. The amount to be shared was determined by the finance commissions. Successive commissions increased the states' shares, which reached high points of 87.5 percent for net income revenues and 47.5 percent of union excise duties in the late 1990s. The central government's response was to increase reliance over time on nonshared revenues, particularly customs duties and the administered prices of public monopolies. The system was changed in 2000, when the Eightieth Constitutional Amendment required all federal revenues to be part of the divisible pool of funds. The Twelfth Finance Commission recommended that 30.5 percent of central tax revenues be shared with the states during the period from 2005–6 to 2009–10 (Rao, 2007b).

There are some purely administrative problems as well. For one, to the extent that the principle of derivation applies or that the grants to states are conditioned on the size of each state's tax base, it is necessary to calculate the collection of tax revenues by state. That may not be an easy task. There may also be a significant time lag between when taxes are levied and the determination of final tax liabilities. For example, the final reconciliation of income tax liabilities can take until several months after the end of the tax year. This will cause a considerable delay in getting the correct amount of revenues to the states. Such a delay can be avoided by a transfer system based on other criteria.[1] If the federal government is better able to bear risks than the states, unconditional formula-based transfer schemes can be preferable to revenue-sharing schemes.

General Revenue Sharing

General revenue sharing refers to systems under which a share of some broad portion of federal revenues is passed on to the provinces. These schemes are more directly comparable with unconditional grant programs

---

[1] Formula-based transfers cannot avoid such delays entirely. For example, to the extent that transfers are based on population, delays in final reconciliation can be significant. Current population estimates may not be that much more accurate than, say, income estimates.

because both are basically financed out of federal general revenues. The main distinction is that the amount of the transfer in the revenue-sharing case is tied directly to federal revenues, whereas there is no such limitation in the case of unconditional transfers. Otherwise, the systems are very comparable. In particular, the allocation of the funds across states can be chosen at will. As well, it would be possible to attach general conditions to the use of the transfers by the states.

The choice between revenue sharing and conditional grant systems seemingly boils down to the desirability of tying transfers to federal government revenues. On the face of it, this seems like an unnecessary restriction, given that state expenditure needs do not evolve in the same way as federal revenues. And, as we have seen, tying state grants to federal revenues implies some cyclical instability in state revenues.

At the same time, there may be some noneconomic arguments for the use of revenue sharing (apart from constitutional stipulations that dictate revenue sharing as a form of transfer). Tying transfers to the states to federal tax revenues ensures that the transfers will be affordable. If the transfers were tied to, say, state expenditures, the federal government might be concerned about the loss of control in the rate at which its payments to the states escalate. Moreover, as we have mentioned, embodying a formula for transfers into a revenue-sharing scheme may result in more sustainability of a formula-based system of transfers.

ASSESSMENT

To complete the discussion of this chapter, we can take stock of the case for and against revenue sharing as part of a system of federal-state fiscal arrangements. The following points summarize the arguments:

1. Revenue sharing applied to one of the broad tax bases is an administratively simple way of getting large sums of money into the hands of the states with little disruption of the tax system. It therefore facilitates the decentralization of expenditure responsibilities.
2. The case for revenue sharing of narrow tax bases is weak. The amount of financing it gets to the states is likely to be small relative to their expenditure needs; the funding is likely to be relatively variable; and the system is likely to influence the incentives of the federal government.
3. General revenue sharing provides a fairly predictable amount of funding to the states and helps ensure that general transfers are

formula based rather than discretionary. That predictability is, however, limited by the fact that revenues being shared are cyclical, so
that the states are faced with the same financial risk as is the federal
government. They may not be as well able to bear that risk.

4. The formula on which revenue sharing is based entails that, for a
given sharing rule, state funding rises at the rate of growth of federal
tax revenues rather than some indicator of provincial expenditure
needs.

5. Revenue-sharing funds can be allocated among the states to achieve
some of the same objectives as federal-provincial transfers. They are
a way to fill the fiscal gap created because the case for decentralization of expenditures is greater than that for taxation. They can be
equalizing, which is important if different states have different
fiscal capacities and needs for public expenditures to finance a
standard level of public services. And they could have broad conditions attached to them to induce the states to use the funds
in ways that recognize or facilitate national economic and social
policy objectives.

6. The main disadvantage of revenue sharing is that it leaves no discretion to the states in terms of revenue raising, even at the margin.
The absence of such discretion detracts from fiscal and political
accountability. This suggests that they should not be the sole or even
the predominant source of revenue to the states. Instead, they should
be accompanied by enough revenue-raising responsibility so that the
states can effectively control the size of their budgets.

7. Among the broad tax bases, the case for revenue sharing is strongest
for the VAT and weakest for direct taxes on income and payrolls. In
the case of income taxes, state surtaxes can be used that not only get
revenues to the states but do so in a way that gives some discretion to
them for the amount of revenues they raise. With payroll taxes, states
can either piggyback onto federal taxes or readily use their own tax
systems. It is considerably more difficult for the states to run their
own VAT systems or to piggyback on the federal VAT. If states are
given direct access to revenue sources, either solely or with the federal government, there needs to be a complementary transfer scheme
that equalizes fiscal capacities of the states and accomplishes the
other objectives of federal-state transfers.

In summary, while revenue sharing may be one useful way to get large
sums of revenues to the states, there are often better alternatives that

will do so in a way that enables decentralized decision making to occur with truly decentralized responsibility. And, when revenue sharing is used, it should be accompanied in the fiscal arrangements by other components that ensure that states have effective discretion for the size of their budgets.

NINE

The Principles of Intergovernmental Transfers

THE TYPES OF TRANSFERS AND THEIR PURPOSE

Federal-state transfers are an important feature of all federations, and their analogue is used in nonfederal countries that have multiple levels of government as well.[1] These transfers form part of a broader system of fiscal relations between the federal and state levels of government. We begin this introductory section by outlining the forms that transfers can take before turning to the rationale for federal-state transfers. In what follows, we use the terms "transfers" and "grants" interchangeably.

Forms of Intergovernmental Transfers

Intergovernmental transfers form part of the system of federal-state fiscal arrangements that are in place to coordinate fiscal decision making at the two highest levels of government, federal and state. Federal-state fiscal relations consist primarily of a set of financial transfers from the federal government to the states and a set of arrangements for coordinating and sharing particular tax bases. There may also be federal-state agreements on fiscal issues, such as agreements on internal trade, agreements to coordinate the exercise of policy responsibilities

---

[1] The distinction between a federation and a nonfederal country with multiple jurisdictions is not a clear one. Virtually all countries have at least two levels of government, a central one and a local one. Federations might best be thought of in terms of the autonomy of the subnational governments. Typically they have independent legislative jurisdiction in some spheres and therefore are not accountable on a detailed basis to the national government. But some multilevel governments are virtually federal in all but name. South Africa, for example, has responsible governments at the state level that have considerable independence of decision making; however, perhaps for political reasons, it eschews the label "federal."

that are jointly occupied by the two levels of government (e.g., environmental polices), and interactions between the governments through regulations. In principle, the two levels of government could be financially independent and separate, but that is typically not the case. The federal government will generally collect more tax revenues than it needs for its own purposes and transfer some of the excess to the states either as grants or by the explicit sharing of tax revenues. This outcome reflects the fact that, while it may be efficient to decentralize expenditure responsibilities to a considerable extent, it is less efficient to decentralize revenue raising. Moreover, in a decentralized federation, there is a need for federal-state transfers in order to allow the federal government to fulfill its national efficiency and equity objectives.

There are some common properties of intergovernmental fiscal instruments that are worth summarizing at the outset.

Instruments of Intergovernmental Finance

Intergovernmental transfers or grants can be broadly classified into two categories: general-purpose (unconditional) and specific-purpose (conditional or earmarked) transfers.

General-Purpose Transfers. General-purpose transfers are provided as general budget support, with no strings attached. These transfers are typically mandated by law, but occasionally they may be of an ad hoc or discretionary nature. Such transfers are intended to preserve local autonomy and enhance interjurisdictional equity. That is why article 9 of the European Charter of Local Self Government advocates such transfers by stating: "As far as possible, grants to local authorities shall not be earmarked for the financing of specific projects. The provision of grants shall not remove the basic freedom of local authorities to exercise policy discretion within their own jurisdiction" (Barati and Szalai, 2000: 21).

General-purpose transfers are termed block transfers when they are used to provide broad support in a general area of subnational expenditures (e.g., education), while allowing recipients discretion in allocating the funds among specific uses. Block grants are a vaguely defined concept. They fall in the gray area between general-purpose and specific-purpose transfers, as they provide budget support with no strings attached in a broad but specific area of subnational expenditures.

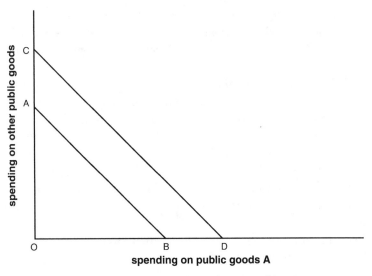

Figure 9.1. Effect of Unconditional Nonmatching Grant

General-purpose transfers simply augment the recipient's resources. They have only an income effect as indicated in Figure 9.1 by the shift in the recipient's budget line AB upward and to the right throughout by the amount of the grant (AC = BD) and the new budget line becomes CD. Because the grant can be spent on any combination of public goods or services or used to provide tax relief to residents, general nonmatching assistance does not affect relative prices (no substitution effect). It is also the least stimulative of local spending, typically increasing such spending by less than fifty cents for each additional dollar of unconditional assistance. The remaining funds are made available as tax relief to local residents to spend on private goods and services.

Conceptually a dollar increase in local residents' income should have exactly the same impact on local public spending as receipt of one dollar of general-purpose transfer. Both tend to shift the budget line outward identically. In fact, all empirical studies show that one dollar received by the community in the form of a general-purpose grant tends to increase local public spending by more than a dollar increase in residents' income – that is, the portion of grants retained for local spending tends to exceed the effective tax rate imposed by local governments on residents' incomes (Rosen, 2005; Oates, 1999; Gramlich, 1977). Grant money tends to stick where it first lands, leaving a smaller-than-expected fraction available for tax relief, a phenomenon referred to as the "flypaper effect." The implication is that for political and bureaucratic reasons, grants to local governments tend to result in more local spending than they would have had the same transfers been made directly to local residents (McMillan, Shah, and Gillen, 1980). An explanation for this impact is provided by the hypothesis that bureaucrats seek to maximize the size of their budgets as it gives them greater power and influence in their local community (Filimon, Romer, and Rosenthal, 1982).

Formula-based general-purpose transfers are very common. The federal and state transfers to municipalities in Brazil are examples of grants of this kind. Evidence suggests that such transfers induce municipalities to under-utilize their own tax bases (Shah, 1991).

Specific-Purpose Transfers. Specific-purpose, or conditional, transfers are intended to provide incentives for governments to undertake specific programs or activities. These grants may be regular or mandatory or discretionary or ad hoc.

Conditional transfers typically specify the type of expenditures that can be financed (input-based conditionality). These may be capital expenditures, operating expenditures, or both. Conditional transfers may also require attainment of certain results in service delivery (output-based conditionality). Input-based conditionality is often intrusive and unproductive, whereas output-based conditionality can advance grantors' objectives while preserving local autonomy.

Conditional transfers may incorporate matching provisions – requiring grant recipients to finance a specified percentage of expenditures using their own resources. Matching requirements can be either open-ended, meaning that the grantor matches whatever level of resources the recipient provides, or closed-ended, meaning that the grantor matches recipient funds only up to a prespecified limit.

Matching requirements encourage greater scrutiny and local ownership of grant-financed expenditures; closed-ended matching is helpful in ensuring that the grantor has some control over the costs of the transfer program. Matching requirements, however, represent a greater burden for a recipient jurisdiction with limited fiscal capacity. In view of this, it may be desirable to set matching rates in inverse proportion to the per capita fiscal capacity of the jurisdiction in order to allow poorer jurisdictions to participate in grant-financed programs.

Nonmatching Transfers. Conditional nonmatching transfers provide a given level of funds without local matching, as long the funds are spent

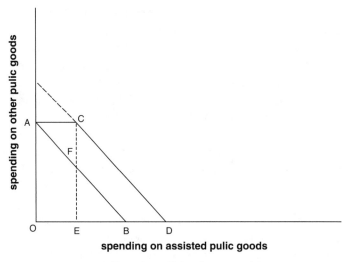

Figure 9.2. Effect of Conditional Nonmatching Grant

for a particular purpose. Following the grant (= AC), the budget line in Figure 9.2 shifts from AB to ACD, where at least OE (= AC) of the assisted public good will be acquired.

Conditional nonmatching grants are best suited for subsidizing activities considered high priority by a higher-level government but low priority by local governments. This may be the case if a program generates a high degree of spillovers up to a given level of provision (OE), after which the external benefits terminate abruptly.

For a given level of available assistance, grant recipients prefer unconditional nonmatching transfers, which provide them with maximum flexibility to pursue their own objectives. Because such grants augment resources without influencing spending patterns, they allow recipients to maximize their own welfare. Grantors, however, may be prepared to sacrifice some recipient satisfaction to ensure that the funds are directed toward expenditures on which they place a priority. This is particularly so when federal objectives are implemented by line agencies or departments rather than through a central agency, such as the Ministry of Finance, with a broader mandate. Federal departments do not want local governments to shift their program funds toward other areas. In this situation, conditional (selective) nonmatching (block) grants can ensure that the funds are spent in a department's area of interest (e.g., health care) without distorting local priorities among alternative activities or inducing inefficient allocations in the targeted expenditure area.

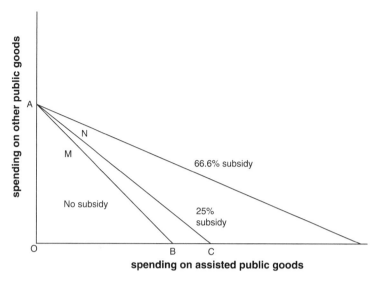

Figure 9.3. Effect of Open-Ended Matching Grant

Matching Transfers. Conditional matching grants, or cost-sharing programs, require that funds be spent for specific purposes and that the recipient match the funds to some degree. Figure 9.3 shows the effect on a local government budget of a 25 percent subsidy program for transportation. AB indicates the no subsidy line – the combination of transportation and other public goods and services a city can acquire with a budget of OA = OB. A federal subsidy of 25 percent of transportation expenditures (i.e., a grant of $1.00 for every $3.00 of local funds spent on transportation) shifts the budget line of attainable combinations to AC. At any level of other goods and services, the community can obtain one-third more transportation services. If the community chooses combination M before the grant, it will likely select a combination such as N afterward. At N, more transportation is acquired.

The subsidy has two effects, an income effect and a substitution effect. The subsidy gives the community more resources, some of which go to acquiring more transportation services (the income effect). Because the subsidy reduces the relative price of transportation services, the community acquires more transportation services from a given budget (the substitution effect). Both effects stimulate higher spending on transportation.

Although the grant is for transportation, other public goods and services may also be acquired, even though they become relatively more expensive, as a result of the substitution effect. If the income effect is sufficiently large, it will dominate, and the grant will increase consumption of other goods and services. Most studies find that for grants of this kind, spending in the specified area increases by less than the amount of the grant, with the remainder going toward other public goods and services and tax relief (see Gamkhar and Shah, 2007). This is the so-called fungibility effect of grants. The fungibility of conditional grants depends on both the level of spending on the assisted public service and the relative priority of such spending. For example, if the recipient's own-financed expenditure on the assisted category exceeds the amount of the conditional grant, the conditionality of the grant may or may not have any impact on the recipient's spending behavior: all, some, or none of the grant funds could go to the assisted function. Shah (1985, 1988b, 1989b) finds that while provincial assistance to cities in Alberta for public transit was partially diverted to finance other services, similar assistance for road transportation improvement was not.

Open-ended matching grants, in which no limit is placed on available assistance through matching provisions, are well suited for correcting inefficiencies in the provision of public goods arising from benefit spillovers, or externalities. Benefit spillovers occur when services provided and financed by a local government also benefit members of other local governments that do not contribute to their provision. Because the providing government bears all the costs but obtains only a portion of the benefits, it tends to underprovide the goods. If the affected communities cannot negotiate compensation, the situation can be corrected by a higher government subsidizing provision of the service, with the extent of the spillover determining the degree of subsidy or the matching ratio.

Matching grants can correct inefficiencies from spillovers, but they do not address uneven or inadequate fiscal capacities across state and local governments. Local governments with ample resources can afford to meet matching requirements and acquire a substantial amount of assistance. States with limited fiscal capacities may be unable to match federal funds and therefore fail to obtain as much assistance, even though their expenditure needs may be equal to or greater than those of wealthier states (Shah, 1991). Other forms of assistance are needed to equalize fiscal capacities in such cases.

Grantors usually prefer closed-ended matching transfers, in which funds are provided to a certain limit, because such transfers permit them to retain control over their budgets. Figure 9.4 shows the effect of closed-ended matching grants on the local budget. AB is the original budget line. When $1.00 of assistance is available for every $3.00 of local funds spent up

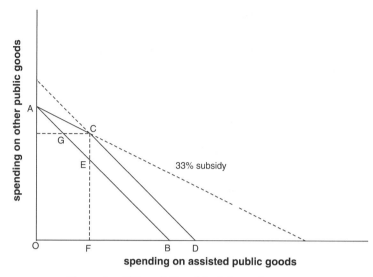

Figure 9.4. Effect of Closed-Ended Matching Grant

to a prespecified limit, the budget line becomes ACD. Initially, costs are shared on a basis of one-third to two-thirds up to a level at which the subsidy limit of CG (= CE) is reached. Expenditures beyond OF receive no subsidy, so the slope of the budget line reverts back to 1:1 rather than 1:3 along the subsidized segment, AC.

Empirical studies typically find that closed-ended grants stimulate expenditures on the subsidized activity more than open-ended grants (Gramlich, 1977; Shah, 1994b; Gamkhar and Shah, 2007). The estimated response to an additional $1.00 of this kind of grant is typically $1.50. Institutional factors may explain this surprisingly large response.

Why are conditional closed-ended matching grants common in industrial countries when they seem ill designed to solve problems and inefficiencies in the provision of public goods? The answer seems to be that correcting for inefficiencies is not the sole or perhaps even the primary objective. Instead, grants are employed to help local governments financially while promoting spending on activities given priority by the grantor. The conditional (selective) aspects of or conditions on the spending are expected to ensure that the funds are directed toward an activity the grantor views as desirable. This, however, may be false comfort in view of the potential for fungibility of funds. The local matching or cost-sharing component affords the grantor a degree of control, requires a degree of financial accountability by the recipient, and makes the cost known to the granting government.

Conditional closed-ended matching grants have advantages and disadvantages from the grantor's perspective. While such grants may result in a significant transfer of resources, they may distort output and cause inefficiencies, because the aid is often available only for a few activities, causing overspending on these functions while other functions are underfinanced. If capital outlays are subsidized while operating costs are not, grants may induce spending on capital-intensive alternatives.

Conditional open-ended matching grants are the most suitable vehicles to induce lower- level governments to increase spending on the assisted function (Table 9.1). If the objective is simply to enhance the welfare of local residents, general-purpose nonmatching transfers are preferable, as they preserve local autonomy.

To ensure accountability for results, conditional nonmatching output-based transfers are preferable to other types of transfers. Output-based transfers respect local autonomy and budgetary flexibility while providing incentives and accountability mechanisms to improve service delivery performance. The design of such transfers is discussed in the next section.

Achieving Results-Based Accountability through Performance-Oriented Transfers

Economic rationales for output-based grants (used interchangeably with performance-oriented transfers in this chapter) stem from the emphasis on contract-based management under the new public management framework and strengthening demand for good governance by lowering the transaction costs for citizens in obtaining public services under the new institutional economics approach. The new public management framework seeks to strengthen accountability for results by changing the management paradigm in the public sector from permanent appointments to contractual appointment and continuation of employment subject to fulfillment of service delivery contracts. It seeks to create a competitive service delivery environment by making financing available on similar conditions to all providers – government and nongovernment.

The new institutional economics approach argues that dysfunctional governance in the public sector results from opportunistic behavior by public officials, as citizens are either not empowered to hold public officials accountable for their noncompliance with their mandates and/or for corrupt acts or face high transaction costs in doing so. In this framework, citizens are treated as the principals and public officials the agents. The principals have bounded rationality – they act rationally on the basis of the incomplete information they have. Acquiring and processing information

Table 9.1. *Taxonomy of grants and their conceptual impacts*

Type of grant	Income effect			Price (substitution) effect			Total effect				Rank by objective function		
	a_1	A	U	a_1	A	U	a_1	A	U	$\partial A/\partial G$	Increases in expenditure	Accountability for results	Welfare
Conditional (input based) matching													
Open-ended	↑	↑	↑	↑	↑	→	↑↑	↑↑	↑↓	>1	1	3 (none)	3
Closed-ended													
Binding constraint	↑	↑	↑	↑	↑	→	↑↑	↑↑	↑↓	≥ 1	2 or 3	3 (none)	4
Nonbinding constraint	↑	↑	↑	n.a.	n.a.	n.a.	↑	↑	↑	≤ 1	3	3 (none)	2
Conditional nonmatching	↑	↑	↑	n.a.	n.a.	n.a.	↑	↑	↑	≤ 1	3	3 (none)	2
Conditional nonmatching output-based	↑	↑	↑	n.a.	n.a.	n.a.	↑	↑	↑	≤ 1	3	1 (high)	1
General nonmatching	n.a.	↑	↑	n.a.	n.a.	n.a.	n.a.	↑	↑	<1	3	3 (none)	1

Note: 1 = highest score, 4 = lowest score. ↑ = positive impact; ↓ = negative impact; a_1 = assisted subfunction; A = assisted function; U = unassisted function; G = grant; n.a. = not applicable.

Source: Shah (2007c).

Program → Objectives	Inputs →	Intermediate →	Outputs →	Outcomes →	Impact →	Reach
Improve quantity, quality, and access to education services	Educational spending by age, sex, urban/rural; spending by grade level, teachers, staff, facilities, tools, books, regulations	Enrollments, student-teacher ratio, class size	Achievement scores, graduation rates, drop-out rates	Literacy rates, supply of skilled professio nals	Informed citizenry, civic engagement, enhanced international competitiven ess	Winners and losers from government programs

Figure 9.5. Results Chain with an Application to Education Services. *Source:* Shah (2005b)

about public-sector operations are costly. Agents (public officials) are better informed than principals. Their self-interest motivates them to withhold information from the public domain, as releasing such information helps principals hold them accountable. This asymmetry of information allows agents to indulge in opportunistic behavior, which goes unchecked because of high transactions costs faced by the principals and a lack of or inadequacy of countervailing institutions to enforce accountable governance. Results-based accountability through output-based grants empowers citizens by increasing their information base and lowering their transactions costs in demanding action.

Output-based transfers link grant finance with service delivery performance. These transfers place conditions on the results to be achieved while providing full flexibility in the design of programs and associated spending levels to achieve those objectives. Such transfers help restore recipients' focus on the results-based chain (Figure 9.5) and the alternate service delivery framework (competitive framework for public service delivery) to achieve those results. In order to achieve grant objectives, a public manager in the recipient government would examine the results-based chain to determine whether program activities are expected to yield the desired results. To do so, he or she needs to monitor program activities and inputs, including intermediate inputs (resources used to produce outputs), outputs (quantity and quality of public goods and services produced and access to such goods and services), outcomes (intermediate- to long-run consequences for consumers/taxpayers of public service provision or progress in achieving program objectives), impact (program goals or very long-term consequences of public service provision), and reach (people who benefit from or are hurt by a program). Such a managerial focus reinforces joint ownership and accountability of the principal and the agent in achieving shared goals by highlighting terms of mutual trust. Thus, internal and external reporting shifts from the traditional focus on inputs to a focus on outputs, reach, and outcomes – in particular, outputs that lead to results. Flexibility in project definition and implementation is achieved by shifting emphasis from strict monitoring of inputs to monitoring performance results and their measurements. Tracking progress toward expected results is done through indicators, which are negotiated between the provider and the financing agency. This joint goal setting and reporting helps ensure client satisfaction on an ongoing basis while building partnership and ownership into projects (Shah, 2005b).

Output-based grants must have conditions on outputs as opposed to outcomes, because outcomes are subject to influence by factors beyond the control of a public manager. Public managers should be held accountable only for factors under their control. Outcome-based conditions diffuse enforcement of accountability for results. Because the grant conditions are concerned with service delivery performance in terms of quality of output and access, the manager is free to choose the program and inputs to deliver results. To achieve those results, he or she faces positive incentives by grant conditions that encourage alternate service delivery mechanisms by contracting out, outsourcing, or simply encouraging competition among government and nongovernment providers. This can be done by establishing a level playing field through at-par financing, by offering franchises through competitive bidding, or by providing rewards for performance through benchmarking or yardstick competition. Such an incentive environment is expected to yield a management paradigm that emphasizes results-based accountability to clients with the following common elements:

- Contracts or work program agreements based on prespecified outputs and performance targets and budgetary allocations
- Replacement of lifelong rotating employment with contractual appointments with task specialization
- Managerial flexibility but accountability for results
- Redefinition of public-sector role as purchaser but not necessarily provider of public services
- Adoption of the subsidiarity principle – that is, public-sector decisions made at the level of government closest to the people, unless a convincing case can be made not to do so

- Incentives for cost efficiency
- Incentives for transparency and competitive service provision
- Accountability to taxpayers

Under such an accountable governance framework, grant-financed budget allocations support contracts and work program agreements, which are based on prespecified outputs and performance targets. The grant recipient's flexibility in input selection – including hiring and firing of personnel and implementation of programs – is fully respected, but there is strict accountability for achieving results. The incentive and accountability regime created by output-based transfers is expected to create responsive, responsible, and accountable governance without undermining local autonomy. In contrast, traditional conditional grants with input conditionality undermine local autonomy and budgetary flexibility while reinforcing a culture of opportunism and rent seeking (Table 9.2).

Output-based grants create incentive regimes that promote a results-based accountability culture. Consider the case in which the national government aims to improve access to education by the poor and to enhance the quality of such education. A common approach is to provide grants to government schools through conditional grants. These grants specify the type of expenditures eligible for grant financing (books, computers, teacher aids, and so forth) as well as financial reporting and audit requirements. Such input conditionality undermines budgetary autonomy and flexibility without providing any assurance about the achievement of results. Moreover, in practice it is difficult to enforce, as there may be significant opportunities for fungibility of funds. Experience has shown that there is no one-to-one link between increases in public spending and improvements in service delivery performance (see Huther, Roberts, and Shah, 1997).

Output-based design of such grants can help achieve accountability for results. As illustrated in Box 9.1, under this approach, the national government allocates funds to local governments according to the size of the school-age population. Local governments in turn pass these funds on to both government and nongovernment providers on the basis of school enrollments. Nongovernment providers are eligible to receive grant funds if they admit students on the basis of merit and provide a tuition subsidy to students whose parents cannot afford the tuition. All providers are expected to improve or at the minimum maintain baseline achievement scores on standardized tests, increase graduation rates, and reduce dropout rates. Failure to do so will invite public censure and, in the extreme case,

Table 9.2. *Features of traditional and output-based conditional grants*

Feature	Traditional grant	Output-based grant
Grant objectives	Spending levels	Quality and access to public services
Grant design and administration	Complex	Simple and transparent
Eligibility	Recipient government departments/agencies	Recipient government provides funds to all government and nongovernment providers
Conditions	Expenditures on authorized functions and objects	Outputs-service delivery results
Allocation criteria	Program or project proposals approvals with expenditure details	Demographic data on potential clients
Compliance verification	Higher-level inspections and audits	Client feedback and redress, comparison of baseline and postgrant data on quality and access
Penalties	Audit observations on financial compliance	Public censure, competitive pressures, voice and exit options for clients
Managerial flexibility	Little or none. No tolerance for risk and no accountability for failure	Absolute. Rewards for risks but penalties for persistent failure
Local government autonomy and budgetary flexibility	Little	Absolute
Transparency	Little	Absolute
Focus	Internal	External, competition, innovation and benchmarking
Accountability	Hierarchical to higher-level government, controls on inputs and process with little or no concern for results	Results-based, bottom-up, client-driven

cause grant funds to be discontinued. In the meantime, reputation risks associated with poor performance may reduce enrollments, thereby reducing the grant funds received. Schools have full autonomy in the use of grant funds and are able to retain unused funds.

Box 9.1 Fiscal Need Compensation through Output-Based Transfers for School Finance: An Illustrative Example

Allocation basis to state or local governments: School age population – population aged fifteen to seventeen.

Distribution basis for service providers: Equal per pupil to both government and nongovernment schools.

Conditions: Universal access toprimary and secondary education. Nongovernment school access to poor on merit. Improvement in achievement scores and graduation rates from baseline. No conditions on the use of funds.

Penalties: Public censure, reduction of grant funds, and risk of termination with persistent noncompliance. Grant funds automatically decrease if parents pull out their children from nonperforming school.

Incentives: Grant funds increase automatically as school attracts more students. Retention of savings for optional use from better management of resources.

Impact implications: Encourages competition, innovation, and accountability to citizens for improving quality and access. Automatic monitoring and enforcement provisions through parental choices.

Source: Shah (2007c).

This kind of grant financing would create an incentive environment for both government and nongovernment schools to compete and excel to retain students and establish reputations for quality education, as parental choice determines grant financing to each school. Such an environment is particularly important for government schools, where staff members have lifelong appointments and financing is ensured regardless of performance. Budgetary flexibility and retention of savings would encourage innovation to deliver quality education.

Output-based grants thus preserve autonomy, encourage competition and innovation, and bring strict accountability for results to residents. This accountability regime is self- enforcing through consumer (parental choice in the current example) choice.

The Role of Federal-State Transfers

We can identify five broad economic arguments for federal-state transfers, each of which is based on either efficiency or equity, and each of which may apply to varying degrees in actual federal economies. All of them have been encountered in earlier chapters. They are the existence of vertical fiscal imbalance, or fiscal gap, arising from the greater degree of decentralization of expenditure responsibilities than of the ability to raise taxes; fiscal inequity resulting from differential net fiscal benefits (NFBs) across states; fiscal inefficiency from the same source; interstate spillovers of the benefits (or costs) of state policies; and the harmonization of state fiscal structures. We consider them in turn.

Vertical Fiscal Gap

A feature of almost all federations is that the federal level of government raises more revenue than it needs and transfers the excess to the states to support their expenditures.[2] This difference in federal revenues and expenditure requirements is referred to as the vertical fiscal gap (VFG).[3] The extent of VFG varies widely across federations, being very large in Australia and Germany and in many developing countries but much smaller in Canada and the United States. There is no established theory to serve as a guide to choosing the right level of VFG. The literature on fiscal federalism has only recently even attempted to analyze the optimal degree of VFG, and then only in very simple models.[4] In general terms, there seem to be two main reasons for a VFG. One involves the strength of the case for decentralizing expenditures versus taxes, and the other concerns the role of a VFG in enabling the federal government to carry out its responsibilities for national economic policy.

The first argument for a VFG then is that it arises simply because the case for decentralizing expenditures to the states is much greater than that

---

[2] Notable exceptions in the past were China and Russia where, for historical reasons, tax collection was highly localized and revenues were passed up to the center. In recent years, both these countries have centralized taxing powers.

[3] The terms vertical fiscal gap and vertical fiscal imbalance have been mistakenly used interchangeably in recent literature on fiscal decentralization. A vertical fiscal imbalance occurs when the vertical fiscal gap is not adequately addressed by the reassignment of responsibilities or by fiscal transfers and other means. Boadway (2005a) argues that vertical fiscal imbalance incorporates an ideal or optimum view of expenditures by different orders of government and is therefore hard to measure.

[4] See, for example, Boadway and Keen (1996) and Boadway et al. (1998). For a more policy-oriented discussion of the VFG and vertical fiscal imbalance (VFI), see Boadway (2005b, 2006a). There, the distinction is drawn between the vertical fiscal gap and vertical fiscal imbalance.

for decentralizing taxes. As we have argued in Chapters 2 and 3, the states might be more efficient at delivering public services to individuals and firms and at targeting transfers on the basis of nonincome characteristics. Major public services in areas like health, education, and welfare constitute a substantial component of public-sector budgets, and in many federations are highly decentralized. On the other hand, as mentioned in Chapter 6, there are strong arguments for not decentralizing taxes to as great an extent. Taxes can readily be administered at the center, where a common tax system can apply with the benefits of a single collection agency. Distortions in the internal economic union due to a fragmented tax system can be avoided by centralized collection, and a uniform standard of redistribution can be applied. A centralized tax system avoids the tax competition and interstate tax distortions that might otherwise exist and which would preclude the states from raising the optimal amount of revenues on their own. Competition to attract capital, business activity, and even labor would induce states to raise too little revenues relative to what would be efficient and to distort the interstate allocation of resources. Some of the benefits of a single tax system can be achieved by tax harmonization agreements, but those too can be more readily supported if the federal government maintains a dominant share of the tax room.

The exact size of the VFG on the basis of these arguments remains a matter of judgment. It is argued that too much VFG reduces the accountability of the states because they are not responsible for raising the revenues that they are spending. The counterargument is that what is important for accountability is the ability to raise revenues at the margin, and state responsibility for marginal revenue raising can be achieved regardless of the degree of VFG. As well, from a technical point of view, greater VFG implies higher federal tax rates and exposes state decision making to larger vertical fiscal externalities. As we discussed in Chapter 2, states will neglect the effects that their tax policies have on federal tax revenues. To the extent that increases in state taxes reduce the tax bases used by the federal government, states will impose a negative fiscal externality on the federal government. States will have an incentive to set tax rates that are too high. The larger the federal tax rate is, the greater is this externality. On the other hand, reducing the VFG by putting more tax authority in the hands of the states leads to greater horizontal fiscal externalities. Where the optimal balance lies is not clear.

There may also be arguments based on stabilization for the federal government's retaining fiscal dominance – specifically, the twin ideas that the federal government needs to control the bulk of the major fiscal instruments to enable its fiscal policy to have bite, and the states can thwart federal fiscal policies by taking actions that undo the effects of federal policies (e.g., they may be procyclical). These arguments are not emphasized much because the efficacy of standard fiscal policy has come to be questioned. Moreover, it can be argued that what might be important for effective fiscal policies is the ability to make marginal changes to fiscal stances, and that is possible even in a decentralized setting. In recent years, fiscal policies have tended to be used more to address just long-run issues, like the control of the debt and the encouragement of growth and innovation. It can be argued that the existence of federal fiscal dominance has been somewhat counterproductive from the point of view of these objectives. For example, in Canada, a substantial part of federal deficit control policy consisted simply of passing the problem on to the states by unannounced cutbacks in transfers. This has led to arguments by the states both for more self-sufficiency and for more say in the way in which federal transfers are determined.

The second argument for a VFG – and, given the current state of knowledge, the more convincing one – is that the federal government needs to make transfers to the states in order to fulfill its responsibility for achieving efficiency and equity in the internal economic union. To assess this argument, we turn to the other roles of federal-state transfers in a decentralized federation.

Fiscal Inequity

Fiscal inequity arises when citizens in two different states within a federation are treated differently by the fiscal system. A federation that considers horizontal equity – the equal treatment of all citizens nationwide – to be a consequence of citizenship will want to correct the fiscal inequity that naturally arises in a decentralized federation. As argued in Chapters 2 and 3, states with their own expenditure and taxation responsibilities will be able to provide different NFBs to citizens within their jurisdictions. Unless these disparities are corrected by a system of transfers, fiscal equity will not prevail in the federation.

These differences in NFBs across states can arise because of differences in state tax capacities, in the cost of providing state public services, and in the need for particular public services within the state. In a fully centralized nation, they would presumably not arise because the national government would provide comparable services to all citizens using a national tax system. Decentralization, however, will lead to states choosing their levels of public services and taxes to suit their fiscal circumstances. States that have lower tax capacities, or greater needs for public services and costs of providing them, could not possibly match other, more fortunate, states in the provision of public services at comparable tax rates. The differences in NFBs are that this inevitably causes results in fiscal inequities among states. Citizens of a given type in better-off states will obtain systematically higher net benefits from their state government than those in less-well-off states.

Federal-state grants can eliminate these differences in NFBs if the transfers to each state depend upon the tax capacity of the state relative to others and upon the relative need for and cost of providing state public services. The need for redistributive federal-state grants will depend especially on how decentralized the tax system is, because differential tax capacity is probably the most important source of fiscal inequity (as well as being the one that is the easiest to measure). Thus, for example, if cost and need differences did not exist, and if state public services were mainly quasi-private goods provided roughly in equal amounts to all, then if the tax system were completely centralized, equal per capita grants to all states would avoid fiscal inequities. As more of the tax system is decentralized, the grants would have to take account of differential tax capacities across states.

More generally, it is useful conceptually to use the unitary state as a benchmark for an optimal equalization scheme. The aim of federal-state equalization transfers can then be viewed as attempting to replicate the financial consequences of a unitary state while allowing for the considerable advantages of fiscal decentralization. This involves designing the grants to enable the states to *potentially* be able to provide comparable levels of public services at comparable tax rates, without obliging them to act identically. This can be thought of as a reasonable way of reaching a compromise between achieving full horizontal equity (as in the unitary state) and obtaining the benefits of decentralization of fiscal decision making to the states. The latter may well entail the states to use their responsibility to deliver different mixes of public services using different tax structures, even though potentially all could provide the same mix of services and employ the same tax structure. In what follows, we usually adopt this notion of potential fiscal equity when we talk of equalizing NFBs.[5] In fact, one of the main policy issues in fiscal federalism, and one that constitutes another possible role for transfers as discussed later,

---

[5] In fact, there is virtually no literature in fiscal federalism that treats the optimal system of equalization when the states have different objectives from each other and, therefore, from the federal government. Allowing state preferences to rule within state jurisdictions seems to be in the spirit of federalism.

is the extent to which the federal government ought to take actions to ensure that states provide comparable levels or structures of some important public services.

Fiscal Inefficiency

The argument for eliminating NFBs using federal-state equalization transfers is reinforced by the fact that the same NFB differentials that give rise to fiscal inequity also cause fiscal inefficiency. As we argued in Chapters 2 and 6, differences in NFBs across states give a purely fiscal incentive for persons and businesses to migrate to the state with higher NFBs. Because this differential does not reflect differences in labor productivity, this fiscally induced migration causes an inefficient allocation of labor across states, with too many workers in high-NFB states. As with fiscal inequity, this can be avoided by equalizing transfers based on differences in tax capacity and need.

Although fiscal equity and fiscal efficiency arguments for equalization are generally reinforcing, there is one area where they might be in conflict. That concerns the treatment of differences in cost of providing public services as opposed to differences in need. Differences in need arise from differences in the composition of the population. If a state has a higher proportion of elderly, it will typically have more need for public services because the elderly tend to use more of them. If one of the policy objectives of the nation is to provide a given level of public services to the elderly financed out of general revenues, equalization would be required to ensure that that objective is being met. If the costs of providing public services were the same in all states, a unitary state would presumably provide the same level of services to the elderly no matter where they reside. In a decentralized setting, states would have different demographic makeups, and equalization transfers would have to be made to ensure that they could provide common levels of the public services at given tax rates.

On the other hand, if the costs of providing public services are different across jurisdictions, then even in a unitary state it is likely that different amounts will be provided (e.g., between urban and rural areas). There will be an equity-efficiency trade-off. In these circumstances, equalizing for differences in costs would not be called for on efficiency grounds. To do so would provide a fiscal incentive for households to remain in high-cost states when it would be more productive for them to move elsewhere. There may be an equity argument for equalizing for cost differences, but even here the equity-efficiency trade-off must be recognized.

The upshot of this discussion of fiscal equity and fiscal efficiency is that, remarkably, both call for similar types of equalization. The arguments apply in different circumstances. To the extent that households are not mobile, the fiscal equity argument applies. To the extent that they are mobile, the fiscal efficiency one does.

Interstate Spillovers

This is the traditional argument for matching conditional grants. Interstate spillovers exist if the benefits from one state's expenditures of a particular type accrue not only to that state's residents but also to the residents of one or more other states. State governments will not have the proper incentive to provide the correct levels of services that yield these spillover benefits. In deciding on service levels, the incentive for the state is to weigh the costs of provision against the benefits to their own residents, neglecting the benefits to the residents of other states. This will result in too low a level of provision. If these spillovers arise in a reciprocal fashion from all states' expenditures on these items, all states will provide too little, and all would be better off if the provision were to increase. A system of matching federal-state grants based on the expenditures giving rise to the spillovers will provide the incentive to increase expenditures. Typically, the extent of the spillover will be difficult to measure so the correct matching rate to use will be somewhat arbitrary.

While this argument based on spillovers is logically correct, it is not clear that it justifies the 50–50 matching grants that have been typically used in many federations. Although there are undoubtedly spillover benefits from the provision of major programs like education, health insurance, welfare, and highways by each of the states, it is unlikely that they are anywhere near the order of magnitude that the usual matching formulas would suggest. The high matching rates may have a better justification as a means of taking differential needs into account across states by basing them on actual expenditures. Matching grants also afford a way by which the federal government can enforce a high degree of accountability of state expenditures to itself. Under matching grant programs, the federal government can retain control over the sorts of expenditures that are eligible for federal matching. They might also be seen as providing an incentive for states to institute such programs in the first place. Whatever the argument, the use of matching grants has been a mainstay of many federations. Unfortunately, the adverse incentive effects of using them are quite high: if states are given matching funds, they have an incentive to overexpand the programs that are being supported by matching grants. The alternative of block conditional transfers can accomplish much of what matching grants are intended to do in terms of providing financial support to particular areas of state expenditures, while affording the states much more discretion in their fiscal decision making.

Expenditure Harmonization: National Standards

One of the most important reasons for federal-state transfers, and one that has been less recognized in the fiscal federalism literature, has to do with the fact that in a decentralized federation the federal government may retain a legitimate interest in the overall design of some state expenditure programs for reasons of national policy objectives. Again, the more decentralized the federation, the more important this role of transfers might be. This leverage can be accomplished by the use of conditional grants – that is, the exercise of the so-called federal spending power. The economic justification for using the spending power is that there are some national objectives that can be attained by encouraging states to incorporate particular federally defined standards into some of the expenditure programs under their jurisdiction, standards that they would not necessarily have an incentive to meet on their own initiative (but which collectively they might agree with).

To be more precise, harmonization of state expenditure programs may be important for two reasons. The first has to do with maintaining the efficiency of the internal common market. There is an advantage to the nation as a whole from harmonizing major state public expenditure programs because uniform expenditure programs will contribute to the free flow of goods and services, labor and capital, and will therefore improve the gains from trade from the internal common market. Thus, use of conditional transfers to ensure portability or accessibility provisions in state programs contributes to the free movement of labor across states. Harmonization may also reduce the possibility of wasteful interstate competition on the expenditure side. Uniformity, as well as portability, might be particularly useful in such areas as health, education, and welfare as ways of encouraging the unimpeded free flow of labor among states.

Harmonization of state expenditure programs may also serve national equity or social policy objectives. Many public services provided at the state level are redistributive in their intent, providing in-kind redistribution, social insurance, or targeted transfers to state residents. To the extent that the federal government is interested in redistribution as a goal, there is a national interest in redistribution that occurs via the provision of these kinds of public services. Because many of the programs that incorporate in-kind redistribution may be provided at the state level for efficiency reasons, the federal government may be restricted to influencing the design of these state programs by conditional grants, where the conditions are intended to achieve national equity objectives.

Expenditure harmonization can be accomplished by the use of conditional grants. In using conditional grants to achieve national purposes in areas of state jurisdiction, there will always be a trade-off between uniformity, which encourages the free flow of goods and factors and equitable access to public services, and decentralization that may encourage innovation, efficiency, and accountability. This suggests that the use of conditions be as nonobtrusive as is necessary to accomplish such objectives. The grants used for this purpose should be block ones. And conditions might be defined in general terms so as to stipulate the coverage of the program, its accessibility, its portability, and so on, rather than including detailed provisions that constitute micromanagement of state programs and priorities. At the same time, the ability of the federal government to use the spending power actually contributes to effective decentralization. The ability to use the spending power increases the case for decentralizing the provision of public goods and services, because it allows the benefits of decentralization to be achieved without unduly compromising national efficiency and equity. By the same token, the more decentralized the federation, the more important the spending power becomes.

In summary, in a decentralized federation, to which many countries aspire, federal-state transfers play an important role. They allow expenditures to be more decentralized than revenue raising. They allow the federal government to correct the inefficiencies and inequities that result from the fact that decentralization would otherwise lead to differing levels of NFBs across states. And they allow the federal government to exercise some influence over the way in which the states design their programs so that national interests are taken into account. Thus, federal-state transfers allow decentralization to be done in a way that achieves its benefits without compromising national efficiency and equity goals.

Some Features of Federal-State Fiscal Arrangements

As mentioned, the set of federal-state fiscal arrangements comprise both the transfers of funds from the federal government to the states through conditional and unconditional grants and arrangements for sharing and harmonizing the raising of revenues through taxation. More generally, fiscal relations may also include negotiated agreements and codes of conduct in other areas of common concern, such as expenditure programs and regulations. The form of the fiscal arrangements depends upon the nature of the federation and the perceived roles of government at the various levels. Some general principles are clear enough.

The first is that the system of fiscal relations must be seen as a whole rather than as a set of unrelated parts. The reason is that each component tends to contribute to more than one objective; equivalently, each objective requires more than one instrument. Moreover, some of the components are quite complementary, and some have equivalent effects. For example, revenue-sharing agreements have similar financial effects to unconditional grants; and equal per capita grants financed out of general revenues have an equalizing aspect to them.

The second principle is that the more decentralized the fiscal system is, the more important is the set of fiscal arrangements. Economists have taken the view that the decentralization of public service provision in a federation is a valuable thing because it increases the efficiency and accountability with which services are delivered. By the same token, some decentralization of revenue raising must accompany expenditure decentralization. However, decentralization also brings the potential for interfering with the efficiency of the internal common market, both through the creation of interjurisdictional distortions and through beggar-thy-neighbor and discriminatory policies, as well as by causing inequities among members of different states. The creative design of fiscal arrangements can offset these induced inefficiencies and inequities while preserving the benefits of decentralized service provision. In particular, the use of the spending power and the coordinating or harmonizing role of the federal government are important.

Third, the design of fiscal arrangements depends critically upon the extent to which economies are dependent upon governments for the allocation and distribution of resources. The greater the role of government is, the more important will be the role of fiscal arrangements. That is, the more will be expected of the federal government in fostering efficiency and equity. In a federation with decentralized fiscal responsibilities, this implies an active role for the fiscal arrangements as a means of ensuring that state decision making conforms to national objectives.

What these general points imply for the particular set of fiscal arrangements depends on the federal institutions of the country in question as well as how decentralized this federation is. Indeed, the same points apply to unitary states in which decentralization applies to local governments. However, there is a set of components that would be beneficial for a wide variety of nations with federal characteristics on the basis of the preceding analysis. The following is a list of some of the more important components, most of which we have already encountered.

Tax Harmonization and Coordination Arrangements

The need for special forms of tax harmonization and coordination will depend on the extent of decentralization of revenue raising in the federation. For federations where state revenue requirements are limited, tax sources for which harmonization is relatively less important can be assigned to the states. These might include excise taxes, property taxes, licenses and fees, and some resource revenues. For these taxes, little explicit harmonization is needed. Tax bases for which harmonization would be more important for equity and efficiency reasons would be assigned to the federal government, such as direct taxes (and transfers), taxes on capital, and even general taxes like payroll and sales taxes.

For more decentralized federations, we must find a way of getting more revenue-raising responsibilities into the hands of the states without jeopardizing national efficiency and equity goals. There are various ways to do this. As discussed in Chapter 8, simple revenue-sharing arrangements between the federal government and the states can be negotiated whereby the federal government retains control of the base, rate structure, and collection, but gives a share to the states. While this is an easy way to get revenue into the hands of the states, the states are essentially passive recipients of revenues with no responsibility for revenue raising and therefore with limited fiscal accountability. As explained in Chapter 4, fiscal accountability can be achieved in various ways. Some broader revenue sources can be assigned to the states either exclusively or alongside the federal government. Payroll taxes would be good candidates for state assignment, as would broad-based sales taxes. In both cases, there may be some benefits from some harmonization of tax bases and their allocation among states, though it is not essential. In the case of the sales tax, its ideal form depends upon the existence of state participation. We have mentioned that it is administratively difficult, though not impossible, to operate multilevel sales taxes at the state level because of the difficulty of accounting for interstate intermediate goods transactions. It is possible to achieve some harmonization between federal- and state-level general sales taxes by coordinating the bases and collaborating on collections. This approach is fully compatible with the state taxes being single-staged and the federal tax being a VAT.

Harmonization is much more important if the states are to have some revenue-raising powers in the direct tax fields. Given federal responsibility for national equity and efficiency and the importance of administrative simplicity, it is desirable that the federal government retain control over the base of direct taxes, and maybe even the rate structure. States could piggyback onto federal direct taxes by levying state-specific surtaxes. In a more decentralized system, the states could even set their own rate structures to the common base in a federally administered income tax system.

Finally, in the case of resource revenues, to the extent that they are decentralized to the states, some harmonization might also be beneficial. If resource taxes were levied on economic rents, resource allocation consequences of state resource taxes would be minimal. However, typically resource taxes are levied on bases that include elements of capital income as well as rents. That being the case, state resource taxes have the opportunity for distorting the allocation of capital across states and for being used as beggar-thy-neighbor policy instruments.

Regulations

Ideally, the regulation of markets for capital, labor, and tradable goods and services should be centralized, to the extent that such regulation is used at all. This has been discussed in Chapter 2. If centralization is not possible, there should be some means of coordinating or overseeing state regulatory outcomes to be sure that the internal common market is not disrupted. There are various ways that such coordination could occur. One way, which is that used in the United States, is for the federal government to have a role in overriding state laws to be sure that they do not violate the free flow of goods and services across internal political boundaries. In other cases, federal-state free-trade-type agreements could be negotiated that preclude governments in a federation firm engaging in distortionary or discriminatory regulations. Such an agreement exists in Canada, although it is not clear that it has teeth. Alternatively, the judicial (or quasi-judicial) system could be relied on to rule on whether state laws are discriminatory or restrictive of interstate trade, although, as we have pointed out earlier, the courts may not be well suited to perform this task.

Closing the Fiscal Gap

Given the greater benefits of decentralizing expenditure relative to revenue-raising responsibilities, a fiscal gap will typically exist that will require transfers from the federal government to states. In the absence of reasons to the contrary, transfers should be unconditional and equal per capita in allocation. As we have just seen, however, there are two important reasons for deviating from this. One is the requirement for transfers to be equalizing. Equalizing transfers are required to reduce NFB differences in order jointly to achieve fiscal efficiency and equity. As we have argued, the general objective of equalizing transfers is to enable the states to provide comparable levels of public services in their jurisdictions at comparable levels of tax rates.

The other reason for deviating from a simple unconditional equal per capita grant formula concerns the use of conditional grants to influence the way in which state governments behave. For one thing, the federal government can use conditional matching grants to induce states to provide certain public services at higher levels than they otherwise would. This might be appropriate where there are significant spillover benefits involved. Matching grants may also be an imperfect way of taking differential need and cost of certain types of services into account. They may be a way of inducing states to introduce certain types of programs to begin with, which they might not otherwise do on an individual basis (e.g., universal health care systems). The federal government may simply want to ensure that state programs do not violate national norms of efficiency and equity, for example, by imposing restrictive state residency requirements. Most of these objectives can be satisfied with a system of block conditional transfers, where the conditions are not too specific, laying out basic criteria that should be followed rather than stipulating program design requirements in detail.

Institutional Control

Finally, an important issue is, Who should be responsible for designing the system of federal-state fiscal arrangements? There are various possible alternatives. The most obvious one is to make the federal government solely responsible on the grounds that it is responsible for the national objectives that are to be delivered through the fiscal arrangements. In many countries, this alternative is the norm. A problem with it might be the natural tendency for the federal government to want to be too involved with state decision making and not to allow the full benefits of decentralization to occur. To some extent, this tendency can be overcome by imposing constitutional restrictions on the ability of the federal government to override state decisions. Alternatively, one can have a separate body involved in the design and ongoing reform and enforcement of the fiscal arrangements. It could be an impartial advisory body, or it could be body comprising both federal and state representatives. It could have true decision-making authority, or it could be purely advisory. In any case, to be effective, it would at the least need to be able to coordinate decision making at the two levels of government.

Above all, it should be remembered that the objective of the exercise is to obtain the benefits of decentralized decision making without sacrificing the integrity of the internal economic union and of national standards of equity.

CONDITIONAL GRANTS

Conditional grants from national to subnational governments are used in virtually every country in the world where there is more than one level of government. This includes not only federations in which lower-level jurisdictions have constitutionally guaranteed independent legislative responsibilities but also unitary states where the lower-level governments (typically local or state governments) have much more limited autonomy. They are especially relevant in nations where the delivery of major public services such as education, health, and welfare services has been decentralized to state or local governments. But they can also be used to provide support and encouragement for more narrowly defined projects, such as infrastructure or administration, as ways of achieving more effective decentralized decision making. The following discussion focuses on the case of federations, where state governments might have considerable discretion. However, similar principles apply to transfers to lower-level jurisdictions in nonfederal nations.

The Rationale for Conditional Grants

The extent to which federal-state conditional grants are used and their design depend very much on the constitutional, institutional, and fiscal circumstances of the nation concerned. In the most general sense, the purpose of conditional grants is to influence the fiscal decisions of the state governments presumably with the express intent of achieving some objective of the federal government, including objectives that are stipulated by the constitution. More specifically, we can identify a number of reasons in principle why conditional grants to the states might be appropriate policy instruments for the federal government in certain circumstances. These reasons parallel those mentioned earlier.

Interstate Spillovers

The traditional argument for conditional grants, especially matching ones, is that one state's spending programs provide spillover benefits to residents of other states. Examples might include transportation facilities that are used by households and firms of neighboring states, education or training provided to households who subsequently change states, or pollution control measures that reduce cross-border pollution. In these circumstances, there is no mechanism for registering the benefits accruing to nonresidents. Conditional grants are meant to be a substitute for that. The spillover benefits can be internalized by a properly chosen matching grant formula, where the rate of matching reflects the share of spillover benefits in the total benefits of the project. Similar arguments could apply to the correction of misperceived marginal cost of public funds (MCPFs) due to tax competition, but matching grants based on revenue sources or on tax effort have not been common.[6]

Although this argument has natural appeal and is fairly noncontroversial, it is unlikely to account for the bulk of intergovernmental transfers in practice. In fact, in some federations (e.g., Canada), matching grants have gone out of fashion, primarily because it has been recognized that many of their alleged objectives could be achieved by conditional block (nonmatching) grants. By avoiding the matching aspect, adverse incentive effects are also avoided. The size of the grants by jurisdiction can be designed to reflect need as well as whatever spillover benefits there were thought to be.

Efficiency in the National Common Market

A related argument is that conditional grants can help to achieve efficiency in the internal common market or economic union, that is, the free and undistorted movement of labor, capital, goods, and services across state borders. If left to their own devices, states may design their programs in ways that distort these cross-border movements, either intentionally or unintentionally. For example, mobility rights may not be guaranteed in state programs, educational and training qualifications may differ from one state to another, different service levels for important public services may deter households or firms from moving between states, or states may engage in beggar-thy-neighbor policies to attract economic activity at the expense of other states.

---

[6] See Dahlby (1996) for an analysis of the theoretical case for this. Grants based on tax effort are like matching grants on the tax side. Their purpose has been quite different from that of correcting misperceived MCPFs.

Grants designed to further national efficiency goals can be conditional block grants, and the conditions that would facilitate these objectives would presumably be fairly general. They might aim to ensure that certain general principles of nondiscrimination, equal access, and mobility rights are guaranteed, or more generally they may attempt to harmonize the design of programs that have implications for interstate exchange. The conditions can be made biting by reducing the size of the grant in the event of noncompliance; however, this solution may not be optimal.

National Standards of Equity

More important, and perhaps more controversial, is the use of conditional block grants to achieve objectives of equity or fairness. The key point to recall and recognize is that many of the expenditure responsibilities that are decentralized to the states are indispensable policy instruments for the pursuit of redistributive objectives. Examples include the main categories of education, health, and welfare services, which together address goals of equality of opportunity, income distribution, and social insurance. While there are good reasons on efficiency grounds for decentralizing their provision to the states, the federal government nonetheless maintains an interest in how these programs are designed. The use of conditional block grants is one effective way for the federal government to discharge its responsibility for national equity objectives while preserving the advantages of decentralized output provision. Of necessity, conditions attached to block grants for the purposes of furthering national equity objectives will be fairly general.

The effectiveness of conditions attached to grants that are used to finance health, education, and welfare services will depend on the proportion of state spending that is financed by grants – the vertical fiscal imbalance. The more financially self-sufficient are the states, the more difficult it might be to assure compliance with general conditions. At the same time, conditional grants to facilitate national standards of equity and efficiency should be seen as complements to equalization and not substitutes. Equalization addresses the particular issues of fiscal inefficiency and fiscal inequity, whereas conditional grants deal with potential violations of efficiency in the internal economic union and interpersonal equity.

Infrastructure

Conditional grants might have a particular role to play in financing state infrastructure projects. These projects tend to be once-over expenditures rather than recurring ones. Moreover, they involve the creation of assets of ongoing use. States might have difficulties in financing them if they have limited access to capital markets. They might also be very important for building up the capacity to provide future services of national importance (schools, hospitals) or for providing assets that build up the economic capacity of a state so that it will be less dependent on future grants (e.g., roads, communications facilities, utilities). These issues are addressed in more detail in Chapter 12.

Building State Administrative Capacity

Related to the infrastructure argument, conditional grants may be important for developing the capacity of states to provide public services. The delivery of an acceptable level of public services requires both physical and human assets. The latter includes both the acquisition of particular skills and the development of management and administrative expertise. Some of this comes with training, and some simply with experience. In either case, extraordinary once-over expenditures will be needed to develop the decision-making capacity of state governments where limited amounts existed before. Once these backlogs of human and physical capital are made up, the capacity of state governments to deliver important public services will be put on a sustainable footing. This is of particular relevance to developing countries.

Strategic Arguments

Yet another related argument for conditional grants is that they are necessary to counter what is referred to as strategic behavior of state governments, the so-called bailout problem or soft budget constraint problem that we encountered in previous chapters. As discussed previously, the idea is that if states recognize that their funding is determined partly by the extent to which their services satisfy the needs of their residents for important public services, they may take actions that exacerbate those needs and result in the federal government increasing its grant. The forms of exploitation by the state government might include overspending or spending in inefficient and unaccountable ways, directing too much of its spending to items of state but not national interest, spending too little on infrastructure or training, and so on. Of course, part of the purpose of the equalization transfer is to remove those adverse incentives from the states. Unfortunately, the system may be less than perfect. Moreover, even if the correct amounts of equalization grants are given to the states, they may nonetheless simply not use them to provide services that meet the federally mandated standards. In these circumstances, the federal government might have no choice but to attach conditions to them, despite the disadvantages of so doing.

These reasons for conditional grants are distinct from, but related to, those for equalization grants. The purpose of the latter is partly to close the vertical fiscal gap that arises because the expenditure responsibilities are more decentralized than revenue-raising abilities. But unconditional grants also serve important national equity and efficiency objectives. They are necessary for ensuring that acceptable standards of public services can be provided at comparable tax rates to citizens no matter where they reside in the nation. This ensures equal fiscal treatment of all citizens (fiscal equity) as well as the removal of artificial fiscal incentives for economic activity to move from one state to another (fiscal efficiency). If an effective system of equalizing grants is in place, making them effective may involve attaching conditions to them.

Difficulties with Conditional Grants

The employment of conditional grants, an example of the use of the spending power by the federal government, can be controversial. The problem is that the federal spending power appears to contradict the independent exercise of state legislative authority. It is not at all clear how to avoid this. If the federal government is seen as the custodian of national equity and efficiency, it is hard to imagine a policy instrument other than the spending power that it might use to achieve its objectives. The spending power is widely used in federations around the world, with varying degrees of intrusiveness.[7] But, compared with other potential policy instruments, such as disallowing state legislation or imposing mandates on the states, it can be relatively nonintrusive.

Despite their usefulness as policy instruments for achieving national objectives in a fiscally decentralized nation, conditional grants have some fundamental potential drawbacks. The main one is that because their intent is to influence the fiscal behavior of states, they necessarily detract from one of the objectives of decentralization, which is to make the states responsible and accountable for their own decisions. If it were possible to set out the conditions such that they clearly reflected national objectives and no more, this interference with state autonomy would be justified. But matters are not so clear-cut.

---

[7] See Watts (1999) for a wide-ranging survey of the use of the spending power in other federations. There is very little economics literature on the spending power. Economists tend to take its use for granted.

On the one hand, it is practically impossible to define general conditions to reflect national objectives in a way that is clear and unambiguous. This means that some discretion is necessary to determine the extent to which states are abiding by the conditions. This inevitably puts the federal government, or in some instances an arm's-length body, in the position of having to hold the states to some extent accountable for the way they spend block grants. In addition to interfering with state autonomy, this also subjects the states to some uncertainty as to whether their policies will be judged to be acceptable or not. Thus, even if the federal government is fully benevolent, it will not be possible in practice to apply general conditions that entirely avoid interference with what may be legitimate state goals. In the end, a compromise must be reached between the benefits of decentralization as achieved through state autonomy and the necessity to ensure that the exercise of state autonomy does not abrogate national objectives. The need to strike an appropriate balance is at the heart of any federal system of government.

On the other hand, federal governments may not be so benevolent as to resist taking the opportunity to use conditional grants to exert undue influence over the priorities of state governments. This temptation to be intrusive suggests that nations should err on the cautious side and not impose conditions on general block grants unless it is absolutely necessary to achieve national objectives. It might be sufficient for the federal government to set out in mandate form the main features of health, education, and welfare programs that states are expected to satisfy. Whether states are satisfying nationally or constitutionally mandated objectives is something for the electorate to judge and for opposition parties to bring to the public's attention. They may be assisted in forming this judgment in some federations by arm's-length institutions that have an advisory role in designing federal-state fiscal arrangements. Such institutions exist in Australia, India, and South Africa and are ideally suited to comment on the degree of success of states in achieving objectives set out for the nation as a whole and to recommend whether mandates need to be reinforced by more specific conditions attached to the grants.

Should such conditions become necessary, their enforcement is not trivial. Penalizing states whose programs do not satisfy national norms and standards could be counterproductive. Such sanctions might make it even more difficult for the states to succeed at meeting those norms, with the result that those most in need of services end up suffering. Thus, the decision to impose conditions on the use of grants that are enforced by financial penalties is a tough call. One would hope that moral suasion would go a long way to ensure compliance, especially if the conditions themselves reflect national objectives that are based on consensus. If the grants are well designed and in accordance with constitutional principles, there should be little need to enforce them.

Specific conditional grants are much easier to implement and enforce. Their objectives can be better defined, and the precise terms of the grants can be negotiated with the recipient states. There is still the temptation that exists for the federal government to intrude excessively in state priority setting and decision making. Unlike with block grants, specific grants tend to be discretionary rather than formula driven, which inevitably puts power in the hands of the federal government, whose exercise may be difficult to resist. If only to ensure that the use of such grants is subject to public scrutiny and debate, the role of watchdog and advisory bodies is critically important.

Grants Based on Tax Effort

Grants may be conditional on revenues raised by the states instead of (or as well as) on expenditures. There are two potential reasons for basing grants on revenue or tax effort. The first one parallels the spillover argument used to support conditional expenditure program grants. Tax setting may involve fiscal externalities imposed on residents of other jurisdictions, and these may be positive or negative.[8] Moreover, they may be horizontal (between states) or vertical (between a state and the federal government). Positive horizontal tax externalities arise as a result of tax competition: an increase in one state's tax rate on a mobile tax base causes some of the tax base to relocate in a neighboring province thereby augmenting the latter's tax revenues. Negative horizontal tax externalities occur because of tax exporting. An increase in one state's tax base is partly borne by residents of another state, who might purchase and import a taxed commodity or who might own a factor of production in the state where the tax is applied. As well, vertical tax externalities can be either positive or negative on balance. A negative vertical tax externality occurs if an increase in a state's tax rate causes a tax base used by the federal government to shrink, thereby reducing federal tax revenues. However, an increase in a state's tax rate can also cause a federal tax base to rise. An example of this is a wage tax. If the federal wage tax base is before-tax wages, an increase in the provincial wage

---

[8] Dahlby (1996) summarizes the various forms of fiscal externalities on the expenditure and taxation sides of state budgets, and discusses their remedies.

tax rate may well cause federal before-tax wages to rise (even if after-tax wages fall). In this case, federal revenues would actually rise.

Making transfers vary positively with tax effort is in principle a way to internalize positive tax externalities, whether horizontal or vertical. With positive externalities, states would select tax rates that are too low. A tax effort grant will induce higher tax rates. Symmetric reasoning suggests that grants should be negatively related to tax effort if negative tax externalities dominate. These arguments are unlikely to form the basis for tax effort grants in practice because it is difficult to be sure whether positive or negative tax externalities will prevail in practice.

The second argument for transfers based on tax effort is concerned more with administrative considerations and applies perhaps with more force in developing countries. The federal government may want to give state governments an incentive to collect more tax revenues from their existing tax bases. This may be partly to give an incentive for the states to collect taxes more efficiently. But it may also serve to offset the disincentive states may have to collect taxes efficiently if they perceive that their grants will be higher the less revenues they collect at given rates. That is, there may be a moral hazard problem associated with the federal-state fiscal arrangements.

In practice, grants based on tax effort are not common. This is probably because governments do not want to give states an incentive to expand tax collection excessively. As well, there would be imprecision about the size of the tax effort incentive that would be appropriate in the event that the preceding arguments were valid.

UNCONDITIONAL TRANSFERS AND EQUALIZATION

Unconditional transfers basically fulfill two objectives. One is simply to get funds into the hands of the states when they do not have the revenue-raising capacity to raise sufficient revenues to finance their expenditure responsibilities, that is, to close the fiscal gap. The other is to equalize the ability of the various states to provide public services. These two objectives are necessarily related. Equalization schemes typically involve differential transfers from the federal government to the states financed out of federal government revenues. That is, they are gross schemes rather than net ones.[9] At the same time, the VFG created by the existence of transfers is

[9] An exception to this rule is the case of Germany, which does operate a net equalization scheme, albeit one that is closely integrated with the system of revenue sharing. But even in the German case, elements of pure federal financing of equalization have crept in with respect to the states (*Länder*) of the former East Germany.

far from a well-defined magnitude. There is no clear-cut notion of what the revenue-raising capacity of the states is. The actual size of the VFG is really a matter of policy choice by the federal government. The amount of transfers it chooses to make effectively determines how much revenue must be raised by the states to finance their desired expenditures. As we have discussed in earlier chapters, there are pros and cons of decentralizing revenue-raising responsibilities.

For the purposes of this section, we essentially take as given the size of the VFG – the amount of funds to be distributed to the states as a whole. Then what becomes relevant is how this amount is allocated among states. The distribution is based on the principles of equalization, which we address in the following section.

In some nations with multiple levels of government, however, the size of the desired VFG must also be calculated. This will be the case when state-level governments have very little revenue-raising capacity or discretion so that the transfers they receive from the federal government effectively determine the size of their budgets. In this case, the VFG must be determined by a notional calculation of the amount of transfers needed to enable the states to provide some desired standard of public services. We consider the elements of that calculation following our discussion of equalization.

Equalization

Equalization transfers are those which are made with the purpose of redistributing revenues from better-off to less-well-off states. This is the case even if the scheme is a gross one financed by the federal government, because the financing itself comes from federal general revenues that are drawn predominantly from relatively well-off states. Equalization is a feature of most federations as well as most nonfederal countries that decentralize expenditure and possibly revenue-raising responsibilities to lower levels of government (e.g., municipalities, prefectures, counties). Thus, the issues involved are general and apply in almost all multijurisdiction nations. There is a substantial literature on the theory of equalization in a federation, as well as on some of the policy issues involved in applying it to actual practice.[10]

---

[10] The role of equalization is discussed in general terms in Boadway and Wildasin (1984). The theoretical underpinnings are developed in Boadway and Flatters (1982a, 1982b) and more recently in Boadway (2004). See also Wildasin (1986), Usher (1995), and the recent summary in Mieszkowski and Musgrave (1999). Policy issues are addressed in Boadway and Hobson (1998) and Shah (1994b).

Equalization transfers exist primarily to offset the NFB differentials that occur in a decentralized federation and that are the sources of fiscal inequity and/or fiscal inefficiency. As we have seen, these differentials can arise because of differences in tax capacity at the state level as well as differences in the need for public expenditures. The precise nature of NFB differentials depends on the type of expenditures and taxes that are decentralized and the extent to which state policies are redistributive. What is appropriate for a given federation thus depends upon the specific features of the federation. It is useful for expository purposes to adopt a benchmark setting in which there should be full equalization of state tax capacities. Using that benchmark, we can then address ways in which actual systems might deviate.

The Benchmark Equalization System

In the benchmark setting, the following features characterize the states:

- State government expenditures are quasi-private and provide equal per capita benefits to all residents in their state.
- States may have access to both source-based taxes and residence-based taxes, and the tax bases for each can vary across states.
- Residence-based taxes (income, payroll, destination-based consumption taxes) are levied on a proportional basis.
- States can differ in their average income levels and in the pattern of income distribution.
- The rates of taxation of residence-based taxes are the same in all states.

Given these features of the federation, state fiscal policies will differ only in the per capita amounts of their public expenditures. States that have larger tax bases per capita will have correspondingly higher tax revenues and expenditures per capita. Particularly relevant for our purposes is the fact that NFB differentials between any two states are the same for all households regardless of their incomes, and this NFB differential is precisely equal to the difference in the level of per capita tax collections in the two states.[11]

The benchmark setting leads to a particularly simple equalization system. Interstate redistribution ought to occur so that per capita revenues in each state are identical. This involves full (100 percent) equalization of differences in tax capacity across states. In principle, this could occur using a "net" scheme in which revenues are taken from the states with higher tax capacity and transferred to those with lower tax capacity. But such a scheme is

[11] This benchmark case is based on Boadway and Flatters (1982b).

typically difficult to implement politically. A "gross" scheme in which the transfers to the less-well-off states come entirely from the federal government is possible if the vertical fiscal imbalance is large enough. Then, the differential transfer made to each state reflects differences in tax capacity.

The full equalization scheme will eliminate the NFB differentials that existed in the decentralized setting without equalization. As such, all fiscal inequities and inefficiencies that might otherwise have existed will no longer apply. In fact, the postequalization outcome will replicate what we can refer to as the unitary state benchmark.

While the benchmark case assumed that all the states applied the same residence-based tax rate in the absence of equalization, that is not a necessary feature of the benchmark. All that is required to ensure that fiscal equity and efficiency are achieved is that the states levy the same tax rates and provide the same level of public services in the presence of full equalization. In practice, the states may choose to behave differently even if faced with the same budgetary opportunities. This is indeed one of the presumed advantages of decentralization. The implication is that even with full equalization, fiscal equity and/or fiscal efficiency will not be fully achieved. For example, if two states choose different levels of public service provision and different tax rates, high-income persons will obtain a lower NFB in the state with the higher tax rate, and vice versa for low-income persons. This cannot be avoided in a federation. The compromise we adopt is to aim for eliminating all potential sources of NFB differentials. In the benchmark setting, this implies equalizing tax capacities of the states so that they could *if they so chose* set common tax rates and provide common levels of public services.

Even in settings that approximate the benchmark one in which residence-based taxes are roughly proportional to incomes and public service benefits are roughly equal per capita, implementing full equalization of tax capacity is not simple. For one thing there are incentive problems. The federal government cannot simply base equalization on actual tax revenues collected by the states, because that would obviously have adverse incentive effects. Instead, they must be based on some notion of tax capacity or the ability to raise revenues. There is no well-defined measure of tax capacity, so many equalization systems use the size of actual state tax bases as proxies.[12] This solution is not perfect because tax bases are not completely exogenous.

---

[12] In the Canadian case, equalization is based on the amount of revenues that would be raised in each province by applying a national average provincial tax rate to the actual provincial base and comparing the result across provinces.

To the extent that state government policies affect their tax bases, their fiscal policies will be affected by equalization. For example, in some federations, state governments have control over natural resource developments. If source-based taxes applicable to resource revenues are available to the states, the equalization system will discourage resource development because it will implicitly diminish state revenues accruing from the development. More generally, to the extent that tax bases are responsive to tax rates, equalization will reduce the MCPF because it will reduce the revenue costs of raising tax rates (Smart, 1998). It is not clear how this design problem can be avoided without compromising the function of equalization.

In addition, there may be measurement issues involved in implementing equalization grants. In the real world, tax systems are complex and contain a myriad of provisions. Decentralized state tax policies will typically result in tax systems that are not uniform. This complicates the implementation of equalization systems that are based on comparisons of tax bases across states. Typically, some standard tax base must be chosen that will differ from those actually used. The more diversity there is in state tax systems, the less perfect will be the equalization system. This constitutes one of many arguments for harmonizing tax systems among state governments.

The benchmark setting has the feature that it calls for full equalization of state tax capacities; indeed, it was chosen for that property. At the same time, it has some fairly strong features, especially the requirement that state expenditures provide equal per capita benefits to all residents and the residence-base tax structure is proportional. It could be argued that from a stylized point of view, this setting is not unreasonable. State expenditure responsibilities in many federations include the provision of public services that are quasi-private, and these services are often provided regardless of income. Moreover, studies of tax incidence typically find that the overall system is roughly proportional. Nonetheless, there may be identifiable circumstances in which these assumptions do not apply. Let us consider how the form of ideal equalization might be affected by deviations from these assumptions.[13]

---

[13] Some authors have even argued that, despite the fact of NFB differentials, the central government need not get involved with equalization at all. The better-off states would voluntarily make equalization payments to the less well-off as a way of internalizing the fiscal inefficiencies from NFB differentials (Myers, 1990). But this argument, which is an analogue of the famous Coase theorem, really applies only in very special circumstances, including where individuals in each jurisdiction are all identical as discussed in Boadway (2004).

Deviations from the Benchmark System

The benchmark setting assumes that state governments provide quasi-private goods on an equal per capita basis to all households. In fact, many public services are quasi-private, but are often provided on a selective basis to particular classes of citizens: education to the young, welfare to the needy, health care to the ill, and so on. In many cases, these services cut across income lines so they do not affect the average progressivity of the fiscal system. But different states might have populations with systematically different demographic makeups, entailing that they have different resource needs for providing a given level of public services. The NFBs available to any given income group will then depend upon differences in these needs across states.

In principle, incorporating different needs into the equalization system is straightforward. If different demographic groups in the population require different resources to provide a given level of public service, these differences can in principle be measured and included in the equalization transfers.[14] In this case, the equalization system would have two components – a tax-capacity-equalizing component and a needs-equalizing component. Notice that this argument for including needs in the equalization system is based on the notion that different demographic groups have systematically different needs for public services. It is different from the idea that given amounts of public services may have different costs of provision in different states. In this latter case, the role of equalization is not clear. Different costs of provision in different states lead to an equity-efficiency trade-off that differs across the two states. It is not obvious that on efficiency grounds one would want to equalize for those types of differences.

Next, suppose that the progressivity assumption of the benchmark case does not apply. For example, suppose that state taxes are progressive rather than proportional. In this case, it is straightforward to show that *tax capacities should be more than fully equalized.* The reason is that a progressive tax will yield relatively more revenues per capita in a high-income state than in a low-income one compared with a proportional tax. By the same token, if the state tax system is regressive, less than full equalization is called for. In the special case where taxation satisfies the benefit principle, no equalization is called for: a given tax system will yield the same tax

---

[14] Various countries include elements of need in their systems of equalizing transfers, including Australia, Japan, and South Africa. All follow some variant of the approach suggested in the text.

liabilities for each type of person in both low- and high-income states so no NFB differentials will accrue. This is a significant caveat to be considered in actual equalization systems. One must make a judgment about how progressive state fiscal policies are relative to the benchmark system in order to come down with a most preferred equalization system. This is obviously not an easy call.

A corollary of the preceding discussion is that some expenditure elements provide benefits that are systematically related to income levels. For example, state governments might provide transfers to low-income persons. These effectively enhance the progressivity of state budgets and would lead to calls for more than full equalization of tax capacities. (Alternatively, such items might be included in the calculation of differences in needs discussed previously.)

It may be that certain types of taxes can be omitted from tax capacity equalization calculations because their revenues finance benefits for those who play the taxes. User fees might be an example of that, or maybe even property taxes. One has to be careful with this argument, however. Some so-called user fees are really no more than excise taxes that apply to the use of some commodity. Automobile license fees might be of this sort. To be a benefit charge, user fees must actually be earmarked to finance the commodity to which the fee applies. More generally, different taxes may have quite different progressivity patterns. Income taxes may be more progressive than payroll or sales taxes, which in turn are more progressive than excise taxes. In principle, the equalization system could treat each tax on its own, with more progressive tax bases being equalized to a greater degree than less progressive ones. This is not the usual practice, no doubt because policy makers are not well enough informed to be able to determine the optimal extent of equalization for various types of taxes precisely.

State public expenditures may not be on quasi-private goods entirely but might include goods that exhibit different degrees of "publicness." In principle, equalization formulas could incorporate this complication by use of a congestion parameter.[15] The qualitative features of the equalization system then change considerably, and no simple formula applies. Most analysts use as a working assumption that state public services are close to being private, given the sorts of items they tend to cover in practice.

---

[15] This is the approach used by Buchanan and Goetz (1972). Boadway and Flatters (1982a) in their development of the theory of equalization include such a parameter.

Yet another caveat to the benchmark argument is that the equity basis for equalization depends on one's accepting the basic value judgment underlying it, that fiscal policies across the entire nation ought to satisfy horizontal equity. The basis for this judgment is that all citizens of a nation ought to "count" equally in the nation's social welfare function. But in nations that are very diverse, it may be that horizontal equity is trumped.[16]

Finally, a secondary function of equalization (other than eliminating NFB differentials) may be to serve as a device by which risk sharing can take place among states. If states are subject to idiosyncratic shocks, an equalization system that transfers to them when their incomes fall and vice versa will act as an insurance device. This has been the focus of some recent literature, which has also emphasized the incentive problems with this form of insurance.[17]

Calculating the VFG

The preceding discussion of equalization implicitly assumes that the states effectively control the size of their budgets. Unconditional transfers are lump-sum – or inframarginal – transfers, and at the margin the states determine their expenditure levels by their discretionary revenue-raising ability. In these circumstances, equalizing for differences in expenditure need is effectively an issue of achieving horizontal balance. National standards of state public services are determined with reference to what states actually spend on average. States with greater need will require more funds to enable them to provide comparable levels of public service to the other states.

In some circumstances, one cannot rely on the level of public services that the states would choose to provide as a basis for equalization transfers. That is because the states might not have enough discretion in revenue raising in order to determine the size of their own expenditure levels. This absence of discretion may reflect the fact that their own revenue sources are very limited, or because they have little discretion to vary the tax rates that can be applied to these revenue sources, even if they are ample.

---

[16] One observer's case against horizontal equity may be found in Usher (1995). Basically, he adopts a different form of horizontal equity from the traditional economic one. He also points out that there may be second-best considerations in actual federations that go against full equalization even if one subscribes to the standard notion of horizontal equity. In particular, policies of the central government may themselves already favor less well-off states.

[17] See especially Persson and Tabellini (1996a, 1996b) and Alesina and Perotti (1998). These authors have also emphasized some of the political economy aspects of decentralization.

The VFG must then be determined not by some average of the level of services that state governments actually provide but by the amount of revenue the states would need to provide a standard level of public services somehow defined. The standard level of services might be that mandated by the federal government itself, perhaps with the input of an advisory body. Alternatively, the federal government might simply determine the amount to be transferred on the basis of what it can afford. Examples of countries that are faced with the requirement to specify a VFG include Australia, Japan, the Scandinavian countries, and Japan.

When the VFG is based on the requirement to provide some standard level of state public services, the calculation of the VFG is in principle straightforward. In fact, it is similar to a needs-based equalization calculation using the mandated standard.[18] For a given type of public service, a standard level of service is defined. The potential user groups are then defined by demographic type. These types might be classified by age, gender, income, and/or any other factors that might make costs of provision different. For each demographic group, the cost of provision of the standard level of service is calculated. Then needs are determined by multiplying the population of each demographic group by the cost. This is done for all the types of public services that the transfers are intended to support. For example, in the case of education, the standard might be defined in terms of a class size and required school supplies at various levels of education. The demographic groups might then be age and income groups, perhaps supplemented by some features of the local community, such as population density or extent of remoteness.

As with equalization calculations, the VFG calculation is meant to lead to a lump-sum transfer per state. Thus, the transfer is not based on the state's actual costs, or on its actual expenditures, but on some measure of costs that is meant to reflect the minimum cost of provision that existing technology will entail. These estimates of cost could be based on some average of the costs incurred by all states. Or they could be based on more sophisticated econometric estimations, as is done in the Australian case. If actual costs of provision by the state itself were used to determine the state's needs, this would have an obvious adverse incentive effect on the state. It would have no incentive to economize on costs of provision because an increased transfer would reward any increases in costs.

[18] A good outline of the detailed procedures involved is found in Financial and Fiscal Commission (2000). This is for the case of South Africa, where responsibilities for health, education, and welfare are devolved to the provinces, but provincial revenue-raising ability is limited.

Because these kinds of calculations are obviously not straightforward, they are difficult to do comprehensively and with accuracy. The estimate of the VFG required by the states may therefore not be regarded as definitive. The federal government might use it more as an indicator than as a deterministic amount. The actual VFG would then be chosen using the estimate of needs as a benchmark, augmented by other qualitative information as well as by fiscal constraints. However, this adds an element of discretion to the determination of grants that is potentially deleterious to the federation. The states will face some uncertainty about the level of transfers they will receive, and the federal government might be tempted to become too intrusive in the way in which grants are accounted for and used by the states.

POLICY COORDINATION AND HARMONIZATION

Federal-state fiscal relations may involve more than financial transfers. They may also involve agreements to harmonize policies. Harmonization serves various purposes: securing efficiency in the internal economic union, implementing common standards of equity, and simplifying the administration of fiscal programs for governments and citizens alike.

The need for harmonization differs by policy area. A high priority is in the area of taxation. The costs of collection and compliance and the transparency of tax laws can be reduced by a tax system that has features of a common base and even has a single tax-collecting authority. In addition, if taxpayers are involved with more than one state, some form of coordination is essential to avoid double taxation. The transfer system might also be simplified by harmonization, especially if it too is administered alongside taxes. Harmonization of public services is perhaps less urgent on administrative grounds, because there tends to be relatively little jurisdictional overlap for users. Of course, possible issues of national efficiency and equity could be addressed by interstate harmonization in the event that the spending power is not used. Finally, harmonization of certain regulations is also desirable, especially where taxpayers operate in different states.

As discussed in Chapters 2 and 4, the manner in which harmonization can be accomplished is controversial. Some might argue that much of it could be achieved by horizontal agreement among the states, with or without the participation of the federal government.[19] But achieving horizontal

---

[19] This view has gained some prominence in Canada, where a recent exponent of this view has been Courchene (1996).

agreement among governments is likely to be difficult. The need for unanimous agreement makes substantive agreements very difficult to negotiate as the threat of veto can be used to obtain one's preferred components. It also restricts the scope of agreements to those in which all states stand to gain. Thus, horizontal agreement over interstate equalization, dividing up a given amount of federal transfers, or many policies involving national equity objectives would be infeasible. The participation of the federal government would not seem to make a difference. If agreement could be secured, enforcement would then be an issue. Dispute settlement mechanisms could be constructed, but their ultimate effectiveness would always run up against the sovereignty of state legislatures.

These considerations make the use of the federal government as facilitator attractive. The federal government has the power of the purse, which allows it to enforce or induce harmonization in a way that not only respects democratic decision making but also avoids the use of the courts. Although harmonizing spending programs involves the use of the spending power, this need not be done in a heavy-handed manner; the conditions attached to its use could be made only as intrusive as necessary for the purpose, and the states could be consulted on an ongoing basis. In the end, though, the need to report to the national electorate is the real check. To harmonize taxes, state participation seems to require a quid pro quo such as a single tax-collecting authority and some state input into tax policy issues, as well as enough federal dominance in the tax field so that the federal government can assume a leadership role in defining the broad parameters of the tax. This has implications for the degree of vertical fiscal imbalance and for the tax mixes used by the federal government and the states.

TEN

The Practice of Intergovernmental Transfers

Intergovernmental transfers finance about 60 percent of subnational expenditures in developing countries and transition economies and about a third of such expenditures in OECD countries (29 percent in the Nordic countries, 46 percent in non-Nordic Europe). Beyond the expenditures they finance, these transfers create incentives and accountability mechanisms that affect the fiscal management, efficiency, and equity of public service provision and government accountability to citizens.

This chapter reviews the practices of intergovernmental finance, with a view to drawing some general lessons of relevance to policy makers and practitioners in developing countries and transition economies. The chapter provides guidelines for grant design. It describes the objectives and design of fiscal transfers in various countries around the world. It shows that in developing countries and transition economies, fiscal transfers focus largely on revenue-sharing transfers, with little attention paid to serving national objectives. It cites examples of simple but innovative grant designs that can satisfy grantors' objectives while preserving local autonomy and creating an enabling environment for responsive, responsible, equitable, and accountable public governance. The concluding section of the chapter highlights some lessons of relevance to current policy debates in developing countries and transition economies. It lists practices to avoid as well as those to emulate in designing and implementing grant programs.

DESIGNING FISCAL TRANSFERS

The design of fiscal transfers is critical to ensuring the efficiency and equity of local service provision and the fiscal health of subnational governments.

A few simple considerations can be helpful in designing these transfers, as indicated in the following guidelines for grant design:

1. *Clarity in grant objectives*. Grant objectives should be clearly and precisely specified to guide grant design.
2. *Autonomy*. Subnational governments should have complete independence and flexibility in setting priorities. They should not be constrained by the categorical structure of programs and uncertainty associated with decision making at the center. Tax-base sharing – allowing subnational governments to introduce their own tax rates on central bases, formula-based revenue sharing, or block grants – is consistent with this objective.
3. *Revenue adequacy*. Subnational governments should have adequate revenues to discharge designated responsibilities.
4. *Responsiveness*. The grant program should be flexible enough to accommodate unforeseen changes in the fiscal situation of the recipients.
5. *Equity (fairness)*. Allocated funds should vary directly with fiscal need factors and inversely with the tax capacity of each jurisdiction.
6. *Predictability*. The grant mechanism should ensure predictability of subnational governments' shares by publishing five-year projections of funding availability. The grant formula should specify ways of alleviating yearly fluctuations, such as by the use of moving averages or floors and ceilings. Any major changes in the formula should be accompanied by hold harmless or grandfathering provisions.
7. *Transparency*. Both the formula and the allocations should be disseminated widely, in order to achieve as broad a consensus as possible on the objectives and operation of the program.
8. *Efficiency*. The grant design should be neutral with respect to subnational governments' choices of resource allocation to different sectors or types of activity unless there are clear efficiency or equity rationales for conditionality of grants.
9. *Simplicity*. Grant allocation should be based on objective factors over which individual units have little control. The formula should be easy to understand, in order not to reward grantsmanship.
10. *Incentive*. The design should provide incentives for sound fiscal management and discourage inefficient practices. Specific transfers to finance subnational government deficits should not be made.
11. *Reach*. All grant-financed programs create winners and losers. Consideration must be given to identifying beneficiaries and those who

will be adversely affected to determine the overall usefulness and sustainability of the program.

12. *Safeguarding of grantor's objectives.* Grantor's objectives are best safeguarded by having grant conditions specify the results to be achieved (output-based grants) and by giving the recipient flexibility in the use of funds.

13. *Affordability.* The grant program must recognize donors' budget constraints. This suggests that matching programs should be closed-ended.

14. *Singular focus.* Each grant program should focus on a single objective.

15. *Accountability for results.* The grantor must be accountable for the design and operation of the program. The recipient must be accountable to the grantor and its citizens for financial integrity and results – that is, improvements in service delivery performance. Citizens' voice and exit options in grant design can help advance bottom-up accountability objectives.

Some of these criteria may be in conflict with others. Grantors may therefore have to assign priorities to various factors in comparing design alternatives (Shah, 1994b; Canada, 2006a).

For enhancing government accountability to voters, it is desirable to match revenue means (the ability to raise revenues from one's own sources) as closely as possible with expenditure needs at all levels of government. However, higher-level governments must be allowed greater access to revenues than needed to fulfill their own direct service responsibilities, so that they are able to use their spending power through fiscal transfers to fulfill national and regional efficiency and equity objectives.

Six broad objectives for national fiscal transfers can be identified. They include bridging the vertical fiscal gap, equalizing state fiscal capacities, setting minimum national standards, compensating for benefit spillovers, influencing local priorities, and dealing with infrastructure deficiencies. Each of these objectives may apply to varying degrees in different countries; each calls for a specific design of fiscal transfers. Lack of attention in design to specific objectives leads to negative perceptions of these grants (Box 10.1). We consider the six objectives in turn.

Bridging Vertical Fiscal Gaps

A vertical fiscal gap is defined as the revenue deficiency arising from a mismatch between revenue means and expenditure needs, a characteristic

Box 10.1 Well-Founded Negative Perceptions of Intergovernmental Finance

Perceptions of intergovernmental finance are generally negative. Many federal officials believe that giving money and power to subnational governments is like giving whiskey and car keys to teenagers. They believe that grant moneys enable these governments to go on a spending binge and the national government then is faced with the consequences of its reckless spending behaviors. Past spending behavior of provincial and local officials also demonstrates that "grant money does not buy anything," meaning that it is treated as a windfall gain and wastefully expended with little to show in service delivery improvements. Citizens perceive the granting of intergovernmental fiscal transfers as the magical art of passing money from one government to another and seeing it vanish into thin air.

These perceptions are well grounded in reality in developing countries, where the primary focus of fiscal transfers is on dividing the spoils. In developing (and nondeveloping) countries, four types of transfers are common:

- *Passing the buck transfers.* These are general revenue-sharing programs that employ multiple factors that work at cross-purposes. Argentina, Brazil, India, the Philippines, and many other countries have such ongoing programs.
- *Asking for more trouble grants.* These are grants that finance subnational deficits, in the process encouraging higher and higher deficits. China, Hungary, and India provide this type of grants.
- *Pork-barrel transfers.* In the past politically opportunistic grants were common in Brazil and Pakistan. They are currently in vogue in India and Western countries, especially the United States.
- *Command and control transfers.* These are grants with conditions on inputs. They are used to micromanage and interfere in local decision making. They are widely practiced in most industrial and developing countries.

more typical of lower orders of government. A national government may have more revenues than warranted by its direct and indirect spending responsibilities; regional and local governments may have inadequate revenues relative to their expenditure responsibilities.

Four causes give rise to vertical fiscal gaps: inappropriate assignment of responsibilities, centralization of taxing powers, pursuit of beggar-thy-neighbor tax policies (wasteful tax competition) by subnational governments, and lack of tax room at subnational levels because of heavier tax burdens imposed by the central government. To deal with the vertical fiscal gap, it is important to deal with its sources through a combination of policies such as the reassignment of responsibilities, tax decentralization or tax abatement by the center, and tax-base sharing (by allowing subnational governments to levy supplementary rates on a national tax base). Only as a last resort should revenue sharing or unconditional formula-based transfers, both of which weaken accountability to local taxpayers, be considered to deal with this gap. Taxation by tax sharing, as practiced in China and India, is particularly undesirable, as it creates incentives for donors to exert less effort in collecting taxes that are shared than they would collecting taxes that are fully retained. In industrial countries, the fiscal gap is usually dealt with by tax decentralization or tax-base sharing. Canada and the Nordic countries have achieved harmonized personal and corporate income tax systems by allowing the central government to provide tax abatement and subnational governments to impose supplementary rates on the national tax base. In developing countries and transition economies, both tax sharing and general revenue sharing are typically used to deal with the fiscal gap.

China, India, Malaysia, Pakistan, Sri Lanka, South Africa, and other countries have in the past provided deficit grants to fill fiscal gaps at subnational levels – with unwelcome results in terms of mushrooming of subnational deficits. These grants are still in vogue in China, Hungary, and South Africa.

Bridging the Fiscal Divide through Fiscal Equalization Transfers

Fiscal equalization transfers are advocated to deal with regional fiscal equity concerns. These transfers are justified on political and economic considerations.

Large regional fiscal disparities can be politically divisive and may even create threats of secession (Shankar and Shah, 2003). This threat is quite real: since 1975 about forty new countries have been created by the breakup of existing political unions. Fiscal equalization transfers could forestall such threats and create a sense of political participation, as demonstrated by the impact of such transfers on the separatist movement in Quebec, Canada.

Decentralized decision making results in differential net fiscal benefits (imputed benefits from public spending minus tax burden) for citizens depending on the fiscal capacities of their place of residence. This leads to both fiscal inequity and fiscal inefficiency in resource allocation. Fiscal inequity arises as citizens with identical incomes are treated differently depending on their place of residence. Fiscal inefficiency in resource allocation results from people in their relocation decisions comparing gross income (private income plus net public-sector benefits minus cost of moving) at new locations; economic efficiency considerations warrant comparing only private income minus moving costs, without any regard to public-sector benefits. A nation that values horizontal equity (the equal treatment of all citizens nationwide) and fiscal efficiency needs to correct the fiscal inequity and inefficiency that naturally arise in a decentralized government. Grants from the central government to states and/or local governments can eliminate these differences in net fiscal benefits if the transfers depend on the tax capacity of each state relative to others and on the relative need for and cost of providing public services. The more decentralized the tax system is, the greater the need for equalizing transfers.

The elimination of net fiscal benefits requires a comprehensive fiscal equalization program that equalizes fiscal capacity (the ability to raise revenues from own sources using national average tax rates) to a national average standard and provides compensation for differential expenditure needs and costs due to inherent cost disabilities rather than differences that reflect different policies. Some economists argue that if public-sector tax burdens and service benefits are fully capitalized in property values, the case for fiscal equalization transfers is weaker, as residents in rich states pay more for private services and less for public services and vice versa in poorer states. According to this view, as argued by Oates (1972), fiscal equalization is a matter of political taste. This view has gained currency at the federal level in the United States and explains why there is no federal fiscal equalization program there. In contrast, local fiscal equalization drives most state assistance to local governments in the United States, especially school finance (Box 10.2).

Conceptually, full capitalization requires a small open area with costless mobility. Most federations and even states in large countries do not fulfill this condition. As a result, criticism of fiscal equalization using the capitalization argument may have only weak empirical support (Shah, 1988a).

In principle, a properly designed fiscal equalization transfers program corrects distortions that may cause fiscally induced migration by equalizing net fiscal benefits across states. A reasonable estimate of the costs and

Box 10.2   Financing Schools in the United States

In the United States, states have taken various approaches to school finance. Hawaii, Idaho, and Washington fully finance primary and secondary education. In contrast, New Hampshire covers only 9 percent of school finance.

Delaware and North Carolina finance education through block grants that are indexed to population, GDP, and inflation growth rates. The grants are derived by calculating equal amounts per unit on the basis of the number of students, teachers, classrooms, courses, classes, and other factors. The units can be standardized using various yardsticks, such as class size and teacher-pupil ratios. Various measures of students, including enrollment, average daily attendance, enrollment weighted by grades, types of programs, and number of students with special needs, are used.

Other states use equalization grants, including foundation grants, percentage equalization grants, and district power equalization grants.

Foundation grants vary inversely with the fiscal capacity of a school board. The grant allocation is based on an application of the representative tax system approach to fiscal capacity equalization per student across school districts. The following formula is used:

foundation grant = maximum per student grant – own school district
contribution per student based on mandated
minimumtax rate applied to per student tax base)
× enrollment

Forty-two states have adopted variants of this approach, with twenty-two states specifying the minimum mandated tax rate. Various measures are used to determine enrollment, including the number of students on the rolls on a specified date, average daily attendance, and average attendance over a period. Most states (thirty-six) use a scheme that weights enrollment by grade, program, and student disabilities.

Rhode Island uses a *percentage equalization grant* – a matching cum equalization grant for school spending based on the following formula:

grant per student = [1 – matching rate × (per capita tax capacity in the
district/state average district tax capacity per capita)]
× district spending per capita

District power equalization grants, used in Indiana and Washington, include incentives for increased tax effort in an equalizing grant. The formula used is:

grant = (per capita average fiscal capacity − per capita fiscal capacity
        of the district) × district tax rate

Source: Vaillancourt (1998).

benefits of providing public services in various states is essential to measure net fiscal benefits. Measures of differential revenue-raising abilities and the needs and costs of providing public services in different states must be developed. Equalization of net fiscal benefits could then be attempted by adopting a standard of equalization and establishing the means of financing the needed transfers.

Measuring Fiscal Capacity

Estimating fiscal capacity – the ability of governmental units to raise revenues from their own sources – is conceptually and empirically difficult. The two most common ways of doing so are with so-called macro indicators and the representative tax system.

Various measures of income and output serve as indicators of the ability of residents of a state to bear tax burdens. Among the better-known measures are the following:

- *State gross domestic product (GDP).* State GDP represents the total value of goods and services produced within a state. It is an imperfect guide to the ability of a state government to raise taxes, because a significant portion of income may accrue to nonresident owners of factors of production. For example, the Northern Territory has the highest per capita income in Australia, but it is treated as the poorest jurisdiction in federal-state fiscal relations.
- *State factor income.* State factor income includes all income – capital and labor – earned in the state. It makes no distinction between income earned and income retained by residents.
- *State factor income accruing to residents only.* This measure represents a more useful measure, provided states are able to tax factor income.

- *State personal income.* The sum of all income received by residents of a state is a reasonable measure of the state's ability to bear tax burdens. It is an imperfect and partial measure of the ability to impose tax burdens, however, and therefore not a satisfactory measure of overall fiscal capacity.
- *Personal disposable income.* Personal disposable income equals personal income minus direct and indirect taxes plus transfers. This concept is subject to the same limitations affecting personal income.

In general, macro measures do not reflect the ability of subnational governments to raise revenues from their own sources. One could argue against the use of macro indicators in an equalization formula on the grounds that a macro formula ignores the fact that fiscal inefficiency and fiscal inequity are the products of the actual mix of taxes chosen by provincial governments (Boadway, 2002). This neglect runs the risk of violating the principles of equalization itself. A second major difficulty in the use of macro indicators is the availability of accurate and timely data at subnational levels. Such data become available only with significant lags, and the accuracy of such data may be questionable. Use of these data may therefore invite controversy (see Aubut and Vaillancourt, 2001, for a Canadian illustration of this point). Despite these problems, both Brazil and India use macro indicators in their federal-state revenue-sharing programs.

The representative tax system approach measures the fiscal capacity of a state by the revenue that could be raised if the government employed all of the standard sources at the nationwide average intensity of use. Estimating equalization entitlements using the representative tax system requires information on the tax bases and tax revenues for each state. Fiscal capacity of the have-not states is brought up to the median, mean, or other norm. Using the mean of all states as a standard, one can determine the state equalization entitlement for a revenue source by the formula:

$$E_x^i = (POP)_x \{[(PCTB)_{na}^i - (PCTB)_x^i] \times t_{na}^i\},$$

where E^i is the equalization entitlement of state x from revenue source i, POP is population, $PCTB^i$ is the per capita tax base of revenue source i, t^i is the national average tax rate of revenue source i, subscript na is the national average, and subscript x is state x. The equalization entitlement for a state from a particular revenue source can be negative, positive, or zero. The total of these values indicates whether a state receives a positive or negative entitlement from the interstate revenue-sharing pool. Because data on major tax bases and tax collections required to implement a representative tax system are usually published regularly by various levels of government, the representative tax system does not impose new data requirements and can be readily implemented in countries that have decentralized taxing responsibility to subnational levels, as most transition economies do. Of course, implementing such a system will not be feasible in countries with limited tax decentralization (very large vertical fiscal gaps) or poor tax administration.

Measuring Expenditure Needs

The case for fiscal equalization rests on eliminating different net fiscal benefits across states that give rise to fiscally induced migration. Such differential net fiscal benefits can arise as a result of decentralization of taxing authority and decentralized public expenditures. Differences in the demographic composition of the population across jurisdictions will result in differential needs for decentralized public services, such as education, health, and social welfare. Differences in age distribution affect the need for schools, hospitals, and recreational facilities. Differences in the incidence of poverty and disease may affect the need for education, training, health, social services, and transfer payments. Jurisdictions with higher need factors would have greater need for revenues to provide comparable levels of public services at comparable levels of taxation. These need differentials are likely to cause substantial variations across jurisdictions in the level and mix of public goods provided, resulting in different net fiscal benefits. A strong case for equalization can be established on grounds of efficiency and equity to compensate for need differentials that give rise to different net fiscal benefits.

The fiscal federalism literature treats differential costs as synonymous with differential needs, but some cost differences may arise from deliberate policy decisions by subnational governments rather than differences in need. One could argue that even for inherent cost disadvantages, such as differences between urban and rural areas, the equity advantage of more equal provision must be weighed against the efficiency costs (Boadway, 2004). If it is more costly to deliver public services in rural areas than urban areas, it is inefficient for an equalization program to neutralize these cost differences. Even in unitary states, the level of public services in remote, rural, or mountainous areas is usually lower than in more densely populated urban areas. Under a decentralized fiscal system, a policy choice must be made about minimum standards, but there is no justification for providing the same level of services in remote and urban areas, as the Australian fiscal need equalization program does. Instead, one could stratify locations in all regions by their costs and equalize across regions within comparable strata. Equalization grants should partially offset only inherent disabilities, disregarding cost differences that reflect deliberate policy decisions or differences in the efficiency with which resources are used.

In practice, expenditure need is more difficult to define and derive than fiscal capacity. The difficulties include defining an equalization standard; understanding differences in demographics, service areas, populations, local needs, and policies; and understanding strategic behavior of recipient states. Despite these formidable difficulties, numerous attempts have been made to measure expenditure need. The approaches can be broadly classified into three main categories: ad hoc determination of expenditure needs, representative expenditure system using direct imputation methods, and the theory-based representative expenditure system.

Ad Hoc Determination of Expenditure Needs. This approach uses simple measures of expenditure needs in general-purpose transfers. The factors used and their relative weights are arbitrarily determined. Germany uses population size and population density adjustments, China uses the number of public employees, and India uses measures of backwardness.

The Canadian provinces use simple measures of expenditure need in their general-purpose transfers to municipalities These include population size, population density, population growth factors, road length, number dwelling units, location factors (such as northern location), urbanization factors (primary urban population and urban or rural class), and social assistance payments (see Shah, 1994b). The most sophisticated of these approaches is the one taken by Saskatchewan, where the standard municipal expenditure of a class of municipalities is assumed to be a function of the total population of the class. Regression analysis is used to derive a graduated standard per capita expenditure table for municipal governments by population class.

An interesting example of the application of this approach is South Africa's use of it in its equitable share transfers to the provinces (South Africa, 2006). The equitable share formula applicable for 2006–2008 focuses almost entirely on need factors, with only a 1 percent weight given to negative needs (per capita GDP). The formula uses the following shares:

- A basic share (14 percent weight) is derived from each province's share of the national population.

- An education share (51 percent) is based on the size of the school-age population (5–17) and the average number of learners (grades K–12) enrolled in public ordinary schools over the past three years.
- A health share (26 percent) is based on the proportion of the population with and without access to medical aid.
- An institutional component (5 percent) is divided equally among the provinces.
- A poverty component (3 percent) is based on incidence of poverty.
- An economic output component (1 percent) is based on data on GDP by region.

The Representative Expenditure System Using Direct Imputation Methods. This approach seeks to create a parallel system to the representative tax system on the expenditure side. This is done by dividing subnational expenditures into various functions, determining total expenditures by each jurisdiction for each function, identifying relative need or cost factors, assigning relative weights using direct imputation methods or regression analysis, and allocating total expenditures of all jurisdictions on each function across jurisdictions on the basis of their relative costs and needs for each function (see Table 10.1 for a compilation of need factors used in industrial countries).

The advantage of this approach is that it obviates the need for the very elaborate calculations and assumptions needed to quantify the provision of services at some defined level. It does so by using the sum of actual total expenditures as the point of departure for measuring expenditure needs, thus reducing the problem to one of allocating total need among subnational governments on the basis of selected indicators of need, including proxies for need if desired. The disadvantage of this approach is that it does not necessarily exclude expenses incurred by any of the provinces that go beyond the concept of a "reasonable level of public service." However, the approach can be adjusted to exclude identifiable excesses from total expenditures (e.g., gold standards for some services or relatively unaffordable benefits provided by some rich states) in respect of which needs are to be allocated.

A sophisticated variant of this methodology is used by the Commonwealth Grants Commission of Australia, which defines expenditure as the cost of supplying average performance levels for the existing mix of state-local programs. Relative expenditure needs are then determined empirically using direct imputation methods for forty-one state-local

Table 10.1. *Measurement of fiscal needs, by service category*

Category	Fiscal need indicator	Per-unit cost	Components of adjustment index
Education, primary and secondary	Population of school ages (e.g., ages 7–18)	National per capita public expenditure on primary and secondary education	Wage index = ratio of wage level in sector to national average; rental cost index = ratio of per-square rental cost to national average; student disability index = ratio of percentage of students with physical disabilities to the national average; poor family index = the ratio of the percentage students from low-income families to national average
Health	Total population	National per capita public expenditure on health care	Health price index = ratio of health care cost to national average; infant mortality index = ratio of infant mortality rate to national average; inverse life expectancy index = ratio of national average life expectancy to life expectancy in region; inverse population density index = ratio of national average population density to density in region
Police and fire	Total population in region	National per capita public expenditure on police and fire protection	Wage index = ratio of wage level to national average; crime index = ratio of per capita crime rate to national average; fire index = ratio of per capita number of fires to national average; urbanization index = ratio of proportion of population in urban areas in region of municipality to national average

(continued)

Table 10.1 (*continued*)

Category	Fiscal need indicator	Per-unit cost	Components of adjustment index
Social welfare	Total population in region	National per capita public expenditure on social welfare	Minimum wage index = ratio of minimum wage level to national average; poverty index = ratio of percentage of low-income population to national average; old-age index = ratio of percentage of old population (e.g., age 60 or older) to national average; unemployment index = ratio of unemployment rate of national average; disability index = ratio of percentage of physically disabled people to national average
Transportation	Total length of roads in region	National per capita public expenditure on transportation	Wage index = ratio of wage level to national average; grade index = ratio of average road grade to national average; snow index = ratio of annual snowfall to national average; inverse population density index = ratio of national average population density to density in region
Other services	Total population in region	National per capita public expenditure on other services	Wage index = ratio of wage level to national average; real cost index = ratio of per-square rental cost to national average; urbanization index of region = ratio of proportion of population in urban areas in region of municipality to national average

Source: Barati and Szalai (2000: 42).

expenditures. The following hypothetical example illustrates the treatment of welfare expenditures using a crude approach similar to that used by the Commonwealth Grants Commission for establishing expenditure needs under a representative expenditure system.

Assume that there are ten states in Grantland, that the unit costs of welfare are equal in all states, and that needs for welfare vary according to the percentage of the working-age population that is unemployed, the percentage of the population that is not of working age, and the percentage of families with a single parent. The independent grants commission assigns a 40 percent weight to the percentage of the working-age population that is unemployed, a 35 percent weight to the percentage of the population that is not of working age, and a 25 percent weight to the percentage of families with a single parent. Assume that expenditures by all states for welfare total $5 billion and that state *A* accounts for 4.8 percent of the ten-state total for the first factor, 3.0 percent of the total for the second factor, and 2.2 percent of the total for the third factor. State *A*'s estimated need for a standard level of welfare expenditure would then equal:

$$\text{\$5 billion} \times (0.048 \times 0.40) + (0.03 \times 0.35) + (0.022 \times 0.25) = \text{\$176 million},$$

or 3.2 percent of all state expenditures.

Shah (1994a) provides an application of the approach using provincial-local expenditure functions for Canada that uses quantitative analysis in selecting and assigning weights to factors for various expenditure functions (see Table 10.2).

This approach is highly subjective and therefore potentially controversial. Recent experience in Australia vividly demonstrates the problems that arise if such an approach is followed in practice as discussed in the following section. Some subjectivity and imprecision can be alleviated by using quantitative analysis in choosing factors and weights, as Shah (1994a) suggests.

The Theory-Based Representative Expenditure System. The theory-based representative expenditure attempts to implement a conceptually desirable view of expenditure needs equalization objectively – that is, with localities to be compensated for inherent cost disabilities rather than for differences that reflect different policies and preferences. If the influences of these latter factors are to be isolated, the representative expenditure system can be significantly improved. A conceptual framework that embodies appropriately defined concepts of fiscal need and properly specified expenditure functions can be estimated using objective quantitative analysis, as

Table 10.2. *Weighting of factors for provincial-local expenditure functions for Canada*

Expenditure category	Need/cost factors	Relative weights
Transportation and Communications	Snowfall (annual – in centimeters) SNOW	0.1020
	Highway Construction Price Index (HCPI)	0.6580
	Paved roads and streets per square kilometer of area (RSPR)	0.0005
	Noncultivatable area as a proportion of total area (NCAR)	0.2357
	Total	1.0000
	Index = (0.10*ISNOW + 0.66*IHCPI + 0.0005*IRSPR + 0.24*INCAR)*ISRP	
Post-secondary Education (PSE)	Full time enrollment in grade 13+(000)(PSS)	0.048
	Percentage of population having a minority language as mother tongue (ML)	0.19
	Provincial Unemployment Rate (UR)	0.018
	Education Price Index (EPI)	0.717
	Help Wanted Index (HWI)	0.010
	Foreign Post-secondary Students (FPS)	0.017
	Total	1.000
	Index = (0.18*IPSS + .70*IML + .08*IUR + .04*IFPS)*IHWI*IEPI	
Elementary and Secondary Education (ESE)	Population under 18 (PO17)	0.014
	Population Density (PD)	0.017
	Education Price Index (EPI)	0.969
	Total	1.000
	Index = (.02*IPD +,98*IEPI)*IP017	
Health (HE)	Alcoholism (hospital separations for alcohol related cases) (ALCO)	0.123
	Urban Population (PU)	0.877
	Total	1.000
	Index = (0.123*IALCO + 0.877*IPU)	
Social Services (SS)	Single Parent Families (SPF)	1.00

Expenditure category	Need/cost factors	Relative weights
Police Protection	Criminal Code Offenses (CCO)	0.39
	Proportion of Population in Metropolitan (PMAR) Areas	0.61
	Total	1.00
	Index = (.39*ICCO + .61*IPMAR)	
General Services (GS)	Private-sector wages (Industrial composite) (AMW)	0.769
	Percentage of population having a minority language as mother tongue (ML)	0.001
	Population Density (PD)	0.023
	Population (POPF)	0.039
	Snowfall (annual - in centimeters) (SNOW)	0.168
	Total	1.000
	Index = (.001*ML + 0.175*ISNOW + .80*IAMW + .024*IPD)*IPOPF	

Note: Calculations based on regression coefficients. The use of a variable prefixed by I means that a relative index of the variable is used.
Source: Shah (1994a).

proposed by Shah (1994a, 1996b) for Canada. Under this refined approach, the so-called theory-based representative expenditure system, the equalization entitlement from expenditure category *i* equals the per capita potential expenditure of state *A* for category *i* based on own-need factors if it had national average fiscal capacity *minus* the per capita potential expenditure of state *A* on expenditure category *i* if it had national average need factors and national average fiscal capacity.

This approach is even more difficult to implement than the less refined approach of direct imputation methods, but it has the advantage of objectivity and it enables the analyst to derive measures based on actual observed behavior rather than ad hoc value judgments. The relative weights assigned to various need factors and their impact on allocation of grant funds are determined by econometric analysis. Furthermore, this approach yields both the total pool and the allocation of fiscal need equalization grants among recipient units. This method requires specifying determinants for each service category, including relevant fiscal capacity and public service need variables. A properly specified regression equation yields quantitative estimates of the influence that each factor has in determining spending levels of a category of public service. Once this information has been analyzed to determine what each state would actually have spent if it had national average fiscal capacity and also actual need factors, it can then be compared to the standard expenditure for each service on the basis of an evaluation of the same equation for determining what each state would have spent if it had the national average fiscal capacity and also national average need factors. The sum of differences of these two expressions for all expenditure categories would determine whether the state had more (if the sum was positive) or less (if the sum was negative) than the average needs (see Shah, 1996b, for a Canadian application of this approach).

The formula for equalization entitlement based on expenditure classification i for state x could be stated as follows:

$$EE_x^i = (POP)_x[(PCSE)_x^i - (PCSE)_{na}^i],$$

where EE_x^i is the equalization entitlement for expenditure classification i for state x, POP_x is the population of state x, $PCSE_x^i$ is the per capita standardized expenditure by state x on expenditure classification i (or the estimated amount the state would have spent to meet actual needs if it had national average fiscal capacity), and $PCSE_{na}^i$ is the national average per capita standardized expenditure for classification i. This is the estimated expenditure for all states, based on national average values of fiscal capacity and need. The equalization entitlement for a particular expenditure classification could be positive, negative, or zero. The total of these entitlements in all expenditure categories is considered for equalization.

A comprehensive system of equalization determines the overall entitlement of a state by considering its separate entitlements from the representative tax system and the representative expenditure system. Only states with positive net entitlements are eligible for transfers of all or some fraction of the total amount, with the fraction determined by the central government on the basis of the availability of funds.

Practical Difficulties in Equalizing Expenditure Needs: Australia's Experience

The Commonwealth Grants Commission of Australia found the theory-based representative expenditure system approach difficult to implement. It opted instead for an alternate representative expenditure system using direct imputation methods that simply equalize what all states on average actually spend. The Australian system seeks absolute comparability for all forty-one state-local services rather than just merit goods (some would question whether this is worth pursuing).

Australia's approach raises several questions. Is equal access to all services in remote areas desirable at any cost? If a rich state decides to buy limousines for its officials, or make higher welfare payments to its aboriginal population, why should equalization payments to poorer states go up? Such an approach diverts states' energies to demonstrate that they "need more to do less" or "money does not buy much" as opposed to "doing more with less," as the equalization grant formula rewards higher spending and discourages cost-saving in delivering improved services. Such a system rewards some bad behaviors, including excessive use of some services by specific groups, tax expenditures by states to attract capital and labor, and state assumption of contingent and noncontingent liabilities.

In addition to conceptual difficulties, the Australian program is plagued with measurement problems. The determinants of expenditure needs for various expenditure categories are arrived at on the basis of broad judgments. Arbitrary procedures are used to derive factor weights and combine various factors into functional forms. State disabilities stemming from various factors are multiplied. For highly correlated factors, disabilities are artificially magnified through double counting and multiplication. The Australian experience highlights the practical difficulties associated with implementing fiscal need compensation as part of a comprehensive fiscal equalization approach (see Shah, 2004b).

Conclusions Regarding the Practice of Fiscal Need Equalization
Fiscal capacity equalization is relatively straightforward to comprehend and feasible (with some difficulty) to implement once a (political) decision is made on the standard of equalization. Fiscal need equalization is a complex and potentially controversial proposition, because by its very nature it requires making subjective judgments and using imprecise analytical methods. An analytical approach such as regression analysis using historical data is inappropriate when underlying structures are subject to change due to technology and other dynamic considerations. Great care is needed to specify determinants of each service.

Australia's Commonwealth Grants Commission makes these calculations using broad judgments and sampling services. With the single exception of the Northern Territory, which has a large aboriginal population, there is little cross-state variation in the expenditure needs of the Australian states. A special grant for the Northern Territory would simplify the Australian program while achieving its equalization objectives.

Very few countries opt for a comprehensive program of fiscal equalization. In contrast, a few industrial countries use fiscal capacity equalization programs, at both the federal-state (Canada, Switzerland) and state-local levels (Canada, Sweden, Switzerland, Denmark). Fiscal need compensation is important, but, for the sake of simplicity and objectivity, rather than implement a fiscal need equalization approach as part of the fiscal equalization program, it may be better instead to achieve fiscal needs compensation on a service-by-service basis through output-based national minimum standards grants. South Africa, however, as discussed earlier, does not use output-based transfers and instead compensates for fiscal needs on a service-by-service basis in determining provincial entitlements for central general-purpose grants to the provinces.

Frequently Raised Concerns in Designing Equalization Transfers

Concerns are often raised about defining the equalization standard, determining whether to include tax efforts provisions, ensuring stability, and forestalling strategic behaviors to qualify for a higher level of transfers. Equalizing net fiscal benefits requires an explicit standard of equalization – the level to which each state is entitled to be raised to provide public-sector net benefits per household that are comparable to other states. Simplicity dictates choosing either the mean or the median of the governmental units involved as the standard. The mean provides a good representation of the data as long as outliers are not present. If sample values have a wide range, the median, or the mean after eliminating outliers, provides a better representation of the sample. The mean is preferable to the median, however, for ease of computation.

An ideal fiscal equalization program is self-financing. Member governments are assessed, as in Germany, positive and negative entitlements that total zero, with the federal government acting as a conduit. If an interstate equalization pool creates administrative difficulties, the equalization program can be financed out of general federal revenues, as is done in Canada, derived in part from the states' receiving equalization.

There is general consensus in the academic literature that an equalization system should enable state governments to provide a standard package of public services if the government imposes a standard level of taxes on the bases at its disposal. State governments or their citizens should, however, be permitted to substitute lower rates of taxation for lower levels of services. In such cases, the equalization payments should be in the form of unconditional grants, which have only income effects. Service areas in which there is a good reason to set minimum national standards are better handled by output-based conditional grants and shared-cost programs. By raising a state's fiscal capacity, unconditional equalization grants enable poorer states to participate in shared-cost programs more easily.

Incorporating tax effort into the formula for determining equalization involves making the equalization entitlement a function of the ratio of actual tax collections in a state to the state's base. Potential nonrecipient states may wish to see such a factor incorporated into the program to prevent states with a positive fiscal deficiency in an area from collecting equalization payments even if they may not levy a tax in the area. Potential recipient states may wish to see tax effort incorporated because, without it, extra tax effort on their part will be relatively unproductive compared with the effort in a wealthy state.

Several problems exist with incorporating tax effort into the program:

- The inclusion of tax effort will cause the program to depart from its unconditional nature. A state should be free to substitute grant funds for revenue from own sources.
- If a state raises taxes to provide a package of services that is more costly than the standard, it should not receive equalization for doing so; other states should not have to pay most of the cost if a state decides to paint its roads.
- Incorporating tax effort ties the federal government to the expenditure philosophies of the various states.
- Some states do not have tax bases in all areas.
- Incorporating tax effort may encourage the employment of strategy by a state.
- In view of the different abilities of the states to export taxes, the measurement of tax effort would be crude.
- Incorporating tax effort could result in an increase in taxes on the poor states.

In view of these considerations, including tax effort would not improve a program of equalization payments.

If equalization payments are based on relative measures of fiscal capacity, they should have a stabilizing effect on state revenues. The level of payments will move in the opposite direction of states' own revenue-raising capacity. Maximum stabilization of state-local revenues will occur when payments are based on all revenue sources, a national average standard of equalization is used, cyclical fluctuations in provincial economies are small, and the time lag in calculating the grants is relatively short. When any large component of the total base, such as natural resource revenues, is volatile, the destabilizing effects can be large. In this case, some sort of averaging formula should be used to ease difficulties associated with provincial budgeting in the face of uncertainty.

Strategy refers to action provincial or state governments can take to influence the level of payments they receive. A program that enables a state to employ strategy is undesirable, because in general the extra payments received may not have any relation to actual disparities. For example, a program employing tax effort could enable states to raise their entitlements by imposing heavy taxes in areas in which they have a tax base below the national average. This problem is less serious in practice than one might expect, because room for additional taxation from sources in which the potential have-not states are not well endowed is extremely limited.

Reflections on Comparative Practices of Fiscal Equalization Transfers

A small but growing number of industrial countries and transition economies have introduced fiscal equalization programs. These include Australia, Canada, China, Denmark, Germany, Indonesia, Japan, Latvia, Lithuania, Poland, the Russian Federation, Sweden, Switzerland, and Ukraine. All equalization programs are concerned with interjurisdictional equity or horizontal fiscal equity, not interpersonal (vertical) equity. Which level of government finances and administers an equalization program is determined either by the constitution (as in Canada, Germany, and Switzerland) or by the legislature (as in Australia) (Table 10.3).

Paternal programs, in which higher-level governments finance equalization at lower levels are common (examples include Australia and Canada). Fraternal or Robin Hood–type (Robin Hood stole from the rich to give to the poor) programs, in which governments at the same level establish a common pool, to which rich jurisdictions contribute and the poor jurisdictions draw, are rare (exceptions include Germany at the *Länder* level and Denmark at the local level). Robin Hood programs are preferred, as they represent an open political compromise balancing the interests of the union and the contributing jurisdictions, as done by the Solidarity Pact II in Germany. Such programs foster national unity, as poorer jurisdictions clearly see the contributions made for their well-being by residents of other

Table 10.3. *Features of fiscal equalization transfers in selected countries*

Feature	Australia	Canada	Germany	Switzerland
Objective	Build capacity to provide services at same standard with same revenue effort and same operational efficiency	Achieve reasonably comparable levels of public services at reasonably comparable levels of taxation across provinces	Equalize differences in financial capacity of states	Provide minimum acceptable levels of certain public services without much heavier tax burdens in some cantons than in others
Legal status	Federal law	Constitution	Constitution	Constitution
Legislation	Federal parliament	Federal parliament	Federal parliament, initiated by Bundesrat	Federal parliament
Paternal or fraternal	Paternal	Paternal	Fraternal	Mixed
Total pool determination	Ad hoc	Formula	Formula	Ad hoc
Equalization standard for pool and allocation	No	Yes	Yes	No
Allocation	Formula	Formula	Formula	Formula
Fiscal capacity equalization	Yes, representative tax system	Yes, representative tax system	Yes, actual revenues	Yes, major macro tax bases
Fiscal need equalization	Yes	No	No (only population size and density)	Some
Program complexity	High	Low	Low	Medium
Political consensus	No (?)	Yes (?)	Yes (?)	Yes
Who recommends	Independent agency	Intergovernmental committees	Solidarity Pact II	Federal government
Sunset clause	No	Yes, five years	No	No
Dispute resolution	Supreme Court	Supreme Court	Constitutional Court	Supreme Court

jurisdictions. Paternal programs lack the discipline of fraternal programs, because, unless enshrined in the constitution (as in Canada), they are guided largely by national politics and the budgetary situation of the federal and state or provincial (for local equalization) governments.

Some countries combine both Robin Hood (fraternal) and paternal components in their grant programs. In Switzerland, effective 2007, the federal government finances two-thirds of the program, with the remaining third financed by the rich cantons. The program has a fiscal capacity equalization component based on factor income, with 59 percent of the financing from the federal government and 41 percent from rich cantons. The cost equalization component is financed solely by the federal government. The German equalization program has a small supplementary component financed solely by the federal government. In Denmark equalization at the local level uses the Robin Hood approach for both fiscal capacity and fiscal need equalization for counties (using 85 percent national average standard) and large cities (90 percent of the national average standard for fiscal capacity and 60 percent of the national average standard for fiscal need); for smaller municipalities, it uses the paternal approach for fiscal capacity equalization (using 50 percent of national average standard as the standard of equalization) and the Robin Hood approach for fiscal need equalization (using 35 percent of the national average as the standard of equalization).

Fiscal equalization programs also differ in terms of how the total pool of resources devoted to such programs is determined. In the Canadian and German programs, both the total pool and its allocation to provinces or states are formula driven. Under the Australian and Swiss programs, the total pool is arbitrarily determined by the federal government through an act of parliament – total proceeds of the general sales tax in Australia and an arbitrarily determined level of funding from the federal government and rich cantons in Switzerland.

The method of equalization also differs across programs. Australia, Canada, and Germany equalize per capita fiscal capacity using the representative tax system. Switzerland uses a macro tax base indicator. It devotes 19 percent of equalization financing to cost equalization using eight factors: population size, area, population density, population older than eighty, number of large cities, number of foreign adult residents for more than ten years, unemployment, and number of people requesting social assistance from the canton. In Germany, actual rather than potential revenues are used in these calculations, as both actual and potential revenues are the same because of the uniformity of state tax bases and tax rates through federal legislation. Germany makes simple expenditure need adjustments based on population size, density, and whether a city is a harbor. China uses potential revenues, although they equal actual revenues, when there is uniformity of tax bases and tax rates as mandated by central government legislation in China. The Canadian program does not include fiscal need compensation. Australia uses a comprehensive equalization program, equalizing fiscal capacity as well as need for all state expenditures. Unlike the Canadian system, the Australian system implicitly equalizes the above-average states down (by adjusting their transfers) as well as the below-average states up. In that sense, it is equivalent to a "net" system. The introduction of expenditure needs compensation introduces complexity and controversy and dilutes political consensus. As a result, the Australian program is the most complex and controversial of all programs and has garnered the least political consensus.

Most equalization programs are introduced as permanent programs; an exception is Canada, where there is a sunset clause for quinquennial review and renewal by the national parliament. Such a clause is helpful in providing a regular periodic evaluation and fine-tuning of the system. Almost all programs in mature federations specify formal mechanisms for resolving disputes regarding the working of these transfers programs.

Overall, the experience of mature federations with fiscal equalization suggests that in the interest of simplicity, transparency, and accountability, it would be better for such programs to focus only on fiscal capacity equalization to an explicit standard that determines the total pool as well as the allocation among recipient units. Fiscal need compensation is best dealt with through specific-purpose transfers for merit goods, as is done in most industrial countries.

Most transition economies have equalization components in their grant programs to subnational governments. China, Latvia, Lithuania, Poland, Romania, the Russian Federation, and Ukraine have adopted transfer formulas that explicitly incorporate either fiscal capacity or expenditure need equalization concerns. For local fiscal equalization, these countries nevertheless use one-size-fits-all approaches to diverse forms of local government, creating equity concerns.

With the exception of Indonesia, developing countries have not implemented programs using explicit equalization standards, although equalization objectives are implicitly attempted in the general revenue-sharing mechanisms used in Argentina, Brazil, Colombia, India, Nigeria, Mexico, Pakistan, and South Africa. These mechanisms typically combine diverse and conflicting objectives into the same formula and fall significantly short on individual objectives. Because the formulas lack explicit equalization standards, they fail to address regional equity objectives satisfactorily. Even in the Indonesian program, total pool is not determined by an explicit equalization standard, and instead the equalization standard is implicitly determined by the ad hoc determination of total funds available for equalization purposes.

Setting National Minimum Standards

Setting national minimum standards in regional-local services may be important for two reasons. First, there is an advantage to the nation as a whole from such standards, which contribute to the free flow of goods, services, labor, and capital; reduce wasteful interjurisdictional expenditure competition; and improve the gains from trade from the internal common market. Second, these standards serve national equity objectives. Many public services provided at the subnational level, such as education, health, and social welfare, are redistributive in their intent, providing in-kind redistribution to residents. In a federal system, lower-level provision of such services – while desirable for efficiency, preference matching, and accountability – creates difficulty fulfilling federal equity objectives. Factor mobility and tax competition create strong incentives for lower-level governments to underprovide such services and to restrict access to those most in need, such as the poor and the old. Attempts to exclude those most in need are justified by their greater susceptibility to disease and potentially greater risks for cost curtailment. Such perverse incentives can be alleviated by conditional nonmatching grants, in which the conditions reflect national efficiency and equity concerns and there is a financial penalty associated with failure to comply with any of the conditions. Conditions are thus imposed not on the specific use of grant funds but on attainment of standards in quality, access, and level of services. Such output-based grants do not affect local government incentives for cost efficiency, but they do encourage compliance with nationally specified standards for access and level of services. Properly designed conditional nonmatching output-based transfers can create incentives for innovative and competitive approaches to improved service delivery. Input-based grants fail to create such an accountability environment.

With a few exceptions, noted later, both industrial and developing countries typically do not use output-based transfers for fiscal need compensation in sectoral grants. However, industrial countries typically keep the design of input-based conditional sectoral grants simple, using relatively basic demographic factors. In contrast, developing countries opt for complex formulas, using state-of-the-art quantitative techniques (Table 10.4).

A good illustration of a simple but effective output-based grant system is the Canadian Health Transfers program by the federal government of Canada. The program has enabled Canadian provinces to ensure universal access to high-quality health care to all residents regardless of their income or place of residence.

Under this program the federal government provides per capita transfers for health to the provinces, with the rate of growth of the transfers tied to the rate of growth of GDP. No conditions are imposed on spending, but strong conditions are imposed on access to health care. As part of the agreement to receive transfers from the federal government, the provinces undertake to abide by five access-related conditions:

1. *Universality, comprehensiveness, and accessibility.* All residents enjoy the same access to a broad range of health coverage.
2. *Portability.* Residents who move to another province retain health coverage in the province of origin for a transition period. Residents and nonresidents have equal access.
3. *Public insurance but public or private provision.* The province agrees to provide universal insurance to all. Both public and private providers are reimbursed from the public insurance system using the same schedule of payments, negotiated by the provincial medical association.
4. *Opting in and opting out.* Providers participating in the system cannot bill patients directly but are reimbursed by the province. All health care providers can opt out of the system, billing patients directly and not following the prescribed fee schedule. Patients of these providers are reimbursed according to a government schedule of payments by submitting claims.
5. *No extra billing.* Charges in excess of the prescribed schedule are not permitted by providers opting into the system.

Breaches in any of these conditions result in penalties. If any of the first four conditions is breached, grant funding can be reduced at the discretion of the federal government. If the last condition is breached, grant funds are reduced on a dollar-for-dollar basis.

Developing countries and transition economies rarely use conditional nonmatching output-based transfers to ensure national minimum standards in merit goods or fiscal need compensation. There are nevertheless a

Table 10.4. *Need factors used for grant financing of health care in selected countries*

Country name	Need factors for health care grants
Need-based top-up for health care in general grants	
Belgium	Age, gender, unemployment, disability
Finland (to local governments)	Age, disability, remoteness, local tax base
Germany	Age, gender
Netherlands	Age, gender, urbanization, income base
Switzerland	Age, gender, region, income
Need-based specific-purpose transfers for core health services	
Denmark	Age, children of single parents
England	Age, sex, mortality, unemployment, elderly living alone
France	Age
Italy (two-thirds)	Age, gender, mortality
Northern Ireland	Age, gender, mortality, low birth weight
Norway (50 percent)	Age, gender, mortality, elderly living alone
Portugal (15 percent)	Burden of illness: diabetes, hypertension, AIDS, tuberculosis
Scotland	Age, gender, mortality, rural costs
Spain	Cross-boundary flows
Sweden	Age, living alone, employment status, housing
Wales	Age, gender, mortality, rural costs
Health transfers using composite indexes based upon principal component analysis	
Brazil	Infant mortality, 1–64 mortality, 65+ mortality, mortality rate by infectious and parasitic diseases, mortality rate for neoplasia, mortality rate for cardiovascular conditions, adolescent mother percentage, illiteracy percentage, percentage of homes without sanitation, percentage of homes without running water, percentage of homes without garbage collection
South Africa	Percentage female; percentage children younger than 5; percentage living in rural area; percentage older than 25 without schooling; percentage unemployed; percentage living in traditional dwelling, shack or tent; percentage without piped water in house or on site; percentage without access to refuse disposal; percentage without access to phone; percentage without access to electricity; percentage living in household headed by a woman

Source: World Bank (2006).

few shining examples of programs that marry equity with performance orientation in grant allocation. These include transfers from the central government to provincial and local governments for primary education and transportation in Indonesia (discontinued in 2001), per-pupil grants to all schools and a 25 percent additional grant as a salary bonus for teachers in the best-performing schools in Chile (P. Gonzalez, 2005), central grants to municipal governments to subsidize water and sewer use by the poor in Chile (Gomez-Lobo, 2002), central per capita transfers for education in Colombia and South Africa, and federal per-pupil grants to states for secondary education and to municipalities for primary education in Brazil (Gordon and Vegas, 2004).

Indonesian education and road maintenance grants to districts before 2001 are examples of good grant design. The operating grant for schools in Indonesia used school-age population (seven to twelve) as the criterion for distributing funds to district and town governments. These operating grants were supplemented by a matching capital grant for school construction (local government matching in the form of land for school) to achieve minimum standards of access to primary schooling (having a primary school within walking distance of every community). The grants enabled Indonesia to achieve remarkable success in improving literacy and achieving minimum standards of access to primary education across the nation.

Before 2001, the Indonesian District/Town Road Improvement Grant used length of roads, condition, density (traffic use), and unit costs as criteria for distributing funds. This grant program helped monitor the health of the road network on a continuing basis and kept roads in good working conditions in most jurisdictions (Shah 1998).

In Chile and the state of Michigan in the United States, school grants finance vouchers for school-age children, giving parents choice in sending their children to public, private, or parochial schools. Grants to municipal governments in Chile for water and sewer access by the poor cover 25–85 percent (means tested) of a household's water and sewer bill for up to 15 cubic meters a month, with the client paying the rest (Gomez-Lobo, 2002).

Brazil has two noteworthy national minimum standards grant programs for primary education and health care. Under the fourteenth amendment to the federal constitution, state and municipal governments must contribute 15 percent of their two principal revenue sources (state value-added tax and state share of the federal revenue-sharing transfers for states, and municipal services tax and the municipal share of the state revenue-sharing transfers for municipalities) to the special fund for primary education (FUNDEF). If the sum of the state and municipal required contributions divided by the number of primary school students is less than the national standard, the federal government makes up the difference. FUNDEF funds are distributed among state and municipal providers on the basis of school enrollments.

Fiscal transfers in support of Brazil's Unified Health System, which operationalizes the constitutional obligation of the universal right to free health services, are administered under a federal program called Annual Budget Ceilings (TGF). The program has two components. Under the first component, equal per capita financing from the federal government that passes through states to municipalities is provided to cover basic health benefits. The second component provides federal financing for hospital and ambulatory care and all registered health care providers – state, municipal, and private – are eligible for grant financing through their municipal government. Under this grant, funding for hospital admissions and high-cost ambulatory care is subject to a ceiling for each type of treatment (World Bank, 2006).

Local governments in the province of Alberta, Canada, use a novel approach to determine the allocation of taxpayers' contribution to school finance. Resident taxpayers designate the education component of their property tax bill to either public or parochial (religious, private) school boards. These declarations determine the total amount of property tax finance available to public and private providers. Schools receive grants on a per-pupil basis, and parents retain the option to send their children to a school of their choosing regardless of the designation on their tax return. This approach encourages competition among schools to attract students and may help explain the better performance of government schools in Alberta and other provinces that use the same approach. In the province of Ontario, higher education financing assigns weights to enrollments in different programs, with medical and engineering education receiving higher weights than the humanities.

In conclusion, while output-based (performance-oriented) grants are best suited to grantor's objectives and are simpler to administer than traditional input-based conditional transfers, they are rarely practiced. The reasons have to do with the incentives faced by politicians and bureaucrats. Such grants empower clients while weakening the sphere for opportunism and pork-barrel politics. The incentives they create strengthen the accountability of political and bureaucratic elites to citizens and weaken their ability to peddle influence and build bureaucratic empires. Their focus on value for money exposes corruption, inefficiency, and waste. Not surprisingly, this type of grant is blocked by potential losers.

Compensating for Benefit Spillovers

Compensating for benefit spillovers is the traditional argument for providing matching conditional grants. Regional and local governments will not face the proper incentives to provide the correct levels of services that yield spillover benefits to residents of other jurisdictions. A system of open-ended matching grants based on expenditures giving rise to spillovers will provide the incentive to increase expenditures. Because the extent of the spillover is usually difficult to measure, the matching rate will be somewhat arbitrary.

Although benefit-cost spillover is a serious factor in a number of countries, such transfers have not been implemented in developing countries other than South Africa. South Africa provides a closed-ended matching grant to teaching hospitals on the basis of an estimate of benefit spillovers associated with enrollment of nonlocal students and use of hospital facilities by nonresidents.

Influencing Local Priorities

In a federation there is always some degree of conflict among priorities established by various levels of government. One way to induce lower-level governments to follow priorities established by the higher-level government is for the higher-level government to use its spending power by providing matching transfers. The higher-level government can provide open-ended matching transfers with a matching rate that varies inversely with the recipient's fiscal capacity. Use of ad hoc grants or open-ended matching transfers is inadvisable. Ad hoc grants are unlikely to result in behavioral responses that are consistent with the grantor's objectives. Open-ended grants may create budgetary difficulties for the grantor.

India, Malaysia, and Pakistan have conditional closed-ended matching programs. Pakistan got into serious difficulty in the late 1990s by offering open-ended matching transfers for provincial tax effort. The central government had to abandon this program midstream, after it proved unable to meet its obligations under the program.

Dealing with Infrastructure Deficiencies and Creating Macroeconomic Stability in Depressed Regions

Fiscal transfers can be used to serve the central government's objectives in regional stabilization. Capital grants are appropriate for this purpose, provided funds for future upkeep of facilities are available. Capital grants are also justified to deal with infrastructure deficiencies in poorer jurisdictions in order to strengthen the common economic union.

Capital grants are typically determined on a project-by-project basis. Indonesia took a planning view of such grants in setting a national minimum standard of access to primary school (within walking distance of the community served) for the nation as a whole. The central government provided for school construction, while local governments provided land for the schools.

South Africa has experimented with a formula-based capital grant to deal with infrastructure deficiencies. The Municipal Infrastructure Grant formula includes a vertical and horizontal division. The vertical division allocates resources to sectors or other priority areas; the horizontal division is determined on the basis of a formula that takes account of poverty, backlogs, and municipal powers and functions. The formula includes five components:

- Basic residential infrastructure, including new infrastructure and rehabilitation of existing infrastructure (75 percent weight). Proportional allocations are made for water supply and sanitation, electricity, roads, and "other" (street lighting and solid waste removal).
- Public municipal service infrastructure, including construction of new infrastructure and rehabilitation of existing infrastructure (15 percent weight)
- Social institutions and microenterprises infrastructure (5 percent weight)
- Nodal municipalities (5 percent weight)
- Final adjustment that includes a downward adjustment or top-up is made on the basis of past performance of each municipality relative to grant conditions

Experience with capital grants shows that they often create facilities that are not maintained by subnational governments, which either remain unconvinced of their utility or lack the means to provide regular upkeep.

Capital grants are pervasive in developing countries and transition economies. Most countries have complex processes for initiating and approving submissions for financing capital projects. These processes are highly susceptible to lobbying, political pressure, and grantsmanship, and they favor projects that give the central government greater visibility. Projects typically lack citizen and stakeholder participation, and they often fail because of lack of local ownership, interest, and oversight. In view of these difficulties, it may be best to limit the use of capital grants by requiring matching funds from recipients (varying inversely with the fiscal capacity of the recipient unit) and by encouraging private-sector participation by providing political and policy risk guarantees. To facilitate private-sector participation, public managers must exercise due diligence to ensure that the private sector does not take the public sector for a free ride or walk away from the project midstream.

Special Issues in Transfers from State or Province to Local Governments

General-purpose transfers to local governments require special considerations, as local governments vary in population size, area served, and type of services offered. In view of this, it is advisable to classify local governments by population size, municipality type, and urban or rural character, creating separate formulas for each class of municipality. The higher-level government could adopt a representative tax-system-based fiscal capacity equalization system and set minimum standards grants for each class and type of municipality. Where the application of a representative tax system is not feasible because of lack of significant tax decentralization or poor local tax administration, a more pragmatic but less scientific approach to general-purpose grants could be used. Some useful components in these grant formulas are an equal per-municipality component, an equal per capita component, a service area component, and a fiscal capacity component. Grant funds should vary directly with the service area and inversely with fiscal capacity (see Shah, 1994b, on examples of state-local transfers from Australia, Brazil, and Canada). South Africa has applied a variant of this approach in central-local transfers (Box 10.3).

Having a formal, open, contestable, and deliberative process for municipal incorporation, amalgamation, and annexation should be a prerequisite for introducing an equal per-municipality component in grant finance. The lack of such a process can create a perverse incentive for the breakup of existing jurisdictions to qualify for additional assistance, as demonstrated by the experience in Brazil (Shah, 1991).

Institutional Arrangements for Fiscal Relations

Who should be responsible for designing the system of federal-state fiscal relations? There are various possibilities. The most obvious one, and the

Box 10.3   South Africa's Equitable Share Formula for Central-Local Fiscal Transfers

South Africa uses an equitable share formula to provide transfers from the central government to local governments. The size of the grant is determined as follows:

$$\text{Grant} = (BS + D + I - R) \pm C,$$

where BS is the basic services component, D is the development component, I is the institutional support component, R is the revenue-raising capacity correction, and C is a correction and stabilization factor.

The purpose of the *basic services component* is to enable municipalities to provide basic services (water, sanitation, electricity, refuse removal, and other basic services), including free basic services to households earning less than R800 (about U.S.$111 a month). (As of April 1, 2006, environmental health care services have been included as a basic service.) Because by its nature environmental health is delivered to everyone in a municipality, this subcomponent is calculated on all households, not only poor ones. For each subsidized basic service, there are two levels of support: a full subsidy for households that actually receive services from the municipality and a partial subsidy for unserviced households, currently set at one-third of the cost of the subsidy, to serviced households. This component is calculated as follows:

BS = [water subsidy 1 × poor with water + water subsidy 2 × poor without water] + [sanitation subsidy 1 × poor with sanitation + sanitation subsidy 2 × poor without sanitation] + [refuse subsidy 1 × poor with refuse + refuse subsidy 2 × poor without refuse] + [electricity subsidy 1 × poor with electricity + electricity subsidy 2 × poor without electricity] + [environmental healthcare subsidy × total number of households].

The *institutional support component* is particularly important for poor municipalities, which are often unable to raise sufficient revenue to fund the basic costs of administration and governance. Such funding gaps make it impossible for poor municipalities to provide basic services to all residents, clients, and businesses. This component supplements the funding of a municipality for administrative and governance costs. It does not fully fund all administration and governance costs of a municipality, which remain the primary responsibility of each municipality.

The institutional component includes two elements: administrative capacity and local electoral accountability. The grant is determined as follows:

$$I = \text{base allocation} + [\text{admin support} \times \text{population}]$$
$$+ [\text{council support} \times \text{number of seats}]$$

where the values used in the formula are $I = R350,000 + [R1 \times \text{population}] + [R36,000 \times \text{councilors}]$.

The "base allocation" is the amount that goes to every municipal structure (except for a district management area). The second term of this formula recognizes that costs rise with population. The third term is a contribution to the cost of maintaining councilors for the legislative and oversight role. The number of "seats" that will be recognized for purposes of the formula is determined by the minister for provincial and local government.

The development component was set at zero when the current formula was introduced on April 1, 2005, pending an investigation of how best to capture the factor in the formula.

The revenue-raising capacity correction raises additional resources to fund the cost of basic services and administrative infrastructure. The basic approach is to use the relationship between demonstrated revenue-raising capacity by municipalities that report information and objective municipal information from Statistics South Africa to proxy revenue-raising capacity for all municipalities. The revenue that should be available to a municipality is then "corrected" by imposing a "tax" rate of 5 percent. In the case of the Regional Service Councils levy replacement grant, the correction is based on the actual grant to each municipality.

Source: South Africa (2006).

norm in many countries, is to make the federal government solely responsible on the grounds that it is responsible for the national objectives that are to be delivered through the fiscal arrangements. A problem with it might be the natural tendency for the federal government to be too involved with state decision making and not allow the full benefits of decentralization to occur. To some extent, this tendency can be overcome by imposing constitutional restrictions on the ability of the federal government to override state decisions. Alternatively, one can have a separate body involved in the design and ongoing reform and enforcement of fiscal arrangements. It could be an impartial body, or it could be a body comprising both federal and state representatives. It could have true decision-making authority, or it could be purely advisory. In any case, to be effective, it would at least need to be able to coordinate decision making at the two levels of government.

For determining the system of grants, one finds four types of models used in practice. The first and the most commonly used practice is for the federal or central government alone to decide on it. This has the distinct disadvantage of biasing the system toward a centralized outcome whereas the grants are intended to facilitate decentralized decision making. In India, the federal government is solely responsible for the Planning Commission transfers and the centrally sponsored schemes. These transfers have strong input conditionality with potential to undermine state and local autonomy. The 1988 Brazilian constitution provided strong safeguards against federal intrusion by enshrining the transfers' formulas factors in the constitution. These safeguards represent an extreme step as they undermine flexibility of fiscal arrangements to respond to changing economic circumstances.

The second approach used in practice is to set up a quasi-independent body, such as a grants commission, whose purpose is to design and reform the system. These commissions can have a permanent presence as in South Africa and Australia, or they can be brought into existence periodically to make recommendations for the next five years, as done in India.. These commissions have proved to be ineffective in some countries largely because many of the recommendations have been ignored by the government and not implemented, as in South Africa. In other cases, while the government may have accepted and implemented all it recommended, it has been ineffective in reforming the system because of the constraints it has imposed on itself, as is considered to be the case in India. In some cases, these commissions become too academic in their approaches and thereby contribute to the creation of an overly complex system of intergovernmental transfers, as has been the case with the Commonwealth Grants Commission in Australia (Shah, 2004b, 2007d).

The third approach found in practice is to use executive federalism or federal-provincial committees to negotiate the terms of the system. Such a system is used in Canada and Germany. In Germany, this system is enhanced by having state governments represented in the Bundesrat, the upper house of the parliament. This system allows for explicit political input from the jurisdictions involved and attempts to develop a common consensus.

The fourth approach is a variation on the third approach and uses an intergovernmental-cum-legislative-cum-civil-society committee with equal representation from all constituent units but chaired by the federal government to negotiate changes in the existing arrangements. The so-called Finance Commission in Pakistan represents this model. This approach has the advantage that all stakeholders – donor, recipients, civil society, and experts – are represented on the commission. Such an approach keeps the system simple and transparent. An important disadvantage of this approach is that because of a unanimity rule, such bodies may be deadlocked forever, as has recently been witnessed in Pakistan.

LESSONS FROM INTERNATIONAL PRACTICES

Review of international practices yields a set of practices to avoid and a set of practices to emulate (Table 10.5). A number of important lessons also emerge.

Negative Lessons: Types of Transfers to Avoid

Policy makers should avoid designing the following types of intergovernmental grants:

1. Do not design grants with vaguely specified objectives.
2. Avoid general revenue-sharing programs with multiple factors that work at cross-purposes, undermine accountability, and do not advance fiscal efficiency or fiscal equity objectives. Tax decentralization or tax-base sharing offers a better alternative to a general revenue-sharing program, as each enhances accountability while preserving subnational autonomy.
3. Avoid grants to finance subnational deficits, which create incentives for running higher deficits in future.
4. Reject unconditional grants that include incentives for fiscal effort. Improving service delivery while lowering tax costs should be public-sector objectives.
5. Do not implement input- (or process-)based or ad hoc conditional grant programs, which undermine local autonomy, flexibility, fiscal efficiency, and fiscal equity objectives.

Table 10.5. *Principles and better practices in grant design*

Grant objective	Grant design	Examples of better practices	Examples of practices to avoid
Bridge fiscal gap	Reassignment of responsibilities, tax abatement, tax-base sharing	Tax abatement and tax-base sharing (Canada)	Deficit grants, wage grants (China), tax by tax sharing (China, India before 2000)
Reduce regional fiscal disparities	General nonmatching fiscal capacity equalization transfers	Fiscal equalization with explicit standard that determines total pool as well as allocation (Canada, Denmark, and Germany)	General revenue sharing with multiple factors (Brazil and India); fiscal equalization with a fixed pool (Australia, China)
Compensate for benefit spillovers	Open-ended matching transfers with matching rate consistent with spill-out of benefits	Grant for teaching hospitals (South Africa)	Closed-ended matching grants

Grant objective	Design recommended	Examples	Practices to avoid
Set national minimum standards	Conditional nonmatching output-based block transfers with conditions on standards of service and access	Road maintenance and primary education grants (Indonesia before 2000) Education transfers (Brazil, Chile, Colombia) Health transfers (Brazil, Canada)	Conditional transfers with conditions on spending alone (most countries), pork-barrel transfers (United States), ad hoc grants
Influence local priorities in areas of high national but low local priority	Conditional capital grants with matching rate that varies inversely with local fiscal capacity	Capital grant for school construction (Indonesia before 2000), highway construction matching grants to states (United States)	Capital grants with no matching and no future upkeep requirements
	Open-ended matching transfers (preferably with matching rate varying inversely with fiscal capacity)	Matching transfers for social assistance (Canada before 2004)	Ad hoc grants
Provide stabilization and overcome infrastructure deficiencies	Capital grants, provided maintenance possible	Capital grants with matching rates that vary inversely with local fiscal capacity	Stabilization grants with no future upkeep requirements

6. Do not design capital grants without assurance of funds for future upkeep, which have the potential to create white elephants.
7. Avoid negotiated or discretionary grants in a federal system, which may create dissention and disunity.
8. Reject one size fits all grants to local governments, which create huge inequities.
9. Do not promote grants that involve abrupt changes in the total pool and its allocation.

Positive Lessons: Principles to Adopt

Policy makers should strive to respect the following principles in designing and implementing intergovernmental transfers:

1. Keep it simple. In the design of fiscal transfers, rough justice may be better than full justice, if it achieves wider acceptability and sustainability.
2. Focus on a single objective in a grant program and make the design consistent with that objective. Setting multiple objectives in a single grant program runs the risk of failing to achieve any of them.
3. Introduce ceilings linked with macro indicators and floors, to ensure stability and predictability in grant funds.
4. Introduce sunset clauses. It is desirable to have the grant program reviewed periodically – say, every five years – and renewed (if appropriate). In the intervening years, no changes to the program should be made, in order to provide certainty in budgetary programming for all governments.
5. Equalize per capita fiscal capacity to a specified standard in order to achieve fiscal equalization. Such a standard would determine the total pool and allocations among recipient units. Calculations required for fiscal capacity equalization using a representative tax system for major tax bases are doable for most countries. In contrast, expenditure need equalization requires difficult and complex analysis, inviting much controversy and debate; as desirable as it is, it may not therefore be worth doing. In view of this practical difficulty, it would be best to deal with fiscal need equalization through output-based sectoral grants that also enhance results-based accountability. A national consensus on the standard of equalization is critically important for the sustainability of any equalization program. The

equalization program must not be looked at in isolation from the broader fiscal system, especially conditional transfers. The equalization program must have a sunset clause and provision for formal review and renewal. For local fiscal equalization, one size does not fit all.

6. In specific-purpose grant programs, impose conditionality on outputs or standards of access and quality of services rather than on inputs and processes. This allows grantors to achieve their objectives without undermining local choices on how best to deliver such services. Most countries need to establish national minimum standards of basic services across the nation in order to strengthen the internal common market and economic union.

7. Recognize population size, area served, and the urban or rural nature of services in making grants to local governments. Establish separate formula allocations for each type of municipal or local government.

8. Establish hold harmless or grandfathering provisions that ensure that all recipient governments receive at least what they received as general-purpose transfers in the prereform period. Over time, as the economy grows, such a provision would not delay the phase-in of the full package of reforms.

9. Make sure that all stakeholders are heard and that an appropriate political compact on equalization principles and the standard of equalization is struck. Politics must be internalized in these institutional arrangements. Arm's-length institutions, such as independent grant commissions, are not helpful, as they do not allow for political input and therefore tend to opt for complex and nontransparent solutions.

Moving from a public-sector governance culture of dividing the spoils to an environment that enables responsive, responsible, equitable, and accountable governance is critical. Doing so requires exploring all feasible tax decentralization options, instituting output-based operating and capital fiscal transfers, establishing a formal fiscal equalization program with an explicit standard of equalization, and ensuring responsible access to borrowing.

PART THREE

FINANCE AND PROVISION OF PUBLIC SERVICES

The goal of decentralized decision making is to ensure that local governments deliver services consistent with local preferences, make the most cost-effective use of tax moneys, provide fair governance, and are answerable to local residents. Structuring fiscal and institutional arrangements to achieve such diverse objectives for merit goods such as education, health, infrastructure, and poverty alleviation while supporting decentralized decision making is the motivation for various chapters in this section.

Health and education expenditures constitute some of the most important public services that governments provide. Their features are also particularly relevant for nations with multiple orders of government. The provision of health care and education services, and sometimes health insurance coverage for individuals, is typically entrusted to subnational governments. At the same time, these services fulfill important national objectives. They contribute to redistributive objectives such as equality of opportunity and social insurance, and they also promote efficiency and growth in the national economy. The result is that, although the provision of health and education services are decentralized, the federal government maintains an interest in how they are delivered and engages in policies to influence that delivery. Chapter 11 is devoted to investigating in more detail some the issues that arise because of this shared responsibility. It discusses conceptual considerations and practices in decentralized assignment of health and education services and financing mechanisms to ensure that equity objectives are not compromised in pursuit of efficiency and matching services with local preferences. The chapter further assesses the use of special-purpose bodies in delivering these services and equity implications of reliance on user fees to finance such services.

Dealing with public infrastructure deficiencies is considered critical to private capital accumulation, economic growth, and poverty alleviation. Under decentralized governance, local governments play a critical role in dealing with infrastructure deficiencies. However durable and shared, the nature of such spending raises special issues in assigning or clarifying responsibility for such shared spending and for raising finance to smooth the sharing of tax burdens across various generations. Chapter 12 discusses the rationale of grant and capital finance for infrastructure capital and the forms of capital grants that would be nonintrusive and the institutional mechanisms to ensure responsible borrowing.

Along with education and health care, poverty alleviation programs constitute the most important social programs in developing countries. The current strategy for development endorsed in many countries involves a two-pronged approach: encouraging private investment and taking advantage of market processes to promote high growth rates, while also reducing the incidence of poverty. Without such corrective intervention, there is a danger of the poorest groups in society falling even further behind. The aim of effective poverty alleviation programs must be to make those most in need productive members of society on a permanent basis. Policy instruments include cash transfers, the provision of services, and getting recipients into the labor force. Because of complex administrative and informational requirements, subnational levels of government must be involved. Yet, at the same time, there are obvious national interests at stake. Thus, all the classic issues involved in fiscal federalism apply. Chapter 13 discusses how these national objectives can be met.

ELEVEN

Finance and Provision of Health and Education

Health and education expenditures constitute some of the most important public services that governments provide. Their features are also particularly relevant for nations with multiple levels of government. The provision of health care and education services, and sometimes health insurance coverage for individuals, is typically entrusted to subnational governments. At the same time, as we have mentioned in earlier chapters, these services fulfill important national objectives. They contribute to redistributive objectives such as equality of opportunity and social insurance, and they also promote efficiency and growth in the national economy. The result is that, although the provision of health and education services are decentralized, the federal government maintains an interest in how they are delivered and engages in policies to influence that delivery. We devote this chapter to investigating in more detail some the issues that arise because of this shared responsibility.

RESPONSIBILITY BY LEVEL OF GOVERNMENT

In discussing the assignment of responsibilities for health care and education and the role of each level of government, it is important to distinguish between the provision of services and their financing.

Provision of Health and Education Services

Both health care and education represent services provided by hospitals, doctors, schools, teachers, and others directly to individuals. By necessity, the provision of these services is decentralized to local agencies or institutions. The assignment issue is concerned with deciding which level of government is responsible for these institutions. It is common practice in nations with multiple levels of government to assign this responsibility to lower levels of government, typically an intermediate level such as the state or regions. Canada, for example, gives provinces exclusive responsibility over education, health care, and hospitals (Knopff and Sayers, 2005). In Germany, education is a *Länder* responsibility (Kramer, 2005). The Belgian federation assigns both education and health care to the language-based communities (Deschouwer, 2005). This assignment is based on the argument, discussed in Chapter 2, that state-level governments are better able to judge the preferences and needs for these services by the local population and can better monitor the behavior of the local institutions – and in this case, local teachers and doctors – that actually deliver these services. As well, accountability might be enhanced and innovation and cost-effectiveness encouraged by decentralized responsibility.

At the same time, state responsibility is often not exclusive. In Belgium, cooperation is necessary as communities are responsible for health policy, while health insurance is a federal task (Deschouwer, 2005). In the United States, education is a state-local responsibility. Local authorities usually provide primary and secondary education, whereas state governments are responsible for higher education. Hospital care is available at state-administered facilities (often attached to educational institutions), as well as in facilities run by municipalities, counties, and special districts (Schroeder, 2006). In Brazil, health and education are shared responsibilities. Since the mid-1990s municipal governments have been responsible for health and primary education services (Souza, 2005). The Mexican constitution lists both education and health care as concurrent responsibilities (J. Gonzalez, 2005). In India, education has always been a concurrent union-state responsibility (Majeed, 2005). In addition, the Seventy-third Constitutional Amendment recognized local governments, whose suggested responsibilities include not only primary and secondary education but also primary health centers, dispensaries, and hospitals. In practice, local government participation depends on enabling state legislation (Alok, 2006). In China, multiple levels of government are involved in education. The national level establishes educational objectives. Provincial governments develop specific policies and regulations in line with these objectives. Local governments provide the nine years of compulsory education. Indonesia decentralized its education system in 1999. The central government retained control of tertiary education. Provincial governments were given responsibility for upper secondary education, while primary and junior secondary schooling became the responsibility of district-level governments. In 2003 further decentralization shifted responsibility for basic education to schools (King and Guerra, 2005). In the Philippines, responsibility for health care is shared across all levels of governments. Basic, primary care is a village responsibility, whereas the primary care facilities themselves are the responsibility of cities and municipalities. Secondary hospitals are provincial responsibilities, while the central health ministry runs most tertiary or specialized hospitals. Health-related research and development is also a responsibility of the central government (Lieberman, Capuno, and Van Minh, 2005).

As noted previously, the services in question have an important national dimension. Consider first the case of education. Education is undoubtedly one of the most important policy instruments for achieving equality of opportunity and for ensuring that all citizens have the ability to participate in the economic and social life of a nation. It is also a key policy instrument for alleviating poverty on a sustainable basis, because it provides the basic literacy, social, and analytical skills that are a prerequisite to productive employment. Indeed, the importance of education is brought out by the fact that it is usually mandatory for all children up to some age. There may be forceful arguments for having some national standards, or some minimal services levels that all state education systems should attain. There may also be good arguments for harmonizing school curricula, for having common professional credentials and remuneration for teachers, and for having comparable teacher-student ratios and access to textbooks, supplies, and information technology.

The argument for such national standards – discussed in more detail in the next section – may be based partly on efficiency considerations. If states have different qualities of education services, this will affect the allocation of economic activity across states, and distortions in the internal economic union can result. Or states acting on their own without regard to national standards may be induced into compromising educational standards by engaging in fiscal competition. States may compete with one another for teachers, or they may engage in tax competition that ends up reducing the resources available for education. Of course, fiscal competition is a two-edged sword. It may well also contribute to efficiency by inducing cost-effective service provision and innovation.

Perhaps stronger arguments for some harmonization of state education policies are those based on equity. The role of education in providing opportunities to all students, no matter where they reside, calls for some minimal standards of education. Putting students on an equal footing may also require some common elements in the curriculum (though perhaps with room for purely local state-specific or culture-specific knowledge). In

Spain, for example, the Ministry of Education defines 65 percent of the material taught in all schools, leaving the remaining 35 to 45 percent of material to reflect regional interests as defined by autonomous communities (King and Guerra, 2005). Thus, elements of national standards are present in most countries. The case for these national standards is stronger for lower levels of education. With mandatory education in effect, virtually all children attend elementary school, where they learn basic skills necessary for entering the labor market and enjoying a fulfilling life. It is at this level that equal opportunity arguments are the strongest. As one moves up to secondary and then postsecondary education, the participation rate declines, and the skills become more advanced and specialized. Moreover, equality of opportunity arguments may lose some of their force at more-advanced education levels: equality of opportunity may be more concerned with giving persons a chance to get to those levels. The case for national standards on equity grounds falls, although the potential for distortionary fiscal competition still exists.

In theory, national education standards might be achieved by interstate cooperation, especially when all have something to gain. Germany, for example, relies on the Education Ministers' Conference to coordinate policy among the *Länder*. The conference ensures that courses of instruction and educational qualifications are virtually identical throughout the country (Kramer, 2005). However, in practice, it is difficult to rely on interstate agreements. By their nature, they must be based on unanimity, and even if there are gains to all participants, such agreements will be difficult to achieve and especially to enforce. As well, common standards of education will almost certainly involve some implicit interstate redistribution, which would hardly pass the unanimity test. Consequently, federal involvement in facilitating national standards in education is almost inevitable.

There are various ways the federal government could do so. At a minimum, it could use its spending power to make grants to the states to give them the wherewithal to provide standard levels of educational services. The grants could have conditions attached to them to ensure that the states' education systems in fact satisfy the standards. The danger is that conditions will be too detailed and too intrusive so as to constrain the states unduly in exercising their discretion. For example, rather than the grants having general, broad conditions attached to them, they may require detailed accounting by the states for the funds expended. This would at least partly defeat the purpose of decentralizing the provision of education to the states in the first place.

Alternatively, if the constitution of the nation allows, the federal government might provide more direct oversight on state educational programs. They might mandate certain features of state programs. Or state programs might be required to comply with federal legislation. Alternatively, the responsibility for various aspects of education may be divided between the federal government and the states. For example, the federal government may be responsible for training and hiring teachers and for designing the curriculum, whereas the states may be responsible for delivering the services. If such a division of responsibilities can be achieved without too much overlap, each level will have a well-defined set of tasks and can be held accountable for them.

Similar sorts of considerations apply with health care. There are strong efficiency arguments for decentralizing the delivery of health care to the states but equally strong arguments for there to be some national standards of care available regardless of state of residence. As discussed in the next section, this might involve a common set of health services that at a minimum are available across the nation, norms with respect to accessibility, portability across state boundaries, and a uniform set of qualifications and training for health care professionals.

As with education, it might be difficult to achieve these national standards without the active participation of the federal government. This participation could involve the use of conditional grants, the setting of mandates, or the division of responsibilities between the two levels of government, analogous to what was discussed for education. Again, the trick is to achieve legitimate national objectives while obtaining the full benefits of decentralization. This would argue in favor of limiting the federal role to one of oversight or setting broad minimal standards, and leaving it to the states to design the details of their own programs.

In India, for example, the union government has taken a coordinating role in health care provision. The government occasionally convenes subject-specific councils to discuss and recommend coordinated policies on topics of interest to multiple state governments or to both the union and state governments. These councils have included the Central Council of Health and the Central Council of Indian Medicine (Majeed, 2005). In Indonesia, the federal role in health care includes setting national policies and minimum service standards, whereas the management and administration of service providers and infrastructure is assigned to the local level (Eckardt and Shah, 2006).

State responsibility for providing education and health services does not preclude private-sector participation. That is, some of the institutions that actually deliver the services on behalf of the state government could be private or public. Hospitals and schools could be privately owned, including by nonprofit or religious organizations. Doctors could be self-employed persons whose services are paid for by the state rather than being state employees. The institutional mode of delivery can be chosen quite independently of the level of government to which responsibility for delivery is assigned. Of course, states might nonetheless expect private providers to abide by whatever norms are deemed necessary. That is, they may not leave the private providers on their own simply to maximize profits.

A somewhat more controversial form of private participation might be to allow private suppliers alongside those of the public sector, particularly if private facilities obtain public support. In Brazil, for example, the central government reimburses both private health care providers and lower-level governments (often municipalities) for health care and the maintenance of hospitals and clinics (Afonso and Araujo, 2006). In the case of health care, private providers may be seen as a way of relieving demand by siphoning off households that are willing to pay extra to have private service. There may be both efficiency and equity advantages to such an arrangement. From an equity point of view, the users of private provision will typically pay for such services, while contributing to the public system through their tax payments. This might also be more efficient to the extent that the private providers must compete for customers and, in turn, will induce public providers to be more efficient. There may be "yardstick competition" effects, whereby private-sector costs of service provide some norm against which to measure what to expect from public providers. On the other hand, there may be disadvantages to private provision as well. From a political economy point of view, it might be argued that if the public health care system applies only to lower-income persons, the political support for it will be eroded, and so will its quality. As well, it may be practically impossible to separate entirely the private from the public sectors. Both may have access to the same hospitals and other facilities. The private users may be able to "jump the queue" with respect to the use of those facilities, thereby reducing the accessibility and fairness of the system to less-well-off persons. Finally, there is a possibility that the private health sector will compete away some of the best health professionals from the public system, driving a wedge in quality between the two systems.

Similar arguments apply to the case of education, though perhaps with less force. Private schools usually do exist alongside public ones. Those who opt for private education still contribute to the public system through taxation (although they may also obtain some tax reduction by virtue of the deductibility of their private education spending). The concerns raised by private participation in education are perhaps less strong than with respect to health care. Almost all countries have mixed private and public education systems, with the latter financed out of general revenues and the former based on fees. In some cases, government support is available for private education. This is the case for Catholic schools in Argentina as well as Islamic schools in Indonesia. Alternatively, government support may be provided to households that choose private schools. This has been the case in the Netherlands since the 1920s, in Chile since 1980, in the Czech Republic and Sweden since the 1990s, and in New Zealand since 1991 (World Bank, 2003).

A special form of private provision of health and education services is provided by nongovernmental organizations (NGOs), which differ from private firms in being not for profit. In most cases, they are run and financed by voluntary, charitable, or religious organizations. Their personnel are typically highly dedicated and have special skills. They bring to developing countries resources and expertise that supplement local resources. They also often provide a valuable service in training local persons to do work in the sector.

The main issue with respect to NGO-provided education and health services concerns coordinating their activities with those of domestic organizations. As well, there might be a presumption that the nature of the services NGOs provide should satisfy the same national standards as apply to domestic institutions. The level of government that is responsible for providing these services – ideally, state governments – should presumably have the task of overseeing the activities of NGOs. In India, the government successfully collaborated with an NGO to create an effective remedial education program in two cities (Mumbai and Vadodara). Local women were hired to teach remedial classes for students falling behind. The inexpensive program was found to be a cost-effective way to improve learning, particularly for poorer students. It has been expanded to twenty Indian cities (World Bank, 2003).

Financing of Health and Education Services

Provision of health and education services is one thing; financing is quite another. Various modes of finance are compatible with federal or state provision and with private or public provision. Indeed, it is quite possible for financing to be at least partly at one level of government and provision at another.

Before considering the role of public financing by level of government, a prior issue is the share of public versus private financing for public services like health care and education. In both cases, the services being provided are essentially private, so it is natural to suppose that the users of the services have at least some responsibility for financing. Private insurance plays a large part in the health care systems of Brazil, Chile, South Africa, and the United States, for example. In all of these cases, it is formal-sector workers who use the private financing system (World Bank, 2005b). In Germany, insurance societies, operating on a not-for-profit basis, purchase health services from both public and private providers (World Bank, 2003). This issue is very difficult to resolve, because both services fulfill social objectives that set them apart from ordinary public services. If they were simply private goods whose benefits accrued solely to the users, the case for public financing would be minimal. There would be no more reason for public support than in the case of ordinary consumer goods. Of course, even in this case, the public sector might have a role.

There might be *efficiency* arguments for intervening in the provision of health and education. In the case of health, inefficiencies can take several forms. There may be market failure in health insurance markets because of asymmetric information involving moral hazard and/or adverse selection. It is well known that insurance cannot be provided efficiently in the presence of these forms of asymmetric information. When unobservable moral hazard is present, households cannot be fully insured. When adverse selection is present, the ideal amount and terms of insurance cannot be provided to households of differing risk classes. Indeed, there may well be no market equilibrium. Whether the government has a role in the face of these forms of market failure is not at all clear. Governments are not likely to be any better informed than the private sector. On the other hand, it is possible that compulsory insurance can yield efficiency improvements in the face of adverse selection. But this form of intervention need not entail any public financing. Inefficiency in health markets can also be caused by the informational and monopoly-type advantages that health care providers enjoy. For example, doctors presumably are better informed about the care needs of their patients. They have the power to prescribe treatment, and in that sense possible overuse of health services may not be demand driven as a result of patient moral hazard as much as supply driven by health professionals. There is also some evidence that the administrative costs incurred by private insurers are much higher than those which would be incurred by a single-payer system, such as a public insurance one. There are also certain elements of health care that have externalities associated with them, especially communicable diseases. The case for public intervention is more apparent in these cases, and it is common for such public health systems to be involved in their provision and financing.

Even if health care and insurance are publicly funded, there might be a role for supplementary private contributions based on efficiency arguments. For example, many countries have a system of user fees, often modest, that users of certain types of health services must pay. This can include visits to doctors, hospitalization, pharmaceuticals, tests, and so on. The Nordic countries of Finland, Norway, and Sweden, for example, have minor fees for primary health care and hospitalization, as well as copayments for pharmaceuticals (Lotz, 2006). Individuals are often able to supplement publicly provided health care and insurance that offer a basic level of care to all households regardless of means with private add-ons that offer them upgraded services.

Efficiency arguments are unlikely to justify the common tendency for health insurance and financing systems to be largely publicly funded. With the exception of the United States, OECD countries tend to treat health care as a type of public service provided more or less universally to all households. The arguments used to support this are based on *equity* considerations. It is argued that health care is a form of social insurance that is uniquely different from private insurance used to deal with other sorts of misfortune (e.g., fire, car accidents, theft). Different persons have different risks of incurring health problems, and these risks are to some extent associated with characteristics that one is born with. Or they may acquire a health condition during their lifetime which puts them at a disadvantage. Either way, because insurance contracts are not written on a lifetime basis, such persons are uninsurable and are therefore left particularly vulnerable in terms of their lifetime well-being. The principle of social insurance says that households ought to be compensated for misfortunes over which they have no control, especially those which may not be fully insurable. It is argued that uniform provision of health insurance is one way of ensuring that all households are covered for unexpected ill health, especially given that the government may not have all the information to be able to redistribute directly on the basis of a propensity for ill health.

This social insurance argument seems to be at least a partial explanation for heavy involvement of the public sector in health care, alongside efficiency arguments mentioned previously. Whatever the ultimate justification, the fact is that health insurance is commonly provided by the public sector. Even countries that lack universal coverage may offer government programs for the poor. In Indonesia, Yogyakarta Province began a new program in 2003 to enable the poor to use public health care facilities by paying their premiums. This program was expanded to the nonpoor in 2004, bringing the government into competition with private providers of benefit packages. The Philippines created a health insurance program in 1995 to target the impoverished. The Philippine Health Insurance Corporation (PHIC) has paying members from both the public and private sectors, and it aggressively recruits families for its indigent program. However, local governments must copay the insurance premium for the poorer constituents; this is viewed as an unfunded mandate (Lieberman et al., 2005). One of the largest federal programs in the United States is the Medical Assistance Program (Medicaid) that pays for the medical care of low-income individuals and families. Both the federal and state governments fund the program. The proportion of costs covered by the federal transfer differs across states, with lower-income states receiving a higher matching rate. Each state government is responsible for designing and administering its own program; in some cases, states have chosen to have local governments (often counties) share the costs (Schroeder, 2006). We return later to a consideration of which level of government ought to be responsible for health insurance.

The case of education is similar. Education is again basically private. In principle, one could ration education services by the pricing mechanism. It can be argued that this would be inefficient to the extent that there are externalities associated with educational services. Society at large may obtain some benefit from a higher degree of literacy among the population. For example, crime might be lower, the private sector might benefit from the agglomeration effects of a highly educated work force, and a given person's productivity may depend in part on the productivity of other workers. Moreover, to the extent that educated workers are more self-sufficient, they will be a lesser burden imposed on society in the future in terms of the need for transfers and public services. To the extent that these arguments are deemed to be valid, there is a case for some public subsidization of private education.

The externalities associated with education may not be the full story. It may not account for the fact that virtually all societies provide public education to the majority of children. As in the case of health care, there might be equity-related reasons for education being treated as a public service provided freely to all. Indeed, in the case of education, not only is it provided free, but it is common to mandate school attendance by school-age children. In the case of education, one can think of it as fulfilling an equal-opportunity objective. Moreover, the public school system might be viewed as an important institution for socialization of children of various backgrounds. In any case, as with health care, we can take it as given that it is provided publicly and that the bulk of the financing will be from the public sector.

As we have already noted, the provision of health and education services are typically decentralized to the state level of government. The issue then is which level of government should be responsible for its financing. It might be argued that, on the basis of accountability, states should be responsible for funding a large part of their own health and education programs. Then their policies and the quality of their implementation would be more transparent to the citizens for whom they are providing the services, especially to the extent that financing is earmarked for these purposes. For example, it is sometimes the case that education is financed by local taxes, such as the property tax, and health care may be financed by premiums of payroll taxes. On the other hand, there is no necessity that earmarked financing be used. To rely on such financing constrains the governments in terms of their tax structures and may make it difficult to spread the costs of providing these important redistributive services fairly across the population. This issue has been raised in the United States, where property taxes are the main source of local revenues for primary and secondary education. These revenues are supplemented by state transfers. The uneven distribution of the tax base has focused attention on the intra-state distribution of funds. In half of the states, courts have mandated that state legislatures design transfers that ensure adequate funding for all school districts in the state. The specific transfer formula varies. A few states provide equal per-pupil transfers or a guaranteed amount of revenue for a given tax effort. The most common approach is a "foundation pro-gram," wherein the state determines a minimal necessary funding amount and a "fair" property tax rate. State transfers are used to fill any gap between the minimum and the estimated tax revenues available. States themselves also receive transfers from the federal government to support education (Schroeder, 2006).

At the same time, there are strong arguments for the federal govern-ment contributing to the financing of these services. On the one hand, the need for financing will typically vary from state to state. If states were fully self-reliant and required to finance these programs on their own, states with higher need might find it difficult to provide standards of service comparable with better-off jurisdictions. Of course, these differences in need can be addressed by an overarching system of equalizing transfers that are based on the needs and fiscal capacities of the states to provide all sorts of public services. Such a system is obviously very important because it does enable all states to provide acceptable levels of health and education services.

China is an example in which the central government reasserted its role in the face of increasing inequalities across jurisdictions. As part of its decentralization reform, the central government reduced subsidies to local schools. Local governments sought alternative funds through taxes, enterprise income, tuition fees, and community and individual contributions. In 1994, however, the central government responded to increasing regional disparities by reducing the taxing authority of local governments. The central government continues to fund teachers' salaries and some capital expenditures. Poor areas receive subsidies from both the central and provincial governments. Nonetheless, interprovincial disparities in per-student spending remain high. The problem is attributed to the lack of a clear equalization mechanism. The existing subsidy to poor areas is a small and ad hoc instrument (King and Guerra, 2005).

In the Philippines, both the central and provincial governments undertake some equalization spending. One of the sources of education funds for local governments is the Internal Revenue Allotment sent to each city and municipality by the central government. Another source is the Special Education Fund (SEF), a 1 percent tax on the assessed value of city- or municipality-owned real property. Half of the SEF is retained locally. The other half is remitted to the provincial local school board, which reallocates the funds among municipalities for educational projects (King and Guerra, 2005).

In Spain, the central government addresses regional inequalities through both block-grant transfers and a revenue-sharing Inter-Territorial Compensation Fund (FCI). For example, in 1996 Madrid received less than 1 percent of redistributed funds, whereas Andalucia received 39 percent of the FCI and 38 percent of state redistributed income (King and Guerra, 2005).

In Brazil, the Fund for the Maintenance and Development of Basic Education and Teacher Appreciation (FUNDEF) was created in the mid-1990s to equalize funding for basic education. Primary schools throughout the country were guaranteed a minimum per-pupil expenditure. Partial equalization within states was also undertaken (King and Guerra, 2005).

In Indonesia, the central government uses earmarked or special allocation grants (DAK grants) to address the special needs of local governments with below-average fiscal capacity. These matching grants typically fund capital expenditures. The components addressing education or health needs take into account such factors as the number of classrooms in poor condition or the number of available health care facilities (Eckardt and Shah, 2006).

Another argument for the federal government to assume a share of the financing of state health and education expenditures is that the federal government might share with the states the responsibility for ensuring that minimum standards of service are available in all states. The federal government might better be able to achieve this if they have some financial leverage over the states. For example, the federal government would be able to credibly impose some conditions on the states with respect to levels and quality of health and education services. In Brazil, for example, local providers are subject to central rules aimed at establishing national programs and minimal standards. The union government uses earmarked federal resources to strengthen its role (Souza, 2005). In the Philippines, the central Department of Health (DOH) administers a conditional matching grant program with the objective of ensuring that local funding is dedicated to core public health programs. An accreditation program (Sentrong Sigla) originally offered grants to local governments that upgraded their health facilities. After it became apparent that the cash awards were being earned by better-off municipalities, the program was revised to give a matching grant to new qualifiers. The certification was also made a prerequisite for other DOH grants (Lieberman et al., 2005).

Of course, as we have stressed throughout, it is important that this power of financial influence not be used in such a way as to defeat the purpose of decentralized decision making in the first place. The conditions ought to be general enough not to interfere with the states' ability to implement programs that best suit the needs of their own citizens.

In Indonesia, educational financing is meant to be a shared responsibility, but some aspects of the central government's funding limit local autonomy. For example, a block grant to districts includes the requirement that a portion is allocated to the salaries of existing teachers. Overall, the funding mechanism for education remains fragmented and diverse, leaving some education officials unclear on the actual amount of moneys available (King and Guerra, 2005). South Africa provides an example of very limited provincial autonomy. Provincial budgets are spent largely on health, education, and social security. They are funded primarily through central government transfers. These transfers include an "equitable share" of nationally raised revenue as well as some discretionary conditional grants. In practice, most provincial spending is determined by the need to meet national standards. About 85 percent of all provincial funds have already been allocated at the national level (Steytler, 2005).

A related argument for some federal financial stake is that the provision of key services may be susceptible to fiscal competition. States may be induced not only to choose their health and education policies to appeal to higher-income persons as well as to firms but also to make it less attractive for heavy users to migrate to the state. Equally important, states may compete for doctors, health care workers, and teachers from one another. Such competition will be especially disadvantageous for needy provinces that might lose key professionals to provinces that are able to bid them away. The central government of the Philippines has initiated several programs that attempt to deal with the difficulty of finding qualified medical staff in remote regions. The Doctor to the Barrios Program was begun in 1993. Centrally paid doctors sign a two-year contract and receive a better package of salary and benefits. Retention has been a problem, however, as employment with the local government offers lower pay. A separate program (the Barangay Health Workers' Benefit and Incentives Act of 1995) trains volunteer workers and provides incentives for them to join the staff of the local health stations. These volunteers perform clerical tasks and minor procedures such as weighing or measuring patients. In Indonesia, the central government initiated a program in the early 1990s to provide doctors to remote areas. The contract doctor program (PTT) hires physicians after medical school. The initial program required three years' service in remote areas as a precondition for advancement. Regulations were changed to allow alternate service, such as working as a civil servant in certain areas or as a private clinic employee in remote regions. After decentralization, many local districts continued to welcome centrally recruited and paid PTT doctors. Concerns are being raised, however, over the ability of the central program to match local supply with local needs (Lieberman et al., 2005).

One final argument for federal financial intervention is that the federal government may be better able to pool the risks associated with social insurance expenditures, which is one of the purposes of an equalization grants system. Otherwise, states that are relatively small may find the possibility of large unexpected shocks in expenditures particularly burdensome.

In the end, the financing of state health and education expenditures might come from a variety of sources, including the following:

1. *State taxes.* States might use general revenues for health and education financing, or they may rely on particular types of taxes earmarked for these purposes. The earmarking might improve transparency and accountability, and it might shelter these funds from shocks to the states' finances. But, on the other hand, earmarked taxes might not serve equity objectives, which are bound to be important in the case of these programs. In fact, earmarked taxes often have a significant benefit taxation element to them.

2. *Federal grants.* Both equalizing grants and block grants with conditions can be important financing instruments for facilitating the decentralization of the provision of health and education, while preserving national efficiency and equity objectives. Equalization grants ensure that all states can provide some minimum standard of services. Block conditional grants can provide the incentive for state programs to abide by common acceptable norms and to avoid some of the adverse consequences of fiscal competition.

3. *User fees.* In the case of both health and education expenditures, user fees might improve the efficiency with which households use the services. Modest user fees for the use of health facilities or for school supplies provide an incentive to avoid excessive or frivolous use. On the other hand, user fees run the risk of reducing accessibility by the poor, thus defeating part of the equity objective of the programs.

4. *Opting out.* Resources can be saved in the public system by allowing persons to opt for private provision. Given that the public system is funded out of tax revenues, those who opt out – presumably the well-off – still contribute to the financing of the public system, as well as bearing the cost of private use (to the extent that this is not subsidized). Thus, the equity properties of the public system are not necessarily compromised. On the other hand, the existence of a private sector might be disadvantageous to the public sector if it attracts scarce resources away from the latter or if it causes an erosion of support. (Of course, this presumes that there is a legitimate public purpose being served by the public system in the first place).

NATIONAL STANDARDS

Although both health and education programs are usually decentralized to lower levels of government, these programs can fulfill important national objectives. The efficiency of the internal economic union, including the allocation of resources across states, can be affected by the manner in which states design the programs. As well, both programs contribute to national equity objectives, especially those involving social insurance and equality of opportunity. The federal government might therefore have an interest in the states abiding by some national norms of program design. Let us consider possible components of national standards for the cases of health and education in turn.

For Health

To the extent the health services are considered to be public services that should be available on comparable terms to all citizens, it may be useful to set out certain common standards that might apply to state health care programs. To avoid intruding excessively into state decision making, these standards might be fairly general. Depending on the country and its political institutions, the standards might be enforced by financial incentives (conditional grants), by the courts, or by legislated mandates by the federal government. Some components of national standards that might be included are:

1. *Portability and mobility.* Citizens ought to be able to receive health care in whatever state they may require. Thus, citizens of one state who are visiting another should be eligible for the same level of services available to residents of the latter state. There may be a financial charge between states in these instances depending on the extent to which states finance their own health care programs. Also, citizens who change location ought to be eligible for health coverage in the state to which they move. Portability provisions ensure seamless access to health care, and remove what might otherwise be a barrier to mobility across states.

2. *Accessibility to health services.* If health care is regarded as a public service that is to be made available to all citizens – that is, a form of social insurance – it should actually be accessible to all residents wherever they reside in the state and without excessive financial discouragement. This is obviously a difficult standard to satisfy perfectly. There may be persons in remote or underpopulated areas for whom it would be very costly to provide identical coverage to persons in urban areas. Thus, some amount of discretion is obviously involved. In addition, to the extent that persons are allowed to supplement their public coverage or opt for private coverage, the

level of service they receive may be higher. The standard of accessibility to the full range of coverage ought to apply with respect to some minimum level of coverage, that is, that offered by the public scheme.

3. *Comprehensiveness of services.* There might be some specified minimum list of services that state health care schemes are expected to provide. These could include particular types of diagnostics, tests, hospital and out-patient services, and pharmaceuticals. The generosity list would depend on affordability by the states. Presumably there would be some leeway for states to determine additional services that might be provided and to decide how best to provide the services.

There may be other components of the standard, such as minimum numbers of hospital beds for the population, restrictions on the use of user fees that might affect accessibility, and criteria for particular types of capital expenditures, such as high-technology machinery.

The federal government might also be involved in harmonizing the amount and quality of health professionals. Doctor training might be a federal responsibility, or there may be a common standard of qualification and certification. Moreover, professionals themselves ought to be mobile between jurisdictions. The federal government might also be involved in broadly monitoring or overseeing the performance of state health care systems. However, detailed cost accounting would entail excessive interference.

In Indonesia, qualification requirements for personnel such as teachers and doctors are established by the national sectoral ministries (Eckardt and Shah, 2006). In both Indonesia and the Philippines, the central health ministries create a list of essential drugs and promote the use of generic medicines. However, poor information distribution and weak enforcement mechanisms make it difficult to ensure drug quality (Lieberman et al., 2005).

Obviously the precise nature of the arrangements for defining national standards and for ensuring that they are enforced will depend on the country in question. What is ultimately important is that such arrangements, as in the case of federal-state arrangements more generally, allow the states enough discretion to ensure the efficient and accountable provision of health services while ensuring that national objectives of efficiency in the internal economic union and equity nationwide are satisfied.

For Education

Similar general principles apply in the case of education, although in this case the range of required services is narrower and better defined. There might be minimum national standards with respect to school curricula, including both its contents and its level. Many countries adopt this approach. The Chinese central government developed standards for eighteen subject areas of the compulsory nine-year education program. In Indonesia, the central government establishes the curriculum and structure for primary and secondary education. The central governments of the Philippines and Chile retain control of the curriculum. In Australia, eight key learning areas are defined in the Curriculum Standard Framework. Similarly, Britain has a national curriculum that specifies objectives for core subjects (King and Guerra, 2005). Portability of students from one system to another should be ensured, along with portability of levels of attainment. Thus, students who complete primary education in one state ought to be able to enroll in secondary institutions in another state without penalty, and the same for secondary completion and postsecondary institutions. There may also need to be some guidelines with respect to accessibility to ensure that education is available to all students regardless of state or place of residence.

Guidelines with respect to classroom size and teacher-student ratios could be formulated. As well, there might be some minimum standards with respect to textbooks used and the extent to which they are provided to students. As in the case of health professionals, there might be common standards with respect to teacher training and qualifications. Moreover, teachers should be mobile across jurisdictions. The extent of the central government's control over teachers varies. In Germany, teachers are public servants whose salaries are set by federal law. The pay scales differ between western and eastern states, but local governments within each region cannot "compete" for employees (Werner, 2006). In Chile and Mexico, there is a standardized national pay scale for teachers, and contracts are centralized. In Indonesia, teachers are civil servants, giving the central government some control over wages and allowances through the civil service law. In the United Kingdom, the central government establishes the qualifications and a minimum pay scale for teachers. Individual schools are responsible for hiring and paying their own staff. Similarly, the central government in China plays a role in teacher education but expects individual school principals to maintain teacher quality through their choices of teachers and of teaching incentives. In Nicaragua, school councils (comprising principals, parents, teachers, and students) can hire and fire teachers (King and Guerra, 2005). In El Salvador, the decision to hire or fire teachers is decentralized to Community Education Associations through the Community-Managed Schools Program (EDUCO). The central Ministry of Education transfers funds directly to the associations, which retain teachers on one-year renewable contracts (World Bank, 2003).

There could be harmonization with respect to monitoring of school performance. For example, common testing might be applied as an instrument for inducing acceptable levels of performance. Again, despite this list of standards that state education systems might be expected to satisfy, the standards should remain general, and the states should be responsible for implementing state education policies consistent with the needs and preferences of their citizens and for the day-to-day functioning of the education system.

An important issue concerns the levels of education for which states would be responsible. It might be argued that states should assume control of education at least up to the secondary level. School-age students typically attend school in the state of their residence. Indeed, elementary school provision might be decentralized further to the local level, with state oversight. In the case of postsecondary education, as we have mentioned earlier, the federal government might have a more direct role. Mobility is higher among students as well as graduates of postsecondary institutions, and part of the output of such institutions might be the creation of knowledge, which benefits the nation as a whole. A federal role in tertiary education has developed in the German system. The central government contributes to the building and expanding of higher-educational institutions, tasks that were originally the sole responsibility of the *Länder* (Kramer, 2005).

USE OF SPECIAL-PURPOSE BODIES

Although state governments might be responsible for providing education and health services, the actual delivery of these services is done by local agencies. These agencies could be local governments who operate the services on behalf of the state, or they may be special-purpose bodies created specifically for the service in question. Thus, local school boards may be responsible for running the schools for local communities, and hospital boards the same for hospital services. Although these special-purpose bodies are accountable to the state, they do have some discretion over the details of administering the services. In fact, the more discretion they have, the more efficient one might expect service provision to be.

In Canada, local, directly elected school boards are responsible for primary and secondary education (McMillan, 2006). Similarly, in the United States, primary and secondary education is often provided through special-purpose school districts. These districts, governed by elected independent boards, can raise some revenues and issue debt related solely to education (Schroeder, 2006). In Brazil, several states have reformed their educational systems by creating school councils, transferring resources directly to schools, and allowing communities to elect their local principal. The EDUCO program in El Salvador gives each elected Community Education Association the legal responsibility to manage a preprimary or primary school. The committees have one-year renewable contracts with the Ministry of Education. The ministry itself oversees basic policy and technical design. In Australia, school councils establish a school charter, essentially a contract between the school and the government (King and Guerra, 2005).

The alternative to special-interest bodies administering the provision of education and health services is for local governments to do so. Local governments already have the administrative overhead to undertake such a task, although they may not have the expertise. Various considerations go into the choice between special-purpose bodies and local governments as providers of education and health services. Local governments have an advantage with respect to accountability and transparency. If governance standards are good, these governments are responsible to their own electorates for performance and can be dismissed in an election if outcomes are not satisfactory. This possibility should make them responsive to local preferences and needs. Because they have revenue-raising ability, they can also be made financially responsible for efficient outcomes. In Brazil, for example, municipal governments have responded to their increased responsibility for health care by forming consortia to share costs, equipment, and personnel (Souza, 2005).

On the other hand, special-interest bodies, by being more specialized, can offer more expertise directly to the operation of schools and hospitals. In principle, they might also be given some revenue-raising responsibilities, such as over local property taxes or user charges. Their board members could also be subject to periodic election, much like local governments. However, accountability is likely to be blurred and resource allocation affected to some extent by the existence of overlapping political institutions in the form of special-interest bodies and local governments. They will be serving common constituencies and drawing resources from the same local pool. Similar issues also arise with respect to local utilities and local water and sanitation services. The ideal resolution will depend on local circumstances and the quality of local governance.

An interesting example of a special-purpose body is the Swiss Universities' Conference. This body, with representatives of the confederation, the university cantons, and the universities themselves, was created specifically to make decisions about tertiary education, a shared responsibility (Schmitt, 2005).

ROLE OF USER FEES

We have already alluded to the possibility of utilizing user fees as a source of revenue to help finance education and health services. These have been controversial in industrialized countries, but they take on possibly added importance in developing countries for two reasons. The first is that developing countries are under tremendous pressure in financing these services. The extent of revenue mobilization is relatively low in these countries compared with that in OECD as reflected in significantly lower tax-revenue-to-GNP ratios. At the same time, the need for these basic services is very high, given the ambition to provide universal education to all children as well as basic health services. The competing requirements for public funds are very high, for such things as poverty alleviation, infrastructure, and, in some case, defense. User fees and other forms of cost recovery are attractive ways of augmenting the limited funds that can be obtained from tax revenues. Of course, attracting external financing from NGOs and aid agencies is also helpful.

The second reason why user fees may be particularly useful is as an aid to governance. Many developing countries have a history of heavy public-sector involvement in the economy with the result that bureaucracies are often large, centralized, and driven by their own objectives. They may also not have effective control over the suppliers of particular services: for example, in some countries, the very high rate of absenteeism among teachers is a symptom of poor managerial control. One of the objectives of decentralization is to transform the orientation of public services from being supply driven to demand driven. That requires that the voice of users be heard and heeded. Decentralization itself can contribute to this objective by locating decisions about health and education closer to those being served. Giving users a financial stake might also be useful, for example, by promoting user fees as an alternative to local taxes.

The choice of user charges as a way of mobilizing additional revenues and giving voice to the process is fraught with some dangers, as we have pointed out earlier. Given that the primary role of the public sector in providing education and health services is a redistributive one, this role can be compromised by the use of user fees. (The same argument does not apply to local services that are more efficiency motivated, such as utilities, water, and sanitation services.) Any system of user fees would have to accommodate the adverse equity effects that would result from imposing charges on the poor. It would also discourage use of basic health services and discourage participation in education (despite its mandatory nature). It could be argued that some extent of user charging might add efficiency to the system, especially in health care, by preventing overuse. However, the onus is on showing that those benefits are substantial enough to warrant the inequities involved with user charges.

Still, ways may be found to take advantage of user fees without incurring the equity problems and discouraging participation. One partial way out of the dilemma would be to restrict fees to levels of service that are above the basic levels needed for all persons. Another would be to attempt to target fees to those who are able to pay them. This might be administratively complex. One would not only have to identify those in need but also have to worry about the stigma effect this might have on the poor. Moreover, it might even be hard to enforce fees on those who are able to pay them. If the final objective were to ensure that the entire population has access to some basic level of education and health care, it would be difficult to deny access to someone who did not pay.

User fees for health services were successfully introduced by the municipal council of Malalag in the Philippines in the early 1990s. The Malalag Revenue Code created a graduated payment scheme, with higher-income families paying a larger share of the fixed service costs. Low-income families were also given priority in receiving services. Once implemented, the fees generated sufficient extra revenues that the government could expand services to include medical, dental, and surgical services (Lieberman et al., 2005).

The financial stringencies that lead to advocating user fees for health and education services raise forceful arguments for private systems parallel to public ones in health and education. Of course, the downside is that a quality wedge is necessarily driven between public and private health services because people would not incur the cost of using private services if public ones of equal quality, but lesser cost, were available.

As with many policy issues in developing countries, the choices between user fees and the private participation option are difficult ones. The benefits and costs need to be weighed in light of local circumstances. A study of user fees for schools in Mali, for example, found that parents were better off paying the charges, because they valued the improvement in school quality more than the fee itself (World Bank, 2003). In China, the central government prohibits user fees, but local governments encourage them. The local government will set a fee scale and retain a percentage of the fee revenue. These funds are then used to compensate other schools in the district, paying for such items as repairs or improvements in facilities (King and Guerra, 2005). On the other hand, eliminating user fees has been linked to higher enrollments in countries such as Kenya, Tanzania, Uganda, and Vietnam (World Bank, 2005b). In 2001 the Philippine central Department of Education prohibited the charging of user fees at the elementary school level. The concern was that fees would cause enrollment to decline (King and Guerra, 2005).

TWELVE

Finance and Provision of Infrastructure

Public-sector capital, including infrastructure, is an important component of public expenditures. The stock of public capital comes in various forms. Some types of public goods are durable by their very nature. Defense spending, for example, includes not only military personnel but also equipment like weapons, tanks, airplanes, and ships. Virtually all public programs, including the provision of public services to citizens, require buildings and associated equipment. The public sector may also be involved to a greater or lesser extent in providing infrastructure for use by the private sector. Examples include transportation facilities (e.g., roads, bridges) and communications installations. As essential components of an efficiently functioning private sector, these forms of infrastructure are well known to contribute to productivity and growth. This chapter addresses the implications for fiscal federalism that result from the significant capital component to public goods and services.

Acquisition of capital gives rise to special issues because of its durable nature. Current capital purchases result in both a stream of benefits and a need for maintenance and replacement in several periods into the future. This has two sorts of implications. First, the decision rules for providing public services must necessarily take account of this intertemporal aspect. Service provision requires not only current expenditures but also the building up of physical capacity to support this provision. Full account must be taken of the likely growth in demand for services in the future. This capacity will have to be maintained and replaced as it wears out. In short, a long-run planning perspective is needed to take full account of the intertemporal nature of capital decisions. Indeed, the hiring of personnel itself has many aspects of a capital decision, because hired employees typically stay in the job for several years. However, there is one important difference, and that leads to the second implication.

Even though the hiring of employed staff has features of a capital decision, its costs can be treated as a current expenditure. That is because employees are paid as they provide services. However, in the case of capital expenditures, the capital is often purchased rather than rented, implying that cash outlays must be made up front. This raises the issue of financing the cash outlays. Current tax revenues could be used, but there are good reasons for financing at least some capital projects using debt. The use of debt can help smooth over the lumpiness in tax revenue requirements that would otherwise occur. As well, for longer-lived capital projects, future taxpayers, many of whom are not included among current taxpayers, are beneficiaries of the capital spending. It might be thought fair that the burden of cost be spread to them. The question of financing must be squarely addressed when considering the need of lower-level governments to make capital and infrastructure acquisitions.

ASSIGNMENT OF RESPONSIBILITY FOR CAPITAL PURCHASES

As we have mentioned, capital purchases include not only capital items that necessarily accompany the provision of public services but also the provision of infrastructure capital that is used by the private sector and members of the public more generally. As in the case of redistributive responsibilities, the responsibility for capital purchases cannot be assigned to one level of government or the other. Indeed, if anything, capital expenditures are relatively more important at the state and local levels of government than at the federal level. Lower levels of government are typically heavily involved in the provision of public services, like health and education, which require fixed capital as inputs (e.g., hospitals and schools). The federal government spends relatively more on transfers and social insurance, which tend to be much less capital intensive. As well, many types of infrastructure and public works are local, including roads and sidewalks, water and sewage, and recreational facilities.

In principle, there is no reason why the lower-level jurisdictions should not assume responsibility for the capital expenditures that necessarily accompany the provision of goods and services for which they are responsible. Indeed, decentralized provision of this type of capital expenditures would seem to be necessary for efficiency. Lower-level jurisdictions are presumably in a better position to know precisely how much capital is needed to ensure that services are provided most efficiently.

In many countries, capital expenditure responsibilities are shared across levels of government. In Indonesia, for example, educational infrastructure is funded by both central and local governments. Primary- and secondary-level infrastructure and school rehabilitation are central responsibilities. Local governments finance and manage this infrastructure. Agricultural and irrigation infrastructure are provided by all three levels of government (central, provincial, and local). Responsibility for transportation infrastructure is separated. The central government funds and manages national infrastructure; provincial governments are responsible for provincial infrastructure; and local governments manage and fund local networks (Eckardt and Shah, 2006). In the Philippines, the central government is responsible for primary infrastructure, including transmission grids for power and primary road networks. Tertiary infrastructure, such as roads and water, is the responsibility of cities and municipalities (Peterson and Muzzini, 2005). In the United States, all levels of government provide transportation infrastructure. Major highways are constructed with funds from both the federal and state governments; maintenance is a state responsibility. Other roads can be built by any level of subnational government. Infrastructure is sometimes provided by special districts, a form of single-purpose local government whose boundaries need not match existing political jurisdictions. Airports, for instance, are usually a local government or special district responsibility. Local transit can be provided by special transit authorities or municipalities. Local public utilities, including sewage and water services, are the responsibility of local governments or special districts (Schroeder, 2006).

Local discretion over investment can be significant. In Nordic countries, local governments determine how services are delivered. Their infrastructure decisions include the number of schools and hospitals and the location of all public infrastructure projects (Lotz, 2006). In Germany, nearly two-thirds of public investment occurs at the local level (Werner, 2006). The management of water resources, including investment decisions, has long been decentralized to the water basin level (World Bank, 1994b). Mexico began a municipal fund program in 1990 that required communities to participate in selecting and executing rural infrastructure projects (World Bank, 1994b). Both Indonesia and the Philippines have investment programs that give local communities the ability to choose small investment projects that the community will manage (Peterson and Muzzini, 2005). In India, rural water service is increasingly delivered by community-managed systems. Local communities help design the systems. The central government provides much of the capital funding, while donor organizations provide technical and organizational support. Local communities manage the systems and bear the costs of operation and maintenance (World Bank, 2003). In Argentina, local governments have increased their role to meet local needs. In Santa Fe, several municipalities formed a highway consortium, a partnership to develop and maintain common highway infrastructure (Asensio, 2006).

However, the lasting nature of capital gives rise to special problems of financing that make managing under true decentralization more difficult than managing current expenditures. The problems arise from both the need to finance a good part of capital acquisitions by borrowing and the temptation to finance even more by borrowing more than is desirable. As mentioned, it is natural to finance a substantial proportion of capital acquisitions by debt. Otherwise, jurisdictions would be faced with huge tax liabilities to be paid by those who will benefit for only a part of the life of the capital. Future generations who inherit the public capital would pay nothing for it. This argument for debt financing should not be taken too far. Numerous assets and liabilities are passed from one generation to another. Only on very few of these assets will there be strict benefit taxation on a cohort-by-cohort basis that will pay for their provision. One could argue that debt policy ought to be a macroeconomic decision that takes account of all forms of intergenerational transfers and smoothes taxes over time appropriately.[1] Unfortunately, rational debt policy is undoubtedly the exception rather than the norm. At least in the case of public-sector capital, a real asset can be set against debt used for financing. In the case of lower-level governments, debt financing might be especially warranted to the extent that the benefit principle is more relevant. In any case, in practice, public capital acquisitions are largely financed by borrowing, especially at the level of state and local governments. In a federal context, such borrowing can give rise to a number of issues.

Borrowing and Vertical Fiscal Gap

Borrowing to finance the capital purchases of lower-level governments can be undertaken either by the relevant government itself or by the federal government on its behalf. The federal government may have easier access to capital markets and so be able to borrow on better terms than lower jurisdictions. For example, financial markets may take federal borrowing to be less risky because the federal government has broader access to revenue sources with which to cover debt servicing. As well, federal

---

[1] The information required to undertake rational debt policies from an intergenerational perspective has recently been greatly enhanced with the innovation of intergenerational accounting. For an overview, see Auerbach et al. (1999).

revenue sources may be less risky because the federal government can pool state-specific shocks to revenue sources. These considerations make it very tempting for the federal government to assume borrowing responsibilities on behalf of states and localities.

However, there are some serious drawbacks to such an arrangement. For one, the federal government does not necessarily have adequate information to properly assess states' borrowing needs. The states (or localities) presumably are in a better position to determine the necessary amount of public capital required to carry out their responsibilities. For another, federal government debt financing of state and local capital projects inevitably leads to closer federal control of those expenditures. Federal funding would be contingent on lower-level capital projects, presumably on a fairly specific and detailed basis. This sort of intrusion may be incompatible with the independence and accountability called for by decentralized decision making.

There would also be a need for ongoing monitoring of capital projects to ensure that adequate depreciation and upkeep expenditures were being made to keep the capital intact. This monitoring too would detract from the kind of decentralized expenditure responsibility that is conducive to efficient decision making in a federation.

In Indonesia and the Philippines, the role of the central government in financing allows it to influence local infrastructure decisions. In Indonesia, local governments can access foreign capital only through on-lending by the central Ministry of Finance (Eckardt and Shah, 2006). In the Philippines, the central government is also the only intermediary between international lenders and local governments. Funds from international organizations are provided at below market rates to two institutions, the Development Bank of the Philippines and the Land Bank of the Philippines. These banks also receive funds from the Philippine National Bank. The loans then made to local governments are secured by the ability to divert intergovernmental revenue-sharing transfers. Because these preferential conditions cannot be met by private lenders, a commercial lending market for local governments has not developed. Both the Indonesian and Philippine central governments can influence local infrastructure decisions through their loan conditions and discretionary loan approval (Peterson and Muzzini, 2005).

Capital Funding as a Component of Federal Grants

Rather than borrowing intrusively on behalf of the lower-level government, the federal government could incorporate the need for capital spending into its general grant formula used for financing state governments.

Ideally, federal government transfers in support of state public goods and services provision could be made on the basis of need. As discussed earlier, measures of need could be estimated on the basis of the costs of providing standard levels of goods and services and measured independently of actual state expenditures. These standard cost measures could incorporate both current and capital costs elements into them, although the latter are admittedly more challenging.

This procedure may get around some of the difficulties outlined previously, such as the informational disadvantage faced by the federal government and the tendency for project-specific financing to be overly intrusive, disrupting state and local autonomy. On the other hand, there are considerable difficulties with incorporating capital financing requirements into a general grant formula. Different states frequently will have different amounts of public capital relative to their needs. For example, in a developing-country context, there will be capital backlogs in important areas such as education (schools) and health (hospitals). A needs-based formula would have to take account of such differences, and resolving them would be fairly difficult to do. Moreover, there are obvious incentives for state and local governments to misinform the federal government about their capital requirements. Above all, given these problems of differential need and backlogs and the resulting requirement to tailor transfers to each state's situation, there will be an obvious incentive for the federal government to use its financial power to interfere excessively with state spending decisions, capital and otherwise.

State-Local Borrowing

Given these disadvantages of the federal government in financing state capital projects, that leaves borrowing by lower-level governments as the remaining alternative worth considering. For this to be a viable alternative, the relevant governments must have adequate revenue-raising powers of their own. Borrowing is simply deferred taxation, so the power to borrow must be accompanied by the responsibility for financing the debt created. Given an adequate level of revenue-raising ability, allowing state and local governments to borrow freely on their own account to finance capital expenditures seems on the surface to be reasonable. More generally, there would seem to be no particular need to tie borrowing to capital projects, because that is not required for the federal government.

At the same time, there are a number of problems alleged to be associated with borrowing by lower levels of government. Indeed, so persuasive are these arguments, at least from the perspective of the federal government, that constraints on such borrowing are commonplace in nations around the world. These constraints can take varying degrees of severity. Borrowing may require approval by higher levels of government, be restricted to capital spending, be restricted to borrowing from the higher level itself rather than from the private sector, or simply be prohibited. What are the arguments that lead to such restrictions?

Riskiness

The solvency of lower levels of government depends on the revenue sources they have. It is quite likely that these sources are riskier than federal government's because they are typically derived from narrower bases and are subject to idiosyncratic shocks at the state level. Some of this extra risk might be insurable, namely, the part of it that is purely idiosyncratic. State governments may be able to self-insure either by enacting fluctuating tax rates or by varying their borrowing over time. However, it seems likely that there is a systematic component of risk that cannot be insured, such as aggregate nationwide shocks or relatively large unanticipated changes in state economic circumstances. Moreover, problems of moral hazard, and possibly adverse selection as well, reduce the extent to which this risk may be insured. Thus, the availability of insurance may induce governments to take more risks or be less vigilant they might otherwise be. Capital markets may not be able to assess fully the riskiness of a given state government, because that depends on the future behavior of the government itself (which is dependent on its identity, the prevailing ideology of the times, and the future economic, social, and political circumstances of the jurisdiction). Given this, it is natural to expect that interest rates charged to state and local governments will be higher than to the federal government, making it more costly for lower-level jurisdictions to finance their own capital spending.

The strength of this effect is disputable. For one thing, if the risks faced by lower jurisdictions actually are systematic, the national government could not insure them either. The real issue is more likely one of default risk. On the other hand, if risks are idiosyncratic, it is true that the federal government could pool risks across jurisdictions. But, then, so could private markets. There should be no risk premium associated with lower-level jurisdictions. Perhaps the real problems are ones of moral hazard, an issue to which we return later.

Even given the existence of systematic risk at the state or local level, it is not clear what the risk really is to the lender. In the case of private loans, insolvency leading to default is a well-defined concept. In the case of governments, the concept of insolvency is not so clear. Governments have the power of coercion over taxpayers in the economy. Public debt ought, in principle, to be payable over time as long as the amount of debt is limited to be less than the present value of expected future GNP. For standard levels of debt, it is not at all clear what default risk involves for public debt. Perhaps what is at stake is simply a refusal to continue burdensome debt payments that have become too onerous, the expectation of which leads to higher interest rates being charged. It is obviously difficult to say with any precision at what point that will occur.

There is a final consideration with respect to risk. To the extent that lower-level jurisdictions are subject to idiosyncratic risks that can be better insured by a higher-level government, this can be, and ought to be, addressed by the equalization system. This is true with respect to the federal and state governments, and it is also true with respect to state and local governments in hierarchical federations. That is, the next higher level of government ought to be able to insure the idiosyncratic risks of the next lower ones. Equalization formulas that are based on some measure of differences in tax capacities should automatically insure against the volatility of lower-level government revenue streams. Of course, it will not be actual revenues but revenue capacities that will be the basis of equalization to avoid well-known incentive problems. By the same token, if expenditure needs are risky, such as those which arise from social insurance programs, these too will be insured by an equalization system that includes a component of needs in its formula.

Governments pursue a number of strategies to help offset the perceived greater risk of lending to subnational governments. Providing loans to establish credit histories, legislating a clear regulatory framework, and undertaking direct oversight and control are some of the tools. In India, the Infrastructure Leasing and Financial Services intermediary of the early 1990s intended to sell its loans to private institutions once credit histories were established. Indonesia used a transitional credit system called the Regional Development Account that lent funds to local authorities at near market rates. The objective was to allow local authorities to create cost-recovery mechanisms and establish credit histories over a three- to five-year period (World Bank, 1994b). South Africa has taken steps to foster municipal borrowing. The 1996 constitution allows municipal debt in a framework of central regulation. The regulatory centerpiece is the 2004 Municipal Finance Management Act. Municipal councils can make binding pledges of security for debt. Failure to meet these obligations can lead to provincial and, if necessary, national intervention. The clarified lending framework may encourage commercial participation. Indeed, almost half of the short- and long-term lending since 1997 came from the Infrastructure Finance Corporation, the specialized municipal lending agency of one of South Africa's major commercial banks (Heymans, 2006).

In India, reliance on the private market to fund urban infrastructure has also increased. Urban municipalities can borrow from the market if they have state approval. State governments typically issue guidelines on such items as the length of the debt, the interest offered on municipal bonds (which must be in line with other government securities), and the provisions for debt servicing. Loans typically are based on the value of lands and buildings assessed for property taxes. Through the mid-1990s, state government guarantees were offered for borrowing through specialized entities such as the Housing and Urban Development Corporation. Since 1996 the municipal bond market has grown, encouraged by both government incentives and the greater use of credit rating agencies. After a positive experience in which one municipality was evaluated and its proposed bond issue approved by a credit rating service, other municipalities have sought access to market funds. Two additional credit rating agencies developed their own criteria for evaluations. The government of India provides a further incentive by allowing eligible issuers to offer tax-free municipal bonds to fund capital investments in urban infrastructure. Conditions include sufficient revenue streams to finance the project and the creation of an escrow account for debt service. There have been no state government or bank guarantees for seven of the nine municipalities that have issued these bonds, reflecting the growing acceptance of municipal bonds as a means to finance urban infrastructure (Mathur, 2006). It is interesting to note that rural panchayats cannot raise loans from public or private sources (Alok, 2006).

Soft Budget Constraints

As explained earlier, state and local governments are often exposed to standard moral hazard problems in the face of creditors. They may have a reduced incentive to raise revenues when needed, they may overextend their expenditures, and they may expose themselves to high debt levels. This tendency may be exacerbated by the shortsightedness that comes with governments being in office for limited terms. In a federation, there is another source of moral hazard besides that which may come about from the imperfection of capital markets. Lower-level governments rely on grants from higher levels. Moreover, at least some of these grants are designed to ensure that state and local governments can meet their expenditure needs. As we have stressed elsewhere, these levels of government deliver many key social programs. In these circumstances, lower-level governments will have more incentive to overextend themselves than would otherwise be the case. This is especially so when grants are based on discretion rather than on formulas.

If lower-level governments can spend excessively and without due diligence and thereby find themselves unable to provide basic public services of acceptable standards, the federal government may feel compelled to come to their financial assistance. Indeed, the federal government may actually be compelled to do so by the constitution. In Germany, for example, a municipality cannot become bankrupt; the federal government must balance all debts completely (Werner, 2006). In Nordic countries, there is a similar legal tradition that municipalities cannot be bankrupted (Lotz, 2006). In other words, state budget constraints may be soft, as we have emphasized from time to time in earlier chapters. Of course, this soft budget constraint problem can occur even in the absence of state or local borrowing. States can let their capital stocks run down and overspend on current items even without the power to borrow. But the ability to borrow provides one more avenue through which the soft budget constraint can be exploited.

It might be argued that the solution to the soft budget constraint problem is to announce a hard budget constraint and stick to it. Unfortunately, commitments to such policies are very difficult for governments. It should be emphasized that this constitutes another forceful argument for formula-based rather than discretionary grants. If formulas are put in place that specify explicitly the determinants of grants and base these grants on objective criteria rather than a state's actual budget, that states will in fact feel bound by the grants is more likely than if there is budgetary discretion involved. Of course, this depends on the presumption that the grant formula itself does not encourage overspending by recipient governments.

Given the potential for a soft budget constraint, a case can be made that state and local governments ought to be responsible for borrowing to finance their own deficit problems. That way they will be faced with the much harder budget constraint imposed by disinterested capital markets. Capital markets will be quick to discipline governments that run up excessive debts, essentially by increasing interest rates. Some OECD countries follow this practice. In Canada, for example, provincial and local governments are essentially free to borrow from capital markets at their own peril. There have been very few instances of financial distress as a consequence.

Of course, for such a system to work, lower-level jurisdictions must have considerable discretion over their own budgetary policies. In many federations, the degree of oversight exercised by the federal government is substantial, especially with respect to the provision of important public services by state and local governments. Given the desire of the federal government to see that these governments do in fact provide public services of acceptable standards, it is a challenge to ensure that they do so without running into soft budget constraint problems.

Government oversight of municipal borrowing in Germany is considerable, which reflects not only the federal responsibility to balance local debts but also the source of most local borrowing. Most direct loans to municipalities are made by public savings banks, which local authorities own and whose credit ratings they guarantee. It is in theory possible for municipal leaders to evaluate their own loans in their capacity as members of a bank's executive board. Laws on local borrowing differ across federal states. In general, borrowing can be used only to fund investments and only after all other revenue sources are tapped. Local budgets must be submitted to the federal Ministry of Finance or its regional agencies. The ministry has the power, in theory, to assume complete control of the local budget (Werner, 2006).

In Nordic countries, where municipalities cannot go bankrupt, there is a traditional "golden rule" restriction on borrowing. While investment is largely funded by loans, current budget revenues are expected to be sufficient for both current expenditures and debt servicing. Bail-out conditions are seen as "humiliating" and are believed to have a deterrent effect (Lotz, 2006).

In the United States, subnational borrowing is kept in check through both legal limits and market discipline. Long-term borrowing is permitted to fund capital infrastructure investment. In some cases, short-term borrowing is also allowed to meet short-term budget needs. Funds are raised directly on the capital market through the sale of bonds. Interest rates are competitive, although state and local governments have the advantage that federal income tax is not applied to interest earned on these bonds. Statutory limits on the volume of bond sales are common. Almost all states limit the amount of bonds guaranteed by tax revenues (full faith and credit bonds) relative to the property tax base. In some cases, voter approval is necessary. Market discipline also limits debt, with higher interest payments required from localities with poorer bond ratings from private institutions (Schroeder, 2006).

Migration
It has been argued that lower-level governments are more prone to running up debts to the extent that their taxpaying populations are more

mobile. Thus, taxpayers in lower-level jurisdictions might be tempted to issue excessive debt if the obligation to participate in its repayment can be avoided by out-migration to neighboring jurisdictions.[2] The importance of this argument can be contested. In most federations, the extent of mobility is unlikely to be large enough to constitute a significant source of incentive to borrow excessively.

Capital–Current Expenditure Mix

Although debt finance might be justified for capital projects that provide benefits of a lasting nature, state and local governments might find it tempting to finance current expenditures by debt. This more general issue of the time horizon of governments seems not to be a problem restricted to lower-level ones. Even so, it might be tempting to deal with the problem at the state and local level selectively. We have pointed out previously that capital expenditures might be relatively more important at the state and local levels of government. Also, while the federal government may well be able to constrain lower-level governments in the amount of debt that they issue and the uses to which it is put, it is not so feasible to put restrictions on the federal government itself. It is possible to legislate balanced-budget restrictions and the like, but these may be rather blunt instruments for restricting potential abuses of debt finance. In the United States, for example, state constitutions or statutes typically prohibit subnational governments from incurring current budget deficits (Schroeder, 2006). Likewise, in Canada, municipalities are not allowed to budget an operating deficit (McMillan, 2006). In the end, the political process and accountability mechanisms, such as effective and independent public auditors, may be the only real protection. In fact, there is no substitute for good governance. If citizens have an effective voice, and politicians are accountable to their electorate, that may be the best way to constrain excessive debt finance. In New York State, for instance, the budgets of the independent local school districts must be approved by local voters each year (Schroeder, 2006).

CAPITAL INVESTMENT AND BUDGETING

Investment

The decision to invest in infrastructure is in principle like any other capital investment decision. It requires comparing the stream of benefits with the

---

[2] This argument has been made in a formal model by Bruce (1995).

stream of costs, both initial capital costs and ongoing replacement, depreciation, and upkeep costs. The standard criterion for deciding where and how much to invest is the net present value (NPV) rule. The NPV is simply the present value of the future stream of benefits less the present value of the stream of costs, discounted at the relevant discount rate and taking risk appropriately into account. If the NPV is nonnegative, the investment is worth undertaking; otherwise, it is not.

In the private sector, the stream of benefits includes the revenues obtained from the sale of outputs, while the stream of inputs includes the cost of capital and current inputs evaluated at market prices. Capital inputs are typically accounted for on an accrual basis, so they include the current value of depreciation, the cost of interest financing, including any risk premium, and any capital losses that have accrued on the capital. The discount rate is the rate at which the owners of the firm discount future versus present funds. Inflation can be accounted for either by evaluating benefits and costs at current prices and discounting using a nominal discount rate or by using constant prices and discounting using a real discount rate. Following this procedure implies that the NPV is a measure of the profits of the project from the point of view of the firm's shareholders.

Public-sector investment decision rules differ from those used in the private sector in a number of ways. Inputs and outputs are evaluated at the shadow or social values. These can differ from market prices because the relevant or related markets are distorted, because there are externalities associated with the use of the input or output, or because the input or output has particular value from a redistributive point of view.[3] As well, the cost of financing the project will reflect the costs associated with the public sector's raising revenues either by taxation or by debt (which is just future taxation). These will include any distortions induced by marginal increases in financing by the public sector. The discount rate will reflect the rate at which the government trades off future versus present funds and can include the weight that the government puts on consumption by future versus present generations. The NPF of a public project reflects its value to society rather than its profitability. Indeed, the two will typically be very different because projects undertaken by the public sector are often ones for which it would be difficult or inefficient to finance by revenues from sales.

Another difference between public- and private-sector decisions arises from the fact that, in the public sector, revenues are not raised for specific

[3] The relevant procedures for shadow pricing, as well as the other technicalities involved in project evaluation, may be found in Boadway (forthcoming).

projects. Instead, investment financing often comes from a fixed pool of funds, and the decision is how to allocate those funds among various projects. This is the problem of capital budgeting. It can be particularly important for subnational governments that may not have access to the capital market but might be faced with a fixed budget imposed by the higher-level government.

Budgeting

Suppose that, for whatever reason, the policy maker has an upper limit on the capital budget that can be used for the projects under consideration. The budget can be used for financing various combinations of projects. In principle, the choice of projects is a straightforward extension of the NPV rule stated previously: choose the combination of projects within the budget limit that maximizes the total NPV of all projects combined, where the NPV calculation is precisely the same as before. This might, of course, entail not undertaking the project that has the highest individual NPV so that the aggregate NPV can be the highest possible.

The discount rate might be thought of as being an issue here. Because the capital budget is fixed, there is no opportunity to borrow and lend, so the interest rate does not reflect the cost of financing projects at the margin. But, in the public sector, it is not necessarily the actual cost of financing that is the appropriate discount rate, or the social discount rate. Rather, it is the rate at which the society – that is, the individuals who make it up and benefit from the projects under consideration – actually discounts future versus present funds, or the consumption to which it gives rise. In the absence of externalities, and if one assumes that households are free to borrow and lend on capital markets, the social discount rate is the after-tax interest rate faced by households on capital markets. Although this can differ from household to household because tax rates differ, that difference is typically not enough to be of quantitative concern.

Although the principles of project evaluation when there are capital budgeting constraints are clear (and not really any different from project evaluation in the unconstrained case), nonetheless a number of conceptual issues must be dealt with in practice.

Unused Capital Funds, Multiperiod Costs, and Future Requirements

If the collection of projects that are chosen does not exhaust the capital budget allotted, the issue of what becomes of the unused funds is relevant.

If they revert to general revenues and serve to relax the government's overall budget constraint, this must be taken into account. In effect, the saving in excess burden of whatever public financing is available must be incorporated into the project evaluation. Projects that use fewer funds will naturally incur less excess burden on this account. In other words, the procedure for taking account of the actual amount of funding for various options is the same as for project evaluation in the absence of the capital budget constraint. The latter simply puts an upper bound on the capital available.

The evaluation will need to take account of the extent to which different projects incur capital costs over a period of years and how the capital budget constraint deals with that. Again, nothing new in principle is involved here. As long as all costs and benefits are appropriately accounted for, including the cost of public funds, the only constraint imposed by the capital budget is a restriction on the amount of funds available over time. The capital requirements for different projects may have different time profiles. As long as they are properly costed in the periods in which they are incurred, there should be no problems. The evaluator must still choose the combination of projects that maximizes the aggregate NPV and does not violate the capital budget allotted.

Similar considerations apply with capital funding that may be required for expansion or replacement investments in future periods. To the extent that capital constraints apply to these investments, they will obviously have to be satisfied.

ACCOUNTABILITY AND GOVERNANCE

The provision of public infrastructure gives rise to particular accountability issues. Because of its durable nature, long-term planning is important. The decision to undertake infrastructure investment today implies a stream of operating and maintenance (O&M) expenditures into the future. If the required O&M is not carried out continually according to a prescribed structure, the infrastructure will not provide the services for which it was intended.

This problem can be particularly important in developing countries, where budgets are extremely limited, and in subnational governments (in whose jurisdictions the responsibility for much of the infrastructure falls) that find it difficult to mobilize their own revenues. If public services are large and bureaucratic and are seen partly as employment-creating institutions, O&M expenditures will be crowded out by wages and salaries.

Moreover, the prevailing attitude in the public sector may be to prioritize public-sector spending on the basis of the interests of the public-sector suppliers rather than the users themselves. Moreover, quite apart from these governance problems, subnational governments may not have built up the management expertise or the proper evaluation, financial accounting, and information procedures to manage infrastructure effectively. Indeed, this lack of expertise may be a consequence of not having had the autonomy to develop the experience needed to fulfill the responsibility.

A challenge for decentralization is to overcome these deficiencies in governance so as to ensure that services of all kinds, including those from infrastructure, are best suited to the needs of potential users. There are several ways that governance can be improved so that the public service is more demand oriented. Above all, because the responsible government must have true ownership of infrastructure projects that are undertaken within their jurisdictions, placing autonomy at the subnational government level is important. The voices of users might be better heard if they have a financial stake in the services being provided. Thus, user charges and reliance on local revenue sources, despite the burden they impose on local residents, might induce public providers to be more accountable to the users. The possibility that user charges might also attract private providers of infrastructure may be particularly valuable given the tight revenue constraints faced by subnational governments. Finally, governance can be improved by putting in place good management and budgeting procedures, and by building the institutional and human capital capacity to manage large infrastructure projects effectively.

USER CHARGES

User charges or other such means of cost recovery for the services provided to households and firms by public-sector infrastructure are often advocated. Not only does this provide a valuable source of revenue to governments to help finance the infrastructure, but it may also serve to ration the use of the infrastructure efficiently among users. In fact, user fees on the use of services provided by infrastructure are but one of many areas in which user charges are employed by governments, especially subnational ones.

Efficient Pricing

Governments are often involved in the supply of products that are essentially private but are provided by the public sector because they have increasing returns to scale, they are monopolies, or they are deemed to have important social values, or for other reasons. There is, of course, considerable debate about what sorts of private products, if any, ought to be provided publicly. For our purposes, we simply note that public provision is common in sectors such as utilities, transportation, communications, water, and sanitation. In many of these cases, user fees are charged that are less than average costs, so the public sector ends up subsidizing the product. A purely efficient pricing scheme would involve pricing at marginal costs, where marginal costs could vary by time of day or season.

However, prices might vary from marginal cost for a couple of reasons. For one, setting a price above marginal cost would be equivalent from the point of view of tax theory to imposing an excise tax on the product. This policy might be legitimate given that the product is being subsidized from general revenues, which themselves entail imposing a tax elsewhere on other products. For another reason, there may be redistributive arguments for setting prices even below marginal costs if the product is viewed as a necessity of life that must be consumed even by the lowest-income persons. Water might be an example of this. There may also be purely administrative reasons for pricing below marginal costs or imposing no price at all. For example, it may be difficult to monitor garbage disposal well enough to warrant instituting a pricing scheme.

It is common to see user fees for infrastructure services at the local level. In the United States, local governments can charge for the use of sewer systems or facilities such as hospitals. Special districts are heavily reliant on user fees. These districts are organized to provide services that are not contiguous with political boundaries, such as airports, transit systems, or water drainage (Schroeder, 2006). In Canada, fees are charged for municipal services such as water, waste collection, and sewerage and drainage. Although transportation networks (roads and streets) are a major municipal expenditure, tolls are limited to specific projects or public transit (McMillan, 2006). In Argentina, municipalities that formed consortiums to build and maintain common highways have in some cases been able to collect tolls (Asensio, 2006). In South Africa, fees from services such as water, sanitation, electricity, and solid waste removal are a major source of local revenue for municipalities (Heymans, 2006). Indeed, Johannesburg, South Africa, had to reorganize service delivery and budgeting systems after the central government refused to bail the city out of a financial crisis in the late 1990s. The city's three-year plan, "iGoli 2002," created semi-independent entities to deliver water, sanitation, electricity, and waste management services. Fees were charged and new user forums were created to allow communities to articulate needs and complaints. Service delivery improved and expanded into previously unserved, poorer outlying communities (World Bank, 2003).

The potential for user fees to improve service provision and maintenance often becomes clearer with experience. Before 1990, Mexican water irrigation systems were run by a parastatal organization. Farmers refused to pay the fees, although they were subsidized, because the service and maintenance were inadequate. Responsibility was then shifted to user associations. These groups voluntarily raised fees to meet maintenance needs. Most of the districts became self-sufficient. In Argentina, drivers initially protested when new fees were imposed on existing road networks after private concessions were awarded with the expectation that fees would fund maintenance. The charges had to be lowered. As the quality of the roads improved, public acceptance of the tolls also increased (World Bank, 1994b).

Governments can pursue explicit policies to have fees fully cover costs. China expects local governments to become more self-sufficient in financing local infrastructure. Toward that end, municipalities are expected to implement full-cost tariffs for water supply, sold waste, and wastewater treatment. The fees are to include the costs of operation and maintenance, debt service, and a return on new capital investment (Peterson and Muzzini, 2005). In the Nordic countries, fees for treating waste and wastewater fully cover the costs of providing these services (Lotz, 2006).

In other cases, fees differ from costs for specific equity reasons. In Argentina, the privatization of water services in Buenos Aires caused initial connection costs to rise to full-recovery levels. Many users could not afford the service, and the issue became a central point in the first major adjustments to the contract (World Bank, 2005b). Indian urban water services are priced below cost. Residential users are charged less than 10 percent of the operating and maintenance costs; industrial users pay more but are still below benchmark cost-recovery levels in the majority of cities. How to adjust these tariffs is an ongoing issue. Some countries pursue targeted subsidies. In Chile, there is a nationally funded household water subsidy. In South Africa, a "national lifeline tariff system" provides a guaranteed minimum quantity of water per household per month (World Bank, 2003). In addition, the Municipal Structures Act requires that rate schedules for services such as electricity and garbage removal facilitate access to basic services for the poor (Heymans, 2006).

There is also a set of important public services that consist of effectively private goods provided by the public sector. These include services often provided by subnational governments, such as education, health, and social services. These are typically provided at well below marginal costs, often at no price at all. The reason, as we have argued earlier, is that they are important instruments for achieving the redistributive and social insurance goals of government.

Charging for Regulatory Services

Another rationale for user fees, especially in more developed economies, is to charge for regulatory services that are provided to firms in particular industries. Thus, food may be inspected for cleanliness and purity, medical products for safety, and industrial outputs for quality and pollution. In this case, the cost of regulation is treated as being a social cost of producing and selling the product concerned. The market value of the product might be enhanced because consumers are better informed. Or costs to consumers might be avoided by regulatory procedures that enhance the safety of the product or the quality of the environment. In any case, to the extent that the regulatory activity is legitimate, efficiency would dictate that its costs are attributed to the producers of the regulated good, even though they may be passed on to consumers in the form of higher prices.

Applying the principle may be difficult. For one thing, it is possible that the regulation is unnecessary and provides no clear benefit to consumers of the product or the general public. Also, there is no mechanism for reinsuring that the regulators go about their jobs in an efficient, thorough, and timely way. Some form of public accountability of the regulatory activity would be beneficial. Finally, even if the regulatory activity is necessary and efficient, it may be difficult to identify the actual costs of the regulation to attribute them to particular firms. A large department of government that is simultaneously engaged in many tasks and has a large overhead component might do the regulating.

Obtaining Rents on Publicly Owned Resources

User charges are often also deployed as devices for obtaining a return on publicly owned resources, such as parks, waterways, and other resources. The charges may take the form of licenses whose cost is not closely related to intensity of use. This rationale is obviously closely related to the first one, where the purpose of the pricing is to ration use of some type of public infrastructure. The same issues apply.

User charges of various sorts are commonly advocated for subnational governments, especially local ones. This is partly because they are the ones that provide the kinds of services that are most suitable for user charges. But there may be further advantage from having local governments use benefit taxation principles for their revenues to as great an extent possible. This will leave the redistributive role to higher levels of government, which can presumably provide a more harmonized national standard of redistribution. As well, to the extent that benefit taxation is used at the local level, problems of fiscal inefficiency and fiscal inequity between jurisdictions will not arise.

CAPITAL AND INFRASTRUCTURE GRANTS

Capital purchases can be financed by current revenues, by borrowing, or, in the case of subnational governments, by grants from the federal government. Moreover, borrowing to finance subnational capital projects may be done by the federal government on their behalf. It is unlikely to be the case that all capital spending will be debt financed. Some, especially replacement investment, is likely to be funded by current sources, including grants from higher levels of government. The exact relationship between debt financing and capital expenditures will be determined by a variety of general factors, such as macroeconomic stability, demographics, and interest rates. Our interest in this section is really more in the role of grants as a source of financing for capital projects.

The Case for Capital Grants

The role and structure of grants are inextricably tied up with the extent of fiscal autonomy exercised by state (and local) governments. In the extreme case in which states are fully responsible for their own fiscal decisions, any grants they receive would be completely unconditional. They would be responsible not only for raising their own-source revenue through both taxes and borrowing but also for the allocation of their spending across programs, as well as for the mix of capital and current expenditures. The case for such an extent of fiscal autonomy has already been made in previous chapters: it is the heart and soul of federal systems of government. State jurisdictions are presumed to be in a better position to assess their program spending needs than the federal government – for example, determining how many hospitals and schools they require, what the maintenance requirements are, or where to locate capital facilities.

The possible use of capital grants presumes that the federal government has some interest in earmarking funds to capital expenditures rather than relying on the states to determine their own capital spending plans. The issue is why that should be a legitimate interest of the federal government. It may, of course, simply be that the federal government is acting in an overly intrusive a manner, micromanaging what the states do rather than relying on the states to manage their fiscal resources and to undertake their responsibilities for themselves. On the other hand, there may be some reasons that on the surface are more defensible.

Accountability

The need for capital expenditures may differ from one state to another. Geographic conditions and the mix and level of public services may vary, the latter because of the demographic makeups of the state populations. In this case, the mix of capital and current expenditures may differ between states, which gives rise to variations in the level of per capita grants to the states. Merely as a matter of accounting, the federal government may want to distinguish between capital and operating grants as a way of differentiating among states.

The federal government may also insist that the states' actual expenditures be divided in the same proportions, although the rationale is not so clear. Needs-based equalization grants to the states are typically derived from estimates of what the states would require in order to provide a package of public services using some standard estimate of unit costs. The grants are then given unconditionally, or at least with minimal general conditions, leaving it up to the states to decide precisely what types of public services to provide in order to meet whatever national standards might be expected of them. Presumably, state responsibility would include determining how to produce the services – that is, with what capital intensity. For example, the size of classrooms in education, the relation between in-patient and out-patient treatment in hospitals, the use of cash transfers versus housing in the social sector, and so on all influence the capital-to-current expenditure ratio. Requiring states to maintain a given ratio determined by the federal government would seem to be too restrictive unless other arguments can be made. Moreover, the actual definitions of capital and current expenditures are vague enough that predetermined ratios would be difficult to enforce. The states should be able to get around them by creative accounting practices.

Access to Capital Markets to Finance Capital Projects

It might be argued that capital grants are appropriate where states have limited access to capital markets, or where the federal government borrows on their behalf. It may be the case that the federal government can obtain finance at more favorable rates than the states, as long as the federal government is responsible for repayment. Presumably state borrowing, if it were used, would go to financing capital expenditures. So, it might be reasonable for a certain amount of federal funding to be earmarked for state capital expenditures.

This argument may not be convincing either. In a federation with fully autonomous state governments with full access to capital markets, there is no reason to insist that there be a particular relation between borrowing and capital expenditures. Simply because the states do not have such access does not imply that they will choose the incorrect mix of capital and current expenditures. In any case, once funds are in the hands of the state governments, it becomes fungible. As long as states are engaging in enough capital expenditures, they can always nominally allocate federal grants to finance such expenditures and use for other purposes the funds that would otherwise have been spent on investment. Moreover, there are good arguments that can be made that states should be responsible for their own borrowing and subject to the discipline of financial markets. This may involve some set-up costs in terms of developing the administrative machinery and human capital to deal with capital markets, but as the experience in some OECD countries has shown, that is feasible.

For the federal government to institute capital grants and insist that they be used for capital spending, it must be the case that there is some reason why states, if left to their own devices, would underinvest. It may be reckoned that state bureaucracies are simply not well enough developed to undertake rational production decisions when it comes to investing in the capital to finance public services. After all, capital decisions involve planning, contracting, and overseeing construction projects, and the states may not have developed the expertise in these areas. This perspective, however, is limited. If one is to take decentralization seriously, the benefits can be achieved only if states are to have discretion over the provision of public services. Those benefits cannot be achieved if the state bureaucracies are the wards of the federal government. In other words, state capacity must be developed to a level such that the states are able to deliver public services in an autonomous fashion with standards being set only from above.

One other possible reason for states' allocating too little of their budgets to capital spending is that the time horizon of state governments may be too short compared with that of the federal government. Current expenditures yield their benefits immediately, whereas the benefits of capital expenditures flow well into the future. In any democratic political system – at federal and state levels alike – politicians serve only as long as the electorate is willing to reelect them. This fact might bias decisions in favor of those based on short time horizons, except to the extent that the electorate cares about the more distant future. The question is whether this problem is expected to be more prevalent at the state rather than the federal level. It may well be true that capital expenditures are a relatively bigger problem at the state than at the local level, so the importance of taking a longer-term view is correspondingly greater. But this in itself does not imply that the federal government should impose its will on the states with respect to capital expenditures, unless it is held that the federal government can take a longer-term view when it imposes capital grants on the states than it does with respect to its own expenditures.

We mentioned previously an argument as to why state governments might have a shorter time horizon than the federal government, and it concerns the interstate mobility of taxpayers. The argument was made to explain why state governments might issue excessive debt. Because the financing cost of that debt is borne in the future, some current state residents perceive that it can be avoided in the future by migrating to other jurisdictions. If all states behave in the same way, excessive debt is issued, and no one can avoid it by migration. A similar argument might be made to explain any other bias toward the present at the expense of the future. Choosing too high a ratio of current to capital expenditures would be an example of that. The significance of this depends on the mobility of taxpayers, especially those who are likely to be influential in determining political outcomes.

Central Objectives
One important reason why the federal government might have a special interest in the public services provided by the states is that some of them might serve interests of a national nature. As we have argued in earlier chapters, the provision of some key public services in the areas of health, education, and social services are typically assigned to subnational governments. Yet these services are important instruments for achieving national goals of equity, equality of opportunity, and social insurance. Thus, the federal government has an interest, often emphasized by the constitution, in ensuring that these services are provided at a satisfactory level in all states. The federal government might attempt to exercise this responsibility by the use of conditional grants both to ensure a harmonized level of provision and to avoid any adverse consequences of fiscal competition.

This rationale for conditional grants is generally regarded as legitimate and necessary. Whether this justifies conditionality extending to the mix of capital and current expenditures is another matter. If federal grants can be made conditional on the states' providing some minimal national standard of services, it is not clear that the states must be constrained in their capital expenditures. One reason might be that standards of service are difficult to observe and monitor, so rougher indicators such as the amount of capital used in providing the services might be used. Another might be that if the states have limited self-interest in the quality of the service that the federal government is funding, they may be prone to excessive current spending at the expense of capital spending because current spending may yield immediate dividends for them such as public-sector employment and bureaucratic preferences.

There might also be some interstate spillovers involved with certain types of infrastructure. For example, state roads, hospitals, or environmental projects might provide significant benefits to out-of-state residents. Or, if local governments are responsible for delivering some of these programs, the spillovers are likely to be more significant. Capital grants may be one way to ensure that the local governments undertake the spillover-generating expenditures.

Backlogs

An important problem in some developing countries is that the various states differ in their level of development. This difference may be particularly true with respect to urban-rural contrasts, but it might also be true for countries that went through a colonial period in which the regions where the colonists clustered became much more developed than other regions. One of the results of such discrepancies is that the relative stocks of public-sector capital differ considerably across regions. A given amount of transfers would provide very different levels of public service given the differing degrees of public capital with which to work.

One way to address this issue is by having a set of capital grants designated to address the backlog issue. The same issues arise with respect to the need to condition such grants on capital expenditures. Presumably, if there are capital backlogs, they will be recognized as well by local residents as by the federal government. The same issues mentioned earlier arise as to why grants must be designated for capital expenditures. The existence of backlogs in capital stocks can certainly be used to justify differences in per capita grants. If state governments and their localities were responsible, they could be relied on to use these grants to select the mix of capital and current expenditures that they see fit. The problem with this argument is that the size of the grants themselves depends on the amount of the backlog. The states will have an incentive not to spend the backlog on capital because doing so would effectively ensure that the backlog component of their grant remains high in the future. Of course, a similar argument may apply more generally. States will have an incentive to let their capital stocks run down if they think this will induce a special backlog grant in the future. This is essentially a version of the soft budget constraint argument.

Soft Budget Constraint

Finally, as we have mentioned previously, state government fiscal decisions can become skewed because of soft budget constraint problems. The most common way this manifests itself is through excessive spending commitments, especially those which might be financed by debt or result in budget deficits that need to be financed. It is conceivable that soft budget constraints can also lead to distortions in the mix of capital and operating expenditures. In particular, there may be an incentive for states to spend too much on the latter relative to the former because thereby they can obtain higher current benefits and rely on the federal government to make up their shortfall on capital spending.

This argument is perhaps the most persuasive one for capital grants. At the same time, it is an argument that arises because states do not have enough financial autonomy in the first place. They are led to rely on the federal government as financer of last resort, rather than their own taxpayers or the private capital markets. As with the soft budget constraint more generally, the remedy may be to address the problem directly by making states more fiscally responsible rather than addressing its consequences by overseeing state expenditure programs more closely.

Forms of Capital Grants

Suppose that state fiscal autonomy is not fully achieved, and that capital grants are part of federal-state fiscal arrangements. What form should they take? The least intrusive grants for capital expenditures would be those which are simply built into the calculations of needs in the equalization formula. A needs-based equalization formula seeks to transfer to each state an amount that is required to provide some acceptable level of public services, given the standard cost of providing each unit of service to various demographic groups. The standard costs would usually be estimated on the basis of average costs borne by all the states rather than the costs borne by a recipient state, so that states could not manipulate their grants.

They would also include both capital and operating cost needs based on some annualized capital costs. If all states were at comparable stages of development, that would be sufficient. If not, a backlogs component would need to be built in reflecting the need for the state to make up for its deficiencies in capital stock relative to other states. As mentioned, it may be necessary to induce states to spend the backlog on capital to avoid them having an incentive to perpetuate their backlog demand in the future. Otherwise, needs-based grants should be unconditional.

Indonesia has a capital grants program that incorporates elements to equalize fiscal capacity and address infrastructure backlogs. The special allocation grants (DAK grants) can fund national priorities or the specific needs of particular regions. Allocation criteria include a measure of the local government's fiscal strength; the program is intended to give priority to the special needs of governments with below-average fiscal capacity. DAK grants are matching grants that require local governments to fund at least 10 percent of total costs. They are usually earmarked for capital expenditures. Funded projects have included road, irrigation, and water infrastructure, as well as the maintenance of health and education facilities. DAK grants are still relatively small compared to the sectoral expenditures of the central government (Eckardt and Shah, 2006).

South Africa is attempting to consolidate and streamline its grant programs for municipal governments. Capital grants have accounted for one-third of direct national transfers. These were allocated through specific sectoral programs and a Consolidated Municipal Infrastructure Program. In March 2003 the decision was made to consolidate all municipal infrastructure grants into a single, decentralized, nonsectoral, multiyear, formula-based capital allocation. This new program is still in its pilot phase. A similar streamlining is happening with operating grants. These were consolidated with the introduction of a constitutional entitlement to distribute equitable shares of the revenue raised at the national level. These unconditional grants are made for a three-year period. The allocations start with a baseline level from the previous budget. The grants reflect the priorities of the national government as well as factors such as developmental needs and backlogs. The objective is to address the fiscal gap at the municipal level, particularly with respect to infrastructure for poor households (Heymans, 2006).

When conditional capital grants are deemed necessary, there are differing degrees of conditionality that can apply. They can be designated for capital expenditures generally, leaving it up to the states to allocate the funds among programs. They can be earmarked to specific programs or sectors, such as transportation, health, or education, again allowing the states to choose the projects in which to invest. Or they can be much more targeted, directed to particular capital projects, like schools, hospitals, or roads. As the degree of specificity increases, states assume less responsibility for their own decisions, thereby detracting from accountability and the advantages gained from decentralized decision making. In the United States, federal highway funds are a specific earmarked transfer. They are allocated by formula and must be used for the building or reconstruction of roads. State and local governments must fund maintenance (Schroeder, 2006). Brazil similarly transfers funds specifically for transportation investment. The federally collected fuel tax is shared with states and municipalities according to nationally legislated criteria (Afonso and Araujo, 2006). In Argentina provincial governments frequently transfer funds to localities as part of agreements on joint provincial-local activities. The provinces contribute the infrastructure funds while the local government is responsible for executing and managing the project. The highway and hydraulic infrastructure of Santa Fe was built and maintained through this type of arrangement (Asensio, 2006).

In federal settings, it is tempting for a federal government, especially one that holds the financial levers, to become involved directly in state decision making. The message here, as in other chapters, is that this can have adverse consequences for the quality of the important services that are delivered by the state governments. A useful general principle is that states should be allowed as much autonomy as possible, unless there are good reasons for federal intervention.

THIRTEEN

Poverty Alleviation in Federations

Along with education and health care, poverty alleviation programs constitute the most important social programs in developing countries. The current strategy for development endorsed in many countries involves a two-pronged approach. On the one hand, a necessary condition for development is an increase in per capita incomes, which is best achieved by encouraging private investment and taking advantage of market processes. The role of developing-country governments in this context is largely one of policy reform – eliminating unnecessary regulations, rationalizing the tax system, deregulating input and output prices, reducing trade protection, and removing public enterprise presence in industrial sectors. These reforms also go hand in hand with better governance by reducing the opportunities for bureaucratic rent seeking in market activities and outright corruption.

At the same time, high growth rates themselves are not sufficient to achieve the objectives of development, which include reducing the incidence of poverty. That is because the fruits of growth do not accrue uniformly across the population. In the absence of corrective intervention, there is a danger of the poorest groups in society falling even further behind. Thus, complementary policies aimed at uplifting the least fortunate in the society are required. In fact, the two objectives of economic growth and poverty alleviation are not conflicting, because higher growth provides the resources for poverty alleviation. Moreover, if poverty alleviation policies are well structured, they need not be a drag on growth: indeed, by improving the well-being of the least well-off, the quality of the work force is improved.

The design of effective poverty alleviation programs remains a difficult and challenging issue for governments. Those most in need must be identified, and means must be found to improve their circumstances in ways that become self-perpetuating. That means that ultimately the aim must be to make them productive members of society on a permanent basis. Not surprisingly, there is no single policy instrument that will suffice. Some involve cash transfers and the provision of services, while others aim to get recipients into the labor force. Given the administrative complexity of these programs and the informational requirements implied by them, it is not surprising that subnational levels of government are involved. Yet at the same time, there are obvious national interests at stake. Thus, all the classic issues involved in fiscal federalism apply.

In this chapter, we begin by discussing the various instruments that governments use to address poverty. Then, the assignment of functions for delivering poverty alleviation policies is considered, followed by a discussion of the relationships between levels of government, and the manner in which national objectives can be met. Finally, coordination of poverty alleviation programs with other policy objectives is considered.

POLICY INSTRUMENTS

The conventional wisdom in public finance about redistribution policy has been that cash transfers constitute the most efficient instrument for improving the well-being of poor households under the assumption that welfare is increased more per rupee transferred if untied cash is used than if transfers are tied to particular uses (e.g., food, shelter). But, even in industrialized countries, where the incidence of poverty is much less and government administrative capacities much better developed than in developing countries, cash transfers (welfare) constitute but one of many approaches to poverty. Various reasons are given for this. First, to the extent that transfers respond to donors' altruism, the latter may depend on how recipients use the funds they receive. Thus, donors may prefer that their donations are tied to, say, food, clothing, and shelter rather than being used for purposes that the recipient might prefer. Second, if the budget is severely limited relative to the number of worthy recipients, as is typically the case in developing countries, it may be felt that a greater benefit can be achieved by focusing on a limited number of truly essential items. Third, given the difficulties in identifying those most in need, in-kind transfers can improve the take-up rate of those most in need. But, fourth, what forms should they take? Which types of transfers ought to be made and by what mechanics? Finally, if the ultimate end of antipoverty policies is to make persons more self-sufficient, programs might go beyond simply transferring cash or kind to the poor. They may involve measures intended to prepare the poor for job market participation or to make it easier for them to help themselves.

Cash Transfers

Cash transfers are relatively little used in developing countries compared with their use in industrialized countries, partly because such transfers are complex, administered either through the income tax system or by welfare agencies that employ skilled professionals (social workers, etc.). In general, high-income countries often use a verified means test to determine eligibility for transfers. This approach has also worked in Eastern Europe. In Latin America, on the other hand, it is more common to rely on proxy means tests, which look at easily observed indicators of wealth. A broader range of cash transfers is used in industrialized countries, but child allowances are popular. In much of Western Europe these programs are universal; child transfers are means-tested in countries such as Italy, Spain, Poland, the Russian Federation, and Argentina (World Bank, 2005b). Cash can be provided for shelter. In England, low-income tenants in both public and private housing receive a means-tested cash benefit. The elderly in private residential homes are also given financial support (King, 2006). In the Nordic countries, disability pensions and social assistance are provided. The Danish government, for example, provides funds for early retirement and social cash benefits (Lotz, 2006). Many developing countries do not have the administrative machinery in place to deliver substantial cash transfers to the poor. More important, in developing countries tax revenue mobilization is much more restricted than in industrialized ones. The proportion of GNP taken as tax revenue is much lower, although the proportion of the population in need is much higher. There are many competing demands for scarce public-sector revenues with the result that the ability to use cash transfers as instruments of redistribution is very limited. If the cash available were spread across all the poor, the amount available per capita would be relatively small, and the number of poor who would receive cash adequate to meet their needs would be limited. Deciding how to ration the funds among the poor would presumably be arbitrary.

Transfer programs do exist for purposes other than addressing persistent poverty. They also serve a social insurance objective. For example, unemployment insurance programs provide income for persons who are temporarily and unexpectedly out of work. While these do not exist on the same scale as in industrialized countries, there are nonetheless unemployment insurance schemes in a growing number of developing countries. However, these are typically directed at persons who are already attached to the formal labor market, thereby precluding the hard-core poor. Similarly, transfers to the elderly, or public pensions, are found in many developing countries. Like unemployment insurance, these are often available on a contributory basis to persons in the work force. Because the poor elderly are an identifiable group, state pension payments to them are viable. Of course, in many societies, transfers to the elderly are traditionally intra-family, which takes some of the weight off government. A number of countries provide social pensions to the elderly without reference to labor force participation. These programs are often means tested, as is the case in South Africa, India, Australia, New Zealand, Italy, and several Latin American countries. In some cases, these programs complement contributory systems that benefit higher-income individuals (World Bank, 2005b).

The fact that social insurance is more prevalent than welfare systems in developing countries is in large part a consequence of its financing by contributions or earmarked taxes, which provide a source of revenue mobilization over and above standard tax revenues. But it also implies that social insurance is out of the reach of the very poor.

In-Kind Transfers

Given the limited financial resources of developing-country governments, it is not surprising that in-kind transfers are prevalent policy instruments for poverty alleviation. In-kind transfers can have a higher impact by taking advantage of two forms of targeting – by commodity and by recipient. In-kind transfers can be restricted to goods considered to be especially crucial in relieving the suffering of the poor. Such goods can be targeted to those considered most in need. Indeed, if the goods are more important to the poor, there will be a tendency for them to self-select into the pool of recipients, thereby easing the administrative burden of identifying them.

One can imagine a variety of commodities as being suitable for in-kind provision. The most common is food, the most basic of requirements for survival, and malnutrition, or even starvation, is a common symptom of poverty. Food also has the advantage that it is often more readily available in developing countries where agriculture is the largest industry. Food-stuffs suitable for in-kind transfers (e.g., grains) are relatively homogeneous and can be distributed readily in identifiable outlets. Other commodities that can be used as part of a poverty alleviation program include water, fuel and cooking oils, shelter, and clothing. Numerous countries make some provision to provide shelter to the elderly or home-less. In England, the government supports residential homes for the elderly. While there is limited public housing stock, local authorities must ensure that the homeless are accommodated (King, 2006). In India, the states of Gao, Karnatka, and Madhya Pradesh have laws requiring urban municipalities to build sanitary dwellings for the poor. In Karnatka, shelter also must be provided for destitute women, orphans, and the disabled. In West Bengal, state law requires municipalities to build and maintain old-age homes, homeless shelters, and low-cost dwellings for the poor (Mathur, 2006). Basic health care needs and medicines play a similar role. These in-kind transfers can also be offered at reduced prices rather than by free provision, perhaps as an attempt to economize on resource costs.

As with any program that attempts to target a particular part of the population, there will be administrative and incentive issues involved with in-kind transfers. There will inevitably be errors of two sorts in targeting. Some poor for whom the program is intended inadvertently are excluded – the case of type I statistical errors. Alternatively, some persons might be included in the net even though they are not part of the intended pop-ulation – type II errors. Type I errors are the most critical forms of error from a poverty alleviation viewpoint, because some deserving poor do not benefit from the transfer. These can occur because of administrative mis-takes or because of geographic circumstances. But it can also occur if take-up rates are too low among the eligible poor. They may not be fully aware of the program benefits to which they are entitled, or there may be a stigma attached to participating in the program. Given that self-selection is often regarded as an important property of the program, the possibility of low take-up rates can be a serious concern. Type II errors also reflect problems with self-selection, when persons are successfully applying for a program for which they are not entitled. A challenge in program design is to min-imize these two types of errors, especially type I errors.

Other administrative problems can arise. To the extent that the good being transferred has resale value, recipients can sell it and use the cash for other purposes. There may be problems with the distribution system, such as inefficiency or outright corruption. In some cases, these can be allevi-ated by using nongovernmental organizations (NGOs) or local communi-ty groups as part of the distribution system. More general problems may be associated with the policies required to implement the in-kind transfer. In the case of food, governments might be tempted to perpetuate systems of protection for agricultural producers in the guise of serving the poor,

thereby clashing with goals of economic liberalization. As well, there will
be a conflict between providing basic services free of charge, such as water,
and advocating more user pricing at the local level, which is a commonly
identified policy objective in developing countries.

Proactive Poverty Programs

It is increasingly recognized that providing current assistance to the poor is
not a permanent solution to the poverty problem. There must also be in
place programs that improve the ability of persons to participate meaningfully in social and economic life. Part of this is achieved by universal
education systems and by basic health care. The provision of nutrition also
improves the capabilities of households for active lives. But many countries engage in more proactive programs.

Some programs involve improving the labor market skills of persons.
This may be through training both on and off the job. Individuals may
have the opportunity to participate in work programs. For example, there
may be public works jobs offered by the public sector. The payment for
such jobs may even be in-kind for similar reasons as discussed previously.
These jobs at least provide work experience that might help in forming
more permanent attachments to the labor force. Public works programs
have succeeded in some middle- and low-income groups in such countries
as Argentina, South Africa, and India (World Bank, 2005b). India now
offers guaranteed employment for adult unskilled manual workers. The
National Rural Employment Guarantee Act of September 2005 ensures
registered workers a minimum of 100 days of employment in a financial
year (Alok, 2006).

Another type of program might be aimed at job creation through local
entrepreneurship. State law in West Bengal, India, requires urban municipalities to "promote income-generating activities" for poor women
(Mathur, 2006). It is often the case that an obstacle to the setting up of
new firms is shortage of credit. Policies that aim to improve the operations
of credit markets, especially at the microlevel, can be effective ways of
unleashing entrepreneurial skills.

As with all government policies that involve intervention in the market
economy, the provision of public-sector jobs and the encouragement of
microcredit markets runs the risk of subverting market processes themselves. In designing these programs, attention must be paid to the possible
disincentive effects that the programs might have on incentives in the
private sector, as well as within the bureaucracy.

ASSIGNMENT BY LEVEL OF GOVERNMENT

Poverty alleviation is widely held to be of national interest, and that is often reflected in the stated objectives of the national governments themselves. At the same time, there are clear arguments for decentralizing the delivery of poverty alleviation programs, for all of the standard reasons that we have already encountered. To the extent that these programs involve in-kind transfers or public services, they must be delivered by agencies located where the poor are being served. If these agencies are under the control of subnational governments, they can design and orient their programs better to those who are most in need. Lower-level governments know local conditions better, and they should be better able to monitor and control the agencies involved in program delivery. The usual arguments about incentives for cost-effective and innovative delivery in a decentralized setting apply. Locally delivered programs are more likely to be responsive to the concerns of the user groups and to be accountable to the electorate.

The key problem then is the classic one of federalism – how to reconcile the desire to obtain the advantages of decentralization in terms of efficient program delivery and responsiveness to user needs with the desire to meet national objectives in these important redistributive programs. This reconciliation involves both a reasonable assignment of functions between levels of government and the establishment of a system of intergovernmental relations that facilitates the achievement of national objectives. This section deals with the assignment of functions, while the next addresses the issue of intergovernmental relations.

Because many of these services are delivered by local agencies and because needs can vary considerably from one locality to the next, it is not unusual for all three main levels of government – national, state, and local – to be involved. Each of them has a distinct role to play in poverty alleviation programs. In Germany, social welfare expenditures are a shared responsibility. The central government sets the broad outlines of policy (criteria and level of spending), while local governments make the determination of social neediness and disburse grants (Werner, 2006). In the United States, public welfare services involve all three levels of government (Schroeder, 2006). In Brazil, the union, state, and local governments are concurrently responsible for social welfare and combating poverty (Souza, 2005). The concurrent list of the Indian Constitution includes social security, employment and unemployment policy, and labor welfare (Majeed, 2005). In South Africa, the central and provincial governments are both responsible for welfare and housing (Steytler, 2005). In China, social welfare expenditures are assigned to all levels of government. In general, the central government sets national policy while local governments design and implement local programs (Qiao and Shah, 2006).

State Government

Many of the advantages of decentralization can be achieved by making state governments responsible for designing and legislating poverty alleviation programs within their boundaries. States generally have different levels of need for public services because of differences in average income, geography, and culture. Decentralizing provision to them allows them to design the parameters of their programs to suit state circumstances. In Belgium, for example, the language-based communities are responsible for personal matters in which language is considered important, including assistance to individuals (Deschouwer, 2005).

At the same time, there are good reasons for not decentralizing all the way to the local level. For one thing, these programs tend to be relatively large expenditure items that are best financed by general sources of revenues, and states are in a much better position to mobilize own-source revenues for that purpose. And accountability is best served by the responsible government having sufficient financial stake in the program being delivered. For another, the population and geographic size of most localities could have detrimental effects on provision if it were fully decentralized to that level. There is likely to be much more mobility between local jurisdictions than between state jurisdictions, and that would adversely affect program design. Many localities are too small to effectively govern these large complex programs. And the existence of a large number of varied localities would make it difficult to achieve the required degree of uniformity in program design.

In Canada, welfare is a provincial responsibility (Knopff and Sayers, 2005). Municipal expenditures on social services and housing are typically small. The exception is Ontario, where spending responsibilities were reassigned in the 1990s. As a result, almost one-quarter of municipal spending is on social services. Provincial transfers fund half the expenditures; the balance comes from own-source revenues (McMillan, 2006).

Nonetheless, localities do have an important role to play in delivering the programs. That implies that the role of the state is not all-encompassing. The state could be viewed as responsible for legislating the main parameters of the program, for monitoring program achievements, and for managing some of its statewide aspects. Thus, in the case of food and nutritional programs, the state could legislate who is eligible, how much they are eligible for, and the mechanism whereby eligibility is determined. As with everything in fiscal federalism, the key assignment issue is how to assign responsibilities to the state in a way that ensures that a well-designed statewide program is possible, while not detracting from the ability of local governments to fulfill their responsibilities in an independent and accountable way.

States will also have an important role in financing poverty alleviation programs. They will have the revenue sources, both own source and transfers from the center, which can be used to support local government implementation. As well, the use of state-local transfers will provide the state government with the leverage to ensure that localities are abiding by overall program design. As always, the transfer system should be designed to be only as intrusive as is necessary to ensure that local governments can deliver the programs with the state standards in place. Detailed conditions and accountability requirements can detract from the efficiency benefits of decentralization.

Given that different localities will have different needs, the state transfer program will have to be designed to reflect those needs. This is not a simple matter because one presumes that the local governments are better informed about the needs of their own residents than is the state government. The states may have to base their transfers on relatively crude indicators of need, such as poverty measures. Ideally, whatever indicators are used, they should not be ones that can be manipulated by the localities or that give rise to adverse incentives. For example, if actual costs of poverty alleviation programs were used, localities would have an obvious incentive to generate excessive costs. Measures based on local behavior should be avoided.

In Germany, each federal state (*Land*) has a local equalization system. The specific equalization programs differ across states. Each *Land* must redistribute part of its own tax revenues (shared from the center). Other possible sources of funds include grants from the *Länder* equalization scheme or revenues from the motor vehicle tax. Hesse, for example, distributes both conditional and unconditional grants to municipalities, rural districts, and incorporated cities. Unconditional grants are given to localities where the local needs indicator exceeds the calculated financial strength. The needs indicator is based on population as well as the number of pupils and unemployed people (Werner, 2006).

Local Government

Local governments are well suited to delivering poverty alleviation programs in a way that best suits the needs of their communities. This means that details of program provision, such as location of agencies, program management, local construction and maintenance, and local hiring can be in the hands of the local government. Because the state government designs the programs, there is a potential problem of incentives and efficiency at the local level. If all they are doing is administering programs dictated from above with limited local discretion and with reliance on state funds, there will be little incentive for cost-effective delivery or for effective delivery according to local needs. More generally, there will be a deficit of accountability, and making local spending accountable to state governments will do little to help.

Consequently, there must be provisions in place that induce local interest and responsibility – that is, that induce local "ownership" of the programs. Discretion over program delivery and accountability to one's own constituents will help. For this purpose, state transfers should not be excessively conditional. It also helps if the local government has some financial stake in the program so that it has to fund it partly out of own-source revenues. Also, institutional mechanisms for community involvement induce local support, especially by users. NGOs are often found to be helpful in this regard, because they can enlist the support of users and mobilize them to participate. Finally, dividing lines of responsibility between state and local governments must be clear so that local governments can be held properly accountable to their constituents.

In the Nordic countries, virtually all welfare services are the responsibility of local authorities, including social assistance, housing assistance, and disability pensions. Central governments give conditional grants, but local authorities are responsible for determining how services are provided. For example, it is a local decision if the elderly are to be cared for through institutional or home care. Local governments control the hiring and firing of staff, although wages are determined in national negotiations. Sweden and Denmark allow free choice among service providers. Indeed, in Denmark services can be obtained from a municipality other than the one of residence. Nordic municipalities have high own-source tax revenues, which include personal income taxes. Municipalities "piggyback" on the national income tax, choosing an annual flat tax rate to apply to taxable income as assessed for the national levy. In Denmark, centrally mandated local expenditures are funded through conditional specific grants. These mandates include early retirement and social cash benefits. Other forms of central government influence include legislation defining minimum quality standards, as is common in Norway (Lotz, 2006).

In Brazil, community councils are intended to increase local control over resource allocations. Councils have been established for policy areas including employment, welfare services, and poverty alleviation. These councils are often required by federal legislation or multinational organizations when programs are funded (Afonso and Araujo, 2006).

Achieving the correct balance of responsibilities between state and local governments is difficult. Moreover, there are two particular problems that must be addressed. The first is that of the capacity of local governments to carry out their responsibilities. In periods of transition to decentralization, local governments will not have had the experience with delivering important public programs. There will be a need to build their institutional capacity through training, infrastructure and management, and budgeting and accounting processes. This development can be facilitated by making use of expertise from the state government or by enlisting NGOs, but eventually local capacity must be developed.

Second, a danger in any setting in which a local government relies on an upper level for financial support is the possibility of a soft budget constraint. Given that local governments are better informed about their needs, it is possible that they will strategically overspend or misspend in anticipation of being bailed out by the higher-level government. This problem is particularly difficult when important programs are involved: the higher government cannot simply respond by cutting off funds. And it would be self-defeating to preempt this problem by imposing onerous accountability requirements. There is no easy solution to this problem, but taking steps to ensure that local governments have ownership of the programs is important.

As a final note, an alternative to local government provision of poverty alleviation programs is through the creation of special-purpose local bodies, analogous to school boards and hospital boards in other sectors. The difficulty with these special-interest bodies is that it is difficult to make them accountable to the local residents. To do so requires that they have duly elected representatives and have some own-source revenues. These bodies have the potential for diluting the accountability that could be achieved if the local government itself were responsible.

Central Government

As mentioned, there are clearly national objectives involved in poverty alleviation. As such, a case can be made for states' providing reasonably common levels of services. There are two prerequisites for this to occur. First, states must have the capacity to do so, and second, there must be mechanisms in place to ensure that they do in fact provide such services. The role of the central government revolves around these two prerequisites.

Equalizing State Capacities

The central government's role in equalizing the ability of states to provide comparable levels of poverty alleviation services is no different in principle than its general equalization role. Different states will have different revenue-raising abilities. They will also have different needs for poverty alleviation expenditures. If these go uncorrected, they will be unable to provide comparable services at comparable state tax rates and fiscal equity and efficiency will suffer.

Because we have discussed at length the principles of ideal equalization systems, there is no need to repeat them here. In applying the principles to the poverty alleviation context, the main specific issue that arises is the measurement of needs. Tax capacity equalization is part and parcel of a more general equalization scheme. The general principle is to define the characteristics of the group that is entitled to assistance and to estimate a standard cost to be applied to the size of the group in each state. (The group might actually be disaggregated by age, gender, etc.) The cost should be one that is independent of the state's own costs so that incentives are not affected. Note that the costs should be full in the sense that they include a component for capital costs. In a transitional period, there may need to be extraordinary costs associated with building institutional capacity and infrastructure.

In practice, the main problem concerns the ability of the central government to obtain the information required to estimate the needs of different states. As we discussed in connection with state transfers to localities, such estimates are liable to be rather crude. However, it would be a mistake to alleviate this crudeness by appealing to actual expenditures in recipient states because that would introduce adverse incentives.

In Nordic countries, equalization of both tax capacity and expenditure needs is undertaken. In most cases, equalization is based on potential tax revenue, measured as taxable income per person. In Sweden, for example, local tax revenue is calculated using actual income figures from two years previously, which are inflated with a national figure to reach an estimate of current-year revenues. In Norway, however, differences in actual tax revenue are equalized. Expenditure needs are calculated in some detail. Most countries use the age distribution of the population. Other criteria can include the number of children in single-parent households (Denmark, Sweden), the number of rental apartments for the elderly (Denmark), the number of unemployed (Denmark, Norway, Sweden), and heating costs (Sweden). The Nordic equalization systems follow a "Robin Hood" model in which resources for poorer municipalities are collected from richer areas. In theory no central government grants are needed. In practice, some supplementary grants from central governments are given (Lotz, 2006).

Inducing Comparable State Poverty Alleviation Programs

Providing states with the capacity to provide comparable programs is necessary but not sufficient to ensure that they actually will provide them. An important role of the central government is to induce that to occur. Of course, it is possible that the states could agree among themselves to provide common standards, but such agreements are difficult to consummate and enforce, given that they require unanimous consent. As a practical matter, there seems no alternative to central government intervention.

There are two main ways the central government could induce states to provide comparable standards. One is to legislate mandates that govern state behavior. In Norway, for example, the central Ministry of Social Affairs and the local government association have a binding agreement on the quality of care for the elderly; the central government has also established minimum standards for housing the homeless (Lotz, 2006). Such mandates would ideally be accompanied by the funding sufficient to abide by the mandates. For example, central governments in the Nordic countries are required to compensate localities for costs imposed by new regulations or legislation at the central level (Lotz, 2006). While mandates are a powerful tool, they are also problematic. Because they are coercive, they can detract from the objectives of decentralization and from state ownership of poverty alleviation programs. Moreover, their enforcement can be problematic. What if the states do not abide by the mandate? What recourse does the central government have? Presumably, the main recourse is through the restriction of transfers to the states. However, this resort makes the use of mandates basically analogous in effect to the second main remedy, which is the use of conditional transfers, what we have referred to as the spending power.

The spending power involves imposing conditions on transfers to the states that, if not satisfied, lead to reductions in transfers. The conditions need not be detailed. They can, and should, be fairly general conditions that lay out the minimum parameters of the programs that are necessary in order that national objectives be achieved. If the conditions are too detailed or too onerous, the ability of the states to exercise discretion is compromised, and the benefits of decentralization put in jeopardy.

Enforcement of the spending power conditions raises some important issues as well. First, if the conditions are stringent and enforcement is tough, there is a danger that the objectives of the program will not be achieved. Thus, if a state is subject to financial penalties for not meeting the conditions of transfers for poverty alleviation, the penalties themselves can make it worse for the poor. This possibility emphasizes again the importance of achieving government ownership of the programs at all levels. There is also the problem of determining when exactly a state is in violation of the conditions. Ultimately, the central government imposes the penalty, so it must agree on when violations have occurred. But clearly the states may disagree with the judgment of the central government, especially because the conditions may be quite general so judgment is necessarily involved. In these circumstances, it is important that there be some means of consultation between the central government and the states about dispute settlement, even if the central government is ultimately the enforcer. Indeed, such consultation could also apply over the setting of the conditions themselves.

National Standards

What kind of national standards might be appropriate in the context of poverty alleviation? This is a difficult issue, given that there will be a general shortage of funds to address the needs of all the poor. National standards might be defined at two levels – the general and the specific.

First, states might be expected to satisfy a set of general principles to be eligible for central funding of poverty programs. Eligibility criteria should be set out clearly. State programs might be required to be equally accessible to all those who satisfy the stated criteria for eligibility. There might be a requirement that benefits be portable in the event of changes in residence and that there be no residence requirements imposed on potential recipients. Special attention might be paid to particular groups of poor, such as children, minority groups, and disadvantaged social groups. In the United States, for example, federal statutes govern most public welfare programs and define the individuals and families who are entitled to receive benefits. State and local governments are responsible for administering the programs and bear part of the costs. The local government share of funding varies from zero to more than 20 percent of program costs (in the four states of California, New York, Virginia, and Wisconsin) (Schroeder, 2006).

Second, more specific stipulations might be imposed on the states, including the minimum level of benefits provided under funded programs and detailed eligibility criteria. The nature of poverty alleviation programs, such as the type of in-kind transfer or the method of distribution; regulations concerning user charges; and the role of the public sector and other potential providers might be stated. Denmark, Norway, and Sweden, for example, have legislated maximum fees for both child care and care of the elderly (Lotz, 2006).

In setting out these standards, attention must be paid to both the pros and cons of central conditions. The conditions should be clear and explicit enough to ensure that national poverty reduction goals are being addressed and that state performance expectations are clear. This is important to ensure accountability, as well as to minimize the frequency of disputes between the central government and the states. At the same time, the conditions must not be so extensive and intrusive that they interfere with the ability of states to exercise discretion in ways that will improve the efficiency of program delivery and the success of outcomes, which, as we have stressed, is the central concern of federal systems of government.

COORDINATION WITH OTHER PUBLIC PROGRAMS

Poverty reduction programs are complicated and multifaceted programs. Their administrative requirements entail a diversity of skills and touch on many aspects of the lives of recipients. The various elements of the programs overlap with those of other public services, or perhaps more to the point, other public services contribute to poverty alleviation. Thus, basic education and literacy skills might be seen as the most effective long-run means for uplifting persons and households out of poverty. Primary health care goes hand in hand with food aid and nutritional programs. The same group of poor persons will be the target of all of these programs. This enhances the importance of proper targeting and of encouraging take-up. As well, it underscores the importance of a coordinated approach among agencies delivering these various services. The highly successful Mexican program Oportunidades (originally PROGRESA) involved careful design and evaluation. Cash transfers were provided directly to mothers, if certain conditions were met. Children had to remain in school, household members had to receive medical checkups, and mothers had to attend nutrition and hygiene information sessions. The program recognized the links between education, health, and nutrition in addressing poverty. Administratively, the program is highly centralized. One woman, chosen by households within the community, acted as an intermediary between program officials and recipients (World Bank, 2003).

Decentralization of the delivery of poverty alleviation programs poses a challenge for this coordination effort. The benefits of efficiency of delivery are achieved by giving local agencies the responsibility for delivering individual programs. They are not in the best position to coordinate with other agencies in other program areas. At the same time, facilitating the information flow among agencies can be important if given individuals obtain the services of different agencies, either at the same time or sequentially. Setting up management information systems to achieve this flow of information might best be viewed as a function of the state-level government. More generally, they might also assume the responsibility for coordinating policies and activities. In India, a coordinating role has been played by the union government. The Central Family Welfare Council was a subject-specific council established to explore issues of interest to multiple jurisdictions and to make recommendations for coordinating actions (Majeed, 2005).

The task of coordination becomes even more complicated when services are contracted out to nongovernment providers, such as NGOs or private firms. Because these are independent institutions whose employees are not directly accountable to government, it is not as easy to integrate them into the information web.

PART FOUR

CHALLENGES AND RESPONSES

Part IV addresses several potential drawbacks to fiscal federalism: macro-economic instability, a race toward the bottom, widening regional disparities, and a higher incidence of bribery and corruption. These claims are scrutinized by having recourse to available conceptual guidance and empirical evidence. In addition, the part also addresses newer challenges to fiscal federalism arising from globalization and the information revolution.

In a flat (globalized) world, "nation-states are too small to tackle large things in life and too large to address small things" (Bell 1987: 13–14). But federal fiscal systems to accommodate either "coming together" or "holding together" pose a threat to macroeconomic stability according to some writers, who argue that decentralized governance structure is incompatible with prudent fiscal management and even regional fiscal equity. Chapter 14 investigates the conceptual and empirical bases of these arguments. More specifically, the chapter questions whether risks of macroeconomic mismanagement and instability are greater with decentralized fiscal systems and assesses macroeconomic management in federal versus unitary countries.

The strengths and weaknesses of fiscal and monetary policy institutions under alternate fiscal regimes are examined, drawing upon neo-institutional economics perspectives on fiscal institutions. A neo-institutional economics perspective aims to reduce transactions costs for citizens (principals) in inducing compliance with their mandates by various orders of governments (agents). A fiscal system that creates countervailing institutions to limit the opportunistic behavior of various agents and empowers principals to take corrective action is expected to result in superior fiscal outcomes. In the context of this chapter, the relevant question, then, is what type of fiscal system (centralized or decentralized) offers greater potential for contract enforcement or rules or restraints to discourage imprudent fiscal management. Contrary to a common misconception, decentralized fiscal systems offer a greater potential for improved macroeconomic governance and regional fiscal equity than centralized fiscal systems Fiscal decentralization is associated with improved fiscal performance and better functioning of internal common markets. This is to be expected, as decentralized fiscal systems require greater clarity in the roles of various players (centers of decision making), transparency in the rules, and greater care in design of institutions that govern their interactions to ensure fair play and to limit opportunities for rent seeking.

Competition among governments at the same level or with similar responsibilities is commonly referred to as *horizontal competition* or interjurisdictional competition in the literature on economics and political science. A related concept of intergovernmental or *vertical competition* refers to competition among governments with different levels and types of responsibilities – for example, among federal, state, and local governments. Chapter 15 is concerned with the interjurisdictional competition (interregional or local-local competition) alone and its implications for the federal government's role in securing an economic union or an internal common market. Competition among state and local governments is quite commonplace in most federal systems. This chapter examines the pros and cons of interjurisdictional competition in a federal system and examines the ways the federal government can play a supporting role to accentuate the positive aspects of this competition while dealing with any negative fallout of unbridled competition. The chapter also evaluates alternate federal policies to deal with regional disparities. The chapter concludes that a paternalist or do-good approach to deal with regional inequities may do more harm than good, while a partnership or do-no-harm approach offers the best policy alternative in regional integration and internal cohesion within federal nations. The question is not whether to compete or to cooperate but how to make sure that all parties compete but do not cheat.

As noted earlier, the world has witnessed a trend toward decentralized governance during the past two decades. This trend is a current source of concern among academic and policy circles worried that localization may adversely affect the quality of public governance through an increase in the incidence of corruption. Chapter 16 examines the conceptual and empirical basis of these concerns by providing analytical perspectives on corruption and its role under decentralized governance. These concerns are evaluated both conceptually and by resorting to available empirical evidence on this subject. The chapter concludes that localization as a means to make government responsive and accountable to people can help reduce corruption and improve service delivery. However, one must pay attention to the institutional environment and the risk of local capture by elites. Localization in the absence of rule of law may not prove to be a potent remedy for combating corruption.

Chapter 17 reflects on the governance implications of globalization and the information revolution and draws implications for the divisions of power in multicentered governance. The chapter states that as a result of globalization and the information revolution, nation-states are fast losing control over some of their traditional areas, such as macroeconomic policy, regulation of external trade, telecommunications, and financial transactions. With the information revolution, governments are experiencing diminished control over the flow of goods and services, ideas, and cultural products. These changes are also strengthening localization which is leading simultaneously to citizen empowerment and the strengthening of local elites. This chapter notes the growing importance of supranational regimes and local governments, the emerging leadership role of national government in social policy, and the diminishing economic relevance yet growing political clout of intermediate orders (states or provinces) in multiorder governance. It highlights emerging conflicts from these shifting divisions of economic powers and local responses to resolve these conflicts. The chapter predicts that local governments and "beyond-government" entities at the local level will assume a pivotal role in improving economic and social outcomes for their residents.

FOURTEEN

Fiscal Federalism and Macroeconomic Governance

Large and growing numbers of countries around the globe are reexamining the roles of various orders of government and their partnerships with the private sector and the civil society with a view to creating governments that work and serve their people (see Shah, 1998c, and Shah and Thompson, 2004, for motivations for a change). This rethinking has led to a resurgence of interest in fiscal federalism principles and practices, because federal systems are seen to provide safeguards against the threat of both centralized exploitation and decentralized opportunistic behavior, while bringing decision making closer to the people. In fact, federalism represents either the "coming together" or "holding together" of constituent geographic units to take advantage of the greatness and littleness of nations, because in a flat (globalized) world nation-states are observed to be "too small to tackle large things in life and too large to address small things" (Bell, 1987: 13–14). However, federal fiscal systems to accommodate "coming together" or "holding together," according to some influential writers, pose a threat to macroeconomic stability. They argue that decentralized governance structure is incompatible with prudent fiscal management and even regional fiscal equity (see, e.g., Prud'homme, 1995; Tanzi, 1996). This chapter investigates the conceptual and empirical bases of these arguments. More specifically, the chapter addresses the following questions:

- Are there greater risks of macroeconomic mismanagement and instability with decentralized fiscal systems (federal vs. unitary countries)?
- What has been the experience to-date in macroeconomic management in federal versus unitary countries? Or what has been the impact of decentralization on fiscal discipline and macroeconomic stability?

To address these questions, the chapter takes a simple institutional-cum-econometric analysis perspective. The strengths and weaknesses of fiscal and monetary policy institutions under alternate fiscal regimes are examined by drawing upon neo-institutional economics perspectives on fiscal institutions (see von Hagen, 2002, 2005, and von Hagen, Hallet, and Strauch, 2002). This perspective aims to reduce transactions costs for citizens (principals) in inducing compliance with their mandates by various orders of governments (agents). A fiscal system that creates countervailing institutions to limit the opportunistic behavior of various agents and empowers principals to take corrective action is expected to result in superior fiscal outcomes. In the context of this chapter, a relevant question then is what type of fiscal system (centralized or decentralized) offers greater potential for contract enforcement or rules or restraints to discourage imprudent fiscal management. To draw some general lessons of public policy interest, a qualitative review of institutional arrangements for monetary and fiscal policy in federal and unitary countries is supplemented by two country case studies and a broader review of available empirical evidence relating to fiscal outcomes under alternate fiscal systems.

Contrary to a common misconception, the chapter concludes that decentralized fiscal systems offer a greater potential for improved macroeconomic governance and regional fiscal equity than centralized fiscal systems .While empirical evidence on these questions is weak, nevertheless it further supports the conclusion that fiscal decentralization is associated with improved fiscal performance and better functioning of internal common markets. This is to be expected as decentralized fiscal systems require greater clarity in the roles of various players (centers of decision making), transparency in the rules, and greater care in design of institutions that govern their interactions to ensure fair play and limiting opportunities for rent seeking. The rest of the chapter discusses the institutional environment for macroeconomic management, which is elaborated separately for monetary and fiscal policies; reviews internal common market and economic union considerations; and draws some general and institutional lessons for enhancing the quality of macroeconomic governance.

INSTITUTIONAL ENVIRONMENT FOR MACROECONOMIC MANAGEMENT

Using Musgrave's trilogy of public functions – namely, allocation, redistribution, and stabilization – the fiscal federalism literature has traditionally reached a broad consensus that while the first function can be assigned to lower levels of government, the latter two functions are more appropriate for assignment to the national government. Thus, macroeconomic management – especially stabilization policy – was seen as clearly a central function (see, e.g., Musgrave, 1983; Oates, 1972). The stabilization function was considered inappropriate for subnational assignment because (1) raising debt at the local level would entail higher regional costs but benefits for such stabilization would spill beyond regional borders, and as a result too little stabilization would be provided; (2) monetization of local debt will create inflationary pressures and pose a threat for price stability; (3) currency stability requires that both monetary and fiscal policy functions be carried out by the center alone; and (4) cyclical shocks are usually national in scope (symmetric across all regions) and therefore require a national response. These views have been challenged by several writers (see, e.g., Scott, 1964; Dafflon, 1977; Sheikh and Winer, 1977; Gramlich, 1987: Walsh, 1992; Biehl, 1994; Mihaljek, 1995; Sewell, 1996; Huther and Shah, 1998; Shah, 1999b, 2006b) on theoretical and empirical grounds, yet they continue to command considerable following. An implication that is often drawn is that decentralization of the public sector, especially in developing countries, poses significant risks for the "aggravation of macroeconomic problems" (Tanzi, 1996: 305).

To form a perspective on this issue, we reflect on the theoretical and empirical underpinnings of the institutional framework required for monetary and fiscal policies.

Institutional Setting for Monetary Policy

Monetary policy is concerned with control over the level and rate of change of nominal variables such as the price level, monetary aggregates, exchange rate, and nominal GDP. Because the control over these nominal variables to provide for a stable macroeconomic environment is commonly agreed to be a primary function, monetary policy is centralized in all nation-states, federal and unitary alike. Nevertheless, there are occasional arguments to add a regional dimension to the design and implementation of monetary policies. For example, Mundell (1968) argues that an optimal currency area may be smaller than the nation-state in some federations, such as Canada and the United States, and under such circumstances the differential impact of exchange rate policies may be inconsistent with the constitutional requirement of fair treatment of regions. Further complications arise when the federal government raises debt domestically, but provincial governments borrow from abroad: this is the case in Canada, as federal exchange rate policies affect provincial debt servicing. Similarly, Buchanan (1997) argues against the establishment of a confederal central bank such as the European Union Central Bank as it negates the spirit of competitive federalism.

In a centralized monetary policy environment, Barro (1996) has cautioned that a stable macroeconomic environment may not be achievable without a strong commitment to price stability by the monetary authority: if people anticipate growth in money supply to counteract a recession, the lack of such response will deepen recession. The credibility of a strong commitment to price stability can be established by consistently adhering to formal rules such as a fixed exchange rate or to monetary rules. Argentina's 1991 Convertibility Law establishing parity in the value of the peso in terms of the U.S. dollar, and Brazil's 1994 Real Plan helped achieve a measure of this level of credibility. Argentine's central bank strengthened credibility of this commitment by enduring a severe contraction in the monetary base during the period December 1994 to March 1995 as speculative reactions to the Mexican crisis resulted in a decline in its foreign exchange reserves.

Alternately, guaranteeing independence from all levels of the government, for a central bank whose principal mission is price stability could establish the credibility of such a commitment (Barro, 1996; Shah, 1998c: 11). Barro considers the focus on price stability so vital that he regards an ideal central banker as one who is not necessarily a good macroeconomist but one whose commitment to price stability is unshakable: "The ideal central banker should always appear somber in public, never tell any jokes, and complain continually about the dangers of inflation" (1996: 58). Empirical studies show that the three most independent central banks (the National Bank of Switzerland – the Swiss Central Bank, Bundesbank of Germany, and the U.S. Federal Reserve Board) over the period 1955 to 1988 had average inflation rates of 4.4 percent compared to 7.8 percent for the three least independent banks (New Zealand until 1989, Spain, and Italy). The inflation rate in the former countries further showed lower volatility. The same studies also show that the degree of central bank independence is unrelated to the average rate of growth and average rate of unemployment. Thus, Barro (1996: 57) argues that a "more independent central bank appears to be all gain and no pain." The European Union has recognized this principle by establishing an independent European Central Bank.

The critical question then is whether independence of the central bank is compromised under a decentralized fiscal system. One would expect, a priori, that the central bank would have greater stakes in and independence under a decentralized system because such a system would require clarification of the rules under which a central bank operates, especially its functions and its relationships with various governments. For example, when Brazil in 1988 introduced a decentralized federal constitution, it significantly enhanced the independence of the central bank (Shah, 1991; Bomfim and Shah, 1994). Yet, independence of the central bank in Brazil remains relatively weak compared to other federal countries (see Huther and Shah, 1998). On the other hand, in centralized countries the role of the central bank is typically shaped and influenced by the Ministry of Finance. In one extreme case, the functions of the central bank of the United Kingdom (a unitary state), the Bank of England, are not defined by law but have developed over time by a tradition fostered by the U.K. Treasury. Only in May 1997 did the newly elected Labour Party government of Prime Minister Tony Blair assure the Bank of England a free hand in its pursuit of price stability. Such independence may still on occasions be compromised as the chancellor of the exchequer still retains a presence on the board of directors as a voting member.

New Zealand and France (unitary states) have lately recognized the importance of central bank independence for price stability and have granted independence to their central banks. The 1989 Reserve Bank Act of New Zealand mandates price stability as the only function of the central bank and expressly prohibits the government from involvement in monetary policy. The People's Bank of China, on the other hand, does not enjoy such independence and often works as a development bank or as an agency for the central government's "policy lending" and, in the process, undermines its role of ensuring price stability (see World Bank, 1995, and Ma, 1995). For monetary policy, it has the authority only to implement the policies authorized by the State Council. The Law of the People's Bank of China, 1995, article 7, states that that its role is simply to "implement monetary policies under the leadership of the State Council" (see Chung and Tongzon, 2004).

For a systematic examination of this question, Huther and Shah (1998) relate the evidence presented in Cukierman, Neyapti, and Webb (1992) on central bank independence for eighty countries to indices of fiscal decentralization for the same countries. Cukierman et al. assess independence of a central bank on the basis of an examination of sixteen statutory aspects of central bank operations, including the terms of office for the chief executive officer, the formal structure of policy formulation, the bank's objectives as stated in its charter, and limitations on lending to the government. Huther and Shah (1998) find a weak but positive association between fiscal decentralization and central bank independence, confirming our a priori judgment that central bank independence is strengthened under decentralized systems. A recent study by Shah (2005b, 2006b) uses a cross section of forty countries for the period 1995–2000 and provides econometric analysis of the impact of fiscal decentralization on central bank independence. The results confirm positive impact of fiscal decentralization and federalism on central bank independence.

Increases in the monetary base caused by the central bank's bailout of failing state and nonstate banks represent occasionally an important source of monetary instability and a significant obstacle to macroeconomic management. In Pakistan, a centralized federation, both the central and provincial governments have, in the past, raided nationalized banks. In Brazil, a decentralized federation, state banks made loans in the past to their own governments without due regard for their profitability and risks, causing the so-called $100 billion state debt crisis in 1995. Brazil, nevertheless later dealt with this issue head on with successful privatization of state-owned banks in the late 1990s and through prohibition of government borrowing from state banks or from the central bank (Levy, 2005). Thus, a central bank's role in ensuring arm's-length transactions between governments and the banking sector would enhance monetary stability regardless of the degree of decentralization of the fiscal system.

Available empirical evidence suggests that such arm's-length transactions are more difficult to achieve in countries with a centralized structure of governance than under a decentralized structure with a larger set of players. This is because a decentralized structure requires greater clarity in the roles of various public players, including the central bank. No wonder one finds that the four central banks most widely acknowledged to be independent (Swiss Central Bank, Bundesbank of Germany, Central Bank of Austria, and the U.S. Federal Reserve Board have all been the products of highly decentralized federal fiscal structures. It is interesting to note that the independence of the Bundesbank is not assured by the German constitution. The Bundesbank Law providing such independence also stipulates that the central bank has an obligation to support the economic policy of the federal government. In practice, the Bundesbank has primarily sought to establish its independence by focusing on price stability issues, as was demonstrated in the 1990s by its decision to raise interest rates to finance German unification in spite of the adverse impacts on federal debt obligations (see also Biehl, 1994).

The Swiss Federal Constitution (article 39) assigns monetary policy to the federal government. The federal government has, however, delegated the conduct of monetary policy to the Swiss National Bank, a private limited company regulated by a special law. The National Bank Act of 1953 has granted independence in the conduct of monetary policy to the Swiss National Bank although the bank is required to conduct its policy in the general interest of the country. It is interesting to note that the Swiss National Bank allocates a portion of its profits to cantons to infuse a sense of regional ownership and participation in the conduct of monetary policy (see Gygi, 1991).

Shah (2005b, 2006b) also examined empirically some additional questions on the impact of fiscal decentralization on monetary stability, including growth of money supply, control of inflation, and inflation and macroeconomic balances. The study concludes that growth of money supply is primarily determined by a central bank's independence and fiscal decentralization has an insignificant positive impact. Similarly, fiscal decentralization has a positive but insignificant impact on price inflation. Finally, the impact of fiscal decentralization on inflation and macroeconomic balances was found to be insignificant.

Monetary Management in Brazil: A Decade of Successful Reforms

Brazil had a long history of state ownership of the banking system and imprudent borrowing by governments from their own banks and subsequent bailouts. This tradition undermined fiscal discipline and macroeconomic stability. More recently, the federal system has been able to come to grips with these issues. To this end, Brazil has given substantial independence to the Central Bank of Brazil and also adopted a variety of institutions to promote arm's-length transactions among governments and the financial institutions. In August 1996 the federal government launched the Program to Reduce State Involvement with Banking Activities (PROES) that offered state governments either support in financing the costs of preparing state banks for privatization, liquidation, or restructuring of state banks, some of which were converted to development agencies, or the voluntary alternative to delegate the control of the overall process of reform to the federal government (Beck, Crivelli, and Summerhill, 2003). Government efforts have successfully led to a reduction in the number of state-owned banks; among some of the ones privatized are former state banks of Rio de Janeiro (BANERJ) in June 1997, Minas Gerias (BEMGE) in September 1998, Pernambuco (BANDEPE) in November 1998, Bahia (BANEB) in June 1999, Paraná (BANESTADO) in October 2000, São Paulo (BANESPA) in November 2000, Paraíba (PARAIBAN) in November 2001, Goiás (BEG) in December 2001, and Amazonas (BEA) in January 2002.

More recently, the Law of Fiscal Responsibility (LRF) enacted in 2000 prohibits government borrowing from own banks or the central bank. It requires that all new government borrowing receive the technical approval of the Central Bank of Brazil and the approval of the Senate. Borrowing operations are prohibited during a period of 180 days before the end of incumbents' government mandate (Afonso and de Mello, 2000). For capital markets, the LRF declares that financing operations in violation of debt ceilings would not be legally valid and amounts borrowed should be repaid fully without interest. Unpaid interests because of nullification constitute a loss to the lender.

Overall, Brazil has achieved monetary discipline since 1997 and sustained price stability since 1995.

Monetary Management in China: Still Muddling Through

China's unitary character is strongly reinforced through its one-party system. China until the early 1980s had an unsophisticated banking system comprised of the People's Bank of China (PBC), along with a few specialized banks such as the People's Construction Bank – an arm of the Ministry of Finance. The central budget and the banking system provided the working capital needed by enterprises and cash used principally to cover labor costs and purchases of agricultural products. The role of the banking system was limited, because most investments in fixed assets in enterprises were financed by direct transfers or grants from the government budget. In 1983, in a major reform, direct grants were replaced with interest?bearing loans to production enterprises. Consequently, the banking system gradually became the primary channel through which investments were financed and the central authority exercised macroeconomic control. In 1984 the PBC was transformed into the Central Bank of China under the State Council and its commercial banking operations were transferred to the Industrial and Commercial Bank of China. A network of provincial branches came to serve as the relays for the central bank's monetary operations. At the same time, other specialized banks and non-bank financial institutions and numerous local branches also emerged. The banks and the central bank established municipal, county, and sometimes township-level branches. The pressure on the central bank to lend originated in investment demand from state-owned enterprises (SOEs).

These developments have made possible a decentralization of enterprise financing, but they have also created a wider financial arena for the scramble after resources and have greatly complicated the management of monetary policy from the center. Under the deconcentrated system, provincial and local authorities have substantial powers in investment decision making and exert great influence on local bank branches' credit expansion. Although provinces are given certain credit ceilings at the beginning of the year, the central bank is often forced to revise the annual credit plans under pressure from localities. Local branches of the central bank were given discretionary authority over 30 percent of central bank's annual lending to the financial sector (see World Bank, 1997: 7.23). Provincial and local governments used this discretionary authority of central bank branches to their advantage by borrowing at will, thereby endangering price stability. According to Qian and Wu (2000), 70 percent of the central bank's loans to state banks were channeled through the central bank's regional branches. Consequently, two-digit inflation occurred in 1988 and 1989 and was followed by a credit squeeze. Monetary (inflation) cycles appeared to be more frequent than during the prereform era and caused significant resource waste. Two-digit inflation reoccurred in 1993, 1994, and 1995, as 1992's credit ceilings were again exceeded by a surprisingly high margin. Given these effects, some studies have identified monetary deconcentration during this period as a mistake (Qian, 2000).[1] As a response, the "Central Bank Law" of 1995 recentralized monetary policy by reassigning supervisory power of the central bank's regional branches uniquely to Central Bank Headquarters. The Chinese monetary authorities have taken steps to promote arm's-length transactions in the banking system, albeit with limited success. They promoted arm's-length transactions in the government-owned banking sector by reducing provincial government influence on the PBC's regional branches (now reorganized into nine regions as opposed to an earlier configuration of thirty-one provincial jurisdictions); limiting subnational influences on state-owned banks, although the SOE's borrowing from these banks could not be restrained and nonperforming portfolio of these banks grew in size; and liberalizing interest rates to encourage market discipline.

These policies have not been very successful. Although state commercial banks are not under the control of local governments and have the authority to decide how to allocate their loans, state banks receive strong pressures from the central government either to fund directly SOEs that could not cover wage payments (Cull and Xu, 2003) or to purchase bonds issued by policy banks (Yusuf, 1997). State banks are willing to comply with these

[1] According to Ma (1995), because of current monetary and fiscal institutions, local government incentives are not aligned with those of the central level. Therefore, significant decentralization reforms in 1989 and 1993 were immediately followed by inflation, forcing the central government back to centralization.

demands on the expectation of a bailout by the central government in case of default. In this vein, Cull and Xu (2003) present empirical evidence that the link between bank loans and profitability weakened in the 1990s, while Shirai (2002) finds empirically that commercial banks' investments in government bonds are associated with lower levels of profitability. Results from both of the aforementioned studies buttress the notion that Chinese reforms have not been successful in promoting arm's-length transactions in the banking system, which is riddled with lending operations of a bail-out-type nature. The central government's use of the banking system to finance subnational governments and SOEs had deleterious effects on price stability governance of the financial sector.

Institutional Setting for Fiscal Policy

In a unitary country, the central government assumes exclusive responsibility for fiscal policy. In federal countries, fiscal policy becomes a responsibility shared by all levels of government, and the federal government uses its spending power (i.e., powers of the purse, or fiscal transfers) and moral suasion through joint meetings to induce a coordinated approach to fiscal policy. The allocation of responsibilities under a federal system also pays some attention to the conduct of stabilization policies, often by assigning stable and cyclically less sensitive revenue sources and expenditure responsibilities to subnational governments. Such an assignment attempts to insulate local governments from economic cycles, and the national government assumes prominence in the conduct of a stabilization policy. In large federal countries, such insulation is usually possible only for the lowest tier of government because the intermediate tier (states and provinces) shares responsibilities with the federal government in providing cyclically sensitive services such as social assistance. These intermediate-tier governments are allowed access to cyclically sensitive revenue bases that act as built-in (automatic) stabilizers.

Fiscal Federalism as a Bane for Fiscal Prudence

Several writers (Tanzi, 1996; Wonnacott, 1972) have argued, without empirical corroboration, that the financing of subnational governments is likely to be a source of concern within open federal systems because subnational governments may circumvent federal fiscal policy objectives. Tanzi (1995) is also concerned with deficit creation and debt management policies of junior governments. Recent studies highlight institutional weaknesses in federal constitutions that may work against coordination of fiscal policies in a federal economy (Weingast, 1995; Seabright, 1996; Saiegh and Tommasi, 2000; Iaryczower, Saiegh, and Tommasi, 2001). These studies note that the institutional framework defining a federal governance structure is usually composed of a body of incomplete contracts.[2] In the presence of undefined or vague property rights over taxing and spending jurisdictions among layers of government, suboptimal policies would emerge because these would represent not an evolution from sound economic principles but the outcome of the intergovernmental bargaining process. They argue that the federal bargaining process is subject to the common property resource problem as well as the "norm of universalism" or "pork-barrel politics," both of which lead to overgrazing. For example, Jones, Sanguinetti, and Tommasi (1998) assert that the problem of universalism manifests itself in Argentina at two levels – first, among provinces lobbying for federal resources and, second, among local governments for greater stakes of the each provincial pool of resources.

Fiscal Federalism as a Boon to Fiscal Prudence

Available theoretical and empirical work does not provide support for the validity of these concerns. On the first point, at the theoretical level, Sheikh and Winer (1977) demonstrate that relatively extreme and unrealistic assumptions about discretionary noncooperation by junior jurisdictions are needed to conclude that stabilization by the central authorities would not work simply because of a lack of cooperation. These untenable assumptions include regionally symmetric shocks, a closed economy, segmented capital markets, lack of supply side effects of local fiscal policy, nonavailability of built-in stabilizers in the tax-transfer systems of subnational governments and in interregional trade, constraints on the use of federal spending power (such as conditional grants intended to influence subnational behavior), unconstrained and undisciplined local borrowing, and extremely noncooperative collusive behavior by subnational governments (see also Gramlich, 1987; Mundell, 1963; and Spahn, 1997). The empirical simulations of Sheikh and Winer for Canada further suggest that failure of federal fiscal policy in most instances cannot be attributed to noncooperative behavior by junior governments. Saknini, James, and Sheikh (1996) further demonstrate that, in a decentralized federation

---

[2] Incompleteness of these contracts arises as unforeseen issues come to the policy agenda. Several of these issues could not possibly be contemplated at the original contract – constitution – or if covered, not fully addressed because of the ever-increasing complexity in public management over time, or because of the prohibitively high costs that designing policy for an immensely large number of future possible scenarios would entail.

having markedly differentiated subnational economies with incomplete markets and nontraded goods, federal fiscal policy acts as insurance against region-specific risks, and therefore decentralized fiscal structures do not compromise any of the goals sought under a centralized fiscal policy (see also Centre for Economic Policy Research, 1993).

Gramlich (1987) points out that in open economies, exposure to international competition would benefit some regions at the expense of others. The resulting asymmetric shocks, he argues, can be more effectively dealt with by regional stabilization policies in view of the better information and instruments that are available at the regional or local levels. An example supporting Gramlich's view would be the effect of oil price shocks on oil-producing regions. For example, the province of Alberta in Canada dealt with such a shock effectively by siphoning off 30 percent of oil revenues received during boom years to the Alberta Heritage Trust Fund, a "rainy day umbrella" or a stabilization fund. This fund was later used when the price of oil fell. The Colombia Oil Revenue Stabilization Fund follows the same tradition.

This conclusion, however, must be qualified by the fact that errant fiscal behavior by powerful members of a federation can have an important constraining influence on the conduct of federal macroeconomic policies. For example, achievement of the Bank of Canada's goal of price stability was made more difficult by the inflationary pressures arising from the province of Ontario's increases in social spending during the boom years of late 1980s. Such difficulties stress the need for fiscal policy coordination under a decentralized federal system.

On the potential for fiscal mismanagement with decentralization, as noted previously by Tanzi, empirical evidence from a number of countries suggests that, while national, central, or federal fiscal policies typically do not adhere to the European Union (EU) guidelines that deficits should not exceed 3 percent of GDP and debt should not exceed 60 percent of GDP, junior governments' policies typically do, in both decentralized federal countries such as Brazil and Canada and centralized federal countries such as Australia and India. Centralized unitary countries do even worse on the basis of these indicators. For example, Greece, Turkey, and Portugal and a large number of developing countries do not satisfy the EU guidelines. National governments also typically do not adhere to EU requirements that the central banks should not act as a lender of last resort.

The failure of collective action in forcing fiscal discipline at the national level arises from the "tragedy of commons" or "norm of universalism" or "pork-barrel politics." But these problems are not unique to a federal system. In their attempts to avoid a deadlock, legislators, in both federal and unitary countries, trade votes and support each other's projects by implicitly agreeing that "I'll favor your best project if you favor mine" (Inman and Rubinfeld, 1992: 13). Such a behavior leads to overspending and higher debt overhang at the national level. It also leads to regionally differentiated bases for federal corporate income taxation and thereby loss of federal revenues through these tax expenditures. Such tax expenditures accentuate fiscal deficits at the national level. In the first 140 years of U.S. history, the negative impact of "universalism" was kept to a minimum by two fiscal rules: the Constitution formally constrained federal spending power to narrowly defined areas and an informal rule was followed to the effect that the federal government could borrow only to fight recession or wars (Niskanen, 1992). The Great Depression and the New Deal led to an abandonment of these fiscal rules. Inman and Fitts (1990) provide empirical evidence supporting the working of "universalism" in post–New Deal United States. To overcome difficulties noted previously with national fiscal policy, solutions proposed include "gatekeeper" committees (Weingast and Marshall, 1988; Eichengreen, Hausman, and von Hagen, 1999), imposing party discipline within legislatures (Cremer, 1986), constitutionally imposed or legislated fiscal rules (Niskanen, 1992; Poterba and von Hagen, 1999; Braun and Tommasi, 2002; Kennedy and Robins, 2001; Kopits, 2004), executive agenda setting (Ingberman and Yao, 1991), market discipline (Lane, 1993), and decentralizing when potential inefficiencies of national government democratic choice outweigh economic gains with centralization. Observing a similar situation in Latin American countries prompted Eichengreen et al. (1999) to propose establishment of an independent "gatekeeper" in the form of a national fiscal council to periodically set maximum allowable increases in general government debt. Although federal and unitary countries alike face these problems, federal countries have demonstrated greater adaptation in limiting the discretionary and unwelcome outcomes of political markets by trying on the solutions proposed previously. It is also interesting to note that fiscal stabilization failed under a centralized structure in Brazil but achieved major successes in this arena later under a decentralized fiscal system. Shah (2005) provides further confirmation of these observations. His results show that debt management discipline (country ratings by the World Bank staff) had a positive but insignificant association with the degree of fiscal decentralization for a sample of twenty-four countries.

Given that the potential exists for errant fiscal behavior of national and subnational governments to complicate the conduct of fiscal policy, what institutional arrangements are necessary to safeguard against such an eventuality? As discussed later, mature federations place a great deal of emphasis on both intergovernmental coordination through executive or legislative federalism and fiscal rules to achieve a synergy among policies at different levels. In unitary countries, on the other hand, the emphasis traditionally has been on use of centralization or direct central controls. These controls typically have failed to achieve a coordinated response because of intergovernmental gaming. Moreover, the national government completely escapes any scrutiny except when it seeks international help from external sources such as the International Monetary Fund. But external help creates a moral hazard problem in that it creates bureaucratic incentives on both sides to ensure that such assistance is always in demand and utilized.

Fiscal Policy Coordination in Mature Federations

In mature federations, fiscal policy coordination is exercised through both executive and legislative federalism and formal and informal fiscal rules. In recent years, legislated fiscal rules have come to command greater attention in both federal and unitary countries alike (see Table 14.1 and Appendix). These rules take the form of budgetary balance controls, debt restrictions, tax or expenditure controls, and referenda for new taxing and spending initiatives. For example, the European Union in its goal of

Table 14.1. *Fiscal rules at a glance*

Country	Operating budget balance requirements	Debt limits	Tax and expenditure restraints	Referenda for new taxes and expenditures	Penalties for noncompliance
EU-GSP	Yes	Yes	No	No	Yes
U.S. states (50 total)	48	41	30	3	Yes
Canadian provinces (10 total)	8	3	2	4	Yes
Germany	Yes	No	No	No	No
New Zealand	Yes	No	No	No	No
Sweden	No	No	Yes	No	No
Brazil	Yes	Yes	Yes	No	Yes (prison)
Argentina	Yes	Yes	Yes	No	No
Argentinean provinces (23 total)	17	17	17	No	No
India	Yes	Yes	No	No	No
Indian states	Yes	Yes	No	No	No

Source: Adapted from Finance Canada (2004).

creating a monetary union through the provisions of the Maastricht Treaty established ceilings on national deficits and debts and supporting provisions that there should be no bailout of any government by member central banks or by the European Central Bank. The European Union is also prohibited from providing an unconditional guarantee in respect of the public debt of a member state (Pisani-Ferry, 1991). These provisions were subsequently strengthened by the Growth and Stability Pact provisions (legislated fiscal rules adopted by the European Parliament). Most mature federations also specify no bailout provisions in setting up central banks with the notable exception of Australia until 1992 and Brazil until 1996. In the presence of an explicit or even implicit bailout guarantee and preferential loans from the banking sector, printing of money by subnational governments is possible, thereby fueling inflation. European Union guidelines provide a useful framework for macroeconomic coordination in federal systems, but such guidelines may not ensure macroeconomic stability because the guidelines may restrain smaller countries with little influence on macroeconomic stability such as Greece but may not restrain superpowers like France and Germany, as demonstrated by recent history. Thus, a proper enforcement of guidelines may require a fiscal coordinating council.

Recent experiences with fiscal adjustment programs suggest that, while legislated fiscal rules are neither necessary nor sufficient for successful fiscal adjustment, they can be of help in forging sustained political commitment to achieve better fiscal outcomes especially in countries with divisive political institutions or coalition regimes. For example, such rules can be helpful in sustaining political commitment to reform in countries with proportional representation (Brazil) or multiparty coalition governments (India) or in countries with separation of legislative and executive functions (the United States, Brazil). Fiscal rules in such countries can help restrain pork-barrel politics and thereby improve fiscal discipline. Von Hagen (2005) based upon a review of EU experiences with fiscal rules concludes that budgetary institutions matter more than fiscal rules. The EU fiscal rules may have encouraged European countries to strengthen budgetary institutions, which in turn had welcome effects on fiscal discipline and fiscal outcomes.

Mature federations vary a great deal in terms of fiscal policy coordinating mechanisms. In the United States, there is neither overall federal-state coordination of fiscal policy nor constitutional restraints on state borrowing, but the states' own constitutional provisions prohibit operating deficits. Intergovernmental coordination often comes through fiscal rules established through acts of Congress, such as the Gramm-Rudman Act. Fiscal discipline primarily arises from three distinct incentives offered by the political and market cultures: the electorates are conservative and elect candidates with a commitment to keep public spending in check; pursuit of fiscal policies perceived as imprudent lower property values, thereby lowering public revenues; and capital markets discipline governments that live beyond their means (see Inman and Rubinfeld, 1994).

In Canada, there are elaborate mechanisms for federal-provincial fiscal coordination that take the form of intergovernmental conferences (periodic first ministers' and finance ministers' or treasurers' conferences) and the Council of the Federation (an interprovincial consultative body). Most direct program expenditures in Canada are at the subnational level, but Ottawa (i.e., the Canadian federal government) retains flexibility and achieves fiscal harmonization through conditional transfers and tax-collection agreements. In addition, Ottawa has established a well-knit system of institutional arrangements for intergovernmental consultation and coordination. Much of the discipline on public-sector borrowing, however, comes from the private banking sector monitoring deficits and debt at all levels of government. Overall financial markets and electorates impose a strong fiscal discipline at the subnational level.

In Switzerland, societal conservatism, fiscal rules, and intergovernmental relations play an important part in fiscal coordination. Borrowing by cantons and communes is restricted to capital projects that can be financed on a pay-as-you-go basis and requires popular referenda for approval. In addition, cantons and communes must balance current budgets, including interest payments and debt amortization. Intergovernmental coordination is also fostered by "common budget directives," applicable to all levels of government, which embody the following general principles: the growth rates of public expenditures should not exceed the expected growth of nominal GNP; the budget deficit should not be higher than that of the previous year; the number of civil servants should stay the same or increase only very slightly; the volume of public-sector building should remain constant; and an inflation indexation clause should be avoided (U. Gygi, 1991:10).

The German constitution specifies that Bund (federal) and *Länder* (state-level governments) have budgetary independence (article 109 (1) GG) but must take into account the requirements of overall economic equilibrium (article 109 (2) GG). The 1969 Law of Stability and Growth established the Financial Planning Council and the Cyclical Planning Council as coordinating bodies for the two levels of government. It stipulates uniform budgetary principles to facilitate coordination. Annual budgets are required to be consistent with the medium-term financial plans. The law further empowered the federal government to vary tax rates and expenditures on short notice and even to restrict borrowing and equalization transfers. *Länder* parliaments no longer have tax legislation authority and Bund and *Länder* borrowing is restricted by the German constitution to projected outlays for capital projects (the so-called golden rule). However, federal borrowing to correct "disturbances of general economic equilibrium" is exempt from the application of this rule. The federal government also follows a five-year budget plan so that its fiscal policy stance is available to subnational governments. Two major instruments were created by the 1969 law to forge cooperative federalism: joint tasks authorized by the Bundesrat, and federal grants for state and local spending mandated by federal legislation or federal-state agreements. An additional helpful matter in intergovernmental coordination is that the central bank (Bundesbank) is independent of all levels of government and focuses on price stability as its objective. Most important, full and effective federal-*Länder* fiscal coordination is achieved through the Bundesrat, the upper house of parliament, where *Länder* governments are directly repre-sented. The German Bundesrat represents the most outstanding institution for formal intergovernmental coordination. Such formal institutions for intergovernmental coordination are useful especially in countries with legislative federalism. The Constitution Act of 1996 of the Republic of South Africa has established such an institution for intergovernmental coordination called the National Council of the Provinces.

Commonwealth-state fiscal coordination in Australia offers important lessons for federal countries. Australia established a loan council in 1927 as an instrument of credit allocation because it restricted state governments to borrow only from the commonwealth. An important exception to this rule was that states could use borrowing by autonomous agencies and local government for their own purposes. This exception proved to be the Achilles' heel for the Commonwealth Loan Council, as states used this exception extensively in their attempt to bypass the cumbersome proce-dures and control over their capital spending plans by the council. The commonwealth government ultimately recognized in 1993 that central credit allocation policy was a flawed and ineffective instrument. It lifted restrictions on state borrowing and reconstituted the Loan Council so that it could serve as a coordinating agency for information exchange so as to ensure greater market accountability. The New Australian Loan Council attempts to provide a greater flexibility to states to determine their own borrowing requirements and attempts to coordinate borrowing with fiscal needs and overall macroeconomic strategy. It further instills a greater understanding of the budgetary process and provides timely and valuable information to the financial markets on public-sector borrowing plans. The process seems to be working well so far.

For the European Union, Wierts (2005) concludes that subnational governments' contributions to consolidated public-sector deficits and debts were relatively smaller as compared to those of the central governments in most EU countries – federal and unitary countries alike.

The Impact of Fiscal Decentralization on Fiscal Management: Econometric Evidence

Econometric analysis presented in Shah (2005b, 2006b) examines the impact of fiscal decentralization on various dimensions of the quality of fiscal management. Econometric evidence presented there supports the hypothesis that fiscal decentralization has a positive significant impact on the quality of fiscal management. The effect of fiscal decentralization on the efficiency in revenue collection is negative but insignificant. Fiscal decentralization leads to prudent use of public resources. Growth in public spending is positively associated with fiscal decentralization, but insignificantly so with the score index of decentralization. Fiscal decentralization is negatively but insignificantly associated with the control of deficits, has a positive but insignificant impact on growth of public debt, and contributes to enhanced transparency and accountability in public management. Finally, fiscal decentralization has a positive yet insignificant association with growth of GDP.

Fiscal Policy Coordination in Brazil, from Fiscal Distress to Fiscal Discipline: A Giant Leap Forward

Tax assignments mandated by the 1988 constitution in Brazil reduced federal flexibility in the conduct of fiscal policies. The new constitution transferred some productive federal taxes to lower-level jurisdictions and also increased subnational governments' participation in federal revenue-sharing schemes. One of the most productive taxes, the value-added tax on sales, was assigned to states, and the Council of State Finance Ministers (CONFAZ) was set up to play a coordinating role. Federal flexibility in the income tax area, however, remained intact. This freedom gives the federal government some possibility of not only affecting aggregate disposable income, and therefore aggregate demand, but also exerting direct influence over the revenues and fiscal behavior of the lower levels of government that end up receiving nearly half of the proceeds of this tax. The effectiveness of such a policy tool is an open question and critically depends upon the goodwill of subnational governments. Consider the case where the federal government decides to implement a discretionary income tax cut. The measure could have a potentially significant effect on the revenues of state and local governments, given their large share in the proceedings of this tax. It is possible that, in order to offset this substantial loss in revenues from federal sources, lower levels of government might choose to increase either the rates and/or bases on the taxes under their jurisdiction or their tax effort. Such state and local government responses could potentially undermine the effectiveness of income taxes as a fiscal policy instrument. Thus, a greater degree of intergovernmental consultation, cooperation, and coordination would be needed for the success of stabilization policies.

An overall impact of the new fiscal arrangements was to limit federal control over public-sector expenditures in the federation. The success of federal expenditures as a stabilization tool again depends upon the cooperation of subnational governments in harmonizing their expenditure policies with the federal government. Once again, the constitution has put a premium on intergovernmental coordination of fiscal policies. Such a degree of coordination may not be attainable in times of fiscal distress.

A reduction in revenues at the federal government's disposal and an incomplete transfer of expenditure responsibilities have further constrained the federal government. The primary source of federal revenues is income taxes. These taxes are easier to avoid and evade by taxpayers and therefore are declining in relative importance as a source of revenues. Value-added sales taxes, which are considered a more dynamic source of revenues, have been assigned to the state level. Thus, federal authorities lack access to more productive tax bases to alleviate the public debt problem and to gain more flexibility in the implementation of fiscally based macroeconomic stabilization policies. According to Shah (1991, 1998c) and Bomfim and Shah (1994), this situation could be remedied if a joint federal-state VAT to be administered by a federal-state council were to be instituted as a replacement for the federal IPI, the state ICMS, and the municipal services tax, whose bases partially overlap. Such a joint tax would help alleviate the current federal fiscal crisis as well as streamline sales tax administration. They argued that federal expenditure requirements could be curtailed with federal disengagement from purely local functions and by eliminating federal tax transfers to municipalities. Transfers to the municipalities would be better administered at the state level as states have better access to data on municipal fiscal capacities and tax effort in their jurisdictions. Some rethinking is in order on the role of negotiated transfers that have traditionally served to advance pork-barrel politics rather than to address national objectives. If these transfers were replaced by performance-oriented conditional block (per capita) federal transfers to achieve national (minimum) standards, both the accountability and coordination in the federation would be enhanced. These rearrangements would provide the federal government with greater flexibility to pursue its macroeconomic policy objectives. Finally, they advocated the development of fiscal rules binding on all levels of government and a federal-state coordinating council to ensure that these rules are enforced.

There has been significant progress on most of these issues in recent years. For example, negotiated transfers have become insignificant because of the fiscal squeeze experienced by the federal government. The senate has prescribed guidelines (Senate Resolution no. 69, 1995) for state debt: maximum debt service is not to exceed 16 percent of net revenue or 100 percent of current revenue surplus, whichever is less, and the maximum growth in stock of debt (new borrowing) within a twelve-month period must not exceed the level of existing debt service or 27 percent of net revenues, whichever is greater (see Dillinger, 1997). More recently, in 1998, pension and civil service entitlements reform have introduced greater budgetary flexibility for all levels of government. Likewise, after the suboptimal results achieved from letting capital markets discipline subnational borrowings, the Brazilian federal government opted for establishing a fairly constraining set of fiscal responsibility institutions. First, Law 9696 of September 1997 set up the framework for a series of debt restructuring contracts between December 1997 and June 1998, whereby a portion of debt (20 percent) should be paid with the proceeds of privatization of state assets, while the remaining portion of state and local debt was restructured with maturities up to thirty years at a subsidized interest rate (equal to 6 percent annual real rate). Debt restructuring contracts become comprehensive in scope as twenty-five out of twenty-seven states and more than 180 municipalities signed debt restructuring agreements (Goldfajn and Refinetti, 2003; International Monetary Fund, 2001). In exchange, the contracts require the subnational governments' commitments to engage in adjustment programs aimed to reduce the debt to net revenue ratio to less than one over a per-case negotiated period of time. Contracts established sanctions for violations to adjustment program agreements, such as increase debt service caps (annual debt service to net revenue ratio of 13 to 15 percent above which service debt is capitalized) and substitutions of market interest rate for the subsidized interest rate. Debt restructuring contracts also impose stringent penalties for non-compliant states and, in the event of a default, authorize the federal government to withhold fiscal transfers or, if this is not enough, to withdraw the amount due to the states from their bank accounts (Goldfajn and Refinetti, 2003: 18). Debt restructuring agreements prohibit further credit or restructuring operations involving other levels of government. This helps to avoid moral hazard incentives from the possibility of intergovernmental bailouts (International Monetary Fund, 2001).

Building upon Law 6996/97 and complementary regulations, the Brazilian federal government adopted a Fiscal Responsibility Law (Lei de Responsibilidade Fiscal, LRF) in May 2000 and its companion law (Lei 10028/2000), binding for federal, state, and municipal or local governments. The LRF is likely the most significant reform after the 1988 constitution in terms of its impact on the dynamics of federalism in Brazil, as subsequent compromises between states and the federal government have continuously increased the negotiation leverage of the latter, while also increasing its effectiveness in macroeconomic management. The LRF establishes ex ante institutions such as a threshold state debt, deficit, and personnel spending ceilings. According to the LRF, states and municipalities must maintain debt stock levels below ceilings determined by the federal Senate regulations. If a subnational government exceeds this debt ceiling, the exceeding amount must be reduced within a one-year period, during which the state or municipality is prohibited from incurring any new debt and becomes ineligible for receiving discretionary transfers (World Bank, 2002). The LRF also regulates that all new borrowing requires the technical approval of the central bank and the approval of the Senate. Borrowing operations are prohibited altogether together during a period of 180 days before the end of an incumbents' government mandate (Afonso and de Mello, 2000). In terms of personnel management, the LRF provisions define ceilings on payroll spending. This should not exceed 50 percent of federal government's net revenues while this ceiling equals 60 percent at the subnational level. The LRF also institutionalized a variety of ex post provisions aimed at the enforcement of its regulations. For governments, violations to personnel or debt ceiling can lead to fines up to 30 percent of the annual salary of those responsible; impeachment of mayors or governors; and even prison terms in the case of violation of mandates regarding election years. For capital markets, the LRF declares that financing operations in violation of debt ceilings would not be legally valid and amounts borrowed should be repaid fully without interest. This provision is aimed at discouraging such lending behavior by the financial institutions.

The Brazilian federation had a remarkable success in ensuring fiscal policy coordination and fiscal discipline at all levels in recent years. By June 2005, the LRF 2000 had significant positive impacts on fiscal performance in Brazil. All states and the federal government have complied with the ceiling on personnel expenditures (50 percent of current revenues). On debt, only five out of twenty-seven states (inclusive of the Federal District) are still above the ceiling of 200 percent of revenues, owing to 2002 currency devaluation. Ninety-two percent of municipalities have reduced debts below 1.2 times revenue levels, and only a handful of large municipalities have unsustainable debt levels. Primary surplus was achieved by all states by 2004 (Levy, 2005).

Fiscal Management in China: An Unmet Challenge

Before 1980, China's fiscal system was characterized by a decentralized revenue collection followed by central transfers – that is, all taxes and profits were remitted to the central government and then transferred back to the provinces, according to expenditure needs approved by the center through bilateral negotiations. Under this system, the localities had little managerial autonomy in local economic development. In 1980 this system was changed into a contracting system. Under the new arrangements, each level of government makes a contract with the next level up to meet certain revenue and expenditure targets. A typical contract defines a method of revenue sharing, which could be a percentage share that goes to the center or a fixed fee plus a percentage share. This contracting system means that the economic interests of each level of government are sharply identified.

Under the fiscal contract system introduced in the early 1980s, the localities have controlled the effective tax rates and tax bases in the following two ways. First, they have controlled tax-collection efforts by offering varying degrees of tax concessions. Second, they have found ways to convert budgetary funds into extrabudgetary funds, thus avoiding tax sharing with the center. As a result, the center has had to resort to various ad hoc instruments to influence revenue remittance from the localities, and these instruments have led to perverse reactions from the localities. On the expenditure side, the center has failed to achieve corresponding reductions in expenditure when revenue collection has been decentralized. The center's flexibility in using expenditure policy has been seriously undermined by the lack of centrally controlled financial resources and the heavy burden of "capital constructions." Between 1978 and 1992, the ratio of government revenue to GNP dropped from 31 to 17 percent. Increasing deficits became a problem, and the lack of funds for infrastructure investment exacerbated bottlenecks in the economy.

Because of the lack of fiscal resources and policy instruments, the central government has found itself in an increasingly difficult position to achieve the goals of macroeconomic stabilization, regional equalization, and public goods provision. In early 1994 the central government initiated reform of the tax assignment system in an attempt to address these difficulties. Under the new system, the center will recentralize the administration and collection of central and shared taxes and will obtain a larger share of fiscal resources as a result of the new revenue-sharing formula. Initially, among the major taxes only the VAT was centralized. Later in year 2002, the administration of Personal Income Tax and the Enterprise Income Tax was also centralized. The VAT is shared according to a 75:25 ratio (center-local), and all extra central revenues above the 1993 levels are then shared 60:40. Revenues are returned to provinces on a derivation or point of collection basis. The central government expected to improve significantly its ability to use tax and expenditure policies in macroeconomic management as a result of these steps. Nevertheless, the new system fails to address a number of flaws in the old system: (1) the division of tax bases according to ownership will continue to motivate the center to reclaim enterprise ownership whenever necessary; (2) the division of expenditure responsibility is not yet clearly defined; (3) the new system impedes local autonomy as the localities are not allowed to determine the bases and/or rates for local taxes; and (4) the design of intergovernmental transfers is not fully settled yet. In 1994 and 1995, the central government also imposed administrative restrictions on investments by provincial and local governments and their enterprises (see Ma, 1995, and World Bank, 1994a for further details) to deal with inflationary pressures. The introduction of the State Council Document No. 29 in 1996 and other measures in 1997 to consolidate budgetary management over extrabudgetary funds sharply restricted the authority of local governments, especially rural local governments, to impose fees and levies to finance their own expenditures (see World Bank, 1998).

The Budget Law 1994 prohibits the central government from borrowing from the Peoples Central Bank of China. The Budget Law also requires local governments to have balanced budgets and restricts subnational governments borrowing in financial markets and in issuing bonds (Qian, 2000). Legal restraints on subnational borrowing and unfunded central mandates have encouraged provincial-local governments to assume hidden debts. Such borrowing is channeled through state-owned entities, such as urban construction and investment companies, that borrow from banks or issue bonds on behalf of the local government (World Bank, 2005a). Such hidden debts pose significant risks for macroeconomic stability.

A combination of unfunded mandates and extremely constrained taxing powers generate incentives for local governments to develop informal channels of taxation. This result is evidenced by the high levels of extra-budgetary funds (self-raised funds) at the subprovincial levels, comprising surcharges, fees, and utility and user charges that are not formally approved by the central government though technically legal. A pilot experiment in Anhui Province identified collection of per capita fees from peasants for local education, health, militia training, road construction and maintenance, welfare for veterans, and birth control (Yep, 2004). This type of quasi-fiscal income accounted for as high as 56 percent of total tax revenues in 1996 (Eckaus, 2003; *China Statistical Yearbook*, 2000: 257, 271) or 8–10 percent of GDP in 1995 (World Bank, 2000). This nontax type of revenue extraction has often imposed excessive burdens in local constituents, generating continuous confrontations between peasants and local officials (Lin et al., 2002; Bernstein and Lu, 2003; Yep, 2004). As noted by Krug, Zhu, and Hendrischke (2005: 11), subprovincial government agencies' de facto control of the property rights of revenues not covered by the tax-sharing system enables "sub-provincial governments at all levels to maintain their residual tax rights over the informal tax system." In fact, institutions ruling subprovincial taxation are shaped as a complex and asymmetric system of contracts between the provincial government and lower layers of government. More recently, the central government has abolished the agricultural income tax and rural fees and charges in 2002 through the "Tax-for-Fee program." These prohibitions have deleterious consequences for county finances as compensating transfers do not fully cover these growing sources of county finance.

Promoting greater fiscal discipline at the subnational level in China remains virtually an impossible task so long as local governments retain ownership of enterprises providing private goods, lack clarity in their spending and taxing responsibilities, and obtain a disproportionate amount of local revenues from ad hoc central transfers. Thus, fiscal policy coordination and fiscal discipline remain an unfinished challenge in China.

Fiscal Policy Coordination: Some Conclusions

Fiscal policy coordination represents an important challenge for federal systems. In this context, fiscal rules and institutions provide a useful framework but not necessarily a solution to this challenge. Fiscal rules binding on all levels can help sustain political commitment in countries governed by coalitions or fragmented regimes. Coordinating institutions help in the use of moral suasion to encourage a coordinated response. Industrialized countries' experiences also show that unilaterally imposed federal controls and constraints on subnational governments typically do not work. Instead, societal norms based on fiscal conservatism such as the Swiss referenda and political activism of the electorate play important roles. Ultimately, capital markets and bond-rating agencies provide more effective discipline on fiscal policy. In this context, it is important not to backstop state and local debt and not to allow ownership of the banks by any level of government. Transparency of the budgetary process and institutions, accountability to the electorate, and general availability of comparative data encourage fiscal discipline.

SECURING AN ECONOMIC UNION

Four dimensions of securing an economic union in a federal system have relevance for macroeconomic governance: preservation of the internal common market, tax harmonization, transfers and social insurance, and regional fiscal equity.

Preservation of the Internal Common Market

Preservation of an internal common market remains an important area of concern to most nations undertaking decentralization. Subnational governments in their pursuit of attracting labor and capital may indulge in beggar-thy-neighbor policies and in the process erect barriers to goods and factor mobility. Thus, decentralization of government regulatory functions creates a potential for disharmonious economic relations among subnational units. Accordingly, regulation of economic activity such as trade and investment is generally best left to the federal or central government. It should be noted, however, that central governments themselves may pursue policies detrimental to the internal common market. Therefore, as suggested by Boadway (1992), constitutional guarantees for free domestic flow of goods and services may be the best alternative to assigning regulatory responsibilities solely to the center.

The constitutions of mature federations typically provide a free trade clause (as in Australia, Canada, and Switzerland), federal regulatory power over interstate commerce (as in Australia, Canada, Germany, the United States, and Switzerland), and individual mobility rights (as in most federations). In contrast, in China, a large unitary country, mobility rights of individuals are severely constrained by the operation of the *hukou* system of household registration, which is used to determine eligibility for grain rations, employment, housing, education, and health care benefits.

Tax Harmonization and Coordination

Tax competition among jurisdictions can be beneficial by encouraging cost-effectiveness and fiscal accountability in state governments. It can also by itself lead to a certain amount of tax harmonization. At the same time, decentralized tax policies can cause certain inefficiencies and inequities in a federation as well as lead to excessive administrative costs. Tax harmonization is intended to preserve the best features of tax decentralization while avoiding its disadvantages.

Inefficiencies from decentralized decision making can occur in a variety of ways. For one, states may implement policies that discriminate in favor of their own residents and businesses relative to those of other states. They may also engage in beggar-thy-neighbor policies intended to attract economic activity from other states. Inefficiency may also occur simply from the fact that distortions will arise from different tax structures chosen independently by state governments with no strategic objective in mind. Inefficiencies also can occur if state tax systems adopt different conventions for dealing with businesses (and residents) who operate in more than one jurisdiction at the same time. This can lead to double taxation of some forms of income and nontaxation of others. State tax systems may also introduce inequities, as mobility of persons would encourage them to abandon progressivity. Administration costs are also likely to be excessive in an uncoordinated tax system (see Boadway, Roberts, and Shah, 1994). Thus, tax harmonization and coordination contribute to efficiency of the internal common market, reduce collection and compliance costs, and help to achieve national standards of equity.

European Union has placed a strong emphasis on tax coordination issues. Canada has used tax-collection agreements, tax abatement, and tax-base sharing to harmonize the tax system. The German federation emphasizes uniformity of tax bases by assigning the tax legislation to the federal government. In developing countries, because of tax centralization, tax coordination issues are relevant only for larger federations such as India and Brazil. In Brazil, the use of ICMS (origin based) as a tool for attracting capital inflow from other regions has become an area of emerging conflict among regions. Despite the fact that the Council of States sought to harmonize ICMS base and rates, there is evidence that some of the tax concessions refused by the council are practiced by many states anyway. States can also resort to tax-base reductions or grant un-indexed payment deferrals (Longo, 1994). For example, some northeastern states have offered a fifteen-year ICMS tax deferral to industry. In an inflationary environment, such a measure can serve as an important inducement for attracting capital from elsewhere in the country (Shah, 1991).

Tax harmonization and coordination are theoretically a nonissue in the context of a unitary country, but substantial use of an informal tax system and tax preferences by local governments in China has elevated them to some prominence.

Transfer Payments and Social Insurance

Along with the provision of public goods and services, transfer payments to persons and businesses constitute most of government expenditures (especially in industrialized countries). Some of these transfers are for redistributive purposes in the ordinary sense, and some are for industrial policy or regional development purposes. Some are also for redistribution in the social insurance sense, such as unemployment insurance, health insurance, and public pensions. Several factors bear on the assignment of responsibility for transfers. In the case of transfers to business, many economists would argue that they should not be used in the first place. Given that they are, however, they are likely to be more distortionary if used at the provincial level than at the federal level because the objective of subsidies is typically to increase capital investments by firms, which are mobile across provinces. As for transfers to individuals, because most of them are for redistributive purposes, their assignment revolves around the extent to which the federal level of government assumes primary responsibility for equity. From an economic point of view, transfers are just negative direct taxes. One can argue that transfers should be controlled by the same level of government that controls direct taxes so that they can be integrated for equity purposes and harmonized across the nation for efficiency purposes. The case for integration at the central level is enhanced when one recognizes the several types of transfers that may exist to address different dimensions of equity or social insurance. There is an advantage of coordinating unemployment insurance with the income tax system or pensions with payments to the poor. Decentralizing transfers to individuals to the provinces will likely lead to inefficiencies in the internal common market, fiscal inequities, and interjurisdictional beggar-thy-neighbor policies. Following this guidance, most federal countries assign unemployment insurance and social security to national levels as do also most unitary countries. An important exception is China, where these are considered provincial-local responsibilities.

Intergovernmental Fiscal Transfers

Federal-state transfers in a federal system serve important objectives: alleviating structural imbalances, correcting for fiscal inefficiencies and inequities, providing compensation for benefit spill-outs, and achieving fiscal harmonization. The most important critical consideration is that the grant design must be consistent with grant objectives, and ad hoc pork-barrel transfers should be avoided. Industrial-country experience shows that successful decentralization cannot be achieved in the absence of a well-designed fiscal transfers program. The design of these transfers must be simple, transparent, and consistent with their objectives. Properly structured transfers can enhance competition for the supply of public services, accountability of the fiscal system, and fiscal coordination, just as general revenue sharing has the potential to undermine it. A comparative look at the design and practice of fiscal transfers suggests that federal countries typically pay greater attention to the incentive effects of these transfers than unitary countries do.

Regional Fiscal Equity

Although we have not addressed the regional equity issue owing to paucity of data, a few casual observations may be in order. As we noted earlier, regional inequity is an area of concern for decentralized fiscal systems, and most such systems attempt to deal with it through the spending powers of the national government or through fraternal programs. Mature federations such as Australia, Canada, and Germany have formal equalization programs. This important feature of decentralization has not received adequate attention in the design of institutions in developing countries. Despite serious horizontal fiscal imbalances in a large number of developing countries, explicit equalization programs are untried, although equalization objectives are implicitly attempted in the general revenue-sharing mechanisms used in Brazil, Colombia, India, Mexico, Nigeria, and Pakistan. These mechanisms typically combine diverse and conflicting objectives into the same formula and fall significantly short on individual objectives. Because these formulas lack explicit equalization standards, they fail to address regional equity objectives satisfactorily.

Regional inequity concerns are more easily addressed by unitary countries but it is interesting to note that the record of unitary countries in addressing these inequities is worse than federal countries (Shankar and Shah, 2003). Von Hagen (2005: 23) also concludes that "surprisingly, perhaps, there is no clear evidence that regional risk sharing is larger in unitary than in federal states."

Fiscal Decentralization and Fiscal Performance: Some Conclusions

Fiscal decentralization poses significant challenges for macroeconomic management. These challenges require careful design of monetary and fiscal institutions to overcome adverse incentives associated with the "common property" resource management problems or with rent-seeking behaviors. Experiences of federal countries indicate significant learning and adaptation of fiscal systems to create incentives compatible with fair play and to overcome incomplete contracts. This explains why that decentralized fiscal systems appear to do better than centralized fiscal systems on most aspects of monetary and fiscal policy management and transparent and accountable governance (see Table 14.2).

Table 14.2. *Fiscal decentralization and fiscal performance: A summary of empirical results*

Fiscal performance indicator	Impact of fiscal decentralization
Central bank independence	Positive and significant
Growth of money supply	Positive but insignificant
Inflation	Negative but insignificant
Management of inflation and macroeconomic imbalances	Positive but insignificant
Quality of debt management	Positive but insignificant
Quality of fiscal policies and institutions	Positive and significant
Efficiency in revenue collection	Mixed but insignificant
Prudent use of tax moneys	Positive and significant
Growth of government spending	Negative and significant
Control of fiscal deficits	Negative but insignificant
Growth of public debt	Positive yet insignificant
Public-sector management: transparency and accountability	Positive and significant
GDP growth	Positive but insignificant

Source: Shah (2005b, 2006b).

SOME LESSONS FOR DEVELOPING COUNTRIES

The following important lessons for reform of fiscal systems in developing countries can be distilled from a review of past experiences.

- Monetary policy is best entrusted to an independent central bank with a sole mandate for price stability. Political feasibility of such an assignment improves under federal systems (decentralized fiscal system).
- Fiscal rules are neither necessary nor sufficient for fiscal discipline. However, fiscal rules accompanied by "gatekeeper" intergovernmental councils or committees provide a useful framework for fiscal discipline and fiscal policy coordination for countries with fragmented political regimes. In this context, one can draw on industrial countries' experiences with "golden rules," Maastricht-type guidelines, and "common budget directives" to develop country-specific guidelines. To ensure voluntary compliance with the guidelines, appropriate institutional framework must be developed. Transparency of the budgetary processes and institutions, accountability to the electorate, and general availability of comparative data on fiscal positions of all levels of government further strengthen fiscal discipline.
- The integrity and independence of the financial sector contribute to fiscal prudence in the public sector. To ensure such an integrity and independence, ownership and preferential access to the financial sector should not be available to any level of government. In such an environment, capital markets and bond rating agencies would provide an effective fiscal policy discipline.
- To ensure fiscal discipline, governments at all levels must be made to face financial consequences of their decisions. This is possible if the central government does not guarantee payment of state and local debt and if the central bank does not act as a lender of last resort to the central government.
- Societal norms and consensus on roles of various levels of governments and limits to their authorities are vital for the success of decentralized decision making. In the absence of such norms and consensus, direct central controls do not work, and intergovernmental gaming leads to dysfunctional constitutions.
- Tax decentralization is a prerequisite for subnational credit market access. In countries with highly centralized tax bases, unrestrained

credit market access by subnational governments poses a risk for macroeconomic stabilization policies of the national government as the private sector anticipates a higher-level government bailout in the event of default and does not discount the risks of such lending properly.

- Higher-level institutional assistance may be needed for financing local capital projects. This assistance can take the form of establishing municipal finance corporations run on commercial principles to lower the cost of borrowing by using the superior credit rating of the higher-level government and municipal rating agencies to determine credit worthiness.
- An internal common market is best preserved by constitutional guarantees. National governments in developing countries have typically failed in this role.
- Intergovernmental transfers in developing countries undermine fiscal discipline and accountability while building transfer dependencies that cause a slow economic strangulation of fiscally disadvantaged regions. Properly designed intergovernmental transfers on the other hand can enhance competition for the supply of public goods, fiscal harmonization, subnational government accountability, and regional equity. Substantial theoretical and empirical guidance on the design of these transfers is readily available.
- Periodic review of jurisdictional assignments is essential to realign responsibilities with changing economic and political realities. With globalization and localization, national government's direct role in stabilization and macroeconomic control is likely to diminish over time, but its role in coordination and oversight is expected to increase as regimes and subnational governments assume enhanced roles in these areas. Constitutional and legal systems and institutions must be amenable to timely adjustments to adapt to changing circumstances.
- Finally, contrary to a common misconception, decentralized fiscal systems offer a greater potential for improved macroeconomic governance than centralized fiscal systems. This is to be expected as decentralized fiscal systems require greater clarity in the roles of various players (centers of decision making) and transparency in rules that govern their interactions to ensure a fair play.

APPENDIX TO CHAPTER 14

Legislated Fiscal Rules: Do They Matter for Fiscal Outcomes?

During the past decade, fiscal rules defined as legislated controls on budgetary balance, debt restrictions, tax and expenditure controls, and referenda for new initiatives on taxing and spending have assumed center stage in policy discussions in attempts to restore fiscal prudence in countries facing fiscal stress. The central question in these discussions is the link between legislated rules and fiscal performance. A growing body of literature on this subject fails to reach any definitive conclusions regarding the causal links (see Kopits, 2004, for a review of experiences with fiscal rules in emerging markets). The literature suggests that some countries with legislated fiscal rules such as Sweden and Italy over the period 1995 to 2003 and Brazil since 2001 had a remarkable turnaround in fiscal performance. India has also shown some progress since 2003. Other countries with legislated fiscal rules such as the United States, France, Germany, and New Zealand did not do so well over the same period. On the other hand, some countries without legislated fiscal rules such as Canada, Australia, and the United Kingdom also succeeded in achieving fiscal adjustment, whereas Japan was less than successful (see Finance Canada, 2004: 74). Noncompliance of France and Germany with the Growth and Stability Pact provisions (legislated fiscal rules) further illustrates the difficulty in binding large constituent units in a federation to fiscal rules.

A closer look at these experiences suggests that successful fiscal adjustment requires sustained political commitment. Such commitment is easier to obtain under a single-party majority rule as in Canada, the United Kingdom, and Australia in recent years. However, such a commitment may not be forthcoming in countries with proportional representation (Brazil) or multiparty coalition governments (India) or in countries with separation of legislative and executive functions (the United States, Brazil. Fiscal rules in such countries can help restrain pork-barrel politics and thereby improve fiscal discipline. A remarkable example of this is the experience in Brazil. Brazil is a large, highly decentralized federation of twenty-six states and a federal district with a population of 182 million (year 2005). By the mid-1990s, price stabilization policies and associated decline in GDP growth contributed to growing fiscal imbalances at federal, state, and local levels. A majority of states faced fiscal crisis as the state debt service to GDP ratio reached 3 percent of GDP and growing personnel expenditures (in some states and local governments reaching 90 percent of operating expenditures) limited their abilities to meet ever-increasing demands for social services. Against this backdrop, federal and state treasury secretaries undertook a study tour of Australia and New Zealand to reflect upon options to arrest the impending fiscal crisis. At a retreat in Auckland, New Zealand, in 1997, they reached a consensus that Brazil must enact fiscal rules binding at all levels to avert the crisis. While initiating a campaign to build consensus for such future legislation, the federal government initiated a state fiscal strengthening program, whereby states were offered incentives to enter into formal contracts on a bilateral basis with the federal government to close down or sell state-owned banks and to undertake expenditure restraints. By the year 2000, political consensus was forged to enact stringent fiscal rules binding on all governments. This legislation, the so-called Fiscal Responsibility Law of 2000, prohibited intergovernmental debt financing, placed stringent limits on debt and personnel expenditure, imposed verifiable fiscal targets and transparency rules and adjustment rules, and mandated institutional and personal sanctions including fines and jail terms for political and bureaucratic officials of all orders of governments. This legislation had a positive impact on fiscal performance – by 2004 all states had achieved primary surplus, all had restrained personnel expenditures to 50 percent of current revenues, and all states and municipalities had reduced debt burdens.

India is a much larger but, compared to Brazil, a relatively less decentralized federation of twenty-eight states and seven union territories with 1 billion people (year 2001). India's fiscal situation paralleled that of Brazil in the 1990s, and it has essentially followed Brazil's lead in dealing with fiscal imbalances at federal and state levels. The state of Karnatka took the lead in enacting fiscal responsibility legislation in August 2002 and established specific targets in reducing revenue and fiscal deficits and introducing fiscal transparency. This was followed by the federal government with its own legislation enacted exactly one year later in August 2003. Subsequently, seven more states have followed suit. In April 2005 the Twelfth Finance Commission in its report to the government of India recommended federal assistance to encourage enactment of state fiscal responsibility legislation and added incentives for states to comply. This inducement proved attractive, and by December 2007 most states had enacted fiscal responsibility legislation. It should be noted that unlike Brazil, legislation in India does not specify institutional and personal sanctions in the event of noncompliance and does not have stringent fiscal rules for spending and debt restraints but instead long-run goals. Such legislation, nevertheless, provides timetables for eliminating revenue deficits and restraining fiscal deficits. While it is too early to judge the impacts of this legislation, initial results appear promising, and several states have been successful in reducing operating deficits (see Howes, 2005, for details). More important, though, this legislation is creating new political dynamics. For example, the chief minister of the state of Orissa has used the legislated fiscal rules to restrain spending demands by his cabinet colleagues and by state legislators.

In conclusion, while legislated fiscal rules are neither necessary nor sufficient for successful fiscal adjustment, they can be of help in forging sustained political commitment to achieve better fiscal outcomes, especially in countries with divisive political institutions or coalition regimes.

FIFTEEN

Interregional Competition and Policies for Regional Cohesion and Convergence

Competition among governments at the same level or with similar responsibilities is commonly referred to as *horizontal competition* or interjurisdictional competition in the literature on economics and political science. A related concept of intergovernmental or *vertical competition* refers to competition among governments with different levels and types of responsibilities, for example, among federal, state, and local governments. Our concern in this chapter is with the interjurisdictional competition (interregional or local-local competition) alone and its implications for the federal government's role in securing an economic union or an internal common market.

Competition among state and local governments is quite commonplace in most federal systems. It occurs through lobbying for employment generation and against hazardous waste location of federal or private-sector projects, including military bases; encouraging foreign and domestic investment; and providing incentives and subsidies for attracting capital and labor, public infrastructure to facilitate business location, a differentiated menu of local public services, one-stop windows for licensing and registration, and endless other ways of demonstrating an open-door policy for new capital and a skilled work force. State and local governments also compete among themselves in erecting barriers to trade and tariff walls to protect local industry and business. They also compete among themselves in exporting tax burdens to nonresidents where feasible.

This chapter examines the pros and cons of interjurisdictional competition in a federal system and examines the ways the federal government can play a supporting role to accentuate the positive aspects of this competition while dealing with any negative fallout of unbridled competition. It further assesses alternate policies to deal with regional inequities.

INTERJURISDICTIONAL COMPETITION AND EFFICIENCY IN A FEDERAL ECONOMY

Matching Public Services with Citizen Preferences

In a decentralized federation, independent decision making by state and local governments may enhance efficiency of the federal system because such uncoordinated decision making promotes competition and innovation in the provision of public services. Citizens are offered a differential menu of tax prices and public services depending on their location choices. They therefore, have the option of "voting with their feet" to locate in a community that matches public services with their preferences. This voting with feet combined with rational voting behavior creates a private-market analogue to public-sector decision making, where uncoordinated behavior of lower-level governments enhances efficiency in a federal economy (see Shah, 1988a, 1989a). For the United States, Oates and Schwab (1998) confirm Stigler's (1957: 216) view that "Competition among communities offers not obstacles but opportunities for various communities to choose the type and scale of government functions they wish." According to this "competitive federalism" perspective (see Breton, 1996), a greater degree of decentralization and relatively unconstrained policies of local governments make the public sector more responsive and accountable to its residents. It puts a premium in the efficiency in use of public funds and restrains the size of governments. Mobility of factors restrains the use of distortionary policies by local governments, and any costs of uncoordinated decision making will be far outweighed by benefits of interjurisdictional competition because intergovernmental competition "impels politicians and public-sector bureaucrats to do what is required to make organizational costs as small as possible, or equivalently, to supply goods and services (including redistribution) in the quantities and qualities desired by citizens" (see Breton, 2000: 1).

Interjurisdictional competition to match local public goods with local preferences enhances the functioning of the internal common market. It allows adaptation of labor laws, environmental standards, product safety laws, highway speed limits, use of local languages, protection of local culture and flora and fauna, regulations, and procurement and fiscal policies to suit local tastes and preferences. Such differential policies for local public goods may represent desired departures from uniform practices in the nation and may not circumvent the efficiency considerations, provided that they use national treatment criterion – that is, that they are applied

equally to all resident and nonresident persons and entities in the jurisdiction (Boadway and Shah, 2007).

Reinforcing Bottom-up Accountability

Interjurisdictional competition encourages governments to compete to
retain the loyalty of their citizens. This is typically achieved by experimenting
and innovating and benchmarking with other governments. These attempts
to better serve their citizens by offering newer services or delivering existing
services at higher quality and lower costs are termed "laboratory federalism"
by Wallace Oates (1999). Benchmarking with the best in the business helps
citizens evaluate the relative performance of their own government with
another better-performing jurisdiction. This enables citizens and politicians
with important electoral platforms to challenge their governments (see Salmon, 2000). Benchmarking has particularly strong political appeal in metropolitan areas with several competing jurisdictions. It encourages managers
to focus on results and, in doing so, facilitates private-sector participation in
the provision of public services. In Malaysia, for example, it is a common
practice for most public agencies to make comparisons of their performance
in achieving results with similar agencies that perform the same functional
activity in another jurisdiction or by market counterparts. In Chile and
Canada, school financing mechanisms encourage informal benchmarking
by private citizens to guide their choice of schools. In Brazil and South
Africa, inter jurisdictional competition leads to improved political competition and greater public participation in decision making at the local levels
(see Willis, Garman, and Haggard, 1999, and Andrews, 2001).

Loosening the Grip of Rent Seekers and the Corrupt

In developing countries, public production processes are often uncompetitive and unaccountable because of the existence of public service monopolies and the lack of any competitive pressures. These uncompetitive
production processes are usually protected by tariffs and by regulatory
and information constraints that provide opportunities for corruption
and self-enrichment to public managers. These situations of unconstrained
inefficiency facilitate rent seeking because barriers provide buffers to external scrutiny and because corrupt gains can easily be passed off as waste
related to inefficient production methods. These two factors limit the
chance of corruption detection and prosecution. Service monopolies have
weak incentives to adjust inefficient production processes. Lack of

competition because of an absence of decentralization leads to entrench-
ment of inefficiencies and adverse incentives. Horizontal competition by
strengthening local autonomy could break this vicious cycle.

Taming the Leviathan

The public sector in some countries is seen by citizens as the "coldest of
cold animals – whatever it says, it lies, and whatever it has, it has stolen";
here, public managers are focused on rent seeking. In such a setting,
competition among governments restrains their taxing powers and limits
the so-called Leviathan in its ability to extract resources from the private
sector (see Oates, 2001). Under such circumstances, Brennan and
Buchanan (1980: 184) argue that "tax competition among separate units
is an objective to be sought in its own right." Tax competition among local
government in the Punjab Province of Pakistan led to tax farming, which
assured local government stability and growth in local revenues. In South
Africa, in Johannesburg metropolitan areas (especially in Sandton and
Rosebank), tax rates on businesses increased markedly in the early
1990s, which resulted in a tax revolt, with many of these businesses relo-
cating to Pretoria, a lower-tax jurisdiction forty-five miles away.

State and local governments typically have access to an increasing array
of benefit charges. The use of benefit charges as an element of fiscal competition poses no risks for an internal common market. These taxes act as
signaling devices for local preferences, and increased reliance on them
leads to more informed choices on location decisions. Tax competition
acts as a useful constraint on policy makers and serves to tame the Leviathan tendencies of such governments. In Switzerland, a highly decentralized multiethnic federation, cantons have access to individual income tax,
a redistributive tax, as a source of revenue. Kirchgassner and Pommerehne
(1996) show that tax competition among cantons neither impacted negatively on public service provision nor compromised redistributive goals.

Improving the Quality, Quantity, and Access
of Local Public Services

Interjurisdictional competition can be a significant source of improvement
in service provision in developing countries. In countries where health care
and education are decentralized, subnational governments have an incentive
to act competitively. In Latin America, a significant degree of competition in
provision of education services exists, leading to differentials in quality and

quantity of education services and access. In Ghana, some competition is observed at the district level in decentralized health care leading to greater citizen satisfaction and support. In Punjab, Pakistan, several municipalities corporatized public hospitals to improve health service delivery. In the Balochistan Province of Pakistan, public school operation and maintenance responsibilities were transferred to community-based organizations.

INTERJURISDICTIONAL COMPETITION: A "RACE TO THE BOTTOM" OR "FEND-FOR-YOURSELF FEDERALISM"

Weakening Internal Common Market

Preservation of an efficient internal common market remains an important area of concern to most nations undertaking decentralization. Subnational governments in their pursuit of attracting labor and capital may indulge in beggar-thy-neighbor policies and, in the process, may wittingly or unwittingly erect barriers to goods and factor mobility.

A significant body of literature sees such interjurisdictional competition as a major source of inefficiency and inequity in a federal economy. State and local governments use their spending, taxing, and regulatory powers to improve local conditions but at the expense of nonresidents. Examples of such behavior include tariff and nontariff protection to local industry and businesses, special incentives to attract investment, and heavier taxation of goods and services used by nonresidents. Differential, standards of services and residency requirements may also impede the free flow of factors across the nation. Tax incentives or differential tax rates may distort firms' location decisions. Differential access to social services limits mobility of individuals. Lack of national minimum standards impedes the flow of goods and services. All these policies wittingly or unwittingly weaken the internal common market and economic union.

Inefficiencies from decentralized decision making can occur in a variety of ways. For one, states may implement policies that discriminate in favor of their own residents and businesses relative to those of other states. They may also engage in beggar-thy-neighbor policies intended to attract economic activity from other states. Inefficiency may also occur because of underprovision of local public services with significant benefit spill-outs. In Brazil, for example, eligibility for municipal health services does not depend on residency. As a result, individuals commute across borders to search for better service. A study of Rio de Janeiro found that the city did not take these externalities into account and that outlying jurisdictions spent less than expected on health care (in both per capita terms and as a share of tax revenues). The end result was a suboptimal level of health care in the greater metropolitan area (Afonso, Ferreira, and Varsano, 2003). Inefficiency may also occur simply from the fact that distortions will arise from different tax structures chosen independently by state governments with no strategic objective in mind. Inefficiencies also can occur if state tax systems adopt different conventions for dealing with businesses (and residents) that operate in more than one jurisdiction at the same time. This can lead to double taxation of some forms of income and nontaxation of others. State tax systems may also introduce inequities as mobility of persons would encourage them to abandon progressivity. Administration costs are also likely to be excessive in an unco-ordinated tax system (see Boadway, Roberts, and Shah, 2000).

Degradation of the Quality of Life

The most egregious cases happen when state or local governments, in order to attract capital and labor, offer an ever-expanding array of tax concessions and lowering of environmental and regulatory standards. In offering lower tax rates, they lower the tax burden not just on new capital but also on old capital, thereby significantly reducing their revenues and the ability to provide quality services. Alternatively, they may still provide businesses with quality services but residential services may be curtailed. This behavior resulting in a downward spiral in public-sector activities is commonly referred to as a "race to the bottom." Such an extreme situation is unlikely to occur in practice as local residents may not accept such a general degradation of their quality of life. But some less extreme examples of competition are observed every day in all societies, developed and less developed alike. For example, in the United States, location of a Toyota Motor Corporation assembly plant attracted a bidding war among several southern states. The Marriott Corporation's head office is currently located in Maryland yet Marriott frequently threatens to move to Virginia to extract greater tax concessions from Maryland. Ford Motor Company ignited a bidding war among localities and provinces in Canada when it announced its decision to locate an assembly plant in Canada but said it was not sure where to locate it (see Breton, 2000).

Underprovision of Merit Goods and Social Policy Fallout

In a federal system, lower-level provision of merit goods such as health and education, while desirable for efficiency, preference matching, and accountability, can create difficulty in attaining equity objectives in the presence of horizontal competition. Factor mobility and tax competition create strong incentives for state and local governments to underprovide such services and to restrict access to those most in need, such as the poor or the old. This response is justified by their greater susceptibility to disease and potentially greater risks for cost curtailment. Such perverse incentives can be eliminated by conditional (conditions on standards of services and access and not on spending or input controls) nonmatching grants from federal government. Such grants do not affect local government autonomy and their incentives for cost efficiency but do ensure compliance with federally specified standards for access and level of services (Shah, 1994b, 2007c).

Expenditure Competition

State or local governments may attempt to attract industry and businesses using firm-specific infrastructure investment or outright subsidies. This practice is common in the United States. Procurement and employment policies may discriminate against nonresidents as done by the Pakistan provinces. Residency restrictions may be put on the use of state or local services such as education, as is the common practice by the American states. In earlier chapters, we have argued that such measures will distort internal economic union if they are effective. If all subnational governments engage in them, however, they are likely to be self-defeating and ineffective.

Erecting Regulatory Impediments

State or local governments sometimes erect regulatory impediments for nonresidents. These include preferential treatment of local capital and labor; labor market regulations to restrict entry by nonresidents; differential entry requirements for access to training and educational programs, as well as cumbersome relicensing programs for nonresidents; and preferential treatment of local languages.

Wasteful Tax Competition

State or local governments may inefficiently compete to drive down taxes for fear of loss of their tax base. In the end, tax rates on mobile factors may be set inefficiently low because of strategic tax competition. If this practice becomes pervasive, then firms faced with competing tax incentives will reap the benefits of such incentives regardless of their location decisions. Thus, from local government perspectives these incentives lead to self-defeating outcomes – namely, reduced reduction in revenues without attracting new capital.

In Brazil, the use of ICMS (origin based) as a tool for attracting capital inflow from other regions has become an area of emerging conflict among states. Despite the fact that the National Council on Fiscal Policy (CON-FAZ, with state finance ministers as members) sought to harmonize ICMS base and rates, there is evidence that some of the tax concessions refused by the council are practiced by many states anyway. States can also resort to tax base reductions or grant payment deferrals that are not indexed (Longo, 1994). For example, some northeastern states have offered a fifteen-year ICMS tax deferral to industry. In an inflationary environment, such a measure can serve as an important inducement for attracting capital from elsewhere in the country (Shah, 1991).

In Pakistan (until 1998) and in India, state and local governments imposed taxes on interjurisdictional trade to provide protection to local industry and to limit internal trade. In India, manufacturing states imposed higher taxation on goods intended for internal trade to pass the tax burden on to nonresidents. Some states allow local urban governments to tax goods entering their jurisdictions. The end result is essentially a series of tariff zones within the country (Rao, 2007b; see also Rao and Shah, forthcoming). In Brazil, industrial states offered tax deferrals for extended periods on state-level VAT. State governments in Brazil often indulge in so-called *guerra fiscal* (fiscal wars), by which they strategically attempt to shift local tax burdens to nonresidents (see Salomao, 2000). Location-specific tax holidays are offered by subnational governments in a large number of countries. These incentives attract fly-by-night, footloose industries. Subnational governments in India, Pakistan, Brazil, Malaysia, Mexico, the Philippines, and elsewhere use the tax system as an active tool for industrial policy. In the United States, state and local governments offer concessions on a range of taxes (property, sales, corporate income, and personal income) as a tool to attract industry. These incentives can be targeted to an individual firm or offered to all firms with particular characteristics (Fox, 2007). Even in China, with a tax system harmonized by unitary tax laws, local jurisdictions manage to offer incentives to attract investment. Richer jurisdictions, easily capable of meeting their assigned "tax revenue task," can waive local taxes or refund the local portion of shared taxes to enterprises in an effort to attract investment (Dong, 2007).

Shifting Tax Burdens to Nonresidents

There may be opportunities to export taxes levied on products and services used by nonresidents. This is especially the case for taxes on business incomes and natural resources. This practice is common in most federations, but there are limits to such a strategy because of mobility of factors in the long run and demand responses.

Encouraging Pork-Barrel Politics

Another source of wasteful competition in developing countries is the competition among subnational governments for greater access to higher-level financing. Shah (1998a) has remarked that, because of a country's lack of focus on service delivery and accountability to its own residents, such competition results in subnational governments contending for scarce public funds to demonstrate ironically that "money does not buy anything." In Brazil, the federal and state governments engage in many specific programs or *convenios*. For many of these programs, pro gram objectives are typically not specified or specified vaguely, and grant objectives in some instances are determined after the funds are released. In 1989 Brazil had 5,000 *convenios*, out of which nearly 3,000 were directed to the home state of President José Sarney (Shah, 1991). In Pakistan, in 1995, Prime Minister Benazir Bhutto directed all of her discretionary funding to her home district of Larkana in the Sindh Province of Pakistan (Shah, 1996c, 1998b). Argentina (Willis et al., 1999), India, China, Pakistan, and Sri Lanka (Shah, 1994b) present interesting examples of provincial competition over national-level funds. National deficit grants were issued during the 1980s to make up for provincial budgetary shortfalls, which created strong incentives for the provinces to run ever-increasing deficits to compete with other provinces for federal financing. In South Africa, provinces administer localized national functions such as health and education, which are fully financed by the center. The provinces in the late 1990s strategically overspent on local functions such as stadiums, parks, and recreation and then claimed there were not enough moneys available to provide nationally mandated services. The national government has been using obtrusive input controls to overcome this problem in recent years, and as a result provincial effort has shifted to more intensive lobbying and cultivation of relationship with national politicians and bureaucrats. South Africa offers some additional examples where local governments competed openly and viciously among themselves for seeking financing of pet development projects. Durban and Richards Bay battled over funding sources for building a bulk container terminal. Durban and Cape Town raced to build a convention center to attain a competitive edge.

ALTERNATIVE APPROACHES TO SECURING AN ECONOMIC UNION

To overcome the undesirable properties of the horizontal competition, various approaches have been followed in federal countries.

Horizontal Coordinating Mechanisms

The Association of Local Governments Ministers (as in Brazil) or Premiers/First Ministers' Conference (Canada and Australia) play important roles in devising rules for self-discipline to avoid the excesses of noncooperative behavior while allowing a substantial degree of free play. Regular meetings at lower levels can also facilitate coordination. The Australian system includes, below the Council of Australian Governments COAG, a network of ministerial councils, as well as intergovernmental meetings of such public officials as parliamentary drafters (Le Roy and Saunders, 2006). In the German federation, experts in various fields meet regularly to exchange information and coordinate decisions. At the administrative level, there are more than 950 working and discussion groups, coordinating policy horizontally and vertically (Kramer, 2005). In Switzerland, larger cantons often help provide complex services, such as sophisticated health care, to smaller ones. Negotiated concordats formalize the cooperation (Linder and Steffen, 2006). An interesting example of intergovernmental cooperation involves university policy. University cantons reached a formal agreement to delegate their powers to a new entity, the Swiss Universities' Conference. The confederation government, in a federal law on university financing, similarly delegated authority. The result is a joint body with real decision-making power over this shared responsibility (Schmitt, 2005). Bilateral agreements can serve the same purpose but at a higher cost. In Germany, the *Länder* can conclude agreements between themselves and with the federation. As long as the subject matter is an exclusive legislative responsibility of the *Länder* (e.g., education or culture), no consent from a federal body is required (Kramer, 2005).

Intergovernmental Bodies

Institutions of vertical cooperation and coordination such as the Bundesrat, the upper house of Parliament in Germany, and the Loan Council, the Council of Australian Governments and the Premier's Council in Australia, and the National Economic Council in Pakistan attempt to achieve a coordinated policy response across all levels of government. The Swiss cantons, seeking greater influence at the national level, created a "Conference of the Cantonal Governments." This group functions as both a lobby for provincial interests and a partner in the central government's discussions in areas in which cantonal interests coincide. An issue for the Swiss is that this group represents cooperation among cantonal governments, but not parliaments (Linder and Steffen, 2006).

Belgium provides an example of extensive coordination and cooperation across government entities. The double-natured federation, with both language-based communities and territorial regions, has been described as the result of "incremental conflict management." There is no hierarchical relationship between regions and communities; both are equally constituent units. The most common form of coordination is a cooperation agreement between two or more bodies. These can be either horizontal or vertical (Deschouwer, 2005).

Role of the Federal Government

The federal governments can also play an important role in securing an economic union. This role varies significantly across countries. As we will see in the following discussion, some federal approaches have proved more helpful than others.

Constitutional Provisions

Constitutional prohibitions against impediments to the free flow of factors and beggar-thy-neighbor policies can be helpful. This, however, brings a strong role for courts to interpret constitutional provisions. Court interventions may prove costly and sometimes not helpful in protecting competitive federalism. The constitutions of mature federations typically provide a free trade clause (as in Australia, Canada, and Switzerland), federal regulatory power over interstate commerce (as in Australia, Canada, Germany, the United States, and Switzerland), and individual

mobility rights (as in most federations). In the United States, two constraints imposed by the Constitution on state powers are (see Rafuse,
1991: 3) the *commerce clause* (article I, section 8: "The Congress shall have
power . . . To regulate commerce with foreign nations, and among the
several states, and with the Indian Tribes") and the *due process clause* (amendment XIV, section 1: "No state shall . . . deprive any person of life, liberty, or
property, without due process of law").

The Indonesian The Indonesianconstitution embodies a free trade and
mobility clause. In China, on the other hand, mobility rights of individuals
are severely constrained by the operation of the *hukou* system of household
registration, which is used to determine eligibility for grain rations,
employment, housing, and health care.

Constitutional restrictions on tax competition have had some success.
The German Basic Law requirement of equivalent living conditions across
the federation effectively eliminates tax competition between *Länder*.
Some *Länder* now argue that this prohibition, combined with substantial
equalization transfers, has removed the incentive for officials to spend
revenues efficiently (Kramer, 2005).

APPROACHES TO A FEDERAL ROLE IN SECURING A COMMON ECONOMIC UNION

Federal countries pursue a wide variety of approaches to curtail regional
disparities and to maintain an internal common market and a sense of
nationhood. These approaches can be broadly classified into two categories: a partnership or do-no-harm approach and a paternalist or a do-good
approach. In the following section, we discuss their effectiveness in dealing
with reducing information and coordination costs and overcoming the
dynamic instability associated with noncooperative competitive behavior
at the subnational level.

A Partnership or Do-No-Harm Approach

Preservation of the Internal Common Market
Preservation of an internal common market remains an important area of
concern for most nations undertaking decentralization. To deal with subnational beggar-thy-neighbor policies, regulation of economic activity
such as trade and investment in most federations is generally left to the
federal or central government. The Canadian government in the Ford
Motor example cited earlier intervened with provincial governments and

was successful in inducing them to avoid a fiscal war to attract the plant. It should be noted, however, that central governments themselves may pursue policies detrimental to the internal common market. Therefore, as suggested by Boadway (1992), constitutional guarantees for free domestic flow of goods and services may be the best alternative to assigning regulatory responsibilities solely to the center.

Tax Harmonization and Coordination
As noted earlier, tax competition among jurisdictions can be beneficial by encouraging cost-effectiveness and fiscal accountability by state and local governments. It can also by itself lead to a certain amount of tax harmonization. At the same time, decentralized tax policies can cause certain inefficiencies and inequities in a federation as well as lead to excessive administrative costs. Tax harmonization is intended to preserve the best features of tax decentralization while avoiding its disadvantages. Thus, tax harmonization and coordination contribute to efficiency of the internal common market, reduce collection and compliance costs, and help to achieve national standards of equity.

The European Union has placed a strong emphasis on tax coordination issues. Canada has used tax-collection agreements, tax abatement, and tax-base sharing to harmonize the tax system. The German federation emphasizes uniformity of tax bases by assigning the tax legislation to the federal government. The Swiss Federal Tribunal will resolve, on request, issues of shared tax bases that cover several cantons or municipalities (Schmitt, 2005). In Australia, the VAT is coordinated using a revenue-sharing mechanism with the commonwealth government collecting the tax and sharing the revenues with the states. In developing countries, owing to tax centralization, tax coordination issues are relevant only for larger federations such as India and Brazil. In Brazil, CONFAZ (National Council on Fiscal Policy) attempts to keep the base of the ICMS relatively uniform across states. These efforts do not always yield the best results because of the unanimity rule. For example, at the CONFAZ meeting held at Foz do Iguacu on September 25, 1997, a consensus emerged among twenty-six of the twenty-seven states to exempt capital goods from the state-level VAT tax (the ICMS) to deal with the inequity that taxes on these goods are levied by the producing states but tax credits have to be provided by the importing states. This measure, however, could not be adopted due the sole opposition from the state of São Paulo.

In the United States, there is no constitutional requirement for states or the federal government to coordinate their tax systems or cooperate with one another (Tarr, 2005). In practice, the systems are linked. The majority of states use federal definitions to calculate their own income tax base, and most states rely on federal administrative systems (databases and audits) to help with collection. States also cooperate among themselves in areas such as compliance. A Streamlined Sales and Use Tax Agreement was reached in October 2005 after a lengthy effort. Nineteen states have enacted the legislation to simplify the sales tax and enable easier collection on remote transactions. Constraints on competition are imposed through court decisions and congressional legislation. For example, a federal court ruling in 2004 (involving Daimler-Chrysler) prevented the use of a number of tax incentives. In particular, a state could not lower a firm's tax burden if activities were expanded in that state while refusing to lower the tax burden if the expansion occurred elsewhere. These limits on competition are not comprehensive, however. There is no broad-based approach to ensure that policies do not disadvantage one state relative to another (Fox, 2007).

Intergovernmental Fiscal Transfers

Federal-state transfers in a federal system serve important objectives: alleviating structural imbalances, correcting for fiscal inefficiencies and inequities, providing compensation for benefit spill-outs, and achieving fiscal harmonization. These transfers allow the use of the spending power of the federal government to overcome some of the undesirable aspects of fiscal competition. Conditional transfers can serve as an important tool to deal with benefit spill-outs and to ensure national minimum standards to secure common economic union. Equalization transfers similarly overcome the inefficiencies and inequities associated with fiscally induced migration.

Properly structured transfers can enhance competition for the supply of public services, accountability of the fiscal system, and fiscal coordination, just as general revenue sharing has the potential to undermine it. For example, transfers for basic health and primary education could be made available to both public and not-for-profit private sectors on an equal basis using as criteria the demographics of the population served, school-age population, and student enrollments. This would promote competition and innovation as both public and private institutions would compete for public funding. Chile permits Catholic schools access to public education financing. The Canadian provinces allow individual residents to choose among public and private schools for the receipt of their property tax dollars. Such an option has introduced strong incentives for public and private schools to improve their performances and be competitive. Such financing options are especially attractive for providing greater access to public services in rural areas.

Protecting David from Goliath or Creating a Level Playing Field

Smaller or fiscally disadvantaged jurisdictions may not be able to compete as a result of having a smaller tax base or a jurisdiction not consistent with fully exploiting the economies of scale and scope. It would be appropriate for the federal government to assist these jurisdictions. Several options are available to render this assistance: bilateral contracts to provide specified services to smaller municipalities (as in Canada, where towns purchase policing services from the Royal Canadian Mounted Police); assumption of an asymmetric federal role in various subnational jurisdictions by common agreement; support for the formation of a consortium to deal with specific issues (e.g., the state of Michigan in the United States establishes bond banks to allow access for bond finance to a group of smaller municipalities); and equalization transfers to ensure subnational governments are able to provide reasonably comparable levels of public services at reasonably comparable burdens of taxation.

Facilitating Local Access to Credit

Facilitating local credit market access can also reduce the need for beggar-thy-neighbor policies by local governments. Local access to credit requires well-functioning financial markets and creditworthy local governments. These prerequisites are easily met in industrial countries. In spite of this, traditions for assisting local governments by higher-level governments are not well established in these countries.

In developing countries, undeveloped markets for long-term credit and weak municipal creditworthiness limit municipal access to credit. Nevertheless, the predominant policy emphasis of the central government is on central controls, and consequently less attention has been paid to assistance for borrowing. In a few countries such assistance is available through specialized institutions and central guarantees to promote municipal access to credit. The menu of choices available to local governments for financing capital projects is quite limited, and available alternatives are not conducive to developing a sustainable institutional environment for such finance because macroeconomic instability and lack of fiscal discipline and appropriate regulatory regimes have impeded the development of financial and capital markets. In addition, revenue capacity at the local level is limited because of tax centralization. A first transitory step to provide limited credit market access to local governments may be to establish municipal finance corporations that are run on commercial principles and to encourage the development of municipal rating agencies to assist in such borrowing. Tax decentralization is also important to establish private-sector confidence in lending to local governments and sharing in the risks and rewards of such lending.

Social Risk Management through Transfer Payments and Social Insurance

Decentralizing transfers to individuals to state and local governments will likely lead to inefficiencies in the internal common market, fiscal inequities, and interjurisdictional beggar-thy-neighbor policies. Thus, the federal government has an important role in unemployment insurance, health insurance, public pensions, and other social safety nets. In the United States, for example, welfare policy was decentralized in 1996 to encourage innovation and give states greater autonomy to determine the level and form of payments. Both the federal government and the courts took steps to ensure that fears of becoming a "welfare magnet" did not lead to drastic cuts in services. Federal grants included the requirement that states maintain their historical levels of welfare spending. Courts ruled that eligibility requirements involving residency periods were unconstitutional. An exception was a program that entitled new migrants only to the level of benefits available in their state of origin for an initial period. Federal courts have also required subnational governments to provide nonresidents equal access to services such as education and health care (see Afonso et al., 2003; Schmitt, 2003; Aroney, 2003; Fox, 2007).

Mitigating Adverse Consequences of Globalization

Mitigating adverse consequences of globalization through skill enhancement may also discourage migration in response to fiscal considerations alone and allow disadvantaged regions to compete in the internal market. Globalization of economic activity poses special challenges to fiscal federalism. In the emerging borderless world economy, interests of residents as citizens are often at odds with their interests as consumers. In securing their interests as consumers in the world economy, individuals are increasingly seeking localization and regionalization of public decision making to better safeguard their interests. With greater mobility of capital, and loosening of the regulatory environment for foreign direct investment, local governments as providers of infrastructure-related services would serve as more appropriate channels for attracting such investment than national governments. In Germany, cross-border institutions can be delegated

Länder functions. This transfer of sovereignty requires federal government consent and is allowed only in fields that are *Länder* responsibilities in the first place. These institutions typically deal with regional planning and traffic management, environmental protection, or joint public services. Examples include the Neue Hansa in the Baltic area and the ARGE-Alp in Bavaria, Austria, Switzerland, and Italy (Kramer, 2005).

Belgium uses a different mechanism to represent regional interests at the international level. A cooperative agreement within the federation allows either a community or regional minister to represent the country in the European Union Council of Ministers. The regions and communities first agree on the position that will be taken. If no consensus can be reached, Belgium abstains from voting (Deschouwer, 2005).

With mobility of capital and other inputs, skills rather than resource endowments will determine international competitiveness. Education and training typically, however, is a subnational government responsibility. Therefore, there would need to be a realignment of this responsibility by giving the national government a greater role in skills enhancement. The new economic environment will also polarize the distribution of income in favor of skilled workers, accentuating income inequalities and regional disparities. Because the national governments may not have the means to deal with this social policy fallout, subnational governments working in tandem with national governments would have to devise strategies in dealing with the emerging crisis in social policy.

In conclusion, federal government by securing economic union through its own policies can help create a level playing field and thereby reduce incentives for state and local governments to follow beggar-thy-neighbor policies.

A Paternalist Approach or a Do-Good Approach

A paternalistic view to deal with horizontal competition with regional inequity calls for an aggressive fiscal and regulatory stance by the central government to mitigate regional disparities not only by discouraging out-migration of factors but also by protecting local industry against competition from the rest of the country. Examples of such policies include regional tax holidays and credits, regionally differentiated social benefits, protection for regional industries, central financing of regional expenditures, and direct central government expenditures. Please recall that, in the partnership approach discussed earlier, the main thrust of policies was on creating an enabling environment for free mobility, competition, and technological diffusion. Here, in contrast, the emphasis is on creating protective barriers to nourish "infant" regions and to slow down, if not to impede, the natural adjustment mechanism. The problem is that such a policy environment may create an incentive structure that could undermine long-run growth potential of a region. This dysfunctional result is termed as "transfer dependency" (see Courchene, 1996). Transfer dependency does not refer to overwhelming dependence of constituent units on central government handouts of revenues without accountability, although such a situation may be a contributing factor. Instead, transfer dependency refers to a situation where the central government's regional policies create incentives for individuals and subnational governments to undertake actions that are not consistent with their long-run interest in the absence of such policies. It also creates incentives for residents to stay in the region in view of the regionally differentiated income transfer policies. For example, recipient states or provinces can provide public-sector wages that are above their productivity levels. They can run persistent trade deficits with other states, but such deficits have little impact on wages and prices within the province, as these deficits are typically financed by central government's redistributive policies. As a result, these policies impede market adjustment responses and lead to either maintaining or even worsening of existing income and employment disparities. Transfer dependency is said to exist when the following conditions hold: regional unemployment rates persistently higher than national average; wages higher than that indicated by labor productivity; and, in extreme cases, personal incomes higher than the GDP.

Atlantic Canada, the Brazilian North and Northeast, Balochistan Province of Pakistan, and southern Italy suffer to a varying degree from the ill effects of such a transfer dependency. Thus, the overwhelming generosity of the regional policies works to the disadvantage of recipient states and undermines their long-run growth potential.

If one examines the country experiences with regional convergence, an obvious conclusion that can be drawn is that, whereas the partnership approach has yielded some degree of success, the paternalistic approach has not worked (see Shankar and Shah, 2003; Shah, 2008). In this context, examples from the U.S. experience are quite instructive. For example, Blanchard and Katz (1992) find that states that experience an adverse shock in demand experience out-migration. The partnership approach to regional disparities undertaken in the United States is highlighted by Lester Thurow (1981) in reflecting upon the New England case. Thurow argues that New England is prosperous today because it went through a painful transition from old dying industries to new growth industries. According to Thurow, if Washington had protected New England's old dying industries, it may still be a depressed and sick region.

CONCLUSION

Preserving intergovernmental competition and decentralized decision making are important for responsive and accountable governance in federal countries. Beggar-thy-neighbor policies have the potential to undermine these gains from decentralized decision making. Short of federal intervention, various solutions are possible. Competing jurisdictions could reach mutual agreements on the rules of the game and a coordination strategy. There may be high coordination costs for reaching such agreement and developing enforcement mechanisms. In the end, such agreements may prove ineffective on issues where stakes may be higher for the competing jurisdictions. Alternately, constitutional prohibitions against local impediments to factor mobility may be helpful. But interpretations of these provisions by the courts may not serve federalism as well as they may unduly restrain the powers of subnational governments.

There is likewise no consensus as to the federal role in preserving horizontal competition while overcoming some negative side effects associated with this competition. A federal government oversight of horizontal competition may prove too obtrusive to respect local autonomy. A federal role, on the other hand, in using its spending power to secure a common economic union appears promising.

This leads us to conclude that a partnership approach that facilitates an economic union through free mobility of factors by ensuring common minimum standards of public services and dismantling barriers to trade, along with wider information and technological access, offers the best policy alternative in regional integration and internal cohesion within federal nations. The question is not to compete or to cooperate but how to make sure that all parties compete but do not cheat.

SIXTEEN

Decentralized Governance and Corruption

In their quest for responsive, responsible, and accountable public governance, numerous countries have recently taken steps to reexamine the roles of their various levels of government. This reexamination has resulted in a silent revolution sweeping the globe that is slowly but gradually bringing about rearrangements that embody diverse features of supranationalization, confederalization, centralization, provincialization, and localization. Note that localization implies home rule – that is, decision making and accountability for local services at the local level. Fundamental elements of home rule are local political autonomy (the ability of elected officials to be accountable to local residents), local administrative autonomy (the ability of local officials to hire and fire local government employees), and local fiscal autonomy (the discretionary ability to raise revenues and authority and flexibility in the use of local resources). The vision of a governance structure that is slowly taking hold through this silent revolution indicates either a gradual shift from unitary constitutional structures to federal or confederal governance for a large majority of people or strengthening local governance under a unitary form of government (twenty-nine federal or quasi-federal and twenty decentralized unitary countries with a combined total of about two-thirds of world population).[1] This trend is a current source of concern among academic and policy circles, worried that localization may adversely affect the quality of public governance through an increase in the incidence of corruption.

This chapter examines the conceptual and empirical basis of these concerns. It first defines corruption and governance and discusses the

---

[1] The total number of countries has risen from 140 in 1975 to more than 200 in 2004. In 2008, there were 28 federal countries with more than 40 percent of the world population (Anderson, 2008), with another 20 decentralized unitary countries with some federal features having 35 percent of world population.

importance of current concerns about corruption,[2] then provides analytical perspectives on corruption; and, in the chapter's later sections, discusses special concerns about corruption under decentralized governance and a synthesis of empirical evidence on this subject.

FUNDAMENTAL CONCEPTS AND CONCERNS

Corruption is defined as the exercise of official powers against public interest or the abuse of public office for private gains. Public-sector corruption is a symptom of failed governance. Here, we define "governance" as the norms, traditions, and institutions by which power and authority in a country are exercised – including the institutions of participation and accountability in governance and mechanisms of citizens' voice and exit and the norms and networks of civic engagement; the constitutional-legal framework and the nature of accountability relationships among citizens and governments; the process by which governments are selected, monitored, held accountable, and renewed or replaced; and the legitimacy, credibility, and efficacy of the institutions that govern political, economic, cultural, and social interactions among citizens themselves and their governments.

Concern about corruption – the abuse of public office for private gain – is as old as the history of government. In 350 B.C., Aristotle suggested in *The Politics* that "to protect the treasury from being defrauded, let all money be issued openly in front of the whole city, and let copies of the accounts be deposited in various wards."

In recent years, concerns about corruption have mounted in tandem with growing evidence of its detrimental impact on development (see World Bank, 2004a). Corruption has been shown to affect GDP growth adversely (Mauro, 1995; Abed and Davoodi, 2000); to lower the quality of education (Gupta, Davoodi, and Tiongson, 2000), public infrastructure (Tanzi and Davoodi, 1997), and health services (Tomaszewska and Shah, 2000; Treisman, 2000b); and to adversely affect capital accumulation. It reduces the effectiveness of development aid and increases income inequality and poverty (Gupta, Davoodi, and Alonso-Terme, 1998). Bribery, often the most visible manifestation of public-sector corruption, harms the reputation of and erodes trust in the state. As well, poor governance and corruption have made it more difficult for the poor and other disadvantaged groups, such as women and minorities, to obtain public services. Macroeconomic stability may also suffer when, for example, the

---

[2] This section draws upon Shah and Schacter (2004).

allocation of debt guarantees on the basis of cronyism, or fraud in financial institutions, leads to a loss of confidence by savers, investors, and foreign exchange markets. For example, the Bank of Credit and Commerce International (BCCI) scandal, uncovered in 1991, led to the financial ruin of Gabon's pension system, and the corrupt practices at Mehran Bank in the Sindh Province of Pakistan in the mid-1990s led to a loss of confidence in the national banking system in Pakistan.

Although statistics on corruption are often questionable, the available data suggest that it accounts for a significant proportion of economic activity. For example, in Kenya, "questionable" public expenditures noted by the controller and auditor general in 1997 amounted to 7.6 percent of GDP. In Latvia, a World Bank survey (2004a: 37) found that more than 40 percent of Latvian households and enterprises agreed that "corruption is a natural part of our lives and helps solve many problems." In Tanzania, service delivery survey data suggest that bribes paid to officials in the police, courts, tax services, and land offices amounted to 62 percent of official public expenditures in these areas. In the Philippines, the Commission on Audit estimates that $4 billion is diverted annually because of public-sector corruption (see Shah and Schacter, 2004). Moreover, a study by Tomaszewska and Shah (2000) on the ramifications of corruption for service delivery concludes that an improvement of one standard deviation in the ICRG corruption index leads to a 29 percent decrease in infant mortality rates, a 52 percent increase in satisfaction among recipients of public health care, and a 30–60 percent increase in public satisfaction stemming from improved road conditions.

As a result of this growing concern, there has been universal condemnation of corrupt practices, leading to the removal of some country leaders. Moreover, many governments and development agencies have devoted substantial resources and energies to fighting corruption in recent years. Even so, it is not yet clear that the incidence of corruption has declined perceptibly, especially in highly corrupt countries. The lack of significant progress can be attributed to the fact that many programs are simply folk remedies or "one-size-fits-all" approaches and offer little chance of success. For programs to work, they must identify the type of corruption they are targeting and tackle the underlying, country-specific causes, or "drivers," of dysfunctional governance.

Corruption is not manifested in one single form; indeed it typically takes at least four broad forms.

1. *Petty, administrative, or bureaucratic corruption.* Many corrupt acts are isolated transactions by individual public officials who abuse

their office, for example, by demanding bribes and kickbacks, diverting public funds, or awarding favors in return for personal considerations. Such acts are often referred to as petty corruption even though, in the aggregate, a substantial amount of public resources may be involved.

2. *Grand corruption.* The theft or misuse of vast amounts of public resources by state officials – usually members of, or associated with, the political or administrative elite – constitutes grand corruption.

3. *State or regulatory capture and influence peddling.* Collusion by private actors with public officials or politicians for their mutual, private benefit is referred to as state capture. That is, the private sector "captures" the state legislative, executive, and judicial apparatus for its own purposes. State capture coexists with the conventional (and opposite) view of corruption, in which public officials extort or otherwise exploit the private sector for private ends.

4. *Patronage or paternalism and being a "team player."* These corrupt practices involve using official position to provide assistance to clients having the same geographic, ethnic, and cultural origin so that they receive preferential treatment in their dealings with the public sector, including public-sector employment. The same assistance can also be provided on a quid pro quo basis to colleagues belonging to an informal network of friends and allies.

It is also known that corruption is country specific; thus, approaches that apply common policies and tools (i.e., one-size-fits-all approaches) to countries in which acts of corruption and the quality of governance vary widely are likely to fail. One needs to understand the local circumstances that encourage or permit public and private actors to be corrupt.

Finally, we know that if corruption is about governance and governance is about the exercise of state power, then efforts to combat corruption demand strong local leadership and ownership if they are to be successful and sustainable.

WHAT DRIVES CORRUPTION?

Public-sector corruption, as a symptom of failed governance, depends on a multitude of factors such as the quality of public-sector management, the nature of accountability relations between the government and citizens, the legal framework, and the degree to which public-sector processes are accompanied by transparency and dissemination of information. Efforts to address corruption that fail to adequately account for these underlying "drivers" are unlikely to generate profound and sustainable results. To understand these drivers, a conceptual and empirical perspective is needed to understand why corruption persists and what can be a useful antidote. At the conceptual level, some interesting ideas have been put forward,[3] which can be broadly grouped together in three categories: principal-agent or agency models, new public management perspectives, and neo-institutional economics frameworks.

Principal-Agent Models

The most widely used modeling strategy involves the principal-agent or agency models. A common thread in these models is that the government is led by a benevolent dictator, the principal, who aims to motivate government officials (agents) to act with integrity in the use of public resources (see Becker, 1968; Becker and Stigler, 1974; Banfield, 1975; Rose-Ackerman, 1975, 1978; Klitgaard, 1988, 1991; Becker, 1983). One such view, the so-called crime and punishment model by Gary Becker (1968), states that self-interested public officials seek out or accept bribes as long as the expected gains from corruption exceed the expected costs (detection and punishment) associated with corrupt acts. Thus, according to this view, corruption could be mitigated by reducing the number of transactions over which public officials have discretion, reducing the scope of gains from each transaction, increasing the probability for detection, and increasing the penalty for corrupt activities. Moreover, because it is costly to increase detection but not to increase penalties (at least if detection is accurate), the most efficient way to eliminate corruption is to impose very high penalties with a relatively low probability of detection. Klitgaard (1988) restates this model to emphasize the unrestrained monopoly power and discretionary authority of government officials. According to him, corruption equals monopoly plus discretion minus accountability. To curtail corruption under this framework, one has to have a rules-driven government with strong internal controls and with little discretion available to public officials. This model gained wide acceptance in public policy circles and served as a foundation for empirical research and policy design to combat administrative, bureaucratic, or petty corruption. Experience in highly corrupt countries, however, contradicts the effectiveness of such an approach because the rules enforcers themselves add an extra burden of corruption,

---

[3] For comprehensive surveys on corruption, see Aidt (2003).

and a lack of discretion is also thwarted by collusive behavior of corruptors. In fact, lack of discretion is often cited as a defense by corrupt officials who partake in corruption as part of a vertically well-knit network enjoying immunity from prosecution.

Another variant of principal-agent models integrates the role of legislators and elected officials in the analysis. In this variant, high-level government officials, represented by legislators or elected public officials, institute or manipulate existing policy and legislation in favor of particular interest groups, representing private-sector interests and entities or individual units of public bureaucracy competing for higher budgets in exchange for rents or side payments. In this framework, legislators weigh the personal monetary gains from corrupt practices and improved chances of reelection against the chance of being caught, punished, and losing an election with a tarnished reputation. Factors affecting this decision include campaign financing mechanisms, information access by voters, the ability of citizens to vote out corrupt legislators, the degree of political contestability, electoral systems, democratic institutions and traditions, and institutions of accountability in governance. Examples of such analyses include the work of Rose-Ackerman (1978), Andvig and Moene (1990), Grossman and Helpman (1994), Flatters and Macleod (1995), Chand and Moene (1997), Van Rijckeghem and Weder, (2001), and Acconcia D'Amato and Martina(2003). This conceptual framework is useful in analyzing political corruption or state capture.

A fine line divides theoretical models that focus on the effects of localization on corruption and those which analyze the decentralization of corruption within a multitier hierarchy from an "industrial organization of corruption" type of framework. In the latter group, a distinction is made between "top-down corruption," where corrupt high levels buy lower levels by sharing a portion of gains, and "bottom-up corruption," where low-level officials share their own collected bribes with superior levels to avoid detection or punishment. The former phenomenon is more likely to exist in a federal system of governance where powers may be shared among various orders of government, and the latter is more likely to prevail under unitary or centralized forms of governance or dictatorial regimes. The impact of governance on the corruption networks is an interesting yet unresearched topic. Tirole (1986) analyzed one aspect of this network by means of a three-tier principal-supervisor-agent model (see also Guriev, 1999). This extension of a conventional principal-agent model assists in drawing inferences regarding the type of corrupt relations that could evolve under a three-tier unitary government structure. These inferences are highly sensitive to underlying assumptions regarding principal-agent relationships under a multitiered system of governance (four-tier hierarchies are modeled by Carillo, 2000, and Bac and Bag, 1998). In Guriev's three-tier hierarchy model, the midlevel bureaucrat supervises the agent and reports to the principal. In comparing the characteristics of equilibria with top-bottom and all-level corruption, Guriev (1999: 2) concludes that top-level corruption "is not efficient, as it redistributes rents in favor of agents, and therefore makes it more attractive for potential entrants," thereby leading to higher total corruption.

Shleifer and Vishny (1993) utilize a conventional industrial organization theory model and conclude that decentralization is likely to increase corruption. In this model, government bureaucracies and agencies act as monopolists selling complimentary government-produced goods, which are legally required for private-sector activity. The main idea behind the model is that under centralized corruption bureaucracies act like a joint monopoly, whereas under decentralized corruption bureaucracies behave as independent monopolies. When bureaucracies act as independent monopolies, they ignore the effects of higher prices on the overall demand for a good and hence drive up the cumulative bribe burden.

Waller, Verdier, and Gardner (2002) define decentralized corruption as a system in which higher-level officials collect a fixed amount of bribe income from each of the bureaucrats who take bribes, without mandating on the bribe size that the bureaucrats charge. In a centralized system, on the contrary, bribe size is determined by the higher level of government officials who collect bribes from bureaucrats and redistribute what remains among them after keeping a share. Waller et al. posit that decentralized corruption leads to lower levels of total corruption in the economy (lower spread), higher levels of bribe per entrepreneur (higher depth), and a smaller formal sector vis-à-vis a centralized corruption equilibrium. Yet, these results vary widely for specific "regimes" in the model, when given parameters satisfy key conditions – for instance, for high-enough wages and monitoring systems, centralized corruption may reduce total corruption and expand the formal economy.

Whereas previously discussed studies centered on the organizational structure of corruption, Ahlin (2001) differs by concentrating on the alternative effects of different types of decentralization, and doing so from a horizontal rather than a hierarchical, perspective. In this model, a country is divided in regions, each with a given number of independent power groups. *Bureaucratic decentralization* affects the political organization in a region by increasing the number of power groups or bureaucracies, while the number of jurisdictions captures the degree of *regional decentralization* (i.e., having a single region and bureaucracy would reflect the maximum degree of centralization). Ahlin's theoretical results suggest that corruption is determined by mobility of economic agents across regions. Under the assumption of no interregional mobility, corruption increases with the degree of bureaucratic decentralization but is independent of the degree of regional decentralization, whereas for perfect interregional mobility corruption decreases with regional decentralization and is independent of bureaucratic decentralization. A key intuition of the model is that corrupt bureaucrats fail to internalize the costs of increases in bribe charges imposed on other bureaucrats.

Arikan (2004) uses a tax competition framework to examine localization-corruption links. In his model, corruption is measured as the proportion of tax revenue appropriated by bureaucrats, whereas decentralization is captured by the number of jurisdictions competing for a mobile tax base. Local governments decide on the levels of tax rates and corrupt earnings in order to maximize a weighted sum of corrupt earnings and citizen's utility. In this framework, higher degree of decentralization is expected to lead to lower levels of corruption.

Bardhan and Mookherjee (2000) shed light upon the determinants of capture of the democratic process. Not surprisingly, they conclude that the extent of relative capture is ambiguous and context specific. Bardhan and Mookherjee find that the extent of capture at the local level depends on the degree of voter awareness, interest group cohesiveness, electoral uncertainty, electoral competition, and the heterogeneity of interdistrict income inequality. A key assumption of this model is that the degree of political awareness is correlated to education and socioeconomic position – in particular, that the fraction of informed voters in the middle-income class is lower than or equal to that of the rich and higher than that of the poor. Uninformed voters are swayed by campaign financing, whereas informed voters favor the party platform that maximizes their own-class utility. The outcome of local and national elections in terms of policy platforms will coincide under four assumptions: (1) all districts have the same socioeconomic composition, and swings among districts (particular district-specific preferences for one of two political parties) are perfectly correlated; (2) national elections are majoritarian; (3) there is an equal proportion of informed voters in local and national elections; and (4) the proportion of rich voters who contribute to their lobby is equal at the national and local levels — the rich are as well organized nationally as locally. Alternatively, capture will be higher at the local level if conditions

(3) and (4) fail – that is, if the proportion of informed voters is lower at the national levels and the rich are less organized nationally than they are locally. On the contrary, greater electoral uncertainty at the local level because of differences in the electoral competition implies lower capture at the local level. If, for example, swings are not identical but rather drawn from the same distribution across districts – under the assumption that this distribution satisfies a regularity condition – heterogeneity on swings will favor different parties, implying less capture of the nationally dominant party.

No definitive conclusions can be drawn regarding corruption and the centralization-decentralization nexus from the agency-type conceptual models. These models simply reaffirm that the incidence of corruption is context dependent and therefore cannot be uncovered by generalized models.

New Public Management Frameworks

The new public management (NPM) literature, on the other hand, points to a more fundamental discordance among the public-sector mandate, its authorizing environment, and the operational culture and capacity. According to NPM, this discordance contributes to government's acting like a runaway train and government officials' indulging in rent-seeking behaviors with little opportunity for citizens to constrain government behavior. This viewpoint calls for fundamental civil service and political reforms to create a government under contract and accountable for results. Public officials would no longer have permanent rotating appointments; instead, they could keep their jobs as long as they fulfilled their contractual obligations (see Shah, 1999a, 2005c).

The new public management paradigms have clear implications for the study of localization and corruption as it argues for contractual arrangements in the provision of public services. Such a contractual framework may encourage competitive service delivery through an outsourcing, purchaser-provider split under a decentralized structure of governance. The NPM goals are harmonious with localization as greater accountability for results reinforces government accountability to citizens through voice and exit mechanisms. Conceptually, therefore, the NPM is expected to reduce opportunities for corruption (see Shah, 1999a, 2005c; Von Maravic, 2003). Andrews and Shah (2005a) integrate these two ideas in a common framework of citizen-centered governance. They argue that citizen empowerment holds the key to enhanced accountability and reduced opportunities for corruption.

Challenges and Responses

Others disagree with such conclusions and argue that the NPM could lead to higher corruption as opposed to greater accountability because the tendering for service delivery and separation of purchasers from providers may lead to increased rent-seeking behavior and enhanced possibilities for corruption (Batley, 1999; Von Maravic, 2003). Further, some argue that decentralized management leads to weaker vertical supervision from higher levels and the inadequacy of mechanisms to exert controls over decentralized agencies (Scharpf, 1997). This loss in vertical accountability is seen as a source of enhanced opportunities for corruption. Of course, this viewpoint simply neglects potential gains from higher horizontal accountability.

Neo-Institutional Economics Frameworks

Finally, neo-institutional economics (NIE) presents a refreshing perspective on the causes and cures of corruption. The NIE approach argues that corruption results from opportunistic behavior of public officials, given that citizens are either not empowered or face high transaction costs to hold public officials accountable for their corrupt acts. The NIE treats citizens as principals and public officials as agents. The principals have bounded rationality – they act rationally on the basis of the incomplete information they have. In order to have a more informed perspective on public-sector operations, they face high transaction costs in acquiring and processing the information. On the other hand, agents (public officials) are better informed. This asymmetry of information allows agents to indulge in opportunistic behavior that goes unchecked because of high transactions costs faced by the principals and a lack or inadequacy of countervailing institutions to enforce accountable governance.[4] Thus, corrupt countries have inadequate mechanisms for contract enforcement, weak judicial systems, and inadequate provision for public safety. This raises the transactions costs in the economy further – raising the cost of private capital as well as the cost of public service provision. The problem is further compounded by path dependency (i.e., a major break with the past is difficult to achieve as any major reforms are likely to be blocked by influential interest groups), cultural and historical factors, and mental models where those who are victimized by corruption feel that attempts to deal

---

[4] Following this line of thought, Lambsdorff, Taube, and Schramm (2005: 14), note that, in fighting corruption from a NIE perspective, policy makers should aim to "encourage betrayal among corrupt parties, to destabilize corrupt agreements, to disallow corrupt contracts to be legally enforced, to hinder the operation of corrupt middlemen and to find clearer ways of regulating conflicts of interest."

with corruption will lead to further victimization, with little hope of corrupt actors being brought to justice. These considerations lead principals to the conclusion that any attempt on their part to constrain corrupt behaviors will invite strong retaliation from powerful interests. Therefore, citizen empowerment (e.g., through devolution, citizens' charters, bills of rights, elections, and other forms of civic engagement) assumes critical importance in combating corruption because it may have a significant impact on the incentives faced by public officials to be responsive to public interest.

EMPIRICAL PERSPECTIVES

The empirical literature on this subject lends support to the NIE perspective elaborated previously but goes beyond it to identify some key drivers on the basis of in-depth country studies – including a recent World Bank look at Guatemala, Kenya, Latvia, Pakistan, the Philippines, and Tanzania – and econometric studies of developing, transition, and industrial countries (see World Bank, 2004a; Tomaszewska and Shah, 2000; Gurgur and Shah, 2002; and Huther and Shah, 2000). The six country case studies by the World Bank examined the root causes of corruption and evaluated the impact of World Bank efforts to reduce corruption in each country. These studies identify four key corruption drivers:

- *The legitimacy of the state as the guardian of the "public interest" is contested.* In highly corrupt countries, there is little public acceptance of the notion that the role of the state is to rise above private interests to protect the broader public interest. "Clientelism" – public office-holders focusing on serving particular client groups linked to them by ethnic, geographic, or other ties – shapes the public landscape and creates conditions that are ripe for corruption. The line between what is "public" and what is "private" is blurred so that abuse of public office for private gain is a routine occurrence.
- *The rule of law is weakly embedded.* Public-sector corruption thrives where laws apply to some but not to others, and where enforcement of the law is often used as a device for furthering private interests rather than protecting the public interest. A common symbol of the breakdown of the rule of law in highly corrupt countries depicts the police as lawbreakers rather than law enforcers – for example, stopping motorists for invented traffic violations as an excuse for extracting bribes. As well, the independence of the judiciary – a pillar

of the rule of law – is usually deeply compromised in highly corrupt countries.

- *Institutions of participation and accountability are ineffective.* In societies where the level of public-sector corruption is relatively low, one normally finds strong institutions of participation and accountability that control abuses of power by public officials. These institutions are either created by the state itself (e.g., electoral process, citizens' charter, bill of rights, auditors-general, the judiciary, the legislature) or arise outside of formal state structures (e.g., the news media and organized civic groups). There are glaring weaknesses in institutions of participation and accountability in highly corrupt countries.
- *The commitment of national leaders to combating corruption is weak.* Widespread corruption endures in the public sector when national authorities are either unwilling or unable to address it forcefully. In societies where public-sector corruption is endemic, it is reasonable to suspect that it touches the highest levels of government and that many senior officeholders will not be motivated to work against it.

How to Formulate a Strategy

So what can policy makers do to combat corruption? Experience strongly suggests that the answer lies in taking an indirect approach and starting with the root causes. To understand why, it is helpful to look at a model that divides developing countries into three broad categories – high, medium, and low – reflecting the incidence of corruption. The model also assumes that countries with high corruption have a low quality of governance, those with medium corruption have fair governance, and those with low corruption have good governance (see Table 16.1).

What this model reveals is that, because corruption is itself a symptom of fundamental governance failure, the higher the incidence of corruption, the *less* an anticorruption strategy should include tactics that are narrowly targeted to corrupt behaviors and the *more* it should focus on the broad underlying features of the governance environment. For example, support for anticorruption agencies and public awareness campaigns is likely to meet with limited success in environments where corruption is rampant and the governance environment deeply flawed. In fact, in environments where governance is weak, anticorruption agencies are prone to being misused as tools of political victimization. These types of interventions

Table 16.1. *One size does not fit all: Effective anticorruption policies specify a pecking order of reforms based upon a recognition of the broader institutional environment in each country*

Incidence of corruption	Quality of governance	Priorities of anticorruption efforts
High	Poor	Establish rule of law, strengthen institutions of participation and accountability, establish citizens' charter, limit government intervention, implement economic policy reforms
Medium	Fair	Decentralize and reform economic policies and public management and introduce accountability for results
Low	Good	Establish anticorruption agencies, strengthen financial accountability, raise public and official awareness, require antibribery pledges, conduct high-profile prosecutions

are more appropriate to a low corruption setting, where one can take for granted (more or less) that the governance fundamentals are reasonably sound and that corruption is a relatively marginal phenomenon.

The model also suggests that where corruption is high (and the quality of governance is correspondingly low), it makes more sense to focus on the underlying drivers of malfeasance in the public sector – for example, by strengthening the rule of law and institutions of accountability. Indeed, a lack of democratic institutions (a key component of accountability) has been shown to be one of the most important determinants of corruption (Gurgur and Shah, 2002). When Malaysia adopted a "client's charter" in the early 1990s that specified service standards and citizens' recourse in the event of noncompliance by government agencies, it helped reorient the public sector toward service delivery and transform the culture of governance (Shah, 1999a, 2005c).

In societies where the level of corruption lies somewhere in between the high and low cases, it may be advisable to attempt reforms that assume a modicum of governance capacity – such as trying to make civil servants more accountable for results, bringing government decision making closer to citizens through decentralization, simplifying administrative procedures, and reducing discretion for simple government tasks such as the distribution of licenses and permits.

Insights into Past Failures

With this model in mind, it is not hard to understand why so many anticorruption initiatives have met with so little success. Take, for example, the almost universal failure of wide-ranging media awareness campaigns and of seminars and workshops on corruption targeted to government officials, parliamentarians, and journalists. As the model shows, this outcome would be expected in countries with weak governance, where corruption is openly practiced but neither the general public nor honest public officials feel empowered to take a stand against it and even fear being victimized. On the other hand, awareness campaigns would be expected to have a positive impact in countries where governance is fair or good and the incidence of corruption is low.

Decentralization provides a further illustration of the importance of understanding the circumstances in which corruption occurs. There is indeed evidence that decentralization can be an effective antidote to corruption because it increases the accountability of public authorities to citizens (for additional references and evidence, see Gurgur and Shah, 2002, and Shah, Thompson, and Zou, 2004). On the other hand, decentralization creates hundreds of new public authorities, each having powers to tax, spend, and regulate that are liable to being abused in environments where governance is weak. As the World Bank's analysis of the Philippines in the 1990s has shown, decentralization may multiply rather than limit opportunities for corruption if it is implemented under the wrong circumstances. This issue is the central theme of this chapter and it is analyzed further in the following sections.

As for raising civil service salaries and reducing wage compression – the ratio between the salaries of the highest- and lowest-paid civil servants in a given country – again, the model provides some insights. The evidence suggests that in environments where governance is weak, wage-based strategies are not likely to have a significant impact on civil service corruption (see Huther and Shah, 2000, for references). Moreover, reducing wage compression may even encourage corruption if public-sector positions are viewed as a lucrative career option. For instance, in corrupt societies, public positions are often purchased by borrowing money from family and friends. Raising public-sector wages simply raises the purchase price and subsequent corruption efforts to repay loans.

How about the establishment of "watchdog" agencies – something most developing countries have done – with a mandate to detect and prosecute corrupt acts? Here, too, the governance-corruption nexus is key.

Watchdog agencies have achieved success only in countries where governance is generally good, such as Australia and Chile. In weak governance environments, however, these agencies often lack credibility and may even extort rents. In Kenya, Malawi, Sierra Leone, Tanzania, Uganda, and Nigeria, for example, anticorruption agencies have been ineffective. In Tanzania, the government's Prevention of Corruption Bureau produces only about six convictions a year, mostly against low-level functionaries, in a public-sector environment rife with corruption. In Pakistan, the National Accountability Bureau does not even have a mandate to investigate corruption in the powerful and influential military. Ethics offices and ombudsmen have had no more success than anticorruption agencies in countries where governance is poor (see Huther and Shah, 2000, and Shah and Schacter, 2004).

REVISITING THE DEBATE ON LOCALIZATION AND CORRUPTION

A brief review of the corruption literature presented previously serves as a useful background to the debate on corruption and decentralization. In the following sections, we briefly review the arguments and the evidence on both sides of the debate and then draw some conclusions based on the simple analytical model presented earlier.

Localization Breeds Corruption

Various arguments have been advanced to support the notion that corruption increases with localization. A few of these are summarized here.

Personalism
Vito Tanzi (1995) argued that localization brings officials in close contact with citizens. This promotes personalism and reduces professionalism and arm's-length relationships. Personalism in his view breeds corruption as officials pay greater attention to individual citizen needs and disregard public interest. Further, a higher degree of discretion at the local level and long tenure of local officials make it easier to establish unethical relationships (Prud'homme, 1995).

Weak Monitoring and Vertical Controls
Impediments to corrupt practices also decrease as local politicians and bureaucrats collude to advance narrow self-interests while the effectiveness

of auditing agencies and monitoring from the central level wane (Prud'-homme, 1995). Localization may increase the motivation for corruption among public officials by creating an impression that they are subject to lower monitoring, control, and supervision.

Fiscal Decentralization and Overgrazing

Treisman argues that decentralized federal systems tend to have higher corruption ratings because of either their larger size or their more likely separation of police forces at both central and subnational levels (which increases corruption because of overgrazing) and their greater propensity to have a regionally elected upper house of parliament with veto power (which also may increase corruption as regional governments may buy off these veto players or have greater leverage to protect their ill-gotten gains). Using cross-country regression analysis, Treisman (1999, 2000a, 2000b, 2007) presents empirical evidence that supports the existence of this negative relationship. Treisman's empirical results, however, are sensitive to the inclusion of other variables in the equation and may have omitted variables bias in view of a lack of underlying framework for corruption.

A recent study by Fan, Lin, and Treisman (2007) provides a more nuanced view of the impact of political decentralization. Combining cross-sectional secondary data for eighty countries with a survey of 9,000 business owners, it finds that "in countries with a large number of government or administrative tiers and (given local revenues) a larger number of local public employees, reported bribery was more frequent. When local or central governments received a larger share of GDP in revenue, bribery was less frequent" (2007: 1). These results suggest that while decentralization in general opens up possibilities for rent seeking by a larger number of individuals, tax decentralization limits such opportunities by bringing greater citizen oversight of local government operations.

Political Decentralization and Lack of Discipline

Political decentralization is seen as a cascading system of bribes by Shleifer and Vishny (1993). They note that "to invest in a Russian company, a foreigner must bribe every agency involved in foreign investment including the foreign investment office, the relevant industrial ministry, the finance ministry, the executive branch of the local government, the legislative branch, the central bank, the state property bureau, and so on" (1993: 15). In the same vein, Bardhan (1997) and Blanchard and Shleifer (2000) have argued that political centralization leads to lower levels of corruption. Blanchard and Shleifer sustain that political decentralization is seen as a source of corruption in Russia but not China, a conclusion that emerges from the contrasting role of local governments in their relations with local enterprises. In China local governments have provided a supporting role, whereas in Russia local governments have stymied the growth of new firms through taxation, regulation, and corruption. The authors note that behavior of Russian local governments can be explained by state capture by old firms, leading local governments to protect them from competition, and rent-seeking behavior of local officials discouraging new firms to enter. The authors attribute this contrasting experience to the presence of political decentralization in Russia and its absence in China. They argue that political centralization in China contributes to party discipline, which in turn reduces the risk of local capture and corruption. However, Blanchard and Shleifer's analysis does not pay sufficient attention to local-enterprise relations in the two countries. Local enterprises in China are owned and run by local governments and even deliver local services such as education, health, and transportation in addition to their economic functions. Thus, local enterprises are part and parcel of the local government. In Russia, on the other hand, a mixed pattern of these relationships has begun to emerge. Therefore, the contrasting experience of the local governments may better be explained by agency problems rather than by political decentralization. In fact, the weakening of party discipline through the emergence of powerful local leaders may be contributing to growth of local industry, as the strong arm of central planning is held at bay by these leaders.

Interest Group Capture

Opportunities for corruption increase because of a greater influence of interest groups at the local level (Prud'homme, 1995). In this regard, Bardhan and Mookherjee (2000) argue that the probability of capture by local interest groups could be greater at the local level if, for example, interest group cohesiveness (fraction of the richest class that contribute to lobby) is higher, or the proportion of informed voters is lower at the local level. Lower levels of political awareness at the local level and less coverage of local elections by media may also impair local democracy and lead to higher capture. The notion of capture at the local levels due to weaknesses of the democratic system has also been raised by Shah (1998a). Concerns about risks of local capture are also expressed in a recent World Bank Study (World Bank, 2004a), which argues that decentralization may increase opportunities for corruption in some developing countries where interference in public administration is the norm, merit culture and management systems in the civil service are weak, and institutions of participation and accountability are ineffective. The issue is significant, for example, in Pakistan and the Philippines and also relevant to Guatemala and Tanzania where more limited decentralization is underway. Pakistan has launched a decentralization program involving the creation of 7,000 local and subnational governments. Given the systemic politicization of public services in Pakistan, decentralization may intensify rather than reduce pressures for political or bureaucratic collusion, although this may be further mitigated by further administrative decentralization, giving elected local officials the power to, hire, fire, and set terms of employment of civil servants in their jurisdiction. Note that administration decentralization in areas under feudal influence is likely to exacerbate the corruption concerns. Identical concerns are pertinent in the Philippines, where legislation in 1991 devolved to regions and localities powers to provide services and raise revenues. A study of local government procurement in the Philippines revealed that (see Tapales, 2001: 21) *"contractors admit to paying mayors of the towns where they have projects, because, they say, the officials can delay the work by withholding necessary permits or harassing the workers. Municipal mayors get seven percent while the barangay (village) captain is given three percent. The heads of implementing agencies – usually the district, municipal or city engineer – get about 10 percent."*

The World Bank study is concerned with the effect of decentralization on corruption when there is a local capture by political and bureaucratic elites. There is little disagreement in the literature that, in such a situation, localization without fundamental electoral and land reforms is likely to increase corruption. On the contrary, the perception of localization as a breeding ground for corruption in the presence of democratic participation and accountability is grounded neither in theory nor in evidence.

Localization Limits Opportunities for Corruption

Localization's ability to curtail corruption opportunities has been commonly based on the potential for greater accountability when the decision making is closer to the people. This line of thought is supported from the following perspectives.

Competition among Local Governments
Competition for mobile factors of production reinforces the accountability culture. Such enhanced accountability has the potential to reduce corruption (Weingast, 1995; Arikan, 2000).

Exit and Voice Mechanisms at the Local Level

There is a general agreement in the literature that localization can open up greater opportunities for voice and choice, thereby making the public sector more responsive and accountable to citizen-voters. Furthermore, because of regional heterogeneity of political preferences, localization may reduce the range of potential capture by a unique nationally dominant party.

Higher Levels of Information

Seabright (1996) argues that accountability is always better at the local level, because local citizens who are better informed about government performance can vote these governments out of office. Under centralization, people vote for parties or candidates partly on the basis of performance in other regions and partly on issues of national interest. As a result, accountability is defused, and potential for corruption increases. Bardhan and Mookherjee (2000) also argue that decentralization of the delivery of anti-poverty programs in developing countries promotes cost-effectiveness and reduces corruption, owing to the superior access of local governments to information on local costs and needs.

Lower Expected Gains from Corruption but Greater Probability of Detection and Punishment

Administrative decentralization causes a loss in control to higher levels, thus curbing their incentives to monitor and detect corrupt activities. However, it also lowers the expected gains from corruption because, following decentralization, the number of individuals who are in charge of a single decision is reduced. It is then more likely that corrupt agents are called to bear the consequences of their actions. This line of thought complements those put forward by Carbonara (1999), who concludes that decentralization, although creating agency problems inside an organization, can help in controlling corruption, and Wildasin (1995), who argues that local officials with limited powers have little scope to engage in massive corruption.

Political Decentralization

Ahlin (2000) has argued that deconcentration has the potential to increase corruption, whereas political decentralization has the potential to contain it because of interjurisdictional competition. This may result from a reduction in the information asymmetry between bureaucrats and the politicians who appoint them vis-à-vis a politically centralized system. Crook and Manor (2000) examined the process of political decentralization in India (Karnatka State), Bangladesh, Côte d'Ivoire, and Ghana and find that such decentralization leads to enhanced transparency. With this enhanced transparency, ordinary citizens become better aware of government's successes and failures and may perceive government institutions as more corrupt than they had before. They observed that in Karnatka, India, political decentralization substantially reduced the amount of public funds diverted by powerful individuals. However, because citizens were not aware of these diversions, they concluded that corruption had increased. Crook and Manor, on the basis of evidence from Karnatka, conclude that political decentralization reduces grand theft but increases petty corruption in the short run, but in the long run both may go down. Olowu (1993) also considers political centralization as a root cause of endemic corruption in Africa. Fiszbein (1997), on the basis of a review of political decentralization in Colombia, concludes that competition for political office opened the door for responsible and innovative leadership that in turn became the driving force behind capacity building, improved service delivery, and reduced corruption at the local level.

Administrative Decentralization

A few studies show that administrative decentralization reduces corruption. Wade (1997) finds that overcentralized top-down management accompanied by weak communication and monitoring systems contributes to corruption and poor delivery performance for canal irrigation in India. Kuncoro (2000) finds that, with administrative decentralization in Indonesia, firms relocated to areas with lower bribes.

Fiscal Decentralization

Huther and Shah (1998), using international cross-section and time series data, find that fiscal decentralization is associated with enhanced quality of governance as measured by citizen participation, political and bureaucratic accountability, social justice, improved economic management, and reduced corruption. Arikan (2004) reconfirms the same result. De Mello and Barenstein (2001), on the basis of cross-country data, conclude that tax decentralization is positively associated with improved quality of governance. Fisman and Gatti (2002) find a negative relation between fiscal decentralization and corruption. Gurgur and Shah's (2002) study is the only one providing a comprehensive theoretical and empirical framework on the root causes of corruption. They identify major drivers of corruption in order to isolate the effect of decentralization. In a sample of industrial and nonindustrial countries, lack of service orientation in the public sector, weak democratic institutions, economic isolation (closed economy), a colonial past, internal bureaucratic controls, and centralized decision making are identified as the major causes of corruption. For a nonindustrial-countries sample, drivers for corruption are lack of service orientation in the public sector, weak democratic institutions, and closed economy. Decentralization reduces corruption but has a greater negative impact on corruption in unitary countries than in federal countries. They conclude that decentralization supports greater accountability in the public sector and reduces corruption.

In all, a small yet growing body of theoretical and empirical literature confirms that localization offers significant potential in bringing greater accountability and responsiveness to the public sector at the local level and reducing the incidence of grand corruption.

CONCLUSIONS

According to Lord Acton, "power corrupts and absolute power corrupts absolutely" (Letter from Lord Acton to Bishop Mandell Creighton, 1887). Localization helps to break the monopoly of power at the national level by bringing decision making closer to people. Localization strengthens government accountability to citizens by involving citizens in monitoring government performance and demanding corrective actions. Localization as a means to make government responsive and accountable to people can help reduce corruption and improve service delivery. In fact, efforts to improve service delivery usually force the authorities to address corruption and its causes. However, one must pay attention to the institutional environment and the risk of local capture by elites. In the institutional environments typical of some developing countries, when, in a geographic area, feudal and industrial interests dominate and institutions of participation and accountability are weak or ineffective and political interference in local affairs is rampant, localization may increase opportunities for corruption. This suggests a pecking order of anticorruption policies and programs, as highlighted in Table 16.1. Thus, establishing rule of law and citizen empowerment should be the first priority in any reform efforts. In the absence of rule of law, localization may not prove to be a potent remedy for combating corruption.

SEVENTEEN

Adapting to a Changing World

Globalization and the information revolution are profoundly influencing economic governance in both the industrial and the industrializing world. Globalization has lifted millions of people out of poverty, and the information revolution has brought about a degree of citizen empowerment and activism in state affairs that is unparalleled in past history. They have also acted as catalysts for "reshuffling" government functions within and beyond nation-states (Friedman, 1999; Courchene, 2001; Castells, 1998) and, in some cases, for creating new states from existing ones. Because of globalization, it is increasingly apparent that "the nation-state is becoming too small for the big problems of life, and too big for the small problems of life" (Bell, 1987: 13–14). In other words, nation-states are gradually losing control of some of their customary areas of authority and regulation, including macroeconomic policy, corporate taxation, external trade, environment policy, telecommunications, and financial transactions. Globalization is also making small, open economies vulnerable to the whims of large hedge funds and polarizing the distribution of income in favor of skilled workers and regions and against those with lower skills and access to information, thus widening income disparities within nations while improving the levels of incomes. Because of the information revolution, governments have less ability to control the flow of goods and services, ideas, and cultural products. The twin forces of globalization and the information revolution are also strengthening localization, reinforcing the consequences of the growing urbanization of population worldwide. They are empowering local governments and "beyond-government" service providers – such as neighborhood associations, nonprofit and for-profit organizations, and self-help groups and networks – to exercise a broader role in improving economic and social outcomes at the local level through greater connectivity to markets and resources elsewhere.

Localization is leading to citizen empowerment in some areas while simultaneously strengthening local elites in others. Courchene (1993, 2001) has termed the overall effect of these changes "glocalization," which implies the growing role of global regimes, local governments, and "beyond-government" entities and changing roles of national and state governments in an interconnected world.

This chapter analyzes the potentials and perils associated with the effect of these mega changes on governance structure in the twenty-first century. The chapter reflects on the governance implications of globalization and the information revolution and draws inferences for the divisions of power in multicentered governance. It highlights emerging challenges and local responses to those challenges. The final section presents a new vision of multiorder governance in which governmental and intergovernmental institutions are restructured to reassert the role of citizens as governors.

GOVERNANCE IMPLICATIONS OF GLOBALIZATION AND THE INFORMATION REVOLUTION

Globalization represents the transformation of the world into a shared space through global links in economics, politics, technology, communications, and law.[1] This global interconnectedness means that events in one part of the world can profoundly influence the rest of the world. Such new links introduce growing decoupling of production in manufacturing and services from location, thereby increasing the permeability of borders and diminishing the influence of national policy instruments. Increasing internationalization of production has decoupled firms from the resource endowments of any single nation. Drucker (1993) noted three fundamental decouplings of the global economy (see also Courchene, 1995a, 2001, 2008): the primary sector has become uncoupled from the industrial economy; in the industrial sector itself, production has become uncoupled from employment; and capital movements rather than trade in goods and services have become the engine and the driving force of the world economy.

As globalization marches on, it is introducing a mega change that exposes the fragility of existing systems of global governance. It is adversely affecting national welfare states that link incentives to national production. The sheer magnitude of this social and economic change makes it difficult for governments and individuals to cope with its consequences, especially

---

[1]   This section is inspired by Courchene (1993, 1995a, 2001) and draws heavily on his works and Shah (1998a, 1998c, 2002).

those nations and individuals who suffer a reversal of fortune as a result of this change. The following sections discuss the implications of this mega change for national governance.

Reorientation of the Nation-State, Emergence of Supranational Regimes, and Strengthening of Localization

Globalization of economic activity poses special challenges to constitutional assignment within nations. Strange (1996: 4) argues that "the impersonal forces of world markets . . . are now more powerful than the states to whom ultimate political authority over society and economy is supposed to belong. . . . [T]he declining authority of states is reflected in growing diffusion of authority to other institutions and associations, and to local and regional bodies." More simply, nation-states are fast losing control of some of their traditional areas of authority and regulation, such as macroeconomic policy, external trade, competition policy, telecommunications, and financial transactions. National governments are experiencing diminished ability to regulate or control the flow of goods and services, ideas, and cultural products. For example, the East Asian financial crisis manifested behavior on the part of financial institutions and hedge funds that would have been subject to regulatory checks within nation-states. The loans made in the precrisis period by banking institutions in industrial countries to Indonesian financial institutions with insufficient collateral and the role of large hedge funds in destabilizing national currencies serve as striking examples of practices that would not have been permitted within a nation-state (see Whalley, 1999).

Similarly, enhanced mobility of capital limits the ability of government to tax capital incomes, especially given the fierce tax competition to attract foreign direct investment that exists in most developing countries. Taxation of capital income is also increasingly constrained by governments' inability to trace cross-border transactions. For example, the government of Japan would have difficulty taxing the income of a stockbroker who trades U.K. securities on the Brussels stock exchange. Opportunities are also expanding for multinational corporations to indulge in transfer pricing to limit their tax liabilities. Although Internet commerce has exploded, bringing those activities within tax reach is a difficult task even for industrial countries. Thus, the ability of governments to finance public goods – especially those of a redistributive nature – may be impaired because governmental access to progressive income taxes (i.e., corporate and personal income taxes) is reduced, while access to general consumption taxes (valued-added taxes, or VATs) is improved with economic liberalization and global integration (Sinn, 2003). Possible erosion of the taxing capacity of governments through globalization and tax competition might be considered a welcome change by citizens of countries with a poor record of public-sector performance in providing public services, as is the case in most developing countries.

Globalization implies that not much is "overseas" any longer and that "homeless" transnational corporations can circumvent traditional host- or home-country regulatory regimes. These difficulties are paving the way for the emergence of specialized institutions of global governance, such as the World Trade Organization and the Global Environmental Facility, with many more to follow – especially institutions to regulate information technology, satellite communications, and international financial transactions. For countries facing economic crises and seeking international assistance, even in areas of traditional economic policy, the power of international development finance institutions to influence local decision making is on the rise. Globalization is therefore gradually unbundling the relationship between sovereignty, territoriality, and state power (see Ruggie, 1993; Castells, 1997). This transformation implies that governance and authority will be diffused to multiple centers within and beyond nation-states. Thus, nation-states will be confederalizing in the coming years and relinquishing responsibilities in those areas to supranational institutions.

The Information Revolution and Citizen Empowerment

With the information revolution, "the ability to collect, analyze, and transmit data, and to coordinate activities worldwide has increased massively, while the costs of doing so have fallen dramatically" (Lipsey, 1997: 76). Firms now have the ability to "slice up the value added chain" (Krugman, 1995b: 333) to gain international competitiveness. The information revolution empowers citizens to access, transmit, and transform information in ways that governments find themselves powerless to block and, in the process, undermines authoritative controls. It also constrains the ability of governments to withhold information from their citizens. Globalization of information – satellite television, Internet, phone, and fax – also serves to enhance citizens' awareness of their rights, obligations, options, and alternatives and strengthens demands for both devolution (power to the people) and localization of decision making. Consumer sovereignty and citizen empowerment through international coalitions on specific issues work as a counterweight to global capital. The influence of such coalitions is especially remarkable on environmental issues, such as building large dams and discouraging the sealing industry (Courchene, 2001).

Consumer Sovereignty and Democracy Deficit

In the emerging borderless world economy, the interests of residents as citizens are often at odds with their interests as consumers. Internationalization of production empowers them as consumers because performance standards are set by the market rather than by bureaucrats. However, it disenfranchises them as citizen-voters because their access to decision making is further curtailed as decision centers in both public and private sectors move beyond the nation-state, thereby creating a democracy deficit. For example, a citizen in a globalized economy has no direct input to vital decisions affecting his or her well-being. Such decisions are made at the headquarters of supranational agencies and regimes such as the International Monetary Fund, the World Bank, and the World Trade Organization or at transnational corporations such as Coca-Cola and McDonald's. Similarly, as noted by Courchene (2001), the European Union Council of Ministers issues hundreds of directives binding on nation-states and their citizens. Friedman (1999: 161) writes, "When all politics is local, your vote matters. But when power shifts to . . . transnational spheres, there are no elections and there is no one to vote for." In securing their interests as consumers in the world economy, individuals are therefore increasingly seeking localization and regionalization of public decision making to better safeguard their interests. To respond to these developments, Castells has argued that national governments will shed some sovereignty to become part of a global order or network of governance and that "the central functions of the nation-state will become those of providing legitimacy for and ensuring the accountability of supranational and national governance mechanisms" (Castells, 1997: 304–305).

Internationalization of Cities and Regions

With greater mobility of capital and loosening of the regulatory environment for foreign direct investment, local governments, as providers of infrastructure-related services, may be more appropriate channels for attracting such investment than are national governments. As borders become more porous and populations concentrate increasingly in urban areas, cities are expected to replace countries in transnational economic alliances in the same way that people across Europe are already discovering that national governments have diminishing relevance in their lives. People are increasingly more inclined to link their identities and allegiances to cities and regions. For example, the Alpine Diamond alliance, which links Lyon with Geneva and Turin, has become a symbol for one of Europe's most ambitious efforts to break the confines of the nation-state and to shape a new political and economic destiny (Courchene, 1995a, 2008). The "decentralization of identity" reduces the solidarity of citizens for one another at the national level and erodes support for the welfare state. Moreover, similar forces can lead to pressures for the breakup of nation-states into smaller, more homogeneous units, pressures that detract from the legitimacy of the national government (e.g., the former Czechoslovakia and Yugoslavia, Belgium, Spain).

Knowledge and International Competitiveness

Because of mobility of capital and other inputs, skills rather than resource endowments increasingly determine international competitiveness. Skilled labor, especially in "symbolic-analytic" services,[2] qualifies for treatment as capital rather than as labor. Courchene (1995b) argues that for resources to remain important, they must embody knowledge or high-value-added techniques. These developments imply that even resource-rich economies must make a transformation to an economy based on human capital, a so-called knowledge-based economy, and that social policy is no longer distinguishable from economic policy. However, education and training are typically a subnational government responsibility. Therefore, this responsibility needs to be realigned by giving the national government a greater role in skills enhancement. The new economic environment also polarizes the distribution of income in favor of skilled workers, thereby accentuating income inequalities and possibly wiping out the lower-middle-income classes. Because national governments may not have the means to deal with this social policy fallout, subnational governments working in tandem with national governments may have to devise strategies to deal with the emerging crises in social policy.

A Potential Source of Conflict within Nations

International trade agreements typically embody social and environmental policy provisions, but these policies are typically the responsibility of subnational governments. These agreements represent an emerging area of

---

[2] Reich (1991) identifies these services as problem-solving, problem-identifying, and strategic brokerage services.

conflict among different levels of government as national decisions in foreign relations affect the balance of power within nations. To avoid these conflicts, these agreements must be, to the extent that they embody social and local environmental policy provisions, subject to ratification by subnational governments, as is currently the practice in Canada.

Reorienting the State as a Counterweight to Globalization

The progress of globalization has created a void in the regulatory environment and has weakened the ability of small open economies to deal with external shocks (Rodrik, 1997a, 1997b). Such external shocks typically lead to major disruptive influences on social safety nets, income distribution, and the incidence of poverty, as witnessed recently in the East Asian crisis. This social and economic disruption leads to enhanced demand for public spending, especially for social protection and redistribution. Globalization also empowers skilled workers to command a greater premium. Courchene (1993, 2001) has argued that the premium on skilled workers will result in the wages of unskilled workers falling to a "global maximum" wage rate as such workers are replaced by cheaper workers elsewhere. Firms may resort to "social dumping" (i.e., to reducing income security and social safety net benefits to retain international competitiveness). Rodrik's (1998) empirical work involving countries of the Organization for Economic Co-operation and Development provides some support for this view. Rodrik finds that economic liberalization is positively associated with public social security and welfare expenditures. With increased globalization, greater social security and welfare expenditures must be made by the public sector to maintain social cohesion (see Rodrik, 1997a, 1997b). The widening gap between the incomes of skilled employees and those of unskilled workers has the potential to create bipolarized incomes and to make the lower-middle-income class disappear. Thus, Rodrik (1997a) has warned that the resulting social disintegration will ultimately erode the domestic consensus in favor of open markets to a point where one might see a global resurgence of protectionism. Some reversals on economic liberalization were observed in response to recent financial crises in several countries. Some governments of developing countries have attempted to dampen these shocks by introducing capital controls (e.g., Malaysia) or by attempting to strengthen social safety nets with international assistance (e.g., Indonesia and Thailand). The role of supranational agencies in dealing with competition policy, regulating short-term capital movements, and overseeing the activities of hedge funds is currently under debate.

The information revolution may allow national governments to be more responsive to the needs of their citizens and to limit demands for decentralization. The information revolution is leading to a decrease in transaction costs and is therefore lowering the costs of correcting for information asymmetries and of writing and enforcing better contracts (see Eid, 1996). Hart (1995) has argued that in such a world, organizational form is of lesser consequence and that therefore the need for decentralized institutions is diminished.

In conclusion, globalization by no means implies a demise of the nation-state; rather, globalization implies a reorientation of the nation-state to deal with the more complex governance structure of an interconnected world. Leaders in some countries might even visualize a more activist state role in smoothing the wheels of global capital markets to deal with social and economic policy fallouts, as experienced in East Asia.

LOCALIZATION

A large and growing number of countries are reexamining the roles of various levels of government and their partnership with the private sector and civil society to create governments that work and serve their people.[3] The overall thrust of these changes manifests a trend toward either devolution (empowering people) or localization (decentralization).

Localization of authority has proved to be a controversial proposition. It is perceived both as a solution to problems, such as a dysfunctional public sector, a lack of voice and exit by people, and as a source of new problems, such as capture by local elites, aggravation of macroeconomic management caused by lack of fiscal discipline, and perverse fiscal behavior by subnational units. Conceptual difficulties arise in choosing the right balance of power among various orders of government, as discussed in Shah (1994b, 1998a, 1998d) and Boadway et al. (1994). Beyond these conceptual issues, a number of practical considerations bear on the quest for balance within a nation. They include the level of popular participation in general elections, feudal politics, civil service culture and incentives, governance and accountability structure, and capacities of local governments.

---

[3] See Shah (1998a) for motivations for such a change and Shah (2007b) for new visions of local governance.

GLOCALIZATION

Emerging Jurisdictional Realignments

The debate on globalization and localization and the growing level of dissatisfaction with public-sector performance are forcing a rethinking of assignment issues and forcing a jurisdictional realignment in many countries. Box 17.1 presents a newer federalism perspective on the assignment of responsibilities by taking into account the considerations noted previously. Functions such as regulation of financial transactions, international trade, the global environment, and international migration have gradually passed upward (centralized) beyond nation-states; some subnational functions, such as training, are coming under greater central government inputs (centralization); and local functions are being decentralized to local governments and "beyond-government" local entities through enhanced participation by the civil society and the private sector. In developing countries, rethinking these arrangements has led to gradual and piecemeal decentralization of responsibilities for local public services to lower levels in a small but growing number of countries. The development and strengthening of institutional arrangements for the success of decentralized policies have significantly lagged. Strengthening of local capacity to purchase or deliver local services has received only limited attention. Even strengthening of the central- and intermediate-level functions required for the success of this realignment has not always

---

Box 17.1 Emerging Rearrangements of Government Assignments: Glocalization

Beyond nation-states: Regulation of financial transactions, corporate taxation, international trade, the global environment, telecommunications, international standards, international migration, surveillance of governance conditions, global security and risk management, transnational production, investment and technology transfer, combating of money laundering, corruption, pandemics, and terrorism.

   Centralization: Social and environmental policy through international agreements, skills enhancement for international competitiveness, social safety nets, oversight, and technical assistance to subnational governments.

   Regionalization, localization, and privatization: All regional and local functions.

materialized. In fact, in some countries, decentralization is motivated largely by a desire to shift the budget deficit and associated debt burdens to subnational governments.

Emerging Governance Structure in the Twenty-first Century

Rearrangements taking place in the world today embody diverse features of supranationalization, centralization, provincialization, and localization. Nevertheless, the vision of a governance structure that is slowly taking hold indicates a shift from unitary constitutional structures in a majority of countries to federal or confederal constitutions. This shift implies that the world is gradually moving from a centralized structure to a globalized and localized (glocalized) one. In such a world, the role of the central government would change from that of a managerial authority to a leadership role in a multicentered government environment. The culture of governance is also slowly changing from a bureaucratic to a participatory mode of operation, from a command-and-control model to one of accountability for results, from being internally dependent to being competitive and innovative, from being closed and slow to being open and quick, and from being intolerant of risk to allowing freedom to fail or succeed. Past global financial crises have hampered this change, but with improved macroeconomic stability, the new vision of governance is gradually taking hold in the twenty-first century (see Table 17.1). Nevertheless, in many developing countries, this vision may take a long time to materialize because of political and institutional difficulties.[4]

Emerging Imperatives for Rethinking Fiscal Federalism

Fiscal federalism is concerned with economic decision making in a federal system of government where public-sector decisions are made at various government levels.[5] Federal countries differ a great deal in their choices about the character of fiscal federalism – specifically, about how fiscal powers are allocated among various tiers and what the associated fiscal arrangements are. For example, Brazil, Canada, and Switzerland are highly decentralized federations, whereas Australia, Germany, Malaysia, and Spain are relatively centralized. The allocation of fiscal powers among

---

[4] See Shah (2007a) for a view on rearrangements in division of powers in decentralized fiscal systems.
[5] This section is based on Shah (2006e, 2007b).

Table 17.1. *Governance structure: Twentieth century versus twenty-first century*

Twentieth century	Twenty-first century
Unitary	Federal or confederal
Centralized	Globalized and localized
Center that manages	Center that leads
Citizens as agents, subjects, clients, and consumers	Citizens as governors and principals
Bureaucratic	Participatory
Command and control	Responsive and accountable
Internally dependent	Competitive
Closed and slow	Open and quick
Intolerance of risk	Freedom to fail or succeed
Focus on government	Focus on governance with interactive direct democracy
Competitive edge for resource-based economies	Competitive edge for human capital-based economies
Federalism as a tool for coming together or holding together	Global collaborative federalism with a focus on network governance and reaching out
Residuality principle, *ultra vires*, "Dillon's rule"	Community governance principle, subsidiarity principle, home- or self-rule and shared rule
Limited but expanding role of global regimes with democracy deficits	Wider role of global regimes and networks with improved governance and accountability
Emerging federal prominence in shared rule	Leaner but caring federal government with an enhanced role in education, training, and social protection
Strong state (province) role	Ever-diminishing economic relevance of states (provinces) and tugs-of-war to retain relevance
Diminishing role of local government	Pivotal role of local government as the engine of economic growth, primary agent of citizens, gatekeeper of shared rule, facilitator of network governance; wider role of "beyond-government" entities
Tax and expenditure centralization with conditional grants (with input conditionality) to finance subnational expenditures	Tax and expenditure decentralization with fiscal capacity equalization and output-based national minimum standards grants

federal members may also be asymmetric. For example, some members may be less equal (enjoy less autonomy because of special circumstances) than others, as in the case of Jammu and Kashmir in India and Chechnya in the Russian Federation. Alternatively, some members may be treated as more equal than others, as in the case of Sabah and Sarawak in Malaysia and Quebec in Canada. Or a federal system may give members a choice to be unequal or more equal, such as the Canadian opting-in and opting-out alternatives, Spanish agreements with breakaway regions, and European Union treaty exceptions for Denmark and the United Kingdom. Further fiscal arrangements resulting from these choices are usually subject to periodic review and redefinition to adapt to changing circumstances within and beyond nations. In Canada, the law mandates such a periodic review (the sunset clause), whereas in other federal countries changes may occur simply as a result of how courts interpret various constitutional provisions and laws (as in Australia and the United States) or through various government orders (as in the majority of federal countries). As noted earlier, in recent years, these choices have come under significant additional strain from the great changes arising from the information revolution and the emergence of a new borderless world economy. The following paragraphs highlight a few important common challenges resulting from division of fiscal powers and emerging local responses in federal countries.

Division of Fiscal Powers

The information revolution and globalization are posing special challenges to constitutional assignment within nations. The information revolution, by letting the sun shine on government operations, empowers citizens to demand greater accountability from their governments. Globalization and the information revolution represent a gradual shift to supranational regimes and local governance. In adapting to this world, various orders of governments in federal systems are feeling growing tension to reposition their roles to retain relevance.

One continuing source of tension among various orders of government is vertical fiscal gaps, or the mismatch between revenue means and expenditure needs at lower orders of government. Vertical fiscal gaps and revenue autonomy at subnational orders remain an area of concern in those federal countries where the centralization of taxing powers is greater than necessary to meet federal expenditures inclusive of federal spending power. Such centralization results in undue central influence and political control over subnational policies and may even undermine bottom-up accountability. This scenario is a concern at the state level in Australia, Germany,

India, Mexico, Malaysia, Nigeria, Russia, Spain, and South Africa. In Nigeria, a special concern exists regarding the central assignment of resource revenues. In Germany, these concerns are prompting a wider review of the assignment problem and a rethinking of the division of powers among federal, *Länder* (state), and local governments. A consensus is yet to be formed on a new vision of fiscal federalism in Germany.

The two emerging trends in the shifting balance of powers within nations are a steady erosion in the economic relevance of the role of the states and provinces – the second (intermediate) tier – and an enhanced but redefined role of local government in multiorder governance.

Diminishing Economic Relevance of the Intermediate Order of Government, or toward an Hourglass Model of Federalism. The federal governments in Brazil, Canada, Germany, India, Malaysia, Russia, and the United States have carved out a large role in areas of federal-state shared rule. In Brazil, entitlements and earmarked revenues are the restraining influences on budgetary flexibility at the state level. In South Africa, the national government has taken over the responsibility for social security financing. In the United States, the federal government is assuming an ever-widening role in policy-making areas of shared rule while devolving responsibilities for implementation to state and local governments. This shift frequently occurs through unfunded mandates or with inadequate financing. In both Canada and the United States, federal governments are partly financing their debts through reduced fiscal transfers to provinces or states.

Another dimension of emerging federal-state conflict is that in countries with dual federalism – as in Australia, Canada, and the United States, where local governments are the creatures of state governments – federal governments are attempting to build direct relationship with local governments and, in the process, are bypassing state governments. In Brazil, Canada, South Africa, and the United States, state governments have increasingly diminished economic relevance in people's lives, although their constitutional and political roles remain strong. This realignment makes vertical coordination more difficult and affects a state's ability to deal with fiscal inequities within its boundaries. In India, the federal government retains a strong role in state affairs through appointment of federal officials to key state executive decision-making positions. Overall, the economic role of the intermediate order of government in federal systems is on the wane, except in Canada and Switzerland. In Canada, provinces have increased their economic roles relative to the federal government. In Switzerland, the cantons have a stronger constitutional role as well as stronger support from local residents. Cantons in Switzerland are similar to local governments in large federations such as Canada, India, and the United States. The political role of states, however, remains strong in all federal nations and even on the rise in some nations such as Germany and Pakistan. In Germany, the *Länder* have assumed a central role in implementing European Union directives and in policy making for regional planning and development. In Pakistan, the newly elected government in 2008 ran on the platform of restoring greater powers and the autonomy for the provinces.

New Vision of Local Governance but Growing Resistance from State Governments. Globalization and the information revolution are strengthening localization and broadening the role of local governments through network governance at the local level. This realignment requires local governments to operate as purchasers of local services and facilitators of networks of government and beyond government providers, gatekeepers, and overseers of state and national governments in areas of shared rule. Nevertheless, local governments are facing some resistance from their state governments in social policy areas. In Brazil, India, and Nigeria, local governments have constitutional status and, consequently, a greater ability to defend their roles. In Switzerland, direct democracy ensures a strong role for local governments, and in both Brazil and Switzerland, local governments have an expansive and autonomous role in local governance. In most other federal countries, local governments are the wards of the state; they are supplicants of federal and state governments that have little autonomy. Their ability to fend for themselves depends on the citizen empowerment engendered by the information revolution. Russia stands out as centralization has proceeded in recent years without resistance from oblasts and local governments or people at large. In Canada, some of the provinces have centralized school finance. In South Africa, primary health care has been reallocated to the provincial order of government. In most countries, local governments lack fiscal autonomy and have limited or no access to dynamic productive tax bases, whereas demand for their services is growing fast. In Canada and the United States, existing local tax bases (especially property taxes) are overtaxed with no room to grow. In the United States, this problem is compounded by limits on raising local revenues and by unfunded mandates in environmental and social spending.

Bridging the Fiscal Divide within Nations

The fiscal divide within nations represents an important element of the economic divide within nations. Reasonably comparable levels of public services at reasonably comparable levels of taxation across the nation foster mobility of goods and factors of production (labor and capital) and help secure a common economic union.

Most mature federations, with the important exception of the United States, attempt to address regional fiscal disparities through a program of fiscal equalization. The United States has no federal program, but state education finance uses equalization principles. In Canada, such a program is enshrined in the Constitution of Canada and is often considered as the glue that holds the federation together. Most equalization programs are federally financed, except for those of Germany and Switzerland. In Germany, wealthy states make progressive contributions to the equalization pool, and poor states receive allocations from this pool. In Switzerland, the new equalization program effective in 2008 has a mixed pool of contributions from the federal government and wealthier cantons.

Institutional arrangements across federal countries to design, develop, and administer such programs are diverse. Brazil, India, Nigeria, Spain, and South Africa take into account a multitude of fiscal capacity and need factors in determining equitable state shares in a revenue-sharing program. Malaysia uses capitation grants. Russia uses a hybrid fiscal-capacity equalization program. Fiscal equalization programs in Canada and Germany equalize fiscal capacity to a specified standard. The Australian program is more comprehensive and equalizes both the fiscal capacity and the fiscal needs of Australian states, constrained by a total pool of revenues from the goods and services tax.

The equity and efficiency implications of exiting equalization programs are a source of continuing debate in most federal countries. In Australia, the complexity introduced by expenditure needs compensation is an important source of discontent with the existing formula. In Canada, provincial ownership of natural resources is a major source of provincial fiscal disparities, and the treatment of natural resource revenues in the equalization program remains contentious. In Germany and Spain, the application of overly progressive equalization formulas results in a reversal of fortunes for some rich jurisdictions. Some rich *Länder* in Germany have in the past taken this matter to the Constitutional Court to limit their contributions to the equalization pool. In Brazil, India, Malaysia, Nigeria, Russia, and South Africa, equity and efficiency effects of existing programs generate much controversy and debate.

Fiscal Prudence and Fiscal Discipline under "Fend-for-Yourself Federalism"

Significant subnational autonomy combined with an opportunity for a federal bailout makes fiscal indiscipline at subnational levels a matter of concern in federal countries. In mature federations, fiscal policy coordination to sustain fiscal discipline is exercised both through executive and legislative federalism and through formal and informal fiscal rules. In recent years, legislated fiscal rules have come to command greater attention. These rules take the form of budgetary balance controls, debt restrictions, tax or expenditure controls, and referenda for new taxing and spending initiatives. Most mature federations also specify "no bailout" provisions in setting up central banks. In the presence of an explicit or even implicit bailout guarantee and preferential loans from the banking sector, hard budget constraints at subnational levels could not be enforced. Recent experiences with fiscal adjustment programs suggest that, although legislated fiscal rules are neither necessary nor sufficient for successful fiscal adjustment, they can help in forging sustained political commitment to achieve better fiscal outcomes, especially in countries with divisive political institutions or coalition regimes. For example, such rules can be helpful in sustaining political commitment to reform in countries with proportional representation (Brazil), in countries with multiparty coalition governments (India), or in countries with a separation of legislative and executive functions (Brazil and the United States). Fiscal rules in such countries can help restrain pork-barrel politics and thereby improve fiscal discipline, as has been demonstrated by the experiences in Brazil, India, Russia, and South Africa. Australia and Canada achieved the same results without legislated fiscal rules, whereas fiscal discipline continues to be a problem even though Germany has legislated fiscal rules. The Swiss experience is the most instructive in demonstrating sustained fiscal discipline. Two important instruments create incentives for cantons to maintain fiscal discipline: fiscal referenda allow citizens the opportunity to veto any government program, and some cantons have legislated the set-aside of a fraction of fiscal surpluses, which puts a brake on debt on rainy days.

Fragmentation of the Internal Common Market

Although preserving the internal common market is a primary goal of all federal systems as well as a critical determinant of their economic performance, removing impediments to such an economic union remains an unmet challenge in federal countries in the developing world. Beggar-thy-neighbor or race-to-the-bottom fiscal policies and barriers to goods and factor mobility have the potential to undermine the gains from decentralized decision making, as recent experience in Brazil, India, Mexico, and Spain indicates. In contrast, the Canadian and U.S. federal systems have successfully met this challenge by securing a common economic union.

Failure of the Fiscal System to Provide Incentives for Responsive and Accountable Governance

In most federal countries, especially in the developing world, intergovernmental transfers focus on dividing the pie without any regard to creating incentives for responsive and accountable service delivery. Revenue-sharing arrangements often discourage local tax efforts and introduce perverse fiscal incentives through gap-filling approaches. Conditional transfers in most federal countries focus on input controls and micromanagement, thereby undermining local autonomy. In a few countries, such as the United States, they serve as a tool for pork-barrel politics. The practice of basing output transfers on national minimum standards to create incentives for results-based accountability is virtually nonexistent.

CONCLUSIONS: THE NEW VISION OF MULTIORDER GOVERNANCE

During the past two decades, globalization and the information revolution have brought about profound changes in the governance structures within and across nations. A few trends discerned from this mega change in division of powers within nations are the growing importance of global regimes in some traditional functions of central and federal governments, such as macroeconomic and trade policies and regulation; a wider federal role in social and environmental policies, which are the traditional domain of provinces and states in federal countries; the diminished economic relevance yet strong and growing political role of the intermediate order (province or state) of government; the growing importance of local government and "beyond-government" entities for improving economic and social outcomes for citizens; and, most important, the growing activism by citizens to reassert their role as governors and principals and to reign in global regimes and governments rather than be treated as subjects and consumers or clients. The growing importance of global regimes has accentuated democracy deficits because the governance structures of these regimes are at present neither responsive nor accountable to citizens at large. Over the coming decades, citizen activism is expected to force these institutions to reform their governance structures to be more responsive to the citizens' voice. Within nations, increasing pressures to realign governance structures are likely to encourage greater bottom-up accountability of government for integrity and service delivery and to reduce transaction costs for citizens in dealing with governments. This trend will mean revamping current inwardly focused government structures and replacing them with structures that are amenable to direct citizen control. It implies an enhanced role of local governments to serve as the primary agent of its citizens. In this role, a local government would serve as a purchaser of local services, a facilitator of a network of government providers and entities beyond government, and a gatekeeper and overseer of state and national governments in the shared rule (see Shah and F. Shah, 2007; Shah and S. Shah, 2006). This role represents a fundamental shift in the division of powers from higher to local governments and "beyond-government" entities and networks. It has important constitutional implications. Residual functions would reside with local governments. State governments would perform intermunicipal services and finance social services. The national government would deal with redistributive, security, foreign relations, and interstate functions, such as harmonization and consensus on a common framework. Supranational regimes would deal with global public goods and would have transparent, responsive, and accountable democratic governance structures. Such rearrangements would reassert the power of citizens as governors and would foster competition and innovation for improving local economies and their connectedness with national and global markets. Globalization and the information revolution support such realignments for citizen empowerment, whereas existing political and economic institutions, as well as security and terrorism concerns, undermine such a paradigm shift. The world's social and economic well-being critically depends on how soon the latter obstacles are overcome.

References

Abbott, Michael G., and Charles M. Beach (1997). "The Impact of Employer Payroll Taxes on Employment and Wages: Evidence for Canada, 1970–1993." In *Transition and Structural Change in the North American Labour Market*, ed. M. G. Abbott, C. M. Beach, and R. P. Chaykowski, 154–234. Corpus Christi, Texas: IRC Press.

Abed, George T., and Hamid Davoodi (2000). "Corruption, Structural Reforms, and Economic Performance in the Transition Economies." International Monetary Fund Working Paper no. 00/132, Washington, DC.

Acconcia, Antonio, Marcello D'Amato, and Riccardo Martina (2003). "Corruption and Tax Evasion with Competitive Bribes." *CSEF Working Papers* no. 112, Centre for Studies in Economics and Finance, University of Salerno.

Advisory Panel on Fiscal Imbalance (2006). *Reconciling the Irreconcilable: Addressing Canada's Fiscal Imbalance*. Ottawa: Council of the Federation.

Afonso, J. R. R., and E. A. Araujo (2006). "Local Government Organization and Finance: Brazil." In *Local Governance in Developing Countries*, ed. A. Shah, 381–418. Washington, DC: World Bank.

Afonso, J. R. R., and L. de Mello (2000). "Brazil: An Evolving Federation." IMF/FAD Seminar on Decentralization. Washington, DC: IMF, November.

Afonso, J. R. R., S. G. Ferreira, and R. Varsano (2003). "Fiscal Competition." In *Federalism in a Changing World: Learning from Each Other*, ed. R. Blindenbacher and A. Koller, 412–431. Montreal and Kingston: McGill-Queen's University Press.

Aghion, Philippe, and Peter Howitt (1998). *Endogenous Growth Theory*. Cambridge, MA: MIT Press.

Aidt, T. S. (2003). "Economic Analysis of Corruption: A Survey." *Economic Journal* 113(491): F632–F652.

Ahlin, Christian (2000). "Corruption, Aggregate Economic Activity and Political Organization." Mimeo, University of Chicago.

  (2001). "Corruption: Political Determinants and Macroeconomic Effects." Working Paper no. 01–W26, Department of Economics, Vanderbilt University

Ahmad, Ehtisham, and Giorgio Brosio, eds. (2006). *Handbook of Fiscal Federalism.* Cheltenham: Edward Elgar.

Ahmad, Ehtisham, and Vito Tanzi, eds. (2002). *Managing Fiscal Decentralization*. New York: Routledge.

557

Akai, Nobuo, Yukihiro Nishimura, and Masayo Sakata (2007). "Complementarity, Fiscal Decentralization and Economic Growth." *Economics of Governance* 8(4): 339–362. Berlin: Springer.

Akai, Nobuo, and M. Sakata (2002). "Fiscal Decentralization Contributes to Economic Growth: Evidence from State-Level Cross-Section Data for the United States." *Journal of Urban Economics* 52: 93–108.

Akai, Nobuo, M. Sakata, and N. Ma (2003). "Complementarity, Fiscal Decentralization and Economic Growth." Paper presented at the 4th International Public Economic Theory Conference, Duke University, June 12–15.

Alderman, H. (1998). "Social Assistance in Albania: Decentralization and Targeted Transfers." LSMS Working Paper no. 134, World Bank, Washington, DC.

Alesina, Alberto, and Roberto Perotti (1998). "Economic Risk and Political Risk in Fiscal Unions." *Economic Journal* 108(449): 989–1008.

Alm, James, Jorge Martinez-Vazquez, and Sri Mulyani Indrawati, eds. (2004). *Reforming Intergovernmental Fiscal Relations and the Rebuilding of Indonesia*. Northampton, MA: Edward Elgar.

Alok, V. N. (2006). "Local Government Organization and Finance: Rural India." In *Local Governance in Developing Countries*, ed. Anwar Shah, 205–231. Washington, DC: World Bank.

Anderson, George (2008). *Federalism: An Introduction*. Don Mills, Ontario: Oxford University Press.

Andrews, Matthew (2001). "Institutional Effects on Local Government Fiscal Outcomes." Mimeo, Syracuse University.

Andrews, Matthew, and Anwar Shah (2005a). "Citizen-Centered Governance: A New Approach to Public Sector Reform." In *Public Expenditure Analysis*, ed. Anwar Shah, 153–82. Washington, DC: World Bank.

(2005b). "Towards Citizen-Centered Local Budgets in Developing Countries." In *Public Expenditure Analysis*, ed. Anwar Shah, 183–216. Washington, DC: World Bank.

Andvig, Jens Chr., and Karl O. Moene (1990). "How Corruption May Corrupt." *Journal of Economic Behavior and Organization* 13: 63–76.

Arikan, Gulsun (2000). "Fiscal Decentralization: A Remedy for Corruption?" Mimeo, Department of Economics, University of Illinois at Urbana-Champaign.

(2004). "Fiscal Decentralization: A Remedy for Corruption?" *International Tax and Public Finance* 11: 175–195.

Aroney, N. (2003). "Fiscal Competition." In *Federalism in a Changing World: Learning from Each Other*, ed. R. Blindenbacher and A. Koller, 492–501. Montreal and Kingston: McGill-Queen's University Press.

Arrow, Kenneth J. (1951). "An Extension of the Basic Theorems of Classical Welfare Economics." In *Proceedings of the Second Berkeley Symposium on Mathematical Statistics and Probability*, 507–532. Berkeley: University of California Press.

Asensio, M. A. (2006). "Local Government Organization and Finance: Argentina." In *Local Governance in Developing Countries*, ed. Anwar Shah, 347–379. Washington, DC: World Bank.

Atkinson, Anthony B., and Joseph E. Stiglitz (1976). "The Design of Tax Structure: Direct versus Indirect Taxation." *Journal of Public Economics* 6: 55–75.

(1980). *Lectures on Public Economics*. Maidenhead: McGraw-Hill.

Atsushi, Iimi (2005). "Decentralization and Economic Growth Revisited: An Empirical Note." *Journal of Urban Economics* 57: 449–461.

Aubut, Julie, and François Vaillancourt (2001). "Using GDP in Equalization Calculations: Are There Meaningful Measurement Issues?" Working paper, Institute of Intergovernmental Relations, Queen's University, Kingston, Ontario, Canada.

Auerbach, Alan J., Laurence J. Kotlikoff, and Willi Leibfritz, eds. (1999). *Generational Accounting around the World.* Chicago: University of Chicago Press.

Ayua, I. A., and D. C. J. Dakas (2005). "Federal Republic of Nigeria." In *Constitutional Origins, Structure, and Change in Federal Countries*, ed. J. Kincaid and G. A. Tarr, 239–275. Montreal and Kingston: McGill-Queen's University Press.

Azfar, O., T. Gurgur, S. Kahkonen, A. Lanyi, and P. Meagher (2000a). *Decentralization and Governance: An Empirical Investigation of Public Service Delivery in the Philippines.* College Park: IRIS, University of Maryland.

Azfar, O., S. Kahkonen, J. Livingston, P. Meagher, and D. Rutherford (2000b). *Making Decentralization Work: An Empirical Investigation of Governance and Public Services in Uganda.* College Park: IRIS, University of Maryland.

Azfar, O., and J. Livingston (2002). *Federalist Disciplines or Local Capture? An Empirical Analysis of Decentralization in Uganda.* College Park: IRIS, University of Maryland.

Bac, M., and P. K. Bag (1998). "Corruption, Collusion and Implementation: A Hierarchical Design." Mimeo, University of Liverpool.

Bailey, Stephen (1999). *Local Government Economics: Theory, Policy, and Practice.* Basingstoke: Macmillan.

Banfield, Edward (1975). "Corruption as a Feature of Government Organization." *Journal of Law and Economics* 18: 587–695.

Banting, K., and R. Boadway (2004). "Defining the Sharing Community: The Federal Role in Health Care." In *Money, Politics and Health Care*, ed. H. Lazar and F. St-Hilaire, 1–77. Montreal: Institute for Research on Public Policy.

Barati, Izabella, and Akos Szalai (2000). "Fiscal Decentralization in Hungary." Centre for Public Affairs Studies, Budapest University of Economic Sciences.

Bardhan, Pranab (1997). "Corruption and Development: A Review of Issues." *Journal of Economic Literature* 35(September): 1320–1346.

Bardhan, Pranab, and Dilip Mookherjee (2000). "Decentralizing Anti-poverty Program Delivery in Developing Countries." Working paper, University of California, Berkeley.

(2003). Poverty Alleviation Effort of West Bengal Panchayats. http://econ.bu.edu/dilipm/wkpap.htm/epwsumm.pdf.

Barro, Robert J. (1996). *Getting It Right: Markets and Choices in a Free Society.* Cambridge, MA: MIT Press.

Batley, R. (1999). "The Role of Government in Adjusting Economies: An Overview of Findings." International Development Department, University of Birmingham, Alabama.

Beck, Thorsten, Juan Miguel Crivelli, and William Summerhill (2003). "State Bank Transformation in Brazil: Choices and Consequences." Paper presented at the World Bank Conference on Bank Privatization and International Society for New Institutional Economics (ISNIE), World Bank, Washington, DC.

Becker, Gary Stanley (1968). "Crime and Punishment: An Economic Approach." *Journal of Political Economy* 76(2): 169–217.

(1983). "A Theory of Competition among Pressure Groups for Political Influence." *Quarterly Journal of Economics* 97(3): 371–400.

Becker, Gary Stanley, and George Stigler (1974). "Law Enforcement, Malfeasance and the Compensation of Enforcers." *Journal of Legal Studies* 3: 1–19.

Bell, Daniel (1987). "The World and the United States in 2013." *Daedalus* 116(3): 1–31.

Bernstein, Thomas P., and Xiaobo Lu (2003). *Taxation without Representation in Contemporary Rural China.* Cambridge: Cambridge University Press.

Besley, Timothy J., and Harvey S. Rosen (1998). "Vertical Externalities in Tax Setting: Evidence from Gasoline and Cigarettes." *Journal of Public Economics* 70: 383–398.

Bewley, Truman F. (1981). "A Critique of Tiebout's Theory of Local Public Expenditure." *Econometrica* 49: 713–740.

Biehl, Dieter (1994). "Intergovernmental Fiscal Relations and Macroeconomic Management – Possible Lessons from a Federal Case: Germany." In *Intergovernmental Fiscal Relations and Macroeconomic Management in Large Countries*, ed. S. P. Gupta, P. Knight, R. Waxman, and Y.-K. Wen, 69–121. New Delhi: EDI, World Bank and Indian Council for Research on International Economic Relations.

Bird, Richard M., and Pierre-Pascal Gendron (1998). "Dual VATs and Cross-Border Trade: Two Problems, One Solution?" *International Tax and Public Finance* 5(3): 429–442.

(2001). "VATs in Federal Countries: International Experience and Emerging Possibilities." *Bulletin for International Fiscal Documentation* 55(7, July): 293–309.

Bird, Richard M., and Thomas Stauffer, eds. (2001). *Intergovernmental Fiscal Relations in Fragmented Societies.* Fribourg, Switzerland: Institute of Federalism.

Bird, Richard M., and Francois Vaillancourt, eds. (1998). *Fiscal Decentralization in Developing Countries.* Cambridge: Cambridge University Press.

Blanchard, Olivier Jean, and Lawrence E. Katz (1992). "Regional Evolutions." In *Brookings Papers on Economic Activity*, ed. William C. Brainard and George L. Perry, 1:1–62. Washington, DC: Brookings Institution.

Blanchard, Olivier, and Andrei Shleifer (2000). "Federalism with and without Political Centralization: China versus Russia." Working paper, no. 7616 (March), 1–14. National Bureau of Economic Research, Cambridge, MA.

Blindenbacher, Raoul, and Arnold Koller, eds. (2003). *Federalism in a Changing World: Learning from Each Other.* Montreal: McGill-Queens' University Press.

Boadway, Robin (1992). *The Constitutional Division of Powers: An Economic Perspective.* Ottawa: Economic Council of Canada.

(2002). "Revisiting Equalization Again: Representative Tax System vs. Macro Approaches." Working paper, Institute of Intergovernmental Relations, Queen's University, Kingston, Ontario, Canada.

(2004). "The Theory and Practice of Equalization." *CESifo Economic Studies* 1: 211–254.

(2005a). "The Vertical Fiscal Gap: Conceptions and Misconceptions." In *Canadian Fiscal Arrangements: What Works, What Might Work Better*, ed. Harvey Lazar, 51–80. Montreal and Kingston: McGill-Queen's Press.

(2005b). "Evaluating the Equalization Program." *Study Prepared for the Expert Panel on Equalization and Territorial Formula Financing*, Ottawa, 40 pp. http://www.eqtffpfft.ca/submissions/EvaluatingtheEqualizationProgram.pdf.

(2006a). "Two Panels on Two Balances." *Policy Options* 27: 40–45.

(2006b). "The Principles and Practice of Federalism: Lessons for the EU?" *Swedish Economic Policy Review* 13(1): 9–62.

(2007a). "Natural Resource Shocks and the Federal System: Boon and Curse?" In *Canada: The State of the Federation, 2006/2007*. Montreal: McGill-Queen's University Press for the Institute of Intergovernmental Relations, School of Policy Studies, Queen's University.

(2007b). "The Practice of Fiscal Federalism in Canada." In *The Practice of Fiscal Federalism: Comparative Perspectives*, ed. Anwar Shah, 98–124. Montreal and Kingston: McGill-Queen's Press.

(forthcoming). "Economic Evaluation of Projects." In *Tools for Public Sector Evaluations*, ed. Anwar, Shah. Washington, DC: World Bank.

Boadway, Robin, and Neil Bruce (1984). *Welfare Economics*. Oxford: Blackwell.

Boadway, Robin, N. Bruce, K. J. McKenzie, and J. M. Mintz (1987). "Marginal Effective Tax Rates for Capital in the Canadian Mining Industry." *Canadian Journal of Economics* 20(1): 1–16.

Boadway, Robin, and Katherine Cuff (1999). "Monitoring Job Search as an Instrument for Targeting Transfers." *International Tax and Public Finance* 6: 317–337.

Boadway, Robin, Katherine Cuff, and Nicolas Marceau (2003). "Agglomeration Effects and the Competition for Firms." *International Tax and Public Finance* 11(5): 623–645.

Boadway, Robin, and Frank R. Flatters (1982a). "Efficiency and Equalization Payments in a Federal System of Government: A Synthesis and Extension of Recent Results." *Canadian Journal of Economics* 15: 613–633.

(1982b). *Equalization in a Federal State: An Economic Analysis*. Ottawa: Economic Council of Canada.

(1993). "The Taxation of Natural Resources: Principles and Policy Issues." Policy Research Working Paper no. 1210, World Bank, Washington, DC.

Boadway, Robin, and Paul A. R. Hobson, eds. (1998). *Equalization, Its Contribution to Canada's Economic and Fiscal Progress*. Kingston: John Deutch Institute for the Study of Economic Policy.

Boadway, Robin, Isao Horiba, and Raghbendra Jha (1999). "The Provision of Public Services by Government Funded Decentralized Agencies." *Public Choice* 100(3–4): 157–184.

Boadway, Robin, and Michael Keen (1996). "Efficiency and the Optimal Direction for Federal-State Transfers." *International Tax and Public Finance* 3: 137–155.

(2000). "Redistribution." In *Handbook of Income Distribution*, ed. Anthony B. Atkinson and François Bourguignon, 1:677–789. Amsterdam: North-Holland.

Boadway, Robin, and Nicolas Marceau (1994). "Time Inconsistency as a Rationale for Public Unemployment Insurance." *International Tax and Public Finance* 1: 107–126.

Boadway, Robin, Maurice Marchand, and Pierre Pestieau (1994). "Towards a Theory of the Direct-Indirect Tax Mix." *Journal of Public Economics* 55(1): 71–88.

Boadway, Robin, Maurice Marchand, and Marianne Vigneault (1998). "The Consequences of Overlapping Tax Bases for Redistribution and Public Spending in a Federation." *Journal of Public Economics* 68: 453–478.

Boadway, Robin, Sandra Roberts, and Anwar Shah (1994). "The Reform of Fiscal Systems in Developing and Emerging Market Economies: A Federalism Perspective." Policy Research Working Paper no. 1259, World Bank, Washington, DC.

(2000). "Fiscal Federalism Dimension of Tax Reform in Developing Countries." In *Fiscal Reform and Structural Change in Developing Countries*, vol. 1, ed. G. Perry, J. Whalley, and G. McMahon, 171–200. London: Macmillan.

Boadway, Robin, and Anwar Shah, eds. (2007). *Intergovernmental Fiscal Transfers.* Washington, DC: World Bank.

Boadway, Robin, and J.-F. Tremblay (2006). "A Theory of Fiscal Imbalance." *Finanz Archiv* 62: 1–27.

Boadway, Robin, and David E. Wildasin (1984). *Public Sector Economics.* 2nd ed. Boston: Little, Brown.

Bodman, Philip, and Kathryn Ford (2006). "Fiscal Federalism and Economic Growth in the OECD." Macroeconomic Research Group, Discussion Paper no. 7, School of Economics, University of Queensland.

Bomfim, Antulio, and Anwar Shah (1994). "Macroeconomic Management and the Division of Powers in Brazil: Perspectives for the 1990s." *World Development* 22: 535–542.

Bordignon, Massimo, Paolo Manasse, and Guido Tabellini (2001). "Optimal Regional Redistribution under Asymmetric Information." *American Economic Review* 91(3): 709–723.

Boskin, Michael J. (1973). "Local Government Tax and Product Competition and the Optimal Provision of Public Goods." *Journal of Political Economy* 81(1): 203–210.

Bowman, Ann, and Richard Kearney (1990). *State and Local Government.* Boston: Houghton Mifflin.

Boyne, George (1998). *Public Choice Theory and Local Government.* Basingstoke: Macmillan.

Braun, M., and M. Tommasi (2002). "Fiscal Rules for Subnational Governments: Some Organizing Principles and Latin American Experiences." Paper presented at the IMF/World Bank Conference on Fiscal Rules, Oaxaca, Mexico, February.

Brennan, Geoffrey, and James Buchanan (1980). *The Power to Tax: Analytical Foundations of a Fiscal Constitution.* Cambridge: Cambridge University Press.

Brennan, Geoffrey, and Loran Lomasky (1993). *Democracy and Decision.* Cambridge: Cambridge University Press.

Breton, Albert (1965). "A Theory of Government Grants." *Canadian Journal of Economics and Political Science* 31: 175–187.

(1994). "Designing More Competitive and Efficient Governments." In *Defining the Role of Government: Economic Perspectives of the State*, ed. Robin Boadway, Albert Breton, and Neil Bruce, 55–98. Kingston: School of Policy Studies.

(1995). *Competitive Governments.* Cambridge: Cambridge University Press.

(1996). *Competitive Governments: An Economic Theory of Politics and Public Finance.* Cambridge: Cambridge University Press.

(2000). "An Introduction to Decentralization Failure." Paper presented at the IMF Conference on Fiscal Decentralization, Washington, DC, November 20–21.

(2006). "Modeling Vertical Competition." In *Handbook of Fiscal Federalism*, ed. Ehtisham Ahmad and Giorgio Brosio, 86–105. Cheltenham: Edward Elgar.

Breton, Albert, and Anthony Scott (1978). *The Economic Constitution of Federal States.* Toronto: University of Toronto Press.

Browning, Edgar K. (1975). *Redistribution and the Welfare System.* Washington, DC: American Enterprise Institute for Public Policy Research.

Bruce, Neil (1995). "A Fiscal Federalism Analysis of Debt Policies by Sovereign Regional Governments." *Canadian Journal of Economics* 28: S195–S206.

Bruce, Neil, and Michael Waldman (1991). "Transfers in Kind: Why They Can Be Efficient and Nonpaternalistic." *American Economic Review* 81(5): 1345–1351.

Brueckner, Jan (1982). "A Test for Allocative Efficiency in the Local Public Sector." *Journal of Public Economics* 19: 311–331.

Buchanan, James M. (1950). "Federalism and Fiscal Equity." *American Economic Review* 40: 583–599.

(1952). "Federal Grants and Resource Allocation." *Journal of Political Economy* 60: 208–217.

(1965). "An Economic Theory of Clubs." *Economica* 32: 1–14.

(1997). *Post-Socialist Political Economy: Selected Essays.* Cheltenham: Edward Elgar.

Buchanan, James M., and Charles Goetz (1972). "Efficiency Limits of Fiscal Mobility: An Assessment of the Tiebout Model." *Journal of Public Economics* 1: 25–43.

Burgess, Robin, Stephen Howes, and Nicolas Stern (1995). "The Reform of Indirect Taxes in India." In *India: The Future of Economic Reform*, ed. Robert Cassen and Vijay Joshi, 113–166. New Delhi: Oxford University Press.

Canada, Government of (2006a). "Achieving a National Purpose: Putting Equalization Back on Track." *Expert Panel Report on Equalization and Territorial Formula Financing, Department of Finance.* Ottawa: Government of Canada.

Caplan, A. J., R. C. Cornes, and E. C. D. Silva (1998). "Pure Public Goods and Income Redistribution in a Federation with Decentralized Leadership and Imperfect Labor Mobility." *Journal of Public Economics* 77(2): 265–284.

Carbonara, Emanuela (1999). "Bureaucracy, Corruption and Decentralization." Department of Economics Working Paper no. 342/33, University of Bologna, Italy.

Carillo, Juan D. (2000). "Corruption in Hierarchies." *Annales d'Economie et de Statistique,* Institut National de la Statistique et des Etudes Economiques (France) 59: 37–61.

Castells, Manuel (1997). *The Power of Identity.* Oxford: Blackwell.

(1998). *End of Millennium.* Oxford: Blackwell.

Caulfield, Janice (2003). "Local Government Reform in Comparative Perspective." In *Reshaping Australian Local Government*, ed. Brian Dollery, Neil Marshall, and Andrew Worthington, 11–34. Sydney: University of New South Wales Press.

Centre for Economic Policy Research (1993). "Making Sense of Subsidiarity: How Much Centralization for Europe?" London.

Chand, Sheetal K., and Karl O. Moene (1997). "Controlling Fiscal Corruption." International Monetary Fund Working Paper WP/97/100, Washington, DC.

China Statistical Yearbook (2000). Beijing: China Statistical Publishing House.

Christiansen, Vidar, Karen P. Hagen, and Agnar Sandmo (1994). "Scope for Taxation and Public Expenditure in an Open Economy." *Scandinavian Journal of Economics* 96(3): 289–309.

Chung, Wee-Wee Connie, and Jose L. Tongzon (2004). "A Paradigm Shift for China's Central Bank System." *Journal of Post Keynesian Economics* 27(1): 87–103.

Cnossen, S. (1998). "Global Trends and Issues in Value Added Taxation, International Tax and Public Finance." *International Tax and Public Finance* 5: 399–428.

Coate, Stephen (1995). "Altruism, the Samaritan's Dilemma, and Government Transfer Policy." *American Economic Review* 85(1): 46–57.

Commission on Fiscal Imbalance (Séguin Commission) (2002). *A New Division of Canada's Financial Resources: Final Report*. Quebec: Government of Québec. http://www.desequilibrefiscal.gouv.qc.ca/.

Courchene, Thomas J. (1993). "Glocalization, Institutional Evolution, and the Australian Federation." In *Federalism and the Economy: International, National, and State Issues*, ed. Brian Galligan, 64–117. Canberra: Federalism Research Centre, Australian National University.

(1995a). "Glocalization: The Regional/International Interface." *Canadian Journal of Regional Science* 18(1, Spring): 1–20.

(1995b). "Macrofederalism: Some Explanatory Research Relating to Theory and Practice." Unpublished paper, World Bank, Washington, DC. Available at www.worldbank.org/wbi/publicfinance.

(1996). "The Comparative Nature of Australian and Canadian Economic Space." In *Reforming Fiscal Federalism for Global Competition: A Canada-Australia Comparison*, ed. Paul Boothe, 7–22. Edmonton: University of Alberta Press.

(2001). *A State of Minds: Towards a Human Capital Future for Canadians*. Montreal, Quebec: Institute for Research on Public Policy.

(2004). "Confiscatory Equalization: The Intriguing Case of Saskatchewan's Vanishing Energy Revenues." *IRPP Choices* 10(3, March): 1–39.

(2008). "Macro Federalism: An Introduction." In *Macro Federalism and Local Finance*, ed. Anwar Shah., 9–76. Washington, DC: World Bank.

Cremer, Jacques (1986). "Cooperation in Ongoing Organizations." *Quarterly Journal of Economics* 101(1): 33–49.

Crook, Richard, and James Manor (2000). "Democratic Decentralization." OED Working Paper Series no. 11 (Summer), World Bank, Washington, DC.

Cukierman, Alex, Bilin Neyapti, and Steven B. Webb (1992). "Measuring The Independence of Central Banks and Its Effect on Policy Outcomes." *World Bank Economic Review (International)* 6(3, September): 353–398.

Cull, Robert, and Lixin-Colin Xu (2003). "Who Gets Credit? The Behavior of Bureaucrats and State Banks in Allocating Credit to Chinese State-Owned Enterprises." *Journal of Development Economics* 71(2): 533–559.

Dafflon, Bernard (1977). *Federal Finance in Theory and Practice: With Special Reference to Switzerland*. Bern: Paul Haupt.

Dahlby, Bev (1981). "Adverse Selection and Pareto Improvements through Compulsory Insurance." *Public Choice* 37: 547–558.

(1994). "The Distortionary Effect of Rising Taxes." In *Deficit Reduction: What Pain, What Gain?*, ed. William B. P. Robson and William M. Searth, 43–72. Toronto: C. D. Howe Institute.

(1996). "Fiscal Externalities and the Design of Intergovernmental Grants." *International Tax and Public Finance* 3(3): 397–411.

(1998). "Progressive Taxation and the Social Marginal Cost of Public Funds." *Journal of Public Economics* 67(1): 105–122.

Dahlby, Bev, and Leonard S. Wilson (2003). "Vertical Fiscal Externalities in a Federation." *Journal of Public Economics* 87(3–4): 917–930.

Davoodi, H., and H. Zou (1998). "Fiscal Decentralization and Economic Growth: A Cross-Country Study." *Journal of Urban Economics* 43(2): 244–257.

Day, Kathleen M. (1992). "Interprovincial Migration and Local Public Goods." *Canadian Journal of Economics* 25: 123–144.

Day, Kathleen M., and S. L. Winer (2006). "Policy-Induced Migration in Canada: An Empirical Investigation of the Canadian Case." *International Tax and Public Finance* 13(5): 535–564.

De Mello, Luis, and Matias Barenstein (2001). "Fiscal Decentralization and Governance - A Cross-Country Analysis." IMF Working Paper 01/71.

Deschouwer, K. (2005). "Kingdom of Belgium." In *Constitutional Origins, Structure, and Change in Federal Countries*, ed. J. Kincaid and G. A. Tarr, 48–75. Montreal and Kingston: McGill-Queen's University Press.

Diamond, Peter A. (1981). "Mobility Costs, Frictional Unemployment, and Efficiency." *Journal of Political Economy* 89(4): 798–812.

Dillinger, William R. (1997). "Brazil's State Debt Crisis: Lessons Learned." *Economic Notes*, no. 14. World Bank, Washington, DC.

Dixit, Avinash, and John Londregan (1996). "The Determinants of Success of Special Interests in Redistributive Politics." *Journal of Politics* 58: 1132–1155.

Dollery, Brian, and Joe Wallis (2001). *The Political Economy of Local Government.* Cheltenham: Edward Elgar.

Dong, Qiu (2007). "China Fiscal Federalism." Unpublished paper, World Bank, Washington, DC.

Downs, Anthony (1957). *An Economic Theory of Democracy.* New York: Harper and Row.

Drucker, Peter (1993). *Post-Capitalist Society.* New York: Harper Business.

Eckardt, S., and Anwar Shah (2006). "Local Government Organization and Finance: Indonesia." In *Local Governance in Developing Countries*, ed. Anwar Shah, 233–274. Washington, DC: World Bank.

Eckaus, Richard S. (2003). "Some Consequences of Fiscal Reliance on Extrabudgetary Revenues in China." *China Economic Review* 14(1): 72–88.

Edwards, Jeremy S. S., and Michael J. Keen (1996). "Tax Competition and Leviathan." *European Economic Review* 40(1): 113–134.

Edwards, Jeremy S. S., Michael Keen, and Matti Tuomala (1994). "Income Tax, Commodity Taxes and Public Good Provision: A Brief Guide." *FinanzArchiv* 51: 472–497.

Eichengreen, Barry, Ricardo Hausman, and Jurgen von Hagen (1999). "Reforming Budgetary Institutions in Latin America: The Case for a National Finance Council." *Open Economies Review* 10(4): 415–442.

Eid, Florence (1996). "Agency Theory, Property Rights, and Innovation in the Decentralized Public Sector." Department of Urban Studies and Planning, Massachusetts Institute of Technology, Cambridge, MA.

Elazar, Daniel, J. (1987). *Exploring Federalism.* Tuscaloosa: University of Alabama Press.

Elhiraika, Adam B. (2007). "Fiscal Decentralization and Public Service Delivery in South Africa." Working paper no.58, African Trade Policy Centre. Addis Ababa, Ethiopia.

Enikolopov, R., and E. Zhuravskaya (2003). "Decentralization and Political Institutions." http://emlab.berkeley.edu/users/webfac/bardhan/e271_f03/oct6.pdf.

Eskeland, G., and D. Filmer (2002). "Autonomy, Participation, and Learning in Argentine Schools: Findings and Their Implications for Decentralization." Policy Research Working Paper no. 2766, World Bank, Washington, DC.

Estache, A., and S. Sinha (1995). "Does Decentralization Increase Spending on Public Infrastructure?" Policy Research Working Paper no. 1457, World Bank, Washington, DC.

Expert Panel on Equalization and Territorial Formula Financing (2006). *Achieving a National Purpose: Putting Equalization Back on Track*. Ottawa: Department of Finance.

Faguet, Jean-Paul (2001). "Does Decentralization Increase Responsiveness to Local Needs? Evidence from Bolivia." Policy Research Working Paper no. 2516, World Bank, Washington, DC.

Faguet, Jean-Paul, and Sanchez, Fabio, (2006). "Decentralizations Effects on Educational Outcomes in Bolivia and Colombia" (March). London School of Economics STICERD Research Paper no. DEDPS47. Available at SSRN: http://ssrn.com/abstract=1127016.

Fan, Simon, Chen Lin, and Daniel Treisman (2007). "Political Decentralization and Corruption: Micro-evidence from around the World." Unpublished paper, Department of Political Science, University of California, Los Angeles.

Filimon, R., T. Romer, and H. Rosenthal (1982). "Asymmetric Information and Agenda Control: The Bases of Monopoly Power and Public Spending." *Journal of Public Economics* 17: 51–70.

Finance Canada (2004). "The Role of Fiscal Rules in Determining Fiscal Performance: The Canadian Case." *International Journal of Public Budget*, no. 56 (December): 51–100.

Financial and Fiscal Commission (2000). *The Financial and Fiscal Commissions' Recommendations for the Allocation of Financial Resources to the National and Provincial Governments for the 2001/2002 Financial Year*. Halfway House, Midrand, South Africa.

Fisher, Ronald (2007). *State and Local Public Finance*. Mason, Ohio: Thomson.

Fisman, Raymond, and Roberta Gatti (2002). "Decentralization and Corruption: Evidence across Countries." *Journal of Public Economics* 83: 325–345.

Fiszbein, Ariel (1997). "Emergence of Local Capacity: Lessons from Colombia." *World Development* 25(7): 1029–1043.

Flatters, Frank R., Vernon Henderson, and Peter Mieszkowski (1974). "Public Goods, Efficiency, and Regional Fiscal Equalisation." *Journal of Public Economics* 3: 99–112.

Flatters, Frank R., and W. Bentley Macleod (1995). "Administrative Corruption and Taxation." *International Tax and Public Finance* 2: 397–417.

Foster, Andrew D., and Mark R. Rosenzweig (2002). "Democratization, Decentralization, and the Distribution of Local Public Goods in a Poor Local Economy." Working paper, Brown University, Providence, RI.

Fox, W. F. (2007). "Fiscal Federalism in the U. S.: A Structure in Continuing Transition." In *The Practice of Fiscal Federalism*, ed. Anwar Shah, 344–369. Montreal and Kingston: McGill-Queen's Press.

Frey, Bruno, and Reiner Eichenberger (1995). "Competition among Jurisdictions: The Idea of FOCJ." In *Competition among Jurisdictions*, ed. Lüder Gerken, 209–229. London: Macmillan.

   (1996a). "FOCJ: Competitive Governments for Europe." *International Review of Law and Economics* 16: 315–327.

   (1996b). "To Harmonize or to Compete? That's Not the Question." *Journal of Public Economics* 60: 335–340.

   (1999). *The New Democratic Federalism for Europe: Functional Overlapping and Competing Jurisdictions*. Cheltenham: Edward Elgar.

Friedman, Thomas (1999). *The Lexus and the Olive Tree: Understanding Globalization*. New York: Farrar, Strauss and Giroux.

Galasso, E., and M. Ravallion (2001). *Decentralized Targeting of an Anti-poverty Program*. Development Research Group Working Paper, World Bank, Washington, DC.

Gamkhar, Shama, and Anwar Shah (2007). "The Impact of Intergovernmental Fiscal Transfers: A Synthesis of the Conceptual and Empirical Literature." In *Intergovernmental Fiscal Transfers: Principles and Practice*, ed. Robin Boadway and Anwar Shah, 225–258. Washington, DC: World Bank.

Goldfajn, Ilian, and Eduardo Refinetti (2003). "Fiscal Rules and Debt Sustainability in Brazil." Technical Note no. 39. São Paulo: Central Bank of Brazil.

Gomez-Lobo, Andres (2002). "Making Water Affordable." In *Contracting for Public Services*, ed. Penelope Brooke and Suzanne Smith, 23–29. Washington, DC: World Bank.

Gonazalez, J. M. G. (2005). "United Mexican States." In *Constitutional Origins, Structure, and Change in Federal Countries*, ed. J. Kincaid and G. A. Tarr, 208–238. Montreal and Kingston: McGill-Queen's University Press.

Gonzalez, Pablo (2005). "The Financing of Education in Chile." Fund for the Study of Public Policies, University of Chile, Santiago.

Gordon, Nora, and Emiliana Vegas (2004). "Education Finance Equalization, Spending, Teacher Quality and Student Outcomes: The Case of Brazil's FUNDEF." Education Sector, Human Development Department, Latin America and the Caribbean Region, World Bank, Washington, DC.

Goss, Sue (2001). *Making Local Governance Work*. New York: Palgrave.

Gramlich, Edward M. (1977). "Intergovernmental Grants: A Review of the Empirical Literature." In *The Political Economy of Fiscal Federalism*, ed. Wallace Oates, 219–239. Lexington, MA: Heath.

   (1987). "Federalism and Federal Deficit Reduction." *National Tax Journal* 40: 299–313.

Grossman, Gene M., and Elhanan Helpman (1994). "Protection for Sale." *American Economic Review* 84(4): 833–850.

   (1996). "Electoral Competition and Special Interest Politics." *Review of Economic Studies* 63(2): 265–286.

Gupta, Sanjeev, Hamid Davoodi, and Rosa Alosno-Terme (1998). "Does Corruption Affect Income Inequality and Poverty?" International Monetary Fund Working Paper 98/76, Washington, DC.

Gupta, Sanjeev, Hamid Davoodi, and Erwin Tiongson (2000). "Corruption and the Provision of Health Care and Education Services." International Monetary Fund Working Paper 00/116, Washington, DC.

Gurgur, Tugrul, and Anwar Shah (2002). "Localization and Corruption: Panacea or Pandora's Box?" In *Managing Fiscal Decentralization*, ed. Ehtisham Ahmad and Vito Tanzi, 46–67. London: Routledge.

Guriev, Sergei (1999). "A Theory of Informative Red Tape with an Application to Top-level Corruption." WP/99/007, New Economic School, Moscow.

Gygi, U. (1991). "Maintaining a Coherent Macroeconomic Policy in a Highly Decentralized Federal State: The Experience of Switzerland." Mimeo, OECD.

Hart, Oliver (1995). *Firms, Contracts, and Financial Structure.* Oxford: Clarendon Press.

Hayashi, Masayoshi, and Robin Boadway (2001). "An Empirical Analysis of Intergovernmental Tax Interaction: The Case of Business Income Taxes in Canada." *Canadian Journal of Economics* 34(2): 481–503.

Heaps, T., and J. F. Helliwell (1985). "The Taxation of Natural Resources." In *Handbook of Public Economics*, vol. 1, ed. A. J. Auerbach and M. Feldstein, 421–472. Amsterdam: North-Holland.

Hettich, Walter, and Stanley L. Winer (1999). *Democratic Choice and Taxation: A Theoretical and Empirical Analysis.* Cambridge: Cambridge University Press.

Heymans, C. (2006). "Local Government Organization and Finance: South Africa." In *Local Governance in Developing Countries*, ed. Anwar Shah, 47–92. Washington, DC: World Bank.

Hirshleifer, Jack, and John Riley (1992). *The Analytics of Uncertainty and Information.* Cambridge: Cambridge University Press.

Hochman, Harold M., and James D. Rodgers (1969). "Pareto Optimal Redistribution." *American Economic Review* 59(4): 542–557. Cambridge: Cambridge University Press.

Howes, Stephen (2005). "Fiscal Responsibility Legislation at the State Level in India: Is It Working?" A Note prepared for the Conference on Fiscal Responsibility and Intergovernmental Finance, Administrative Staff College of India, Hyderabad, June 22–24.

Humes, Samuel, IV (1991). *Local Governance and National Power.* New York: Harvester/Wheatsheaf.

Huther, Jeff, Sandra Roberts, and Anwar Shah (1997). *Public Expenditure Reform under Adjustment Lending: Lessons from World Bank Experiences.* Washington, DC: World Bank.

Huther, Jeff, and Anwar Shah (1998). "Applying a Simple Measure of Good Governance to the Debate on Fiscal Decentralization." Policy Research Working Paper no. 1894, World Bank, Washington, DC.

(2000). "Anti-corruption Policies and Programs: A Framework for Evaluation." Policy Research Working Paper no. 2501, World Bank, Washington, DC.

Iaryczower, Matias, Sebastian Saiegh, and Mariano Tommasi (2001). "Coming Together: The Industrial Organization of Federalism." Working Paper no. 30, Centro de Estudio para el Desarrollo Institucional, Fundacion Gobierno y Sociedad, Buenos Aires.

Ingberman, D., and D. Yao (1991). "Presidential Commitment and the Veto." *American Journal of Political Science* 35: 357–389.

Inman, Robert P. (2006). "Financing Cities." In *A Companion to Urban Economics*, ed. Richard Arnott and Daniel McMillen, 311–332. Malden, MA: Blackwell.

(2007). "Federalism's Values and the Value of Federalism." *CESifo Economic Studies* 53: 522–560.

Inman, Robert P., and M. A. Fitts (1990). "Political Institutions and Fiscal Policy: Evidence from the US Historical Record." *Journal of Law, Economics and Organization* 6: 79–132.

Inman, Robert P., and Daniel L. Rubinfeld (1994). "The EMU and Fiscal Policy in the New European Community: An Issue for Economic Federalism." *International Journal of Law and Economics* 14: 147–162.

International Monetary Fund (2001). "Brazil: Report on Observance Standards and Codes (ROSC) – Fiscal Transparency." IMF Country Report 01/217. International Monetary Fund, Washington, DC.

Isham, J., and S. Kähkönen (1999). "What Determines the Effectiveness of Community-Based Water Projects? Evidence from Central Java, Indonesia on Demand Responsiveness, Service Rules, and Social Capital." Mimeo, University of Maryland, College Park.

Johnson, William R. (1988). "Income Redistribution in a Federal System." *American Economic Review* 78(3): 570–573.

Joumard, I. (2003). "Problems of Equalisation in Federal Systems – The Concept of Equalisation." In *Federalism in a Changing World: Learning from Each Other*, ed. R. Blindenbacher and A. Koller, 471–480. Montreal and Kingston: McGill-Queen's University Press.

Kanbur, Ravi, and Michael Keen (1993). "Jeux Sans Frontières: Tax Competition and Tax Coordination When Countries Differ in Size." *American Economic Review* 83: 877–892.

Keen, Michael (1998). "Vertical Tax Externalities in the Theory of Fiscal Federalism." *IMF Staff Papers* 45(3): 454–485.

Keen, Michael, and Christos Kotsogiannis (2002). "Does Federalism Lead to Excessively High Taxes." *American Economic Review* 92(1): 363–370.

Keen, Michael, and Maurice Marchand (1997). "Fiscal Competition and the Pattern of Public Spending." *Journal of Public Economics* 66: 33–53.

Keen, Michael, and S. Smith (2000). "Viva VIVAT!" *International Tax and Public Finance* 7: 741–751.

Kehoe, P. J. (1989). "Policy Cooperation among Benevolent Governments May Be Undesirable." *Review of Economic Studies* 56(2): 289–296.

Kennedy, S., and J. Robins (2001). "The Role of Fiscal Rules in Determining Fiscal Performance." Canadian Department of Finance Working Paper 2001-16, Ottawa.

Kenyon, Daphne, and John Kincaid, eds. (1996). "Fiscal Federalism in the United States: The Reluctance to Equalize Jurisdictions." In *Finanzverfassung im Spannungsfeld zwischen Zentralstaat und Gliedstaaten*, ed. Werner W. Pommerehne and George Ress, 34–56. Baden-Baden: Nomos Verlagsgesellschaft.

Khaleghian, P. (2003). "Decentralization and Public Services: The Case of Immunization." Policy Research Working Paper no. 2989, World Bank, Washington, DC.

Khemani, Stuti (2004). "Local Government Accountability for Service Delivery in Nigeria." World Bank, Development Research Group, Washington, DC.

Kincaid, John (1967). "Municipal Perspectives in Federalism." Unpublished paper. Cited in Ann O. Bowman and Robert C. Kearney, *State and Local Government*, Boston: Houghton Mifflin.

King, David (2006). "Local Government Organization and Finance: United Kingdom." In *Local Governance in Industrial Countries*, ed. Anwar Shah, 265–312. Washington, DC: World Bank.

King, E. M., and S. C. Guerra (2005). "Education Reforms in East Asia: Policy, Process and Impact." In *East Asia Decentralizes: Making Local Government Work, World Bank Report*, 179–207. Washington, DC: World Bank.

King, E. M., and B. Ozler (1998). "What's Decentralization Got to Do with Learning? The Case of Nicaragua's School Autonomy Reform." Development Research Group Working Paper, World Bank, Washington, DC.

Kirchgassner, Gebhard, and Wener Pommerehne (1996). "Tax Harmonization and Tax Competition in the European Union: Lessons from Switzerland." *Journal of Public Economics* 60: 351–371.

Klitgaard, Robert E. (1988). *Controlling Corruption*. Berkeley: University of California Press.

(1991). "Gifts and Bribes." In *Strategy and Choice*, ed. Richard Zeckhauser, 211–240. Cambridge, MA: MIT Press.

Knopff, R., and A. Sayers (2005). "Canada." In *Constitutional Origins, Structure, and Change in Federal Countries*, ed. J. Kincaid and G. A. Tarr, 103–142. Montreal and Kingston: McGill-Queen's University Press.

Kopits, G. (2004). *Rule-Based Fiscal Policy in Emerging Markets: Background, Analysis and Prospects*. New York: Palgrave Macmillan.

Kramer, J. (2005). "Federal Republic of Germany." In *Constitutional Origins, Structure, and Change in Federal Countries*, ed. J. Kincaid and G. A. Tarr, 143–178. Montreal and Kingston: McGill-Queen's University Press.

Krug, Barbara, Ze Zhu, and Hans Hendrischke (2005). "China's Emerging Tax Regime: Devolution, Fiscal Federalism or Tax Farming?" Paper presented at the annual meeting of the European Public Choice Society, Durham, UK, March.

Krugman, Paul (1993). *Geography and Trade*. Cambridge, MA: MIT Press.

(1995a). *Development, Geography, and Economic Theory*. Cambridge, MA: MIT Press.

(1995b). "Growing World Trade: Causes and Consequences." *Brookings Papers on Economic Activity* 1: 327–362.

(1998). "What's New about the New Economic Geography?" *Oxford Review of Economic Policy* 14(2): 7–17.

Kuncoro, Ari (2000). "The Impact of Licensing Decentralization on Firm Location Choice: The Case of Indonesia." Mimeo, Faculty of Economics, University of Indonesia.

Lambsdorff, Johann (1999). "Corruption in Empirical Research – A Review." Mimeo, Transparency International, Berlin.

Lambsdorff, Johann, Markus Taube, and Mathias Schramm (2005). *The New Institutional Economics of Corruption*. London: Routledge.

Lane, Timothy D. (1993). "Market Discipline." Staff Papers, *International Monetary Fund* 40(March): 53–88.

Le Roy, I., and C. Saunders (2006). "Australia: Dualist in Form, Cooperative in Practice." In *Dialogues on Legislative, Executive, and Judicial Governance in Federal Countries*, ed. R. Blindenbacher and A. Ostien, 6–10. Forum of Federations and International Association of Centers for Federal Studies. Montreal and Kingston: McGill-Queen's University Press.

Levy, Joaquim Vieira (2005). "Fiscal Rules and Fiscal Performance." Unpublished manuscript, Ministry of Finance, Brazil.

Lieberman, S. S., J. J. Capuno, and H. Van Minh (2005). "Decentralizing Health: Lessons from Indonesia, The Philippines, and Vietnam." In *East Asia Decentralizes: Making Local Government Work, World Bank Report*, 155–178. Washington, DC: World Bank.

Lin, Justin Yifu, and Z. Liu (2000). "Fiscal decentralization and economic growth in China." *Economic Development and Cultural Change* 49(1): 1–22.

Lin, Justin Yifu, Ran Tao, Mingxing Liu, and Qi Zhang (2002). "Urban and Rural Household Taxation in China: Measurement and Stylized Facts." CCER Working Paper, Peking University.

Lindbeck, Assar, and Jorgen W. Weibull (1993). "Balanced-Budget Redistribution as the Outcome of Political Competition." *Public Choice* 52(3): 273–297.

Linder, W., and I. Steffen (2006). "Switzerland: Cooperative Federalism or Nationwide Standards?" In *Dialogues on Legislative, Executive, and Judicial Governance in Federal Countries*, ed. R. Blindenbacher and A. Ostien, 32–35. Forum of Federations and International Association of Centers for Federal Studies. Montreal and Kingston: McGill-Queen's University Press.

Lipsey, Richard G. (1970). *The Theory of Customs Unions: A General Equilibrium Analysis.* London: Weidenfeld & Nicholson.

——— (1997). "Globalization and National Government Policies: An Economist's View." In *Governments, Globalization, and International Business*, ed. John H. Dunning, 73–113. Oxford: Oxford University Press.

Lockwood, Ben (1999). "Inter-regional Insurance." *Journal of Public Economics* 72: 1–37.

——— (2001). "Tax Competition and Tax Co-ordination under Destination and Origin Principles: A Synthesis." *Journal of Public Economics* 81: 279–319.

Longo, Carlos Alberto (1994). "Federal Problems with VAT in Brazil." *Revista Brasileira de Economia* 48: 85–105.

Lotz, J. (2006). "Local Government Organization and Finance: Nordic Countries." In *Local Governance in Industrial Countries*, ed. Anwar Shah, 223–263. Washington, DC: World Bank.

Ma, Jun (1995). "Macroeconomic Management and Intergovernmental Relations in China." Policy Research Working Paper no. 1408, World Bank, Washington, DC.

Majeed, A. (2005). "Republic of India." In *Constitutional Origins, Structure, and Change in Federal Countries*, ed. J. Kincaid and G. A. Tarr, 180–207. Montreal and Kingston: McGill-Queen's University Press.

Martinez-Vazquez, Jorge, and Robert M. McNab (2003). "Fiscal Decentralization and Economic Growth." *World Development* 31(9): 1597–1616.

——— (2005). "Fiscal Decentralization, Macrostability, and Growth." International Studies Program Working Paper Series at Andrew Young School, no. 0506. Georgia State University.

Martinez-Vazquez, Jorge, and Bob Searle, eds. (2007). *Fiscal Equalization: Challenges in the Design of Intergovernmental Transfers.* New York: Springer.

Mathur, O. M. (2006). "Local Government Organization and Finance: Urban India." In *Local Governance in Developing Countries*, ed. Anwar Shah, 169–204. Washington, DC: World Bank.

Mauro, Paolo (1995). "Corruption and Growth." *Quarterly Journal of Economics* 110(3): 681–713.

McLure, Charles E., Jr. (2000). "Implementing Subnational Value Added Taxes on Internal Trade: The Compensating VAT." *International Tax and Public Finance* 7: 723–740.

McMillan, Melville (1995). "A Local Perspective on Fiscal Federalism." Unpublished paper, Policy Research Department, World Bank. Available at www.worldbank.org/wbi/publicfinance.

(2006). "Local Government Organization and Finance: Canada." In *Local Governance in Industrial Countries*, ed. Anwar Shah, 41–81. Washington, DC: World Bank.

(2008). "A Local Perspective on Fiscal Federalism: Practices, Experiences, and Lessons from Developed Countries." In *Macro Federalism and Local Finance*, ed. Anwar Shah, 245–289. Washington, DC: World Bank.

McMillan, Melville, Anwar Shah, and David Gillen (1980). *The Impact of Provincial-Municipal Transportation Subsidies*. Alberta Transportation, Edmonton, Alberta, Canada.

Mieszkowski, Peter M., and Richard A. Musgrave (1999). "Federalism, Grants, and Fiscal Equity." *National Tax Journal* 52: 239–260.

Mihaljek, Dubravko (1995). "Hong Kong's Economy Two Years before 1997: Steady Sailing, Prosperous Voyage." *IMF Survey* 25: 109–112.

Mintz, Jack, and Henry Tulkens (1986). "Commodity Tax Competition between Member States of a Federation: Equilibrium and Efficiency." *Journal of Public Economics* 29(2): 133–172.

Mirrlees, James A. (1971). "An Exploration in the Theory of Optimum Income Taxation." *Review of Economic Studies* 38(114): 175–208.

Mitsui, Kiyoshi, and Motohiro Sato (2001). "Ex Ante Free Mobility, Ex Post Immobility, and Time-Consistent Policy in a Federal System." *Journal of Public Economics* 82: 445–460.

Molander, Per, ed. (2003). *Fiscal Federalism in Unitary States*. New York: Springer.

Moore, Mark (1996). *Creating Public Value*. Cambridge, MA: Harvard University Press.

Morris, Alan (2007). "Commonwealth of Australia." In *The Practice of Fiscal Federalism: Comparative Perspectives*, ed. Anwar Shah, 43–72. Montreal and Kingston: McGill-Queen's Press.

Mountfield, E., and C. P. W. Wong (2005). "Public Expenditure on the Frontline: Toward Effective Management by Subnational Governments." In *East Asia Decentralizes: Making Local Government Work, World Bank Report*, 85–105. Washington, DC: World Bank.

Mueller, Dennis C. (1989). *Public Choice II*. Cambridge: Cambridge University Press.

Mundell, Robert A. (1963). "Capital Mobility and Stabilization Policy under Fixed and Flexible Exchange Rates." *Canadian Journal of Economics and Political Science* 29(4): 475–485.

(1968). *International Economics*. New York: Macmillan.

Muramatsu, Michio, and Farrukh Iqbal (2001). "Understanding Japanese Intergovernmental Relations: Perspectives, Models, and Salient Characteristics." In *Local*

Government Development in Postwar Japan, ed. Michio Muramatsu and Farrukh Iqbal, 1–28. Oxford: Oxford University Press.

Musgrave, Richard A. (1959). *The Theory of Public Finance*. New York: McGraw-Hill.

(1983). "Public Finance, Now and Then." *FinanzArchiv*41(1): 1–13. Reprinted in R. A. Musgrave (1986), *Public Finance in a Democratic Society* I (New York: New York University Press), 89–101.

Myers, Gordon M. (1990). "Optimality, Free Mobility and Regional Authority in a Federation." *Journal of Public Economics* 43: 107–121.

Niskanen, William A. (1992). "Political Guidance on Monetary Policy." *Cato Journal* 12: 281–286.

Oates, Wallace (1969). "The Effects of Property Taxes and Local Public Spending on Property Values: An Empirical Study of Tax Capitalization and Tiebout Hypothesis." *Journal of Political Economy* 77: 957–971.

(1972). *Fiscal Federalism*. New York: Harcourt Brace Jovanovich.

ed. (1998). *The Economics of Fiscal Federalism and Local Finance*. Cheltenham: Edward Elgar.

(1999). "An Essay on Fiscal Federalism." *Journal of Economic Literature* 37(September): 1120–1149.

(2001). "Fiscal Competition and European Union: Contrasting Perspectives." *Regional Science and Urban Economics* 31: 133–145.

(2005). "Towards a Second Generation Theory of Fiscal Federalism." *International Tax and Public Finance* 12(4): 349–373.

Oates, Wallace, and Robert Schwab (1988). "Economic Competition among Jurisdictions: Efficiency Enhancing or Distortion Inducing?" *Journal of Public Economics* 35: 333–354.

Olowu, Dele (1993). "Roots and Remedies of Government Corruption in Africa." *Corruption and Reform* 7(3): 227–236.

Olson, Mancur (1969). "The Principle of Fiscal Equivalence: The Division of Responsibilities among Different Levels of Government." *American Economic Review* 59(2): 479–487.

Pauly, Mark V. (1973). "Income Redistribution as a Local Public Good." *Journal of Public Economics* 2: 35–58.

Persson, Torsten, and Guido Tabellini (1996a). "Federal Fiscal Constitutions: Risk Sharing and Redistribution." *Journal of Political Economy* 104(5): 979–1009.

(1996b). "Federal Fiscal Constitutions: Risk Sharing and Moral Hazard." *Econometrica* 64: 623–646.

Peterson, G. E., and E. Muzzini (2005). "Decentralizing Basic Infrastructure Services." In *East Asia Decentralizes: Making Local Government Work*, World Bank Report, 209–236. Washington, DC: World Bank.

Phillips, K., and G. Woller (1997). "Does Fiscal Decentralization Lead to Economic Growth?" Working paper, Brigham Young University.

Pisani-Ferry, J. (1991). "Maintaining a Coherent Macro-economic Policy in a Highly Decentralized Federal State: The Experience of the EC." Paper presented at the OECD Seminar on Fiscal Federalism in Economies in Transition, Paris, April 2–3.

Poschmann, F., and S. Tapp (2005). *Squeezing Gaps Shut: Responsible Reforms to Federal-Provincial Fiscal Relations*. Toronto: C. D. Howe Institute.

Poterba, James, and Jürgen von Hagen, eds. (1999). *Fiscal Institutions and Fiscal Performance*. Chicago: University of Chicago Press.

Prud'homme, Remy (1995). "On the Dangers of Decentralization." *World Bank Research Observer*, August, 201–210.

Qian, Yingyi (2000). "The Institutional Foundations of China's Market Transition." In *Annual World Bank Conference on Development Economics, 1999*, ed. Boris Pleskovic and Joseph Stiglitz, 289–310. Washington, DC: World Bank.

Qian, Yingyi, and Gerard Roland (1998). "Federalism and the Soft Budget Constraint." *American Economic Review* 88: 1143–1162.

Qian, Yingyi, and Jinghian Wu (2000). "China's Transition to a Market Economy: How Far across the River?" Working Paper no. 69, Center for Research on Economic Development and Policy Reform, Stanford University.

Qiao, B., and Anwar Shah (2006). "Local Government Organization and Finance: China." In *Local Governance in Developing Countries*, ed. Anwar Shah, 137–167. Washington, DC: World Bank.

Rafuse, R. W. (1991). "Revenue Raising Powers, Practice and Policy Coordination in the Federal System of the United States." Mimeo, Advisory Commission on Intergovernmental Relations, Washington, DC.

Rao, M. Govinda (2007a). "Resolving Fiscal Imbalances: Issues in Tax Sharing." In *Intergovernmental Fiscal Transfers*, ed. Robin Boadway and Anwar Shah, 319–337. Washington, DC: World Bank.

(2007b). "Fiscal Federalism in India: Emerging Challenges." In *The Practice of Fiscal Federalism*, ed. Anwar Shah, 151–177. Montreal and Kingston: McGill-Queen's Press.

Rao M. Govinda, and Anwar Shah, eds. Forthcoming. *States' Fiscal Management and Regional Equity in India*. New Delhi: Oxford University Press.

Ravallion, Martin (1998). "Reaching Poor in a Federal System." Policy Research Working Paper no. 1901, March. World Bank, Washington, DC.

Reich, Robert (1991). *The Work of Nations*. New York: Alfred A. Knopf.

Rezende, Fernando (2007). "Fiscal Federalism in the Brazilian Federation." In *The Practice of Fiscal Federalism*, ed. Anwar Shah, 73–97. Montreal and Kingston: McGill-Queen's Press.

Rhodes, R. A. W. (1997). *Understanding Governance: Policy Networks, Governance, Reflexivity, and Accountability*. Buckingham: Open University Press.

Riker, H. William (1964). *Federalism: Origin, Operation, Significance*. Boston: Little, Brown.

Rodden, Jonathan, Gunnar Eskeland, and Jennie Litvack, eds. (2002). *Fiscal Decentralization and the Challenge of the Hard Budget Constraints*. Cambridge, MA: MIT Press.

Rodrik, Dani (1997a). *Has Globalization Gone Too Far?* Washington, DC: Peterson Institute for International Economics.

(1997b). "Trade, Social Insurance, and the Limits to Globalization." NBER Working Paper 5905, National Bureau of Economic Research, Cambridge, MA.

(1998). "Why Do More Open Economies Have Bigger Governments?" *Journal of Political Economy* 106(5): 997–1032.

Rodríguez-Pose, A., and A. Bwire (2003). "The Economic (In)efficiency of Devolution." Department of Geography and Environment, London School of Economics.

Rose-Ackerman, S. (1975). "The Economics of Corruption." *Journal of Public Economics* 4(February): 187–203.

(1978). *Corruption: A Study in Political Economy.* New York: Academic Press.

Rosen, Harvey S. (2005). *Public Finance.* 7th ed. Boston: McGraw-Hill/Irwin.

Ruggie, J. G. (1993). "Territoriality and Beyond: Problematizing Modernity in International Relations." *International Organization* 47(1): 139–174.

Sachs, J. D., and A. M. Warner (1999). "The Big Push, Natural Resource Booms and Growth." *Journal of Development Economics* 59: 43–76.

(2001). "The Curse of Natural Resources." *European Economic Review* 45(4): 827–838.

Saiegh, Sebastian, and Mariano Tommasi (2000). "An Incomplete-Contracts Approach to Intergovernmental Transfer Systems in Latin America." In *1999 World Bank Conference on Development in Latin America and the Caribbean: Decentralization and Accountability in the Public Sector,* ed. J. Burki, G. Perry, F. Eid, M. Freire, V. Vergara, and S. Webb, 127–144. Washington, DC: World Bank.

Saknini, Humam, Steven James, and Munir Sheikh (1996). "Stabilization, Insurance and Risk Sharing in Federal Fiscal Policy." Mimeo, Department of Finance, Ottawa.

Salikov, M. (2005). "Russian Federation." In *Constitutional Origins, Structure, and Change in Federal Countries,* ed. J. Kincaid and G. A. Tarr, 276–310. Montreal and Kingston: McGill-Queen's University Press.

Salmon, Pierre (2000). "Decentralization and Supranationality: The Case of European Union." Paper presented at the IMF Conference on Fiscal Decentralization, November 20–21.

(2006). "Horizontal Competition among Governments." In *Handbook of Fiscal Federalism,* ed. Ehtisham Ahmad and Giorgio Brosio, 61–85. Cheltenham: Edward Elgar.

Salomao, Miguel (2000). "Fiscal Federalism and Tax Competition in Brazil." Paper presented at the First Conference in Cooperative Federalism, Brasilia, D. F., May 9–11.

Salop, Steven C. (1979). "A Model of the Natural Rate of Unemployment." *American Economic Review* 69(1): 117–125.

Samuelson, Paul (1954). "Pure Theory of Public Expenditures." *Review of Economics and Statistics* 36(4): 387–389.

Sandmo, Agnar (1998). "Redistribution and the Marginal Cost of Public Funds." *Journal of Public Economics* 70: 365–382.

Santos, B. D. S. (1998). "Participatory Budgeting in Porto Alegre: Toward A Redistributive Democracy." *Politics and Society* 26(4): 461–510.

Sato, Motohiro (1998). "Three Essays in Fiscal Federalism." Ph.D. diss., Queen's University, Kingston, Canada.

Saunders, C. (2005). "Commonwealth of Australia." In *Constitutional Origins, Structure, and Change in Federal Countries,* ed. J. Kincaid and G. A. Tarr, 12–47. Montreal and Kingston: McGill-Queen's University Press.

Scharpf, Fritz W. (1997). *Games Real Actors Play: Actor-Centered Institutionalism in Policy Research.* Boulder, CO: Westview.

Schmitt, N. (2003). "Problems of Equalisation in Federal Systems – Revenue Equalisation versus Cost Equalisation." In *Federalism in a Changing World: Learning from Each Other*, ed. R. Blindenbacher and A. Koller, 481–491. Montreal and Kingston: McGill-Queen's University Press.

(2005). "Swiss Confederation." In *Constitutional Origins, Structure, and Change in Federal Countries*, ed. J. Kincaid and G. A. Tarr, 347–380. Montreal and Kingston: McGill-Queen's University Press.

Schroeder, Larry (2006). "Local Government Organization and Finance: United States." In *Local Governance in Industrial Countries*, ed. Anwar Shah, 313–358. Washington, DC: World Bank.

Scott, Anthony (1964). "The Economic Goals of Federal Finance." *Public Finance* 19: 241–288.

Scottish Office (1998). "The Constitutional Status of Local Government in Other Countries." Unpublished report, Central Research Unit, Edinburgh, Scotland.

Seabright, Paul (1996). "Accountability and Decentralization in Government: An Incomplete Contracts Model." *European Economic Review* 40: 61–89.

Sen, Amartya K. (1977). "Social Choice Theory: A Re-examination." *Econometrica* 45: 53–89.

(1985). *Commodities and Capabilities*. Amsterdam: North-Holland.

Sewell, David (1996). "'The Dangers of Decentralization' According to Prud'homme: Some Further Aspects." *World Bank Research Observer* 11(1): 143–150.

Shah, Anwar (1985) "Provincial Transportation Grants to Alberta Cities: Structure, Evaluation, and a Proposal for an Alternate Design." In *Quantity and Quality in Economic Research*, ed. Roy Chamberlain Brown, 1:59–108. New York: University Press of America.

(1988a). "Capitalization and the Theory of Local Public Finance: An Interpretive Essay." *Journal of Economic Surveys* 2(3): 209–243.

(1988b). "An Empirical Analysis of Public Transit Subsidies in Canada." In Quantity and Quality in Economic Research, ed. Roy Chamberlain Brown, 2:15–26. New York: University Press of America.

(1989a). "A Capitalization Approach to Fiscal Incidence at the Local Level." *Land Economics* 65(4): 359–375.

(1989b). "A Linear Expenditure System Estimation of Local Response to Provincial Transportation Grants." *Kentucky Journal of Economics and Business* 2(3): 150–168.

(1991). *The New Fiscal Federalism in Brazil*. World Bank Discussion Paper no. 557. Washington, DC: World Bank.

(1992). "Empirical Tests for Allocative Efficiency in the Local Public Sector." *Public Finance Quarterly* 20(3): 359–377.

(1994a). "A Fiscal Needs Approach to Equalization Transfers in a Decentralized Federation." Policy Research Working Paper no. 1289, World Bank, Washington, DC.

(1994b). *The Reform of Intergovernmental Fiscal Relations in Developing and Emerging Market Economies*. Policy and Research Series 23. Washington, DC: World Bank.

(1996a). "On the Design of Economic Constitutions." *Canadian Journal of Economics* 29(1): 614–618.

(1996b). "A Fiscal Need Approach to Equalization." *Canadian Public Policy* 22(2): 99–115.

(1996c). *Fiscal Federalism in Pakistan: Challenges and Opportunities*. Washington, DC: World Bank.

(1997). "Federalism Reform Imperatives, Restructuring Principles and Lessons for Pakistan." *Pakistan Development Review* 36(4): 499–536.

(1998a). "Balance, Accountability and Responsiveness: Lessons about Decentralization." Policy Research Working Paper no. 2021, World Bank, Washington, DC.

(1998b). "Indonesia and Pakistan: Fiscal Decentralization – An Elusive Goal?" In *Fiscal Decentralization in Developing Countries*, ed. Richard Bird and François Vaillancourt, 115–151. Cambridge: Cambridge University Press.

(1998c). "Fostering Fiscally Responsive and Accountable Governance: Lessons from Decentralization." In *Evaluation and Development: The Institutional Dimension*, ed. Robert Picciotto and Eduardo Wiesner, 83–96. New Brunswick, NJ: Transaction Publishers.

(1999a). "Governing for Results in a Globalized and Localized World." *Pakistan Development Review* 38(4): part I, 385–431.

(1999b). "Fiscal Federalism and Macroeconomic Governance: For Better or Worse?" In *Fiscal Decentralization in Emerging Economies: Governance Issues*, ed. K. Fukusaku and L. De Mello Jr., 37–54. Paris: OECD.

(2000). "Federalism and Regional Equity: Building Partnerships or Transfer Dependencies." Paper presented at the Conference on Cooperative Federalism, Globalization and Democracy organized by the Presidency of the Federative Republic of Brazil, Brasillia, May 9–11.

(2001). "Interregional Competition and Federal Cooperation – To Compete or to Cooperate? That's Not the Question." Paper presented at the International Forum on Federalism in Mexico, Veracruz, Mexico, November 14–17.

(2002). "Globalization and Economic Management." In *Public Policy in Asia: Implications for Business and Government*, ed. Mukul Asher, David Newman, and Thomas Snyder, 145–173. London: Quorum Books.

(2003). "Fiscal Decentralization in Transition Economies and Developing Countries: Progress, Problems and the Promise." In *Federalism in a Changing World: Lessons from Each Other*, ed. R. Blindenbacher and A. Koller, 432–460. Montreal and Kingston: Queen's University Press.

(2004a). "Fiscal Decentralization in Developing and Transition Economies: Progress, Problems, and the Promise." Policy Research Working Paper no. 3282, World Bank, Washington, DC.

(2004b). "The Australian Horizontal Fiscal Equalization Program in the International Context." Presentation at the Heads of Australian Treasuries Forum, Canberra, Australia, September 23.

(2005a). "A Framework for Evaluating Alternate Institutional Arrangements for Fiscal Equalization Transfers." Policy Research Working Paper no. 3785, World Bank, Washington, DC.

(2005b). "Fiscal Decentralization and Fiscal Performance." Policy Research Working Paper no. 3786, World Bank, Washington, DC.

(2005c). "On Getting the Giant to Kneel: Approaches to a Change in the Bureaucratic Culture." In *Fiscal Management*, ed. Anwar Shah, 211–229. Washington, DC: World Bank.

(2006a). "Corruption and Decentralized Public Governance." In *Handbook of Fiscal Federalism*, ed. Ehtisham Ahmad and Giorgio Brosio, 478–498. Cheltenham: Edward Elgar.

(2006b). "Fiscal Decentralization and Macroeconomic Management." *International Tax and Public Finance* 13(4): 437–462.

ed. (2006c). *Local Governance in Industrial Countries*. Washington, DC: World Bank.

ed. (2006d). *Local Governance in Developing Countries*. Washington, DC: World Bank.

(2006e). "Comparative Reflections on Emerging Challenges in Fiscal Federalism." In *Dialogues on the Practice of Fiscal Federalism*, ed. Raoul Blindenbacher and Abigail Ostien Karos, 40–46. Montreal: McGill-Queen's University Press.

ed. (2007a). *The Practice of Fiscal Federalism: Comparative Perspectives*. Montreal: McGill-Queen's University Press.

(2007b). "Rethinking Fiscal Federalism." *Federations*: 6(1): 9–11, 25.

(2007c). "A Practioner's Guide to Intergovernmental Fiscal Transfers." In *Intergovernmental Fiscal Transfers: Principles and Practice*, ed. Robin Boadway and Anwar Shah, 1–53. Washington, DC: World Bank.

(2007d). "Institutional Arrangements for Intergovernmental Fiscal Transfers and a Framework for Evaluation." In *Intergovernmental Fiscal Transfers*, ed. Robin Boadway and Anwar Shah, 293–317. Washington, DC: World Bank.

ed. (2008). *Macro Federalism and Local Finance*. Washington, DC: World Bank.

ed. (forthcoming). *Environmental Federalism and the Taxation of Natural Resources*. Washington, DC: World Bank.

Shah, Anwar, and Tugrul Gurgur, (2002). "Localization and Corruption: Panacea or Pandora's Box." In *Managing Fiscal Decentralization*, ed. Ehtisham Ahmad and Vito Tanzi, 45–67. London: Routledge.

Shah, Anwar, and Mark Schacter (2004). "Combating Corruption. Look before You Leap." *Finance and Development* 41(4, December): 40–43. Washington, DC: IMF.

Shah, Anwar, and Furhawn Shah (2007). "Citizen Centered Local Governance: Strategies to Combat Democratic Deficit." *Development* 50: 72–80.

Shah, Anwar, and Sana Shah (2006). "The New Vision of Local Governance and the Evolving Roles of Local Governments." In *Local Governance in Developing Countries*, ed. Anwar Shah, 1–46. Washington, DC: World Bank.

Shah, Anwar, and Theresa Thompson (2004). "Implementing Decentralized Local Governance: A Treacherous Road with Potholes, Detours and Road Closures." In *Reforming Intergovernmental Fiscal Relations and the Rebuilding of Indonesia*, ed. James Alm, Jorge Martinez-Vazquez, and Sri Mulyani Indrawati, 301–337. Northampton, MA: Edward Elgar.

Shah, Anwar, Theresa Thompson, and Heng-fu Zou (2004). "The Impact of Decentralization on Service Delivery, Corruption, Fiscal Management and Growth in Developing and Emerging Market Economies: A Synthesis of Empirical Evidence." *CESifo Dice Report, a Quarterly Journal for Institutional Comparisons* 2(Spring): 10–14.

Shah, Anwar, and John Whalley (1991). "Tax Incidence Analysis of Developing Countries: An Alternative View." *World Bank Economic Review* 5(3): 535–552.

Shankar, Raja, and Anwar Shah (2003). "Bridging the Economic Divide within Countries: A Scorecard on the Performance of Regional Policies in Reducing Regional Income Disparities." *World Development* 31(8): 1421–1441.

Shapiro, Carl, and Joseph E. Stiglitz (1984). "Equilibrium Unemployment as a Worker Discipline Device." *American Economic Review* 74(3): 433–444.

Sheikh, M. A., and Stanley L. Winer (1977). "Stabilization and Nonfederal Behavior in an Open Federal State: An Econometric Study of the Fixed Exchange Rate, Canadian Case." *Empirical Economics* 2(3): 195–211.

Shirai, S. (2002). "Banking Sector Reforms in the People's Republic of China: Progress and Constraint." In *Rejuvenating Bank Finance for Development in Asia and the Pacific, United Nations Economic and Social Commission for Asia and the Pacific and the Asian Development Bank*, 49–92. New York: United Nations.

Shleifer, Andrei, and Robert W. Vishny (1993). "Corruption." *Quarterly Journal of Economics* 108(August): 599–617.

Sinn, Hans-Werner (1995). "A Theory of the Welfare State." *Scandinavian Journal of Economics* 97: 495–526.

(2003). *The New Systems Competition*. Oxford: Blackwell.

Smart, Michael (2005). *Federal Transfers: Principles, Practice, and Prospects*. Toronto: C. D. Howe Institute.

(1998). "Taxation and Deadweight Loss in a System of Intergovernmental Transfers." *Canadian Journal of Economics* 31: 189–206.

South Africa, Government of (2006). *Budget, 2006: National Budget Review*. Pretoria: Government Printing Service.

Souza, C. (2005). "Federal Republic of Brazil." In *Constitutional Origins, Structure, and Change in Federal Countries*, ed. J. Kincaid and G. A. Tarr, 76-102. Montreal and Kingston: McGill-Queen's University Press.

Spahn, Paul Bernd (2001). "Maintaining Fiscal Equilibrium in a Federation: Germany." University of Frankfurt, Germany, August.

Stansel, Dean (2005). "Local Decentralization and Local Economic Growth: A Cross-Sectional Examination of US Metropolitan Areas." *Journal of Urban Economics* 57(1): 55–72.

Steytler, N. (2005). "Republic of South Africa." In *Constitutional Origins, Structure, and Change in Federal Countries*, ed. J. Kincaid and G. A. Tarr, 311–346. Montreal and Kingston: McGill-Queen's University Press.

Stigler, George (1957). "The Tenable Range of Functions of Local Government." In *Federal Expenditure Policy for Economic Growth and Stability*, ed. Joint Economic Committee, Subcommittee on Fiscal Policy, U. S. Congress, 213–219. Washington, DC: U.S. Government Printing Office.

Stoker, Gerry, ed. (1999). *The New Management of British Local Governance*. London: Macmillan.

Strange, Susan (1996). *The Retreat of the State: The Diffusion of Power in the World Economy*. Cambridge Studies in International Relations. Cambridge: Cambridge University Press.

Switzerland, Government of (2003). *The Swiss Confederation – A Brief Guide*. Bern: Bundeskanzlei.

Taliercio, R. R. (2005). "Subnational Own-Source Revenue: Getting Policy and Administration Right." In *East Asia Decentralizes: Making Local Government Work, World Bank Report*, 107–128. Washington, DC: World Bank.

Tanzi, Vito (1996). "Fiscal Federalism and Decentralization: A Review of Some Efficiency and Macroeconomic Aspects." In *Annual World Bank Conference on Development Economics*, ed. by Michael Bruno and Boris Pleskovic, 295–316. Washington, DC: World Bank.

Tanzi, Vito, and Hamid Davoodi (1997). "Corruption, Public Investment, and Growth." International Monetary Fund Working Paper 97/139, Washington, DC.

Tapales, Proserpina (2001). "Corruption and Decentralization in Philippines." Unpublished paper, Operations Evaluation Department, World Bank.

Tarr, G. A. (2005). "United States of America." In *Constitutional Origins, Structure, and Change in Federal Countries*, ed. J. Kincaid and G. A. Tarr, 381–408. Montreal and Kingston: McGill-Queen's University Press.

Technical Committee on Business Taxation (Mintz Committee) (1998). *Report.* Ottawa: Department of Finance.

Ter-Minassian, Teresa, ed. (1997). *Fiscal Federalism in Theory and Practice.* Washington, DC: International Monetary Fund.

Thiessen, U. (2000). *Fiscal Federalism in Western European and Selected Other Countries: Centralization or Decentralization? What Is Better for Economic Growth?* DIW Discussion Paper no. 224. Berlin: DIW.

Thornton, John (2007). "Fiscal Decentralization and Economic Growth Reconsidered." *Journal of Urban Economics* 61(1): 64–70.

Thurow, Lester (1981). "The Productivity Problem." In *Policies for Stagflation: Focus on Supply*, ed. Ontario Economic Council, 2:11–34. Toronto: Ontario Economic Council.

Tiebout, Charles M. (1956). "A Pure Theory of Local Expenditures." *Journal of Political Economy* 64: 416–424.

Tirole, Jean (1986). "Hierarchies and Bureaucracies: On the Role of Collusion in Organizations." *Journal of Law, Economics and Organization* 2: 181–214.

Tomaszewska, Ewa, and Anwar Shah (2000). "Phantom Hospitals, Ghost Schools and Roads to Nowhere: The Impact of Corruption on Public Service Delivery Performance in Developing Countries." Working paper, Operations Evaluation Department, World Bank.

Treisman, Daniel S. (1999). "Decentralization and Corruption: Why Are Federal States Perceived to Be More Corrupt?" Paper presented at the annual meeting of the American Political Science Association, December.

   (2000a). "Decentralization and the Quality of Government." Working paper, Department of Political Science, University of California, Los Angeles.

   (2000b). "The Causes of Corruption: A Cross National Study." *Journal of Public Economics* 76(3, June): 399–457.

   (2007). *The Architecture of Government: Rethinking Political Decentralization.* Cambridge: Cambridge University Press.

Usher, Dan (1995). *The Uneasy Case for Equalization Payments.* Vancouver: Fraser Institute.

Vaillancourt, François (1998). "Financing Formulas for Public Primary-Secondary Educations in the United States: Presentation and Evaluation." World Bank, Economic Development Institute, Washington, DC.

Van Rijckeghem, Caroline, and Beatrice Weder (2001). "Bureaucratic Corruption and the Rate of Temptation: Do Low Wages in Civil Service Cause Corruption?" *Journal of Development Economics* 65: 307–331.

von Hagen, Jürgen (2002). "Fiscal Rules, Fiscal Institutions and Fiscal Performance." *Economic and Social Review* 33(3): 263–284.

   (2005). "Budgetary Institutions and Public Spending." In *Fiscal Management*, ed. Anwar Shah, 1–29. Washington, DC: World Bank.

von Hagen, Jürgen, Andrew Hughes Hallet, and Rolf Strauch (2002). "Budgetary Institutions for Sustainable Public Finances." In *The Behavior of Fiscal Authorities*, ed. B. Marco, J. von Hagen, and C. Martinez-Mongay, 94–114. New York: Palgrave.

Von Maravic, Patrick (2003). "How to Analyse Corruption in the Context of Public Management Reform?" Paper presented at the first meeting of the Study Group on Ethics and Integrity of Governance, Lisbon, September.

Wade, Robert (1997). "How Infrastructure Agencies Motivate Staff: Canal Irrigation in India and the Republic of Korea." In *Infrastructure Strategies in East Asia*, ed. Ashoka Mody, 109–130. Washington, DC: World Bank.

Wajidi, Muhammad (1990). "Origin of Local Government in the Indo-Pakistan Sub-continent." *Journal of Political Science* 13(1–2): 131–139.

Wallack, Jessica, and T. N. Srinivasan, eds. (2006). *Federalism and Economic Reform: International Perspectives*. Cambridge: Cambridge University Press.

Waller, Christopher J., Thierry A. Verdier, and Roy Gardner (2002). "Corruption: Top-Down or Bottom-Up." *Economic Inquiry* 40(4): 688–703.

Walsh, Cliff (1992). "Infrastructure Funding and Federal-State Financial Relations." Discussion Paper no. 21, Federalism Research Center, Australian National University.

Watson, William G. (1986). "An Estimate of the Welfare Gain from Fiscal Equalization." *Canadian Journal of Economics* 19(2): 298–308.

Watts, Ronald L. (1999). *Comparing Federal Systems*. 2nd ed. Montreal and Kingston: McGill–Queen's University Press.

Weingast, Barry R. (1995). "The Economic Role of Political Institutions: Market Preserving Federalism and Economic Growth." *Journal of Law, Economics, and Organization* 11(1): 1–31.

   (2006). "Second Generation Fiscal Federalism: Implications for Decentralized Democratic Governance and Economic Development." Discussion draft, Hoover Institution, Stanford University.

Weingast, Barry R., and W. Marshall (1988). "The Industrial Organization of Congress: Why Legislatures, like Firms, Are Not Organized like Markets." *Journal of Political Economy* 96(1): 132–163.

Werner, Jan (2006). "Local Government Organization and Finance: Germany." In *Local Governance in Industrial Countries*, ed. Anwar Shah, 117–148. Washington, DC: World Bank.

Werner, Jan, and Anwar Shah (2005). "Horizontal Fiscal Equalization at the Local Level: The Practice in Denmark, Norway, and Sweden." Unpublished paper, World Bank, Washington, DC.

West, L., and C. Wong (1995). "Fiscal Decentralization and Growing Regional Disparities in Rural China: Some Evidence in the Provision of Social Services." *Oxford Review of Economic Policy* 11(4): 70–84.

Whalley, John (1999). "Globalization and the Decline of the Nation State." Paper presented at the First International Conference on Federalism, Forum of Federations, Mont Tremblant, Quebec, October 6–7.

Wierts, Peter (2005). "Federalism and the EU: Fiscal Policy Coordination within and between EU Member States." International Conference on Federalism, Brussels, March 1–5.

Wildasin, David E. (1986). *Urban Public Finance*. Chur, Switzerland: Harwood Academic.
 (1991). "Income Redistribution in a Common Labor Market." *American Economic Review* 81(4): 757–774.
 (1995). "Comment on 'Fiscal Federalism and Decentralization.'" Seventh Annual World Bank Conference on Development Economics, 323–328. Washington, DC, May 1–2.
 (1997). "Externalities and Bailouts: Hard and Soft Budget Constraints in Intergovernmental Fiscal Relations." Policy Research Working Paper no. 1843, World Bank, Washington, DC.
Williamson, Oliver (1985). *The Economic Institutions of Capitalism*. New York: Free Press.
Willis, Eliza, Christopher da C. B. Garman, and Stephan Haggard (1999). "The Politics of Decentralization in Latin America." *Latin American Research Review* 34(1, Winter): 7–46.
Wilson, John D. (1999). "Theories of Tax Competition." *National Tax Journal* 52: 269–304.
Wilson, L. S. (2003). "Equalization, Efficiency and Migration – Watson Revisited." *Canadian Public Policy* 29(4): 385–395.
Winer, Stanley L., and Denis Gauthier (1982). *Internal Migration and Fiscal Structure: An Econometric Study of the Determinants of Interprovincial Migration in Canada*. Ottawa: Economic Council of Canada.
Winkler, D., and T. Rounds (1996). "Municipal and Private Sector Response to Decentralization and School Choice." *Economics of Education Review* 15(4): 365–376.
Wonnacott, Paul (1972). *The Floating Canadian Dollar*. Washington, DC: American Enterprise Institute for Public Policy Research.
World Bank (1994a). "China: Budgetary Policy and Intergovernmental Fiscal Relations." Report no. 11094-CHA, Washington, DC: World Bank.
 (1994b). *Infrastructure for Development*. World Development Report, 1994. Washington, DC: World Bank.
 (1995). *China: Macroeconomic Stability in a Decentralized Economy*. Washington, DC: World Bank.
 (1997). *World Development Report, 1997 – The State in a Changing World*. Washington, DC: World Bank.
 (1998). *China: Public Expenditure Management Review*. Washington, DC: World Bank.
 (2000). "China: Managing Public Expenditures for Better Results." Report no. 20342-CHA, World Bank, Washington, DC.
 (2002). "Brazil: Issues in Fiscal Federalism." Report no. 22523-BR, Brazil Country Management Unit, World Bank, Washington, DC.
 (2003). *Making Services Work for Poor People*. World Development Report, 2004. Washington, DC: World Bank.
 (2004a). *Mainstreaming Anti-corruption Activities in World Ban, Assistance – A Review of Progress since 1997*. Washington, DC: World Bank.
 (2004b). *Devolution in Pakistan: An Assessment and Recommendations for Actions*. Washington, DC: World Bank.
 (2005a). "China Quarterly Update." World Bank Office Beijing, February.
 (2005b). *Equity and Development*. World Development Report, 2006. Washington, DC: World Bank.

(2006). "Capitation Financing Options in the Health Sector: International Experience. Uzbekistan Programmatic Public Expenditure Review." *Europe and Central Asia Region*, Washington, DC: World Bank.

Xie, D., H. Zou, and H. Davoodi (1999). Fiscal Decentralization and Economic Growth in the United States. *Journal of Urban Economics* 46: 228–239.

Yep, R. (2004). "Can 'Tax-For-Fee' Reform Reduce Rural Tension in China? The Process, Progress and Limitations." *China Quarterly* 177: 42–71.

Yusuf, Shahid (1997). "China's State Enterprise Sector: Problems and Reform Prospects." Mimeo, World Bank, Washington, DC.

Zhang, T., and H. Zou (1997). "Fiscal Decentralization, the Composition of Public Spending, and Regional Growth in India." Development Research Group Working Paper, World Bank, Washington, DC.

(1998). "Fiscal Decentralization, Public Spending and Economic Growth in China." *Journal of Public Economics* 67(2): 221–240.

Zheng, Yingpin, and Fan Wei, eds. (2003). *The History and Civilization of China.* Beijing: Central Party Literature Publishing House.

Index

Abbott, Michael G., 186
Abed, George T., 518
absence of markets, 20–21
Acconcia, Antonio, 522
accountability, fiscal and political
  corruption and, 528, 535
  decentralized governance, 73–75
  expenditure assignment, 130
  infrastructure, 432–433, 438
  intergovernmental transfers, 314–320,
    353
  local governance, 262
  regional competition and cohesion,
    500, 534–535
  revenue assignment, 165–166
Acton, Lord, 537
administration
  conditional grants building state
    administrative capacity, 336
  corporate income tax, 176–177
  corruption
    decentralization of administration
      affecting, 535, 536
    petty, bureaucratic, or
      administrative, 520
  expenditure assignment,
    administrative capacity of
    subnational governments for,
    131–132
  harmonization of taxes to reduce cost
    of, 197
  in-kind transfers, 450

local governance, administrative
  feasibility criterion for, 251
revenue assignment, administrative
  costs of
  collection and compliance, 164–165
  corporate income tax, 176–177
  excise taxes, 185
  factor, as, 170–171
  harmonization of taxes to reduce,
    197
  sales taxes, 179, 183
adverse selection, 22
Afonso, J. R. R., 400, 444, 455, 471, 484,
  503, 513
age, universal transfers by (demogrants),
  143
agglomeration
  economies of, 53
  network externalities and, 19
Aghion, Philippe, 145
agriculture
  infrastructure for. *See* infrastructure
  land taxes, 189
Ahlin, Christian, 523, 535–536
Aidt, Toke S., 521
Akai, N., 121
Albania, 119
alcohol, taxes on. *See* excise taxes
Alderman, H., 119
Alesina, Alberto, 347
Alok, V. N., 396, 426, 450
Alonso-Terme, Rosa, 518

fiscal transfers. *See* intergovernmental transfers
Fisman, Raymond, 536
Fiszbein, Ariel, 536
Fitts, M. A., 476
Flatters, Frank R., 47, 49, 187, 208, 220, 226, 341, 342, 346, 522
FOCJ (functional, overlapping, and competing jurisdictions), 244
Ford, Kathryn, 121
Foster, Andrew, 119
Fox, W. F., 142, 154, 155, 156, 176, 177, 189, 192, 505, 511, 513
France
decentralized governance in, 5
fiscal policy in, 478, 495
health care, grant financing of, 378
intergovernmental transfers, 279
local governance in, 242, 268–269, 272–274, 275, 276, 279
monetary policy and central banking in, 468
fraternal fiscal equalization programs, 372
free trade clauses, 488, 508
free-rider problem, 133
Frey, Bruno, 244
Friedman, Thomas, 538, 542
functional, overlapping, and competing jurisdictions (FOCJ), 244
fungibility effect of grants, 312

Gabon, 519
Galasso, E., 119
gambling, taxes on. *See* excise taxes
Gamkhar, Shamah, 312, 313
Gardner, Roy, 523
Garman, Christopher, 500, 506
gas resources. *See* natural resources ownership and management
gasoline taxes. *See* excise taxes
Gatti, Roberta, 536
Gauthier, Denis, 49, 226
GEF (Global Environment Facility), 541
Gendron, Pierre-Pascal, 117, 180, 181, 239
general sales tax. *See* sales taxes

general-purpose or unconditional transfers, 305–306, 309, 315, 340–341
Germany
cooperative federalism, 7
decentralized governance in, 6, 122
economic union in, 488
equalization program, 552
expenditure assignment in, 142, 147, 150, 152, 153
extent of federalism in, 547
federal status of, 5
fiscal policy in, 478, 479–480, 495
globalization and the information revolution in, 513, 550, 551, 552
health and education expenditures in, 378, 396, 398, 402, 412, 413
infrastructure in, 420, 428
intergovernmental transfers in, 279, 340, 361, 372, 373, 374
local governance in, 269, 272–274, 275, 276, 279
monetary policy and central banking in, 467, 469
natural resources ownership and management in, 241
poverty alleviation, governmental responsibility for, 451, 453
regional competition and cohesion in, 507–508, 509, 510, 513
revenue assignment in, 157, 187, 196
revenue sharing in, 199, 294
subnational governments
federal influence on, 8
influence on federal government, 8
tax harmonization in, 489
VFG in, 321
Ghana, 502, 536
Gillen, David, 309
Global Environment Facility (GEF), 541
globalization and the information revolution, 538–539
citizen empowerment by, 541–542
competitiveness, international, 543
consumer sovereignty resulting from, 542

Kenya, 417, 519, 527, 531
Kenyon, Daphne, 7
Khaleghian, P., 120
Khemani, Stuti, 120
Kincaid, John, 7
King, David, 447, 449
King, E. M., 119, 397, 398, 406, 407, 412,
    413, 414, 417
Kirchgassner, Gebhard, 501
Klitgaard, Robert E., 521
Knopff, R., 142, 146, 150, 153, 396, 452
knowledge culture, 543, 581. *See also*
    globalization and the information
    revolution
Kopits, G., 476, 495
Korea, 5
Kotsogiannis, Christos, 43
Kramer, J., 142, 147, 151, 153, 188, 199,
    396, 398, 413, 507, 509, 514
Krug, Barbara, 487
Krugman, P. R., 53, 212, 541
Kuncoro, Ari, 536

laboratory federalism, 500
Laffer curve, 43
Lambsdorff, Johann, 526
Lane, Timothy D., 476
Latin America. *See also specific countries*
    cash transfers in, 447, 448
    regional competition and cohesion in,
        502
Latvia, 372, 375, 519, 527
layer cake model of dual federalism, 6–7
Le Roy, I., 507
leadership commitment and corruption,
    528
Leo XIII (pope), 245
Leviathan model, 16, 28, 56, 130, 255, 501
Levy, Joaquim Vieira, 469, 485
Lieberman, S. S., 397, 404, 407, 408, 411,
    416
Lin, Chen, 532
Lin, Justin, 121
Lindbeck, Assar, 28
Linder, W., 507, 508
Lipsey, Richard G., 31, 541
Lithuania, 372, 375

Liu, Z., 121
Livingston, J., 120
loans. *See* borrowing, governmental
local governance, 3–4, 242–243
    accountability of, 262
    administrative feasibility criterion, 251
    ancient history, 267
    citizen-centered, 260, 262
    comparative perspectives on 267, 581.
        See also under specific countries
    alternative national/regional models,
        267–272
    developing economies, 290
    OECD countries, 272–281
    correspondence principle, 244
    corruption and localization. *See under*
        corruption
    credit, local access to. *See under*
        borrowing, governmental
    decentralization theorem for, 245
    defined, 242–243
    dual supervision model of, 268
    economic efficiency criterion for, 248
    expenditure assignment
        developing economies, 286
        OECD countries, 277
    fiscal equivalency, principle of, 244
    fiscal need/revenue adequacy criterion,
        251
    FOCJ (functional, overlapping, and
        competing jurisdictions), 244
    globalization and the information
        revolutionincreasing importance
        of, 243, 542–551
    handmaid to higher governance orders
        in traditional fiscal federalism,
        246–253
    health and education expenditures,
        responsibility for, 414
    home rule principle, 244, 271
    infrastructure borrowing, 429–521
    integrated analytical framework for,
        262
        citizen-centered local governance,
            260, 260–262
        implications of, 260–265
        new and old views compared, 266

judicial interpretation of constitution
in, 549
local governance in, 242, 246, 254, 274,
276, 271, 272, 273, 279–280
Medicare and Medicaid, 142, 145, 404
monetary policy and central banking
in, 466, 467, 469
natural resources ownership and
management in, 211, 240
poverty alleviation, governmental
responsibility for, 451, 458
regional competition and cohesion in,
499, 503, 504, 505, 508–509, 510,
512, 515
revenue assignment in, 157, 171, 176,
186, 187, 188, 191, 192, 196
subnational governments, federal
influence on, 8
subnational influence on federal
government, 8
TANF (Temporary Assistance for
Needy Families), 145
VFG in, 321
universalism, 475–476
user fees, 10
health and education expenditures,
409, 415–418
infrastructure, 437
revenue assignment, 170, 190–191
Usher, Dan, 341, 347
utilities, public. *See* infrastructure

Vaillancourt, François, 359
value-added tax (VAT)
accountability issues, 166
feasibility in federal systems where
states have discretion over tax
rates, 239
natural resources ownership and
management, 239, 241
responsibility for, 115–118
revenue assignment, 166, 171,
178–183
revenue sharing, 229–300
surtaxes on federal taxes, 202
Van Minh, H., 397, 404, 407, 408, 411,
416

Van Rijckeghem, Caroline, 522
Varsano, R., 503, 513
VAT. *See* value-added tax
Vegas, Emiliana, 379
Venezuela, 5
Verdier, Thierry A., 523
Verreira, S. G., 503, 513
vertical competition. *See* regional
competition and cohesion
vertical equity in federal states, 54, 56
vertical fiscal [im]balance
natural resources ownership and
management, 232–234, 236–240
VFG distinguished, 321
vertical fiscal externalities, 46, 169–170
vertical fiscal gap (VFG)
calculating, 347–349
defined, 293
infrastructure borrowing and, 421–422
intergovernmental transfers and,
321–323, 341, 347–349, 353–355
vertical fiscal imbalance distinguished,
321
VFG. *See* vertical fiscal gap
Vietnam, 191, 417
Vishny, Robert W., 523, 532
voice and choice, opportunity for,
corruption affected by, 535
Voltaire, 268
von Hagen, Jurgen, 465, 476, 478, 492
Von Maravic, Patrick, 525–526

Wade, Robert, 536
wagering, taxes on. *See* excise taxes
wages
corruption, wage-based strategies to
combat, 530
globalization and the information
revolution affecting, 544
taxes on. *See* income taxes; payroll
taxes
Wajidi, Muhammad, 270
Waldman, Michael, 23, 146
Wales. *See* United Kingdom
Waller, Christopher J., 523
Wallis, Joe, 243, 255, 257, 258
Walsh, Cliff, 466